# THE
# ILLUSTRATED
# REFERENCE BOOK
## OF

# MODERN HISTORY

GENERAL EDITOR JAMES MITCHELL

# Picture Credits

*The Illustrated Reference Book of Modern History*
This edition published in 1982 by
**WINDWARD**
an imprint owned by W. H. Smith & Son Limited
Registered No. 237811 England, Trading as WHS Distributors St John's House East Street Leicester LE1 6NE

© Mitchell Beazley Encyclopaedias Limited 1980, 1982

Pages 2-171 © Mitchell Beazley Encyclopaedias Limited 1976 and 1977
Artwork © Mitchell Beazley Publishers Limited 1970, 1971, 1972, 1973, 1974, 1975 and 1976
　　　　　© International Visual Resource 1972
　　　　　© Mitchell Beazley Encyclopaedias Limited 1976

ISBN 0 7112 0237 0

Phototypeset in Great Britain by Filmtype Services Limited, Scarborough
Printed in Yugoslavia by Mladinska Knjiga

The Joy of Knowledge

# THE
# ILLUSTRATED
# REFERENCE BOOK
## OF
# MODERN HISTORY

GENERAL EDITOR JAMES MITCHELL

WINDWARD

# Preface

## How to use this book

*Modern History* is an important section of *The Joy of Knowledge*. It contains all the general knowledge my editors and I think most interesting about man's innovative progress from the mid-nineteenth century to the modern world – the period during which machines have come increasingly to influence our lives.

**The spread system**
Every topic in *The Joy of Knowledge* takes the form of an article that occupies two facing pages of text and pictures; what we call a "spread". Each two-page spread in the book is organized in the same way. It is the heart of our approach to explaining things.

The spread system is a strict discipline but once you get used to it we hope you'll find the structure to be systematic and reassuring. You should start to feel at home in all sorts of unlikely areas of knowledge with the spread system to guide you. It works like this.

Each two-page spread in *Modern History*, as throughout *The Joy of Knowledge*, tells a self-contained story. It explains all the essential facts you need to know about its subject in as efficient a manner as possible. We believe that the discipline of having to get in all the essential and relevant facts in this comparatively small space actually makes for better results than a rambling essay could achieve – text that has to get straight to the point, pictures and diagrams that illustrate the salient points in a clear and comprehensible fashion, and captions that really work and explain the point of the pictures.

The spreads are, in a sense, the building blocks of knowledge. Like the various circuits and components that go to make up a computer, they are also systematically "programmed" to help the reader find out things more easily and remember them better. Each spread, for example, has a main article of about 850 words summarising the subject. This article is illustrated by an average of ten pictures and diagrams, the captions of which both complement and supplement the basic information in the main article. Each spread, too, has a "key" picture or diagram in the top right-hand corner. The purpose of this picture is twofold: it summarises the story of the spread visually and it is intended to act as a memory stimulator to help you recall all the integrated facts and pictures on a given subject.

**Where to start**
A good way to begin acquiring knowledge from this particular part of *The Joy of Knowledge* is initially to read the Introduction. The Introduction provides a useful framework for the information contained in the following pages. If, however, you prefer to plunge straight into the book (but don't have much basic general knowledge on the subject) I suggest you look first at the spreads "The impact of steam" beginning on page 44, "The foundations of 20th-century science" on page 46, "Industrialization 1870–1914" on page 48 and "Political thought in the 19th century" on page 60. Once you have absorbed the information on these spreads you can build up a more comprehensive general knowledge by exploring the rest of the book.

*Modern History* is a book about the people, the events and the discoveries which have shaped our present lifestyle on the planet Earth. I hope you will find it both stimulating and helpful.

# Contents

# Editor's introduction

All historical statements are subject to revision. They are all controversial. Especially vulnerable are statements about the recent past. The more recent the event, the more difficult it is for an historian to place it in perspective, to create a persuasive pattern of the past. The importance that future generations will attach to, say, the Castro-led revolution in Cuba, the invention of the telephone, or the twelve-tone musical theory of Arnold Schoenberg is impossible to foretell. On a more sweeping scale, it is too early to say whether the last 150 years have seen the beginning of the demise of Christianity as one of the world's major religions, or whether the Christian Church has simply been in a slough of despond from which it will arise with renewed vigour and influence.

The historian of modern times has, however, one compensating advantage over the historian of the more remote past. He has at his disposal a wealth of material to investigate. The first national census was compiled in Great Britain in 1801, and as the role of central governments expanded throughout the countries of the world, so the size, diversity and detail of official government records also increased. The nineteenth century was truly the beginning of the age of statistics and, in addition, nineteenth-century politicians and officials were copious letter-writers. Samuel Wilberforce, the flamboyant Bishop of Oxford in mid-century, was accustomed to receive more than 150 letters each week. Such wealth of documents can be a burden and an embarrassment to the modern historian, who despairs of his researches ever scraping more than the surface of the evidence available to him. But it is an embarrass-

ment which ancient as well as medieval historians would gladly share with him.

This volume could well be called The Age of Technology. Every age, of course, has its tools, its own technology peculiar to its own requirements. The plough satisfied the needs of the early farming communities. The past two hundred years have been the age of industrial technology. Machines of all kinds have come to influence the way people live in the developed world. Industrial technology has, since its hesitant beginnings in the middle of the eighteenth century, always been dependent upon non-renewable sources of energy, chiefly coal and petroleum. We now know that this first industrial phase of man's history is drawing to its close and it is appropriate that we should attempt to clarify in our minds what the prevailing tendencies of our history were during this brief, but revolutionary, phase.

In the first place, as is reflected in many parts of this wide-ranging book, the last two hundred years have seen the great strides forward made by the working classes. Socialist theory, the chief contribution of the nineteenth century to political and economic thought, pointed the way, and where socialists led, non-socialists found that they had to follow. Once western Europe had conceded the inevitability of universal suffrage and democratically elected parliaments, it became the interest of governments to frame their policies, both social and economic, with one eye fixed on the working-class electorate. Side by side with the development of democratic politics went the advance of trade unionism, bitterly opposed by the old ruling elites at the outset, but by the end of the nineteenth century accorded its legitimate place within the law of democratic constitutions. Nevertheless, as the experience of the twentieth century has made plain – in Nazi Germany, Fascist Italy and, more mildly, in McCarthyite America – the course of true democracy never does run smooth. Totalitarianism, with its intolerance of dissenting minorities, has played as conspicuous a part as liberal democracy in the industrial era. The French writer Albert Camus went so far in his *Reflections on the Guillotine* as to describe our age as the first in history in which every individual could imagine being imprisoned or put to death for his political opinions.

Future generations may, indeed, look back upon the democracy of the West as its own peculiar institution, incapable of transplant to other parts of the world. For the second major theme of the recent past is the continued expansion of Europe's global influence in the nineteenth century, followed by its retreat in the twentieth century. The frenzied imperialist scramble for Africa in the 1880s and 1890s was the last expression of Europe's insatiable appetite for control of world markets. In the twentieth century the economic and military power of the Soviet Union and the United States made those countries the new arbiters of world affairs. And at the same time, the extensive overseas empires of the European powers broke against the aroused national and racial consciousness of their subjects in the Third World.

While many parts of the world strive to follow in Europe's wake, to become industrialized economies and, in some places, political democracies, the West itself has had to adjust to the new style of life which industrial technology introduced. As the efficiency and diversity of machines increased during the past two hundred years, town populations came greatly to outnumber rural populations. The 1851 census in Great Britain showed that for the first time in British history more people lived in towns and cities than in the countryside. In America the last frontier had disappeared by 1900. Urbanization has meant wealth, and wealth has led to more leisure time, "space for living", in the current jargon. That space has been filled by the popular press, the cinema, television, organized sport grown so large as to become big business, and all the other outlets for a pleasure-seeking consumer society. The result is a radical transformation in man's social functioning. For the entire span of man's previous history, his labour was almost exclusively devoted to the production of food and commodities. Art and learning were the precious preserve of a tiny elite. No longer is that true, at least in the developed countries of the West. In Great Britain in 1980 almost two-thirds of the working population was employed in service and communication industries. And the coming of the silicon chip, an electronic circuit in miniature, promises to release even greater numbers of people from the manufacture of essential goods and thereby to produce a dramatic expansion of the information services. The world is fast becoming a place in which people no longer make things for one another, but rather one in which they pass on information to one another.

Finally, the Age of Technology has been a time of war and revolution. Ever since the cataclysmic upheavals of the French Revolution, which broke out in 1789, the cry for freedom and equality has been raised by oppressed peoples and nations all over the world. And ever since the twenty-year struggle of the Napoleonic Wars (which may be considered as the first world war in history), scarcely a year has gone by in which somewhere in the world one nation has not been at war with another. The illustrious *Pax Britannica* of the nineteenth century never really existed. Small wars in places of strategic interest to the great powers broke out everywhere; the rival claims of the imperialist powers led to a succession of crises and skirmishes; European fears of Russian aggrandisement and the nationalist aspirations of the various Slavic peoples turned the Balkans into the powder-keg of the world. Eventually, the strains and the tensions became insupportable and the destructive severity of modern warfare was unleashed on the world. The two "total wars" of the twentieth century ended with the explosion of that miracle of technological sophistication, the atom bomb. Since 1945 mankind has trembled under its ominous and omnipresent shadow. Present-day thermonuclear weapons are capable of destruction on a scale that makes the first explosion to be dropped on a populated area, the city of Hiroshima, seem insignificant by comparison. And the neutron bomb, which destroys human and animal life only, is well within the capability of modern technology. Technology, which has brought man to the brink of discovering how to create life, has brought him also the power utterly to destroy it. It is up to everyone, therefore, to ensure that technology is used only for the benefit of mankind.

# The British labour movement to 1868

Craft organizations had existed for centuries in Britain, usually protected by a framework of paternalistic legislation that determined terms of apprenticeship and wages. With the growth of towns and industry during the Industrial Revolution in the eighteenth century, the old craft regulations came under pressure from employers who sought to free industry from rigid restrictions and to introduce labour-saving machinery.

## Unrest and the Combination Laws

The wars with revolutionary France, which opened in 1793, were marked by high prices and labour unrest. Fearing the growth of radical ideas among the lower classes, the government passed the Combination Laws of 1799–1800 [Key]. These were the culmination of a series of laws against "combinations" in specific trades. The Combination Laws prohibited any association between two or more workmen to gain either an increase in wages or a decrease in hours. Unions were forced to operate in secret or under the guise of "non-political" Friendly Societies, which were recognized as legal in 1793.

The economic warfare between Britain and France in the latter part of the Napoleonic Wars brought trade depression and hardship to the growing industrial areas. In 1810–12 there occurred the most serious wave of Luddite disturbances [3], in which workmen under a mythical leader, "King Ludd", destroyed machinery which they saw as threatening their livelihood.

This violence was in large part the traditional reaction of workmen threatened with a decline in their living standards. The degree of union organization in the Luddite outbreaks is obscure, but some elements of union organization were undoubtedly present in Nottinghamshire. Further outbreaks of machine-breaking in 1816–17 and 1826 were also firmly repressed.

In the post-war years, continued distress and radical agitation for parliamentary reform made the government suspicious of trade union activities. Strikes in the factory districts took place in spite of the Combination Laws, most notably in Lancashire where the cotton spinners and weavers conducted an extensive strike in 1818. Elsewhere brick-makers and carpenters secured wage advances without being prosecuted.

Postwar agitation came to a climax in the St Peter's Fields meeting in Manchester of August 1819 [5]. The Peterloo Massacre, as it was dubbed by the radical press, helped to create a more sympathetic attitude towards working-class organizations. The writings of men such as William Cobbett (1763–1835) [4] were also creating a more self-conscious desire for improvement among workmen.

## Growth in union membership

In the easier economic climate after 1820, the Combination Laws were attacked. A former tailor, Francis Place (1771–1854), devoted himself to the legalization of trade unions and, with the support of radical MPs, secured the repeal of the Combination Laws in 1824. Unions could now bargain about conditions although still surrounded by some restrictions. Attempts, in 1830 and 1833 to form a single national union failed. Many unions turned to "new model unionism", emphasizing their respectability and rejecting militant activity.

**1 Thomas Paine's** (1737–1809) *The Rights of Man* (1791–2) was published in reply to Edmund Burke's (1729–97) criticisms of the French Revolution. It did much to stimulate popular radicalism. However, threat of prosecution forced Paine to flee the country for France in September 1792.

**2 Disturbances** broke out in England between 1830 and 1832 in which agricultural labourers protested against unemployment, low wages and the introduction of threshing machines. The unrest was not politically motivated, but was a reaction to growing poverty. Nine labourers were hanged and 457 transported.

— MERRY ENGLAND

**3 Luddite rioters** of 1810–12 and 1816–17 smashed factory machinery in protest against the introduction of new equipment in the hosiery and woollen cloth industries. The protesters claimed to be led by a "Ned" or "King Ludd" whose name was attached to public letters denouncing the introduction of the new machinery. The riots caused a series of harsh measures to be enacted by the government.

**4 William Cobbett** was the most influential of the radical critics and writers in the parliamentary reform movement. Of humble origin, he published a number of radical newspapers including, in 1816, the weekly *Political Register*, which soon had an estimated sale of 60,000 copies a week among working men. His hatred of the new industrialism is evident in his documentary *Rural Rides* (1830).

**5 The Peterloo Massacre**, so-called, was a tragic fracas that took place in August 1819. Manchester reformers called a meeting at which the radical demagogue "Orator" Henry Hunt (1773–1835) was to speak. But the local magistrates, fearing trouble, ordered the yeomanry to arrest Hunt at the meeting. When this failed, Hussars were sent in against the crowd of 60,000, and in the ensuing confusion 11 people were killed and more than 400 injured, including women and children. The incident was used by the government as a pretext for introducing a fresh wave of repressive legislation, the Six Acts, against "seditious assemblies" and politically "subversive" literature.

By the 1840s most unions consisted of skilled workmen and the bulk of semi- and unskilled workers still lay outside union organization. The conviction of the "Tolpuddle Martyrs" in Dorset in 1834 [6] for administering unlawful oaths showed the obstacles that could still face unskilled workers who tried to organize themselves.

Many unions took an ambivalent attitude towards the Chartist demands for the vote contained in the People's Charter [7]. Elite craft groups, such as the engineers or potters, were reluctant to align themselves with a movement tainted with violence and disorder. Some of the declining crafts, however, such as the handloom weavers, participated in Chartism in a desperate attempt to reverse their deteriorating situation.

With the decline of Chartism after 1848, the craft unions continued to consolidate their position. By 1852, the Amalgamated Society of Engineers had 12,000 members, centralized control, and high rates of subscription, which enabled it to wage successful strikes. Unskilled workers formed organizations, such as the Miners' Association of 1842, but still lacked the solidarity and strength of the skilled workmen.

From the period of model unionism, there was an improvement in the public image of the trade union movement. The Friendly Societies and Co-operative Movement, founded at Rochdale in 1844, were aided by middle-class sympathizers [9].

## Co-ordination of union activities

In 1866–7, a short trade slump in the midst of improving conditions led to a number of strikes and some violence, notably at Sheffield. The "Sheffield Outrages" [10] led to a Royal Commission in 1867 on trade unions. The Commission recommended putting trade unions upon a firm legal basis and allowing them to secure their funds. These gains were established in the Trades Union Act of 1871. In 1868 the Trades Union Congress (TUC) was founded in Manchester with 34 delegates. In 1869 in Birmingham, quarter of a million trade unionists were represented at the TUC by 40 delegates and a "Parliamentary Committee" was established to represent trade union interests.

KEY

A FREE BORN ENGLISHMAN!
THE ADMIRATION of the WORLD!!!
AND THE ENVY of SURROUNDING NATIONS!!!!

**Repressive measures** were adopted by the government against radical societies which arose following the French Revolution. Habeas corpus was suspended in May 1794, and some radical leaders were charged with high treason. In 1795, following an attack upon the king's coach in October, the Two Acts were passed. These restricted the right of free assembly and extended the law of treason to cover acts of speech and writing. The laws against combinations restricted the growth of trade unions. After 1815 the government again resorted to laws against meetings and radical propaganda, in the "gagging" Acts of 1817 and the Six Acts of 1819.

**6 The precarious legal status** of early trade unions was illustrated when six Dorset labourers were arrested in 1834 for swearing men into a union at the village of Tolpuddle. All were sentenced to seven years transportation. After demonstrations such as this, they were pardoned in 1836.

**7 Chartism,** expressed in the People's Charter, owed its origins to the failure of the 1832 bill fully to enfranchise the working man. The Charter demanded male suffrage, secret ballot, annual parliaments, equal electoral districts, an end to property qualifications for MPs and the introduction of official payment for them.

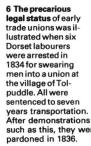

Centres of Chartism
Major areas of support
Riots
1st petition 1839
2nd petition 1842
3rd petition 1848

Glasgow
Newcastle
Padiham
Leeds
Plug riots 1842
Manchester
Nottingham
Leicester
Birmingham riots 1838
Ipswich
Newport
Rebecca riots 1842–3
Bath
Trowbridge
London
Food riots 1847

0    100km

**8 The Anti-Corn Law League,** which was mainly composed of industrialists, was founded in 1839 to oppose the duties on imported corn that protected domestic producers. Although the League was campaigning for cheaper food in opposition to the power of the landed classes, the Chartists and the working classes did not fully support it. The Chartists argued that in reality the League wanted wages reduced by the amount that corn prices would fall if the Laws were repealed.

**9 The first Co-operative shop,** a non-profit making retail store, was one of a number of co-operative ventures in the 1830s and 1840s. By selling cheap and pure food it was the most successful.

**10 The "Sheffield Outrages",** a series of violent incidents directed at non-union members, led to the establishment of a Royal Commission to investigate the status of trade unions. In 1867 union status was further put into question by a ruling that they were defenceless against officials who absconded with union funds. Unions were represented on the Commission which recommended that they be given a legal basis.

THE SHEFFIELD HEROES.

Mr R...... PITY THE SORROWS OF A POOR OLD MAN.
WORKMAN. IT'S NO USE OLD BOY, WE'RE NOT TO BE CAUGHT WITH CHAFF, YOU'VE DECEIVED US LONG ENOUGH, MUNDELLA IS THE MAN OF OUR CHOICE.

# Social reform 1800–1914

The rapid increase in population and new industrial towns during the Industrial Revolution created immense social problems in Britain. The new towns had grown uncontrolled, many lacked basic amenities such as sanitation and water supply, and the problems of poverty, ill-health, crime and bad housing were widespread. There was almost no schooling for most of the population. Child and female labour was regularly used in factories and mines [1], even for the most arduous and dangerous tasks. The prevailing ethic of laissez-faire that the state should not interfere with the workings of the economy or society held back any far-reaching legislation to improve working conditions.

## Poverty and social concern

During the course of the nineteenth century some of these evils were diagnosed and brought to public notice by social commentators [8] and novelists such as Charles Dickens (1812–70), Mrs Gaskell (1810–65) and Charles Kingsley (1819–75). In addition, parliamentary enquiries were set up to examine social questions. The result was a considerable body of social legislation.

The Poor Law was a source of concern to nineteenth-century reformers. The existing system of "outdoor" relief, levied from parish rates, burdened the propertied classes, and Thomas Malthus (1766–1834) in his influential *Essay on the Principle of Population* (1798) had argued that it perpetuated poverty by encouraging population growth. Under the Speenhamland system, introduced in 1795, labourers' wages were subsidized out of parochial funds on a scale linked to the price of bread. But in the large industrial towns, the parochial organization of poor relief was totally inadequate to meet the strains of heavy unemployment.

In 1834 the New Poor Law was passed. It much reduced "outdoor relief". Instead of receiving charity, all able-bodied people requiring relief were forced to go into the workhouse, where a strict regime, including segregation of the sexes, even of married couples, was intended to deter all but the truly destitute [5]. In addition, poor law authorities were amalgamated to spread the burden of poor relief evenly.

The insanitary conditions of the great towns gave rise to considerable concern about public health. In the 1840s an inquiry showed that more than half the major towns in Britain had an insufficient or impure water supply. The cholera epidemics of the mid-nineteenth century acted as a spur to the public health movement. Edwin Chadwick's (1800–90) famous *Report on the Sanitary Conditions of the Labouring Population* in 1842 led to the creation of a central Board of Health under the Public Health Act of 1848. Individual towns were empowered to set up local Medical Officers of Health. In 1875 a Public Health Act laid the foundations for an overhaul of public sanitation.

## Legislation on housing

Housing reform was left to piecemeal action. Lord Shaftesbury's (1801–85) [2] Lodging Houses Act of 1851 checked the worst abuses of "doss-houses". More important, however, was the Artisans' Dwelling Act of 1875 which gave local authorities the power to clear slums. A number of reforms of local government, especially the Municipal

1 The use of child and female labour in factories and mines during the Industrial Revolution was widespread. In the early 1830s, nearly half the labour force in the cotton mills was under 21, and of the adults more than half were women. Hours and conditions were regulated only by the benevolence of employers, and a working week exceeding 90 hours was common until the 1833 Factory Act became effective.

2 Lord Shaftesbury was an evangelical churchman and a dedicated reformer. He is associated with the 1833 Factory Act and with legislation to prohibit the employment of children by chimney sweeps, in 1840, and of women and children in the mines, in 1842. But his overriding paternalism made him unsympathetic to franchise extension in 1867 and to too much state involvement in welfare.

4 No free public libraries existed before 1845. From the mid-century, however, many towns set up rate-assisted public libraries to provide access to books and newspapers for all classes.

5 Under the New Poor Law of 1834, workhouse conditions were to be made inferior to those of the poorest labourer outside, in order effectively to deter "laziness" and "vagrancy" among the poor.

3 The Corn Laws of 1815 protected British agriculture by prohibiting the importation of foreign wheat until the domestic price exceeded 80 shillings per quarter. These laws were widely opposed by the urban poor and also by the industrialists because it was generally thought that they forced up the price of food and wages. In the long term too, it was argued that protectionism would harm exports. In 1839, the Anti-Corn Law League was founded by Richard Cobden (1804–65) and John Bright (1811–89) to agitate for repeal. In attacking the privilege and sectional interests behind the laws, the league took on a reformist appearance. The Corn Laws were repealed in 1846.

Corporations Act of 1835 and the Local Government Act of 1888, provided the administrative machinery necessary to implement these measures on a local level.

Factory legislation began as early as 1802 when Robert Peel senior (1750–1830), introduced an act to limit the employment of children to under 12 hours a day. The 1819 Factory Act forbade the employment of children in cotton mills under the age of nine. Lord Shaftesbury's 1833 Factory Act further limited the working hours of all children under 18 years old and appointed factory inspectors to enforce this. Safety regulations and limitations on women's working hours were introduced by an act in 1844. This legislation was extended in the course of latter part of the nineteenth century to include all types of factories. In 1891, a consolidating act raised the minimum age for the employment of children to 11 years.

### The rise of state education
Education remained a patchwork of private initiative and philanthropic effort for much of the nineteenth century. The Royal Lancaste-rian Association (1810) and the Anglican National Society (1811) founded hundreds of schools without any government involvement. State intervention began in the 1830s and the first government grant to education was made in 1833. In 1839 an education department was set up to inspect grant-receiving schools [6].

In 1870, Forster's Education Act provided virtually free elementary education for anyone who wanted it by setting up local boards empowered to establish schools financed, in part, from the rates. Education up to the age of ten years was made compulsory in 1880. In 1902, the Balfour Education Act created Local Education Authorities and thoroughly reformed the whole system of secondary education.

The growth of state responsibility for social welfare was embodied in the legislation of the Liberal governments after 1906, which went a considerable way towards creating a rudimentary "welfare state", with important, new measures such as the Old Age Pensions Act of 1908 and the National Health Insurance Act of 1911 [10].

**Chronic over-crowding** and grossly inadequate facilities characterized the new industrial towns that mushroomed during the Industrial Revolution. The sheer scale and complexity of the problems were quite unprecedented, and unnoticed until social reformers, philanthropists and the unavoidable pressure of events forced them upon public notice.

**7 The Salvation Army,** founded by "General" William Booth (1829–1912) in 1865, aimed at social as well as spiritual welfare. It provided soup kitchens, night shelters and many facilities for the destitute. Booth was particularly concerned at the adverse effects of urbanisation and the depopulation of the countryside. He hoped that through a system of rural re-education he could reverse this trend.

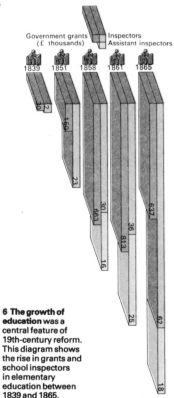

**6 The growth of education** was a central feature of 19th-century reform. This diagram shows the rise in grants and school inspectors in elementary education between 1839 and 1865.

Government grants (£ thousands)  Inspectors  Assistant inspectors
1839 1851 1858 1861 1865

**8 John Ruskin** (1819–1900) art critic and reformer argued that art, ethics and social conditions were inextricably linked. Many of his proposals, such as pensions and state education, were later adopted.

**10 The National Insurance Act** of 1911 provided unemployment pay and free medical treatment in return for graduated weekly contributions to be paid by employers, employees and the state.

**9 Private philanthropy** in the 19th century very often preceded state action by many years. Port Sunlight, shown here, was built by the industrialist Lord Leverhulme (1851–1925) in 1888. It was the first village to be built on the garden city principles, then advocated as a means to eliminate the physical and moral effects of urban overcrowding by Ruskin and other social reformers. This is shown in the planned houses, open spaces, and the provision of public amenities.

**THE RIGHT TICKET FOR YOU!**
YOU ARE TRAVELLING ON A SAFE LINE
GOVERNMENT LINE 1913
MALE WORKER PAYS 4ᵈ
EMPLOYER PAYS 3ᵈ
STATE PAYS 2ᵈ
YOUR RETURN DURING ILLNESS
10/- Per Week FOR 26 WEEKS
5/- AFTERWARDS (TILL 70) WHILE INCAPABLE OF WORK
FREE DOCTOR & MEDICINE
30/- Maternity Grant
SANATORIUM BENEFIT
AND ARE ASSURED A SAFE RETURN

# The revolutions of 1848

In an age of revolution 1848 was the year of revolution. The governments of France, Italy and central Europe were all shaken by insurrection. Contrary to the belief of contemporaries, there was no overall plan, however, and lack of co-ordination was fatal for the revolutionaries.

## Political reform through revolt

The roots of the risings throughout Western Europe were remarkably similar. The Industrial Revolution had unrooted traditional patterns of life and had created a new urban proletariat and a much enlarged bourgeoisie intent upon political power. Economic and social unrest was aggravated by the autocratic rule that was a legacy of the Vienna Settlement of 1815 and which provided a focus for the intellectuals who were agitating for political reform. People were hungry as a result of crop failures in 1845, 1846 and 1847 when bad corn harvests coincided with potato blight. Famine drove desperate mobs onto the streets prepared to demand any changes that offered hope.

Significantly, the centres of unrest were the great cities [2]. Many areas of Europe had recently experienced the Industrial Revolution and thousands had flocked to the cities only to live in squalor and work in conditions of frightening degradation. These people were hit by the second crisis of 1848 – an international credit collapse, which led to wholesale bankruptcies and unemployment. The unemployed joined the hungry on the streets. Finally, there was a psychological catalyst. The epidemic of revolution was accompanied by an epidemic of cholera, which spread panic and anger [7].

## Wave of early successes

The first revolts erupted in Italy [5]. Once Louis-Philippe (1773–1850) had abdicated from the French throne in February [3] revolution took hold. In March the resignation of the apostle of European stability, Prince Metternich (1773–1859), Chancellor of the Hapsburg Empire, boosted the morale of the revolutionaries. Caught by surprise and overwhelmed by the extent of the outbreak, governments could not call on each other for help. Their only hope seemed to be to make concessions. Liberal constitutions [1] were granted everywhere and the Hapsburg emperor, the pope and the kings of France and Prussia fled from their capitals.

Simultaneously with the liberal revolts came an upsurge of nationalism. The Hapsburg Empire with its spheres of influence in Italy and Germany [4] seemed doomed. Hungary declared her independence, the Bohemians formed a nationalist movement and a Slav Congress met to consider a new deal for Slavs in the empire. In Italy, Giuseppe Mazzini (1805–72) called for a rising to form a new Italian state. At the same time King Charles Albert of Piedmont (1798–1849) sent an army to help the Lombards drive out the Austrians, hoping to form a north Italian kingdom. In the German Confederation an assembly met at Frankfurt to decide on a policy to unite Germany. These political moves showed the degree of hostility to the Vienna Settlement of 1815 and its legacy of repression.

In spite of all this, by the middle of 1848 the tide of revolution was stemmed. Early successes proved illusory. The Hapsburg

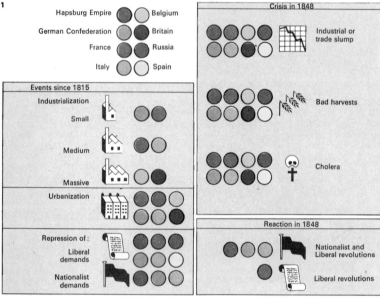

1 Uprisings occurred in most European countries in 1848, with similar causes but varying in intensity and effect. In Russia and Spain, political dissent lacked the concentrated support of the factory or city, while Belgium and Britain had already made political concessions in the face of heavy industrialization and urbanization, avoiding the violent confrontations of 1848.

2 The revolutions of 1848 were urban; the peasants were apathetic or conservative. Political ideas spread quickly along the new railways, attracting city intellectuals, workers and businessmen.

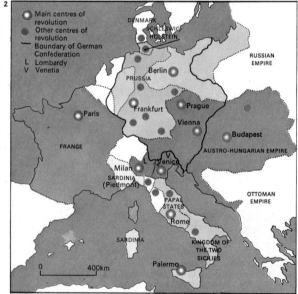

3 Paris barricades in March 1848 were manned by middle-class liberals, working-class socialists and the unemployed. Shattered by his unpopularity, Louis-Philippe abdicated within a few days.

4 Liberal revolts in the 39 German states won constitutions that did not survive the repression of 1849. The impotence of nationalists in the Frankfurt Assembly was shown when they called Austrian and Prussian troops in to keep order.

Empire followed its historic policy – divide and rule – by exploiting deep divisions between the revolutionaries. Croats and Romanians who resented Magyar domination rose against Hungary's new leader, Louis Kossuth (1802–94). Their armies helped to do the Hapsburgs' work for them. In Italy, Charles Albert's forces were smashed by the Austrian army in two campaigns. Traditional loyalty to existing separate states deprived him of wide Italian support. Catholics hesitated to disobey the pope, who had forbidden violence against the Catholic Hapsburgs.

In Germany, at the Frankfurt Assembly, the intellectuals wrangled interminably and failed to decide on a form for the new Germany until it was too late. Everywhere the middle classes, who had provided the impetus and leadership for the revolution, were horrified by the forces they had unleashed [8]. Having seen revolution degenerate into anarchy, they welcomed the restoration of law and order. By 1849 all was quiet again. The forces of reaction seemed triumphant. Disorganized mobs [Key] stood no chance against the professional armies [6]

of Austria, Prussia, Russia and France. The Hapsburg tradition of garrisoning each province with troops from other provinces had prevented any chance of soldiers siding with the revolution. In every area there was little hope of successful revolution since most of the population – the peasants – rejected it.

**The legacy of 1848**
There were a few significant gains, however. Serfdom was abolished in the Hapsburg Empire. Piedmont and Prussia kept their constitutions and eventually led Italy and Germany to unity in 1871. Governments learned to pay more attention to the material interests of their subjects and to pay lip service at least to more democratic processes.

But nationalists had learned that idealism and popular enthusiasm would not be enough. Their hopes would be fulfilled only if they could match their opponents' military strength. The revolutions of 1848 were followed by a period of cynicism and opportunism in politics and a use of armed force to settle grievances. Bismarck's age of "blood and iron" had begun.

WOMEN ON THE BARRICADE, NEAR THE PORTE ST. DENIS.

**Women on the barricades**; the tricolour, symbolizing hopes of liberty, equality and fraternity; the red flag of socialist revolution; the flags of German, Italian, Hungarian or Bohemian nationalism – all these made a heroic display in 1848. But heroic slogans such as "Bread or Death" did not match an army.

**5 Italian revolts** for state constitutions, for republics in Rome and Venice and for a north Italian kingdom all collapsed by 1849.

**6 Military saviours of the Hapsburgs** (caricatured left to right) were Jellačić (1801–59), who led Croats against Magyars in independent Hungary, Radetzky (1766–1858), who successfully ended the Italian revolts, and Windischgrätz (1787–1862), who subdued Vienna and Bohemia.

**7 The Paris sewers** begun by Baron Haussmann (1809–91) during the 1850s were a response to criticism of governmental failure to stop cholera spreading in 1848, when fear of the disease acted as a catalyst in the revolutions. Haussmann also created wide boulevards to facilitate cavalry charges against future revolutionary barricades.

**8 Karl Marx** (1818–83), shown as Prometheus chained to his printing press, and Friedrich Engels (1820–95) published the *Communist Manifesto* early in 1848 as a doctrine and strategy for the Communist League. Although this made no contribution to the outbreaks of 1848, fear of socialism inhibited the revolution.

# German and Italian unification

Italy and Germany were created in spite of limited popular support, strong communal loyalties to existing units and the proximity of two powers whose interests were endangered by their emergence as strong nations – the Austrian Hapsburg Empire and France. The new nations were the fruit of the ambitions of their strongest components, Piedmont and Prussia, and of the outstanding practitioners of the new *Realpolitik*, Camillo Cavour and Prince Otto von Bismarck.

## The birth of modern Italy

As Prime Minister of Piedmont from 1852, Cavour (1810–61) [5] built up his state as a magnet to attract the rest of Italy. He made the new parliamentary democracy work, encouraged up-to-date agriculture and industry and linked the Piedmontese economy to that of Europe through a railway network and the modernized port of Genoa. He created a fair legal system and an efficient bureaucracy. With a competent small army and a king, Victor Emmanuel (1820–78), known to be a genuine Italian patriot, Piedmont became the focus of national hopes.

Outside help was vital to drive out the Austrians. France became a pawn in Cavour's game. In the Pact of Plombières (1858), Louis Napoleon – the French Emperor Napoleon III (1808–73) – promised him help in a future war. Cavour engineered an attack against Piedmont by Austria in 1859 and French troops were sent in. After triumphs at Magenta and Solferino, Louis Napoleon had second thoughts and withdrew his support from Cavour, but his help had been decisive. In the excitement of the victories, Parma, Modena, Tuscany and the Romagna demanded amalgamation with Piedmont. In return for the acquisition of Nice and Savoy, Napoleon backed plebiscites in Emilia and Tuscany and Cavour won an overwhelming majority in favour of the formation of a north Italian kingdom.

Matters might have rested there but for Giuseppe Garibaldi (1807–82). When the Sicilians rose in revolt against Naples in 1860, Garibaldi and 1,000 men went to their help. Within weeks, the Neapolitan army had been swept out of Sicily and Garibaldi marched in triumph through Naples itself. Rome

was his next objective. But if Garibaldi attacked Rome then France and Austria might intervene to defend the pope, so Cavour sent a Piedmontese army to forestall any further advance. Garibaldi, in a dramatic gesture, gave up the south to Piedmont [6].

Only two areas of Italy now remained unintegrated. Venetia was held by Austria and Rome and its surrounding territories were held by the pope and a garrison of French troops [3]. In 1866, Victor Emmanuel joined Prussia in the Austro–Prussian war and was given Venetia. In 1870, France withdrew her troops from Rome to fight the Prussians and Victor Emmanuel became king of a united Italy [7].

## Prussia and the "Iron Chancellor"

In northern Europe Bismarck (1815–98) had become Chancellor of Prussia in 1862, where he was faced with a Liberal majority hostile to his aims. But he managed to manipulate them and finally gain their support for unification and his policy of *Realpolitik*.

Together, the customs union, or Zollverein [2], and the growth of railways had

1 **Kaiser Wilhelm I** of Prussia was acclaimed German Emperor at Versailles in 1871. He called it "The unhappiest day of my life"; he had wanted the less democratic title "Emperor of Germany" and left the room without glancing at the architect of the new Germany, Bismarck. Bismarck [centre] had crushed all opposition to German reunification by "blood and iron". It was his skill and vision that had created Germany; as Chancellor until 1890 he moulded its institutions and laboured to make it inviolable. Von Moltke (1800–91) [on Bismarck's left], Chief of the Prussian General Staff, was the strategist of the triumphs against Austria and France.

2 **A potpourri of 39 states**, the German Confederation, was united in the customs-free Zollverein in 1844. The Confederation was further extended by the Austro-Prussian War of 1866. Thuringia and Mecklenburg sided with Prussia, and joined; Hesse-Darmstadt and Saxony were annexed on Austria's defeat.

3 **This caricature of Pope Pius IX** expresses the disappointment felt at his failure to support liberalism consistently. As papal lands were lost, he increased the spiritual claims of the Holy See. In 1864 he condemned contemporary political doctrines and in 1870 went on to proclaim papal infallibility.

Map legend:
- North German Confederation 1867
- Joined German Confederation 1871
- Ceded by France 1871
- German Empire 1871

0    200km

already removed most natural and artificial impediments to German integration and prosperity. Bismarck was determined to remove Austrian influence and unite Germany, and despite opposition in the Catholic south to the dominance of Protestant Prussia, in three wars he succeeded.

Bismarck's diplomatic skill ensured that each war was fought against an isolated opponent. In the Danish war of 1864, he fought ostensibly to free the two-German-speaking duchies of Schleswig and Holstein from Danish control. But by setting up a joint control of the duchies with Austria, the principal obstacle to German unification, he created an ideal situation for picking a quarrel with her.

The time was ripe in 1866. France's neutrality had been bought by vague promises of territorial concessions and Louis Napoleon had no time to realize his mistake [Key]. In a war lasting only seven weeks, the Austrian army was smashed at Sadowa. In 1867, Prussia dominated a north German confederation. A southern confederation was set up, but without Austria.

France realized too late the emerging danger on her eastern frontier. Vital reforms to her army had come too late and Louis Napoleon was outmanoeuvred by Bismarck in a diplomatic game over rival candidates for the throne of Spain. The hysterical reaction in both countries to the candidature of a nephew of the Hohenzollern king of Prussia provoked France to declare war on Prussia in July 1870. On 1 September, the French army capitulated at Sedan and all resistance collapsed by January 1871.

A wave of enthusiasm swept the south German states for unity with the north. On 18 January 1871, Wilhelm I, King of Prussia, was proclaimed German Emperor [1].

**Death of a dream**
Before 1848, Italian and German nationalists had dreamed of new states that would free their citizens, release their stifled talents and regenerate Europe. The new states of 1871 were created at a price. Liberalism was sacrificed to nationalism; cynicism opportunism and violence had triumphed – not idealism and liberty.

**Napoleon III, Emperor of France,** was exploited and outwitted first by Cavour, then Bismarck, in the unification of Italy and Germany. By offering help to Cavour, he hoped to gain Savoy and Nice and create a weak client state. In the event he almost missed his reward and saw the creation of a unified Italy. He was outmanoeuvred by Bismarck, realizing the threat too late, after Prussia had defeated Austria. By staking his authority on an attempt to force Bismarck to give up any future plans to put a Hohenzollern on the Spanish throne, he led France into the war with Prussia that brought his own empire to an end.

**4 Mazzini's proclamation** of a Roman Republic in 1849 left a legend of heroism to Italy. Giuseppe Mazzini (1805–72) had founded "Young Italy" to lead his countrymen towards democracy without outside help or compromise, and dreamed of a state that would "evoke the soul of Italy".

**5 Camillo Cavour** was never able to inspire the sense of moral crusade that was brought to the *Risorgimento* by Mazzini and Garibaldi. But he understood the politics, grasped the international context and had the skill to exploit the possibilities. Without the exertion of his skills Italy could not have been unified.

**6 At an historic meeting** in 1860 on the Naples road, Garibaldi gave to Victor Emmanuel the gift, in effect, of a unified nation – in exchange he took a sack of seedcorn.

**7 Although Italy was united by 1870,** political and economic development was uneven. Despite Garibaldi's dramatic exploits, southern Italy remained backward compared with Piedmont.

9

# Victoria and her statesmen

Queen Victoria's reign, from 1837 to 1901, lasted longer than that of any other British monarch. During that time the party system and parliamentary democracy came to their maturity. The monarchy itself moved out of the arena of active politics, but achieved a new status as the neutral guardian of national stability. In 1830 even *The Times* had found it difficult to mourn the death of George IV; republicanism was a serious radical cry. By 1897, the year of the Diamond Jubilee [9], republicanism had been drowned in popular royalist enthusiasm.

## The changing style of politics

Ten prime ministers served Queen Victoria [Key]. None of them was chosen by her in defiance of the wishes of the Commons. Each came to power by virtue of being the leader of his party, and cabinets were composed of members of the same party. That was a marked though gradual change from the eighteenth-century politics of connection. Party had replaced the Crown as the source of political power. After the 1832 Reform Act, both the Whigs and the Conservatives took steps to organize themselves into national parties. Elections lost much local colour and acquired national meaning.

## The first half of the reign

It was not easy for the 18-year-old princess to step with confidence onto the crowded political stage. Victoria was fortunate to find a devoted tutor in her first prime minister, the debonair Lord Melbourne (1779–1848), then mellowed with age. To the man whom Caroline Ponsonby had flattered to deceive in marriage, Victoria brought a late spring in the autumn of his career. To her, he became as a father.

She was loath to part with Melbourne. But the weakness of her constitutional position was brought home to her by the Conservative victory at the 1841 elections. Loving Melbourne, she had learned to love the Whigs. Losing him, she learned to work as closely and fairly with his successor. Throughout her reign she kept herself fully informed on political developments; her opinions could never be treated lightly by her ministers.

Robert Peel, from 1841 to 1846 the first prime minister of a Conservative (as opposed to a purely Tory) Party, was a new breed of prime minister. His roots were commercial and his forte was economics. He had no sentimental attachment to the landed aristocracy. The squires on the back-benches, the heart of his party, found him uncommunicative and arrogant. He tried to turn the Tories into a party that worked to balance the claims of competing interests [1], instead of seeking to defend the exclusive interests of the land and the Church. He failed, split his party, and left it a minority for a generation.

Viscount Palmerston (1784–1865) was the beneficiary of this Conservative misfortune. He was prime minister for all but 14 months between 1855 and 1865. England was then enjoying the mid-Victorian boom; the standard of living was generally high and social problems unobtrusive. Palmerston believed that a government did best by doing as little as possible. His great interest was foreign affairs, the one sphere where the royal will still counted for something. He

**1 Robert Peel** (1788–1850) sought an undoctrinaire approach to the problems of industrialization that brought violent Chartist unrest, and in 1846 after the Irish famine he alienated the traditionally Tory landowners by removing tariffs on imported corn, thus reducing the price of bread.

**2 The Great Exhibition** (1851) at the Crystal Palace, asserted Victoria's international standing early in her reign. Rulers from many parts of the world attended the festivities, which were originally conceived by Prince Albert to celebrate the wonders of industry and to promote peace.

**3 Prince Albert** (1819–61), married Victoria in 1840, and rebuilt much of the Kensington district of London for the Great Exhibition. Among the monuments erected to him was the Albert Bridge, shown here.

**4 Disraeli became Conservative leader** in the Commons in 1849. He passed the 1867 Reform Act in an attempt to outbid the Liberals for popular appeal, and founded the Conservative Central Office (1868) to organize the party in the country.

and Victoria clashed often and she sometimes won. In 1857 Palmerston made light of the Indian Mutiny; Victoria knew better, and it was on her initiative that troop reinforcements were sent to India which saved the British presence there.

### Gladstone and Disraeli

Palmerston's death in 1865 allowed William Ewart Gladstone (1809–98) [6] to assume the leadership of the Liberal Party. He was the first prime minister to form four governments (1868–74, 1880–85, 1886, 1892–4). He was too single-minded, too earnest, and too radical to earn anything but Victoria's habitual distrust. But he was beyond question the giant of Victorian politicians. Under his premiership the Irish Church was disestablished (1869), secondary education made universal (1870), the secret ballot introduced (1872), and the agricultural labourer enfranchised (1884). His mission, he said, was to pacify Ireland, but his Home Rule Bill of 1886 was defeated by Liberal Unionists, led by Joseph Chamberlain (1836–1914), perhaps the greatest Vic-

torian statesman never to be prime minister.

Gladstone's great rival was Benjamin Disraeli (1804–81) [4], already a tired man at the start of his main ministry (1874–80). His achievement was to help swell the tide of imperial sentiment by his rhetoric and, by making Victoria Empress of India in 1876, to exalt in the popular imagination the person and office of the monarch. And she for six years found in "Dizzy" an unfailingly courteous and amusing companion. He was her favourite prime minister. It was an extraordinary end to the career of one who, from his Jewish descent, his landless status, and suspect literary connections, had never become quite acceptable even to his own Conservative party.

His successor as Conservative leader, Lord Salisbury (1830–1903) [7], was in the purest Tory mould, the last great representative of the Cecil family that had risen to prominence under Elizabeth I. He was the ideal minister to preside over the Jubilee celebrations. He formed three administrations (1885–6, 1886–92, 1895–1902), and left politics just after the queen's death.

**The queen, as head of state,** appointed each new prime minister. Here she is shown giving the seals of office to Lord John Russell (1792–1878) in 1846 after the fall of Peel's ministry on the controversial issue of the repeal of the Corn Laws. In the 18th century, the monarchs chose their own ministers and exercised real discretion over dissolutions of Parliament. Victoria's power was less direct but her personal relations with her prime ministers were of great importance to the history of her reign.

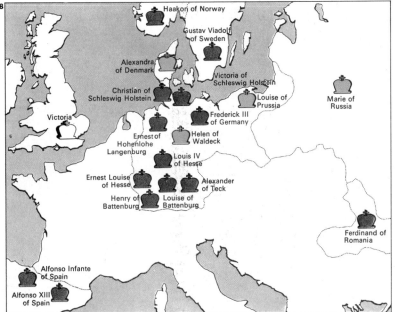

**5 The death of Albert** in 1861 led Victoria to withdraw from social life and dress in mourning for many years. At this point her popularity reached its lowest ebb, but revived by the 1880s. She never recovered from the loss of her German-born husband.

**6 Gladstone** was the son of a Liverpool cotton merchant and retained a radical and evangelical outlook throughout his career. His stirring oratory made him the darling of the industrial masses, but he was a highly intellectual man who was MP for Oxford University (1847-65). His political career, like that of Disraeli, began in The Conservative Party, in Peel's ministry; but he joined the Liberals in 1859.

**7 Lord Salisbury was enigmatic and shy** and an implacable foe of Irish Home Rule. He made the Conservative Party into the most powerful party in the state by 1902.

Grandchildren

Daughters-in-law

Sons-in-law

**8 Queen Victoria was related** to most of the royal houses of Europe by the marriages of her children and grandchildren. At her death there were 37 of her great-grandchildren living, and she became popularly known as the "grandmother of Europe". Her intimacy with foreign courts gave her a knowledge of diplomacy. But her constitutional position prevented her from exercising real influence over foreign affairs. She was restricted to the Crown's ancient right to be consulted, to encourage and to warn.

Map labels:
Haakon of Norway
Gustav Viadolf of Sweden
Alexandra of Denmark
Victoria of Schleswig Holstein
Christian of Schleswig Holstein
Louise of Prussia
Marie of Russia
Victoria
Frederick III of Germany
Ernest of Hohenlohe Langenburg
Helen of Waldeck
Louis IV of Hesse
Ernest Louise of Hesse
Alexander of Teck
Henry of Battenburg
Louise of Battenburg
Ferdinand of Romania
Alfonso Infante of Spain
Alfonso XIII of Spain

**9 The Diamond Jubilee** of 22 June 1897 was a grand imperial festival which was attended by representatives of Victoria's 387 million subjects. The queen was 78 and suffered from rheumatism and failing eyesight. The short service at St Paul's, which marked the halfway point of the royal procession from Buckingham Palace, was held outside the cathedral to avoid carrying the queen up the steps in a wheelchair. Like the jubilee of 1887 the Diamond Jubilee provided an occasion for a colonial conference.

# Victorian London

In the nineteenth century, London became the biggest and richest city in the world, its population quadrupling to reach 6,586,269 by 1901 in Greater London (a term first used in the 1881 census). Its growth as the heart of a great commercial and military empire presented a spectacle both imposing and appalling. Between the plush and cut-glass elegance of the West End and the fever-ridden slums of Dickensian description lay a gulf the century could not bridge. Overwhelmed by the squalor in which many of the people lived, the critic John Ruskin in 1865 called London "rattling, growling, smoking, stinking – a ghastly heap of fermenting brickwork pouring out poison at every pore".

## Commerical expansion

The port of London was central to the economic growth of the capital. The first large enclosed docks were completed in 1802. In 1885 the expansion of trade was marked by the completion of the Victoria Dock, 2 kilometres (1.2 miles) long. Although challenged by ports such as Hull and Liverpool, London remained the premier port, and 13 million tonnes of goods passed through it in 1880.

London was the centre of a host of industries associated with trade, refining and processing imported goods for distribution to the rest of the country or for re-export. In addition to brewing, distilling, tanning and food-processing the capital supported a shipbuilding industry that was overtaken by Newcastle and Glasgow only in the closing years of the century. By 1851 there were almost half a million workers engaged in manufacturing. Service industries employed nearly one million by 1861.

Even before the end of the eighteenth century, London had begun spreading out into rural areas of Surrey and Kent. The nineteenth century saw a rapid extension of this process as the City proper, the "square mile" formerly confined by the city wall, was given over to shops, offices and warehouses. In the West End, fashionable squares and town houses were completed. The growing middle classes built houses in suburbs such as Camberwell, Paddington and Clapham. Although the East End, [7] including Whitechapel, Bethnal Green and Stepney, continued to grow, the working classes too began moving to districts on the edge of the built-up area, such as Hammersmith.

## Railways and transport

The growth of suburban London was greatly accelerated by the coming of the railways [1], which soon spread out into a dense network. The first underground line in the world, from Paddington to Fenchurch Street, was opened by the Metropolitan Railway Company in 1863 and in the first six weeks carried an average of 26,000 passengers a day. A first-class fare between Edgware Road and King's Cross was sixpence. In 1864 special workmen's trains were introduced with a maximum return fare of only threepence. Other lines soon connected the main line stations and all important parts of the metropolis. The first electrified line opened in 1890. By the end of the century horse-drawn buses and trams provided alternative transport [Key].

The central area of the capital was refurnished with a series of new public buildings,

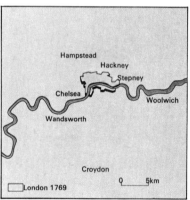

**1 Railways grew out of urban expansion** but also created it. The London and Greenwich line, opened in 1836, was London's first steam-powered railway. By 1852, most of today's mainline stations were in being and there were several suburban lines. From 1863 the Underground system provided rapid transport in the metropolitan area. In 1880, between 150 and 170 million rail journeys were made in the city annually.

Hampstead
Hackney
Stepney
Chelsea
Woolwich
Wandsworth
Croydon
0   5km
London 1769

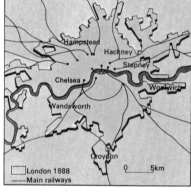

Hampstead
Hackney
Stepney
Chelsea
Woolwich
Wandsworth
Croydon
0   5km
London 1888
— Main railways

**2 Cholera epidemics** in the 1830s and 1840s gave an important stimulus to the public health system. Royal Commissions of inquiry led to the creation of a General Board of Health and a Medical Officer of Health in 1848, in spite of opposition from the City of London. Improvements in water supply and sanitation followed. Until the 1860s, London's sewers were discharged into the Thames.

FATHER THAMES INTRODUCES HIS OFFSPRING TO THE FAIR CITY OF LONDON
(A Design for a Fresco in the New Houses of Parliament.)

**3 A professional police force** for London was created under the Metropolitan Police Act of 1829. Until then, London had only a few hundred professional police. The security of the capital largely depended upon an unco-ordinated band of watchmen and constables under several different authorities. The Act enabled a unified policing of the whole metropolitan area, with the exception of the City proper, using about thousand professional police officers

**4 The Bank of England,** established in 1694 to finance a war with France, was subsequently granted a monopoly of joint stock banking. While smaller banks were restricted to only six partners between 1708 and 1826, it became government banker and reserve bank for the whole country – a status ratified in the Bank Charter Act (1844). The fine buildings, completed in 1827, are imposing examples of the many public buildings erected in London during the 19th century. Others, in Victorian neo-Gothic style include St Pancras Station (1865–71) and the Royal Courts of Justice (1871–82).

**5 London fashion** set the pattern of taste and consumption for the country as a whole. The mass market in the capital stimulated the rise of large department stores in the 1880s along bustling streets such as Regent Street, shown here. During the 19th century small, family-run shops began to disappear. They either developed as chain stores, such as J. Sainsbury's, which first opened in Drury Lane in 1869, or they were replaced by large, independent department stores.

including the rebuilt Houses of Parliament (1836–67), the Royal Courts (1871–82), the Bank of England (1795–1827) [4] and the great museums in Kensington. Trafalgar Square was completed in the 1840s. Widened streets, notably the Embankment [8], imitated the boulevards of Paris and some of the old slums were cleared to make way for new streets such as Charing Cross Road. Sewerage [8], lighting, paving and water supply were gradually brought under control after the cholera epidemics of the 1830s and 1840s [2]. The establishment of a Metropolitan Board of Works in 1855 was important for unified planning.

## Social reforms

The vitality and commercial prosperity of the capital were reflected only slowly in social reforms. As people crowded into the terrace houses thrown up by speculative builders around gasworks, breweries or warehouses, the parishes of the East End became spawning grounds for crime and disease. General William Booth (1829–1912), who founded the Salvation Army in 1878 to reconvert the slum dwellers called them the people of "darkest England". In that year, while many landowners were earning £100,000 a year and paying tax of only 2d in the pound, the average labourer's income was £70. Fashionable strollers [5] wore hand-sewn garments created by sweated labour paid at a rate of only 2d an hour.

In 1885, it was estimated that one in four Londoners still lived in abject poverty. Only after 1880, when primary education became compulsory, were the streets cleared of ragged children living on their wits.

Despite the ferocious penalties for even petty crime, an estimated 100,000 in London lived by thieving or swindling in the 1860s, and another 80,000 were prostitutes. Sensational stories of crime and capture by the Metropolitan Police Force [3] could be read daily in the "penny dreadfuls". This was the fog-shrouded city of Sweeny Todd the Barber and Jack the Ripper. Violent riots by the unemployed in 1886 and 1887 gave belated vent to the distress that went hand-in-hand with the music halls [6], gin palaces and imperial pomp of Victorian London.

KEY

**St Paul's Cathedral,** erected in more spacious days, looks down on the Fleet Street of 1900 when vehicles thronged London's streets and traffic jams had become common. In 1850 there were more than 1,000 horse-drawn buses at work in the capital as well as countless carts and wagons. Congestion was one indication of the need for a new form of urban planning. London was the first industrial metropolis to have to cope with the problems of public health, urban transport, housing and other services on a mass scale. The unprecedented difficulties created by its growth necessitated a dramatic increase in the powers of local government.

**6 Music halls became immensely popular** in the 19th century. After a licensing Act in 1843, music halls, unlike theatres, could serve alcohol. The first commercial halls were the Canterbury in Lambeth (1852) and the Oxford Music Hall in Oxford Street (1861). Forty halls were taking in custom in London in 1868, and as the century progressed, music halls came to be more widely accepted as an alternative to the theatre.

**7 The East End of London** remained notorious for its poverty and bad housing well into this century. Many of its inhabitants were immigrants who had come from Ireland and continental Europe.

**8 Construction of the Embankment** (started 1867) with railways, sewerage and other services was a rare example of unified planning for growth. An efficient London system of drainage and sewerage was delayed by a lack of centralized authority. In 1858, work began on a complete system of sewerage for the capital. This great engineering feat was completed in 1865 and cost £4 million, with 131km (82 miles) of pipe carrying 1,703 million litres (420 million gallons) of sewage each day.

**9 London was the social centre** of Britain. The London "season" attracted wealthy families up from the country to reside in the substantial houses they kept in town. Hyde Park (shown here) was a fashionable place of recreation.

# Colonizing Oceania and Australasia

The voyage of Ferdinand Magellan across the "Peaceful Sea" in 1520 brought the Pacific Ocean to the attention of Europe. But it was 1565 before the Spaniard López de Legaspi (died 1572), sailing west from the New World, settled the Philippines, where Magellan had died [1]. Spanish rule, although challenged, was uninterrupted until the Spanish-American War of 1898, when the Philippines were ceded to the United States.

## The Indies and Australia

Meanwhile to the southeast, as Portuguese power declined, the ships of the Dutch East India Company, founded in 1602, routed the pirates of the Malay Archipelago, seized control of the lucrative spice trade and paved the way for a Dutch colonial empire extending from Sumatra, Java and Borneo to Celebes, the Moluccas and western New Guinea [9]. The prosperity of the new colonies, largely derived from cloves, nutmeg, pepper and coffee, was set against a background of repression and bloodshed. In Borneo, where gold and diamond mining attracted Chinese immigration, Dutch rule was precarious; and

not until 1701 did the British East India Company, formed in 1600, establish a factory or trading post in what later became a permanently divided island.

Commissioned by East Indies Governor Anthony van Diemen (1593–1645) to chart the western and southern shores of New Holland (Australia), Abel Tasman [2] in 1642–3 discovered Van Diemen's Land (later Tasmania), skirted New Zealand and later sailed along the southern coast of New Guinea into the Gulf of Carpentaria. More than a century passed before the British Admiralty dispatched James Cook (1728–79) [5] to take possession of any land in the south in the course of a scientific expedition to the South Seas. By sailing during 1768–71 from Cape Horn to New Zealand (which he charted as two islands) Cook finally exploded the theory that a great southern continent balanced the land mass of the Northern Hemisphere. He sailed up the east coast of Australia, claiming it for Britain, showed that New Guinea was a separate island and, in two later voyages, made other significant Pacific discoveries.

Britain was left to colonize the vast

subcontinent of Australia in 1787, first as a penal settlement, later as rich sheep and cattle country. Population was concentrated in the east and south where Brisbane, Sydney, Melbourne and Adelaide were founded. Sparse settlement spread out as explorers trekked across the vast deserts of the interior [6]. The principal victims of white expansion were the nomadic Aborigines, their Stone Age culture based entirely on hunting, their clubs, spears and boomerangs ineffectual against firearms. Introduced diseases had an even more devastating impact. Guns and epidemics wiped out the native population of Tasmania and sharply reduced that of the mainland. The Aborigines were to have no share in new Australian prosperity, accelerated by later gold rushes [7].

## New Guinea and New Zealand

Rumours of gold also drew prospectors to the great island of New Guinea in the mid-nineteenth century. Mineral resources proved negligible but traders and speculators stripped coastal forests of timber. In the mountainous interior, inhabited by plumed

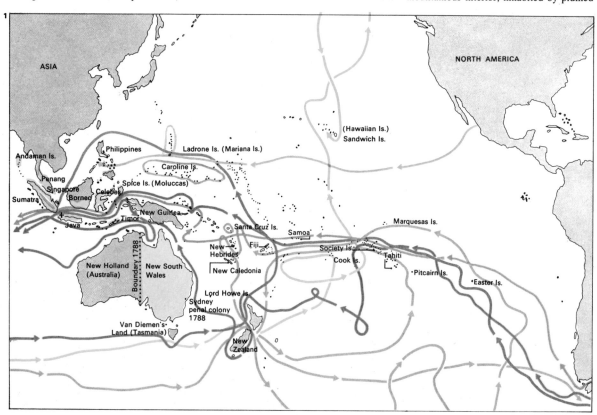

Legaspi 1564–5
Tasman 1642–4
Bougainville 1766–9
Cook 1767
Cook 1768–71
Cook 1772–5
Wallis 1776–9
British possessions 18th cent.
Dutch possessions 18th cent.
Spanish possessions 18th cent.
Batavia—headquarters of the Dutch East India Co

1 **Imperial ambition,** commercial rivalry and the search for a legendary southern continent motivated navigators of the great European maritime nations – Spain, Portugal, Holland, England and France – to explore the Pacific between the 16th and 18th centuries. They included Legaspi, who conquered the Philippines, Tasman, the discoverer of Tasmania and New Zealand, Bougainville, first Frenchman to sail round the world, Wallis, the English discoverer of Tahiti, and Cook, whose three voyages opened up most of the Pacific.

2 **Abel Tasman** (1603– c. 1659), an employee of the Dutch East India Company, touched on the southern shore of an island he named Van Diemen's Land (after the Indies' Governor-General). In 1865 the island was renamed Tasmania. He was deterred from landing in New Zealand by warlike Maoris. After discovering Tonga and the Fiji Islands he returned to Batavia where he was rebuked for "having been negligent in investigating the situation, conformation and nature of the lands and peoples discovered".

3 **William Dampier** (1652–1715), formerly an English buccaneer, explored the coasts of Australia, New Guinea and New Britain, vividly describing lands and people. An equally frosty reception greeted his second voyage along the south coast of New Guinea and north Australia.

4 **Louis de Bougainville** (1729-1811) set out on a round-the-world voyage of discovery in November 1766 in the frigate *La Boudeuse.* He sailed through the Straits of Magellan to the Tuamotus and Tahiti, which he claimed for France, unaware that Samuel Wallis (1728–95) had found it ten months earlier. He sighted and named islands in the Samoa and New Hebrides groups and would have reached the unknown east coast of Australia had he not been diverted by the Great Barrier Reef. Despite starvation and scurvy he had lost only seven men by the time he returned home in 1769. He also founded a settlement in the Falkland Islands.

5 **The voyages of Captain James Cook** were supplemented by careful and perceptive accounts of lands he visited and by scientific observations of great practical value. During his first voyage in *Endeavour* in 1768–71 he circumnavigated the two main islands of New Zealand, charted and claimed the east coast of Australia and returned home through the Torres Strait. In the second voyage he took *Resolution* to the Antarctic and discovered or rediscovered many

Pacific islands. Finally, he visited Australia and New Zealand again in *Resolution* and discovered Hawaii, where he was killed in 1779.

and painted head-hunters, civilizations made little impact even when Holland, Germany and Britain annexed the island in 1884–5.

In New Zealand the Maoris, more advanced socially and culturally, were treated with more respect by European settlers. Whalers [10] and sealers were initially welcomed by the local population although disease took a terrible toll. The early nineteenth-century arrival of traders and missionaries in the North Island was followed by British annexation with Maori agreement in 1840 and rapid settlement of both islands. But misunderstandings over tribal rights to sell land to the colonists led to disputes as the Maoris realized the threat to their lands. They resisted in a series of fierce wars, particularly in the 1860s [8] but were defeated, lost most of their land despite nominal consultation and thus faced the future with a great deal of misgiving.

The Maoris had left their original homelands in Polynesia several centuries earlier. Other peoples – Micronesians, Melanesians and Polynesians – still inhabited the island groups of Oceania that were sighted (and

often colonized) by Europeans between the sixteenth and nineteenth centuries [3, 4]. Dried coconut (copra), used for animal feeding and later for the extraction of edible oil, was the staple export crop. A few islands were commercially more rewarding – notably British Fiji with its forests of sandalwood; French New Caledonia, where nickel was found; and Hawaii, where a combination of American missionary work and enlightened local rule led to independence as early as 1843; a prosperous economy based on sugar and pineapples thereafter developed.

## Cultural impact
Elsewhere, repression, missionary conversion, disease and "blackbirding" – the forced transport of native labour to work in the sugar and cotton plantations of Fiji and Queensland – all helped to destroy local cultures and tribal structures as white civilization spread. Colonialism also put a stop to more savage rituals – cannibalism, head-hunting and blood feuds – with a promise of improved education and a share in economic wealth and political power.

**The Maoris of New Zealand,** whose Polynesian ancestors paddled some 3,300 kilometres (2,000 miles) across the Pacific in about the 13th century, were unsurpassed craftsmen of dugout canoes, of which a model is shown here. Their war canoes, carrying up to 100 men, were elaborately carved by sculptors who also taught their pupils the magical and religious ritual associated with the craft. Paddled at full speed, they could overtake European sailing ships.

**6 Explorers** during the first half of the 19th century sailed round the uncharted coasts of Australia and probed the interior from settled areas in the southeast. They journeyed up the great rivers and across mountains and deserts in search of fertile land and an inland sea which they believed to exist. Later explorers, mostly from Europe, established that the heart of the Australian continent was barren.

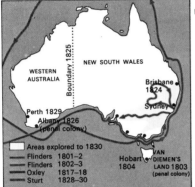

6 A

WESTERN AUSTRALIA
NEW SOUTH WALES
Boundary 1825
Brisbane 1824
Perth 1829
Albany 1826 (penal colony)
Sydney

Areas explored to 1830
Flinders 1801–2
Flinders 1802–3
Oxley 1817–18
Sturt 1828–30

Hobart 1804
VAN DIEMEN'S LAND 1803 (penal colony)

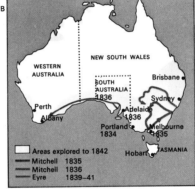

B

WESTERN AUSTRALIA
NEW SOUTH WALES
Perth
Albany
SOUTH AUSTRALIA 1836
Adelaide 1836
Portland 1834
Brisbane
Sydney
Melbourne 1835

Areas explored to 1842
Mitchell 1835
Mitchell 1836
Eyre 1839–41

Hobart
TASMANIA

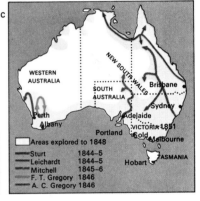

C

WESTERN AUSTRALIA
NEW SOUTH WALES
Perth
Albany
SOUTH AUSTRALIA
Adelaide 1851
Portland
Brisbane
Sydney
VICTORIA 1851 Gold
Melbourne

Areas explored to 1848
Sturt 1844–5
Leichardt 1844–5
Mitchell 1845–6
F. T. Gregory 1846
A. C. Gregory 1846

Hobart
TASMANIA

7
10,000 immigrants
125,441
10,000 live births
68,731
67,776
20,030
1840   1860   1880   1900

[1840] 0·2
1860   1·1
1880   2·2
1900   3·8

Total white population (millions)

**7 Australia** relied initially on immigration to build up its population. An assisted immigration scheme was introduced in 1829 and up to 1860 immigrants accounted for over three-quarters of the population growth. The gold rushes of 1851–6 brought an even greater immigrant surge. Thereafter, the Australian birth-rate began to rise and overshadow a reduced flow of immigrants.

8

**8 Maori gallantry** against superior weaponry marked many battles during the 1860s when Crown attempts to satisfy the land hunger of New Zealand settlers without disrupting Maori tribal rights broke down in bitter disputes over land sales. Maoris defended redoubts such as this one above the Katikara Stream near Mt Egmont. In 1863 the fort was battered by naval guns and 350 troops routed 600 Maoris.

**9 The fortress port of Batavia** was the trade centre of the Indies in the 17th century when Aelbert Cuyp (1620–91) painted "The Return Fleet of the East India Company on the Roads of Batavia". Dutch naval supremacy and commercial enterprise, backed when necessary by guns, led to the establishment of a colonial empire that lasted 300 years. Batavia eventually reverted to its former name of Jakarta as the capital of the independent nation of Indonesia.

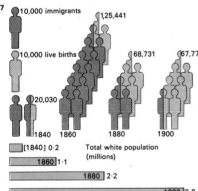

9

10

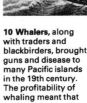

**10 Whalers,** along with traders and blackbirders, brought guns and disease to many Pacific islands in the 19th century. The profitability of whaling meant that fishing grounds were rapidly depleted, although the industry survived for many years. This somewhat fanciful print entitled "The North Cape New Zealand and Sperm Whale Fishery" may exaggerate the density of the whale population but typifies the old-style shore whaling practices which led to many coastal settlements.

# Australia & New Zealand to 1918

Australia began as a penal colony for the overflow from British gaols, after the American War of Independence had closed off the main area for convict transportation. The First Fleet, under Captain Arthur Phillip (1738–1814) [1], arrived in Botany Bay on the eastern Australian coast on 18 January 1788, but the settlement soon shifted to a much better anchorage in nearby Port Jackson. There, at Sydney Cove, the colony of New South Wales was established on 26 January, which was subsequently commemorated as Australia Day.

## The early colonies

Convicts provided the initial labour force for erecting a settlement and scratching a living from the poor soil in and around Sydney, but by 1815 a way had been found through the Blue Mountains to the fertile plains in the west. Free settlers, capital accumulated from shrewd trading or imported from England, illegal squatting on Crown lands, and merino sheep all contributed to a developing wool export industry. Wool and wheat exports paid for the necessary manufactured goods and, with land sales, helped to subsidize the passage of new settlers.

New settlements were established partly to pre-empt the French, partly by adventurers without authority, at points along the coast, on Norfolk Island, and in Van Diemen's Land (renamed Tasmania in 1853). The vast distances involved required colonial administrations separate from Sydney. These were set up in Van Diemen's Land in 1825, Western Australia in 1829, South Australia in 1836, Victoria in 1851 and Queensland in 1859.

New Zealand lies 1,920 km (1,200 miles) southeast of Australia. Its fertile, well-watered land had been occupied by Maori Polynesian tribes for more than 400 years by the time the colony was established at Sydney. Sealers, whalers, freebooters and missionaries soon made their way across the Tasman Sea, establishing coastal trading settlements among a warlike people numbering perhaps 200,000. Apart from the inroads of European diseases, the sale of muskets had a devastating impact on the Maoris, intensifying fierce inter-tribal wars in the 1820s.

Britain annexed New Zealand in 1840 with the assent of most North Island chiefs at the Treaty of Waitangi [3] and made it a separate colony from New South Wales in 1841. Systematic settlement followed, inspired by the evangelical ideas of Edward Gibbon Wakefield [2]. Disputed land titles impeded initial development until Governor (later Sir) George Grey (1812–98) established order, although in the North Island the way was cleared for massive settler purchases only after Maori chiefs hostile to sales were crushed (1860–65). In the emptier South Island, pastoral settlement increased, boosted by a gold rush to Otago in 1861. Six provincial councils set up in 1852 gave way to centralized administration by a general assembly in Wellington, which replaced Auckland as the capital in 1865.

## Expanding economies

In Australia, the discovery of gold [5], especially in Victoria in 1851, brought an influx of migrants, expanded domestic capital and investment, assisted social mobility and created problems of law and order [6]. It also

**1 Captain Arthur Phillip** was the first governor of the colony of New South Wales (1788–92). He had to deal with the dregs of humanity sent to him from overcrowded British prisons, long, uncertain supply lines, and sandy soil unsuitable for crops. With such unpromising material he managed to set the fledgling colony on its feet. In spite of his repeated appeals for free settlers, Britain still sent more convicts.

**2 Edward Gibbon Wakefield** (1796–1862) developed in England a theory of colonization that was subsequently applied, with varying success, in New South Wales and Port Phillip district (1832–42), South Australia (after 1836) and New Zealand (after 1839). Crown lands were sold for agriculture to young people of good character, representing a cross-section of British society, from the nobility to labourers.

**3 The Treaty of Waitangi,** concluded on 6 February 1840 between Captain William Hobson RN (1793–1842) and Maori chiefs of New Zealand's North Island, gave Britain formal possession of both major and off-shore islands, while recognizing Maori land rights. Britain had been reluctant to declare sovereignty but by 1838 accepted the need for orderly relationships between Maoris and settlers.

**4 A proclamation** to the Australian Aborigines, dated 1816, asserted equal rights and punishments for black and white. But in general the aboriginal population of Australia suffered from the advent of the Europeans. Not only did they suffer hitherto unknown diseases, but encroachment of farming and mining on to their old hunting lands went unchecked. By 1900 Aborigine numbers had been dramatically reduced.

**5 The discovery of gold in Australia** in the 1850s brought a rush of immigrants, many of whom came from California after the end of its gold rush. And during the next 100 years Australia was one of the world's major gold producers. In the decade after the first important discoveries in New South Wales and Victoria in 1851, output, at nearly 25 million ounces, was 39% of the world total. Gold is found in all states, the largest producers being Victoria and Western Australia.

stimulated the founding of colonial constitutions for New South Wales, Victoria, Tasmania and South Australia and the achievement, between 1853 and 1860, of a large measure of democratic government by lower houses, restrained by upper houses with property qualifications. Frontiers were pushed inland; sheep flocks and wheatfields expanded rapidly and agricultural exports to Britain were increasingly supplemented by mineral products. In New Zealand, the Corriedale cross-bred sheep produced good meat as well as wool and refrigerated ships [7] carried meat and dairy produce on regular voyages to London.

## Political developments
During the 1880s, falling export prices, the effects of over-borrowing for expansion, bank failures and a general depression produced strikes and class bitterness which encouraged the entry of labour into politics in both countries. With protective tariffs, industry was expanded rapidly in Sydney and Melbourne. New Zealand, under vigorous Liberal rule from 1891 to 1912 led the world

in some aspects of social legislation, namely votes for women (1893), compulsory state industrial arbitration (1894) and old age pensions (1898).

The six Australian colonies became states in the federal Commonwealth of Australia on 1 January 1901, with responsible government based on universal suffrage. The second Prime Minister, Alfred Deakin (1856–1919) [8], like Richard John Seddon (1845–1906) [9] of New Zealand a staunch nationalist and imperialist, launched many of the policies of the new nation: restrictive immigration based on race; protectionist tariffs with British preferences; industrial arbitration by a court empowered to fix minimum wages; old age pensions, and naval and military defence.

Australia and New Zealand sent forces to South Africa to support Britain during the Anglo-Boer War (1899–1902). In World War I their troops again fought together under British command in the Dardanelles [10] and in France, both countries making a contribution out of all proportion to their size and forging for the first time, a mature sense of national identity.

**"Shearing the Rams"** by Tom Roberts (1856–1931) shows a sheep-shearing scene in Australia in the 1890s. Spanish merino sheep were first imported from South Africa in the late 1700s, and later from England. Since that time, the Australian economy has developed largely "on the sheep's back".

6

**6 The "Eureka Stockade"** of 1854 began when a group of gold miners on the Eureka field near Ballarat, Victoria, reacted violently to the police and military who were harshly enforcing the law requiring miners to be licensed. They built a rough wooden stockade which was easily overcome by the troops. But the incident captured public attention and the organization of mining and electoral legislation were reformed. Licences became easier and cheaper to obtain, simmering discontent between the Irish and English communities was revealed (the rebel leaders were mostly Irish) and every miner thereafter became eligible to vote.

7

**7 The refrigerated ship Dunedin** was commissioned in 1882 by the New Zealand and Australian Land Company to carry about 5,000 frozen lamb carcases from New Zealand to London. This followed an earlier successful trial shipment from Australia. As a result, trade from both New Zealand and Australia was opened up, and New Zealand lamb has been widely sold in Britain for nearly a century.

8

**8 Alfred Deakin,** journalist and statesman, initiated the irrigation movement in Australia and helped to form the Australian federation. He was a minister in the first federal government and prime minister intermittently between 1903 and 1910.

9

**9 Richard John Seddon** was Premier of New Zealand from 1893 until his death in 1906. A Liberal, he facilitated the granting of women's suffrage, old age pensions, free places in secondary schools and the passage of other social legislation.

10

**10 Australia and New Zealand** came of age at Gallipoli on 25 April 1915 when the Australian and New Zealand Army Corps (ANZAC) went ashore at Anzac Cove. The cliff-face dugouts the troops occupied for eight months can be seen on the right. The campaign cost the Anzacs 44,822 casualties.

# South Africa to 1910

Southern Africa is historically a conventional term for the countries lying south of Zaïre and Tanzania, and it is not a separate entity from the rest of the African continent. Many of its peoples stem ultimately from Cameroon, filtering through Angola and Zaïre. There, in the fourteenth and fifteenth centuries, a number of kingdoms began to evolve. And, as populations increased and land grew scarcer, so a steady trickle of migrants set up new national groups from west to east right across Africa.

## Early trade and commerce
In many areas the people mined copper and iron, and today Rhodesia and Transvaal are pitted with old workings. The Karanga Empire of the Monomotapa in present-day Rhodesia was especially favoured; by the twelfth century that region had begun to export gold – chiefly to Arabia and India – in return for cloth, beads, pottery and porcelain [4]. Slavery existed among Africans as it did among other peoples, but there was no extensive trade until slaves began to be exported in numbers by the Portuguese from Angola in the sixteenth century, despite frequent bans by the papacy. Although the Mani Kongo (King of Kongo) protested, by about 1530 some four or five thousand slaves were being shipped annually.

The Portuguese had established a fort at Sofala, Mozambique, in 1505 to control their gold trade. In 1507 they built a hospital, church, factory, warehouse and fort on Mozambique Island to serve primarily as a stop-over station for ships and their crews on the way to India.

Europeans did not occupy the Cape until the Dutch took it in 1652, to serve as a victualling station on the route to the East Indies. The British occupied the Cape on behalf of the exiled Prince of Orange from 1795 to prevent the Cape, like Holland, from falling into French hands. In 1802, the Cape was restored to The Netherlands under the Peace of Amiens. But the British returned in 1806, this time making their occupation effective.

It was at that time that Britons migrating to the Cape began an uneasy co-existence with the Afrikaners who had also absorbed Huguenot refugees in 1688 and 1689. Reaction to British rule took shape in the Great Trek of 1835, with Boer republics being set up beyond the frontiers. In 1843 Natal was annexed by the British, and in 1852 the independent Transvaal was set up; this was followed in 1854 by the establishment of the Orange Free State.

## European exploitation
The real turning-point was reached with the gold and diamond rushes of 1869, out of which Cecil Rhodes (1853–1902) and his friends soon developed powerful controlling companies – De Beers and Consolidated Gold Fields. Rhodes was prime minister of Cape Colony 1890–96. Britain annexed the Transvaal in 1877, and also fought a series of small wars with Bantu peoples, of which the Zulu War (1879) was the hardest [6]. The annexation of the Transvaal led to war with the Boers in 1881, following which Britain recognized the republic. Shortly after, in 1883, Germany set up a post at Lüderitz Bay, and in 1884 annexed the whole of South West Africa.

**1 The Iron Age building of Zimbabwe,** the most famous of its kind in Rhodesia, was built by the Karanga, a Bantu-speaking people, in stages between the 4th and 15th centuries AD. They used patterned dry-stone walling and they modelled soapstone bowls and ceremonial bird figures. Zimbabwe was probably the religious centre for the *mwari* (spiritualist) cults, as well as the commercial centre — organizing mining and the gold, copper and ivory trades together with the Swahili middlemen. Relics recovered from the ruins include Chinese and Persian ceramics, 16th or 17th century Venetian beads and Arab glass and numerous African gold and iron ornaments.

**2 Jan Anthonisz van Riebeeck** (1619–77), first governor of the Cape, landed in Table Bay with about 90 men on 7 April 1652. The first winter months were testing ones for the little band. Illness laid low about half the work force, and there were many deaths. Also, food was extremely scarce for some time. In spite of setbacks, the first permanent fort was soon planned, and 100 men were engaged in its building. By 1662, when Van Riebeeck finally departed, the Cape had not only a fort but also a hospital, workshops, a mill, a granary, houses and fertile land under cultivation. Van Riebeeck and his companions are justly regarded as the founders of the Afrikaner nation.

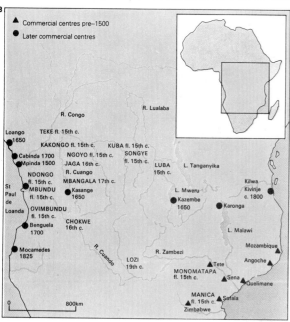

**3 The river systems in southern Africa** played an important part in the movements of early migrants. As early as the 10th century, Swahili settlements already existed on the east coast. In the 14th century, fresh waves of immigrants set up a series of kingdoms in the region of the present-day republics of the Congo and Zaïre and in northern Angola, which gradually extended from the west coast to the shores of the Indian Ocean.

**4 Cape Town** had a purely Dutch appearance until the mid-19th century. This picture dates from about 1888; the stucco-fronted brick houses were massively dominated by Table Mountain, 3.2km (2 miles) long and 1,070m (3,500ft) high.

The "scramble for Africa" was now at its height. There were minor British annexations in 1884. In 1885 Bechuanaland (now Botswana) was proclaimed a Crown colony, and part of Zululand was annexed in 1886. The Nyasaland Protectorate (now Malawi) was proclaimed in 1889, the flag was raised in what is now Rhodesia in 1890, Swaziland was annexed to Transvaal in 1893, Britain claimed Pondoland in 1894, and took over what was later Northern Rhodesia, now Zambia, in 1895.

**The Boer Wars and after**
None of this took place without African resistance nor friction between Boer and Briton and war broke out in 1899. Fewer in numbers and less well-equipped, the Boers showed themselves masters of guerrilla warfare, and only by resorting to a scorched-earth policy was Lord Kitchener (1850–1916) able to overcome them in 1901. The Peace of Vereeniging (31 May 1902) marked the end of the Boer Wars.

The Boers accepted British sovereignty and Britain promised them representative government and £3 million for restocking their farms. In the meantime, the British took over the valuable resources in gold and diamonds. An enlightened policy aimed at the conciliation of the Boers led to self-government in Transvaal and the Orange River Colony in 1906.

On 31 May 1910 the Union of South Africa came into being as a federal state [9] and was given the status of a self-governing dominion on 1 July. The first parliamentary elections were won by the South African Party, and Louis Botha (1862–1919), a prominent Boer general, took office as the first prime minister.

Of the countries of southern Africa, the Union of South Africa stood alone with its wealth in gold and diamonds and, in the wetter regions near the Cape, a flourishing agriculture. By comparison, the Portuguese establishments in Angola and Mozambique were primitive and backward: and the British establishments in Southern and Northern Rhodesia and in Malawi, together with Bechuanaland, Basutoland and Swaziland, were at a pioneering stage.

**The earliest inhabitants** encountered by Europeans at the Cape were Khoisan (Hottentot) cattle herdsmen, who moved in search of grazing, together with groups of San (Bushmen) hunters under their protection, Both adapted to Afrikaner penetration.

**5**

**5 Fort St Sebastian,** on Mozambique Island, was begun by the Portuguese in 1558 and completed by them after 1595. Beyond the ramparts is the Church of Our Lady of the Bulwark, which was built about 1505.

**6 British forces were crushed at Isandlwana,** Natal, during the Zulu War. In January 1879, a mixed British and African contingent was overwhelmed by 24,000 Zulus. Almost all the 800 Europeans were killed. The next day, about 4,000 Zulus attacked some 110 men of the 24th Regiment at nearby Rorke's Drift. The Zulus were heroically beaten off, with 350 dead; the British lost only 17 men in the day's battle.

**6**

**7**

**8**

**9**

**7 Johannesburg, by about 1900,** was already a handsome city. First surveyed in 1886, the site was rocky, lacking in water, and uninhabited. But following the discovery of gold, it developed rapidly. By 1905, it had some 23,000 municipal voters.

**8 Stephanus Johannes Paulus Kruger** (1825–1904), was elected President of the Transvaal in 1883 and served until 1900. He was a consistently uncompromising fighter for Boer independence, and a lifelong and bitter opponent of the British.

**9 The growth of South Africa** can be traced on this map, from its beginnings in Cape Colony under the Dutch East India Company to when it became the Union of South Africa on 31 May 1910 — a country with a parliament subject only to Westminster.

The South African Republic of the Transvaal that had been set up after the Great Trek was ruled by a Boer patriarchy hostile to the British, and Cecil Rhodes tried to install a more amenable régime by supporting the abortive Jameson raid of 1892.

Cape Colony 1854, 1895
Natal 1854, 1895
Orange Free State 1854 boundary
Orange Free State 1895
S. African Rep. 1854, 1895
Boundary Union of South Africa 1910

# Imperialism in the 19th century

The nineteenth century saw a major expansion in European control and influence over the rest of the world. Earlier, important empires had existed in the ancient world and the Spanish, Dutch and Portuguese had established extensive trading empires in the sixteenth and seventeenth centuries. But the nineteenth century was the period of Europe's greatest overseas expansion when European influence was introduced for the first time to a wide variety of races and peoples [Key]. By 1914, more than 500 million people lived under imperial rule [1].

### The rise of Britain
In the course of the eighteenth and early nineteenth centuries, the older empires of Spain, Portugal and Holland entered a decline. A series of revolts freed the Latin American republics from Spanish domination and virtually ended the economic importance of the Spanish Empire. After a sequence of wars in the eighteenth century, culminating in 1815 with the defeat of Napoleonic France, Britain emerged as the strongest maritime nation with substantial colonies and many island possessions.

During the middle years of the nineteenth century, colonial expansion was relatively limited; Britain concentrated on consolidating her hold upon the colonies she already possessed, partly by conceding self-government to the most developed and responsible, such as Canada, and also by military force [7], as in the suppression of the Indian Mutiny of 1857–8. During this period Britain pursued a policy of "informal control", attempting to limit her commitments to those essential to the maintenance of trade, while avoiding large-scale involvements in governing new territories. Thus characteristic British acquisitions of the mid-nineteenth century were positions of strategic or commercial significance, such as trading rights in Singapore, purchased in 1819 from the sultan of Johore, and trade settlements on the African Gold Coast, bought from Denmark in 1850. The British attitude to India was somewhat anomalous. Although many Englishmen were prepared to contemplate the eventual secession of most of her white colonies, the prospect of

India's becoming independent was never actively supported. After the suppression of the Indian Mutiny, the maintenance of India as a vital part of Britain's overseas interests became the lynch-pin of imperial policy.

### The scramble for Africa
By 1870, there were stirrings in several parts of the world that had remained beyond European influence. Africa was being opened by the journeys of the great missionaries and explorers. Technological developments in weaponry and transport and advances in tropical medicine made it easier to penetrate the "dark continent". Once explorers had charted the routes it was inevitable that further European involvement in Africa would follow. The "scramble for Africa" began when, mainly for strategic reasons of safeguarding the main route to India, Great Britain occupied Egypt in 1882 [6]. Within 20 years almost the whole continent had been divided up between the major powers. Economic incentives, strategic concerns, and diplomatic rivalry all played a part in the expansion of European influence. However,

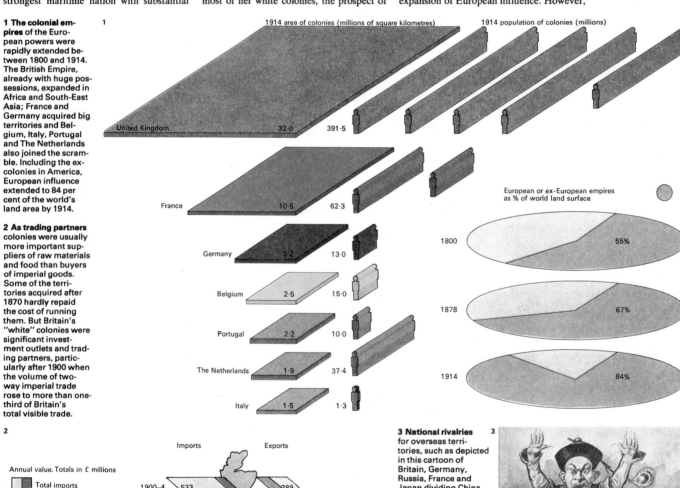

**1 The colonial empires** of the European powers were rapidly extended between 1800 and 1914. The British Empire, already with huge possessions, expanded in Africa and South-East Asia; France and Germany acquired big territories and Belgium, Italy, Portugal and The Netherlands also joined the scramble. Including the ex-colonies in America, European influence extended to 84 per cent of the world's land area by 1914.

1914 area of colonies (millions of square kilometres) | 1914 population of colonies (millions)

| | area | population |
|---|---|---|
| United Kingdom | 32·0 | 391·5 |
| France | 10·5 | 62·3 |
| Germany | 3·2 | 13·0 |
| Belgium | 2·5 | 15·0 |
| Portugal | 2·2 | 10·0 |
| The Netherlands | 1·9 | 37·4 |
| Italy | 1·5 | 1·3 |

European or ex-European empires as % of world land surface

1800 — 55%
1878 — 67%
1914 — 84%

**2 As trading partners** colonies were usually more important suppliers of raw materials and food than buyers of imperial goods. Some of the territories acquired after 1870 hardly repaid the cost of running them. But Britain's "white" colonies were significant investment outlets and trading partners, particularly after 1900 when the volume of two-way imperial trade rose to more than one-third of Britain's total visible trade.

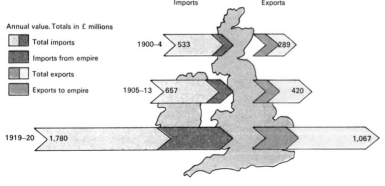

Annual value. Totals in £ millions

Total imports
Imports from empire
Total exports
Exports to empire

Imports | Exports
1900–4  533 | 289
1905–13  657 | 420
1919–20  1,780 | 1,067

**3 National rivalries** for overseas territories, such as depicted in this cartoon of Britain, Germany, Russia, France and Japan dividing China, were often fanned by attitudes at home. In the 1870s the word "jingoism" was coined to describe a belligerent attitude fostered by the rise of mass-circulation papers. British disputes with Russia on the North-West Frontier of India and with France over Sudan in 1898 led to popular support for war, although ultimately it was averted.

the degree to which economic motivation accounts for the rapid expansion of the European empires between 1870 and 1914 has often been overstated. In contrast to the earlier phase of European colonialism, trade [2] now tended to follow the flag rather than act as a direct cause of territorial annexation.

**Strategic and political considerations**
In 1865, a British Parliamentary Committee was prepared to concede influence in the economically important area of West Africa in favour of strategic benefits in the economically poorer East Africa, with its ports on the Indian Ocean. In France, colonial development was largely a preoccupation of the government, a minority of businessmen, the military, and exploration groups, with little active support from the electorate. Similarly in Germany, Bismarck pursued a colonial policy for diplomatic and internal political reasons. As a result, the new territories acquired after 1870 tended to take only a limited part of the export of European capital [4] and population, and provided a relatively small volume of trade, supplying mainly trop-

ical products such as rubber, cocoa and hardwoods.

Although the new imperialism was motivated primarily by political and strategic imperatives, it was fostered by a climate of approval for the "civilizing mission" of the European races. The benefits of trade, Christianity and European rule were considered obvious by many educated people in the imperial nations, providing powerful self-justification for the extension of colonial rule over "primitive" peoples. By the late nineteenth century, the glamour of imperial adventure [5] was taken up by the emerging mass-circulation press to foster "jingoism" and bring pressure to bear on politicians to support aggressive imperialism [3]. But until 1914, in spite of periods of acute tension and rivalry, the partition of Africa and expansion elsewhere was conducted without a major conflict between the European powers. A series of agreements and treaties defined areas of control and spheres of influence, leaving Great Britain with the largest overseas empire, followed in size by those of France and Germany.

**European supremacy overseas** was symbolized by Queen Victoria when she became Empress of India. The greatest imperial expansion of the 19th century, however, took place in Africa.

**4 The growth of European** investment overseas was a major aspect of imperialism after 1870. The most important exporters of capital were Britain, France and Germany. By 1914 they had invested over US 30,000 million dollars in foreign and colonial loans throughout the world. Although some commentators, such as Lenin, saw the search for markets and investment areas as a primary motive for imperial expansion, relatively little European capital went to territories acquired in the period of greatest expansion between 1870 and 1914. France and Germany invested most of their capital outside their colonies, especially in eastern Europe. Half of Britain's overseas capital went to the empire, but it was invested mainly in the "old" empire of the white colonies and India, where it brought in a large revenue which helped pay for Britain's imports of raw materials and food.

Foreign investments 1914 ($1,000 millions)
- North America
- Africa
- Asia
- Oceania
- Latin America
- Europe

**4**
Total 19·8
7·0
2·4
3·5
2·2
3·7
1·0
United Kingdom

Total 9·0
0·5
0·9
1·2
0·1
1·6
4·7
France

Total 5·7
1·1
0·5
0·7
0·9
2·5
Germany

**5 The death of Charles Gordon** (1833–85), a British general, at the hands of Sudanese religious fanatics in Khartoum led to public outrage in England against governmental bungling. Gordon's bravery epitomized the romantic appeal of imperialism, which was seen as providing an outlet for heroism and adventure in exotic parts of the world, whether in seeking new colonies or in garrisoning and protecting existing ones.

**6 The Suez Canal** provided Britain with a reason to add Egypt to its empire in 1882. Constructed by a Frenchman, Ferdinand de Lesseps, the canal was opened in 1869, making a short route from Europe to India. Britain acquired the canal shares in 1875, following the bankruptcy of the Egyptian khedive. A nationalist revolt prompted Britain to intervene and take Egypt under effective control to safeguard the canal.

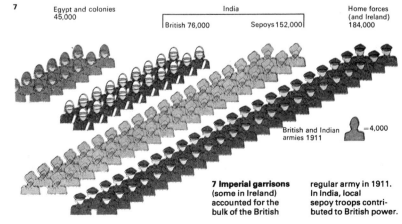

**7**
Egypt and colonies 45,000
India — British 76,000 Sepoys 152,000
Home forces (and Ireland) 184,000

British and Indian armies 1911 = 4,000

**7 Imperial garrisons** (some in Ireland) accounted for the bulk of the British regular army in 1911. In India, local sepoy troops contributed to British power.

# The British Empire in the 19th century

In 1815 Britain was the world's greatest colonial power. Although it had lost the American colonies in the 1700s, it had asserted its claims elsewhere: in British North America, in India, in Southern Africa, and in the valuable sugar islands of the Caribbean. Outposts had also been established in Australasia; the New South Wales's penal colony began in 1788 and missionaries made contact with New Zealand Maoris in 1814.

### The imperial debate

However interested missionaries and merchant traders were in the Empire, government circles and the population as a whole were doubtful of its value. The loss of the American colonies in 1776 and the successful rebellions of Spain's Latin American colonies in the 1820s suggested the notion that as colonies ripened to maturity they fell naturally from the mother tree.

The spectacular growth of trade between the United States and Britain after 1783 demonstrated that trade did not have to follow the flag. From 1815 until the 1870s, it was orthodox opinion that Whitehall should

not impede the gradual devolution of the empire, and only in the last decades of the nineteenth century did Britain once more become a self-consciously imperialist power.

Lord Durham's epoch-making report of 1839, advocating a measure of self-government for Canada [2], set the tone of the early Victorian colonial debate. That debate was conducted not between imperialists and anti-imperialists, but between those who argued for an active policy of dismemberment and those who preferred to leave matters to the course of time. Even Benjamin Disraeli (1804–81), who in the 1870s was to sound the note of the new imperialism, in 1849 described the colonies as a millstone around the mother country's neck.

Between 1815 and 1870 only one-sixth of the £1,000 million in credit accumulated abroad was in the colonies. The cost of their defence lay heavily on the Exchequer, and the abolition of the slave trade in 1807 and of slavery in 1833 ended the triangular trade between Britain, Africa and the New World which had proved so lucrative in the eighteenth century. After the repeal of the Corn

Laws in 1846, therefore, and the decline of protectionism, the old mercantilist system was dismantled.

In other ways, too, colonial ties were weakened. In 1852 New Zealand was granted a self-governing constitution and the Church establishment there was abolished. In Canada, a year later, the lands set aside for the support of the Church were given over to the disposal of the colonial assembly. In 1867 the four provinces of British North America became the united, self-governing confederation of Canada. In South Africa, responsible government was granted to Cape Colony in 1872 and to Natal in 1893.

### India and the new colonies

The exception to this process of relaxation was India. After the Mutiny of 1857, the East India Company lost its share in the government of India, which was placed directly under the Crown department, the Board of Control. Indeed, there was everywhere a sharp distinction drawn between the white settlement colonies, extensions of British stock [3], and the coloured colonies, acquired

**1 The Colonial Office** was established as a separate department in 1812, but began to exert great influence in government only with the appointment of "Mr Over-Secretary", James Stephen (1789–1859) in 1836. He remained there until 1847 as permanent under-secretary, and took the prevailing mid-century view that the colonies were a trust to be upheld, but also a liability bringing the mother country great difficulties and few rewards.

**2 In 1849 English Canadians** burned their parliament building in protest against the Rebellion Losses Bill, which compensated French rebels as well as English loyalists for the loss of property incurred in the Lower Canada rebellion of 1837. That rebellion, and its counterpart in Upper Canada, had been the occasion for Lord Durham's famous report (1839), which recommended granting responsible government to Canada.

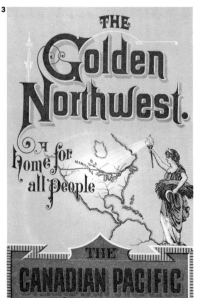

**3 Emigration**, encouraged by reformers such as Edward Gibbon Wakefield (1796–1862) and Thomas Carlyle (1795–1881), eased the population problems in Britain. Most emigrants went to the Americas. The peak decades were the "hungry forties", when more than 1.5 million people left Britain, and the fifties, when the figure was more than 2 million. Many of the emigrants were people driven from Ireland by the great famine of 1845–7 and by the pressure of population in a rural subsistence economy.

**4 Cecil Rhodes**, the greatest imperialist-entrepreneur, built up a huge diamond and gold empire in southern Africa. He also established Southern and Northern Rhodesia as new colonies.

**5 Rudyard Kipling was the bard of the Empire.** His novels and poems were inspired by the glory of imperialism, yet "The White Man's Burden" stressed the awesome responsibility of empire.

by conquest and attracting few permanent emigrants [6].

There was also a distinction between the "formal" empire built up in the eighteenth century and the "informal" empire of the nineteenth century. Missionaries, traders and explorers went into Asia and Africa [Key], and governments were drawn, usually reluctantly, to follow them. The necessity of protecting British commercial interests lay behind the acquisition of Egypt, British New Guinea and North Borneo in the 1880s.

By the 1880s the private companies that carried British influence into the tropical zone had a semi-official sanction. Imperial administration then followed in the wake of commercial penetration. It was the financial empires of men such as Cecil Rhodes (1853–1902) [4] that drew Britain deeper into the whirlpool of southern Africa. The area west of the Transvaal became British in 1885, and the territories that became Southern and Northern Rhodesia were taken over. Kenya and Uganda became British protectorates in the 1890s.

Much of the impetus for this new era of expansion derived from the threat posed to Britain's former trading supremacy by the industrial competition from Germany, France, Belgium and America. Moreover, surplus industrial capital brought a quicker return in Africa than in Britain.

### Consolidation and evolution
The imperial revival, sounded by Rudyard Kipling (1865–1936) [5] and cloaked in the language of civilizing mission, was not an issue that sharply divided the political parties. Voices were raised to argue that the trend of self-government in the white settlement colonies should be halted and the old empire consolidated as a bulwark against foreign competition. Proposals for a permanent imperial council and a revived scheme of colonial preferential tariffs came to nought. Six colonial conferences held between 1887 and 1911 marked the beginning of the general evolution of the Empire [8] into a commonwealth of self-governing states. The value of the conferences was shown by the speed with which the Dominions entered the war on behalf of the Empire in 1914.

The Empire-building of the 19th century was the product of a complex mixture of motives. It was often the work of private individuals – traders, business investors and missionaries, such as this one in Africa – who induced political control to follow in their wake. Quarrels between missionaries, who tended to defend native interests, the less selfless traders and the local populace, drew the government into official supervision of places such as Guinea and Bechuanaland which they would rather have left alone. Imperial ideas at home were very different from those of men overseas.

6 Malay House, photographed in the 1880s, gave governors a residence in the native style. British interest in Malaya began with the East India Company's acquisition of Penang Island in 1786 in search of goods to trade with China. In 1819 Thomas Stamford Raffles (1781–1826) set up a settlement in Singapore. This finally came under the official control of the Colonial Office in 1867.

7 The white colonies assisted Britain in the South African (Boer) War of 1899–1902. Australia became federated and self-governing in 1901. Its states are shown here as cubs supporting the British lion.

8 The British Empire at its greatest extent in 1914 was the largest empire in the history of the world. Although many of the smaller colonies were of little financial benefit to Britain, the larger colonies, especially the "white" ones, were important sources of cheap raw materials for the mother country. There were therefore many vital sea routes to be protected; many of the small islands and African coastal territories acquired in the course of the century had this strategic importance. The most important of these routes was the Suez route to India, which became central to British imperial strategies after Disraeli bought a controlling interest in the Canal for the country in 1875.

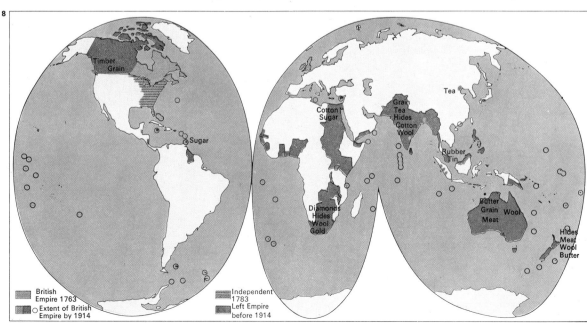

Timber
Grain
Sugar
Cotton
Sugar
Grain
Tea
Hides
Cotton
Wool
Tea
Rubber
Tin
Diamonds
Hides
Wool
Gold
Butter
Grain
Meat
Wool
Hides
Meat
Wool
Butter

British Empire 1763
Extent of British Empire by 1914
Independent 1783
Left Empire before 1914

# The story of the West Indies

During the four voyages of Christopher Columbus (c. 1451–1506) to the Caribbean (1492–1504) Spain asserted its sole right to colonize the region. At first this monopoly, sanctioned by the pope, went unchallenged; Spain settled Cuba, Puerto Rico, Jamaica and Hispaniola (now Haiti and the Dominican Republic). By the 1530s, French, Dutch and English seamen questioned the notion of the Caribbean as a Spanish domain. They began to trade illegally and attacked Spanish shipping and settlements.

## Piracy and colonization

Prominent among the English interlopers were Sir John Hawkins (1532–95), who made three West Indian voyages (1562–8) with African slaves to begin England's involvement in the slave trade, and Sir Francis Drake (c. 1540–96), the most successful raider of all, who sacked Nombre de Dios in Panama (1572) and Santo Domingo in Hispaniola (1585). No attack, however annoying, seriously threatened to undermine Spanish hegemony, but they left a legacy of piracy and buccaneering [2].

Early seventeenth-century treaties with a war-weary Spain gave her confident rivals, so they believed, the right to colonize unoccupied islands without fear of molestation by Spain. These islands were in the eastern Caribbean and their fierce Carib inhabitants did not deter the new colonizers. The English settled in St Kitts in 1624 (sharing it with the French until 1713), Barbados (1627), Nevis (1628), Antigua and Montserrat (1632). The French took Martinique and Guadeloupe (1635); the Dutch, Danes and Brandenburgers settled elsewhere.

These islands had to provide tropical produce for the mother country, a duty they kept until independence. Originally they grew tobacco, cotton and indigo on small holdings worked by a farmer with a few white indentured servants, often Irishmen. But society changed drastically when Dutch entrepreneurs introduced the colonists to Brazilian techniques of large-scale sugar production using slave labour. By the 1660s lucrative plantation slavery [3] was ousting the small farmer and his indentured servants many of whom emigrated to North America; the West Indian population became predominantly African and the islands were bound to the fortunes of a single crop.

## European exploitation

England's capture of Jamaica (1655) [1] attracted capital and planters to this largest British possession in the West Indies. At the same time the French were infiltrating western Hispaniola. Their new colony, St Dominique, became the world's largest sugar producer until its downfall in the Haitian revolution (1791–1803). These sugar colonies became the most prized imperial possessions in the eighteenth century. The remaining Windward Islands were settled in that period: Dominica, Grenada and St Vincent by Britain; St Lucia by France. By 1815 Britain had gained St Lucia, Spanish Trinidad and the mainland Dutch colonies of Berbice, Demerara and Essequibo – the last-named becoming British Guiana (now Guyana) in 1831.

Plantation life was remarkably similar in all sugar colonies. A planter or his deputy, supported by a few white or black overseers,

1 **The British captured Jamaica** with ease in 1655. Oliver Cromwell (1599–1658) had begun a policy of open aggression against Spanish possessions in the Caribbean for the first time since Drake. He first sent a force to attack Santo Domingo, capital of Hispaniola, but the expedition became a fiasco and ended in defeat. To atone for their crushing defeat the commanders decided to attack Jamaica, the most weakly garrisoned Spanish island. A week after they landed, a capitulation was signed. The Spanish troops retreated to the mountains and in alliance with the Maroons, bands of escaped slaves, kept up guerrilla warfare against the English until 1660.

2 **Pirates and buccaneers** terrorized Caribbean shipping in the 17th century. Pirates preyed on any ship but buccaneers usually attacked only Spanish vessels. The buccaneers waged unofficial war even in peacetime, as well as enriching themselves, for England, France and The Netherlands, who supplied their manpower. Henry Morgan (c. 1635–88), one of the most notorious British buccaneers, looted and burnt Spanish-controlled Panama City in 1671. Three years later he was made Lieutenant-Governor of Jamaica. Around the year 1700 policies changed: the buccaneers were suppressed although piracy lingered on.

3 **The plantation** or great house where the proprietor or his deputy, the attorney, lived was usually the only substantial building on an estate, apart from the mill. The plantation houses that were built in the 18th century at the height of West Indian prosperity were often elegant mansions noted for their ostentatious and flamboyant hospitality. They were staffed by numerous house slaves. At a discreet distance from the planter's mansion and hidden from view were the crude huts and barracks that the field slaves retired to at the end of a gruelling day's toil.

4 **The English Harbour, Antigua,** was the largest of the two English naval bases in the West Indies in the 18th century. With Port Royal, Jamaica, it provided an important base for repairs and taking on fresh supplies that the French fleet lacked. This proved a serious handicap in the many wars that England and France fought over the sugar islands and trade in the 18th century. Many islands changed hands several times and nearly all of them were attacked by raiding forces in the bitter fighting.

ruled despotically over an enslaved workforce. There were field slaves, house slaves and craftsmen. Some arrived directly from Africa but an increasing proportion were "Creoles", born in the Caribbean. Uneasily in the middle were mulattos (the offspring of one white parent and one black).

## Periods of adjustment

Humanitarian pressure [5] by reformers such as William Wilberforce (1759–1833) and, perhaps, more profitable opportunities elsewhere for British capital led to the ending of the British slave trade in 1807 and of slavery itself in 1833. There was stiff opposition from planters, who already faced competition from Brazil and Cuba and a new and efficient rival, European beet sugar. The planters sought a new source of labour [6] and finally found it in India. Between 1845 and 1917, 380,000 East Indians, as they are called, went as indentured labour to British Guiana and Trinidad. By 1970 they accounted for 51 per cent of the Guyanese population and 38 per cent of Trinidad's.

In the late nineteenth century, popula-tion pressure mounted as public health measures improved, West Indians began to emigrate. They went to Panama to build the canal and railways, to the plantations of Central America and Cuba, to the oilfields of Venezuela and to the USA.

Persistent poverty in the 1930s, made worse by world depression, led to rioting throughout the British West Indies and stimulated nationalist movements [9]. After World War II and the granting of universal suffrage the territories moved towards independence. A short-lived federation (1958–62) broke up through internal rivalries and countries became independent on their own: Jamaica and Trinidad (1962); Barbados and Guyana (1966); and Grenada (1974). The rest are self-governing with some powers still reserved to Britain.

Meanwhile the former British colonies, now members of the Commonwealth, have been re-defining their political positions. The sugar-producing nations were members of a cartel, formed to guarantee crop prices. Jamaica, Trinidad and Guyana are also members of the non-aligned nations.

Sugar production is both an agricultural and industrial process. Because the sucrose content declines rapidly, harvested sugar cane must be processed without delay. A sugar mill is therefore usually on the estate or near by. The molasses is separated and used in the manufacture of rum. Today, as for the last three centuries, sugar is the major crop in the Caribbean.

5 The Anti-Slavery Society, founded in 1823, brought order and direction to the efforts of religious sects and humanitarian reformers who led the early campaign against slavery. The society was one of the first pressure groups to be formed and more than 200 branches were set up. The society produced a lively magazine, and organized lecture tours by fiery campaigners and returned missionaries kept enthusiasm alight.

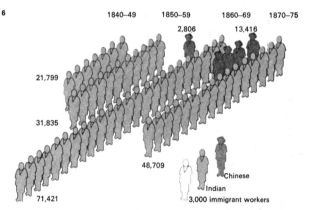

6

| 1840–49 | 1850–59 | 1860–69 | 1870–75 |
|---|---|---|---|
| | | 2,806 | 13,416 |
| 21,799 | | | |
| 31,835 | | | |
| | 48,709 | | Chinese |
| 71,421 | | | Indian |

3,000 immigrant workers

6 Immigrants came from a variety of places to take up jobs in the West Indies after the abolition of slavery led to a shortage of labour. East Indians were the most numerous, but there were also Africans liberated by the Royal Navy from ships smuggling slaves to Cuba and Brazil; Portuguese from Madeira; Chinese and freed blacks from the United States; and West Indians from overcrowded Barbados and the small islands. The Chinese and Madeirans soon moved from the estates mostly into commerce, while the Africans merged with the Creole population after about a generation.

7 About 115,000 West Indians arrived in Britain in the 1950s. After World War II the West Indies had too few jobs for its expanding population. It became increasingly difficult to migrate, as earlier generations had done, to foreign Caribbean islands or the United States because of new restrictions there. But from the mid-1960s West Indian immigration was reduced by restrictions introduced by the British government.

9 Norman Manley, (1893–1969) typified a generation of nationalists who helped their countries to gain independence. Like Eric Williams (1911–  ) of Trinidad and Forbes Burnham (1923–  ) of Guyana, he was educated at an English university. He returned as a barrister to Jamaica where the unrest of the 1930s encouraged him to enter politics. In 1938 he formed the People's National Party, based on Fabian socialism, while a cousin, Alexander Bustamente, founded the rival Jamaican Labour Party. Since then these parties have been the main forces in Jamaican politics. Manley's son, Michael (1923–  ), followed him into politics and became Prime Minister of Jamaica in 1972.

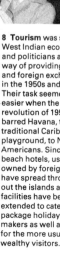

8 Tourism was seen by West Indian economists and politicians as a way of providing jobs and foreign exchange in the 1950s and 1960s. Their task seemed easier when the Cuban revolution of 1959 barred Havana, the traditional Caribbean playground, to North Americans. Since then beach hotels, usually owned by foreigners, have spread throughout the islands and facilities have been extended to cater for package holiday-makers as well as for the more usual, wealthy visitors.

# The story of Canada

Indians and Eskimos inhabited Canada for thousands of years before the first Europeans set foot on its soil. The Indians, migrant from Asia perhaps 20,000 years ago, hunted and fished the vastness of the continent. In the Arctic region the life of the Eskimos, a branch of the same stock, revolved around seals, from which they obtain food, clothing, light and heat. These were the first human inhabitants, and the name of Canada itself comes from the Huron-Iroquois word *Kanata* which Jacques Cartier (1492–1557) noted during his explorations of 1534–5 [1].

## The French influence

About AD 1000 the Vikings became the first Europeans to land in Canada. Little is known about these forays and some 500 years elapsed before details of frequent European contact began to be recorded. In 1497 John Cabot (*c.* 1450–*c.* 1500) under English patronage explored Newfoundland's coastline. He was followed by Cartier who explored the mouth of the St Lawrence River in 1534 and set up the first French settlements, but it was not until after 1600 that permanent bases

were established. Samuel de Champlain (1567–1635) founded a base at Port Royal (present-day Annapolis, Nova Scotia) in 1605 and built a fort at Quebec three years later, thus laying the foundations for French settlement of what was known as New France. The new colony, however, was troubled by Indians and British settlers.

The rivalry between Britain and France in Europe and the Caribbean was also evident in North America, where both had colonies and trading posts [2]. The contest came to a head during the Seven Years War (1756–63). The British wrested Quebec [3] and then Montreal from the French whose position in the continent rapidly worsened. The Peace of Paris (1763) ratified the cession of all France's North American possessions east of the Mississippi, except for Louisiana.

Although the former French colonies now became British possessions, the French-speaking people of Quebec were allowed to keep their Roman Catholic religion and French civil law. British loyalists had flooded northwards during the American Revolution (1776–83) and in an attempt to avoid further

friction between the two communities the British in 1791 created Upper Canada (present-day Ontario) and Lower Canada (present-day Quebec). Upper Canada was predominantly British, Lower Canada predominantly French.

## The road to federation

Politically Canada resulted from a shotgun marriage of English-speaking and French-speaking settlers, but the English were more numerous and had the ear of the British governors. Furthermore, the nineteenth century saw a great influx of immigrants, most of whom came from Britain and the United States; few came from France.

Uprisings in Upper and Lower Canada in 1837 reflected social tension and growing frustration at the restrictions imposed by a system of government with officials appointed for life. Chosen to investigate, Lord Durham (1792–1840) recommended the granting of self-government in local matters and that Upper and Lower Canada be reunited, a union effected in 1840. Eventually, in 1867 the British North American Act

1 **Recorded European exploration of Canada** began with Cabot exploring the eastern coast and Cartier the St Lawrence River. Henry Hudson (*d.* 1611) in 1610 entered the great bay that bears his name. Samuel Hearne (1745–92) was the first white man to go overland from Hudson Bay to the Arctic Ocean. Anthony Henday reached the Rocky Mountains and Alexander Mackenzie (1755–1820) crossed to the Pacific coast in 1793.

Cabot 1497–8
Cartier 1534–5
Hudson 1609–10
Hearne 1770–
Henday 1754–5
Mackenzie 1789–93

0 500km

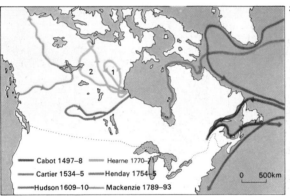

2 **Hudson Bay was** the first site of the company that dominated the early economy of Canada. Founded in 1670, the Hudson's Bay Company had a charter from King Charles II (*r.* 1660–85) to seek a northwest passage to Asia, occupy land around the bay and trade with Indians. The company made huge profits in furs and also served as an outpost of the British Empire, extending its sway throughout the Canadian northwest.

3 **The capture of Quebec in 1759** by Major-General James Wolfe (1727–59) led to the defeat of France and bolstered the British position in North America. Wolfe was only 32 when given command of an expedition to attack Quebec from the St Lawrence and gain it for Britain. He laid siege to the town in June but an assault in July failed. Yet on the night of September 12, British boats eluded the notice of the French sentries and more than 4,000 of Wolfe's men were able to scale the bluff overlooking the river to meet the French in battle next day on the Plains of Abraham. The contest was short and savage, and both Wolfe and the French commander, General Louis Montcalm (1712–59), were mortally wounded.

4 **Canada came into being in 1867** with the union of Upper Canada (Ontario), Lower Canada (Quebec), Nova Scotia and New Brunswick. The western lands, bought from the Hudson's Bay Company, were organized as the North-West Territory and governed from Ottawa. Saskatchewan and Alberta were later created out of it. Newfoundland was more attached to Britain than to Canada and stayed separate until 1949.

Provinces 1867
Added by 1898
Added by 1949
Boundaries 1949
Disputed area
To Canada 1870, 1880

DISTRICT OF FRANKLIN
NORTHWEST TERRITORIES
YUKON TERRITORIES
BRITISH COLUMBIA
ALBERTA
SASKATCHEWAN
MANITOBA
ONTARIO
QUEBEC
NEWFOUNDLAND
PRINCE EDWARD ISLAND
NOVA SCOTIA
NEW BRUNSWICK

0 500km

5 **John A. Macdonald** (1815–91) first prime minister of federal Canada, is regarded as its architect. Born in Scotland, he combined a strong sense of nationhood with political opportunism. He survived a major scandal over receiving campaign funds from a railway contractor to win the 1878 election. He campaigned for a "national policy" of protection for industry by imposing high tariffs, a transcontinental railway and systematic development of the Canadian west.

set up a federal structure for the new nation [4] that was to enjoy a large measure of self-government and dominion status.

### The growth of nationhood

In the twentieth century Canada has come to take an independent stance in international affairs. Recurrent fears of annexation by the United States had been an early spur to the evolution of a distinctive identity. The policies of such prime ministers as Wilfrid Laurier (1841–1919), Robert L. Borden (1854–1937), William Lyon Mackenzie King (1874–1950), Louis St Laurent (1882–1973) and Lester Pearson (1897–1972) were in sympathy with this development.

Canada was the first of the British colonies to assert its claim to full independence this century. In 1919 Canadians were forbidden to accept British titles; in the 1920s Canada opened its first diplomatic post abroad; when asked by Britain to send troops to Chanak in 1922, Mackenzie King refused to do so without first consulting parliament; Canada delayed its entry into World War II to stress the independent nature of the de-

cision; and appeals to the Privy Council in Britain were brought to an end in the 1940s.

There has been a positive dimension to Canada's participation in world affairs. Canada was a founder member of the United Nations (1945) and the North Atlantic Treaty Organization (1949), and Prime Minister Pearson inspired the idea of a UN peacekeeping force in Suez in the mid1950s. Canada established diplomatic links with communist China in 1971, before most nations, and in July 1976 became the wealthiest non-member country to sign a trade agreement with the European Economic Community.

Domestically Indian agitation since 1945 for social and political recognition has led to a number of much-needed reforms including granting the vote to all Indians in 1960. In 1976 the victory of the Parti Québecois in Quebec's provincial elections brought to power a party with an avowedly separatist leadership. The possibility that Quebec may yet secede presents the most significant constitutional challenge to the federation since it was formed a century ago.

**Pierre Trudeau** (1919– ) [right] addressed Congress during his visit to the United States in February 1977. It was an historic occasion: never before had a Canadian Prime Minister been invited to speak before both houses of Congress in assembly. Trudeau was able to assure his audience that he was implacably opposed to Quebec's secession, and that as long as the Canadian people desired it, the unity of the confederation would remain unimpaired. Trudeau's trip took place just one month after the inauguration of US President Jimmy Carter (1924– ) [left] and the leaders discussed Canadian-American matters and broader world issues.

**6**

**6 The Canadian Pacific Railway,** completed in 1885, linked Montreal and Vancouver, quickened settlement and development in the west and helped to instil a spirit of national unity. A stupendous feat by any standards, the line was built by a private firm aided by bank loans and government land grants.

**7 Fewer than 500,000 people** lived in the British North American colonies in 1815, yet by 1850 the population boosted by immigrants topped 2 million. By 1901 it was 5 million. By 1971 it had reached 21.5 million, of which 18.2 million were Canadian-born, including (270,000 Indians, 17,500 Eskimos). Those born in Britain numbered 933,000.

**7**

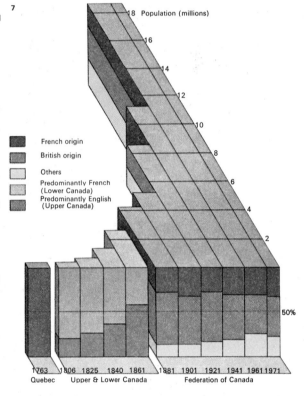

Population (millions)

French origin
British origin
Others
Predominantly French (Lower Canada)
Predominantly English (Upper Canada)

50%

1763 — Quebec
1806  1825  1840  1861 — Upper & Lower Canada
1881  1901  1921  1941  1961  1971 — Federation of Canada

**8 Canada was the sixth largest** trading nation in the world in 1971 but her pattern of trade has changed dramatically during the century. In 1900 more than 50 per cent of exports went to Britain and only 38 per cent to the United States. By the mid-1970s 70 per cent went to the United States and 7 per cent to Britain. Japan and other EEC countries took as much as Britain. The United States supplies 70 per cent of Canada's imports; no other nation provides more than 5 per cent. The largest export earners for Canada are newsprint, wheat, lumber, wood pulp, nickel, aluminium, petroleum, iron ore and copper. Major import items include machinery, car parts, electrical goods, cars and tractors.

**8**

UK
USA
Other Europe
Asia
Other

Imports

| | | | |
|---|---|---|---|
| 6.7% | 12.1% | 10% | 13.2% |
| 3.5% | 2.5% | 3.6% | 7.4% |
| 6.5% | 2.1% | 5.2% | 7.6% |
| 65.7% | 72.9% | 72.9% | 68.7% |
| 17.6% | 10.4% | 8.3% | 3.1% |

Exports

| | | | |
|---|---|---|---|
| 38.6% | 25.8% | 17% | 4.9% |
| | | | 67.8% |
| 36.1% | 38.4% | 58.5% | |
| | 14.5% | | |
| 10.7% | 5.6% | 11.3% | 10.6% |
| 5.9% | 15.7% | 4.3% | 8.7% |
| 8.7% | | 8.9% | 8% |

**9**

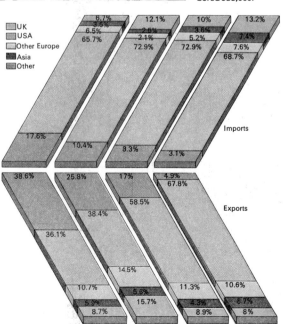

**9 A major diplomatic crisis** developed when President De Gaulle (1890–1970) of France raised the issue of separatism within Canada in 1967. On a visit to Montreal, he addressed a crowd with the slogan: "Vive le Quebec libre". This delighted supporters of the separatist parties, but the government and many more Canadians were simply affronted. In this satirical view of the separation issue, the Parti Québecois leader, René Levesque, is depicted using separatism as a saw cutting through Canada.

# The expansion of Christianity

The spread of Christianity across the world has taken place in stages. The first saw the new religion spread from its birthplace in Palestine into the wider Roman world during the first few centuries of its existence. The second was the early medieval period when the faith survived the tumult of the Dark Ages and most of Europe became Christian. The third stage began in the fifteenth century when European civilization and Christianity turned to the oceans and the lands beyond Islam in the Near East.

## The instrument of conquest

The founding of the Portuguese and Spanish empires in the Americas in the fifteenth century, and along the coastline of Africa, the Indies and the Pacific, gave an immense impetus to the advance of Roman Catholicism. The world was divided by a papal bull in 1493 into spheres of influence for the Catholic crowns of Portugal and Spain and the Church itself became an instrument of conquest and colonization.

In some instances whole populations in the newly discovered lands were forcibly converted and there were other abuses of colonial power. Often the Catholic missions were outspoken critics of these abuses, none more so than the Protector General of the Spanish Caribbean, Bartolomé de las Casas (1474–1566). Catholic advances were not, however, confined to territories formally ruled by Spanish or Portuguese governors.

The foremost Jesuit missionary, Francis Xavier (1506–52), was Papal Nuncio over the Portuguese Indian settlements. He went on to found a mission in Japan and died near Macao, in China. Another Jesuit, Matteo Ricci (1552–1610), was responsible for bringing Catholicism to China, where for a time it enjoyed the protection of the emperors and made many converts. Only in the eighteenth century did squabbles within the Church bring it into disrepute, so that Catholicism was repressed and by the end of the century the numbers of Catholics in China had become much reduced.

The success of the mission to Japan was less impressive. For 50 years from 1587 the Church was severely persecuted, and few Christians survived.

Protestant forms of Christianity were taken to those parts of the world where large numbers of Europeans settled – notably North America (except in French Canada, where the settlers were Catholics), and later South Africa, Australia and New Zealand; but the seventeenth and early eighteenth centuries were a time of dormant missionary activity. The main exception to the lack of interest was the work of the Moravian and other German Pietist groups; these were to inspire later Protestant missionaries.

## Christianity and colonial activity

The second great spurt of missionary activity took place at the end of the eighteenth century and throughout the nineteenth, and was closely connected with the Protestant revival in northwestern Europe. The new Christian advance coincided with the increase of European colonial activity in the generally densely populated, tropical parts of the world, notably India and Africa, and with the ferment of the French and Industrial Revolutions. A spate of well-organized and often financially powerful societies were formed – the British

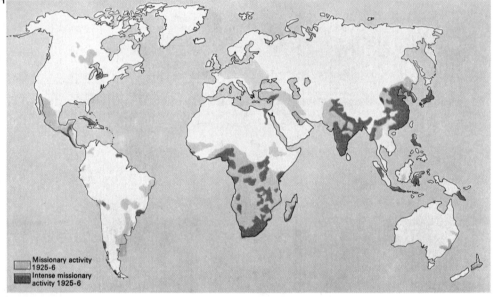

1 **Christian missionary work** greatly expanded from 1815 into the 20th century. As well as a revival of Roman Catholic missions there was an upsurge of Protestant activity, characterized by a notable degree of co-operation. This culminated in the International Missionary Council set up in 1921, which assisted and stimulated missionary activity throughout the world until it merged with the World Council of Churches in 1961. This map shows its activity in the mid-1920s. More than 1,000 million people were claimed to be Christians, in 1965 divided as follows: North America, 226 million; South America, 200 million; Europe, 515 million; Asia, 90 million; Africa, 90 million; Oceania, 7 million.

Missionary activity 1925-6
Intense missionary activity 1925-6

2 **The Church in Brazil,** as in the Spanish colonies, was closely linked to the state despite Rome's influence over the Jesuits. Portuguese churches, such as this one in Salvador, tended to be less oppulent than those built by the Spaniards.

3 **This roadside shrine** in Otovalo, Ecuador, symbolizes the assimilation of religion at grass roots level. The Church, although concerned with Indian welfare, aided their cultural decline by supporting their employment in the mines.

4 **Christianity in Japan** arrived with the Portuguese in the mid-16th century, but its presence became a source of suspicion within a few decades. In 1637, many thousands of Christian converts were massacred. The succeeding isolation of Japan was finally broken in 1858 and missionary work resumed, making notable contributions to education. Hugh Foss, one of the first missionaries, became Bishop of Osaka in 1899. He is seen here [left] with native clergy.

Baptist Missionary Society in 1792, which sent missionaries to India; the Nonconformist London Missionary Society in 1795; The Netherlands Missionary Society in 1797; the Church of England Church Missionary Society in 1799; the American Board of Commissioners for Foreign Missions in 1810; and the Wesleyan Methodist Missionary Society in 1813 (various Scottish Presbyterian societies came together about the same time). The interdenominational Basel Missionary Society, with support from Germany and Switzerland, was founded in 1815. Some of the great names associated with these Protestant missionary societies in Britain were the Baptist William Carey (1761–1834), William Wilberforce (1759–1833), who was also leader in the successful campaign for the abolition of slavery, and David Livingstone (1813–73).

### Catholic revival in the nineteenth century

By the end of the nineteenth century, more than 300 such societies or boards existed. Catholic missionary activity, at first slow to revive, produced an effect as large as that of the Protestants – perhaps, in terms of numbers of converts, even larger. One of the foremost Catholic missionary societies was the mainly French White Fathers.

The result of all these remarkable missionary efforts, which continued from the nineteenth century into the twentieth, was the spread of Christianity over much of the tropical world. It did not make great advances in areas where other religions with claims to universality, particularly Islam, were strong. Indeed, at the same time as the spurt of Christian missionary activity at the end of the 1700s there was a revival of Islam, which made gains on the periphery of the older heartlands of the religion, especially in Indonesia and Africa [5].

Although most of the nineteenth-century missionary societies were rivals, the decline of European imperialism after World War I brought a wider, more international approach. These resulted in the formation of the World Council of Churches in 1948. This body did not include the Roman Catholic Church, but ties between Catholicism and the Council have grown increasingly close.

**The Ibo of southeastern Nigeria**, like a number of ethnic groups in Africa, were receptive to Christianity and education under British colonial and missionary influence in the 19th century. The Christian faith was often merged with existing faiths, which included belief in a creator god as well as numerous other deities and spirits. The mask illustrated reflects this assimilation. Carved in wood it depicts Christ on the cross flanked by angels. The Ibo mask is the basis of a long tradition still vigorously maintained. It is employed in various dramas such as the invocation of the gods, or initiation, as well as specifically Christian festivals.

**5 A mosque in Malawi** [A] stands in stark contrast to its Christian counterpart [B] and marks one point where Islam and Christianity competed for the souls of inhabitants in central Africa.
The church built by the Church of Scotland mission in Blantyre, Malawi, in the late 19th century, symbolizes the permanence of its missionaries' work in the old British central Africa.

**7 British dominions in India** were the focus of increasing missionary endeavour in the late 18th and 19th centuries, initially centred on the work of medical doctors. After the pioneering work of Alexander Duff (1806–78) in Calcutta in the 1830s, Christianity became a central force in the education system established by the British. But it failed to make large inroads into the native religions, especially after the mutiny of 1857–8 led to a new realization of the importance of indigenous culture. Here St Thomas's Cathedral in Madras reflects the uncompromising application of Christianity in the Victorian mould.

**6 Christian spires** dominate the waterfront of Canton, in southern China. It was here that Jesuits arrived in 16th-century China after the successful pioneering work of Matteo Ricci. Canton became an important port of entry into China for later missionaries, who were able to establish colleges and hospitals there.

# India in the 19th century

By the end of the nineteenth century most Englishmen regarded India as being as indissolubly linked to Britain as Yorkshire or Wales. The idea of an independent India was so remote as to be almost unimaginable. The creation of the great Indian Empire was largely accomplished between 1800 and 1860 and many Victorians saw it as Britain's supreme achievement, an essential part of Britain's rise to world power [Key].

## British territorial conquests

After 1800 the British deliberately set about enlarging the territorial conquests that Clive had begun in the mid-eighteenth century [1]. By 1820 they had greatly expanded their holdings in south India and secured their position against the revival of native princes such as Tipu Sultan [2]. In the north of India the same process was carried on more slowly, but no less relentlessly, culminating in the conquest of the Punjab from the Sikhs in 1849 and the annexation of Oudh in 1856.

These great conquests were not inspired by simple avarice. They seemed to follow logically from the efforts of the East India Company (which was the instrument of British power in India until the British government's takeover in 1858) to protect itself against the threats to its trade. For with the decay of the Mogul Empire new states arose more unstable and less friendly to the company, forcing it to rely not on diplomacy but on its own armed strength. Once this process began it was difficult to stop. Raising armies in India required the company to control more land and more people, and to extract more revenue, the main source of which was the tribute traditionally paid by cultivators to their ruler. Thus each new war led to new annexations of land to pay for the company's armies and to ensure that the defeated rajahs and nawabs would not have another opportunity to attack.

Once India was fully under their control the British used its resources, and above all its army (paid for by the Indian taxpayer), for their own wider purposes in Asia, compelling the Chinese to open their ports to British trade [3]. Possession of India became indispensable to Britain's position as a great power east of Suez. But in India itself the British had to devise a system that would enable them to govern its vast area and huge population efficiently and cheaply. It was a novel problem: nowhere else had they attempted to rule people so different in language, culture and religion. And it had to be accomplished using only a very small number of British administrators [5].

The result was that for all the appearance of despotic power the British relied upon the co-operation of Indians: village administration was largely delegated to lesser Indian officials while the good will of rural notables – upon whom fell the main burden of keeping order in the countryside – was vital. This meant turning a blind eye to minor irregularities and preserving, where possible, the existing structure of local power.

## Indian Mutiny: causes and effects

The extension of British control was not accomplished without violent reaction on the part of their Indian subjects, most notably in the mutiny of 1857–8 [4]. Although the mutiny arose initially from the refusal of Indian sepoys (soldiers) to bite open car-

**Map legend:**
British possessions 1805
British acquisitions by 1858
British acquisitions by 1914
Dependent Indian states 1914
Area of mutiny 1857

KASHMIR, PUNJAB, BALUCHISTAN, RAJPUTANA, Delhi, OUDH, ASSAM, SIND, GUJARAT, BIHAR, BENGAL, BURMA, CENTRAL PROVINCES, HYDERABAD, CARNATIC, CEYLON

0 — 800km

1 **British control of India** developed from modest beginnings in small coastal trading stations into an empire that made Britain one of the greatest powers in Asia. Apart from direct administration of the great provinces Britain supervised nearly 600 princely states which were allowed wide autonomy but were carefully prevented from befriending imperial rivals or threatening the basic authority of the British.

2 **Tipu Sahib, Sultan of Mysore,** was an aggressive, expansionist ruler who was a thorn in the side of the British in south India, even allying himself with Napoleon. He died fighting the British in 1799.

3 **Indian opium** was bought by the British in exchange for manufactures and sold in China for silks, spices and tea demanded by British consumers.

4 **The Indian Mutiny of 1857–8** was marked by several fierce battles before British reinforcements arrived and suppressed the sepoys. Although the rising failed from a lack of concerted leadership it took Britain completely by surprise and left a legacy of distrust as well as denting the complacency of British attitudes towards the Indians.

tridges greased with animal fats forbidden to Muslims and Hindus, it swiftly became a much wider rebellion against the side-effects of company dominance: heavier taxation, displacement of Indian magnates from positions of authority and the introduction of laws that abruptly altered the old systems of landholding, rent-paying and tenancy.

For a time British authority all over north and central India swayed in the balance; Lucknow was overrun and Cawnpore besieged. The British restored their authority through the deployment of a large army, the systematic destruction of the hostile sepoy forces and savage punishment for those they considered rebels. But they learned their lesson. They realized that the mutiny had resulted from too rough a handling of the Indian gentry, from the anxieties that too much rapid change had aroused in the Indian population and from Indian fears that the British were planning to attack religious customs and practices.

After the mutiny the British were more careful and administration by the company was replaced by government rule. Headlong changes in law and in the economic character of rural life through new systems of taxation were slowed down or stopped altogether. The wholesale demolition of the remaining princely states was halted and the rajahs and princes were promised security in return for their swearing allegiance to Queen Victoria.

## Stirrings of independence

By the later nineteenth century the whole spirit of British rule in India had changed. The British gave up the hope that social change and education would quickly and smoothly turn Indians into "brown Englishmen" and India into a modern society. Administrators [7] concentrated on keeping the status quo so as not to risk their power. This could not work for long. India had been opened up to the outside world and flooded with British goods and British ideas. In the big towns, economic change produced Westernized Indians who wanted a say in government. In 1885 men such as these founded the Indian National Congress and in doing so began, unwittingly, the long struggle for independence.

**Stable British rule in India** was underlined when Queen Victoria became Empress of India in 1876, at Benjamin Disraeli's suggestion. The event was depicted in a contemporary cartoon.

**5 A British magistrate on tour** represented a focal point of authority. Great value was attached to keeping in touch with local headmen and other important Indians in rural districts.

**6 British and Indian troops** on the North-West Frontier were deployed in large numbers in attempts to check the historical incursions of mountain tribesmen into the plains of northern India. When the British became rulers of India they were determined to subdue the unruly hillmen. They also feared that their great rivals in central Asia, the Russians, would try to undermine their power in India using Afghanistan as an ally. Desperate rear-guard actions, such as that depicted in W. B. Wollen's painting "Last Stand of the 44th Foot at Gandamuk", followed some Afghan campaigns.

**7 Lord Curzon, Viceroy of India** from 1898 to 1905, symbolized the pomp and circumstance of British rule. Although an untiring administrator he found the task of governing India frustrating and his autocratic ways were resented.

**8 Indian economic life** continued largely unchanged in villages during British rule. Better communications, however, did help to combat the scourge of famine and to stimulate the growth of large cities such as Calcutta and Bombay.

**9 Simla became the summer capital** of the British central administration in India after 1864. Lying in the Himalayan foothills, its bracing climate was a relief from the heat of the plains. It became a resort where British administrators, army officers and their families, isolated in their districts for most of the year, could enjoy a wider (and sometimes disreputable) social life. The hilly site became a status key: senior officials lived higher up.

# Africa in the 19th century

The nineteenth century was a period of great and often rapid change for much of Africa, set in motion either by Africans themselves or by outsiders, especially Europeans. The partition of almost the whole continent among seven European states took place in the last 20 years of the century. The previous 80 years saw largely a continuation of trends already long established. Tiny trading "factories" (or castles) set up by European slave traders dotted the west coast of Africa, from Cape Verde to the Congo estuary [1]. On the southern tip of the continent, Britain had taken over the settlement of the Dutch East India Company at the Cape.

## Foretaste of expansionism

The extension of European influence was gradual: in 1820–22 Egypt, technically an Ottoman dependency, conquered the Nilotic Sudan; in 1830 the French invaded the Ottoman dependency of Algiers and began the long, costly process of conquering it; and in the late 1830s Dutch farmers known as Boers trekked deep into the interior of southern Africa, away from British control.

With the abolition of the slave trade by most European countries late in the 1800s, trade in palm oil and other tropical products largely replaced it in West Africa. Only the French on the River Senegal expanded fairly deep into the interior; but missionaries were active, especially in areas settled by freed slaves, such as Sierra Leone [7].

Islam had so long penetrated what is known as the Sudanic belt of Africa that by the beginning of the nineteenth century it was thoroughly "Africanized". Much of this region was swept, from the eighteenth century on, by a wave of religious revival, spearheaded by holy wars, *jihads*, waged against black Muslims as much as against pagans. A *jihad* in 1804 rapidly conquered all the old Hausa city states (such as Kano) and beyond and led to the establishment of a huge new empire, the Sokoto caliphate, which survived until taken over by the British in northern Nigeria in 1903. Other Muslim empires were created on the middle Niger and in what is now Guinea and the Ivory Coast, where prolonged opposition was encountered by French invaders in the

1880s. South of the Sudanic belt, several great kingdoms, such as Ashanti and Dahomey, continued to expand and prosper (and offered vigorous resistance to the British and French respectively), while others began to disintegrate.

## Rise of Ethiopia and the Zulus

In Ethiopia, the ancient Christian Amhara Empire, after a period of prolonged feebleness, slowly and painfully recovered during the reigns of three forceful emperors – Theodore (reigned 1855–68), Johannes IV (reigned 1868–89) and Menelik (reigned 1889–1911). These rulers asserted their power against that of the mighty landed aristocracy and the Coptic Church. Menelik [5] not only maintained his position against the powerful northern barons and greatly expanded the boundaries of Ethiopia in the south, but beat off an Italian attempt to conquer his state, at the Battle of Adowa (1896).

In 1818 in southern Africa, Shaka (c. 1787–1828) became king of a small group, known as the Zulu and, by revolutionizing the military and social structure of his people,

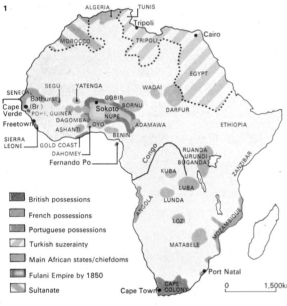

1 **European possessions in Africa in 1830** were few. France had invaded Algeria (1830) and some Boer (Dutch) settlers were trekking out of the British Cape Colony into the hinterland of South Africa. Britain and France had a few tiny colonies in West Africa – Senegal, Sierra Leone and Gold Coast. Apart from Europeans on trading posts, only the Portuguese had old-established colonies – in coastal parts of Angola and up the Zambezi valley of Mozambique. Although the Egyptians had conquered the Nilotic Sudan in 1821, the rest of the continent consisted of African empires, kingdoms and peoples who still maintained their independence.

British possessions
French possessions
Portuguese possessions
Turkish suzerainty
Main African states/chiefdoms
Fulani Empire by 1850
Sultanate

2 **An idealized view of European influence** appears in this picture of the British explorer John Speke (1827–64) with King Mutesa of Buganda. Men like Speke, who found the source of the Nile in 1858, played an essential role in opening up Africa to Europeans. Two Scottish explorers were James Bruce (1730–94) who went to Ethiopia and the Sudan, and Mungo Park (1771–1806) in West Africa early in the 19th century. Heinrich Barth in northern and western Africa, David Livingstone in central and eastern Africa and H. M. Stanley, who found Livingstone in 1872 and journeyed down the Congo, were dominant in the middle of the century.

3 **The storming of Magdala,** a mountain citadel in Ethiopia by British forces in 1868 was one of the most extravagant episodes in the history of relations between Europeans and Africans in the 19th century. An expedition under General Napier invaded Ethiopia to punish its emperor, Theodore (or Tewodoros) for briefly holding prisoner a British consul and some Europeans. After Magdala fell, the emperor dramatically committed suicide and the expedition then withdrew.

4 **This Ethiopian village** has hardly changed at all since the last century. Then, as a community of peasant cultivators producing little more than what was necessary for subsistence, it would have been typical of rural Africa.

fashioned a formidable and ruthless military state which rapidly conquered surrounding people. Offshoots of the Zulu, and other groups who copied their techniques, rampaged over much of southern and central Africa in mass population movements and tribal regroupings, known as the *mfecane*, the Time of Troubles.

### Explorers and imperialists

During the middle years of the nineteenth century Africa was gradually becoming better known to Europeans through the efforts of many courageous travellers [2], such as the German scientist Heinrich Barth (1821–65), in the Sudanic regions, and the Scotsman David Livingstone (1813–73), whose travels were partly motivated by his concern over the ravages of the Arab slave trade in central and east Africa. The Welsh-American explorer Henry Morton Stanley (1841–1904) was more concerned with exploitation. In 1877 he completed an epic journey down the River Congo – and then sold his services to King Leopold II of the Belgians (1835–1909).

By this time bitter trading rivalries had grown up between Britain and France in West Africa, stimulated by British occupation of Egypt in 1882. Motivated largely by politics, a rush for African colonies began with Britain and France in the forefront, followed by Belgium and Germany, and with Portugal, Spain and Italy bringing up the rear. In many areas the conquest of Africa met with intense opposition and vicious wars of "pacification" were mounted. But resistance [3] was seldom more than local, and could be dealt with piecemeal.

In southern and central Africa the main impetus for British expansion was provided by Cecil Rhodes (1853–1902), who, from a base in the Cape Colony, appropriated a vast private empire for himself (as did King Leopold in the Congo/Zaïre). The two independent Boer republics of the Transvaal and Orange Free State were annexed in a war that fully extended the power of the British Army (the Anglo-Boer War, 1899–1902). By the turn of the century the whole of Africa, except for Ethiopia and Liberia, had been conquered by Europeans [9].

**Moshweshwe** (*c.* 1786–1870) was the founder of the Sotho nation (Lesotho) in southern Africa, and an example of how African rulers adopted practices and ideas introduced by Europeans. Moshweshwe emerged as leader of the Sotho, a small group of people who found refuge in the Drakensberg Mountains from the devastation produced in the interior of southern Africa by the Zulu and other warrior kingdoms in the 1820s. He was a man of peace, and ensured the protection of his people through wise diplomacy. Lesotho rapidly increased in prosperity, making use of European techniques. It was a British protectorate from 1868 until its independence in 1966.

**5 Emperor Menelik** (1844–1913) successfully maintained the independence of Ethiopia against European encroachment. In 1896 his forces defeated an Italian invasion at the Battle of Adowa.

**6 Mochudi in Botswana** was one of several large towns to develop long before the coming of Europeans – notably in the Sudanic belt, Yorubaland in West Africa, Botswana and southern Africa.

**7 Freetown, capital of Sierra Leone,** was typical of European coastal towns in tropical West Africa. It was built in colonial style with churches, business centres and separate areas for whites and blacks.

**8 Johannesburg in South Africa** grew from a farm on the veld to a sprawling city by 1900. The discovery of gold in the Boer Republic of the Transvaal in the mid-1880s led to rapid development.

**9 A map of Africa in 1914** shows how it had become partitioned among seven European countries. This partition was a rapid process taking place during the last 20 years of the 19th century. Only Ethiopia and Liberia remained independent of European rule. Although some territories were termed protectorates (like Uganda and Morocco) rather than colonies, Europeans were firmly in control. The four white-ruled colonies in South Africa had formed a Union in 1910 but remained a British dominion. Colonial boundaries drawn up entirely by Europeans were often merely straight lines on the map. This caused great problems when Africa regained independence.

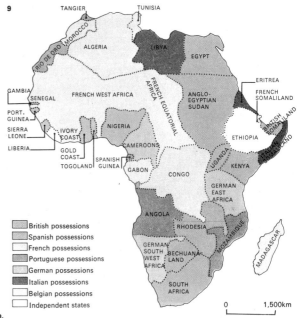

**9**

Map legend:

- British possessions
- Spanish possessions
- French possessions
- Portuguese possessions
- German possessions
- Italian possessions
- Belgian possessions
- Independent states

0   1,500km

# The opening up of China

Two changes in China during the nineteenth century gave that country an impetus towards the revolution that flowered in the twentieth century. One that was not new in Chinese history was the decay of a dynasty – the Manchu (Ch'ing), founded in 1644. What was new, confusing and finally explosive was the challenge of Western power and technology.

## The "unequal treaties"

The opening up by the West of the closed, Confucian, agrarian society of China began with the first "Opium War" of 1839–42, during which Britain crushed a Manchu attempt to stop illegal trade in opium through Canton, then the only point of Chinese contact with the money economy of the West. The resulting Treaty of Nanking (which also gave Britain a foothold in Hong Kong) was the first of the so-called unequal treaties. They eventually forced China to grant trade and territorial rights to Western powers, legalize the trade in opium and permit missionaries [4] to spread Christianity throughout the country. After pressure by France and Britain in 1856–60, China even

had to grant Europeans a diplomatic quarter in Peking, implying equality with a country whose emperor had been a guardian of civilization for a thousand years and had always received tribute from inferior "barbarian" countries.

The disruptive impact of the West on the traditional pattern of Chinese life coincided with a chaotic situation in the countryside. Rural misery was accentuated by the massive population rise of the eighteenth century [1] combined with a weak and corrupt administration which neglected its duties to maintain grain reserves and irrigation. In reaction, China was swept by a series of risings against the Manchus, beginning with the Taiping Rebellion (1850–64). Virtually a civil war, this rising was suppressed only with the deaths of at least 25 million people in the lower Yangtze provinces [2]. Other rebellions soon followed, such as those of the Nien in north-central China and the Chinese Muslims in the southwest and northwest, which were suppressed by 1875.

Meanwhile, the Western-administered treaty ports, and the foreign missions

spreading all over the country, steadily eroded Chinese sovereignty. In the 1860s a serious attempt was made to reinvigorate the dynasty. But this "restoration" failed to transform the conservative thinking of a court already influenced by the autocratic and dogmatic Tz'u Hsi (1835–1908) who became the Empress Dowager.

## Slow technological progress

The "self-strengthening movement" that accompanied the restoration period began with the construction of arsenals, railways and dockyards in the 1860s [3] and went on with early moves for industrialization in the 1870s. But compared with Japan's speedy industrialization, China's was slow and unsure of its direction. Anti-Western feeling grew, often heightened by antagonism to Chinese "rice Christians" who took their own pickings from the privileges exacted by foreigners. Incidents in which Westerners were attacked embittered relations between the Chinese government and foreign powers. The need to learn from the West and to introduce fundamental changes was widely recog-

**1 China's population growth** between 1750 and 1850 was immense, although the figures are unreliable. Growing land hunger in an overwhelmingly peasant economy coincided with worsening administration.

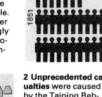
1 Pop. in 20 millions
1741
1851

**2 Unprecedented casualties** were caused by the Taiping Rebellion (1850–64), two Muslim risings and a north China drought in 1876–9 which led to famine and millions of deaths by disease.

2 Deaths in 3 millions
1850-64 : 25 million
1856 and 1862-75 : 8 million
1876-9 : 13 million

**3 A "self-strengthening" movement** aimed at increasing military strength to overcome Western power was launched in 1860. The build-up of armaments and improvement of railways were continued during the 1870s with moves to lay the foundation for a modern industry run by the mandarin class. Textile mills, a shipping company and an iron and steel works were established as well as smaller industries.

**4 Some missionaries** aroused Chinese hatred and stimulated nationalism. But some, such as the Welsh missionary Timothy Richard, also brought new ideas and won respect for their dedicated help.

4 Missionaries to China
1870 350 missionaries
1910 4,000 missionaries

**5 Chinese students** began to go to America in 1872 but the real flow to Western universities began only after 1919. Until then, Japan was the source of modern thought for a generation of Chinese.

5 Students to Japan
1900 500
1910 10,000

**6 Li Hung-chang** (1823–1901) became China's Foreign Minister after the former "Office for Barbarians" gave way to an office for "foreign matters" in 1861. He made his reputation commanding an army against the Taiping rebels and later revealed a talent for diplomacy which was acknowledged by Western powers with whom he negotiated from a position of weakness. Founder of the Chinese navy, he advanced China's interests by visiting Europe.

7 ☐ Russian influence
☐ British
☐ French
☐ Japanese
☐ German
▨ Russian possessions
▨ British
▨ French
▨ Japanese
☐ German
⌇⌇ The Great Wall
— Boxer Rebellion 1900
⋯⋯ Railways
  First treaty ports 1842
• Later treaty ports
+ Christian missions

1900
RUSSIAN EMPIRE
MANCHURIA
OUTER MONGOLIA
SIN KIANG
INNER MONGOLIA
Peking
Niu-chuang
Tientsin
Lu-ta
KOREA
Chefoo
Weihaiwei
Tsingtao
TIBET
NEPAL
Nanking
Chinkiang
Ichang
Hankow
Wuhu
Soochow
Shanghai
Shasi
Hangchow
Ningpo
Yangtze
Chungking
Kiukiang
Wenchow
BHUTAN
Foochow
Tengchung
Hungshui-Ho
Mengtsz
Lungchow
Amoy
Formosa
Szemao
Canton
Swatow
Pescadores Islands
BURMA
Nanning
Macao (Port.)
Kowloon
Hong Kong
Pakhoi
Kiungchow
INDOCHINA
SIAM
Hainan
0    750km

**7 Foreign influence** never extended to rule over China. But "treaty ports" such as Shanghai, Tientsin and others inland were administered, policed and taxed by foreigners. Chinese living in them were outside their government's jurisdiction. The diplomatic quarter of Peking itself was foreign administered until 1947. Towards the end of the 19th century key areas were divided up into "spheres of influence". Foreign missions and consulates abounded. While the coastal cities prospered, China's peasant economy suffered from foreign imports. Rural areas were drained of talent and the exactions of absentee landlords increased.

nized only in 1895 when China was humiliatingly defeated by Japan [8].

In the treaty ports new middlemen in foreign trade were, those patriots who knew what changes were needed. Sun Yatsen (1866–1925), educated in Hawaii and Hong Kong, preached nationalism, and mandarins such as K'ang Yü-wei (1858–1927) backed the young Kuang Hsu Emperor (reigned 1875–1908) in reform edicts in 1898. But the Empress Dowager imprisoned her son and assumed power.

**The end of the old China**
Competing European imperialists now threatened to partition China – a scramble halted only by an American-inspired "Open Door" policy by which the Western powers agreed to restrain their territorial ambitions in return for open trade. Meanwhile fierce anti-foreign rioting broke out in 1900 when the court diverted a rising by the secret society of the "righteous and harmonious fist" against Westerners. Known as the Boxer Rebellion, this cost the lives of nearly 250 missionaries and thousands of Chinese

Christians before it was suppressed by an international army.

The old China was finished however, outmoded and discredited. The archaic civil service examination system was abolished in 1905 and the Manchu dynasty hastily abdicated after a provincial revolt in 1911. The formula for a viable Chinese republic did not yet exist. A parliament headed by Sun Yatsen immediately gave way to rule by a former Manchu commander, Yüan Shih-k'ai (1859–1916). A decade of rule by rival warlords followed.

The intellectual consensus needed for change was emerging, however. Sun Yat-sen [10] refounded his movement as the Kuomintang Party and thousands of students educated overseas [5] or at new universities were influenced by liberal teachers such as Ch'en Tu-Hsiu (1879–1942) and Hu Shih (1891–1962) [11]. When China's weak government accepted concessions to Japan imposed after World War I (in which China had taken little part), student protest on 4 May 1919 launched a revolutionary nationalism [11] that set China alight.

**A common Western attitude to China** in the nineteenth century was summed up in a cartoon of the Western powers shaking the corpulent body of China. After the 1840 Opium War contempt for the China of the Manchu emperors began to replace the admiration held by eighteenth-century Europe for the achievements of Chinese civilization. By the 1890s when nations such as Germany, Russia, Japan, Britain and France were scrambling for territorial rights, most Europeans thought "this rotten old hulk" would break up and be remade by Western enterprise. Few perceived the enduring strength of Chinese civilization beneath the decay.

**8 After the Sino-Japanese War** of 1894–5 China sued for peace (as seen in a Japanese drawing). Joining the Western powers in their demands on China, the Japanese had disrupted China's sphere of influence in Korea. In the war that followed, the Chinese were easily beaten and had to cede Formosa to Japan. This stimulated Chinese shame and nationalism more than earlier defeats inflicted by Britain and France because the Chinese had always regarded the Japanese as inferiors who had adopted Chinese culture a thousand years before. But Japan's modernization after 1868 sent its military and industrial power far ahead.

**9 Chinese dislike of foreigners** is shown in an 1891 cartoon of a pig as a Chinese Christian and goats as foreigners being slaughtered. Earlier in the nineteenth century, foreigners were almost unknown; most Chinese lived and died without seeing one. Christianity made little appeal to the Chinese.

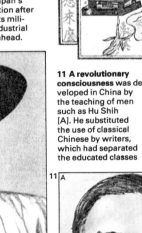

**10 Intellectual leaders** played a vital role in changing Chinese attitudes to the structure of government and society after the old China was swept away in the turbulence that followed the death of the Empress Dowager in 1908. The next decade brought together strands of nationalism, cultural change and revolution. Sun Yatsen [A] was an outsider to the Chinese classical tradition and the world of the mandarin. Affected by Victorian progress he wanted to modernize China. His magnetic personality built up a mixed following in the secret societies. Supported in Japan and welcomed in the West where his Christianity and good English helped, his tenacity finally won mass backing after 1919. Ch'en Tu-Hsiu [B] was a more revolutionary intellectual. When he founded the influential "New Youth" in 1915, he favoured "Mr Science and Mr Democracy" but by 1921 he had emerged as the first leader of the rising Chinese Communist Party.

**11 A revolutionary consciousness** was developed in China by the teaching of men such as Hu Shih [A]. He substituted the use of classical Chinese by writers, which had separated the educated classes from others, with the vernacular. A pragmatic thinker who studied in America, he remained the spokesman of Western liberalism but influenced the future communist leader of China [B], the young Mao Tse-tung (1893–1976), who was snubbed by professors when he went to Peking University as a library assistant. For Mao's generation of students 1919 was the year of revolutionary awakening.

# Japan: the Meiji Restoration

Until the middle of the nineteenth century Japan had been closed to the outside world for more than 200 years. Only the Chinese and the Dutch were allowed limited trading access to one port, Nagasaki. It was Commodore Matthew Perry in command of a squadron of United States warships who, during visits in 1853 and 1854, cajoled a reluctant shōgunate – Japan's military government – into opening two ports to American shipping. Other powers soon followed the American lead; within a few years Japan's self-imposed seclusion was over.

## Civil war and a new capital

The intrusion into Japan by the Western world mortally harmed the prestige of the Tokugawa Shōgunate which, under pressure, signed treaties granting extraterritorial rights and tariff privileges to the foreign powers [3]. The imperial court at Kyōto, universally revered but possessing no effective power of its own, became the focus of loyalty for those samurai (warriors) who called for the expulsion of the alien "barbarians". After some years of complicated domestic strife the shōgunate was overthrown in 1868 by an alliance of provincial lords and warriors from domains in southwest Japan. Their successful civil war was fought in the name of the youthful ´Emperor Meiji – "enlightened rule". He was installed in the shōgun's castle at Yedo which was renamed Tokyo and made the new capital.

By this political upheaval, known as the Meiji Restoration, governing powers were restored, although in name only, to the imperial house. It marked the beginning of Japan's transformation from a feudal society to a modern state. The new government, an oligarchy of relatively young samurai, resolved to bring Japan up to the technological level of Europe and the United States.

## Japan's industrial revolution

Foreign teachers and specialists of every kind, skilled in the techniques of Western civilization, were invited to Japan; and Japanese in large numbers went abroad to study [2]. Remarkable progress in modernization was made within two decades [1]. The cotton-spinning industry provides a striking example. In the 1870s annual production, increasing yearly, barely exceeded 2,000 bales, but the figure for 1889 was 142,000 bales; ten years later it was 750,000 bales. Comparable growth occurred in many other sectors of manufacturing industry. Almost none of this early expansion was financed by borrowing abroad – instead the cost fell heavily on the rural areas.

Japan's industrial revolution was broadly completed by the eve of World War I and within the lifetime of some of the leading figures of the Meiji Restoration. Political change was symbolized by the Constitution of 1889 which established a diet (parliament) of two chambers. But the Meiji Constitution was authoritarian in letter and spirit. The upper house of the diet was non-elected and until after World War I members of the lower house were elected on a limited suffrage. Cabinet ministers were responsible only to the emperor, not the diet, and the war and navy ministers were always generals and admirals representing services strongly imbued with the samurai martial spirit.

The same spirit was also perceptible

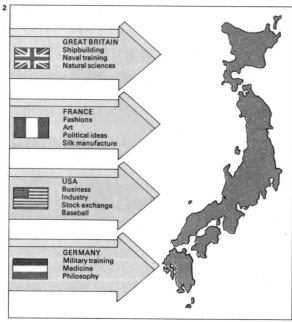

**1 The first Japanese railway line,** completed in 1872, was built by British engineers and covered the 29km (18 miles) between the capital, Tokyo, and Yokohama. Railways played a particularly important role in the modernization of Japan for in pre-Meiji days there was very little wheeled traffic along the roads. Commerce between the main centres of the country was mainly seaborne. The growth of the railway system in 32 years was rapid: in 1886 there were 692km (430 miles) of track; in 1896, 4,007km (2,490 miles) and in 1906, 8,494km (5,278 miles). By 1918 the total was more than 14,480km (9,000 miles) of working track.

**2 The greatest contributions** to Japan's modernization were made by Great Britain, the USA, Germany, France, Russia and Italy. Britain trained the Japanese navy and influenced other maritime activities. The USA influenced such areas as business and education. France and Germany trained the army; Russia and Italy influenced the arts.

GREAT BRITAIN
Shipbuilding
Naval training
Natural sciences

FRANCE
Fashions
Art
Political ideas
Silk manufacture

USA
Business
Industry
Stock exchange
Baseball

GERMANY
Military training
Medicine
Philosophy

**3 Japan's first important diplomatic** mission abroad in 1871 was led by Prince Iwakura. In the United States and Europe the aim of the mission was to persuade the Western powers to revise the "unequal treaties" they had signed with Japan. But the Japanese had to wait nearly 30 years before they could secure treaty revision and thereby obtain tariff autonomy and the abolition of extraterritorial privileges. This picture of Iwakura's departure to Yokohama illustrates Japanese society obviously in a state of transition. Some of the men are wearing Western suits, while their companions still favour the traditional "top-knot" hairstyle and carry the samurai (warrior) sword.

among the people at large for the state education system gave great importance to loyalty and patriotism. The effectiveness of such indoctrination was illustrated by the events of the Sino-Japanese War of 1894–5 and the Russo–Japanese War of 1904–5.

## Military and naval supremacy

In both struggles the Japanese surprised the world with their victories on land and sea, of which the most dramatic was the destruction of the Russian fleet off Tsushima in May 1905 by Admiral Togo (1847–1934) [5]. This masterly demonstration of naval supremacy won Japan acceptance as a great power.

The Sino-Japanese War had arisen from rivalries in Korea. Japan's victory gave her possession of Formosa and eliminated Chinese influence in Korea. In 1904 the reason for war was again largely Korea. Russia, occupying key points in Manchuria, seemed about to penetrate Korea, still nominally an independent state, although then dominated economically and politically by Japan. By the Treaty of Portsmouth (New Hampshire) in the United States, which

ended the Russo-Japanese War, Japan acquired south Sakhalin and inherited Russia's lease of Port Arthur and her valuable rights and interests in south Manchuria. This setback for Russian power in the Far East sealed the fate of Korea, which was finally annexed by Japan in 1910 [7].

Emperor Meiji died in 1912 [6]. Due to ill health the new ruler (Taisho) was a mere figurehead. The Anglo-Japanese Alliance, first concluded in 1902 as a gesture of solidarity against Russian ambitions in Asia, brought Japan into World War I on the British side. Japanese forces captured Germany's leased port in China, Tsingtao, and occupied her island possessions in the Pacific. While the European powers fought each other, Japan partly extended its influence over a weak and divided China.

At the 1919 Paris Peace Conference, Japan was given a permanent seat on the Council of the newly created League of Nations, which amounted to full recognition of Japan's status as a world power. In the space of 50 years the aims of the early Meiji modernizers had been achieved.

KEY

The Japanese battleship *Kashima* (16,660 tonnes; four 12in guns) was built by Elswick shipyard and launched at Newcastle in 1905. Until the Russo-Japanese War all Japan's larger warships were built abroad, the majority of them in Britain.
The last was the battlecruiser *Kongo* (27,500 tonnes; eight 14in guns) launched by Vickers Armstrong, Barrow-in-Furness, in 1913.

4 Japanese aggression against Russia and Japan's reliance on foreign military aid was ridiculed in this Russian cartoon of 1904. Although Britain supported Japan, diplomatically and with arms, the United States was not in fact directly involved and in the following year President Roosevelt (1858–1919) acted as mediator between the two belligerents. Despite the confidence of the Russian defenders in this picture, their fleet was destroyed in May 1905.

5 Admiral Togo Heihachiro, a national hero after his annihilation of the Russian Baltic fleet at Tsushima in 1905, was revered almost as much in Britain as in Japan. Trained in England in HMS *Worcester*, he based his signal at Tsushima – "On this battle will depend the fate of our empire" – on Nelson's famous signal at Trafalgar exactly one century earlier. He was created count in 1907 and died in 1934, aged 87.

6 The death of the Emperor Meiji in 1912 marked the end of Japan's "Victorian age". The funeral procession in Tokyo took place at night, the coffin being carried on an oxwagon from the palace to Tokyo Station. Enormous silent crowds kneeled respectfully as it passed. Interment was at Momoyama near Kyōto. A detachment of Royal Marines took part in the funeral procession.

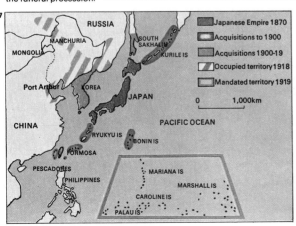

7 The expansion of Japanese territory at the end of the 19th and in the early part of the 20th century was a result of both war and treaties. In 1875 the Kurile Islands were acquired from Russia by treaty in exchange for abandonment of Japanese claims on Sakhalin. Formosa was won in the Sino-Japanese War; south Sakhalin, lease of Port Arthur and rights in south Manchuria in the Russo-Japanese War. Korea was annexed in 1910.

Japanese Empire 1870
Acquisitions to 1900
Acquisitions 1900-19
Occupied territory 1918
Mandated territory 1919

0        1,000km

RUSSIA
MANCHURIA
MONGOLIA
SOUTH SAKHALIN
KURILE IS
Port Arthur
KOREA
JAPAN
CHINA
PACIFIC OCEAN
RYUKYU IS
BONIN IS
FORMOSA
PESCADORES
PHILIPPINES
MARIANA IS
MARSHALL IS
CAROLINE IS
PALAU IS

8 The Yawata Ironworks in northern Kyushu (completed in 1901) was for many years the main steel-producing plant in Japan. Production of iron and steel on a large scale began relatively late because Japan was deficient in natural resources such as iron ore and coking coal. The need for these materials, essential to Japan's industrialization, was one of the reasons for Japan's aggressive interest in both Manchuria and China.

# USA: the opening up of the West

During the first half of the nineteenth century, the United States grew from a small cluster of 13 states huddled against the Atlantic coast into one of the largest nations on earth, extending from the shores of the Atlantic to the shores of the Pacific, and from Canada in the north to Mexico and the Gulf of Mexico in the south [Key].

### Frontiersmen and settlers

The opening of the West began as a scattered penetration by hunters and explorers into the areas immediately adjacent to the coastal settlements. Even before the Revolution, men such as Daniel Boone (1734–1820), who crossed the Appalachians to scout out Kentucky, blazed trails through unknown regions. They and their successors drifted into the Shenandoah valley, the Alleghenies and the wooded wilds of Vermont. Probing ever deeper inland, frontiersmen reached the River Mississippi, the western limit of the territory won from Britain in the revolution.

Settlers followed, venturing westwards in search of land, livelihood and living space. Their numbers were swelled by migrants from Europe who, in addition, sought religious and political freedom. The settlers – their lives often imperilled by the Indians whose land they were appropriating – dotted the new areas with cabins, forts [4], communities, then towns. Gradually the western territories took shape.

To avoid a land scramble among the states Congress promulgated its precedent-setting North-West Ordinance of 1787. This was designed to promote an orderly development of self-government in the newly settled regions. Each "territory" was empowered to elect a legislature when its free male population reached a total of 5,000 and to claim statehood when its population had increased to the figure of 60,000.

### From sea to shining sea

In 1803, the United States, barely two decades old, doubled in area. Napoleon, embroiled in a war with Britain, sold the vast Louisiana territory – extending from the Mississippi to the Rocky Mountains and from Canada to the Gulf of Mexico – to the American government for 15 million dollars.

President Thomas Jefferson (1743–1826) immediately dispatched Meriwether Lewis (1774–1809) and William Clark (1770–1838) to explore this enormous acquisition [1], as well as the Oregon territory to the west. The prospect of a nation's extending "from sea to shining sea" began at last to materialize.

Pioneers penetrated beyond the Mississippi in ever-growing numbers. Among them were resourceful, independent, nomadic hunters who chose to make the western wilderness their home. Known as "mountain men", they ranged far and wide through the West, often acting as intermediaries between the Indians and white settlers and officials. They also served as scouts for the wagon trains of settlers who had to make long, hazardous journeys across Indian territory to lush, fertile valleys in the Far West [2].

To the south, thousands of Americans settled in the Mexican province of Texas. Refusing to accept Mexican authority, they rebelled in 1835 [7], setting up a provisional government. This paved the way for the American annexation of Texas a decade later

**1 Lewis and Clark** set out up the Missouri River, crossed the Rockies with the aid of Sacagawea, a young Shoshone, and reached the Pacific in their 1804–6 expedition to map the vast American heartland acquired from France in the Louisiana Purchase. The maps and drawings they made served both to establish American claims to the area and to encourage pioneers, although they failed to find the hoped-for portage route.

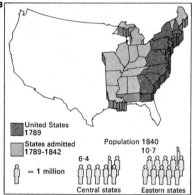

**4 Forts were built** along commonly traversed pioneer routes such as the Oregon Trail to protect travellers and scattered communities and provide refuge in the event of attack by Indians. Some forts, such as Hall and Bridger, had begun as trading posts; others, such as Fort Yuma on the southeast edge of the Rockies, became posting stations for mail routes. Manned by US Cavalry, the forts were rectangular enclosures up to 152m (500ft) long with timber walls up to 5m (18ft) high. Plank walks for sentries and combat positions were placed 1.2m (4ft) from the top with loopholes offering protected firing positions. Two blockhouses, at diagonally opposite corners, provided the main defence. Some forts became centres of thriving communities in the West as time passed.

**2 Covered wagons** were the main vehicles used for long-distance travel by settlers penetrating the West. Wagon trains often consisted of more than 100 canvas-draped wood-framed "prairie schooners", which were usually drawn by from two to six yokes of oxen. A journey of migration up the Oregon Trail could take six months or more. Wagons crossed the central Rockies before turning north to reach Portland. Caravans would form in towns on the Missouri and the Mississippi. Seeking safety in numbers to cross dangerous territory, groups would elect leaders to consult with hired scouts about the route and to settle any disputes.

**3 By 1842 the westward movement was** well under way, opening up the fine farmlands of the new states. Meanwhile, a steady stream of European immigrants, particularly from Britain and Germany, converged on the northeast.

United States 1789
States admitted 1789-1842
Population 1840
= 1 million
6·4 Central states
10·7 Eastern states

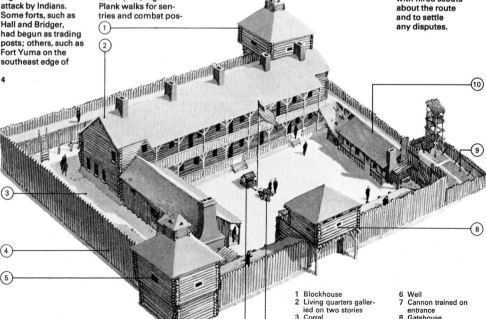

1 Blockhouse
2 Living quarters galleried on two stories
3 Corral
4 Palisade
5 Loophole for small cannon
6 Well
7 Cannon trained on entrance
8 Gatehouse
9 Garden
10 Storehouse and kitchen

**5 The Mormons,** persecuted for their religious beliefs in the state of Illinois, set out in 1847, led by Brigham Young (1801–77), to found Salt Lake City.

and the Mexican War (1846–8), as a result of which the United States acquired vast areas of territory including New Mexico, Arizona and California.

Few events provided greater impetus for the opening up of the West than the discovery of gold in the Sacramento valley in 1848. Tens of thousands scurried to California to seek their fortunes [10], and communities sprang up overnight.

Impelled by different objectives, 148 Mormons had branched southwestwards from the Oregon Trail in 1847 to claim the inhospitable area around the Great Salt Lake [5]. There they sought a sanctuary to practise their newly founded faith without harassment. They transformed the stark Utah territory into flourishing communities by modern irrigation methods.

### Dispossessed Indians

Sporadic settlement had left large areas thinly populated. In order to attract settlers to the Great Plains, Congress passed the Homestead Act of 1862, promising farmers free land for cultivation. Within five years of

this significant event the settlement of the American heartland was well under way [6].

The relentless westward expansion was a disaster for the Indian peoples [9]. The 1830 Indian Removal Bill (authorizing removal of eastern Indians to locations west of the Mississippi) merely confirmed the right of settlers to dispossess Indians wherever they found them, including the regions beyond the Mississippi. Some tribes, notably the Creeks, Comanches, Apaches and Sioux, resisted the invasion, terrorizing isolated communities, attacking wagon trains and battling with the US Cavalry. Outnumbered and outgunned, they were swept aside, slaughtered or pressed back. Tribes were sometimes induced to cede their land for territory farther west – from which, later on, they were also expelled. They were relegated to reservations, and farmers, cattlemen [8] and miners moved in.

The coming of the railways sharply accelerated westward flow and settlement. In 1869 the first transcontinental rail link was completed [11] and the West's open spaces became significantly less remote. The frontier had passed into history and legend [12].

KEY

1 United States territory 1783
2 Louisiana purchased 1803
3 Ceded by Great Britain 1818
4 Florida purchased 1819
5 Texas annexed 1845
6 Oregon Country ceded 1846
7 California, Arizona and New Mexico ceded 1848
8 Gadsden Purchase 1853

**By annexation, war, purchase or treaty,** the United States increased its territory to include the whole subcontinental expanse in the space of 90 years between 1763 and 1853. In so doing, it prevented a resurgence of British or French influence and gave effect to the Monroe Doctrine of 1823 that America was no territory for colonization by any other power.

United States 1842
States admitted 1842-76

Population 1870
⌐ = 1 million
1·0

19·4    18·4

Western states    Central states    Eastern states

**6 By 1876 Florida,** the central and far western states had joined the Union as the spread of railroads allowed for more concentrated settlement. California, acquired in 1848, had achieved statehood two years later as the 1849 gold rush swelled its population to well over the 60,000 minimum required. At the same time rapid immigration continued from Europe (more than six million from 1840 to 1870), many of whom had fled from the Irish famine.

**7 The Alamo,** an old Spanish chapel in San Antonio, was the fortress in which about 150 Texans, rebelling against Mexican rule, held out for nearly two weeks in 1836 until all but two women and two children were killed. The Texans made good their independence later that year.

**8 Cowboys,** a hard-riding, hard-working breed, built the Texas cattle empires. Later they opened the range of the Wyoming, Montana and Colorado pastureland.

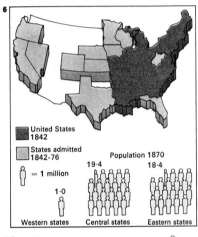

9 A
—Proclamation Line 1763
- United States territory 1783
☐ Tribal lands lost by 1784

B
UNITED STATES
☐ Tribal lands lost by 1870

**9 Indian land cessions** were integral to westward expansion. The Proclamation Line of 1763 protecting Indian hunting between the Alleghenies and the Mississippi was soon passed by land speculators [A]. After independence, treaties with the Indians pushed them farther and farther west. By 1890 no Indian titles to land were left and the Indian population had been largely confined to reservations on poor land [B] or goaded to resistance and suppressed in the many Indian wars. A major campaign, in which General Custer was killed in 1876, followed a Sioux uprising led by Chief Sitting Bull [C] who attacked US Cavalry invading his hunting grounds.

**10 The California gold rush** (1849) led to a frantic search for "pay dirt", which drew prospectors and then settlers to remote regions of the West. Miners alone numbered more than 5,000 by 1850.

**11 The continent was spanned by rail** in 1869 when the Central Pacific and Union Pacific railways were linked by a golden spike at Promontory Point, Utah. By 1870 85,000km (52,800 miles) of rail existed.

**12 By 1912 the American frontier,** which had been so central a feature in the life of the nation, had ceased to exist and the country had turned from territorial expansion to concentrated industrial and agricultural production, as the mineral deposits of the West stimulated the growth of new towns. Meanwhile, European immigration to the teeming cities of the eastern states reached a record figure of 5.2 million in the decade 1880–90. By 1910 the total population was 91,972,266.

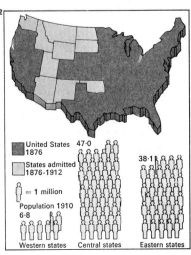

United States 1876
States admitted 1876-1912

⌐ = 1 million

Population 1910
6·8    47·0    38·1

Western states    Central states    Eastern states

# The American Civil War

The Civil War from 1861–65 was the bloodiest and bitterest conflict the United States has ever experienced. It was, President Abraham Lincoln said, a test of whether America could endure. Although the nation emerged from it intact, the "war between brothers" left a legacy of grief and hatred. It remains a vital formative influence on one of the strongest nations in the world.

## Regional interests
The Civil War was kindled by a conflict of interests between the northeastern and southeastern sections of the country at a time when most of the West was still being settled. The North was a major manufacturing and commercial region while the South was overwhelmingly agricultural with "King Cotton" providing most of its wealth [2]. The North believed in strong central government to nourish its economic growth; the South insisted on "states' rights" to guard its regional interests. Tariffs, which the North demanded to protect its industries, were opposed by the South because they raised the prices of manufactured goods. Northern

industrial expansion was able to accommodate growing numbers of free labourers, despite extremes of poverty and wealth. The South's plantation economy depended on a large workforce of black slaves [1] and it was on the slave question that North–South differences gradually came to focus.

By 1850 slavery had become the most important issue in American politics. The South considered the system proper as well as necessary; many in the North considered it abominable and held it responsible for the South's comparative economic backwardness. Congressional compromises patched up differences and delayed an open break, but the South continued to press for the extension of slavery into western territories. In the North abolitionists, of whom William Lloyd Garrison (1805–79) was the most eloquent, agitated against the "peculiar institution" of human bondage. The influential novel of Harriet Beecher Stowe (1811-96), *Uncle Tom's Cabin* (1852), dramatizing the brutalities of slavery, won support for the anti-slavery movement. The drift towards a violent resolution of sectional differences

gathered momentum as hatred was whipped up by inflammatory speeches on both sides.

Both the Democratic and Whig parties, the two major national political organizations, were badly split over slavery and the Whigs proved unable to survive the internal divisions. From the ruins of their party there emerged in 1854 a new Republican Party whose presidential candidate six years later was a former Illinois congressman, Abraham Lincoln [Key]. Lincoln opposed the spread of slavery and foresaw its eventual disappearance as an economic and social system.

A month after Lincoln was elected president South Carolina, fearing an attack on the fabric of Southern society, seceded from the Union and was followed by Mississippi, Florida, Alabama, Georgia, Louisiana and Texas. On 8 February 1861 the secessionist states proclaimed the existence of a new nation, the Confederate States of America.

## The war begins
Lincoln refused to recognize the dismemberment of the United States and appealed to the Confederate states to reconsider. Their

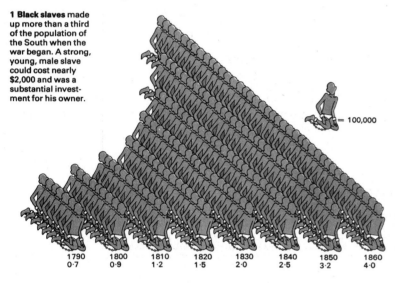

**1 Black slaves** made up more than a third of the population of the South when the war began. A strong, young, male slave could cost nearly $2,000 and was a substantial investment for his owner.

= 100,000

| 1790 | 1800 | 1810 | 1820 | 1830 | 1840 | 1850 | 1860 |
|------|------|------|------|------|------|------|------|
| 0·7 | 0·9 | 1·2 | 1·5 | 2·0 | 2·5 | 3·2 | 4·0 |

Totals in millions

**2 A stately mansion** with stucco columns and verandas on the ground and first floors was the focal point of many Southern plantations. House slaves acted as servants while field slaves tilled the surrounding soil. Although there were fewer than 10,000 plantation owners who had 50 or more slaves in the 1850s, they wielded overwhelming political and social influence throughout the South.

**3 Loyalties to South or North** crossed state lines and divided families during the Civil War. Three of Abraham Lincoln's brothers-in-law died fighting for the Confederacy. Of the 23 states, including California and Oregon, which were loyal to the Union, the most difficult decision fell to the "border states", the slave states of Kentucky, Maryland and Missouri. Their allegiance to the "Stars and Stripes" proved to be stronger than their purely regional interests. Although Virginia joined the Confederacy, the western part of the state chose the Union instead and gained statehood as West Virginia before the end of the war.

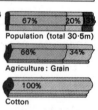
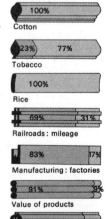

4

| 67% | 20% | |
Population (total 30·5m)

| 66% | 34% |
Agriculture : Grain

| 100% |
Cotton

| 23% | 77% |
Tobacco

| 100% |
Rice

| 69% | 31% |
Railroads : mileage

| 83% | 17% |
Manufacturing : factories

| 91% | 9% |
Value of products

$ | 80% | 20% |
Finance : bank deposits

☐ North  ☐ South

■ Slaves

**4 Outmatched** in industrial capacity, and with a much smaller population, the South counted in vain on a collapse of Northern morale.

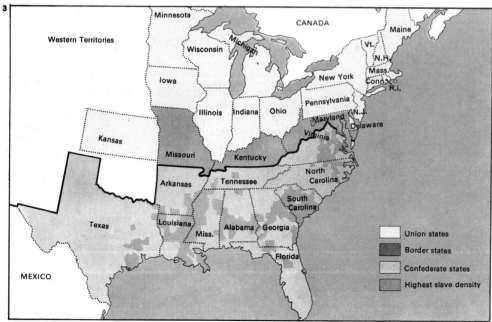

Union states
Border states
Confederate states
Highest slave density

Western Territories

CANADA

Minnesota · Maine · Michigan · Wisconsin · Vt. · N.H. · Iowa · New York · Mass. · Conn. · R.I. · Illinois · Indiana · Ohio · Pennsylvania · N.J. · Maryland · Delaware · Kansas · Missouri · Kentucky · Virginia · Arkansas · Tennessee · North Carolina · South Carolina · Texas · Louisiana · Alabama · Georgia · Miss. · Florida · MEXICO

reply came at dawn on 12 April when Southern guns opened fire on Fort Sumter, a federal outpost in Charleston, South Carolina. Virginia, Arkansas, North Carolina and Tennessee soon joined the Confederacy [3]. Both sides mobilized. The Civil War had begun.

The North had distinct advantages because its industrial capacity was far greater [4]. The South's free population was less than a quarter of that of the North. The North controlled the navy and imposed an increasingly effective blockade of the South. The South's only, dubious, advantage, apart from the quality of its fighting men, was that it was defending its home ground, while the North had to launch an assault.

The first major battle quickly showed that there would be no easy Northern victory. Union troops tried to crash through Confederate lines at Bull Run, Virginia, and were driven back in panic to Washington. But Northern superior numbers and equipment soon began to tell. After a major Northern victory at Antietam Lincoln issued an Emancipation Proclamation, effective from 1

January 1863, declaring all slaves in the Confederate states to be free.

Southern attempts to rally to preserve slavery and the Confederacy met with increasingly confident and effective Northern onslaughts [6]. There was no recovery from a devastating Confederate setback at Gettysburg in July 1863 [7, 8]. General William Sherman's (1820–91) "March to the Sea" in Georgia the following year undermined the South's remaining capacity to fight.

## Victory and its aftermath

With victory inconceivable and the bulk of his forces cut off, the Confederate commander General Robert E. Lee (1807-70) surrendered to the Union commander General Ulysses S. Grant (1822–85) at Appomattox, Virginia, on 9 April 1865.

The Civil War had cost the lives of 360,000 Union and 260,000 Confederate men as well as thousands of civilians. The South was in ruins. Despite Lincoln's plea for "malice towards none", the seeds of enduring bitterness had been sown.

**Abraham Lincoln (1809–1865),** United States president during the Civil War, believed the country could not survive "half slave and half free" but was determined to prevent the break-up of the Union. A self-taught lawyer of humble birth but great shrewdness, sincerity and common sense, he gained national recognition through public debates on slavery and was elected in 1860. Mild-mannered but strong-willed, he led the North with firmness and urged "charity for all" after the South was defeated. He was assassinated by an actor, John Wilkes Booth, in Washington on 14 April 1865, soon after starting his second term of office.

**5 Jefferson Davis (1808–89),** the champion of "states' rights" and the extension of slavery to western territory, was elected president of the Confederacy in 1861 and led the South until its surrender.

He suffered from poor health and his relations with other Southern leaders were often strained. Although taken prisoner after the war and indicted for treason, Davis was never tried.

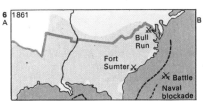

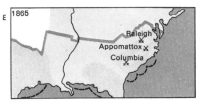

**7 Gettysburg** marked the turning point of the war in 1863 when a daring Confederate invasion of Pennsylvania was blocked in a ferocious three-day battle. General Lee, the Confederate commander, intended to await a Northern repulse near Cashtown. But a chance encounter between rival patrols precipitated the battle near the small town of Gettysburg on 1 July. Successful probing assaults on Union positions led Confederate officers to misread the situation and cavalry that was engaged elsewhere failed to scout the terrain. Finally three divisions of Confederate troops were sent into a withering barrage of artillery and rifle fire.

**6 Erosion of Confederate territory** was steady after an initial stalemate [A] in 1861 when the North realized it must blockade the South. In 1862, after victories westwards, the Union advanced from the north [B]. By May 1863 it controlled the Mississippi [C]. By the end of 1864 Sherman had split the South in two [D]. Surrender became inevitable in 1865 after further Union gains [E].

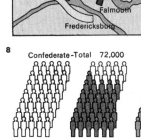

**8 Battle statistics at Gettysburg** are the subject of controversy, but it is likely that about 72,000 Confederate troops faced nearly 90,000 Union troops. This disparity need not have been decisive in view of earlier Confederate

successes. While about 23,000 Union men were killed or died of wounds the South's losses were about 28,000 (higher than the official figure given at the time). The strength of the Union was not undermined significantly. But although

its surviving forces escaped back to the South, the Confederacy had suffered a crippling and irrevocable loss. By 1865, with both sides conscripting men, the North had 960,000 under arms and the South only 450,000.

**9 Union troops** with a battery of 32-pounders near Fredericksburg were photographed by Matthew Brady (c. 1823–96), one of the first war photo-

graphers in history. The Civil War was also the first conflict in which telegraphy and railroad transport were used widely and the first in which ironclad

naval vessels went into battle; in March 1862 the USS Monitor and the Confederate Merrimac fought each other at Hampton Roads, Virginia. An early

submarine attack was launched by the Hunley which rammed its torpedo into the USS Housatonic off Charleston in 1864, with the loss of both ships.

**41**

# USA: reconstruction to World War I

The United States developed from a predominantly rural nation at the end of its Civil War (1861–5) into the world's largest and wealthiest urban industrial power by the time of its entry into World War I (1917). Among the key factors responsible for this major transformation were a huge population increase; discovery and exploitation of enormous supplies of mineral resources; consolidation of the settlement of the Great Plains and most of America's vast western hinterland; and the sprouting of far-flung railway networks to service industrial, agricultural and population growth.

## Problems of the South

America's development during this period was blighted by serious problems. Reconstruction of the defeated and devastated South after the Civil War [2] was retarded by residual North-South hostility. Northern military units policed Southern states to suppress lingering vestiges of rebellion. Carpetbaggers (northerners who migrated southwards for opportunistic or idealistic reasons) sought to govern and con-

trol sections of the ravaged South aggravating Southern animosity.

In the rest of the country, however, industrial development was rapid. Rich coal veins were worked along the Appalachian mountain spine and in the Monongahela, Ohio and Allegheny valleys. Vast deposits of iron ore were mined in the Great Lakes region. Copper, lead and other minerals were discovered and hungrily tapped [Key], as was oil.

Industrial growth was further intensified by a host of inventions [8] including commercially viable electric lighting, the telephone and rubber vulcanizing. The mechanization of agriculture through the invention of the reaper, thresher, mechanical harvester and other farm machinery enabled farmers to expand land cultivation. Between 1860 and 1910 farm acreage more than doubled and farm production more than trebled. Cattle kingdoms flourished on a wide stretch of open range from Texas to Montana.

A complex of railway networks reached out across the country linking industry, agriculture and their respective markets. By 1900, 310,000km (193,000 miles) of track

criss-crossed the United States – more than in all of Europe at that time. By 1916 the figure was 425,000km (250,000 miles).

The rapid pace of development lent itself to the activities of aggressive entrepreneurs [5]. Men such as Scottish-born Andrew Carnegie (1835–1919), instrumental in consolidating the American steel industry, and John D. Rockefeller (1839–1937) who concentrated on oil, built personal fortunes through huge companies that could overwhelm competition, fix prices and benefit from large-scale marketing and speculation beyond the resources of smaller firms.

## Population explosion

The giant companies [6] played a major role in the surge in America's gross national product, which rose from $7,000 million in 1870 to $91,000 million in 1920, despite economic fluctuations. The country's pool of labour, provided by a rapidly growing population, seemed bottomless. The number of Americans grew from 40 million in 1870 to 92 million in 1910. A flood of immigrants [3] from Europe throughout the period contri-

**1 Members of the Ku-Klux-Klan,** hooded and robed, hold elaborate initiation ceremonies. The society was originally organized by former Confederate soldiers in 1866 at Pulaski, Tennessee, to maintain white supremacy in the Southern states after emancipation of black slaves had been confirmed by the defeat of the South in the Civil War. The Klan attracted many recruits to its ranks but its night-riding vigilante violence against blacks and northerners led to its dissolution in 1869. When it was revived in 1915 its anti-black policies were supplemented by anti-Catholic, anti-Jewish and anti-alien emphasis.

**3 Health checks were largely superficial** for the more than 20 million immigrants who settled in the USA between the Civil War and World War I. At first they came mainly from Britain, Germany and Scandinavia, and later mostly from southern and eastern Europe, seeking religious or political freedom or escape from poverty. They formed German-American, Scandinavian-American and other intermixed ethnic islands in Great Plains agricultural regions; or they mined the natural resources, chopped down the forests and laid the rail tracks for the burgeoning American economy. By 1920 one out of every eight American citizens was of foreign birth.

**2 In the unsettled years** after the Civil War, bands of outlaws roamed across the central states. One of the best-known figures was Jesse James (1847–82), here seated front left. He led a gang of bank and train robbers that included his brother Frank [front right] and four brothers of the Younger family – Coleman [rear left], James, Robert [rear right] and John. Jesse and Coleman had been members of Quantrill's Raiders – a band of Confederate mounted guerrillas – and they had no respect for Northern-controlled banks and railways. The James–Younger gang left a blood-soaked trail of robberies across the Midwest. After John Younger was shot dead in a bank raid his brothers were captured and imprisoned. Badly shaken, the James brothers went into hiding. Three years later they went back to robbing trains. In 1882 Jesse was killed by Robert Ford, a new member of his gang who was tempted by the $10,000 reward.

buted substantially to this increase and amounted to almost one million a year between 1900 and 1910.

Housing was frequently inadequate in congested urban centres, wages were low and poverty widespread. These conditions gave rise to the American trade union movement. The Knights of Labor, founded in 1869, was superseded by the American Federation of Labor, founded in 1886, which was to become a potent industrial and political force. Similar action was needed in the rural sector to combat the damaging aspects of the rapid growth of agriculture – overproduction, soil exhaustion, droughts, dust storms and railways that offered bargain rates to favoured clients. Farmers formed protective associations, known as Granges, that became the basis for the Populist movement and for the success in promoting legislation to further farmers' interests.

A burgeoning campaign against social injustice established a tradition of investigative journalism. The novels of Theodore Dreiser (1871–1945) and Frank Norris (1870–1902) described the often unsavoury machinations of big business. New laws limited the length of the working day, regulated railway rates and prohibited the sale of "deleterious" foods and medicines. President Theodore Roosevelt (1858–1919) put an end to the indiscriminate exploitation of America's natural resources.

**War against Spain**
The country was already looking outside itself. Aroused by sensational press reports of the brutal suppression of a Cuban revolt against Spanish rule, and provoked by the sinking of the USS *Maine* by a mine in Havana harbour, the United States took up arms against Spain in 1898. It emerged victorious from the Spanish-American War in less than three months; Cuba was freed from Spanish rule and became independent. A more far-reaching consequence from the American point of view was that the United States, by annexing the Philippines, Guam and Puerto Rico, became a colonial power. By 1900 the United States was an economic giant; by 1914 she had become a fully fledged international power.

KEY
● Coal in million tonnes
○ Steel in million tonnes
○ Manufactures in million dollars

**Coal and steel production** increased phenomenally in the closing decades of the 1800s and the opening years of the 1900s to feed the American industrial boom. Augmented by substantial quantities of other important minerals such as copper, aluminium, lead, zinc and tin, the groundwork was laid for the major industries that are now the pillars of the US economy. In 1860 the North already had a huge lead over the South in industrialization with, for example, more than 80% of the country's factories; the South was slow to recover from the ravages of the Civil War and so industrial growth was at first confined almost entirely to the North.

---

4

**4 A revolution in urban building** was the Carson, Pirie, Scott store in Chicago completed in 1904. Its architect, Louis Sullivan (1856–1924), had worked on the world's first skyscraper – the 10- storey Auditorium building in Chicago – 15 years earlier. The discovery that a steel frame could support the weight of skyscrapers permitted cities to expand upwards as well as outwards.

5 Assets: 5 financiers and allies 1901

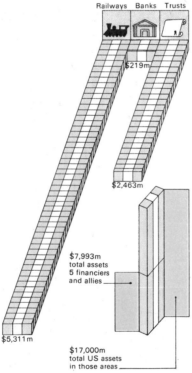

Railways  Banks  Trusts

$219m

$2,463m

$7,993m total assets 5 financiers and allies

$17,000m total US assets in those areas

$5,311m

6

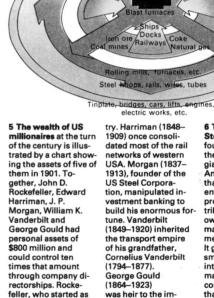

Blast furnaces
Ships
Docks
Iron ore / Railways / Coke
Coal mines / Natural gas
Rolling mills, furnaces, etc.
Steel hoops, rails, wires, tubes
Tinplate, bridges, cars, lifts, engines, electric works, etc.

**5 The wealth of US millionaires** at the turn of the century is illustrated by a chart showing the assets of five of them in 1901. Together, John D. Rockefeller, Edward Harriman, J. P. Morgan, William K. Vanderbilt and George Gould had personal assets of $800 million and could control ten times that amount through company directorships. Rockefeller, who started as a book-keeper, formed the Standard Oil Company to dominate America's oil industry. Harriman (1848–1909) once consolidated most of the rail networks of western USA. Morgan (1837–1913), founder of the US Steel Corporation, manipulated investment banking to build his enormous fortune. Vanderbilt (1849–1920) inherited the transport empire of his grandfather, Cornelius Vanderbilt (1794–1877). George Gould (1864–1923) was heir to the immense rail holdings of his unscrupulous father Jay Gould (1836–92).

**6 The United States Steel Corporation,** founded in 1901, was the first of the giant "vertical" American companies that dominated the entire process of production and distribution through ownership of raw material sources and means of transport. It gained control of smaller firms and integrated them into massive, profitable, corporate structures that were capable of eliminating competition, fixing prices and manipulating markets.

---

7

8

**7 New York 1911** had a population of almost four million and was already a sprawling metropolis. It was a major cultural and business centre, threaded together by a network of streetcar and subway lines, tunnels and bridges. Extremes of rich and poor were seen in the contrast between the elegant mansions of "Millionaires' Row" and the grim immigrant slums. The automobile industry rapidly expanded about this time, as the number of cars here, in Herald Square, indicates.

**8 Thomas Alva Edison** (1847–1931) became America's most prolific inventor. His formal education amounted to three months' schooling at the age of seven. Edison is credited with inventing the phonograph, automatic telegraph receiver and the first commercially viable incandescent lamp. He had over 1,000 patents and amongst them was the world's first plant for distributing electric power for lighting to a surrounding area, built in New York City, 1882.

# The impact of steam

The application of steam power in the course of the nineteenth century to land and water transport and to manufacturing and agriculture [5] transformed the world trading system. Steam power also enormously increased the mobility and economic dominance of the most advanced Western nations over the economically backward territories of the earth. Of all the agencies of change, railways had the largest impact.

## Nationalism and the railways
In the first stage of their development, until about 1870, railways served to strengthen and enlarge national markets and to consolidate national states. The opening of the first transcontinental railway in 1869 linked with "hoops of iron" the state of California to the rest of the USA. The unification of both Germany and Italy and the growth of their national economies were accelerated by means of the railway. The condition laid down by the Maritime Provinces (Nova Scotia, New Brunswick, Prince Edward Island and Newfoundland) for their acceptance of Canadian Confederation in 1867 was that a railway should be built to link them with the provinces of the interior. A similar condition was laid down by British Columbia when it joined the confederation in 1871.

Later railway developments had a bigger impact on the world economy, especially in greatly increasing the volume of commodity exchange. The extension of railways into the prairies of North and South America through such agencies as the Canadian Pacific Railway and the Argentine Railway, the opening of the "western windows" of Russia – Riga and Odessa – through railways stretching into their wheat-growing hinterlands, and the construction of lines into the fertile plains of the Punjab and of Bengal, all contributed handsomely to the expansion of world markets in basic commodities.

Before the railway age national economies were largely self-sufficient, but in the age of steam the importation of vast quantities of basic foodstuffs and essential raw materials by the advanced industrial nations enabled them to concentrate on the large-scale, steam-powered production of standardized manufactured goods.

The raising of funds for building steam railways was one of the most important reasons for the growth of a world capital market, with London as its leading centre before 1914. Of the £4,107 million British investors had placed overseas by 1914, £1,531 million was in railway securities.

## Migration and colonialism
Steamship and railway companies both stood to gain by encouraging the mass migration of labour. Many companies preferred to carry migrants, who loaded and unloaded themselves, rather than cargo that did not. The steerage fare from Liverpool to New York in the 1880s was only £3. More than 20 million people emigrated to the United States between 1865 and 1914.

Without the aid of the gunboat [4] and the railway, military and political domination of colonial territories by the metropolitan powers would have been impossible [2]. In the 1880s the French sent several military expeditions to Algeria to suppress a serious insurrection under Bu Amama. The uprising was eventually subdued by the building of a

**1 Small steamboats** played an important part in the exploration of Africa between c. 1855–85, and thereafter in the policing and administration of colonial territories. In this steam launch, the *Ma-Robert*, David Livingstone explored the Zambezi in 1850. He explored the River Rovina in the steam launch *Pioneer* in 1860. Four years later H. M. Stanley used the steam launch *Lady Alice* to circumnavigate Lake Victoria and help in the search for the source of the Congo. Colonial administrators in West Africa used steam launches between railheads up and down the Senegal and Niger rivers.

**2 Steam-powered warships** were used by Western powers to drag Japan out of her long sustained policy of isolation. In July 1853, fearing that unless he acted quickly Russia would forestall him, the President of the USA sent Commodore Matthew Perry with four warships (two were steamers) to Uraga with a letter addressed to the shōgunate demanding trade concessions, including coaling stations. In February 1854, Perry returned with seven ships, insisting on a reply. Overawed by the "black ships" in the harbour, the shōgunate yielded. The Treaty of Kanagawa, signed on 31 March 1854, opened two ports to US ships.

**3 The *Great Eastern*** of 18,915 tons, 210.9m (685ft) long and powered by paddle, screw and sail, was too large for weak contemporary marine engines. In July 1866 she laid the first successful transatlantic telegraph cable.

**4 Gunboat *Foxhound*** served in the Royal Navy from 1877–90. Built to a length of 38.1m (41.5ft), a beam of 7.16m (8ft) and tonnage of 445, she carried two 60-pounder and two 20-pounder guns and could sail towards trouble faster than major capital ships. Small frigates steamed into harbours and even up estuaries to devastate enemies. It was ships of these relatively small sizes that made Britain mistress of the seas in the years before 1914.

railway through the heart of the troubled area. Following the suppression of an Ashanti rebellion by the British in 1900, the pacification of the Gold Coast was sealed by building a railway. Once colonial rule was established, railways reduced administrative expenses in the transport of personnel and stores. A train of the 1890s could do the work of 13,000 porters at five per cent of the cost.

Before the 1860s steamships had a voracious consumption of coal, which limited their range of economic operations to coastal and short sea routes. (The North Atlantic, with a large passenger traffic, was an exception.) Technical improvement came more slowly to the marine engine than the locomotive. In 1840 the 1,139-ton *Britannia* carried only 90 passengers and only 225 tonnes of goods because it needed 640 tonnes of bunker fuel for the Atlantic crossing. But the introduction of the compound marine engine in the 1860s made a 40 per cent saving in fuel consumption. In 1914 the 4,556-ton Cunarder *Bothnia* carried more than three times as much cargo as coal and had room for 340 passengers. With the opening of the Suez

Canal in 1869 it was profitable to use compound-engined steamships in the Far East trade.

The use of steel in ship construction in the 1880s and the introduction of the steam turbine in the following decade drove sailing vessels off the sea lanes to Australia and New Zealand. These advances also led to the increase of freight carried in the world's steamships from 27 million tonnes in 1873 to 63 million tonnes in 1898.

**Industry and agriculture**

Before 1914 the use of steam power for driving textile machinery was still heavily concentrated in Western Europe and the USA, which together accounted for 80 per cent of factory textile production. But its dispersion had produced rapid advances in industrialization in India, Japan, Australia and Egypt. Steam power was used at all stages in the production of iron and steel, but dispersion of steam power outside the older industrial areas was slow. Steam's biggest impact agriculturally was on the processing of agricultural produce as in threshing [Key].

**This steam-driven threshing machine** displaced the primitive flail during the 1830s. This was steam's most dramatic contribution to agriculture – the one important incursion of steam power into an industry that remained largely unmechanized until the introduction of the petrol engine.

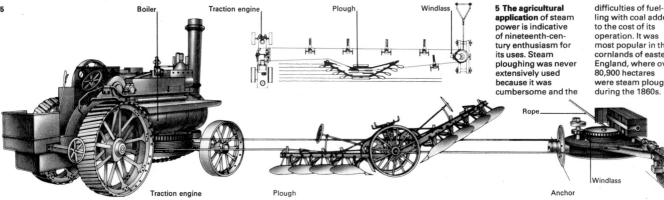

5 | Boiler | Traction engine | Plough | Windlass
Traction engine | Plough | Rope | Windlass | Anchor

**5 The agricultural application** of steam power is indicative of nineteenth-century enthusiasm for its uses. Steam ploughing was never extensively used because it was cumbersome and the difficulties of fuelling with coal added to the cost of its operation. It was most popular in the cornlands of eastern England, where over 80,900 hectares were steam ploughed during the 1860s.

**6 The American Civil War** (1861–5) was the first major war in which railways played a decisive role. Here, a train bringing Union reinforcements to General Johnston has run off the track in the forests of Mississippi (1863). In Virginia, some railway tracks were blown up and relaid as many as six times during the fighting. The repair gangs worked in sight of the enemy's artillery.

**7 The Chilean railway** from Valparaiso to Santiago was built between 1853 and 1864 and was the first important South American railway. Its construction through the Andes represented a great engineering feat, and was financed largely by British investment. Such railways brought development to remote areas, encouraged greater administrative centralization in previously disunited countries and focused nationalist aspirations.

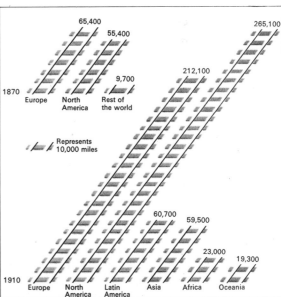

8 | Represents 10,000 miles

1870 | Europe 65,400 | North America 55,400 | Rest of the world 9,700

1910 | Europe 265,100 | North America 212,100 | Latin America 60,700 | Asia 59,500 | Africa 23,000 | Oceania 19,300

**8 Steam railways** were pioneered by Great Britain and the USA. The world's first fully locomotive-powered public railway, the Liverpool and Manchester (1830), was quickly followed by the Baltimore and Ohio and other lines. For the next 40 years railway building was mainly concentrated in Europe and North America, where capital and engineering skill were available, linking centres of industry and commerce. From 1832–8 railways were started in France, Belgium, Bavaria, Austria and Canada. After 1870, railways on the American continent were often built to open up new land and to develop its commercial potential. Railways in Japan and India dominated rail construction in Asia.

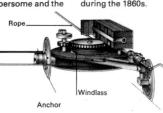

45

# The foundations of 20th-century science

Many fields of science in the nineteenth century seemed to be marked by orthodox progress – that is, a series of discoveries that could be fitted into the existing view of nature. Yet, in retrospect some of these discoveries were to lead to fundamental changes in the scientific picture. The new fields of thermodynamics and electromagnetism suggested new concepts of energy, and the mathematical work of the German Karl Gauss (1777–1855) and Georg Riemann (1826–66), although purely academic in the 1850s was by the 1920s used as a means of describing the very nature of space.

## Biology and medicine
The biological world also seemed straightforward until it was upset by Charles Darwin (1809–82) and Gregor Mendel (1822–84) [4]. When Darwin produced his *Origin of Species* in 1859, placing man among the animals in an evolutionary process that worked by natural selection, a storm of controversy broke that did not completely subside for more than a century. Mendel's work in the 1860s on inheritance factors went unnoticed

at the time but in the 1900s was to help lay the foundations of genetics.

Medical science also progressed; Claude Bernard (1813–78) studied the chemical properties of the digestive system and the treatment of infection improved with the new bacteriological ideas of Louis Pasteur (1822–95) [3]. These studies, together with the introduction of antiseptics and anaesthetics, were to lead to advances in surgery and in the understanding of new ways to combat disease. Medical scientists also began to explore the realms of the mind, virtually uncharted until the late nineteenth century, and in the work of Sigmund Freud (1856–1939) [8] the foundations of psychoanalysis were laid and the important concept of the unconscious introduced.

## The atomic theory
Chemistry finally broke its remaining ties with alchemy and its mysticism, becoming a true practical and scientific study according to the principles laid down by Antoine Lavoisier (1743–94). Its central advance was the atomic theory. Introduced in its modern

form at the beginning of the nineteenth century by John Dalton (1766–1844), the theory propounded the view that all chemical changes were merely rearrangments of individual and indestructible atoms.

It took some time before the theory was accepted, since a considerable amount of independent evidence was deemed necessary, yet in the work of Amadeo Avogadro (1776–1856), Stanislao Cannizzaro (1826–1910) and Jöns Berzelius (1799–1848), the desired correlations and experimental proofs were found and the theory of the atomic nature of matter became established. Other discoveries followed not least in the field of organic chemistry. These advances were due especially to the work of Justus von Liebig (1803–73) on agricultural chemistry and fertilizers, and Friedrich Kekulé (1829–96) who discovered the ring-like structure of the atoms in a molecule of benzene and similar compounds. This has led to the development of plastics and many other petrochemical products, to the development of modern synthetic drugs and explosives and to a better understanding of

---

**1 Faraday's "ring"** was constructed for a central experiment in the work of Michael Faraday (1791–1867) on the nature of electromagnetism, in London in 1831.

He knew that electricity flowing along a wire had an associated magnetic field and he argued that a magnet should create (by induction) an

electric current in a wire placed near it. He showed that this could happen if the magnet was moving, and with this apparatus discovered self-induction.

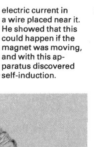

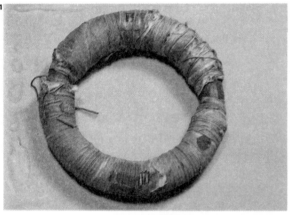

**3 This illustration of Louis Pasteur** is from a cartoon published in *Vanity Fair* in 1887. Pasteur worked on fermentation, on the souring of milk, on putrefaction and then on a disease in silkworms. He showed that all were due to

the presence of micro-organisms and proved that these were airborne. He then studied other animal diseases and devised a method of immunization by inoculating a toxin to raise the host's resistance to more virulent types of the organism.

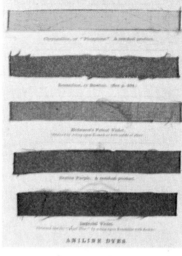

**4 Gregor Mendel** was dissatisfied with current explanations of how the many different changes in, and varieties of, living things occurred. In the 1860s he began experiments in cross-breeding peas and found the existence of dominant and recessive characteristics (now called genes). Thus crossing tall and dwarf types gave him a tall hybrid, not one half as tall, as current theory predicted. Tallness was the dominant characteristic. The next generation gave a quarter that were short; the recessive characteristic (dwarfness) had returned. Continued breeding showed the dwarf strain interbred as dwarfs. Mendel showed how proportions changed in later generations.

**2 In the middle of the 19th century** William Henry Perkin (1838–1907), in his laboratory, carried out research in organic chemistry and in particular into quinine and a substance derived from the coal-tar product aniline. By

chance this led him to discover a mauve dye. Previously purple colours could be produced only from an expensive natural product. Other aniline dyes followed – some early samples are shown from the *Popular Science Review* (1864).

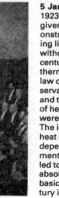

**5 James Dewar** (1842–1923) could not have given this demonstration of pouring liquid hydrogen without the 19th century's work on thermodynamics. The law of the conservation of energy and the identifying of heat as energy were vital advances. The idea that the heat of an object depends on the movement of its molecules led to the concept of absolute zero and is basic to the 20th-century idea of matter.

the chemistry of food and of all living things.

In physics important advances were made in the understanding of electricity. This began in 1800 with the construction of a cell or battery – the "voltaic pile" – by Alessandro Volta (1745–1827), by means of which a continuous flow of electricity was obtained for the first time. There was also research by others, especially Humphry Davy (1778–1829), on the chemical effects of electricity and Michael Faraday [1] on the connections between electricity and magnetism. His ideas were taken up and carried further by James Clerk Maxwell (1831–79) who studied the mathematical properties of the electromagnetic field, and predicted the existence of types of electromagnetic radiation other than light.

**Experiments with light**

Maxwell used the theory that light moves in waves, which had been developed by the experiments in interferometry by Thomas Young (1773–1829). Interest in the nature of life was intensified by the invention of spectroscopy, too, by Joseph von Fraunhofer

(1787–1826) and later developed by Gustav Kirchhoff (1824–87). This proved to be a delicate means of chemical analysis and it soon became a revolutionary tool of astronomical research. In the nineteenth century it was generally assumed that light travelled through an invisible substance known as the ether, although no proof of its existence was available. An experiment conducted in 1887 by A. Michelson (1852–1931) and E. W. Morley (1838–1923) indicated that this substance did not exist. This experiment left physics in a state of confusion until the publication of the special theory of relativity by Albert Einstein (1879–1955) in 1905 [9].

In other fields, too, new studies at the end of the nineteenth century brought important breakthroughs. Work on the discharge of electricity through gases, in particular, led to astonishing results. William Crookes (1832–1919) discovered cathode rays and J. J. Thomson (1856–1940) [Key] the electron – together with the quantum theory of Max Planck (1858–1947), the cornerstone of atomic and nuclear physics.

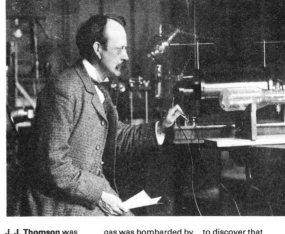

**J. J. Thomson** was director of the Cavendish Laboratory at Cambridge. With a brilliant research student, Ernest Rutherford, he found that when a rarefied gas was bombarded by X-rays it became able to conduct electricity. From this Thomson was led to consider the nature of cathode rays, and this led him to discover that they were composed of electrons, the first sub-atomic particles, thus proving that atoms were not the smallest units of matter.

**6 From 1800–09 Thomas Young** revived the wave theory of light, which opposed Newton's particle theory. In the 17th century the Dutch physicist Huygens suggested light was due to waves pushing outwards (longitudinal waves) from a source; Young however used up-and-down (transverse) waves [1], illustrated in his *Course of Lectures on Natural Philosophy and the Mechanical Arts* (1807). Interference patterns [2] were explained by the wave theory of light.

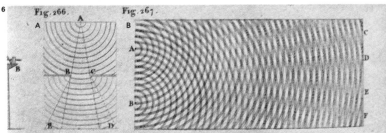

**7 In 1896 it was discovered that uranium** constantly emitted rays more penetrating than X-rays; such rays also made gases conduct electricity. This field was next studied by Marie and Pierre Curie. They found that other heavy substances emitted such rays (gamma rays). They analysed pitchblende, a uranium compound, and found it contained polonium and radium, the latter being a strong emitter. They realized the emission must be caused by some behaviour of the atoms in the materials; they called this behaviour "radioactivity". The illustration shows Marie Curie's hand photographed using a gamma-ray source.

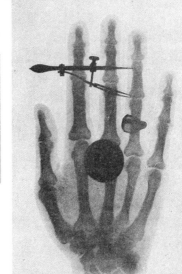

**8 Sigmund Freud**, a Viennese, developed a theory of the "psyche", at first through the use of hypnosis in the treatment of hysteria and later through the technique of free association. Both probed the unconscious and its power to affect conduct. He also stressed the sexual motivation behind much human behaviour. Freud's ideas, which included the analysis of dreams, were taken up and modified by others, particularly Carl Jung.

**10 The University of Göttingen**, famous for its mathematics and physics faculties, produced some of the leaders in the massive expansion of physical science studies in late 19th-century Germany.

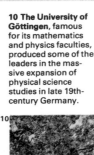

**9 Albert Einstein's** paper in 1905 on special relativity showed that not all physical quantities are capable of absolute measurement, but are relative to the same frame of reference. This did not take account of gravitation. But in 1915 he published his general theory of relativity which extended the idea to include gravitation and accelerated motion. Einstein's theory profoundly affected the outlook of modern science on the natural world.

47

# Industrialization 1870–1914

The most striking feature of the latter half of the nineteenth century was the growth and spread of industrialization through Europe and into other parts of the world such as Japan and the United States. The rise of industrial economies in Western Europe had profound social and political consequences. With the rapid growth of cities and towns came the development of a more complex political society in which new groups of people – the middle and working classes in particular – began to group themselves and exert greater political influence than before.

## Spread of industrialization

In 1850 the only country that could be described as having an industrial economy was Britain [3]. But industrial development spread to Belgium, France and Germany by 1870, and in the last decades of the century was becoming established in countries such as Sweden and Russia.

Belgium industrialized rapidly and by 1870 had one of the leading economies in Europe. French commerce, iron production and textile output were flourishing by the latter part of the century and between 1870 and 1890 French technical innovation played an important part in the development of many engineering products.

By 1900 the most important industrial economy to emerge on the continent of Europe was that of Germany. Her unification by 1871 was accompanied by an accumulation of capital and development of the transport network. From 1850 to 1880 Germany increased coal production tenfold and, with the acquisition of the iron ore fields of Alsace-Lorraine from France in 1871, output of iron and steel rapidly expanded [1]. Other countries, such as Sweden, Russia, Switzerland and Austria, began to share in these developments by 1900.

## Technology and trade

European industrialization rested upon the application of a technology pioneered in Great Britain, but made use of more advanced techniques. The Bessemer process for making steel, invented in 1856, enabled the cheap production of a material that was stronger than iron. Steelmaking from the phosphoric ores common in Europe was made possible by the Thomas-Gilchrist process after 1878. Cheap steel could be used for machinery, shipbuilding and many other items of general use and provided the basis for the rapid expansion of engineering industries throughout Europe. By 1900, with scientific inquiry into chemical and electrical phenomena, other new industries appeared. The first electrical apparatus and industrial chemicals began to emerge, especially in Germany. Development of the internal combustion engine was well under way by the turn of the century and refinements in mechanical engineering provided the impetus for a flood of labour-saving products ranging from sewing-machines and vacuum cleaners to typewriters.

Trade expanded rapidly during the late nineteenth century, facilitated by the increasing use of iron and steel steamships. Imperialism stimulated the search for new markets and raw materials but the bulk of trade occurred between European and American markets. Cheap foodstuffs from North America after 1870 played an impor-

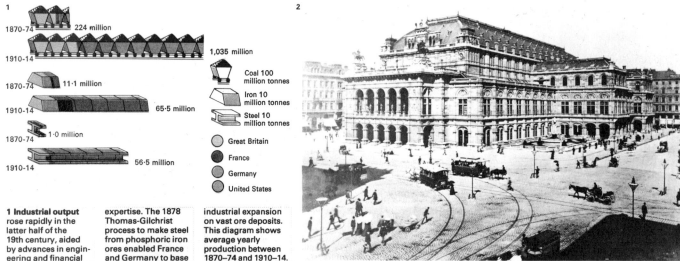

**1 Industrial output** rose rapidly in the latter half of the 19th century, aided by advances in engineering and financial expertise. The 1878 Thomas-Gilchrist process to make steel from phosphoric iron ores enabled France and Germany to base industrial expansion on vast ore deposits. This diagram shows average yearly production between 1870–74 and 1910–14.

Coal 100 million tonnes
Iron 10 million tonnes
Steel 10 million tonnes

Great Britain
France
Germany
United States

**2 Opera houses** such as that of Vienna were part of an impressive urban culture created by the growing wealth of many European cities, which built concert halls, art galleries and museums together with municipal buildings and better systems of sanitation, lighting and street paving. Improved housing for better-off workers and the middle classes led to the first suburbs and mass transport by tram and railway.

**3 A population shift** from the country to the cities proceeded rapidly as industrialization spread. In 1850, Britain apart, nearly three-quarters of Europe's people still lived on the land. But as Germany industrialized, its population ratio began to alter in the direction of Britain's – a trend followed by France towards the end of the century.

**4 London celebrated** the relief of Mafeking in 1900 during the Boer War with an outburst of national pride fuelled by widespread reporting of the war in the popular press. The rise of mass newspapers helped to create a powerful and excitable public opinion in the last decades of the century, when imperial adventures and colonial rivalry gave birth to "jingoism" expressed in bellicose literature, spirited demonstrations and songs.

**5 The bicycle** was the first "luxury" consumer product to gain a mass market. Heavily promoted by colourful advertisements such as this from the Michelin Building, London, it was sold in such numbers that manufacturers realized a huge new market had been suddenly created. Other mass-produced goods developed through advances in engineering and metallurgy, including sewing-machines, gramophones, typewriters and motor cars.

PARIS-BREST 1891    CH. TERRONT

tant part in reducing European food prices while at the same time depressing local agriculture in what was called the "Great Depression". Established industries, too, were exposed to fluctuations with the rise of competing industrial economies. To protect their newly established industries France and Germany imposed tariffs. A more complex economic structure emerged with large trusts and cartels grouping related industries into large combines; joint stock companies supplanted many family firms and banking and investment institutions became more sophisticated. By 1914 London was the financial centre of the world, with large stakes in shipping, insurance and investment.

### Far-reaching social changes
Industrial development and the continued rise of Europe's population associated with European urbanization [7] brought fundamental social changes. There was a great increase in middle-class wealth, often derived from investment in stocks and shares [8]. But even the poorest classes benefited from rising real wages. Living conditions in

the growing towns and cities of Europe were often harsh and difficult, but were improving at record rates. Social welfare measures began to be adopted by some states, as in Bismarck's Germany, and philanthropy in countries such as Britain provided some relief for the most deprived. Emigration was widespread from the poorest countries, especially Ireland, Russia and the Austro-Hungarian Empire. Most migrants went to North America, although some went to British colonies, in particular to Australia.

An advance in living standards by 1900 was reflected in the emergence of the first aspects of mass consumer society [Key]. The rise of cheap newspapers, widespread advertising and selling of consumer goods such as bicycles [5], and the growth of mass entertainment in sport, music hall and holiday excursions, showed that the working classes were beginning to enjoy some of the fruits of industrialization. This was certainly the case with the large middle-class families [6] who gave the latter part of the nineteenth century a somewhat staid character that belied the changes at work in society.

**Growing wealth** for all sections of society in the late 19th century led to the first mass con- / sumer market with the development of advertising and the growth of "chain" stores, among them / Marks & Spencer, who opened a "penny bazaar" in Stretford Street, Manchester, in the 1890s.

**6 Victorian families** of all classes tended to be large because of a high birth-rate and declining mortality / due to improved medical care, diet and general living standards. Among poorer sections of the community in- / fant deaths from infectious diseases continued to be high and there were usually more pregnancies than survi- / ving children. But upper-class family life was based on large units with many servants as well as children. / Two or three servants were a bare minimum for a solid middle-class family. In the aristocratic households of the / great country estates it was not unusual to find over 100 house-servants, kitchen staff and gardeners. / The rambling Victorian house was often a viable living unit only when it could be maintained by numerous staff.

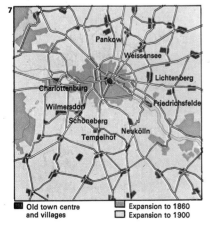

7 Old town centre and villages / Expansion to 1860 / Expansion to 1900

**7 The growth of Berlin** was typical of many nineteenth-century cities. Up to 1860 its expansion was mainly around the old city centre, but with the growth of the German state, and the development of Berlin as a capital city and industrial centre, it grew into a major European metropolis. As with many other cities, Berlin's rising population spread out to create surrounding suburbs, incorporating villages that had once been separate.

8 / Income below £100 / 87·2 / £100 – £1,000 / 9·4 / £1,000 – £5,000 / 2·3 / £5,000 – £10,000 / 0·4 / £10,000 – £25,000 / 0·5 / £25,000+ / 0·2

1% total population over 25 years old

Proportion of total capital

**8 Much of the wealth** created by the Industrial Revolution was concentrated in the hands of the upper classes. In Britain in 1911, as shown here, a tiny group of wealthy industrialists and aristocrats still disposed of a large share of the national income, although a growing proportion was held by the lesser industrialists and professional men.

# The fight for the vote

The early nineteenth-century parliamentary system in Britain contained many anomalies. The right to vote was governed by a complex system of traditional rights and privileges that had hardly changed since the mid-seventeenth century. Many boroughs elected their MPs on a tiny franchise; some had become so reduced that they were known as "rotten" boroughs and election to the seat lay almost entirely within the power of the local landowner. Moreover, the dramatic growth and redistribution in population during the Industrial Revolution created an anomalous situation where large, thriving towns had no representation whatsoever in Parliament.

### Twin aspects of reform

Parliamentary reform, therefore, had two major aspects; the progressive extension of the franchise, to encompass all men, and later women; and the redistribution of seats to rectify the anomalies of the "unreformed" House of Commons. In addition, the conduct of elections, the use of bribery, and the decisive power of individual patrons in the many "pocket" boroughs all formed part of the long-standing unreformed system.

Movements for reform began in the second half of the 1700s, when the radical demagogue John Wilkes (1727–97) whipped up much popular support in London in the 1760s and 1770s. Fear of disorder, following the French Revolution, and the vested interests of many existing MPs, held back reform for another generation. But reform and "radical" ideas were kept alive by men such as Henry Hunt (1773–1835), William Cobbett (1763–1835), John Cartwright (1740–1824), and Francis Place (1771–1854).

The growth of the manufacturing towns during the Napoleonic Wars created a demand for representation, seen in the formation of political unions in towns such as Birmingham and Manchester. Discontent with the Tory administrations brought the Whigs to power in 1830.

A bill was introduced in 1831 but was rejected by the House of Lords. This caused widespread unrest, including riots at Derby, Nottingham and Bristol. Under threat of the creation of new peers, the Reform Bill was passed in 1832. The First Reform Act replaced the existing confusion of voting qualifications with a more regular system. But the electorate rose to only 652,000 and power remained vested in the hands of the upper and middle classes. More significant was the redistribution of 143 seats from the worst of the insignificant rotten boroughs to the larger manufacturing towns, London, and the counties [1, 2].

The 1832 Reform Act was in many ways conservative. Even many Whigs regarded it only as a measure to cure the anomalies of the existing electoral system. Attempts by the Chartists to coerce Parliament into a further programme of radical reform was resisted by the propertied classes. Three mass petitions in 1839, 1842 and 1848 [3] in support of the Charter were ignored.

### The vote for the working man

Growing prosperity brought more people within the 1832 franchise qualifications by the 1860s. With the increasing inevitability of a further measure of reform, the Conserva-

**1 The post-1832 "reformed" Parliament** had members from the previously unrepresented manufacturing towns at the expense of the small "rotten" boroughs and some "pocket" boroughs.

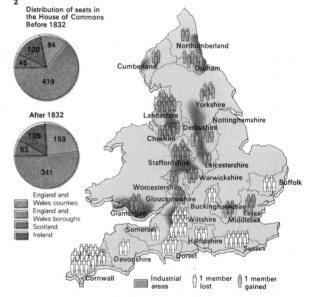

**2 The First Reform Bill** was essentially a conservative measure. It rectified the anomalies created by the population changes in the previous hundred years and enfranchised the upper middle classes.

**3 The Chartists,** here shown at their last great meeting in 1848, demanded sweeping electoral reforms; but the movement died because of dissension and poor leadership.

**4 Disraeli leads** "the race for electoral reform" in this Punch cartoon. The Second Reform Bill was passed in 1867 by the Conservatives under Derby and Disraeli.

tive leaders, Lord Derby (1799–1869) and Benjamin Disraeli (1804–81), and the Liberal leader, William Gladstone (1809–98), juggled with the new proposals to win advantage for their parties. It was Disraeli who finally managed to keep his party together and who is credited with the Second Reform Act in 1867 [4]. This act extended the vote to about one million urban working men, a further redistribution of seats.

The Ballot Act of 1872 introduced secret ballot, and in 1883 the worst aspects of electoral corruption were made illegal. In 1884 the Third Reform Act was passed by the Liberals, which enfranchised agricultural labourers and increased the electorate from about three million to about five million. In the following year, another redistribution of seats removed the last proprietary boroughs. Finally, in 1918 all men over the age of 21 received the vote [8].

### The suffragette movement

Women had been excluded from the vote in all the reform acts up to 1918. They still had very insecure property rights and were widely regarded as unfit to exercise the responsibilities of political power [6]. The Women's Social and Political Union was founded in Manchester in 1903 to fight for the vote, headed by Mrs Emmeline Pankhurst (1858–1928) [7]. Known as "suffragettes", they gradually gave up normal methods of demonstrations and propaganda and turned to violence, breaking windows, setting building on fire, chaining themselves to railings, and resisting arrest.

With the defeat of a moderate proposal for female suffrage in 1912, the campaign for women's rights was temporarily frustrated. World War I, however, advanced the status of women. They played an immense part in the war effort, working in munitions factories and previously male-dominated jobs. In 1918 women over 30 were given the vote; and this franchise was extended to all women over 21 in 1928.

Plural voting, through property or businesses in more than one constituency, was abolished in 1906; it finally disappeared in 1948 with the removal of university seats at Oxford and Cambridge.

**The introduction of secret voting** (1872) was one of the several reforms that had removed the worst abuses from the electoral system by the end of the 1800s. But women – half the population – still did not have the vote. After 1884, more than half the adult males were eligible to vote: the redistribution of seats had corrected the worst imbalances produced by the growth of the industrial towns that occurred during the Industrial Revolution. One result of these and other reforms, such as the abolition of a property qualification for MPs (1858), was the rise of the Labour Party.

**5 Ramsay Macdonald** (1866–1937) [centre] formed the first Labour government in January 1924. The Labour Party achieved an electoral breakthrough in the 1906 general election, when they formed a pact with the Liberals. Labour's 30 seats at that election were a recognition of the growing power of a party that represented the interests of the newly enfranchised working classes.

SHE. IT IS TIME I GOT OUT OF THIS PLACE, WHERE SHALL I FIND THE KEY?

CONVICTS AND LUNATICS HAVE NO VOTE FOR PARLIAMENT

Should all Women be classed with these?

**6 The question of votes for women** became a prominent issue in the ten years prior to 1914 when women's groups were formed to campaign for the "suffrage". This was not fully achieved, for women over 21, until 1928.

**7 Mrs Emmeline Pankhurst**, leader of the suffragettes, is carried away by the police during a demonstration. After 1905, the suffragettes pursued a militant policy, which led to a number of arrests and imprisonments.

UNDER WHICH FLAG?

THE PEOPLE'S BUDGET

Which is your side in the great fight—

PEERS OR PEOPLE?

**8 The electorate** only gradually increased with the passing of the Reform Acts of 1832, 1867 and 1884. Growing economic prosperity brought many within the franchise qualifications without the need of legislation. In 1918, men over 21 and all women over 30 years old were granted the vote. In 1928 all women over 21 were given the vote. In 1948 the last remnant of plural voting was abolished and, as a result, the number of the electorate fell to some extent.

8 ▢ Voters as % population 20+ yrs
▢ Voters as % population 17+ yrs

| Pre-1832 | 1832 | 1867 | 1884 | 1918 | 1928 | 1948 | 1970 |
|---|---|---|---|---|---|---|---|
| 5 | 7 | 16 | 28 | 74 | 96.9 | 96.7 | 96.5 |

**9 A contemporary election poster** graphically portrays the conflict in 1909 between the Conservative-dominated House of Lords and the Liberal government; it reached a climax when the Lords rejected the government's budget. Two elections were forced, and on each occasion the Liberals were returned. In 1911 the primacy of the elected assembly was established when, under threat of the creation of more peers, a bill was passed restricting the powers of the Lords.

# Ireland from Union to Partition

The legislatures of Dublin and London were combined on 1 January 1801 for reasons of state – British reasons, although the Union also suited those Protestants of the Irish Ascendancy who feared the rising forces of Catholicism and democracy. Other Irish Protestants opposed the measure, distrusting Westminster's will to preserve Protestant privileges, while Catholic leaders tended to favour Union, accompanied as it was to be by legislation to grant Catholics the right to sit in the Union Parliament.

## Consequences of the Union
In the event, Protestant fears of the Union turned out to be as unfounded as Catholic hopes. Protestants continued to represent Irish constituencies in Parliament, the Anglican Church remained established and the separate Irish administration continued to favour Protestant interests.

To Catholics, the Union provided scant blessing. Their right to sit in Parliament was not conceded, the prime minister, the younger William Pitt (1759–1806) preferring to resign rather than jeopardize the war effort against France by provoking a constitutional crisis over King George III's (reigned 1760–1820) opposition to Catholic emancipation. Emancipation became, therefore, a principal issue of the Union Parliament: its denial completely disenchanted Catholics with the Union [1].

## The land problem and Home Rule
The Great Famine of 1845–49 [2] stressed the enduring problem of nineteenth-century Ireland – the imbalance of its land and people. The Irish population had grown alarmingly from five-and-a-half million in 1800 to more than eight million by 1845. Crowded together in smallholdings subdivided into uneconomic units, increasingly dependent upon a potato diet, the Catholic labourers and tenant farmers presented a desperate spectacle. Without industrial alternatives, the peasantry had to remain on the land, exposed to periodic crop failures.

At Westminster, tenant and Catholic spokesmen tried to co-ordinate Irish MPs to deal with Irish issues, but, in practice, allegiance to the Liberal and Tory parties prevailed. But after the false start of Isaac Butt's (1813–79) Home Rule League (1873), Charles Stewart Parnell (1846–91) [5] welded together a disciplined Irish Party in pursuit of Home Rule.

As a result of the long-felt grievance over ownership, unsatisfactory tenancy arrangements, misguided legislation, a further series of bad harvests from 1877, and the organization of the Irish National Land League, rural discontent was brought to a new focus between 1879–82 [4]. Parnell yoked this to his parliamentary demands, while the shadowy Irish Republican Brotherhood (the Fenian movement) begun by James Stephens (1825–1901) in 1858 and now given direction by John Devoy (1842–1928) from America, lent clandestine support. Coercion proved an insufficient government response but the Liberal leader, William Gladstone (1809–98), accepting the logic of Parnell's position, attempted in vain to devolve a Home Rule parliament to Dublin [6].

Meanwhile, the Home Rule Party, split in 1890 and discredited by internal feuds, was being outflanked by other movements

**1 Daniel O'Connell,** (1775–1847), the first politician in the British Isles to mobilize mass support behind his cause, won Catholic emancipation in 1829. As MP for Clare, he alternately bargained for reforms amd attacked the Union itself. But support for his Repeal Association declined after 1843 when he refused to risk bloodshed in opposition to Westminster and the Union.

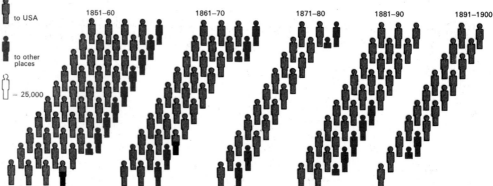

**3 Inhibitions against emigration** were broken by the Famine and a steady flow of emigrants began to leave Ireland. By 1911, when the population stabilized at nearly four-and-a-half million, more Irish lived in North America, Britain and the Empire than in Ireland. Their departure made possible a better standard of living in Ireland, and added an international dimension to Irish nationalism.

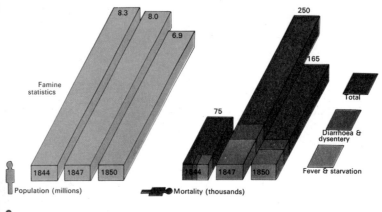

Famine statistics

Population (millions): 1844, 1847, 1850
8.3  8.0  6.9

Mortality (thousands): 1844, 1847, 1850
250  165  75
Total  Diarrhoea & dysentery  Fever & starvation

**2 The Great Famine of 1845–9** was a disaster on an unprecedented scale in Irish history. Total figures for deaths and disease disguise the famine's uneven impact, most severe in the West and least damaging in the North East. In 1845–6 government action relieved starvation, but renewed crop failure overwhelmed the shadowy administrative structure. The ensuing horror generated intense hatred against Britain.

to USA
to other places
= 25,000

1851–60    1861–70    1871–80    1881–90    1891–1900

**4 Eviction of tenants was common** in the 1870s and 1880s when conflicts between tenant farmers and landlords were at their sharpest. Landlords did not consolidate sufficiently, being effectively restrained by popular opposition, but with tenants of tiny holdings unable to live, let alone pay rent, amalgamation into viable farms was the only economic solution. The Land League seized on the evictions to focus mass resentment against the landlord system.

**5 Charles Stewart Parnell,** MP for Meath from 1875, led 59 Irish MPs at Westminster by 1880, soon moulding them into a disciplined, salaried party (86 strong at its height), pledged to support Home Rule. Backed by constituency branches, mass Land League support and secret Fenian co-operation, he made Home Rule credible, and in 1886 won the Liberal Party over to this cause. Parnell lost Catholic support after he was cited in a divorce case in 1890.

working to "de-Anglicize" Ireland and to win complete independence. In 1906 Arthur Griffith (1872–1922) succeeded in mobilizing disparate political groupings into his own movement, Sinn Fein, dedicated to economic self-sufficiency and political withdrawal from the Union.

Yet, even while Sinn Fein gathered strength, the Home Rule Party, shamed into unity in 1900 under the leadership of John Redmond (1856–1918), received renewed authority from political circumstances in Britain. The return of the Liberals there in 1906 made Home Rule again a possibility.

### Ireland divided

From 1912 onwards, tension grew first with the Protestant Unionists arming [7], then Home Rulers – the one to prevent, the other to enforce a bill expected to become law in 1914. Only the outbreak of World War I subsumed this minor quarrel within a mightier conflict. The operation of Home Rule was postponed until the end of the war.

Before that, however, republicans, socialists and other separatists had risen in 1916 [8]

to proclaim an independent Irish Republic. They were quickly crushed and their leaders executed, but these groups re-formed in 1917 to merge under the Sinn Fein banner.

The Home Rule Party, compromised by its attachment to the British war effort and the indecisive leadership of the dying Redmond, could not be saved from humiliation in the post-war elections. But Sinn Fein, while winning 73 seats to the Party's 6, could not prevent the Unionists from winning 26 in the North East.

Prime minister Lloyd George (1863–1945) belatedly turned again to Ireland in 1919. In 1920 he created two Home Rule parliaments: one in Dublin for 26 of Ireland's 32 counties; the other in Belfast for the remainder in the North East. Reluctantly, Northern Unionists accepted this compromise, although they had been committed to preserving the 9-county Province of Ulster from Dublin rule. Contemptuously, Southern Nationalists, by now sworn to win a 32-county Irish Republic, refused either to accept the limited powers offered or the partition of the island involved.

**On Easter Monday** 24 April 1916, Irish republicans, socialists and other separatists rose in armed revolt against British rule in Ireland. The rebellion was quickly crushed, the last rebel strongholds surrendering to British troops six days after the republic had been proclaimed (the proclamation is shown here). In the fighting, 100 British troops and 450 Irish were killed. The rebel leaders were executed, notably Patrick Pearse (1879–1916) and James Connolly (1870–1916). Only Eamon de Valera (1882–1975) survived because he had been born in the USA. However these measures, in the aftermath of the rebellion, won Irish opinion to the republican cause.

**6 William Gladstone,** seen in the cartoon struggling with the Irish question, became absorbed with Irish affairs after 1886 and his unsuccessful first Home Rule Bill. Prior to that, in 1869, he had disestablished the Irish Church and passed Land Acts, in 1870 and 1881, which gave tenants greater security and legally fixed rents. In 1893 he introduced the second Home Rule Bill, which was rejected by the House of Lords.

**7 Edward Carson** (1854–1935) led the Ulster Unionists from 1910–20, pledging and arming them to resist Home Rule in any form. In 1914 his offer to accept Home Rule with the exclusion of Ulster was rejected. In 1916 he reduced this demand to only the six most Protestant Ulster counties. Although Carson preferred continued integration with the United Kingdom, he accepted the creation of a separate parliament for the six counties in Belfast in 1920.

**8 The Easter Rising** of 24–29 April 1916, led by the Irish Volunteers and the Irish Citizen Army, seized several public buildings in the centre of Dublin before surrendering to the British army. Although many Irish people were out of sympathy with the insurrection itself, support for the republican cause grew after the secret execution of the seven signatories of the Proclamation of the Irish Republic and eight other rebel leaders, and widespread arrests.

**9 Michael Collins** (1890–1922) (right) was a leader of the Irish struggle for independence. After 1916 he became involved in Sinn Fein politics and was elected to the Dail in 1919, becoming a leading member of the provisional government. Eamon de Valera (left) was the senior surviving officer of the 1916 rising and principal Irish leader. He became President of Sinn Fein in 1917, and President of the Republic and of Dáil Eireann (Irish lower house) in 1919.

# Scotland in the 19th century

The political framework of nineteenth-century Scotland continued to be union with England but, by the end of the century, in place of the handful of privileged voters who had elected MPs under the old regime, something approaching a democracy based on adult male suffrage had been achieved. This had been the work of successive Reform Bills in 1832, 1867 and 1884. Eventually Scotland was electing 72 MPs from constituencies that gave weight to the Scottish urban population, and its share of the Westminster parliament – 670 MPs – fairly reflected the Scottish proportion of British population.

## The beginnings of socialism

Following the triumph of the Whigs under Francis Jeffrey (1773–1850) and Henry Cockburn (1779–1854) at the time of the Great Reform Bill of 1832, Scotland settled down to become loyally Liberal – 53 MPs were elected under William Ewart Gladstone's colours compared to seven Conservatives in 1880, although the split in the party over Irish Home Rule in 1886 shook this allegiance seriously. At the same time

there was a Scottish radical tradition to the left of this mainstream.

It surfaced at the time of the so-called Radical War in 1820, which was really a combination of a strike and a small abortive rising in the Glasgow area. It was seen again with the Chartists between 1838 and 1848, although the Scottish Chartists mainly disapproved of physical force and sought reformation through temperance and democracy. And in 1888 socialism struck root with the foundation of the Scottish Labour Party and the rise of Keir Hardie (1856–1915) [9] who later became the leader of the British Independent Labour Party (ILP) in 1893. Trade unionism grew rapidly, especially in skilled trades and among the cotton spinners and miners, although a Scottish Trades Union Congress (with 40,000 members) was not founded until 1897.

Generally speaking, there was little dissatisfaction over union with Britain, although because Westminster was increasingly obliged to legislate for Scottish affairs as the problems of industrial society became more complex (by reforming the Poor Law in

1845 and the school system in 1872, for example) there was more demand for specifically Scottish experts in the government. This was met in 1885 by the creation of a Secretary of State for Scotland and a Scottish Office based in London and Edinburgh. A small nationalist movement arose at the end of the century; few took it seriously, although Hardie and other early socialists also favoured Home Rule. For many Scots, Church politics were more significant than national ones; the Disruption of the Church of Scotland in 1843 [5] into the Established Church and the Free Church over the question of who should choose the ministers generated enormous excitement.

## The prosperity of heavy industries

The Scottish economy in the nineteenth century was highly successful: to the original base of cotton textiles an important iron industry in the West Central Belt was added in the 1830s, and after 1870 the vitality of the shipyards and steelworks of Clydeside and of jute round Dundee prevented the country from slipping into recession [3]. A third of all

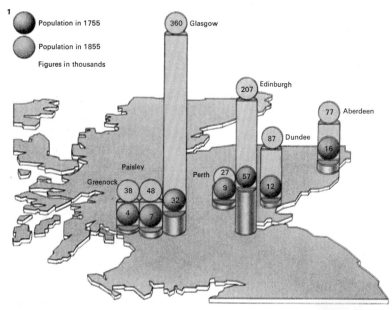

**1 Industrialization in Scotland** was accompanied by rapid urbanization, not so much in the foundation of new towns as in the very rapid growth of old ones: Glasgow, for example, had 23,000 inhabitants by about 1750, when it was already the second town of Scotland, but it had 329,000 by 1851. Nevertheless there were new towns, which often grew very fast. Airdrie, for instance, had a population of 1,200 in 1755, but with the development of iron and coal in Lanarkshire, it exceeded 13,000 by 1851. But primitive sanitation, unimproved from a previous era, menaced the growing towns and ominously increased mortality.

**2 The Highlands' economy collapsed** in the early 1800s and this resulted in a grim outlook for crofters such as these. Prices for three of their four main staples – cattle, kelp and fish – had fallen disastrously, and only wool was still viable. This meant that wealthy sheep farmers from the Lowlands began to introduce their animals into the crofters' fertile plots. As a result, the green summer pastures were quickly overcropped. The crofters themselves were usually evicted to the outskirts. Such evictions were sometimes executed considerately, but at other times the action was ruthless, causing great hardship.

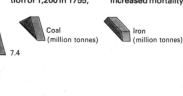

**3 Economic growth** in early Victorian Scotland was firmly based on Scottish natural resources, but with the invention of cheap steel after 1870 many of the ores had to be imported from various countries. The soaring indices of production point to an economy increasingly dependent on a narrow base of heavy industry. For example, by 1900 much of the metal went into the great ships being built in the yards along the Clyde.

| | |
|---|---|
| 1850 | Coal (million tonnes) 7.4 |
| | Iron (million tonnes) 0.5 |
| 1870 | 14.9 |
| | 1.2 |
| 1890 | 24.3 |
| | 0.7 |

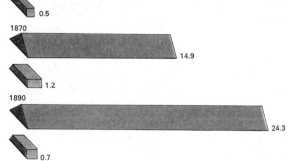

**4 The new castle at Balmoral** was the apotheosis of Queen Victoria's love of the romantic. In 1856 she wrote of it in her diary: "Every year my heart becomes more fixed in this dear Paradise . . . and so much so now, that *all* has become my dear Albert's *own* creation . . .". The castle, standing about 80km (50 miles) west of Aberdeen on the banks of the River Dee, was bought by Prince Albert for the royal family in 1852.

ships built in Britain were being built on the Clyde by 1913. The Scots had earned much lower incomes than the English in 1800, but by 1900 the average working man on the Clyde was probably at least as well paid as the average English worker. This sense of prosperity made Glasgow an enormously self-confident business capital – few Scottish firms were controlled from elsewhere – but concealed the fact that Scottish wealth rested on a narrow base of heavy industries.

## The improverished Highlands
The reverse side of the coin was the patchy nature of the wealth. Throughout the Highlands people were very poor: the population increased until 1841, far outstripping the growth of resources, and then collapsed after the potato famine of 1846. Thousands of small-scale tenants were evicted in the "clearances" to make way for sheep [2]; tens of thousands emigrated [6]. By the 1870s and 1880s over-intensive sheep farming had run down the fertility of the land and this, coupled with a dramatic slump in grain and wool prices, led to even further depopulation

of the Highlands regions through migration.
Meanwhile those who left were partly balanced by those who arrived. These were Irishmen immigrating into the coalfields and factories of central Scotland where they generally had to take the lowest paid labouring jobs. The urban poor had a hard time; the slums of the great cities were probably the worst in Europe even when the economy was booming [Key, 1].

To the outside world, however, there were perhaps two main symbols of nineteenth century Scotland: Balmoral [4], where Queen Victoria gloried in a romantic view of the Highlands far removed from the unpleasant realities of the black houses of the Isle of Lewis; and Scottish science and medicine at the universities. Men such as Lord Kelvin (1824–1907) at Glasgow, or James Clerk Maxwell (1831–79), the physicist who was professor at Aberdeen, King's College, London and Cambridge, vied in their reputations with Joseph Lister (1827–1912) [7] and James Simpson (1811–70) who made surgery comparatively safe and painless.

KEY

**The industries and slums of Clydeside** were the central paradox of 19th-century Scotland. On the one hand they produced the greatest wealth Scotland had ever known – by 1906 wage rates were higher than in most of England. On the other hand, they had a population whose housing conditions were worse than any in Britain: even in 1911 two-thirds of the population lived in houses that had only one or two rooms.

**5 Thomas Chalmers (1789–1847)** was a widely influential theologian and preacher. He was for years head of the evangelical wing of the Church of Scotland, and then founded the Free Church which broke off at the Disruption of 1843. He abandoned the established church because of its traditional method of choosing ministers – he preferred democratic elections. Within Britain he was celebrated for his book, *Christian and Civic Economy of Large Towns*, which encouraged the middle classes to believe that the problems of poverty could be cured by generous philanthropic action with a rigorous inquiry into the personal and moral condition of the individual poor.

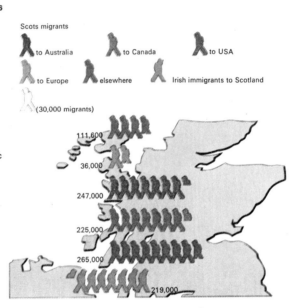

Scots migrants

to Australia    to Canada    to USA

to Europe    elsewhere    Irish immigrants to Scotland

(30,000 migrants)

111,600

36,000

247,000

225,000

265,000

219,000

**6 Nineteenth-century Scotland** was like a bath with the taps full on and the plug out. There was a rapid natural increase accompanied by an inrush of Irish immigrants to the looms, mines and ironworks of the Central Belt. At the same time, many native Scots, especially Gaelic-speaking Highlanders unwilling to move to an unfamiliar urban life, chose to go to Canada, and also to Australia, the USA and New Zealand. This outflowing tide resulted not so much from lack of opportunity at home as from the enticement of kinfolk already abroad. Few European nations apart from Ireland and Norway lost so much of their natural increase.

**7 Joseph Lister (1827–1912)** founded modern antiseptic surgery. When he went to work at Glasgow Infirmary in 1861 he found that nearly half the amputation cases died of postoperative gangrene. Lister eventually began to realize that pus formed as a result of infection by germs. He ensured that hands, instruments and dressings were sterilized. This, together with his introduction of sterilized catgut and carbolic acid as an antiseptic, after 1865, dramatically reduced surgical mortalities.

**8 The decision of a handful of crofters** to resist eviction by force in 1882 alarmed the government, who sent a gunboat to Skye to put down the "rising". It was cheered by the peasants, who believed that Queen Victoria had come to hear their grievances.

**9 Keir Hardie** (shown here) and R. B. Cunninghame Graham (1852–1936) were the fathers of socialism in Scotland. Hardie became leader of the British ILP and was described as "the best-hated and the best-loved man in Great Britain".

In 1928 Cunninghame Graham helped to found the Scottish National Party. Hardie was a confirmed pacifist and was fervently opposed to the Boer War. He also favoured women's suffrage, and founded *The Labour Leader*, a Scottish newspaper.

# Wales 1536–1914

The Acts of Union (1536–43) decreed that Wales henceforth was to be governed "in like form" to England. Wales was given a definite administrative boundary and was also unified politically within itself [Key]. The most progressive of the Welsh gentry were happy to be subsumed in a common British citizenship and voiced their gratitude to the Tudors for bringing order, stability and prosperity to Wales.

## The power of the gentry

The gentry were the most powerful element within society and the task of administering local government remained in their hands for some 350 years. Traditionally conservative, they supported the Crown through every event. During the English Civil Wars (1642–6, 1648) they fought for the king in order to protect their prosperity and security and, after the Restoration in 1660, they reestablished a monopoly of influence on the society, economy and politics of Wales. Until the mid-nineteenth century political power lay in the hands of a narrow circle of landowning families, and the mass of society remained deferential to their will. Three developments – the growth of Nonconformism, the Industrial Revolution and the spread of political radicalism – undermined the foundation of this society.

From the sixteenth century onwards successive waves of Protestantism lapped over Wales. Much was achieved: Welsh became the language of religion, and the translation of the scriptures into the vernacular [1] fostered the growth of a Bible-reading public. With the coming of Methodism in the 1730s, Reformation ideas were propagated far more intensively [3]. In 1811, the Methodist movement was forced to sever its connection with the Anglican Church and, in the company of fellow Dissenters, spread widely into rural and industrial areas. Noncomformity became a popular movement so that by 1851 about 80 per cent of practising Christians in Wales were Nonconformists.

## The Industrial Revolution in Wales

The second major factor that created modern Wales was the Industrial Revolution. Until the end of the eighteenth century Wales displayed the main features of a pastoral, pre-industrial economy: a primitive technology, a slow rate of technical development and a lack of capital. But the arrival of the Industrial Revolution after 1760 transformed the social and economic life of Wales. Financed largely by English entrepreneurs, industrial development focused on the chain of ironworks on the periphery of the South Wales coalfields and in northeast Wales, on the copper mines of Anglesey and the slate quarries of Caernarvonshire. The spread of canals and railways improved communications and hastened large-scale industrial expansion.

At the same time, population growth began to accelerate dramatically. It rose from 370,000 in 1670 to 586,000 in 1801. Small villages grew into booming towns: in 1801, Merthyr Tydfil, with a population of 7,705, was the largest town in Wales [4]. By 1861, 60 per cent of the Welsh people lived in industrial areas. The decline of the iron industry after 1850 was followed by the growth of new steelmaking processes and the massive expansion of the coal industry.

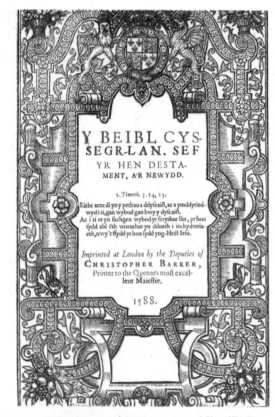

1 **The first Welsh Bible** (1588) resulted from a statute in 1563 which ordered that the translation of the Bible into Welsh should be undertaken forthwith. The work was duly completed by an erudite Denbighshire vicar, William Morgan (c. 1545-1604). The translation provided a literary standard for future generations and ensured that Protestantism would be propagated in the Welsh language.

2 **The Sker House,** a large, bleak edifice close to the Kenfig Burrows in Glamorgan, is a good example of the many new or remodelled buildings which were constructed by the Welsh gentry in the 16th century. The house was built on a former monastic grange by the Turberville family. The economic and political power of the gentry at that time was reflected in their imposing country homes.

3 **Howel Harris** (1714–73) was the moving spirit behind the growth of Welsh Methodism. A fiery evangelist, Harris provided the movement with inspired leadership and an efficient organization.

4 **The massive Cyfarthfa ironworks,** founded in the mid-18th century, became the focal point of the iron-smelting town of Merthyr. In keeping with much of the Industrial Revolution in Wales, the works were financed by English capital.

As the unparalleled resources of the Rhondda valleys were plundered, coal came to dominate the Welsh economy. By 1912, coal output in the mining valleys of South Wales was more than 50 million tonnes.

## Nationalism and political radicalism

The third factor was the growth of political radicalism, inspired by the revolutionary ideals formulated in France. Many processes hastened these ambitions: the Welsh press created an articulate and informed body of public opinion; acute economic distress in rural and industrial communities encouraged class awareness and a growing interest in political reform; and a slanderous government report – *The Treason of the Blue Books* in 1847 – injected new life into radicalism and awakened a sense of nationhood. The extension of the franchise in the nineteenth century gave radical Nonconformists the opportunity to undermine the landowning monopoly, to remove religious disabilities, and to create cultural and educational institutions attuned to Welsh circumstances and aspirations. Between 1868 and 1918

Welsh Liberals voiced the ambitions of a new Nonconformist middle and working class, and the response which they evoked from the electorate enabled them to erode the power of the old Anglican squirearchy and to capture the overwhelming majority of parliamentary seats in Wales.

As political nationalism spread in from Europe and Ireland, a new effort was made to emphasize the distinctiveness of Wales and to press for national equality and justice [7]. In Parliament, a ginger-group of young Liberals, led by Thomas Ellis (1859–89) and David Lloyd George (1863–1945) [8], called for religious equality, educational opportunity and land reform. Eventually, many gains were achieved: the Church in Wales was disestablished in 1920; Welsh universities, a National Library at Aberystwyth and a National Museum at Cardiff were established; a Welsh department was created within the Board of Education; and the concept of Wales was firmly established. By 1914 it was no longer considered to be a mere geographical term with neither institutions nor pride in its own nationhood.

KEY
Boundaries of Welsh shires 1536
Shires formed from March Lordships

FLINT
ANGLESEY
DENBIGH
CAERNARVON
MERIONETH
MONTGOMERY
RADNOR
CARDIGAN
BRECKNOCK
CARMARTHEN
MONMOUTH
PEMBROKE
GLAMORGAN

0    40km

**The Acts of Union** incorporated Wales into England in order to achieve a more effective governance of Wales and the border area (Marches). Welshmen henceforth were to enjoy the rights and privileges of Englishmen; land was to be inherited according to the practice of primogeniture; and the whole of Wales was divided into shires — a framework that persisted until April 1974. English became the official language of law and government and English common law and methods of local administration were introduced. In return the new Welsh shires and boroughs could send 24 MPs to represent them in the English Parliament.

**5 The Merthyr riot of 1831** developed from three main causes. First, discontent with the system of compelling workers to spend part of their wages in the expensive, company-owned shops; secondly, unemployment and the harsh provisions of the Poor Law; and thirdly unrest at the delay in passing the 1832 Reform Bill.

**6 The Rebecca riots in the early 1840s** occurred in separate places across southwest Wales. Disguised as women, small farmers protested against abuses of the turnpike system. They attacked the hated toll gates, burnt haystacks and threatened local magistrates. A government inquiry in 1844 resolved many of their grievances.

**8 David Lloyd George,** MP for Caernarvon boroughs from 1890, made his mark in politics as an enthusiastic champion of the rights of Welshmen, an enemy of privilege and as a "man of the people". As Chancellor of the Exchequer (1908-15) he introduced crucial social reforms, and his 1909 budget provoked an important constitutional crisis with the Lords. In 1916, he became the first Welshman to be appointed prime minister, which he remained until 1922. He earned a reputation as a courageous and decisive war leader, and a constructive peace-maker after World War I. His fertile mind and oratorical genius aroused widespread devotion and, equally, widespread dislike.

**7 Michael D. Jones** (1822–98) was one of the principal Welsh nationalists of the 19th century. He strove valiantly to persuade Welshmen to embrace a new, radical philosophy, to agitate for their political rights and to recover their self-respect and confidence. His determination to preserve national identity prompted him to establish a Welsh colony in Patagonia, South America, in 1865; this colony still exists as an isolated Welsh-speaking outpost today.

# Russia in the 19th century

In Russia, since the time of Peter the Great (1672–1725), fundamental reforms have followed in the wake of war. For many years after the Crimean War (1854–6) [1], Russia was no longer regarded as a friendly power by Britain and France. Despite the fact that it had the largest land forces on the continent of Europe this war showed that Russia was no match for the Anglo-French alliance and that its effort to insulate itself from the political changes in the rest of Europe had proved to be a source of weakness rather than of strength. Finally, its economy and social order could not withstand the war. Russia if it wished to regain its position as a leading nation, had to imitate the Western powers and adopt their forms of government.

## The emancipation of the serfs

Alexander II (1818–81), who came to the throne in 1855, was willing to introduce reforms. He warned the nobility that if reform did not come from above it would come from below. In February 1861 the Emancipation Act was ready.

The Act ensured personal freedom for millions of peasants and introduced the elective *zemstvo*, an organ of local government, which was to have an important say in the countryside. Other major reforms followed: in 1864 equality before the law, trial by jury and independence of courts and judges were introduced; legislation of 1863 and 1864 broadened the basis of education; the 1870 Government Act set up new municipal institutions; the 1874 army reforms established the principle of universal military service and reduced actual service from 25 years to six. But the peasants were still subject to customary law and had special courts; their freedom of movement was limited and they still paid poll taxes. Moreover, the Tsar did not grant a parliament

The emancipation disappointed most of the peasants and their supporters. Population increased from 70 million in 1863 to 155 million in 1913 (excluding Finland and Poland), aggravating rural poverty. Migration eased the situation slightly, but the problem of land hunger was exacerbated by the failure to introduce modern agricultural methods, obstructed by the communal system of land ownership. Much peasant dissatisfaction also stemmed from the poor quality of the land that they were allotted, and the high level of repayments they were forced to make to the government to compensate the former owners of the land.

## Seeds of revolution

The inadequacy of Alexander's reforms aroused moral revulsion and anger among many sons and daughters of the gentry and others who had acquired some education. Disillusionment over the reforms at first encouraged nihilism. The nihilists believed that the existing order could not successfully reform itself and in Russia they contributed significantly to the tradition of revolutionary political movements. During the 1870s a more positive populism [5] or agrarian socialism developed which glorified the peasant as the repository of pure, untainted wisdom. Those who had received an education felt that they owed a debt of gratitude to the toilers who had made it possible.

Agrarian populism was difficult to convert into political action and the onset of

1 **Following the capture of Sevastopol** and her defeat in the Crimean War, Russia became little more than a second-rate power. Britain and France had turned against her and exposed the backwardness of her economy and the brittleness of her army. The new tsar, Alexander II, was convinced that Russia had to imitate the Western powers if she was to beat them and so he favoured sweeping reforms.

2 **Peasants received insufficient land** as a result of the Emancipation Act (here being read out to Georgian peasants). They did not receive land freely, most of them having to pay a fixed annual amount to the state which in turn compensated the landlords with state bonds. Repayments were to extend over 49 years and were higher than the market value of the land warranted. The result was that the peasants had less land than before – in fact about 20% less in total – 23% of this in the black earth lands and 31% in the Ukraine. Former state and crown peasants received the best terms.

4 **Georgy Plekhanov** (1857–1918), the father of Russian Marxism, started his political life as a populist. He opposed terrorism, but had to flee the country for Geneva in 1880 during a wave of political repression and did not return to Russia until 1917. A brilliant writer and polemicist, his influence within Russia in the 1890s was immense. He initially supported Lenin, then opposed him.

5 **Populism** became the leading philosophical attitude in the 1870s. Its most significant leader was Peter Lavrov (1823–1900). Populism rejected the Industrial Revolution and favoured rural life.

3 **The execution of terrorists** who planned the assassination of Tsar Alexander II by a bomb in March 1881, in the hope that the whole imperial edifice would collapse, sums up the impotence of revolutionary politics in 19th-century Russia. The acute disappointment felt by the peasants and intelligentsia after the Emancipation Act led to pessimism concerning the possibility of reform from above. Many radicals, known as populists or agrarian socialists, believed the peasantry would rise *en masse* and sweep away the hated autocracy. Some believed in the gradual awakening of peasant consciousness, moulded by radical idealists. Others were unwilling to wait for the uprising of the masses and adopted terrorist methods.

industrialization in the late 1880s and the boom of the 1890s made it less relevant. Marxism, placing its faith not in the rural worker but in the urban, industrial worker, became a doctrine more in tune with contemporary Russian conditions. The Social Democratic Party, the forerunner of the Communist Party, emerged, although it still appealed for the most part to intellectuals rather than to the working classes.

The terrorist wing of the populist movement finally resulted in the assassination of Alexander II. But instead of collapsing, the autocracy struck back at its tormentors.

### The end of the era
Alexander III (1845–94), who came to the throne in 1881, was ultra-reactionary. His policies reversed many of the liberal reforms of his predecessor and began a tradition of conflict between the *zemstvos* and central government that came to a head in 1905.

The succession in 1894 of Nicholas II (1868–1918) [8] occurred at a time of rapid economic advance [6]. The dynamic thrust of Sergei Witte (1849–1915), minister of finance from 1892–1903, kept the economy moving until the first years of this century. Then harvest failures and industrial crises produced civil unrest. The revolution of 1905-6 shook the autocracy to its foundations [10]. It could be suppressed only when the war against Japan had been lost and troops were released for internal duties.

The years 1903-13 were a golden era for industry and agriculture and this helped the government, led by Peter Stolypin (1862–1911), to resist the growing demands for political and social reforms, which were voiced in the Duma (a parliament forced on the Tsar by the crisis of 1905) by the Social Democratic and Kadet (liberal) parties. Thwarted in the Far East, Russia turned after 1906 towards the Balkans where, throughout the nineteenth century, it had supported Slav states against the decaying Ottoman Empire. But the Great Powers stepped in and blocked Russia's progress to the Mediterranean. The empire of Austria-Hungary was the main rival power in the Balkans and therefore Russia felt obliged to support Serbia against the empire in August 1914.

**Servile labour** was typical of the life of millions of Russians in the 19th century, but with industrial development and the population explosion, changes occurred. There were 412,000 barge hauliers on the Volga in 1830, but by 1851 this number had been reduced to 150,000. The steamship had gradually replaced them. There were approximately 40 million peasants (80% of the population) in Russia on the eve of emancipation and about half were in personal bondage to the gentry. Their plight dominated economic life in Russia.

**6 In the 1890s** the industrial development of Russia was improved by the opening up of new oil fields, including this one at Baku. Russia was the world's largest producer of oil until 1900, when the USA took the lead. Railway building was another dynamic force; by 1874 there were 18,220km (11,320 miles) of railway. A by-product of this was Russia's emergence as a major grain exporter. From the 1880s the state began to play an important role in the economy, guided by the policies of Sergei Witte. Development was concentrated in railway construction and in heavy industry.

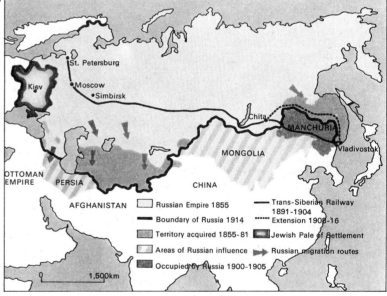

**7 Russia's imperial advance** was spectacular in the later 19th century. She colonized Central Asia and acquired territory which the Chinese still claim as their own. Russia's population explosion caused seven million peasants to move eastwards and cross the Urals. Meanwhile two million Jews emigrated to the USA and 200,000 more to Britain between 1880 and 1914. The Trans-Siberian Railway (built between 1891 and 1904) made a more active policy feasible in the Far East – that is, towards Japan – with the secondary aim of securing an ice-free port on the Pacific. Russia's eastward push and her influence in Manchuria alarmed the Japanese to the point of their going to war in 1904. Apart from her Far Eastern ambitions, Russia also greatly extended her influence in the regions on her southern borders.

Russian Empire 1855
Boundary of Russia 1914
Territory acquired 1855-81
Areas of Russian influence
Occupied by Russia 1900-1905
Trans-Siberian Railway 1891-1904
Extension 1908-16
Jewish Pale of Settlement
Russian migration routes

1,500km

**8 The last of the Romanovs,** Nicholas II, was a reluctant tsar. He came to the throne unusually young and made an inauspicious start in 1894. His mind lacked the cutting edge necessary to evolve a coherent policy and to see it through. Although Russia changed rapidly during his reign he did not move with the times and listened instead to reactionaries, including the monk Rasputin (1871–1916) who mystically influenced the empress. Here Nicholas [2nd from left] is with the Prince of Wales [far right].

**9 An outstanding statesman,** Peter Stolypin (1862–1911) introduced agrarian reforms. He swept away the commune and encouraged the peasants to consolidate their holdings and become farmers. But his autocratic methods lost him liberal support.

**10 "Bloody Sunday"** began as a peaceful demonstration on which troops opened fire in St Petersburg on 22 January 1905. Discontent had grown as the industrial boom of the 1890s gave way to a slump during the early years of the 20th century. Harvest failures aggravated the problem compounded by the defeat in war with Japan. Although unsuccessful, the subsequent revolution of 1905–6 did produce a constitution and a parliament (Duma).

# Political thought in the 19th century

In the mid-nineteenth century most people with any political awareness would almost certainly have described themselves as either "liberals" or "conservatives". The conservatives would have had little difficulty in explaining what they were and what they stood for, namely the established order. They were firmly against radical change and followed the line laid down by Edmund Burke (1729–97) in his *Reflections on the Revolution in France*, published in 1790. This insisted that state and people alike were products of imperceptible, natural and organic growth and that artificial change based on general theories was self-defeating.

In the realm of practical politics, however, it was not quite so easy to preach and practise conservatism – particularly after the fall of the Austrian statesman Prince Metternich (1773–1859) in the revolution of 1848. Metternich refused to concede that any kind of change was permissible, if only as a tactical manoeuvre to prevent more radical developments, and was ultimately obliged to take refuge in England.

Metternich's downfall was one of the factors that encouraged the British prime minister, the astute Benjamin Disraeli (1804–81), to present the country with a Second Reform Bill. Meanwhile in Germany Prince Otto von Bismarck (1815–98) introduced universal suffrage and limited social welfare legislation. In France, Napoleon III (1808–73) had embarked on similar action.

## The decline of liberalism

Liberals were distinguished by the belief that progress could be achieved by means of "free institutions". In Britain and France this usually referred to a freely elected parliament, with ministries responsible to it, an independent judiciary, freedom of speech and religion, freedom from arbitrary arrest and freedom to acquire and safeguard property.

In Russia a "liberal" might merely be someone who advocated a strong state council to advise the tsar. But even in France there were "liberals", including François Guizot (1787–1874), the statesman and historian, who believed that institutions were already as free as possible – a belief that made them seem highly conservative.

One of the most interesting themes of nineteenth-century European history is the decline of liberalism as a real political force. The main reason for the collapse was that, although the liberal ideal of making a framework of free institutions was born of the Enlightenment, once erected it became a bastion behind which the propertied classes defended their vested interests. The Continental turmoil of 1848 saw middle-class liberals deserting their ideals when faced with the prospect of sharing power with the lower-paid and less-educated sections of society.

## The rise of socialism

The creed that began to appeal to many of those apparently abandoned by liberalism was socialism, and the greatest socialist thinker of the century was without doubt Karl Marx (1818–83) [Key]. The young Marx of the first half of the century drew his ideas from a wide variety of sources but the foundation of his beliefs was the conviction, derived from the German philosopher Georg Hegel (1770–1831), that history was progressive, had objective meaning and

**1 Appalling social conditions** existed in 19th-century Europe as a result of the development and concentration of industry and a boom in population. By 1848 the "social question" was causing concern. Neither government nor individuals did much to tackle the problem. Chartism emerged as a force in Britain, while in Europe the old spirit of revolution was again showing signs of revival. But in the long term, a steady if slow increase in living standards was brought about not by political organization and agitation, as might be supposed, but by the unexpected growth of the economy.

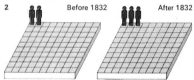
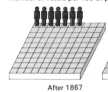

Number of voters per 100 of population

Before 1832 · After 1832 · After 1867 · After 1884

**2 A new British electoral system** was created between 1832 and 1885, based on a series of Acts of Parliament. The result was that by 1886 two-thirds of the adult male population of England and Wales, and three-fifths in Scotland, had the right to cast their vote in secret. The measures that brought this about were three Representation of the People Acts, a Ballot Act and two Acts to redistribute the seats and prevent corruption.

**3 The world's first trade unions** were founded in Britain where they were legalized in 1825. This was well in advance of other countries – trade unions were first tolerated in France in 1864 but not made legal until 1884, while Germany did not permit them until the 1890s. Membership of the early British unions such as the Friendly Society of Iron and Steel Founders was restricted to local skilled artisans. The first large union was the Amalgamated Society of Engineers, founded in 1851, but it had more interest in social benefits than in trade disputes. By 1875 unions were well established and the laws on strikes, picketing and contractual obligations had been clarified.

**4 Mikhail Bakunin** (1814–76), a Russian aristocrat, resigned his commission in the Imperial Guard to become Europe's leading anarchist. Not surprisingly his life was eventful: he was sentenced to death by the Austrians and the Prussians and was sent to Siberia by his own country. He escaped in 1861 and spent the rest of his life advancing anarchism in western Europe. Unlike the socialists, he believed that society could only be overthrown through individual revolt.

would reveal this meaning through a series of revolutionary jumps.

The *Communist Manifesto* of 1848 reflected Marx's faith in the success of the European revolutions of that year, but with their ultimate failure he laid more stress on the deterministic aspects of his thought. He predicted that bourgeois society would collapse as a result of its own internal contradictions. Capital, he said, would become concentrated in fewer hands until the oppressed workers would be forced to revolt against their exploiters. A "dictatorship of the proletariat" would then emerge, paving the way for such social harmony that the state could wither away. The Paris Commune [7] revived his faith in revolutionary activity and in the 1870s he even toyed with the possibility of a peaceful overthrow of the social system through the ballot box with the aid of a fully enfranchised proletariat.

### The development of nationalism

It was not the thoughts of Marx, however, that dominated the nineteenth century. By far the greatest force was nationalism, which conquered both the liberals and the socialists.

In 1815 nationalism was still weak in Europe, but only 45 years later the philosopher and economist John Stuart Mill (1806–73) was to write that it was "in general a necessary condition of free institutions that the boundaries of government should coincide in the main with those of nationalities".

Meanwhile nationalism had developed in many ways. The German philosopher Johann Herder (1744–1803) had insisted before the end of the eighteenth century that men's minds were conditioned by their cultural environment and, especially, by their language. Other thinkers took up this theme at the beginning of the new century and subsequently gave rise to many linguistic revivals. European scholars compiled dictionaries and grammars; folk-songs and folk poetry were collected; national histories were written. This, in turn, stimulated political demands and national wars radically redrew the map of Europe. The rest of the world did not escape: frustrated nationalism led to adventures overseas and the great wave of imperialism.

**Karl Marx** was the father of modern socialism. His political views are outlined in the *Communist Manifesto*, his views on political economy in *Das Kapital* (*Capital*).

6

**6 The Geneva Convention** of 1864 established the International Red Cross. This was a humane reaction to the suffering of soldiers in the wars of the 1850s but also reflected concern about the problems of war itself. Other aspects of this were the continuing attempts to regulate war by law and the strength of the international pacifist movements. Peace congresses were held frequently from the middle of the century onwards. By 1900 there was a belief current in Europe that some genuine progress had been made towards achieving permanent peace.

7

**7 Napoleon's statue was overturned** in 1871 to signal the founding of the Paris Commune, one of the significant events of 19th-century Europe. Socialists saw it as a vindication of their belief that only by resorting to force could workers hope to overthrow the rule of the bourgeoisie. Yet the truth, in retrospect, is more complex than legend and it must be conceded that national and sectional interests were involved in the tragedy. Paris had declared itself independent of the rest of France and had to be brought back into line before peace with Prussia was possible. The end of the Commune brought vengeance and bloodshed: 20,000 were killed and 50,000 arrested.

5

**5 "The Republic"**, a symbolic painting by Daumier (1808–79), shows the idealism often attributed to such government. Before the French Revolution republics were considered as legitimate as any monarchy but after 1815 they went "out of fashion" and Europe grew more monarchical. As new states such as Belgium, Greece, Romania and Bulgaria were created, so too were new monarchies. Although monarchy was no longer divine it was the system of government most comprehensible to the ordinary man. It was argued that only monarchy could unite all groups and all classes. Even France was little different. It was ruled by kings or emperors for most of the century and the Third Republic was established by one vote in 1875 as the regime that "divided Frenchmen least".

# Masters of sociology

The development of sociology in nineteenth-century Europe was stimulated by the need to understand the birth of industrial society [1]. The traditional agrarian social order, apparently based on the squire and the Church, was in the process of dissolution. In its place a new order was emerging whose symbols were the factory and the vast, anonymous urban proletariat [2]. A previously integrated structure of culture and authority was giving way to a series of sharply differentiated economic cultures and to class warfare. In this atmosphere of uncertainty intellectuals began to search for explanations of what was happening to society.

## The British tradition

In Britain the path of industrialization generally caused little concern. Until the end of the century most Englishmen felt that the factory represented an unequivocal force for good, which was taking their society towards perfection. This largely unquestioning acceptance of the notion of "progress" meant that Britain produced no original sociological theory. Indeed, the main British theoretical

tradition was inherited uncritically from the optimistic Enlightenment of the previous century. Its tenets were that society consisted of autonomous individuals each of whom was naturally good; that an "invisible hand" lay behind human activity and pushed it towards conditions of freedom in which the individual could express his innate goodness; and that social science should proceed by reason to discover the objective laws by which the hand worked and so facilitate its operation.

The one man who added something new to these ideas was Herbert Spencer (1820–1903) [3C] who recognized that the orthodox interpretation of society assumed but did not explain change. Spencer, however, did not abandon the ideas of the Enlightenment but regarded them in relation to a model of social change owing much to Darwin's *Origin of Species*. He argued that societies were driven forward to more complex and higher forms by the struggle for survival between individuals, and that the struggle had produced in Britain a *laissez-faire* industrial society which was as yet the highest social form. Although Spencer's

conclusions were controversial, his methodology was influential. For the next 50 years British sociologists sought to explain social institutions by their "history".

## The French tradition

In France the aftermath of the Revolution produced a reaction against Enlightenment thinking. The Vicomte de Bonald (1754–1840) argued that society ought to be seen not as a collection of individuals but as an organic whole. Change in one part (as by one social group) was bound to upset the entire organism.

The organic tradition was continued by Auguste Comte (1798–1857) [3B], not only to order and control change but also to understand it. Comte held the Enlightenment view that there were objective, discoverable laws of social progress. But he insisted that these laws operated in the context of whole societies and not individuals. Men, through their conditioning in society, were made by laws they could not alter. They should recognize this fact and accept their assigned social position.

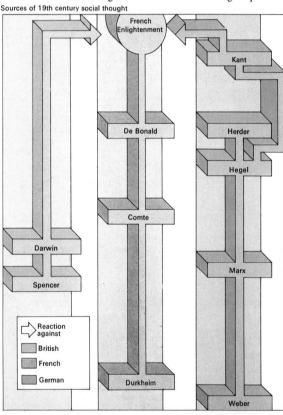

1 **The common origin** of European sociology was the Enlightenment. Different national traditions reacted to the Enlightenment in different ways. The only British innovation was Spencer's adaptation of Darwin's model of biological evolution to provide explanations of social change. In France, however, the conservative reaction to the French Revolution rejected atomistic models of society (centred on the individual) and questioned the validity of empirical inquiry (based on experience). But with Auguste Comte, Enlightenment empiricism was brought back into French sociology. In Germany, Kant and Hegel added new insights to these ideas. Man was no longer to be seen as an object moved around by impersonal laws and social forces: his own consciousness created the social relationships in which he participated.

Sources of 19th century social thought

French Enlightenment — Kant — De Bonald — Herder — Hegel — Comte — Marx — Darwin — Spencer — Durkheim — Weber

Reaction against

British
French
German

2 **The Industrial Revolution** dramatically changed the environment of European society. Millions of people were crowded into filthy, disease-ridden towns and were obliged to move to the new social and economic rhythms of factory labour. The obvious horror of mid-19th century urban life, illustrated by this Manchester slum interior, caught the attention of many early sociologists – Friedrich Engels (1820–95) for example – and produced some of the first exercises in applied sociology. Sociologists surveyed specific situations in the hope of finding remedies for major problems.

3 **Major 19th-century sociologists** included: Max Weber [A], who attempted to combine empiricism and neo-Kantianism in his *Protestant Ethic and the Spirit of Capitalism* (1905). Auguste Comte's [B] doctrine of positivism (to organize all knowledge into a consistent philosophy) is contained in *Système de Politique Positive* (1851–4). Herbert Spencer [C] amalgamated atomistic sociology and Darwinian evolution in *The Principles of Ethics* (1879–93).

Comte's "positivism" was most highly refined by one of the most influential individuals in all sociology, Emile Durkheim (1858–1917). The distinctive characteristics of French sociology included "methodological collectivism", which studied only phenomena that would reveal how men were conditioned by their society. There were also functional explanations whereby social institutions were described in terms of their functions within the entire social system rather than by their history. Lastly there was an emphasis on the need for order where change was regarded as the result of a malfunction in society.

**The German tradition**
In Germany the inheritance of Enlightenment rationality was joined by two other intellectual elements. The Kantian philosophical revolution (after Immanuel Kant [1724–1804]) held that the laws of nature existed only in men's minds; and the Romantic movement of Johann Herder (1744–1803) stressed the creative importance of language and culture.

The first great German theorist was G. W. F. Hegel (1770–1831), who saw social change as the product of human reason driven forward by its need to know and overcome the world around it. Hegel's theme was further developed by Karl Marx (1818–83) [4] who is perhaps best seen as a sociological Hegelian. Marx shared Hegel's view that the force behind social change was man's pursuit of rational understanding and control of his environment. But Marx's most important work resulted from his belief in the economic basis of social structure and in his suggestion of a sequence of social development.

The third major German theorist was Max Weber (1864–1920) [3A] who complemented Marx by adding an appreciation of the role of cultural values to Marx's work.

The principal achievements of the German tradition were "methodological individualism": an approach to society from the viewpoint of self-conscious human subjects; a combination of explanations from history and explanations from function; and the development of a theory of knowledge of the social sciences.

**These men on strike in 1889** at the East and West India Docks in London symbolize the class and culture conflict produced by industrialization, which sociologists of the period tried to understand. It aggravated the division of culture along class lines and led to strife in every nation.

Primitive    Patriarchal    Feudal    Capitalist    Socialist

**4 Karl Marx** argued that human society developed in response to man's desire to satisfy his material needs. But needs themselves continued to develop. Eventually the prevailing form of social structure would no longer be able to accommodate these growing needs and so would break down, giving way to a new structure that permitted the continuation of need satisfaction. The final stage would be reached when bourgeois capitalism succeeded in concentrating wealth in a few hands and in impoverishing the masses. The starving proletariat, whose basic needs were not being met, would rise up and take over the means of production and create a society in which the forces of production and the social structure were no longer in conflict.

B

**5 The interpretation** of the European revolutions of 1848 and 1870 brought out the different perspectives of French, English and German sociology. For the French the revolutions (particularly the Commune of 1870 [A]) represented evidence of a deep-seated malfunction in society. For the British, they represented the just struggle of European society for individual, bourgeois freedoms against the tyranny of anachronistic, feudal governments. For the German Marxists the revolutions were a sign of the imminent destruction of the whole capitalist order: the cartoon [B] shows the French President Thiers (1797–1877) with a Prussian soldier looking down on the cauldron of Paris.

# Europe 1870–1914

The period after the unification of Italy and Germany witnessed the consolidation and growth of the major nation states. Rising population, growing industrialization and stronger governments created a period of immense dynamism, but also intense national rivalry. The rise of democratic institutions in many parts of Europe and the development of trade unions encouraged more social legislation, such as welfare programmes. By the outbreak of World War I, socialist parties had appeared in many countries.

### The rise of German power and influence
In terms of population, trade, industry and armed forces Imperial Germany was clearly the most powerful European state [4]. Its easy conquest of France in the Franco-Prussian War of 1870–71 testified to its military strength [1]. Following the war the German Chancellor, Count Otto von Bismarck (1815–98), sought to create a stable diplomatic environment in which a "satiated" Germany would be able to consolidate its gains and build up its international power and prestige. Germany's Dual Alliance with Austria-Hungary (1879) and the Reinsurance Treaty with Russia (1887) were designed to prevent those two countries clashing in the Balkans. Bismarck's diplomatic system survived recurrent crises over this issue [3] until his resignation in 1890.

The Dual Alliance became the Triple Alliance with the addition of Italy in 1882, and was faced by the Franco-Russian alliance of 1891. Great Britain joined France in the *Entente Cordiale* in 1904 and an Anglo-Russian treaty was signed in 1907, forming the Triple Entente. Bismarck's bequest became a dangerous system of alliances which was put under severe strain by imperial rivalry, Balkan crises and the instability of the Austro-Hungarian Empire.

Domestically many European states made considerable advances. In Britain extension of the franchise in 1867 and 1884 gave votes to many working men. France also operated a parliamentary democracy. Although still largely an autocratic state, Imperial Germany had the façade of constitutional government and political groups were developing rapidly, including a powerful socialist party. In northern Europe, the Scandinavian countries evolved along a largely peaceful path, often pursuing progressive social legislation.

In southern Europe parliamentary democracy existed only to a limited extent. Italy [8] was threatened by its own poverty and frequent periods of disorder and political instability. In the Iberian Peninsula a small middle class and the powerful hold of the Roman Catholic Church meant that politics remained oligarchic and backward. In eastern Europe, Austria-Hungary [5] remained an essentially monarchial state, troubled by severe national rivalries.

### The conflict between Church and state
The growing power of the nation states and an increasing degree of state intervention in the areas of public education and welfare brought conflict with the Roman Catholic Church. The Church was attacked in many countries for political conservatism and opposition to liberal and national aspirations. In France the conflict was mainly about education, where the Church had great influ-

**1 The entry of Prussian troops** into Paris at the end of the Franco-Prussian War of 1870–71 illustrated the power of the newly unified German state under the rule of the Hohenzollern dynasty and the direction of Bismarck. Domination of Europe by France as the greatest continental power was rudely supplanted by the growing industrial might of Imperial Germany, whose armies made efficient use of the German railways and artillery built by Krupps. In France defeat toppled Napoleon III's Second Empire and, after the Paris Commune, ushered in the Third Republic.

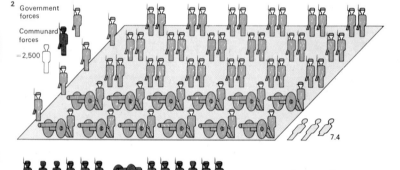

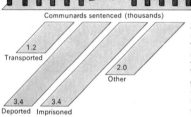

**2 The Paris Commune** followed privations endured in the siege of Paris during the Franco-Prussian War. When a new government at Bordeaux called in Paris rents, the lower middle classes and workers revolted and, although greatly outmanned and outgunned, they held the city from March to May 1871. They introduced a semi-socialist regime until savagely suppressed by government troops.

**3 The great powers** all attended the Congress of Berlin in 1878. A major source of conflict was the fate of the decaying Ottoman Empire and its Balkan dependencies, in which the interests of Austria-Hungary (represented by Karolyi, far left), and Russia (Shuvalov, right foreground, shaking hands with Germany's Bismarck), were deeply involved. The Congress recognized the independence of several Balkan states but denied them some of the territory they had just won from Turkey with Russia's help. Austria was allowed to occupy Bosnia-Hercegovina while France and Britain also made gains. The Congress however left all parties unsatisfied.

ence. Republican aims were advanced by the French statesman Jules Ferry (1833–93), who secularized education through legislation in 1882 and 1886. In spite of a period of relative amity between Church and state in the period that followed, known as the *Ralliement*, the Dreyfus affair [7] once again revealed the old tensions and led to bitter anti-clerical feeling. As a result, the concordat between the Papacy and the state was ended in 1905.

In Germany, too, between 1870 and 1880, Bismarck waged the *Kulturkampf* in which the Jesuits were expelled, religious orders dissolved, civil marriage made compulsory and other anti-Catholic legislation introduced [6]. In Italy, Belgium and other Catholic countries similar clashes occurred, although on a lesser scale.

Tariff reform became a pressing political issue in an era of growing rivalry in international trade and an influx of cheap foodstuffs from outside Europe. France protected its manufacturers by the Meline Tariff of 1892 and Germany built up its industry behind protective barriers. Even *laissez-faire* Britain

witnessed a tariff reform campaign in 1902–5 by Joseph Chamberlain (1836–1914) which, however, failed to secure majority support among the electorate for protection of British and colonial goods.

**Appeals to patriotism and nationalism**
Several states sought to appease growing working-class demands by social legislation. In Britain, Benjamin Disraeli (1804–81) and later David Lloyd George (1863–1945) introduced social welfare. The latter copied the comprehensive social insurance schemes of Bismarck. In France, although anti-clericalism and other issues of the past could still create great passion, politics essentially constituted the safeguarding of vested interests and social legislation lagged. Governments everywhere tended to rally public opinion by stimulating patriotic feeling. Growing literacy, prosperity and communications also fostered intense nationalism. Conscript armies, equipped with the weapons of modern industrial economies, created war machines [Key] capable of unprecedented warfare.

**A growing armaments industry** towards the end of the 1800s produced weapons such as this German howitzer, which fired a 45kg (100lb) shell. Consolidation of nation states and the emergence of an intense patriotism was translated by conscription and industrialization into mass armies with which the nations of Europe faced each other in 1914.

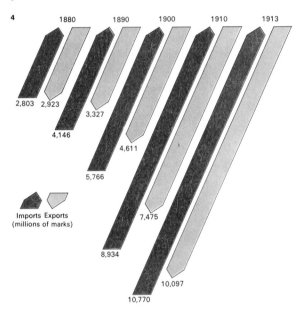

4

| 1880 | 1890 | 1900 | 1910 | 1913 |

2,803  2,923
4,146
3,327
4,611
5,766
7,475
8,934
10,097
10,770

Imports Exports
(millions of marks)

**4 The unified German Empire** became the greatest industrial power in Europe in the years before World War I, surpassing Great Britain in many branches of manufacture by 1900. From 1880 Germany's trade soared and both imports and exports increased more than threefold by 1913.

**5 Elegant women, dashing officers** – the outward glitter of "Gay Vienna" in the late 19th-century – masked a rich intellectual and artistic life that stemmed not only from the polyglot Austro-Hungarian Empire but also from much of eastern Europe. The culture it produced influenced the whole of Europe.

5

**8 Giovanni Giolitti** (1842–1928), five times prime minister of Italy between 1892 and 1921, managed to achieve periods of near stability and considerable industrial progress at a time when Italy was socially and economically backward. Parliamentary democracy was often difficult to introduce in recently unified states and in Italy political strikes and hunger riots were common before 1914.

6

7

8

**6 Count Bismarck** was a master of diplomatic chess, countering the interdicts of Pope Pius IX (1792–1878) with anti-monastic legislation, as shown in this cartoon of the day. He presided over the unification of Germany, conducting both foreign and domestic policy with ruthless cunning until his resignation as Chancellor in 1890 after disagreement with the new kaiser, Wilhelm II. Groups such as the Catholics and socialists were subordinated to the interests of the state.

**7 Caricatured as a traitor to France,** Captain Alfred Dreyfus (1859–1935) was the centre of a bitter controversy after 1896, when it emerged that an army court had unjustly convicted him of spying for Germany. Dreyfus was a Jew and both anti-semitic and ultra-conservative groups tried to block a fair retrial. Anti-clerical and radical groups supported him with ultimate success and the issue showed the deep divisions underlying the apparent stability of France.

# British foreign policy 1815–1914

The years between the final British victory over the French at Waterloo in 1815 and the outbreak of European war in 1914 are known by the British as the *Pax Britannica*. They were not years in which Britain was entirely free from war, but, defended around the globe by the world's most powerful navy, it faced no direct threat to its security. During this period, Britain's foreign secretaries played upon a world stage, able to take an enlarged view of their duties and so to weave into their strategic considerations matters of very wide political import.

## Protecting free trade and the empire

For most of the century Britain was able to conduct its foreign affairs with mere deference to the views of other powers. Britain's main strategic aims were to protect the empire, in particular the trade route to India, and to maintain the balance of power in Europe. Liberal statesmen tried to encourage the progress of liberal nationalist movements in various parts of the world. But in general, foreign secretaries did not interfere in foreign disputes.

Britain was, of course, favourably placed by the conquests of the eighteenth century and the strength of the navy [5] to look upon the world as its oyster. The idea of free trade came to dominate not only the Exchequer, but also the Foreign Office. British statesmen considered the world as a place in which all nations, freely trading with one another, would learn that commercial interdependence had made war obsolete as an instrument of national policy.

Only as a result of mounting fear of Russian influence in the Mediterranean did Britain intervene in the war of Greek independence [1] in the 1820s and the Turko-Russian quarrel that led to the Crimean War (1854–6) [2, 3]. The nascent power of Russia and the debility of Turkey, the "sick man of Europe", were eventually to turn the Balkans into a powder keg. For a century the "Eastern question" smouldered.

## British liberalism abroad

The tendencies of the age were revealed in the 1820s, during the foreign secretaryships of Viscount Castlereagh (1769–1822) and

George Canning (1770–1827). Their main achievement was to disengage Britain from the conservative Holy Alliance of the despotic northern powers – Prussia, Austria and Russia. At the Congress of Verona (1822) Britain refused to support intervention in Spain to put down the liberal constitutional government that had toppled the Spanish Bourbons. Nor would it aid the "reactionary" cause in Sicily and Portugal. In Latin America Canning gave his blessing and recognition to the revolts against Spanish and Portuguese rule that ended in the establishment of the independent nations throughout the continent. Canning also lent his support to the Greek patriots who fought to gain their independence from the Ottoman Turks. He died two months before the British navy destroyed the Turkish and Egyptian fleets off Navarino (Pilos, Greece) in October 1827, but in 1830 Greece became a fully independent nation.

In that year Palmerston [Key] began his first stint at the Foreign Office (1830–41), during which his most notable achievement was to assist Belgium to win independence

**1 The revolt of the Greeks,** epitomized in this painting by Delacroix, was the first liberal cause of the century that took England away from the alliance that had defeated Napoleon. Whereas Austria and Russia opposed Greek freedom, Castlereagh and Canning supported the revolt, and English sympathizers went to fight for the Greeks against the Turks – among them the poet Byron (1788–1824), who died there.

**3 The Crimean War** revealed the inefficiency of the army's organization and command. More soldiers died from disease than in battle. William Russell (1820–1907) reported the chaos in *The Times*.

**2 A Quaker deputation** led by Joseph Sturge on the eve of the Crimean War (1854) paid a special visit to Tsar Nicholas I to plead for peace. This was unofficial, and although the British cabinet was divided on the issue, public opinion clamoured for war. Radical MPs who denounced it, including John Bright (1811–89) and Richard Cobden (1804–65), lost their seats at the election of 1857, in which Palmerston was safely returned.

**4 Giuseppe Garibaldi** (1807–82), the Italian nationalist leader, visited London in 1864 and received a great popular welcome, addressing crowds of 20,000 at the Crystal Palace. Several other Continental revolutionaries and nationalists had a similar reception, including the Hungarian Louis Kossuth (1802–94), who fled to England after the Russians had invaded Hungary following Kossuth's proclamation of Hungarian independence from the Hapsburgs early in 1849. Despite his dubious political ambitions, Kossuth was entertained by the foreign secretary, Palmerston. Support for Continental nationalist movements was a potent force in domestic politics in the 19th century; sympathy for the Italians' struggle against the Austrians took Gladstone, who had previously been a Conservative, into the Liberal Party in 1859. Garibaldi's visit to London in 1864 quickened the demand for parliamentary reform; this was met in 1867.

from the Netherlands. (British guarantees to Belgium had fateful consequences in 1914). In the East, Palmerston sought to uphold the territorial rights of Turkey. For a time peace was maintained, but in 1854 Russia and Turkey went to war and Britain and France entered on the side of Turkey.

**The Crimean War and after**
The Crimean War was ostensibly about the tsar's claim to protect Christians under Turkish rule in Europe; in fact it was about whether Turkey should maintain its empire in Europe as a bulwark against Russian aggrandizement in the Balkans. The British army suffered terrible losses, but, in the end, Constantinople and the Black Sea were preserved from Russian control.

Twenty years later, when Turkish misrule in Bulgaria threatened war once more, Benjamin Disraeli (1804–81) went to the Congress of Berlin (1878) and brought back "peace with honour". The *status quo* was upheld without war, but Turkey's failure to learn the lesson and put its house in order and the rising appeal of Slav nationalism throughout the Balkans was a bleak omen.

By the 1880s British security was being undermined. The scramble by European powers for colonies in Africa had begun and in 1882 Britain occupied Egypt. Germany was cutting into Britain's trading and manufacturing supremacy, and was politically worrying France. At the end of Victoria's reign, Germany started building up its naval strength.

As the German threat grew, fears of Russia receded. The Foreign Office was led to recast its priorities, and "splendid isolation" became a thing of the past. In 1904 Edward VII's diplomacy was instrumental in securing the Entente Cordiale with France. There were many people, among them Joseph Chamberlain (1836–1914), who hankered after a German partnership, but the current was flowing in the opposite direction. France was the ally of Russia and in 1907 Britain joined them in the Triple Entente. In 1908, when Bosnia-Hercegovina was annexed by Germany's ally, Austria-Hungary, against the wishes of Russia, the ground was prepared for World War I.

**Viscount Palmerston** (1784–1865) presided over British foreign policy longer than any other man in modern history. As foreign secretary (1830–41, 1846–51) and prime minister (1855–8, 1859–65), his policy rested on confidence in the global pre-eminence of mid-Victorian Britain. His forthright defence of British interests was expressed in the Don Pacifico debate (1850), when he used warships to protect a British citizen against the Greek government, and defended himself with the phrase *"Civis Brittanicus sum"* (I am a citizen of Britain), echoing the *"Civis Romanus sum"* of Imperial Rome. From that day until his death Palmerston was a national hero.

**5**

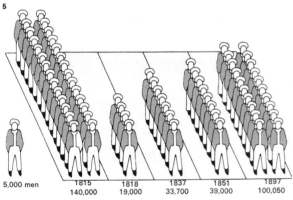

5,000 men | 1815 140,000 | 1818 19,000 | 1837 33,700 | 1851 39,000 | 1897 100,050

**5 The British navy** was the basis of the nation's power throughout the century. But the overwhelming victory at Trafalgar meant that the navy did not need to be large to maintain its ascendancy. It was only with the introduction of steam-driven battleships in the 1880s, and the start of the naval building race with Germany that the navy again employed as many men as in the time of Nelson.

**6**

**6 The use of gunboats** to quell local disturbances throughout the world, as in this expedition up the Nile to relieve Khartoum in 1884, was typical of the *Pax Britannica* as maintained by Palmerston.

**7**

THE COLOSSUS OF WORDS.

**7 William Ewart Gladstone** (1809–98) is depicted here as the "Colossus of Words", whose policies of peace and liberalism serve as an inspiration for reform at home. His stirring opposition to the Bulgarian atrocities of 1876, when the Turks violently put down a nationalist revolt, was typical of the high moral tone of his political feelings, and led to his overthrow of the Conservative government four years later.

**8 Edward VII's visit to Paris in 1903**, and his meeting with the French foreign secretary, won him great affection from the French. It also paved the way to the signing of the Entente Cordiale in 1904, so ending the enmity between the nations.

**8**

**9**

**9 Naval strength** was an important issue in the election of 1910, as this poster shows.

HMS *Dreadnought* first of a powerful new class of battleship, was completed in 1906.

# Balkanization and Slav nationalism

Austria-Hungary and Russia were the chief protagonists in the struggle to supplant the once powerful Turkish Empire, "the sick man of Europe" [3], as the dominant power in the Balkans in the second half of the nineteenth century. For Russia, the mastery of the Balkans would have served its historic aim: to gain control of the Straits of Bosporus and the Dardanelles with the city of Constantinople, and thus gain access to ice-free seas. Austria-Hungary's main concern was to prevent Russia from establishing itself in the Balkans as the protector of a cluster of small states, some claiming territory within the Hapsburg Empire. The Austro-Hungarian policy of blocking Russia's advance towards the Mediterranean was supported by both Germany and Britain.

## Russian hopes dashed

In 1877–8, Russia fought Turkey on the side of Serbia and Montenegro in support of Slav Christians in the province of Hercegovina who had clashed with the Turkish authorities because they refused to pay taxes or to perform the customary labour services. A Tur-

kish force sent against them in 1875 had been defeated with the aid of sympathizers from Serbia and Montenegro as well as from Austria-Hungary's Croat province of Dalmatia. The insurrection had then spread in 1876 to Bulgaria, where an estimated 12,000 to 30,000 Bulgarians were killed by Turkish irregulars in atrocities that aroused indignation throughout Europe.

Although Russian armies reached the outskirts of Constantinople in 1878, the diplomacy of Britain and Austria-Hungary frustrated Russia's main aim. At the Congress of Berlin [1], Russia secured territorial enlargement for Serbia and Montenegro and independence for Bulgaria. Austria-Hungary (which had stayed neutral) was allowed to occupy Bosnia-Hercegovina, Bulgaria was denied access to the Aegean, and the province of Macedonia, to which both Serbia and Bulgaria [2] aspired, was handed back to Turkey.

Serbian and Montenegrin successes in the war fired the imagination of all Slavs in the Austro-Hungarian Empire, but particularly those in the south: Croats, Slovenes and

Serbs living outside Serbia proper in Bosnia, Croatia and Hungary. In Serbia itself the government covertly, and various non-official bodies overtly, gave money and encouragement to groups working for south Slav union. Serbian politicians and intelligentsia saw Serbia as the nucleus of a greater southern Slav nation [Key].

## Revolutionary societies

Croats and other Slavs living in the Hungarian half of the Hapsburg Empire originally viewed the idea of a union with Serbia with suspicion, preferring a south Slav state under Hapsburg leadership. But alienated by Magyar dominance in Hungary, many of them became revolutionary towards the 1900s. Sensing the nationalist threat to their multi-national empire, the Hapsburgs redoubled efforts to control and subdue Serbia, in their view the originator of the monarchy's troubles. The annexation of Bosnia-Hercegovina in 1908 was the result. It was an attempt to pre-empt south Slav nationalism by simply incorporating a disputed area into the empire and thus, hopefully, neutralizing

2 **San Stefano**, the name on the girl's flag in this Bulgarian poster, summed up Bulgaria's efforts to regain from her neighbours what she had won in the San Stefano treaty but lost at Berlin. To that end, Bulgaria fought and defeated Serbia in 1885, but was forced to withdraw after Austrian intervention. In October 1915 Bulgaria, allied to Austria and Germany, again fought Serbia.

1 **The Congress of Berlin** in 1878 drew up a Balkan settlement that was to last a generation. Dominant personalities were the British Prime Minister, Benjamin Disraeli (1804–81) and the German chancellor, Otto von Bismarck (1815–98). Under a treaty signed in July, Russia had to agree to the scrapping of the Treaty of San Stefano, made in March, giving her and her Balkan allies huge territorial gains. Under pressure from Britain, Austria-Hungary and Germany, victorious Russia agreed to limit itself to taking a strip of Bessarabia from Romania, Batum and Kars in the Caucasus and a part of Armenia. Romania's independence was formally recognized. Bosnia and Hercegovina were handed over to Austria-Hungary to administer. Britain was given Cyprus to keep as long as Russia kept Kars and Batum. Serbia and Montenegro received land that Bulgaria had gained earlier but remained cut off from the Aegean. Macedonia was returned to Turkey.

3 **At Constantinople in 1876**, Sultan Abdul-Hamid II (1842–1918) proclaimed a constitution under pressure from Western-educated officials to reform the reactionary Turkish Empire. But he soon abrogated the constitution and it was only in 1908 that the Young Turk movement forced him to reissue it, summon parliament and abolish press censorship. When he prepared a counter-coup in 1909 he was overthrown and replaced.

4 **The German Kaiser, Wilhelm II** (1859–1941), here visiting Constantinople, played a major role in Germany's moves to acquire influence in Turkey as part of a larger extension of power in central Europe and the Mediterranean. Based on a concession granted in 1899 by Turkey to the German company of Anatolian Railways, a rail system was to be built all the way from Berlin to Constantinople and Baghdad as the key to a new German Empire.

it. Russia's weakness after her defeat in the disastrous war against Japan in 1904–5 enabled Austria-Hungary to escape without Russian retaliation.

## The Balkan Wars

The Bosnian annexation initially turned the main thrust of Serbian nationalism south towards Albania and southeast Macedonia which Serbia, Bulgaria and Greece all claimed but which the Congress of Berlin had handed back to Turkey. Exploiting Turkey's preoccupation with its war against Italy in 1911–12, the four Balkan states – Greece, Bulgaria, Serbia and Montenegro – set up the so-called Balkan League and declared war on Turkey in October 1912 [6, 8] (the first Balkan War 1912–13). But the victorious anti-Turkish forces were again frustrated by great power diplomacy.

Germany saw Turkey as the strategic base of its own future thrust into the Middle East and beyond [4] to challenge its greatest rival, Britain. Under Austrian pressure the Serbs were denied access to the Adriatic by the establishment of Albania as a separate state.

Serbia in turn quarrelled with Bulgaria over Macedonia and war broke out between them in June 1913 and lasted a month. Bulgaria was defeated by an alliance of all her neighbours including Romania.

But Hapsburg hopes of the situation becoming calmer in the wake of the Bosnian annexation were disappointed. Nationalist agitation [6] for a union of all south Slavs was boosted by Serbia's successes in the Balkan Wars. Assassinations by members of secret societies in Bosnia and elsewhere became commonplace. The apparent political impasse made Austria-Hungary's leaders think once again of a military solution. The idea was that if only Serbia, the hotbed of nationalistic agitation, could be subdued and neutralized, the rest of Europe would calm down. Germany's virtually unlimited backing of Austria-Hungary's policies strengthened the resolve of certain Austrian military and civilian leaders. The assassination of the heir to the Hapsburg throne, Archduke Franz Ferdinand, in Sarajevo in Bosnia in June 1914, by a revolutionary group based in Serbia, gave them the pretext for war.

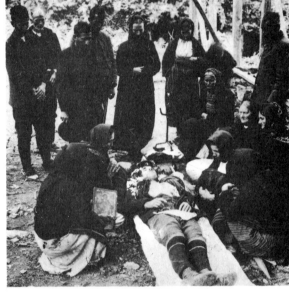

**The spirit of Slav nationalism** is captured in "The Illyrian Revival" by a 19th-century Croatian painter, Vlaho Bukovac. Illyria was a hoped-for independent union of south Slavs under Croat leadership. But the Serbs, who managed to free themselves from Turkish rule in 1830 and became a kingdom in 1882, took the upper hand while Croatia and Slovenia remained part of Austria-Hungary.

**5 The new Balkan states,** formed as a result of Turkey's retreat from Europe, were in dispute with each other: Serbia and Bulgaria over Macedonia; Romania and Bulgaria over Dobruja; and Romania and Austria-Hungary over Transylvania. But the most explosive dispute was between Serbia and Austria-Hungary because of Serbia's support of terrorist activity among Slavs living under Austro-Hungarian rule. This was greatest in Bosnia-Hercegovina, a province of Croats, Serbs and Slav Muslims, which Austria-Hungary had taken over in 1878 and formally annexed in 1908 in order to prevent Serb agitation. Austria-Hungary also frustrated Serbia's attempt to gain direct access to the Adriatic by encouraging the formation of a separate Albanian state, which was proclaimed in 1912.

| | |
|---|---|
| **1878** | |
| Ottoman Empire | |
| Bulgaria | |
| Romania | |
| Greece | |
| Serbia | |
| Montenegro | |

Thessaly to Greece 1881
East Rumelia to Bulgaria 1878
To Greece 1908

To Greece 1913
Occupied by Austria-Hungary 1870–1909
Boundaries 1903

0 ———— 300km

**6 The first Bulgarian soldier to be killed** in the first Balkan War is surrounded by mourners. Although fighting did not begin until October 1912, the seeds of the conflict were sown in a secret treaty concluded between Serbia and Bulgaria in March. They planned to attack Turkey and divide the spoils. According to this, Serbia was to have been given most of Albania. The war started when Montenegro attacked Turkey on 8 October. Bulgaria, Serbia and Greece then joined in, and soon the Turks were reeling under the combined onslaught. They asked for a truce in December.

**7 Peoples of many different races** and religions inhabit the Balkans. The Croats have a Latin script and are Roman Catholics. The Serbs, Bulgarians, Montenegrins and Macedonians received their Cyrillic script, Orthodox religion and political tradition from Byzantium. Under Turkish rule the Orthodox Church retained its autonomy and was influential in the national revival of the Balkan peoples. Turkey left two enclaves of Islam in Europe: Bosnia and Albania.

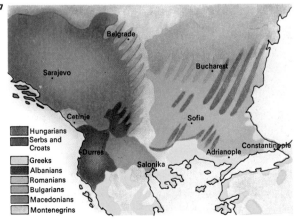

| | |
|---|---|
| Hungarians | |
| Serbs and Croats | |
| Greeks | |
| Albanians | |
| Romanians | |
| Bulgarians | |
| Macedonians | |
| Montenegrins | |

**8 Bulgarian troops** (here shown near the Serbian border) moved against Serbia in June 1913, so starting the second Balkan war. The attack pre-empted Serbia's designs on parts of Macedonia, held by Bulgaria since the settlement to the first war. By August, however, Bulgaria had been defeated by an alliance of all her neighbours. In the settlement, Serbia gained most while Turkey, Greece and Romania also made teritorial gains.

# Causes of World War I

During the 1890s Germany's ruling class, headed by the intelligent but vacillating German Kaiser, Wilhelm II (1859–1941), abandoned Bismarck's cautious foreign policy in favour of a more dynamic one designed to reflect Germany's industrial and military strength. Germany wanted a large colonial empire, not only for economic reasons but to enhance its prestige. To this end a law to expand the German navy, the first of many such laws, was enacted in 1898. The new navy was designed ultimately to challenge British naval supremacy [1] and to force Britain, faced with seemingly perpetual Franco-Russian hostility, to collaborate in a wholesale reallocation of colonial territory.

## German diplomatic set-backs

The first set-back to Germany's "world policy" came in 1904 when Britain and France settled their colonial differences. Then, in 1907, Britain resolved its long-standing central Asian disputes with Russia, France's ally since 1894. In 1905 Germany, taking advantage of Russia's defeat by Japan, challenged France's increasing strength in Morocco [2] and coerced it into participating in an international conference in January 1906 at Algeciras to settle the Moroccan question on Germany's terms. However, Germany suffered a diplomatic defeat, for its plans for Morocco were supported only by Austria-Hungary. Moreover Germany's assumption that the Anglo-French *entente* would be wrecked by Britain's failure to support France proved to be similarly erroneous. Britain co-operated closely with France during the conference and, alarmed by Germany's aggressive policy, initiated unofficial Anglo-French military discussions.

Germany next proceeded to alienate Russia. In 1909 it insisted with a veiled threat of war that Russia recognize Austria-Hungary's 1908 annexation of Turkish Bosnia-Hercegovina and abandon support for Serbia's claim for compensation. International tension was further increased when, in a bid to secure colonial compensation from France, now almost in control of Morocco, Germany sent a gunboat to the Moroccan port of Agadir on 1 July 1911. Although during the following months Britain and France came close to war with Germany over the Moroccan issue, a Franco-German colonial compromise was signed in November. The crisis left a legacy of bitterness and hatred in both countries. As a result Germany, in 1912, further increased its naval strength and began to expand its army. It was followed inevitably in this action by every other Continental great power [3].

## Instability in the Balkans

The causes of World War I were, however, more directly connected with events in the Balkans. In 1912 the Balkan League (Serbia, Greece, Montenegro and Bulgaria) drove Turkey out of most of its remaining possessions. The following year Bulgaria was defeated by its former allies, Greece and Serbia, and lost its Macedonian gains of 1912 to Serbia. Austria-Hungary was thus faced with a greatly enlarged and ambitious Serbia, determined that the Slavs within the Hapsburg Empire should come under this rule.

The cumulative effect of all these crises was to increase preparations for war: indeed, Germany had long since devised its blueprint

1 **The British fleet** in the 1890s aimed to equal those of the two next biggest naval powers, France and Russia. When this two-power standard was challenged by the rise of the German navy in the 1900s, Britain settled her differences with France and Russia and concentrated on maintaining naval superiority over Germany. As a result, Anglo-German relations became increasingly embittered. The launching of the *Dreadnought* (faster and better armed than any ship before it) by Britain in 1906 opened a new stage in naval rivalry as each country tried to build more such vessels than its neighbours. But Britain kept its lead.

2 **Visiting Tangier** in March 1905, the Kaiser pledged to uphold Morocco's independence. He hoped to protect German interests in Morocco (rapidly falling under French control) and to force France to recognize that its future lay in alliance with Germany. While the independence of Morocco was thus preserved until 1911, Germany's clumsy diplomacy drove France and Britain closer together.

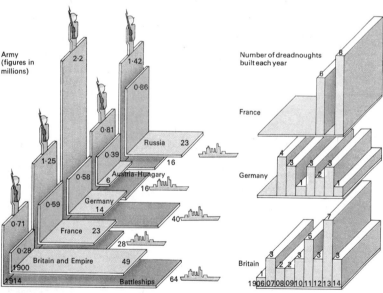

Army (figures in millions)

2·2
1·42
0·86
0·81
Russia 23
0·39
1·25
16
Austria-Hungary
0·58
16
6
Germany 14
0·59
France 23
40
0·71
28
Britain and Empire 49
0·28
1900
1914
Battleships 64

Number of dreadnoughts built each year

France

Germany

Britain

1906 07 08 09 10 11 12 13 14

3 **An armaments race** between the Great Powers before 1914 both reflected and heightened European tension. In addition to building a large navy, Germany possessed the most formidable army in Europe. Although its size remained fairly stable from 1900–10, Germany's deteriorating diplomatic situation led in 1912–13 to increases in army strength which provoked the other Great Powers, except Britain (the only one with a volunteer army), to increase their own forces.

4 **The Schlieffen Plan** was based on a two-front war with Russia and France, which had been allies since 1894. It provided for a massive German assault through Holland (later excluded) and Belgium to outflank the French army. Meanwhile, Austro-German forces would defend the east until the main German army, having knocked out France, could be rapidly moved to meet the slowly advancing Russians. Violation of Belgian neutrality would risk British intervention.

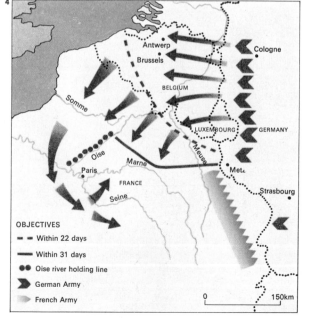

Antwerp
Brussels
Cologne
BELGIUM
Somme
LUXEMBOURG
GERMANY
Oise
Paris
Marne
Meuse
FRANCE
Metz
Seine
Strasbourg

OBJECTIVES
- – – Within 22 days
- —— Within 31 days
- ●● Oise river holding line
- German Army
- French Army

0        150km

for victory, perfected by Count Alfred von Schlieffen (1833–1913), Chief of Staff, in 1905, and amended by his successor, Helmuth von Moltke (1848–1916). The Schlieffen Plan [4] relied on the slowness of Russian mobilization and provided for a rapid thrust through Belgium to defeat France, leaving the German army free to move rapidly east to meet the Russians.

The assassination of the heir to the Hapsburg throne, Franz Ferdinand (1863–1914), at Sarajevo on 28 June 1914 [8] was the climax of a series of Serbian provocations towards Austria. Berlin feared that if Austria-Hungary failed to take the opportunity provided by the murder to bring Serbia within its orbit, its multi-national empire would collapse, leaving Germany isolated. Thus Austria was under German pressure to act against Serbia, with the promise of German military support should war ensue. Successive German diplomatic defeats, a sense of "encirclement" by Britain, France and an increasingly strong Russia, and deep divisions within German society all combined in 1914 to convince the German ruling élite of the desirability of war partly to preserve the idea of a German-dominated "*Mittel Europe*". Although apprehensive, German Chancellor Theobald von Bethmann Hollweg (1856–1921) gambled on both Russian and British neutrality [6] and hoped that the Austro-Serbian dispute could be localized, in spite of the rigid system of alliances that divided Europe.

### The final steps to war
Austria finally [7] presented an ultimatum demanding the right to investigate Serbian terrorists and, when Serbia rejected this, declared war on 28 July 1914. Russia could hardly stand aside and, faced with growing pro-Slav feeling, Tsar Nicholas II (1868–1918) ordered mobilization. British mediation failed to persuade Austria-Germany to compromise. When France refused to leave Russia to fight alone, the Schlieffen Plan was activated and events proceeded rapidly [9] towards war between the Central Powers (Germany, Austria-Hungary and Turkey) and the Allies (Russia, Serbia, France, Belgium and Great Britain).

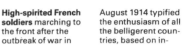

**High-spirited French soldiers** marching to the front after the outbreak of war in August 1914 typified the enthusiasm of all the belligerent countries, based on intense nationalism and a belief that the war would be short and glorious.

**5 A wartime photograph** of the Kaiser (centre) and his generals reflects his fondness for military life. Responsible for Germany's foreign policy, the ultimate decision to mobilize on 1 August was his alone.

**6 Germany's Chancellor** Bethmann Hollweg [left] and Foreign Minister Gottlieb von Jagow (1863–1935) misjudged the willingness of Britain to go to war over a "scrap of paper" guaranteeing the neutrality of Belgium. They gambled on diplomatic victory for the Central Powers when, with the promise of German military support, they encouraged Austrian action against Serbia in July 1914.

**7 Count Leopold von Berchtold** (1863–1942), the Austrian Foreign Minister, was convinced that the multi-national Hapsburg Empire would collapse unless Serbia was crushed. His opportunity was provided when Franz Ferdinand was murdered but although promised full German support, he encountered considerable opposition to his plans from the Hungarian government. This partly accounted for the delay in presenting the Austrian ultimatum to Serbia.

**8 Gavrilo Princip** (1893–1918) precipitated the chain of events leading to war when he shot the heir to the Austro-Hungarian thrones, Archduke Franz Ferdinand, and his wife while they were visiting Sarajevo, capital of Bosnia, on 28 June 1914. He was one of a group of Bosnian conspirators with Serbian support.

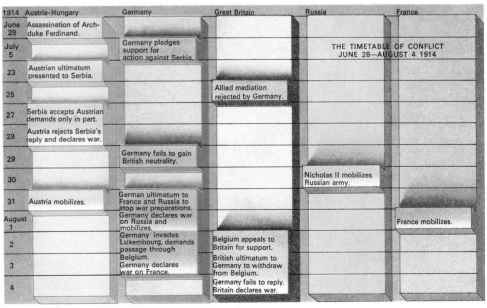

| 1914 | Austria-Hungary | Germany | Great Britain | Russia | France |
|---|---|---|---|---|---|
| June 28 | Assassination of Archduke Ferdinand. | | | | |
| July 5 | | Germany pledges support for action against Serbia. | | THE TIMETABLE OF CONFLICT JUNE 28—AUGUST 4 1914 | |
| 23 | Austrian ultimatum presented to Serbia. | | | | |
| 25 | | | Allied mediation rejected by Germany. | | |
| 27 | Serbia accepts Austrian demands only in part. | | | | |
| 28 | Austria rejects Serbia's reply and declares war. | | | | |
| 29 | | Germany fails to gain British neutrality. | | | |
| 30 | | | | Nicholas II mobilizes Russian army. | |
| 31 | Austria mobilizes. | German ultimatum to France and Russia to stop war preparations. | | | |
| August 1 | | Germany declares war on Russia and mobilizes. | | | France mobilizes. |
| 2 | | Germany invades Luxembourg, demands passage through Belgium. | Belgium appeals to Britain for support. | | |
| 3 | | Germany declares war on France. | British ultimatum to Germany to withdraw from Belgium. | | |
| 4 | | | Germany fails to reply. Britain declares war. | | |

# World War I

On 28th June 1914, the heir to the Austro-Hungarian throne, Archduke Franz Ferdinand (1863–1914), was assassinated in Sarajevo, Bosnia, by a pro-Serbian student, Gavrilo Princip (1893–1918), precipitating a chain of diplomatic manoeuvres that ultimately led to war. The Balkans had long been a centre of conflict. Serbian nationalism threatened the shaky Austro-Hungarian Empire, whose collapse would isolate her ally, Germany, in Europe. Russia, Serbia's ally, was also involved in the Balkans because whoever controlled them would be in control of Russia's main trade route.

### The first battles on both fronts

Germany pressed her ally to take firm action and on 28 July Austria-Hungary declared war on Serbia. Two days later, Russia mobilized and Germany responded by declaring war on Russia on 1 August. Germany's Schlieffen Plan, drawn up to avoid a war on two fronts, necessitated an all-out attack through Belgium to knock out France, Russia's ally, quickly. Germany therefore declared war on France on 3 August and invaded Belgium the next day. As a result, Great Britain came to Belgium's defence.

By 9 September German forces had advanced to the Marne where the British and French were able to halt them. At the end of October each side faced the other in trenches running from the English Channel to the Swiss frontier. In the east, the vast, ill-equipped Russian army had lumbered into East Prussia where it was crushingly defeated on 20 August at the Battle of Tannenberg.

Throughout 1915 the Germans remained on the defensive in the west, allowing the Allies to exhaust themselves in a series of futile attacks, while launching a summer offensive in the east that hurled the Russians back more than 480km (300 miles).

Turkey had entered the war on the side of the Central Powers in October 1914. After a costly naval attack by the Allies, 75,000 Australian, New Zealand, British and French troops tried to open a new front at Gallipoli at the mouth of the Dardanelles. The expedition failed to achieve surprise, scarcely advanced from the beaches and suffered heavy casualties until withdrawn in December. Thus Russia was effectively cut off from Allied supplies.

By the end of 1915 both sides realized that the war was going to be a prolonged affair. On 21 February 1916, the Germans assaulted Verdun in an offensive calculated by General Erich von Falkenhayn (1861–1922) to exhaust the French, rather than to achieve a breakthrough. By the end of June nearly 600,000 men had died in this action, but the French managed to hold on. The Russians under General Alexei Brusilov (1856–1926) launched an offensive that gained some territory with terrible loss of life and the British under Field-Marshal Sir Douglas Haig (1861–1928) attacked on the Somme, suffering 20,000 dead on the first day and gaining less than 8km (5 miles) in five months' fighting.

### The war at sea

At the beginning of the war, the Royal Navy had begun a blockade of German ports, turning back neutral shipping [6]. The Germans replied with submarine attacks [8], but had little success in 1915 and 1916 because

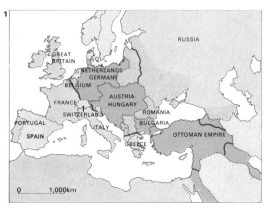

Entente Powers and allies

Central Powers and allies

Neutral Powers

Greatest advance of Central Powers

Front lines November 1918

**1 Most of the fighting** took place in Europe; the main battlefields were in northern France and Belgium, Poland, Russia and Italy. Overseas campaigns were fought in Mesopotamia and the Middle East and in the German colonies in Africa.

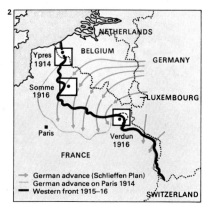

**2 The Western front** was the decisive battleground of the war. Once the Schlieffen Plan had failed to eliminate France, it was here that the bloodiest battles were fought, as both sides poured in men and materials to achieve the vital breakthrough. In 1918 the impetus of a new Allied offensive backed by the fresh American armies convinced the Germans that the war was lost even before the Allies reached them.

German advance (Schlieffen Plan)

German advance on Paris 1914

Western front 1915–16

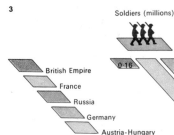

| | Soldiers (millions) | Battleships | Cruisers | Submarines |
|---|---|---|---|---|
| British Empire | 0.16 | 16 | 14 | 6 |
| France | 1.2 | 16 | 12 | 23 |
| Russia | 1.4 | 28 | 34 | 29 |
| Germany | 2.2 | 40 | 57 | 64 |
| Austria-Hungary | | 64 | 121 | 73 |

**3 The strength of the two alliances** was reasonably well-balanced, as what Britain lacked in troops she made up in naval strength. It was this balance that made World War I a war of attrition that was to result in horrific loss of life and massive destruction. Figures for troops quoted here are those of the standing armies. Mobilized forces were approximately: Britain 711,000; France 3.5 million, Russia 4.4 million, Germany 3.8 million (in emergency a maximum of 8.5 million could be raised), Austria-Hungary 3 million.

**4 The generals of 1914** had been trained to think of mobile offensive warfare, but the relatively new British Vickers medium machine gun with its lethal effect on exposed infantry was among the armaments that upset their view. Once the exhausted armies had dug in, artillery and machine guns ensured that trench warfare would continue. Commanders tried for the rest of the war to break the stalemate, but massive infantry attacks proved hideously ineffective.

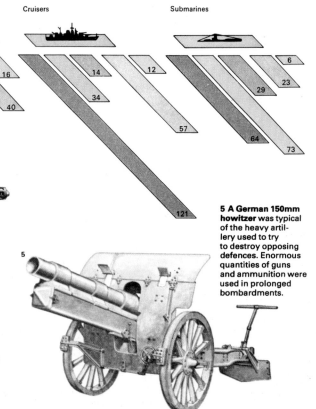

**5 A German 150mm howitzer** was typical of the heavy artillery used to try to destroy opposing defences. Enormous quantities of guns and ammunition were used in prolonged bombardments.

sinking neutrals was banned. The two great battle fleets fought only one major action, at Jutland on 31 May 1916. The outcome was inconclusive, but the German surface fleet remained in harbour for the rest of the war. During 1916 the blockade caused severe food shortages in Germany, which led to widespread unrest. On 31 January 1917, the Germans launched unrestricted submarine warfare, and by sinking US shipping pulled the United States into the war. Only the new convoy system prevented Britain from being economically strangled.

**The final offensive and Allied victory**
On the Western front the French began a series of unsuccessful offensives; elements of their army mutinied in May 1917, but were brought under control during June by Marshal Henri Pétain (1856–1951).

Tanks were used *en masse* at Cambrai on 20 November, but their initial successes were not followed up. Italy had entered the war on the Allied side on 26 April 1915 and fought inconclusively against Austria-Hungary until a massive defeat at Caporetto on 24 October

1917 almost knocked her out of the war.
In Russia the unpopularity of the war led to the overthrow of the tsar in March 1917. A provisional government launched another offensive but, after that had been thwarted, the Bolsheviks seized power in November and sued for peace. The Treaty of Brest-Litovsk in March 1918 gave Germany huge territorial gains in western Russia.

Aware that they must follow up success in the east with victory in the west before American help could arrive in force, the Germans opened a series of offensives under General Erich Ludendorff (1865–1937) from March to July 1918. They drove the Allies back to the Marne, but were again halted there. Then, strengthened by American troops, the Allies counter-attacked during August. A massive offensive launched on 26 September convinced the German High Command that the war was lost and they sued for peace. In early November anti-war and pro-Bolshevik risings took place, the kaiser abdicated on 9 November and an armistice was signed on 11 November. Austria-Hungary also collapsed in November after an Allied offensive.

**For future generations** World War I was to become a symbol of senseless slaughter and destruction. Not only did more than 10 million soldiers die, but the war affected every level of society in all combatant countries. Wholesale conscription was introduced and governments took dictatorial powers to control economies and to ration food and supplies. The war radically changed the map of Europe, sweeping away the German, Austro-Hungarian and Russian empires and setting up smaller states in Eastern Europe.

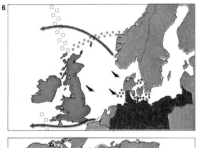

6

:·: British minefields
·:·: German minefields
← U-boat routes
◁ Convoy terminals
◻◻ British blockade
· Naval battles

▮ Central Powers
German raider activity
● Aug 1914-Mar 1915
U-boat attacks
February 1917 onwards
Main trade routes

▮ Allied Powers
▬ Naval blockade 1914-18
Convoy routes May 1917 onwards
Main trade routes

7

**6 The two great fleets** had only one major battle during the war. The Germans used longrange raiders and submarines, while British warships mounted an effective blockade of German ports.

**7 Cavalry, like this German troop,** found few outlets other than the Eastern front, where the war was more fluid and the trench system never evolved. There cavalry was used chiefly for reconnaissance.

11

figures in millions

200,000

Prisoners of war

Wounded

Dead

4·2
3·6
2·2
1·8
1·2
0·9

Germany | Austria-Hungary

Italy | British Empire | France | Russia

0·5 | 0·5 | 0·2 | 0·4
0·9 | 0·9
1·4
1·7
2·1 | 2·0
2·5
4·9

United States

8

**8 Germany had more submarines** than Britain at the beginning of the war. This is one of the Class 31-37 U-boats. It was 64.7m (212ft) long and fully submerged it weighed 880 tonnes. It was armed with 24 500mm (20in) torpedoes fired through four tubes. The attacks on British shipping were relatively ineffective during 1915–16. However, after 1917 the Germans came close to starving Britain into submission.

9

**9 German Gotha IIIs** were used for armed reconnaissance over the battlefields as well as for bombing. Developed to take over the Zeppelins' role in bombing English cities, they

arrived too late in the war to make a significant difference. After their attacks on England (in which they claimed 857 lives) the Gothas were switched to the French theatre.

10

**10 Gas** was first used in 1915 by the Germans to try to break the trench stalemate. It proved inefficient, difficult to control and easy to detect. The masks these soldiers wear were early attempts at protection.

**11 The military casualties** of the major powers were vast. France suffered the greatest destruction and the heaviest civilian and military losses. Never had a war killed so many people in so short a time, removing a whole generation of young men and scarring Europe for the next 20 years.

# World War I: Britain's role

Britain's small but professional expeditionary force of 100,000 men, commanded by Sir John French (1852–1925), landed in France on 14 August 1914, ten days after the declaration of war. With an insight that ran contrary to popular opinion, the War Minister, Lord Kitchener (1850–1916), was already telling the Cabinet that they would have to be prepared for a long struggle.

## Initial reverses

After an initial clash at Mons, the BEF retreated. It stood fast at Le Cateau on 26 August, but suffered heavy casualties. On 5 September the Battle of the Marne began, with the Germans only 48km (30 miles) from Paris. The battle raged for seven days – by 14 September the Germans had withdrawn to the River Aisne and Paris had been saved. In October each side tried to outflank the other – the so-called "race to the sea" merely extended the line of trenches. By the end of 1914 the trenches ran from the North Sea to Switzerland; the British part of them from Ypres in Belgium to the River Somme [1]. That 80-mile strip was to account for almost 90 per cent of the 2,883,000 casualties the war cost Britain.

By 1918 the four original divisions had grown to more than 60 and from 1916 onwards Britain increasingly became the dominant partner.

Under pressure from both Germany and Turkey, Russia appealed to the British at the end of 1914 for some action to distract the Turks. The result was the Gallipoli campaign [4] which lasted eight months, cost 100,000 British casualties, and ended in evacuation of the peninsula. While the Allies were on Gallipoli, Bulgaria joined the Central Powers. On 5 October 1915, in anticipation of an invasion of Serbia [2, 3], one British and one French division landed at Salonika, in neutral Greece. They finally moved in September 1918, forcing the Bulgarians to sign an armistice.

## The desert campaign and war in Africa

The Mesopotamian campaign [4, 5] at first made good progress. Sent out from India to protect oil interests in Kuwait, a force under Gen. Charles Townshend (1861–1924) got to within 28km (18 miles) of Baghdad, but then heat, disease and enemy harassment forced it into a defensive position at Kut-al-Imara. After holding out for five months, Townshend surrendered his force of 10,000 Indians and 2,000 British in April 1916.

From Egypt Gen. Archibald Murray moved into the Sinai and by the end of 1916 was close to Gaza, the nearest point of Turkish-held Palestine. He was twice beaten back and in June 1917 was replaced by Gen. Sir Edmund Allenby (1861–1936). A month later Capt. T. E. Lawrence (1888–1935), with a force of Arabs, captured Akaba.

Baghdad had fallen to an army under Gen. Sir Stanley Maude (1864–1917) on 11 March 1917, at a cost of 92,500 casualties. Instead of reinforcing Gaza, the Turks decided to counter-attack at Baghdad, and Allenby mounted a two-pronged attack against Beersheba and Gaza. By 9 December he was in Jerusalem. There was then a prolonged pause. In September 1918 Allenby advanced again, sweeping up through Damascus to Aleppo; Gen. William Marshall (1865–1939), who had taken over after

**1 British infantry** had to endure trench-feet, lice, flies and monotonous rations as well as regular shellfire when in the trenches. Out of the line they spent their time in working parties. Combat consisted of small-scale raids into enemy trenches and large set-piece battles. In the Battle of the Somme in 1916 (this is the front line at Ovillers), there were 420,000 British casualties in four-and-a-half months.

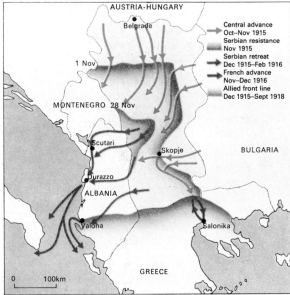

**2 Serbia repulsed Austrian attacks** three times in 1914. In October 1915 the Central Powers tried again, Austria and Germany attacking from the north and Bulgaria from the east. The Serbian army was forced to retreat across the Albanian mountains in appalling conditions. Of its 300,000 men, only 135,000 reached the Adriatic. Of 500,000 civilian refugees who accompanied the army, only 200,000 survived.

**3 Belgrade was taken by the Austrians** on 2 December 1914, but recaptured by Serbs under Gen. Radomir Putnik (1847–1917). Ten months later it finally fell. This painting by Oscar Laske shows the last day's resistance. One consequence of WWI was the creation, in 1918, of what became modern Yugoslavia.

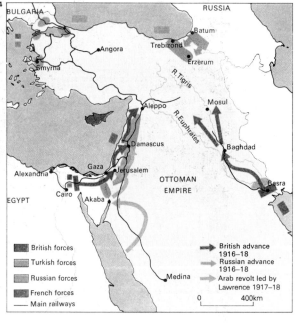

**4 In the Middle East** disease caused more casualties than enemy action. From January 1915 to the Armistice, 503,377 British troops went down with malaria, cholera, dysentery and other fevers, whereas only 51,500 were lost by enemy action. The eight-month campaign at Gallipoli in the Dardanelles, where the troops also suffered from disease, was an attempt to open a route to Russia via the Black Sea. An important consequence of its failure was that Russia was cut off from its foreign markets. One aspect of the desert war, later to be highly romanticized, was the exploits of T. E. Lawrence, who led an Arab revolt and led guerrilla raids against Turkish positions and the main railway.

Maude's death headed for Mosul. On 30 October Turkey surrendered.

Three weeks after the war began, a small British force accepted a German surrender in Togoland. In German Southwest Africa, Gen. Louis Botha (1862–1919), the Premier of the Union of South Africa, forced the Germans to surrender on 9 July 1915.

## War in Europe

In August 1917 a decision by the German High Command to take the offensive on the Italian front [7] led to the Battle of Caporetto, fought between 24 October and 12 November. The Italians lost 305,000 men, 275,000 of whom surrendered, and five British divisions had to be pulled out of the Western Front and rushed to their support.

Cambrai, the first battle in which tanks were successfully used on a large scale, was yet another Allied attempt to break the deadlock that had existed since the beginning of 1915. In the three years since the Marne, the British had fought the First Battle of Ypres (October 1914, 58,000 casualties); Neuve-Chapelle (March 1915, 13,000);

Second Ypres (April 1915, 59,000); Loos (September 1915, 60,000); the Somme (July-November 1916, 420,000); and Third Ypres (July-November 1917, 245,000).

The stalemate on land in those years had been offset to some extent by success at sea and in the air. The British blockade of Germany was extremely effective, whereas the German submarine campaign was restricted until late in 1916 by the fear of provoking the United States. When unrestricted submarine warfare was introduced, the British countered with the convoy system (the first sailed from Gibraltar on 10 May 1917) and improved anti-submarine technology. In the air, the Royal Flying Corps [6] received its first aircraft with synchronized guns in April 1916, and ended a ten-month period in which the German Air Services' 425 Fokker *Eindeckers* had created a reign of terror.

By 31 December 1917 there were 177,000 American troops in France, and less than a year later, at the Battle of Amiens (August 1918, 22,000 casualties) the end was in sight. At 11am on 11 November 1918 the shooting stopped.

**KEY**

■ Principal areas of conflict
Other engagements

**Britain's major concerns in WWI** were France, Egypt, Gallipoli and Mesopotamia, but British and empire troops fought in the Pacific, Africa and even in China, where in November 1914 they joined the Japanese in the capture of Tsingtao. New Zealand took Samoa and Australia took New Guinea in the first two months; in November the raider *Emden* was sunk off the Cocos Islands. Other naval engagements included one at Dogger Bank in 1915, the historic Battle of Jutland in 1916, and the raid on the U-boats in Zeebrugge in 1918.

**5 Australian and New Zealand cavalry,** were part of Allenby's expedition to Gaza. The ANZACs (Australian and New Zealand Army Corps) also fought at Gallipoli, moving to the Western Front in 1916.

**6 Captain Albert Ball, VC,** was photographed in this SE5 at London Colney, Herts, in March 1917 and killed in it on 7 May. He was 20 years old. Ball shot down 44 German aircraft and, like

Major Mick Mannock, VC, who with 73 victories was Britain's top World War I ace, was killed by machine-gun fire from the ground. The Royal Flying Corps sent 48 reconnaissance aircraft to France in 1914: by the end of the war the Royal Air Force (formed on 1 April 1918) had 22,171 serviceable aircraft. The war cost the air services 16,823 killed, of whom 12,782 were officers.

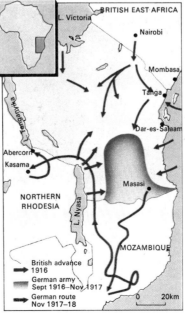

**7 Italy joined the Allies** in April 1915 and declared war on Austria-Hungary on 23 May 1915. Not until 1916 did it declare war on Germany. Many of the clashes between the Italians and the Austrians took place in the Alps: this Austrian gun is at a height of 3,860m (12,545ft). Of the five British divisions rushed to the Battle of Caporetto, two were withdrawn nine months later, but the troops who remained joined an Italian assault on the anniversary of Caporetto, in 1918, which led to the Austrians' seeking an armistice.

British advance 1916
German army Sept 1916–Nov 1917
German route Nov 1917–18

**8 The East African campaign** cost the British 19,000 casualties. That it was so protracted was due to the military genius of the German commander, Paul von Lettow-Vorbeck. who, with drastically outnumbered forces, fought on until November 1918.

**9 Shorts and topees were standard uniform** for troops in East Africa, and provided some relief from the intolerable heat. The torment of tsetse flies, fever and dysentery made conditions as bad, in their own way, as they were on the Western Front.

# The Peace of Paris

The Paris Peace Conference, formally opened on 18 January 1919, was dominated by the five leading victorious powers of World War I – the United States, France, the British Empire, Italy and Japan. The defeated nations and Russia were excluded.

## Conflicting demands

The French delegation, led by Prime Minister Georges Clemenceau (1841–1929), was obsessed with the long-term threat posed to France by Germany's larger population and superior industrial potential and demanded the imposition of a harsh treaty that would prevent any further German aggression against France. The French aims conflicted with those of the President of the United States, Woodrow Wilson (1856–1924) who, in his Fourteen Points (accepted with certain reservations by Britain and France on 4 November 1918), called for a peace settlement based on national self-determination and a League of Nations [2].

Britain's major demands had already been met with the surrender of the German fleet and the British occupation of most of

Germany's colonies and the bulk of the Turkish Middle East. Despite pressure from Wilson that these areas should be administered directly by the League, they were retained by the British Empire under a complex League mandate system [4]. Thus the British Prime Minister, David Lloyd George (1863–1945), was in a position to mediate between the French and the Americans.

Italy demanded the satisfaction of its claims under the 1915 Treaty of London to the Tyrol, Trieste and a large part of the Slav-populated Dalmatian coast, including Fiume. The Italians were unable to persuade Wilson to agree to their claim to Fiume, which was assigned to Yugoslavia, leaving Italy with Trieste and the Tyrol [6].

Despite strong opposition from Wilson and the Chinese, Japan secured the former German concessions in Chinese Shantung promised to it by the entente in 1917.

## Wilson's ideals compromised

The Republican victory in the November congressional elections in America undermined Wilson's prestige and he was forced to

compromise on some of the Fourteen Points in order to secure the adherence of the other leaders to his League of Nations Covenant. However, neither he nor Lloyd George would accept France's demand for a Rhineland buffer state under French military control. This would have been a clear breach of the principle of national self-determination and, in Lloyd George's view, was likely to breed lasting German resentment. The French accepted a compromise on 14 April whereby the Allies were to occupy a demilitarized Rhineland, including the Rhine bridgeheads, for 15 years, with an Anglo-American guarantee to protect France against German aggression. The French were also given permission to exploit the valuable Saar coalfields.

Despite Wilson's strenuous opposition France also demanded massive reparations from Germany, not only to compensate for the immense destruction inflicted during the war but also as a means of weakening the German economy [7]. Lloyd George was, by the end of March, becoming concerned at the increasing severity of the Allied demands on

**1 The new East European states** emerged from the wreckage of the German, Austro-Hungarian and Russian empires. Although founded on the basis of national self-determination, they also included

alien minorities like the Germans in Czechoslovakia. They were a source of constant unrest after 1919. Britain and France divided the former Ottoman Middle East between them, but both faced

rising Arab nationalism and, in Britain's case, increasing Arab-Zionist conflict in Palestine. In the Ottoman empire nationalists formally established the Republic of Turkey in 1923.

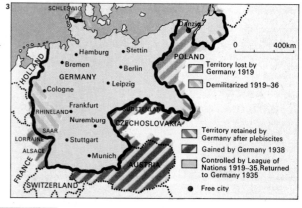

**2 The Allied leaders** (from left to right) Lloyd George, Orlando, Clemenceau and Wilson, were bitterly divided by conflicting policies and temperamental differences. The peace settlement they eventually imposed on Germany was soon condemned by their countrymen and they did not remain in office for long after it. The treaty was signed in 1919 by all the great powers except the United States.

**3 Germany's losses and gains** from 1919 to 1938 are shown on this map. The Supreme Council had endeavoured to settle Germany's frontiers on the basis of nationality. Its territorial losses, in the east particularly, were a cause of Germany's detestation of the treaty. Allied disunity and weakness in 1938 enabled Hitler to incorporate Austria into the Reich and to annex the German Sudetenland.

Territory lost by Germany 1919
Demilitarized 1919–36
Territory retained by Germany after plebiscites
Gained by Germany 1938
Controlled by League of Nations 1919–35. Returned to Germany 1935
Free city

**4 Germany lost all its colonies** at the end of World War I. Woodrow Wilson hoped that the captured German colonies would be administered directly by the League of Nations. This idea was opposed by the British Dominions and Japan, which had conquered them. A compromise was reached by a system of "A", "B" and "C" mandates: "C" was virtually indistinguishable from annexation. Thus Wilsonian idealism was again frustrated by the other powers.

German territories mandated by League of Nations after 1919

British mandate
Australian mandate
Japanese mandate

British mandate
French mandate
Belgian mandate
Union of South Africa mandate

New Zealand mandate
Held by Germany until 1914. Occupied by Japan 1914–22. To China 1922–3

Russian Empire 1914
Germany 1914
Austro-Hungarian Empire 1914
Ottoman Empire 1914
Boundaries 1920
French mandate 1920
British mandate 1920
Emirate under British suzerainty 1923
Serb-Croat-Slovene kingdom created 1918 Name changed to Yugoslavia 1929

Germany which he feared would hinder Germany's economic recovery and lead to the creation of a Bolshevik Germany.

Eventually a compromise was reached that left the total sum owed by Germany to be determined by an inter-Allied reparation commission by 1921. Meanwhile Germany was forced to accept responsibility for causing the war. The Allies also imposed a substantial measure of disarmament on the German army, navy and air force.

### The eventual compromise

The three leaders could not agree about the settlement of Germany's eastern borders. France supported large territorial gains at Germany's expense by the newly established East European states, especially Poland. After a long struggle Lloyd George managed to reduce Poland's acquisitions by insisting on a League-controlled free port of Danzig, the reduction of the Polish corridor and a plebiscite in Upper Silesia. Czechoslovakia retained the German Sudetenland. Austria, stripped of its former empire, was forbidden to unite with Germany. In 1920 Hungary lost all its non-Magyar lands to its neighbours and a severe peace was imposed on Turkey [1].

The Allies finally presented the draft treaty to Germany on 7 May, giving her 15 days to draw up counter-proposals, the bulk of which were rejected. After further delays Germany signed the treaty at Versailles on 28 June 1919. It was widely regarded in Germany as a dictated peace and a betrayal of Wilsonian principles. Failure to apply the principle of self-determination to the distribution of the German countries of the former Austrian Empire, in particular, was a major German grievance and one that gave the German nationalists and Hitler's Nazi Party valuable propaganda against the Weimar Republic in the 1920s [3].

The United States Senate rejected the treaty and the League covenant, and the United States retreated into isolationism. France thus lost the Anglo-American guarantee and became even more determined to insist on German compliance with the treaty, especially the reparations clauses. This intransigent attitude led to considerable friction with Britain.

**The armistice was signed** on 11 Nov 1918 at the French headquarters in the Forest of Compiègne. Marshal Foch signed for the Allies. It secured Germany's evacuation of occupied territories and a complete cessation of all hostilities.

**5 British troops** marched along Whitehall, London, in July 1919 in a "Peace Procession" that marked the signing of the Treaty of Versailles. But disillusionment soon replaced enthusiasm.

**6 A quick conclusion to the peace conference** was essential, to pemit European reconstruction. Although attended by most nations and governments, it was soon dominated by Britain, France and the USA.

| | |
|---|---|
| 11 Nov 1918 | German armistice |
| 18 Jan 1919 | Paris Peace Conference opens |
| 22 Jan | Council of Ten sets up League of Nations Commission |
| 3 Feb | League of Nations Commission meets |
| 14 Mar | Formation of Council of Four |
| 10 Apr | Council of Four appoints Reparation Commission |
| 22 Apr | Italians withdraw |
| 26 Apr | Conference accepts League of Nations Covenant |
| 6 May | Italians return |
| 7 May | Draft treaty is presented to Germans |
| 29 May | Germans present counter-proposals |
| 16 June | Allies reject most of the counter-proposals |
| 28 June | Treaty of Versailles |

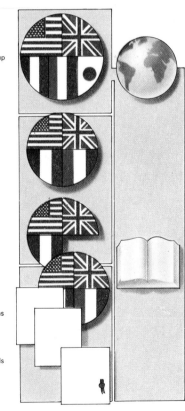

**7 Germany's reparations payments were** a major obstacle to her economic reconstruction and weakened the entire European economy in the 1920s. But after the French invasion of the Ruhr and the dramatic German inflation in 1923 the need for a strong German economy was recognized, leading to increased investment, especially from the USA. Much of this investment however, was spent on public buildings.

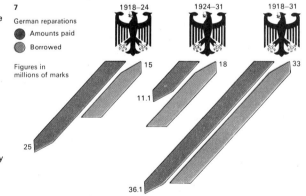

7

German reparations
- Amounts paid
- Borrowed

Figures in millions of marks

1918–24    1924–31    1918–31

15    18    33

11.1

25    36.1

**8 The League of Nations** was intended by Woodrow Wilson to be the foundation of a new and peaceful world order. However, the USA's refusal to join in 1920 and the exclusion of both Germany and Soviet Russia (until 1934) reduced its prestige. After the admission of Germany in 1926 the League was fairly successful, until its failure to prevent the Japanese conquest of Manchuria in 1931–2 and the Italian conquest of Ethiopia, 1935–6.

**9 Hitler's rise to power** in 1933 and the Treaty of Versailles are not directly connected, but the treaty was used as an important element in Nazi propaganda against the Weimar Republic and the Social Democrats in the 1920s. Hitler's appointment as chancellor was the product both of luck and calculation. His opportunity was provided by general discontent and the economic depression, and the inability of Weimar politicians to cope with either.

# What World War I meant to Britain

World War I is seen as one of the turning-points in British history — but it would be wrong to suggest that before the war all was tranquillity and security, a last "golden age", and that after it all was uncertainty and depression. Major political, economic and social changes were already taking place in Britain and the empire before 1914. They would have overturned the old way of life anyway; the war merely speeded them up, and made their effects far more shattering than they would otherwise have been.

## Optimism and disillusionment

In 1914, Britain had effectively been at peace for almost a century; the Crimean (1854–6) and Boer wars (1899–1902) had had little effect on the population, and had seemed only minor interruptions in the growth of Britain's power. Several generations had grown up who knew little of war and were convinced of the superiority of their country and race. But all levels of British society were becoming more aware of the German threat to British naval and commercial supremacy in the years before 1914, and

the hostility that this caused goes some way towards explaining the enthusiasm with which war was greeted. More than 500,000 men volunteered in the first few weeks, and during the following year 125,000 men a month went gladly to the front [1].

Early hopes that the war would be over by Christmas 1914 faded as both sides dug in. A static war of attrition ensued. By mid-1916 the fighting men were disillusioned by the squalor of the trenches and the mass slaughter. Because new battalions were formed on a geographical basis, whole towns and villages in Britain were almost depopulated by the fighting. On 1 July 1916, the first day of the Battle of the Somme, nearly 20,000 British soldiers were killed: individual battalions suffered heavily, the 10th West Yorkshires, for example, losing almost 60 per cent of its strength. At home there were some shortages and a few air raids [4], but the civilian population never really understood what it was like at the front. At the start of the war the government established a Press Bureau with the task of censoring newspaper reports and the true progress of

the war was concealed from the public. Instead, the mass of public opinion was coloured by propaganda stories of atrocities.

## The economy and government control

The unforeseen demands that the war placed on the British economy forced the state to intervene more actively than ever before. Although attempts were made after the war to retreat from this, active state involvement was never lost. The need for vast supplies of munitions, and the inability of private industry to produce them, led to the creation of a Ministry of Munitions in May 1915 with considerable directive powers. In 1916 British Summer Time was introduced to prolong daylight working hours. The need to ensure adequate food supplies led, in December 1916, to the establishment of county committees to direct agriculture and the creation of a Ministry of Food. In 1918 rationing was introduced.

The war brought an end to the free trade policy that Britain had struggled to maintain since the 1840s. The McKenna duties of 1915, putting a tariff on luxury imports,

**2 These women working in a factory** in 1917 testify to the sexual revolution that took place on the home front during the war. As more and more men volunteered or were drafted into the forces, their places in the munitions factories, shops, offices, voluntary services, hospitals, schools and transport were taken by women. By thus ably replacing men or working beside them, women's claims for equality of status and rights were so widely accepted that in 1918 an Act giving the vote to women over the age of 30 was passed with very little opposition. After so many women had gained social and economic independence, there was no way for the conventional barriers to be re-erected once the war was over. This radical change in attitudes was reflected later, in the 1920s, in extremes of fashion and a degree of permissiveness in social behaviour

**1 Voluntary recruiting** at first resulted in more men than could be adequately trained or equipped. The outbreak of war was greeted with overwhelming enthusiasm by all classes. Hatred of the Germans was whipped up by an almost hysterical press, and the chance of adventure and glory after long years of peace brought men flocking to join the forces. With no conscription, Britain had to rely on volunteers and, in spite of massive losses, the supply of new recruits was adequate for more than a year. But the authorities felt obliged to introduce conscription by May 1916 in order to reinforce the depleted ranks.

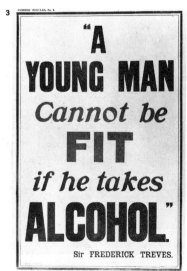

**3 Watered beer and afternoon closing** of the pubs were introduced by the government because it was felt that the national consumption of alcohol was impairing the war effort.

**4 Barrage balloons,** thinly spread over London, served as token protection rather than forming any serious deterrent to German air attacks. London was first bombed by Zeppelins (1915) but these were vulnerable and soon replaced by aeroplanes.

**5 Wilfred Owen** (1893–1918) and other young poets such as Siegfried Sassoon (1886–1967) and Robert Graves (1895–    ), who had fought in the trenches, wrote about the horror and despair of the experiences through which they had passed.

were retained after 1918, and were followed in 1921 by a Safeguarding of Industry Act to protect certain industries against foreign competition. On the outbreak of war, the Bank of England was authorized to issue banknotes not backed by gold, and there was a rapid and lasting rise in rates of income tax, which themselves had a much more progressive structure. The national debt rose from £650 million in 1914 to more than £7,000 million in 1918.

Shortages of labour caused by the demand for troops made workers realize their strength. Trade union membership rose from 4.1 million in 1913 to 6.5 million in 1918 and 8.3 million in 1920. Similarly, the widespread recruitment of women into industry broke down prejudices and strengthened the cause of the suffragettes [2]

### The peacetime boom and slump

In November 1918 there was little evidence of any widespread demoralization caused by wartime losses – rather a pride in having come through an unprecedented trial. David Lloyd George (1863–1945), who had be-

come prime minister of a Liberal-Tory coalition in 1916, took the opportunity to hold a general election which swept the coalition back into office. There was a brief restocking and rebuilding boom, but by spring 1920 it had degenerated into speculation and collapsed [6]. The economy slumped and the numbers of those unemployed rose to more than two million in June 1921 [8].

The government attempted to correct the economy by cutting public spending, wages and prices, all of which only made the problem worse. The war had accelerated the decline of Britain from the industrial and commercial supremacy it had once enjoyed. Traditional export markets had developed their own industries and major exporting sectors of the British economy, such as cotton, coal and shipping, were permanently reduced [7]. The war had given impetus to some new industries, such as chemicals and motor car manufacturing. But these tended to be developed in new regions, far from the traditional centres of industry where the misery and hopelessness of long-term unemployment were at their worst.

## The "Scrap of Paper"

This document is a translation and facsimile of signatures from the original treaty of 1831 guaranteeing the independence and neutrality of Belgium, which was confirmed by the six Powers in the famous treaty of 1839, the breaking of which by Germany is responsible for the present war with the British Empire.

ARTICLE II.
Her Majesty the Queen of the United Kingdom of Great Britain and Ireland, His Majesty the Emperor of Austria, King of Hungary and Bohemia, His Majesty the King of the French, His Majesty the King of Prussia, and His Majesty the Emperor of all the Russias, declare, that the Articles mentioned in the preceding Article, are considered as having the same force and validity as if they were textually inserted in the present Act, and that they are thus placed under the guarantee of their said Majesties.

ARTICLE VII.
Belgium, within the limits specified in Articles I., II., and IV., shall form an independent and perpetually neutral State. It shall be bound to observe such neutrality towards all other States.

PALMERSTON
British Plenipotentiary
SYLVAN DE WEYER
Belgian Plenipotentiary
SENFT
Austrian Plenipotentiary
H. SEBASTIANI
French Plenipotentiary
BÜLOW
Prussian Plenipotentiary
POZZO DI BORGO
Russian Plenipotentiary

**The little "scrap of paper"** was a contemptuous phrase used by the German Chancellor in 1914 to describe the 1839 treaty that guaranteed Belgium's neutrality. As a gesture, the Germans asked permission to go through Belgian territory on their way to Paris. King Albert I (r. 1909–34) of the Belgians replied: "Belgium is a nation, not a road", but German troops had already crossed the frontier. During the critical days before the Germans invaded, some sections of British opinion were opposed to Britain's participation in a continental war. But this act of aggression against "brave little Belgium" united the country in its determination to forcibly intervene against Germany.

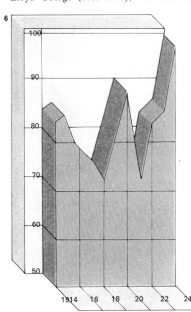

**6 Britain's gross national product** enjoyed a brief boom immediately after the war as industry restocked and changed over to peacetime products. But drastic cuts in government expenditure, the loss of export markets and the erosion of favourable economic conditions, such as free trade, led to a severe slump.

**7 Cotton production and exports** in the decade from 1912 to 1922 show a postwar slump that was typical of several major British industries. After the war they discovered that many of their markets had disappeared forever. It was a failure to replace the jobs in these industries that was the basic cause of lasting unemployment.

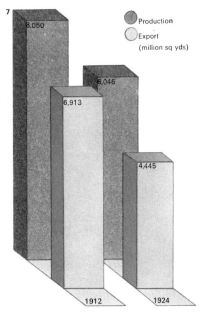

Production
Export
(million sq yds)

8,050
6,913
6,046
4,445
1912
1924

**8 Unemployment** was non-existent during the war, but after 1920 an intricate system of reliefs had to be built up in response to a fundamental change in the attitude of the public. Before the war the unemployed had been resigned to their fate as an inevitable fact of life. But after the war men expected the government to find them jobs, or to support them adequately until the necessary employment was available.

**9 Ex-servicemen hawking their wares** in the streets in 1920 symbolized the disillusionment and despair that broke down all the old certainties of British society. There was a dawning and bitter realization that the prodigious feats of government organization and direction that had helped to win the war did not seem to be winning the peace. The poor no longer accepted their fate as inevitable or unalterable, while the middle classes saw their income and status being steadily eroded by higher taxes. The frivolities of the "Gay Twenties" stemmed from a widespread desire to ignore doubts and difficulties that seemed insoluble. It amounted to enjoying life for the moment and letting tomorrow look after itself.

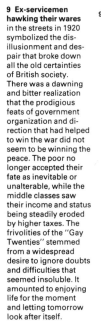

**10 Striking coal miners in Wigan** formed part of a "triple alliance" of miners, engineering and transport unions who were prepared to call a national strike. There was little industrial strife early in the war, but various government Acts, such as the Munitions of War Act of 1915 (which set wage levels and enforced arbitration), led to widespread strikes in 1917. The government modified its approach, but when in 1921 rising unemployment coincided with a withdrawal of government subsidies, support for a minimum wage, and removal of state control over the mines, the triple alliance was born. But the government compromised, the transport and engineering workers withdrew their support, and the threat of a general strike was ended. The miners came out alone, but within three months they were defeated, and returned under worse conditions than could have been reached by negotiation. This was followed by the political excitement over the collapse of Lloyd George's coalition government in October 1922.

# The Russian Revolution

Russia went reluctantly to war in 1914. Her army was in no condition to face imperial Germany and early enthusiasm for the war waned with a shattering defeat by the Germans at Tannenberg within a month of hostilities commencing. But only the Bolsheviks vehemently opposed the war, the five Bolshevik deputies in the Duma (Parliament) being banished to Siberia. Their leader, Vladimir Ilyrich Lenin (1870–1924), nevertheless saw the defeat of imperial Russia as the surest way of furthering revolutionary goals.

## Impact of the February Revolution

The longer hostilities lasted, the more incompetent the imperial administration appeared. It was astonished by the revolution in March 1917 (dated as February by the old-style calendar), but then so were its opponents. Power was transferred, by hungry peasants, disenchanted aristocracy and mutinous troops, from Tsar Nicholas II (1868–1918) [3] to a provisional government that was intended to be a temporary, caretaker administration until a Constituent Assembly adopted a constitution and appointed a legal government. The first provisional government (there were four in all) fell because of its failure to end the war.

Peace and the redistribution of land were closely connected. If Russia left the war, the soldiers (who were mostly peasants in uniform) would descend on the countryside and demand more land; if the peasants were granted land while war continued, the soldiers would desert to seize their portion. The government had also to contend with the emergence of genuinely democratic institutions, the soviets (councils). The most famous of these were in Petrograd and in Moscow, but they sprang up spontaneously everywhere after the revolution. Despite support from the moderate socialists – the Mensheviks and the Socialist Revolutionaries (SRs) – the provisional governments were violently opposed by Lenin and the Bolsheviks. During July, armed workers and soldiers tried to seize power in Petrograd [4, 5]. Denounced for accepting German money, Lenin was forced to flee to Finland when the demonstrations were unsuccessful. On 22 July, Alexander Kerensky (1881–1970) became premier and tried to restore order in the capital [2, 6]. But Leon Trotsky (1879–1940), a leading figure in the Petrograd soviet, organized armed insurrection under the cover of soviet legitimacy. Lenin slipped back into Russia and on 7 October (25 November, old style) he and his Bolsheviks [7] swept away Kerensky.

## The October Revolution and after

Some workers hoped that the new Russia would be ruled by the soviets but events soon dictated otherwise. Given their narrow political base (there were fewer than 300,000 Bolsheviks in November 1917), Lenin and his supporters faced widespread opposition on every front [8]. There were those who advocated a revolutionary war to advance socialism in the rest of Europe; there were Bolsheviks who wanted money abolished and a socialist economy overnight; there were the peasants who wanted to be left alone with the land now redistributed; and there were the dispossessed of the former regime.

The treaty of Brest-Litovsk in March 1918 ended the war with Germany; in the

**1 Russia paid a fearful price** in human life for her incompetence in waging a long modern war. More than 15 million men had been mobilized by mid-1917. About 1.7 million men perished on the battlefield, 4.9 million were wounded and 2.4 million were taken prisoner. Russia was superior in strength to Turkey, Bulgaria and Austria-Hungary, but was outmatched by their ally, Germany.

**2 Alexander Kerensky** played a major role in shaping policies of the provisional governments in 1917. He was a minister in the first two provisional governments, prime minister from July onwards, and after he had suppressed an army revolt in September he also took over as commander-in-chief. His failure to solve the twin problems of land and peace paved the way for Lenin's victory in October.

**3 On 15 March 1917** Tsar Nicholas II, shown here with his family, was persuaded to abdicate and the first provisional government was formed in Petrograd.

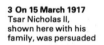

**4 Demonstrations** during the "April Days", 1917, against the war led to the fall of the first provisional government and the resignation of Foreign Minister Milyukov (1859–1943). But Russia's war effort continued, and in the soviets support for the Bolsheviks grew at the expense of the moderates. Calling for peace and a complete transfer of power to the soviets, further demonstrations in June showed the growing influence of the Bolsheviks and the declining support for the provisional government.

**5 Clashes broke out in Petrograd** on 16–18 July 1917 when armed workers demonstrated for "All power to the soviets" but were suppressed by the government.

**6 General L. G. Kornilov** (1870–1918), Kerensky's commander-in-chief, marched his troops on Petrograd in August 1917. This was seen by Kerensky as a right-wing attempt to take power and he turned to the Bolsheviks for help. The plot dissolved but it emphasized the growing political divisions that Kerensky could no longer bridge.

**7 The Winter Palace** was taken by the Bolsheviks on 7 November 1917. Lenin had secretly returned to Petrograd to forward Bolshevik plans for the overthrow of the provisional government, the collapse of which seemed imminent as unrest mounted. With the almost bloodless seizure of the palace, Kerensky fled and other members of the provisional government were arrested.

summer of the same year civil war broke out between the "Reds" (the Bolsheviks) and the "Whites" (anti-communists). In the autumn, the Allies intervened in an attempt to re-establish the eastern front [9], and soon began assisting the Whites. Hostilities lasted until the end of 1920 and revealed two victors, the Red Army and the Communist Party. During this time the Bolsheviks murdered the imprisoned tsar and his family. The Reds had the advantage of a claim that they were defending Russia from invasion. The desperate measures needed to secure military victory alienated many workers and peasants. Although desertions from the Red Army were frequent, Trotsky was successful in forging Soviet military might, but democracy fell victim to the needs of the hour. Lenin fashioned a new force to rule the country, the Communist Party of the Soviet Union. Aided by the feared Cheka (a secret police force), the Party and the military were willing to obey Lenin and his colleagues, while the soviets would not.

The bloodshed and exhaustion of seven years of war left Soviet Russia racked by

revolt. Lenin gave way to the peasants and in 1921 introduced the New Economic Policy (NEP) which temporarily relaxed socialism in favour of some private ownership. The "commanding heights of the economy" stayed in state hands but agriculture, employing 80 per cent of the population, was on a market basis. The economy thus gradually recovered under the NEP.

### The emergence of the new Russia

Soviet Russia had to be satisfied with less territory than the old empire held. The borderlands – Finland, Estonia, Latvia, Lithuania, Poland, part of the Ukraine and Bessarabia – were lost. But in the three independent Transcaucasian republics, following the British evacuation of Transcaucasia in December 1919, the way was clear for the Bolsheviks to take over. By April 1921 Transcaucasia was back in the fold thanks to the activities of the Red Army.

There remained the problem of succession. Lenin expected Trotsky to succeed him but ultimately Joseph Stalin (1879–1953) proved the more ruthless politician.

**Vladimir Ilyich Ulyanov** (known as Lenin) was born in Simbirsk (now Ulyanov) on the Volga. He was mainly in exile from 1900, but returned for the Revolution of 1917.

8

Тов. Ленин ОЧИЩАЕТ землю от нечисти.

**8 "Comrade Lenin sweeps the world** of its rubbish" in this early Soviet cartoon. Peace and land were the two major demands Lenin promised to meet and immediately on seizing power the Bolsheviks put into effect the land policy they had adopted from the Socialist Revolutionaries. Land was later nationalized, but in 1917 most peasants still regarded it as their own. During the civil war grain was forcibly requisitioned to feed the Red Army and the cities. The peasants planted less and there was famine and disease. Finally Lenin capitulated and introduced the New Economic Policy in 1921.

9

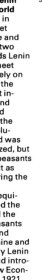

**9 Civil war divided Russia from 1918–20,** threatening Bolshevik rule. In March 1918 Germany had forced Russia to a disadvantageous peace settlement at Brest-Litovsk. However, Allied troops then came to Russia to prevent German forces occupying key centres. After Germany's defeat they stayed and aided the Whites during the civil war. The Bolsheviks, who had demobilized the imperial army by granting land to the peasants and seeking a separate peace, had to create a new force, the Red Army. Trotsky, the father of the Red Army, was a brilliant military leader. The Reds had to contend with Greens (anarchists), Poles and dissident nationalities and the British, Americans, Japanese and French scattered around the country. The cartoon shows Uncle Sam about to release the dogs of war: the White leaders Denikin, Kolchak and Yudenich.

10

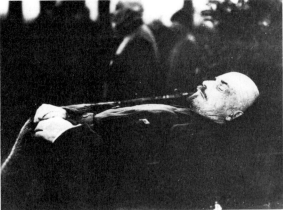

**10 The famine** that devastated the Volga region in the winter of 1921–2 claimed about 5 million lives and came on top of a virtual collapse of the Russian economy in 1921. By the end of 1920, the defeat of the Whites and the withdrawal of the Allies was complete. But seven years of war had left Russia in chaos, and popular unrest was fermented by inflation, shortages of food and fuel and the increasingly autocratic measures introduced to deal with internal and external threats to the infant Soviet state. Lenin introduced the New Economic Policy in 1921 to stimulate economic reconstruction and to placate the peasants by allowing a limited market economy with greater freedom of production. The period of the NEP was also one of considerable freedom expressed in the arts.

11

**11 Lenin's death** in 1924 followed a stroke in 1922, at which time a troika of Zinoviev (1883–1936), Kamenev (1883–1936) and Stalin had been established to continue the leadership. Lenin distrusted Stalin, whose main rival for the succession was Trotsky. But by skilfully playing off various factions and by control of the party mechanism, Stalin isolated Trotsky by 1925 and moved towards personal domination and ultimate dictatorship.

# Stalin's Russia

The Soviet Union's evolution between 1917 and 1953 was dominated by two men, Vladimir Ilyich Lenin (1870–1924) and Joseph Stalin (1879–1953) [Key]. While Lenin was alive he was the main driving force behind events. Nevertheless there were other important personalities such as Leon Trotsky (1879–1940) [1], Nikolai Bukharin (1888–1938) [2], Mikhail Tomsky (1880–1936), Grigori Zinoviev (1883–1936) and Anatoli Lunacharsky (1875–1933), to name only a few. All made an original contribution to Soviet development. Lenin, a man of outstanding intellectual ability, would listen to an opposing point of view if it came from one of his supporters, but had noticeably less respect for the views of his outspoken political opponents.

## The policies of Stalin
Lenin realized the importance of consolidating the revolution, Stalin developed and extended the means. He sanctioned the revolutionary violence of the Cheka and extended the primacy of the party in state affairs. His doctrine of "Socialism in One Country" meant that all foreign communist parties became subservient to Soviet interests through the Comintern (Communist International). Furthermore, he continued to hold the show trials of a number of so-called counter revolutionaries. The first took place in 1922 and were directed at the Socialist Revolutionaries.

Nevertheless, there were major differences between the two men. Stalin was an intuitive anti-intellectual. His intellectual insecurity did not permit him to envisage a policy and then take on his opponents in open debate. Instead he sought to outmanoeuvre them in labyrinthine intrigue. Lenin was good at placing labels, often misleading ones, on his opponents; Stalin was a past master at the art. Lenin used the Cheka and the show trial against non-Bolsheviks; Stalin used them against the Communist Party as well.

## The achievement of power
Stalin built up his power by his administrative skills and filled the leading party bodies with workers, but he did take the precaution of first briefing them on how to vote.

Stalin's journey on the way to supreme power can be divided into three stages, the completion of each marking a significant step forward. The first, terminating in 1928–9, saw him with almost total control over the apparatus of the Russian Communist Party which, because of the events of the immediate post-October period, had inherited the dominant role in the state. Victory over the party was not sufficient to permit Stalin to reach out to every corner of the Soviet Union. This he did during the 1930s when collectivization and industrialization transformed the scene. The peasants lost their land and their livestock and were brought under complete state control [3]. The foundations of great industrial advance were laid with heavy industry, vital for defence, receiving top priority [4]. A terrible massacre of real, putative, imaginary and potential opponents of Stalin's dictatorship took place. No one was secure, whether top party official (a major target were the Old Bolsheviks, those who had seized power with Lenin in October 1917), military leader, writer, peasant, worker, engineer or foreign

**1 An outstanding theorist**, Trotsky was, however, a poor politician, ill at ease with the minutiae of government. Although expected to succeed Lenin, he was inept at intrigue and was defeated. It was his failure to perceive the machinations of his fellows that soon led to his exile and death. He was an unequalled speaker, but his independent, critical attitude was not tolerated by Stalin.

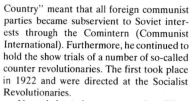

**2 Lenin called Bukharin** "the darling of the whole party" and its "most valuable and most powerful theorist". Bukharin was the leading party writer on economic subjects. He sided with Stalin against Trotsky, Kamenev and Zinoviev and was a leading defender of the New Economic Policy. He was swept aside at the end of the 1920s when collectivization became the new official policy.

1927 Total peasantry 120,000,000
Total households 25,000,000

**3 The New Economic Policy** was a compromise on the way to socialism. It permitted the blossoming of private farming and since four out of five Soviet citizens lived in the countryside there was a risk of the capitalist ethic proving attractive. Lenin had preached co-operation and Bukharin ably elucidated his views after 1924. When agricultural production climbed back after 1924 to the level of 1913, the Soviets were faced with a choice – allow private agriculture to develop and provide the basis for overall economic growth, or socialize agriculture and base economic growth on industrial development. They chose the latter out of fear that private agriculture could overturn the socialist state and Stalin wanted food supplies for the urban worker.

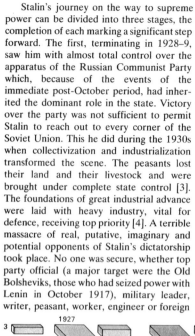

**4 Soviet power** was insecure without a strong industrial and military base. Ambition ran riot as the first Five Year Plan got under way in 1928. Production goals were pushed up in the belief that a revolutionary spirit could perform miracles. Heavy industry was favoured at the expense of light industry and agriculture. Wonders were performed, but at appalling cost. Enthusiasm waned after the first plan and labour discipline became severe with saboteurs and counter-revolutionaries unmasked everywhere. Living standards dropped as millions flooded to the cities where accommodation was primitive. Both food and clothing were also in short supply.

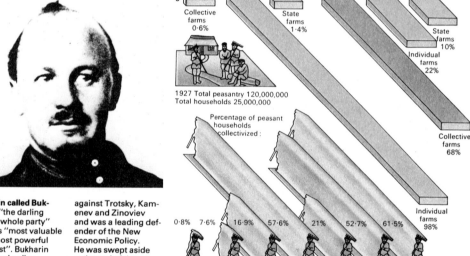

**5 The tractor was the symbol** of Soviet power in the Russian countryside. The collective farm or *kolkhoz* became the dominant enterprise in socialist agriculture after 1928. Much virgin land was brought into cultivation in the 1930s and *sovhozes* or state farms were usually set up in new areas. Collective farm peasants were permitted a small, private plot and some animals. They received a share of the produce in proportion to the net income of the *kolkhoz*.

communist leader living in exile in the USSR. More than ten million people perished, including the great majority of the class of *kulaks* (well-to-do peasants).

When this period ended Stalin was master of all he surveyed in Soviet Russia; he controlled the party, the government and the police. Through the agency of foreign communist parties he could influence the internal politics of other countries. The third phase, which began with the outbreak of World War II and ended with Stalin's death in March 1953, saw Stalinist Russia reach the peak of world influence.

Stalin exhibited great tactical skill in the 1920s in overcoming his competitors one by one. In 1923–4 he allied himself with L. V. Kamenev (1883–1936) and Zinoviev against Trotsky; in 1925 he sided with Bukharin against Kamenev and Zinoviev; in 1926–7 still with Bukharin (who realized too late that Stalin's allegiance was merely tactical) against Trotsky, Kamenev and Zinoviev and finally in 1928–9 he was strong enough to oppose Bukharin, Tomsky and Rykov (1881–1938) by himself. By 1929 Trotsky

was in exile and the others living on borrowed time. Most were to perish in the purges of 1936–8 [6, 7]. Trotsky, exiled in Mexico, was murdered by Stalin's executioner in 1940.

## Russia's development

Russia's industrial effort in the 1930s made great progress. The bases of a thriving heavy industry were established and were to prove of vital importance when war came. Stalin took a long time to learn foreign affairs [11]. He indirectly helped Hitler gain power in Germany; then saw the danger and launched the Popular Front, inviting the collaboration of all democratic forces. He again put his faith in National Socialist Germany in 1939 and almost paid with the annihilation of the USSR after the German attack of June 1941.

Stalin's war record, except for the opening days of the war when he lost his nerve, is admirable. He led by example and his ruthlessness steadied his armies. Stalin played a vital role in the victory of the Allies. But had he allied Soviet Russia with Britain and France in 1939, it is possible that Germany would not have attacked Poland.

**"Lenin is the Marx of our time"** was the slogan when Vladimir Ilyich Lenin [left] was alive. Soon a new form appeared: "Stalin is our Lenin". Stalin became the main interpreter of Marx's chief Russian disciple. Those who threatened his supremacy were soon removed from positions of power.

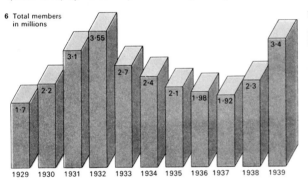

6 Total members in millions

1·7 — 1929
2·2 — 1930
3·1 — 1931
3·55 — 1932
2·7 — 1933
2·4 — 1934
2·1 — 1935
1·98 — 1936
1·92 — 1937
2·3 — 1938
3·4 — 1939

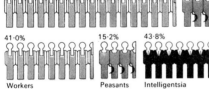

Class composition of recruits 1929
81·2% Workers 17·1% Peasants 1·7% Intelligentsia

1936–9
41·0% Workers 15·2% Peasants 43·8% Intelligentsia

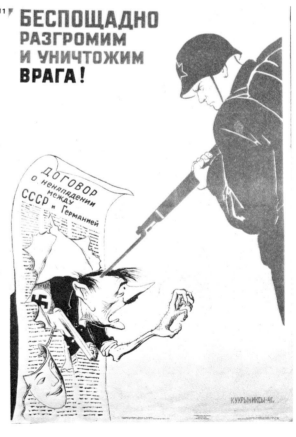

**7 The "purges of the 1930s"** were in fact composed of many different operations; these gathered momentum and reached a crescendo in the "Yezhovschina" (named after Yezhov, the head of Internal Affairs) of 1937–8. The first purge was launched by the party in January 1933. In 1935 a "verification of party documents" was ordered. About one member in five was expelled, including recent workers and peasant recruits. About 9% had been purged before the "show trials" ushered in the devastating Great Purge of 1936–8, when millions perished in the party and populace alike.

Party members
Purged
New members

1933 2·7 million
1938 2·3 million

**6 The composition of the Communist Party's** membership changed markedly between 1929 and 1939. In 1929 four-fifths of party members were workers; ten years later that proportion had dropped to two-fifths. The difference was made up by a massive recruitment of the intelligentsia, partly because of a campaign to recruit the "best" people, partly because a party card was needed to qualify for a number of important posts in industry and the administration. The proportion of peasant members remained fairly constant. The dramatic change in membership reflects the policy behind the 1933–8 purges as well as their effects.

**11 Stalin misjudged fascism** in the early 1930s but when he realized the danger he launched the "Popular Front" policy in 1935. All progressive forces were to unite against the common enemy and posters declared "Let's mercilessly rout and destroy the enemy". This policy did not deter Germany, and Stalin, thinking he understood Hitler, signed the pact of August 1939. Stalin intended to intervene opportunely in the impending war when Hitler had become over-committed on the Western Front. Stalin was so thunderstruck by the invasion of June 1941 that he lost his nerve and failed to provide resolute leadership during the first days of the war. The failure of the German *Blitzkrieg* in 1941–2 to overrun the USSR meant that the war of attrition, which Germany could not win because of inadequate resources, became inevitable. Major battles were Moscow and Stalingrad.

БЕСПОЩАДНО РАЗГРОМИМ И УНИЧТОЖИМ ВРАГА!

ДОГОВОР о ненападении между СССР и Германией

КУКРЫНИКСЫ-41.

**8 Vyacheslav Molotov** (1890– ) became a full member of the Politburo in 1926. He was instrumental in shaping the non-aggression pact with the Nazis and he remained a loyal servant to Stalin. He was also involved in party construction.

**9 Nikita Khrushchev** (1894–1971) was on the Moscow party committee between 1932 and 1938, when he took the key post of First Secretary of the party in the Ukraine. He became a member of the Politburo in 1939 where he backed Stalin.

**10 Lazar Kaganovich** (1893– ) became a full member of the Politburo in 1930. He headed the Moscow party committee 1930–35 and was minister of transport 1935–44. A loyal supporter of Stalin, he retained favour during the years 1930–53.

# The twenties and the Depression

The years from 1919–38 were dominated by an economic depression that troubled Europe for most of the time and affected the rest of the world most heavily in the 1930s. The aftermath of World War I was notable for an attempt to return to "normalcy", a term coined by the American President Warren Harding (1865–1923), and in Britain the immediate postwar years witnessed a boom in industrial production and living standards. After 1922, however, trade and industrial activity fell off, creating unemployment in the major heavy industries of the British economy [1]. Germany, the other great industrial economy of Europe, was unable to recover from the effects of the war and the impositions of the peace settlement [2]. The result was to depress the economy of Europe, which needed the prosperity of German industry. With the problems of inflation, political instability and the heavy reparations to contend with, the German economy did not begin to make a major recovery until the mid-1920s.

The war had left the United States as the major creditor nation, supplanting the position Britain had once held. A large proportion of the world's gold reserves had accumulated in Fort Knox, providing the basis for a large-scale expansion in American output. The growth in credit and consumption which these gold reserves allowed enabled a boom in manufacturing output to take place [3].

The twenties saw a wave of prosperity in the United States. It combined with a sense of release after war years to create the hectic atmosphere of the "roaring twenties". To a lesser extent this was felt in Europe towards the end of the decade, when an economic revival helped to popularize American music, dances and films.

## Aspects of social life

Socially, the twenties had a paradoxical air. On the one hand, the end of the war heralded new freedoms, particularly for women. They had worked in many new occupations during the war and began to reap the benefits in terms of political and social emancipation. Fashions became more practical, there was a greater knowledge about birth control and

there was a wider range of job opportunities. The twenties in America also saw Prohibition, which restricted the sale of alcohol, and created a boom in illicit alcohol.

## Crisis and deflation

The more optimistic economic climate of the late twenties was, however, brought to an end by the Wall Street Crash of October 1929. The American boom had already begun to falter by the summer of 1929 with a downturn in the economic indices. The slide in share prices that followed became a panic [5]. In America, unemployment soared as credit dried up, consumption declined, and bankruptcies and redundancies multiplied. Compounding the Depression, agricultural prices fell disastrously for farmers in many other countries. World unemployment doubled within a year; in the United States it reached six million by the end of 1930.

For two years the Depression deepened throughout the industrialized world. By 1932, more than 12 million people were out of work in the United States and whole communities were at a standstill. The impact of

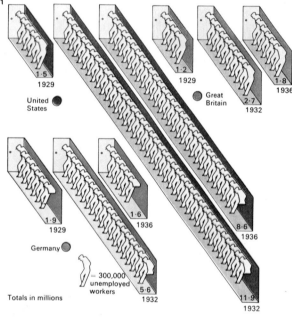

**1 After World War I** Britain suffered from the decline of her basic industries and the rise of competition, while Germany needed several years to recover from the war and reparations. The USA enjoyed a boom period in the twenties, which was brought to a halt by the Great Crash of 1929 and the decline in financial confidence and world trade. It brought a dramatic rise in unemployment in the industrial West, as shown here.

United States
Great Britain
Germany

= 300,000 unemployed workers

Totals in millions

1929 1·5
1929 1·2
1936 1·8
1932 2·7
1929 1·9
1936 1·6
1936 8·6
1932 5·6
1932 11·9

**3 The American economy boomed** in the twenties with a rapid growth of heavy industries. The industrial production index here shown is based on an average index of 100 for 1935–9. Rising consumption and easy credit fuelled the boom until 1929.

**4 The motor car industry** grew to major importance in the interwar period. Although invented and produced before 1914, cars remained expensive luxuries.

By 1932, the assembly lines and conveyor belts, which had created the cheap, popular cars for a wider market, had come to a halt, leaving thousands jobless.

3
| 1921 | 1923 | 1925 | 1927 | 1929 | 1931 | 1933 |
|---|---|---|---|---|---|---|

110
95
90
88
100
75
69
58
American industrial production

**2** German paper marks equivalent to one gold mark

1757
16 46 75

Jun 1921  Dec 1921  Jun 1922  Dec 1922

**2 The German economy** was thrown into severe difficulties by the effects of the war and the peace settlement. The loss of major industrial areas and reparations depressed the economy and created preconditions for inflation. With French occupation of the Ruhr because of Germany's default of reparation payments, massive inflation was triggered off, wiping out all savings, until a loaf of bread cost millions of marks.

**5 Thousands rushed to sell** their shares on Wall Street in the panic selling of 1929. In two months share values had declined by a third and a paper loss of $26 million was registered. The growth in the American economy had been accompanied by a major speculative boom in share prices, involving small investors and large trusts. By 1929 industrial production began to peak and share prices slumped, causing the panic.

the Great Crash was equally disastrous on European economies, many of which depended on United States credit.

Current economic thinking decreed that a crisis of this kind could be cured only by a harsh dose of deflation, to balance budgets, reduce surplus capacity, and ride out the storm. In Germany the government of Franz von Papen (1879–1969) applied ever tougher doses of deflation and this pattern was followed in Britain, under the National Government of Ramsay MacDonald (1866–1937), and in the United States under President Herbert Hoover (1874–1964). Although the British economist J. M. Keynes (1883–1946) was in the process of formulating alternative policies, in which emphasis would be placed upon increased government spending and rising consumption to revive economic activity, his radical views were not generally available.

**Political repercussions**

The Depression had important political repercussions. In the United States dissatisfaction with the performance of Presi-

dent Hoover and his management of the economic crisis was reflected in the victory of Franklin D. Roosevelt (1882–1945) with his promise of a "New Deal" [7]. In Britain, the effects of the deepening depression in 1930 brought about a financial and political crisis for the Labour Government of Ramsay MacDonald. A National Government was formed after the 1931 general election, with a massive Conservative majority, but under the leadership of MacDonald and a small group of Labour followers. In Germany, the mounting unemployment and fear of social breakdown engendered support for the Nazi Party and undermined the basis of the Weimar Republic [8]. France was affected later than the rest of Europe because her large agricultural sector disguised unemployment and her industrial base was smaller than that of other countries.

Although the Depression dominated the thirties in Europe and the United States, recovery began in 1933, so that by the outbreak of World War II some considerable advances had been made in living standards in the period as a whole for those in work.

**Drought and low prices** for farm produce forced many farmers and their families to migrate from the American Midwest to California. Their hardships, immortalized in John Steinbeck's *The Grapes of Wrath*, symbolized the Depression.

6

7

**6 In Britain**, the Depression led to "hunger marches", such as that of 1936 when 200 men from Jarrow marched to London seeking work. In America, unemployed ex-servicemen marched to Washington in 1932. The action of police in dispersing them and leaving some dead caused much resentment.

**7 Under Roosevelt's "New Deal"** a number of ambitious projects were started to bring work to the unemployed and to stimulate the economy. The Tennessee Valley Authority sought to revitalize the economy and living conditions of a whole region by prestige projects such as the Hoover Dam, shown here.

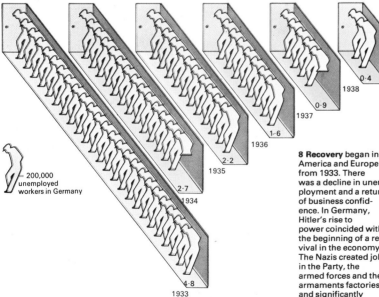

8

200,000 unemployed workers in Germany

0.4
1938

0.9
1937

1.6
1936

2.2
1935

2.7
1934

4.8
1933

Totals in millions

**8 Recovery** began in America and Europe from 1933. There was a decline in unemployment and a return of business confidence. In Germany, Hitler's rise to power coincided with the beginning of a revival in the economy. The Nazis created jobs in the Party, the armed forces and the armaments factories, and significantly reduced unemployment, as shown here.

9

**9 Franklin D. Roosevelt** brought a new period of prosperity to the United States after the worst years of the Depression when he became President in 1933. He won a landslide victory over Herbert Hoover on a programme for a "New Deal" for America, consisting of welfare legislation, public works, agricultural aid and planning, and an end to Prohibition. Roosevelt's confident style was almost as important as his legislation, bringing a measure of optimism and stability to the business and commercial world. His "fireside chats" on the radio helped to reassure the public that the government was acting to help the ordinary people. He went on to be elected for a second and third term. He died in office in 1945.

# The British labour movement 1868–1930

The driving force behind the British labour movement in the latter half of the nineteenth century was the trade unions, which had been given restricted legality in 1825. Until the advent of the so-called "new unionism" in the 1880s, most trade unions were associations of skilled workers of varying political allegiance. Nonetheless, by the 1880s they had established a relatively secure position for themselves. In 1871 trade unions had been given legal recognition and in 1875 peaceful picketing was legalized.

### New unionism

The period from 1875 to 1900 saw rapid growth in trade unions. This resulted partly from the rising prestige of the Trades Union Congress (TUC) which was founded in 1868, and partly from the efforts of a generation of "new unionists" who preached a much more militant form of trade unionism and organized semi-skilled and unskilled workers, such as dockers and gas workers, into new, industrial unions [Key]. These unions were prepared to take strike action with much less hesitation than before [2]. The result

was the growth of working-class solidarity, an increasing dissatisfaction with the Liberal Party and the spread of genuinely socialist ideas among working men.

The growth of socialism had been demonstrated in 1888 when James Keir Hardie (1856–1915) and R. B. Cunninghame Graham (1852–1936) founded the Scottish Labour Party. It was given national expression in 1893 when Hardie [3] founded the Independent Labour Party (ILP) with the aim of encouraging trade unionists and socialists to join forces for the creation of an independent political party with working-class representation in Parliament. A non-revolutionary path to socialism was also sought by the Fabian Society which was founded in 1884. Among its best known exponents were Sidney (1859–1947) and Beatrice (1858–1943) Webb and the writer George Bernard Shaw (1856–1950). In 1900 the Fabians, with the ILP, the Marxist Social Democratic Federation and trade unionists, set up the Labour Representation Committee (LRC). Its aim, to quote Hardie, was to form a distinct Labour

group in Parliament. Its first secretary was James Ramsay Macdonald (1866–1937).

The LRC's programme was a moderate one – it avoided commitment either to socialism or to the class war. As a result, in 1901, it lost the support of the Marxist Federation, but it did gain considerable trade union support, largely in reaction to the Taff Vale decision by the House of Lords in 1901 which found trade unions liable for losses incurred through strikes. In 1906, therefore, the LRC saw 29 out of 50 of its candidates elected to Parliament; later that year, the LRC was renamed the Labour Party.

### The growth of the Labour Party

From 1906 to 1914 the Labour Party supported the social reforms of the Liberal governments, which in turn passed legislation benefiting the trade unions. The Trade Dispute Act of 1906 reversed the Taff Vale decision of 1901 and the Trade Union Act in 1913 allowed trade unions to support the Labour Party financially. Nonetheless from 1910 to 1914 trade union militancy increased [4] as a result of rising prices and the spread,

1 **The London match girls** came out on strike in 1888. Their appalling working conditions had previously been exposed by the Fabian lecturer Mrs Annie Besant (1847–1933) in her paper *The Link*. With her help and that of other socialists, the match girls were eventually victorious and won recognition for their union. This was one of the first examples of the wave of "new unionist" activity and organization that spread among the semi-skilled and unskilled workers from 1889. It clearly indicated the bad conditions that had to be endured by these people who made up by far, the bulk of the British working class.

2 **The London dock strike** (1889), the first major action of its kind by unskilled workers, lasted five weeks. It ended in victory for the dockers who won their claim for a basic 6d (2$\frac{1}{2}$p) an hour (the "dockers' tanner"). The most significant aspect of the strike, however, was the widespread support won by the dockers from skilled workers and other sectors of the community. The dockers advertised their case skilfully and thus notably advanced the cause of working-class solidarity. Their militancy also highlighted the spread of socialism among British workers.

3 **James Keir Hardie** was one of the leading and best-loved figures in the British labour movement. Born in Lanarkshire, Scotland, he worked as a coal miner from the age of ten, and in 1886 formed the Scottish Miners Federation. He was the first chairman of the Scottish Labour Party (1888), and in 1892 became the first workers' representative in Parliament when he was elected as an independent Labour MP. Through his tireless efforts he was involved in the foundation of the Independent Labour Party in 1893, and the Labour Representation Committee, in 1900. He lost his seat in 1895, but was re-elected in 1900 as Labour MP for Merthyr Tydfil, south Wales, which he held until his death.

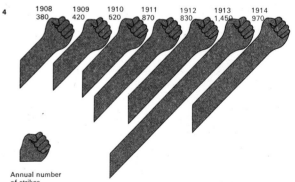

| 1908 | 1909 | 1910 | 1911 | 1912 | 1913 | 1914 |
|------|------|------|------|------|------|------|
| 380 | 420 | 520 | 870 | 830 | 1,450 | 970 |

Annual number of strikes

4 **Industrial unrest** characterized the years 1911–14. In 1908 there were 380 strikes; in 1913 there were 1,450. Dockers, seamen, railwaymen, and miners all struck between 1911 and 1914. There were militant and bitter conflicts and the men often held out for long periods in support of their demands. The strikes were prompted by various factors – the restoration of trade unions' legal immunity in 1906, falling standards of living, the apparent failure of the Labour Party to protect the interests of the working class, and the growth of Marxist and syndicalist ideas among working men. With the onset of the war in 1914, unrest declined because most union leaders and members chose to back the war effort.

from France and the United States, of syndicalist ideas that advocated a general strike to destroy capitalism.

The Labour Party continued to co-operate with the Liberal Party in Parliament and during World War I Arthur Henderson (1863–1935), who succeeded MacDonald as leader of the Labour Party in 1914, sat in the war cabinet of the coalition government. Various other Labour members also held administrative posts. By 1918, however, the Labour Party stood for a more independent policy, and influenced by events in Russia, adopted a more socialist constitution.

After the war the Labour Party soon became the second party in the country. Disillusionment, unemployment, and political strife within the Liberal Party meant that the Labour Party became the official opposition in Parliament in 1922. In 1924 Ramsay MacDonald became prime minister at the head of a minority government. His administration lasted only ten months. Publication of the so-called "Zinoviev letter" – instructions for a communist uprising in Britain apparently sent by Gregori Zinoviev

(1883–1936), chairman of the Communist International – severely damaged the Labour Party. Although the letter was later proved to be forged, Labour fell before the Conservatives in November 1924.

**The second Labour Government**
In 1926 the trade unions challenged Conservative rule when the TUC supported the General Strike on behalf of the miners [7] but the government successfully resisted the challenge and in 1927 outlawed general strikes and attempted to reduce trade union subscriptions to the Labour Party.

In 1929, with the onset of the Depression, Labour returned to office with Ramsay MacDonald once again at the head of a minority government. His cabinet was divided over economic policy. Because socialist legislation was impossible in the midst of the economic slump, in 1931 MacDonald formed a coalition national government. In doing so he forfeited the support of the Labour Party, whose parliamentary representation dropped sharply in the 1931 general election.

By the 1870s trade unions had achieved legal recognition. Until that time unions had followed no specific political viewpoint, but from the 1880s the movement took a new turn. Disillusioned with the Liberal Party and influenced by socialist ideas, the "new unions" increasingly stressed the political role. They demanded a legal minimum wage, an 8-hour day, and the right to work. Although union militancy continued until well after World War I – until its defeat in the General Strike of 1926 – with the establishment of the Labour Party by 1906 union activity increasingly followed more conventional, parliamentary channels.

5 Tom Mann (1856–1941) was one of the leading "new unionists" of the late 19th century. In 1881 he joined the Amalgamated Society of Engineers and by 1886 had become involved in the socialist movement. In that year he published a pamphlet arguing that a more militant attitude should be taken by trade unionists. In 1889 Mann helped to organize the London dock strike and from 1894–7 was secretary of the Independent Labour Party. He emigrated, and in 1902 was active in the Australian labour movement. In the 1920s, after his return to England, he became a founder of the British Communist Party, feeling that the existing unions could not be militant enough.

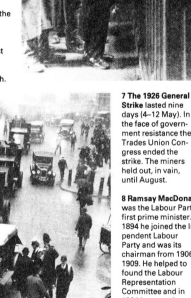

6 Labour exchanges were introduced into Britain in 1910 by Winston Churchill (1874–1965), then Liberal President of the Board of Trade. Advocated by the Poor Law commission of 1909 and by the economist William Beveridge (1879–1963), labour exchanges were intended to provide a service for workers seeking employment and for employers seeking labour. They also prepared the way for a national system of social insurance. Initially, they were not as effective as had been hoped. Registration of unemployment was not compulsory so that only one-third of vacancies were filled through the nationwide exchanges.

7 The 1926 General Strike lasted nine days (4–12 May). In the face of government resistance the Trades Union Congress ended the strike. The miners held out, in vain, until August.

8 Ramsay MacDonald was the Labour Party's first prime minister. In 1894 he joined the Independent Labour Party and was its chairman from 1906 to 1909. He helped to found the Labour Representation Committee and in 1924 became the first Labour Party premier. In 1929 he again became prime minister but was rejected by the Labour Party when he formed a coalition national government in 1931, the only way he saw of keeping Labour in power.

# Socialism in the West

Socialism developed from a group of thinkers, especially Robert Owen (1771–1858), Henri de Saint-Simon (1760–1825) and Charles Fourier (1772–1837), who criticized industrialism because of the suffering and hardship it caused the working class. But it was not until the mid-nineteenth century that socialism developed a mass following as a direct result of the growth of industry in different parts of Europe and the related rise of an urban working class.

### Early developments
As the first industrial nation, Great Britain took the lead in the development of workingmen's organizations [7]. Despite legal restrictions and occasional persecution, such as the transportation to Australia of the Tolpuddle Martyrs in 1834 for trade union activity, unions flourished by the middle of the nineteenth century, especially among skilled workers. The political ideas of this "labour aristocracy" were largely Owenite, emphasizing co-operation and reformist political activity. Attempts to establish a Grand National Consolidated Trades Union

had failed by 1834, and following this the Chartist movement attempted to enlist the mass of factory operatives in the cause of political rights, which were enshrined in the "People's Charter", presented to Parliament and rejected three times. Under reformist leaders British trade unions concentrated upon securing gradual concessions in the political and social sphere during the period of prosperity after 1851.

In Europe the slower progress of industrialization hampered the growth of organized socialist movements. Trade unions remained illegal in France until the middle of the nineteenth century and socialist support was divided between the followers of revolutionary leaders, reformists and anarchists. Although workers participated in the overthrow of Louis-Philippe (1773–1850) in 1848, there was no organization to unite them. In Germany, too, the workers who supported the revolution of 1848 remained divided and dominated by middle-class liberals. The German risings of 1848 did, however, see the emergence of Marxism in the *Communist Manifesto*. Written by Karl Marx

(1818–83) and Friedrich Engels (1820–95), the manifesto provided a coherent intellectual basis for many later socialists.

### The First International
Although socialist ideas played little part in the revolutions of 1848, and Chartism was defeated in Britain in the same year, they did mark the emergence of the first important mass movements of workers in Europe. In 1864 socialist groups came together in the First International. Although racked by dissension, the International provided a vehicle for Marxist ideas and encouragement to socialist groups throughout Europe. In France in 1871 the rising of Parisian workers and the lower middle classes in the Commune was proof of the growing strength of socialist ideas. The International was liquidated in 1876, following quarrels between the anarchists and Marx. In the less developed parts of Europe, especially Spain, Italy and Russia, anarchist ideas propagated by Mikhail Bakunin (1814–76) had a strong appeal and led to risings in Spain and terrorist acts in Russia [2].

1 **Two reformers,** Sidney (1859–1947) and Beatrice Webb (1858–1943), adapted socialism to the cause of social reform which they sought to achieve gradually through democratic procedures. They formed the Fabian Society in 1884. It attracted many middle-class and intellectual figures such as George Bernard Shaw. The British Labour Party adopted the ideals of "Fabianism" for its philosophical basis.

2 **In Russia, anarchism inspired** the opponents of the tsarist regime in a campaign of terrorism, including the assassination of Alexander II in 1881. Anarchism grew out of the ideas of Pierre Proudhon (1809–65) among others. It rejected all authority in its search for a self-governing ideal in which men could totally fulfil themselves. The most famous 19th-century exponents were Russians, especially Mikhail Bakunin and Prince Peter Kropotkin (1842–1921). In France, anarchism became blended with trade unionism, and in Spain anarchist groups played an important part in the political upheavals of the early 20th century, including the Spanish Civil War.

3 **The years before World War I** were marked by labour militancy and violent strikes throughout Europe and the USA. In Britain there was a wave of bitter disputes and troops had to be called out in South Wales during the coal strike of 1912. The trouble was caused by the rise of organized labour, the spread of militant ideas and a slight downturn in living standards after a period of improvement.

4 **Jean Jaurès** (1859–1914) was a most eminent French socialist. A successful politician and moderate Marxist, he brought unity to the fragmented socialist groups in France before being assassinated by a fanatic for opposing the war with Germany in 1914.

5 **Polish-born Rosa Luxemburg,** with Karl Liebknecht, led the Marxist "Spartacist" movement which sought to end the 1914–18 war through revolution. They were both assassinated by reactionary troops in Berlin during the revolt of 1918–19.

6 **Like these Londoners,** liberals everywhere protested in 1927 at death penalties imposed on two US anarchists, Nicola Sacco (1891–1927) and Bartolomeo Vanzetti (1888–1927). Many believed their conviction, for murder, was politically motivated.

After 1870 the German socialist movement became the most powerful in Europe. In 1890, in spite of laws restricting its operation, the Social-Democratic Party was the largest in the Reich. Although divided between Marxist and "revisionist" groups, the socialists continued their rise up to 1914. In the aftermath of Germany's defeat an alliance between the social-democrats and the army was formed to set up the Weimar government and to frustrate the challenge from the Marxist "Spartacists" led by Karl Liebknecht (1871–1919) and Rosa Luxemburg (1871–1919) [5]. In France the socialist movement remained fragmented. French workers turning aside from party politics were attracted to syndicalist ideas of control being achieved by workers through strikes.

**The Second International**
The Second International, formed in 1889, was severely divided between reformist and revolutionary groups, and was not strong enough concertedly to oppose World War I. Nonetheless, by 1914 socialism was a powerful political force in Europe and had also

spread to Latin America and the United States. Although it was never as strong in the USA as in Europe, a socialist candidate for the presidency, Eugene Debs (1855–1926), polled 900,000 votes in 1912, while the militant Industrial Workers of the World (IWW) mounted a series of bitter strikes. The war caused a breakup of the international socialist movement because its members had to choose between patriotism and allegiance to the socialist ideals.

The Russian Revolution led to a revival of left-wing militancy in the aftermath of World War I, but the inter-war period saw the socialist parties of Britain, France and Germany playing a prominent part in parliamentary politics, and the triumph of socialist parties in Scandinavia. Although the Depression and the rise of fascism led to suppression, as in Germany, Italy and Spain, they also led to a revival of socialism in middle-class and intellectual circles. The Spanish Civil War [9, 10] provided a rallying point for the left and the triumph of the Allies in World War II left socialist parties in a prominent position in nearly all the countries of Europe.

By 1914 the trade union movement, representing millions of working people, was a growing force in the major industrial countries. The years between 1900 and 1914 saw an increase in the number and intensity of union strikes. Generally, employers still disputed the right to strike and often still challenged the unions' right to exist. Bitterness and hostility underlying strikes often led to open violence. However, trade unions were often narrowly sectional in their interests while generally supporting a socialist political stance. Contribution cards, such as this for the Carmen's Trade Union, were proof of full union membership.

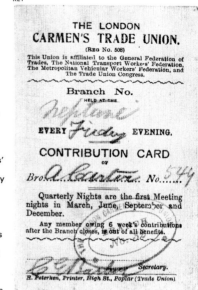

THE LONDON
**CARMEN'S TRADE UNION.**
(Reg No. 508)
This Union is affiliated to the General Federation of Trades, The National Transport Workers' Federation, The Metropolitan Vehicular Workers' Federation, and The Trade Union Congress.

Branch No.
HELD AT THE *Neptune*
EVERY *Friday* EVENING.
**CONTRIBUTION CARD**
OF
Bro *A. Carter.* No. *549*

Quarterly Nights are the first Meeting nights in March, June, September and December.

Any member owing 6 week's contributions after the Branch closes, is out of all benefits.

*Secretary.*
H. Peterken, Printer, High St., Poplar (Trade Union)

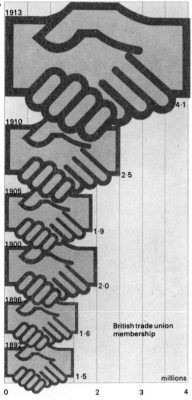

**7** Before 1914 there was a surge in trade union membership because of industrial development. In Britain the number of unionists more than doubled between 1905 and 1914, mainly as a result of the organization of unskilled and semi-skilled workers such as the dockers and railway workers, as opposed to the "labour aristocracy" who had created the unions.
In 1893 the Independent Labour Party (ILP) was formed, later to become the Labour Party (1906).

1913 · 4·1
1910 · 2·5
1905 · 1·9
1900 · 2·0
1896 · 1·6
1892 · 1·5
British trade union membership
0   2   3   4   millions

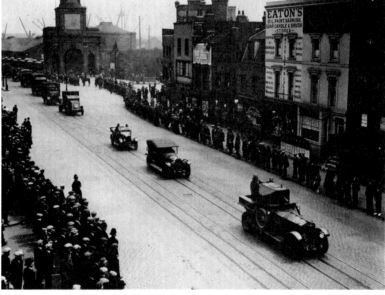

**8 The concept of the general strike** became widespread in the early years of the 20th century under the influence of syndicalist ideas. In Britain, the reformist character of the Trades Union Congress, formed in 1868, made it reluctant to use the general strike as a weapon, but in 1926 it called the General Strike in support of a bitter dispute in the coal industry. After a tense confrontation with the Conservative Government of Stanley Baldwin (1867–1947) the strike was defeated. Because of the Government's fear that food supplies would be looted, imports were collected from the London docks by armed convoys.

**9 The Spanish Civil War** (1936–9) was a rallying point for left-wing forces in Europe. The attempt by Franco's Nationalist forces to topple the Spanish Republic with aid from Italy and Germany resulted in co-operation between many divided communist and socialist parties. Although the war was a complex battle between various Spanish groups, it seemed to many socialists to symbolize the threat of fascism and the need for a united front.

LA GARRA DEL INVASOR ITALIANO PRETENDE ESCLAVIZARNOS

**10 As a result of widespread concern** for the Spanish Republic among left-wing groups, the International Brigade was formed to fight in Spain. It was drawn from many different nationalities and consisted mainly of Communist Party members, trade unionists and sympathetic intellectuals. The Brigade was recruited through the Communist Party, which organized training, equipment and transport to Spain. The volunteers played an important part in preventing an early victory by Franco's forces and his German and Italian allies, but they suffered heavy casualties. Their role symbolized the wider significance of the civil war and its emotive appeal for a whole generation.

French 10,000
German/Austrian 5,000
Italian 3,400
American 2,800
British 2,000
Yugoslavian 1,500
Czechoslovakian 1,500
Canadian 1,000
Hungarian 1,000
Scandinavian 1,000
Russian 500–1,000     = approx 500

89

# East Asia 1919–45

The history of East Asia from 1919 to 1945 is dominated by two related themes: the rise of Chinese nationalism in the 1920s and the spread of Japanese imperialism after 1931. Both developments were influenced by Western imperialist presence in the region. Chinese nationalism was complicated by the diverging interests of the two major political parties, the Nationalist Kuomintang (KMT) and the Chinese Communist Party (CCP).

## Rise of Chinese nationalism

The year 1919 is a watershed in Chinese history. Demonstrations against the Paris Peace Conference's granting of former German concessions in China to Japan – which the Chinese government accepted – developed into an unprecedented national movement [1]. Sensing the revolutionary mood, Sun Yat-sen (1866–1925) reorganized his Nationalist Party into the disciplined KMT. With both a socialist ideology and a party-dominated army under Chiang Kai-shek [Key], the KMT received help from the Comintern and collaborated with the fledgling CCP formed in 1921. Both parties

sought to end the division of China and its exploitation by foreign powers.

These privileges were little diminished by the Washington Conference (1921–2) which achieved only partial withdrawal by Japan. Chinese dissatisfaction coalesced with labour unrest, particularly in the treaty ports, culminating in a 15-month strike and boycott of foreign trade in Hong Kong in 1925–6. Against this background, Chiang Kai-shek led a northern expedition to unite China under the National Government set up in Canton. In 1927 Chiang clashed with party leftists, especially the communist bloc within the KMT. Purging the areas under his control [3], he succeeded in reunifying the KMT at the expense of the left and the CCP, setting up his own government in Nanking and bringing Peking and much of China under his control in 1928.

By 1930 extension of Nationalist authority put Chinese nationalism and Japanese imperialism on a collision course. Japanese privileges secured in Manchuria since 1905 were threatened by China's reassertion of its sovereignty there. Not only

was Manchuria a buffer against Soviet ideology and military power, it also represented a considerable economic investment and had a million Japanese subjects.

## Japanese imperialist expansion

Japan of the 1920s was characterized by paternalistic capitalism with limited democracy at home and co-operation with the great powers abroad. But in the 1930s ultra-nationalism and militarism fostered ideas of an autonomous economic empire as an answer to the Depression, which had exacerbated tensions in Japanese society. As confidence in politicians waned, popular support grew for the militarists who were close to Emperor Hirohito [5]. Japanese officers in Manchuria used the Mukden Incident of 1931 [4] to create a situation that led to the establishment of a Japanese puppet state, Manchukuo, in 1932. Expansion southward in 1935–6 was designed partly to create a subservient North China to protect Japan's rear in the event of war with the USSR.

Japan's encroachment brought a temporary truce between the KMT and CCP in

**1 The May 4th Incident** in 1919 was a demonstration by 3,000 students in Peking, protesting at the Paris Peace Conference that left Japan in control of German possessions it had seized in China. Spreading protest forced government changes and foreshadowed a new Chinese nationalism.

**2 Japanese naval power** grew rapidly in east Asia after 1919 despite the 1922 Naval Treaty limiting replacement of capital ships by the US, Britain and Japan to a 5:5:3 ratio. Ratios for auxiliary ships set in 1930 were: heavy cruisers 10:10:6; light cruisers and destroyers 10:10:6; submarines, parity.

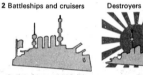

2 Battleships and cruisers        Destroyers        Submarines

Built by Japan 1919–20
4    17    9

Built 1921–24
12    34    32

Built 1925–28
8    21    19

Built 1929–32
7    17    12

**3 Communists were massacred** in Shanghai on 12 April 1927 when Nationalist troops, police and secret agents disarmed workers and pickets and dissolved labour unions. The culmination of a power struggle between the left and right wings of the KMT, the purge spread elsewhere with more massacres of the Chinese left-wing and communists.

**4 Japanese troops** marched into Manchuria after the Mukden Incident of 18 September 1931. Acting without the authority of their government, Japanese forces occupied Mukden using the pretext of a bomb on the Japanese-run South Manchurian railway and a skirmish with Chinese patrols. The speedy occupation of Manchuria (shown here) followed.

1936. Chiang had dislodged the communists from their southern rural bases and forced them to undertake the Long March [6]. But the CCP leader, Mao Tse-tung (1893–1976), urged on by Russia, now sought a united front against Japan and Chiang was forced to agree. When full-scale fighting broke out in 1937, the powerful Japanese army forced the KMT to retreat to Changking in the south-west. The fall of Nanking in December [7] was followed in 1938 by the announcement of Japan's "New Order" with Japanese army rule in occupied parts of China and a puppet government in Nanking (1940).

## Japan's empire in World War II

To secure access to South-East Asian raw materials and to block Western aid for Chiang, Japanese troops entered Indochina in 1940 and moved southward in 1941. America, Britain and Holland responded with a near total embargo on exports to Japan in July 1941, reducing oil supplies by 90 per cent. Japan soon put into operation its contingency plan to achieve economic self-sufficiency by force. Allied to Germany and

Italy, and envisaging the imminent collapse of Britain and China, it tried to eliminate American interference by sinking the Pacific Fleet at Pearl Harbor on 7 December 1941.

By August 1942 Japan had seized a vast oceanic and continental empire [8]. It was not until early in 1944 that Allied sea power reversed these successes. While the Chinese Nationalists and communists tied down large numbers of Japanese troops in a war of attrition and Allied supply lines were restored in Burma, American amphibious offensives in the Philippines and Gilberts established bases from which air power could be brought to bear on Japan itself. In 1945, after atomic bombs had destroyed Hiroshima (6 August) and Nagasaki (9 August), Japan agreed to unconditional surrender on 2 September [9].

Japan's defeat left China divided between a Nationalistic administration gravely weakened by the war and the communists who had gained in strength. Japan was transformed under American occupation into a democratic state. In east and southeast Asia, the old empires were never to recover their shattered prestige and power.

Chiang Kai-shek (1887–1975) was the leading military aide of Sun Yat-sen by 1919. After Sun's death in 1925 he dominated the Kuomintang and became president of a largely reunited Republic of China in 1928. But his authority was contested by the Communist Party and threatened by the Japanese. Recognized by the Allies as China's wartime leader, he secured the abolition of extra-territorial rights in China in 1943 and in 1945 a seat for China in the UN Security Council. Renewed postwar conflict with the communists led to his defeat and the withdrawal of his government to Formosa (now Taiwan) in 1949.

5 Emperor Hirohito (1901– ) came to the Japanese throne in 1926, having been named regent in 1921. Under the Meiji constitution his position was both sacred and sovereign, although there is little evidence to show the part actually played by the Emperor in Japanese policies.

6 In the Long March, about 85,000 communist soldiers and 15,000 officials left Kiangsi province under pressure from Chiang Kai-shek, in 1934. A year later 30,000 survivors regrouped near Yenan after a march of 8,000km (5,000 miles). The communist 2nd and 4th armies also had to regroup in the north.

| Communist areas 1927–34 |
| The Long March 1934–35 |
| Second Army 1935–36 |
| Fourth Army 1935–36 |
| Communist Yenan 1937 |

0 _____ 850 km

7 The fall of Nanking, Chiang Kai-shek's capital, on 12 December 1937, was followed by the massacre of some 100,000 people by Japanese troops. Known as the "rape of Nanking", this atrocity was revealed at the International War Crimes Tribunal in Tokyo. The city's fall came after three months of stubborn opposition by Chiang's army to the advance of the Japanese.

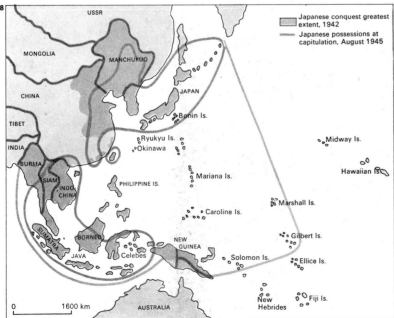

Japanese conquest greatest extent, 1942
Japanese possessions at capitulation, August 1945

0 _____ 1600 km

8 Japan's territorial acquisitions in World War II reflect its initial aims: to conquer China before dealing with the USSR and to control the south-west Pacific. Later the military priority shifted to include invading India in preference to defending Pacific islands. Before the Allies entered the war against Japan, China traded space for time. Once deep in Chinese territory, Japanese troops, although controlling most industrial areas, were surrounded by a hostile countryside.

9 Japan's surrender was signed aboard the USS *Missouri* in Tokyo Bay on 2 September 1945 with General Douglas MacArthur representing the Allies. The Japanese decision to surrender on 14 August 1945 came from the Emperor.

# Indian nationalism

In 1900 British rule in India appeared more secure and more permanent than ever. Lord Curzon's years as viceroy (1898–1905) emphasized the determination of the British to remain the governors of India. The greater efficiency of the administration, the maintenance of peace and order, and the spread of railways [3] and the telegraph, all seemed to confirm Britain's grip on India, while in the wider world British foreign policy was geared to the retention of the Indian empire as the second great base (after Britain itself) of British world power. Yet within fifty years that same Indian empire had been split up and the British rulers dismissed.

## Growth of nationalism

Part of the reason for this reversal lay in the growth of a nationalism which drew support from Indians all over the subcontinent. This nationalism had risen from modest beginnings in the late nineteenth century with the foundation of the Indian National Congress Party and was at first approved by the British for its attempt to break through the divisions of caste, religion and region that stifled

efforts to modernize India. But before long they came to see it as a potent threat to British power and a stimulant to disorder and anarchy. Anti-British terrorism before 1914 made many officials deeply hostile to the call of nationalists for more Indian participation in government. The British believed that the Congress was the tool of ambitious and unscrupulous westernized Indians, seeking not independence and unity but self-advancement, regardless of the poor.

The first great triumph of Indian nationalism came in the years immediately following World War I when Mahatma Gandhi (1869–1948) [Key] emerged as a charismatic leader pioneering the technique of non-co-operation and non-violent resistance to the government through peaceful demonstrations and refusal to pay taxes. Gandhi was helped in showing the British that many Indians rejected their authority by the effects of India's involvement in World War I. Higher taxation, the recruitment of thousands of Indians for the army, and the use of that army to defend Britain in northern France united Indians of diverse interests in

the belief that the British were placing new and unfair burdens upon them and breaking the terms on which British rule was accepted. They turned for protection to the Congress Party. To the British, Gandhi's campaign was deeply worrying. Some of them believed a second mutiny was imminent (the first mutiny in 1857–8 had resulted from unrest amongst the sepoys [soldiers], but was suppressed by the British): and it was in a climate of panic that the notorious shooting of unarmed Indian demonstrators – the Amritsar Massacre [1] – occured in 1919.

## Divisions among the Indians

For all its successes between 1918 and 1922, Indian nationalism faced enormous problems in trying to destroy British power. Once India had settled down after the war and its aftermath, non-co-operation fizzled out. Many Indians were profoundly suspicious of the politicians who ran the Congress Party. The rural landowners who wished to keep the social status quo disliked the urban and westernized Indians who dominated the nationalist movement. They feared that if

**1 At Amritsar** on 13 April 1919, British troops shot dead over 300 unarmed Indians during an illegal demonstration. The Indians were forced to apologize publicly after the riot because the British thought this would encourage them to be orderly and respectful. Here a Sikh is arrested.

**2 By origin, Gurkha soldiers,** still a distinctive element in the British army, were mountain tribesmen from Nepal who were defeated by the British in the Gurkha wars of 1814–16. They became famous for their endurance, loyalty and courage, and for their *kukri,* deadly broad-bladed curved knives that they carry.

**3 By 1948,** India had the fourth largest railway system in the world. The railways had originally been constructed to serve British purposes, to help control India's vast expanses cheaply and

efficiently, and to open up the hinterland to trade. But they also helped to unify India economically and politically and thus lay the foundations for an Indian nationalism on the subcontinent.

**4 Jawaharlal Nehru** (1889–1964) was the first prime minister of independent India. Educated in England, he emerged as a leading figure in the Congress Party in the 1930s and as Gandhi's heir.

**5 Mohammed Jinnah** (1876–1948) was the architect of Pakistan, which resulted from the partitioning of the old unified India into two states. He believed this was the only way to safeguard Muslim interests.

**6 As well as the provinces** which they ruled directly, the British retained ultimate power over nearly 600 autonomous princely states. The Victorians adopted the durbar (traditionally in India a gathering of vassals to do homage to their ruler) to symbolize the allegiance of the Indian princes to the British monarch. The 1911 durbar was attended by King George V in person.

such men became strong enough to throw out the British their next target would be the conservative gentry, still so powerful in the countryside. And not all Indians wanted democracy and one man, one vote. Hindus living in areas where the majority was Muslim, and vice versa, were fearful that popular government would threaten their interests and maybe their lives.

This meant that the British still had an advantage. They were willing to give Indians a greater say in running their internal affairs so as to avoid trouble; and they found that delegating some power to some Indians was a convenient method of preventing all Indians from combining against them. They hoped by this to keep India united in a federation which in international matters would still be tightly bound to Britain; and they wanted to go on using the Indian army.

These clever calculations were swept away by two "accidents". The first was the outbreak of World War II – once again involving India – which aroused more resentment among Indians than World War I. Meanwhile British prestige was undermined by humiliating defeats by the Japanese. The second "accident" was the resolve of the leaders of the large Muslim communities of north India to insist upon the creation of Pakistan as a separate Muslim state.

## Independence

Thus India gained independence in a way quite unintended by the British. The division of the subcontinent wrecked the delicate mechanisms of federalism through which they had planned to influence India in her international role as a pillar of the Empire-Commonwealth. Deprived of Indian help, the British Empire east of Suez withered away in less than 20 years. In India itself, independence left vast problems unsolved: the overpopulation of the countryside; the failure to increase food production sufficiently; the desperate poverty of village and city alike. The British had lacked the means and the nerve to modernize Indian society properly. The victory won by Indian nationalism in 1947 was, therefore, only a beginning. The building of a modern nation state lay ahead.

**Gandhi** adopted the symbol of the spinning wheel in 1920. He believed that India should make her own cloth, thus threatening British textile exports to India and giving Indians the self-confidence necessary for independence.

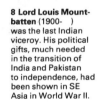

**7 The Indian Army** was an enormous asset for the British in the defence of their vast empire. In World War I, Indian troops fought on the Western Front, while in the period 1939–45 they were used in Burma, the Middle East, the Mediterranean and North and East Africa. The loss of their services after independence in 1947 placed a great strain on Britain's own military resources.

**8 Lord Louis Mountbatten** (1900-   ) was the last Indian viceroy. His political gifts, much needed in the transition of India and Pakistan to independence, had been shown in SE Asia in World War II.

**9 Political democracy** in India was extended in the reforms of 1919 and 1935 when the British gave the Indians the right to participate in government. Universal suffrage was achieved in 1947.

**10 As independence drew nearer,** the tensions between different communities in India became acute. The most serious were those between Hindus and Muslims, especially in areas where their numbers were almost equal and the proposed partition caused great bitterness. The aftermath of bitter riots in Calcutta in 1946, when at least 4,000 people died in the communal fighting, is illustrated here.

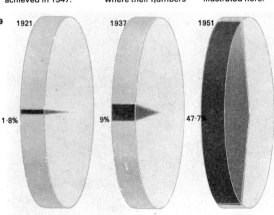

9  1921    1937    1951

1·8%    9%    47·7%

Registered voters as a percentage of total population

# British foreign policy since 1914

Britain's aim in World War I (1914–18) – to prevent the domination of Europe by any single power – was achieved by the peace treaties imposed in 1919 on Germany and its allies. But then the Allied coalition that won the war dissolved: the United States withdrew into isolation, Russia, under communist control, campaigned against the West, and France disagreed with Britain on the treatment of Germany [1]. Between 1925 and 1930 British governments welcomed a short-lived reconciliation between France and Germany, helped by the flow of American money into Europe. But by 1931 the world was hit by a grave economic crisis.

## The age of appeasement

The economic slump propelled Adolf Hitler (1889–1945), leader of the National Socialists,' into power in Germany in 1933 and ended the liberal regime in Japan. This provided Britain with two major foreign-policy problems in the 1930s: the satisfaction of German pressure for revision of the Treaty of Versailles 1919, especially its reparation and disarmament clauses, and the expansion of Japanese militarists into Manchuria, which they annexed in all but name in 1931–2, and into China proper in 1933–7.

Britain was handicapped in dealing with these problems by three factors: First its economic weakness, expressed in long-term unemployment; second, a public opinion stunned by the losses in World War I and nervous about rearmament; finally the sheer inability of Britain and France, with no help from isolationist America, to control Germany and Japan, as well as a restless Italy under Benito Mussolini (1883–1945).

A confrontation became unavoidable after the Munich Agreement in September 1938 [5]. Britain and France thereby agreed to German occupation of the Sudetenland, which was Czech territory accepting that this was Hitler's "final" demand; but on 15 March 1939 German forces cynically abrogated the agreement by taking over the rest of Czechoslovakia. Almost the only benefit derived by Britain from this short-sighted policy of appeasement was time to build up its pitiably weak defences. When Hitler confidently invaded Poland on 1 September 1939, the British government finally honoured their treaty obligations and declared war on Germany two days later.

## Policy during World War II

After the collapse of France in June 1940, Britain faced Hitler's Europe alone. The military situation was transformed when Germany invaded the Soviet Union on 22 June 1941 and when the United States entered the war after the Japanese attack at Pearl Harbor on 7 December 1941. But the diplomatic situation was complicated. The United States' President, Franklin Roosevelt (1882–1945) agreed with the British Prime Minister, Winston Churchill (1874–1965) on general war aims in the Atlantic Charter, signed in August 1941, but had no interest in preserving the British Empire. At the Yalta conference (4–11 February 1945) the two met Soviet leader Joseph Stalin (1879–1953) and Roosevelt seemed to side with Stalin on imperial questions against the British.

Churchill, an old opponent of communism, willingly accepted Stalin's territorial claims in eastern Europe, but he was worried

1 On 11 January 1923, French and Belgian forces, despite British protests, occupied the German industrial Ruhr (until August 1925) as a penalty for alleged non-payment by Germany of coal reparations. In the aftermath of World War I, Britain and France disagreed over the treatment of Germany. Britain, intent upon economic recovery, wanted Germany leniently treated; France demanded strict enforcement of the Treaty of Versailles.

2 At the League of Nations, Geneva, in March 1925, Britain rejected a major attempt to enforce the peaceful settlement of international disputes in refusing to sign the Geneva Protocol. France sought to strengthen the League's powers of collective action against aggression by providing for compulsory arbitration of disputes. But Britain was wary of the protocol's absolute commitment to armed intervention.

5 The Munich Agreement of 29 September 1938 typified Britain's policy of appeasement. Britain, France and Italy agreed that the Sudeten region of Czechoslovakia should be ceded to Germany. British Prime Mini-ster Neville Chamberlain (1869–1940), shown here on his return from Munich, made an agreement with Hitler to consult on any future Anglo-German questions. A year later Britain and Germany were at war.

3 Winston Churchill was a backbench MP during the 1930s, and an outspoken critic of the National Government's policy of appeasement towards Germany. Public opinion favoured a vague pacifism in the face of German rearmament and growing Italian and German aggression. Such was the desire for, if not faith in, peace, that British rearmament did not seriously begin until after 1938.

4 The Spanish Civil War was fought between the Nationalist rebels on the one hand, helped by Hitler and Mussolini, and the Spanish Republican Government on the other, from 1936 to 1939. The war seems to have presaged the later conflict waged between Fascism and democracy in World War II. But in 1936, the British Government was chief sponsor of an international agreement for non-intervention which was signed by all the major powers. This was adhered to by all countries except Italy, Germany and the Soviet Union – the last-named sent some aid to the Republican forces. Public opinion in Britain was divided: some, illegally, went to Spain to fight, mostly for the Republicans, whose British International Brigade numbered about 2,000 men.

how far into western Europe Soviet influence would penetrate and whether the United States would help to resist it.

## Loss of world power

Britain's Labour government of 1945–51 hoped fervently for co-operation between the Soviet Union and the West after the war. But when the East-West cold war developed with disagreements about the revival of Germany and about Soviet communization of Eastern Europe, Labour ministers took Britain first into the Brussels collective defence pact of March 1948 with France and the Benelux states – Belgium, Holland and Luxembourg – and then into the North Atlantic Treaty Organization (NATO), signed on 4 April 1949, with Canada, the United States and nine other states of Western Europe. At the same time, Britain received economic assistance from the United States through a £1000 million loan in December 1945 and then through the Marshall Aid programme of 1948–52.

Britain strove continuously to moderate East-West tensions, by urging restraint on the United States during the cold war, but its credibility was undermined by recurrent balance-of-payments difficulties, and later by severe unemployment and inflation. These called into question the basic assumption of British policy after 1945: that Britain remained a world power, not with the strength of the United States or the Soviet Union, but still with an assured presence at conference "top tables".

In January 1968 the Labour Prime Minister, Harold Wilson (1916– ), decided to terminate the East-of-Suez role by December 1971, ie, the maintenance of British forces in the Persian Gulf and at Singapore. The effect of this was to reduce Britain to the level of an essentially European and Mediterranean power.

The change in Britain's international position was symbolized in January 1973 by its entry into the European Economic Community. By that time Britain's empire, which once embraced a quarter of the world's population, had been gradually transformed into a loosely knit Commonwealth of politically independent states.

**6 British troops were sent to Korea** in 1950 as part of a United Nations force to repel a North Korean communist invasion of South Korea. The UN force had been formed despite the opposition of the Soviet Union, which supported North Korea's claims to South Korea. At that time the cold war had reached its height and the UN was deeply divided by the East-West tensions that had emerged since 1945.

**Anti-British feeling in Cyprus** (1955–60) typified the strains of decolonization in areas where Britain's handover of power after World War II was complicated by divisions in the local community. In other colonies, the transition to independence was often peaceful. But areas of violence included mandated Palestine, India, Egypt, Kenya, Malaya and Aden.

**7 The nationalization of the Suez Canal** in July 1956 by the Egyptian Government was part of a policy that aimed to unite the Arab world and end foreign control. Britain and France tried to internationalize the Canal and when this failed they attempted to seize the Canal by armed force. The troops seen here were landed in November, but as a result of US pressure a ceasefire took place within two days. The incident was a major blow to the international prestige of Britain and France. Anthony Eden (1897–1977), the British prime minister, who had pressed for the use of force, resigned in the following January.

**9 Ian Smith** (1919– ), Prime Minister of Rhodesia, unilaterally declared independence from Britain on 11 November 1965 after rejecting British terms for granting independence. Smith, shown here following discussions with British Prime Minister Harold Wilson in October 1965, wanted to maintain white supremacy in Rhodesia, although the white population was outnumbered 22 to 1 by black Africans.

**8 The Anglo-American "special relationship"** was a principal feature of British foreign policy after 1945. Two of its chief exponents were Harold Macmillan (1894– ) [left], British Prime Minister (1957–63) and John F. Kennedy (1917–63) [right], US President (1961–63). Here they are shown after talks in Washington in 1961 that were aimed at controlling the spread of the H-bomb and increasing unity among the countries of the Western alliance.

**10 The leaders of France and Britain,** Georges Pompidou (1911–74), [right] and Edward Heath (1916– ) [left] cleared the way for Britain to enter the EEC, in January 1973. When the Community was first formed in 1957 Britain refused to join, fearing the EEC's supranational powers. Two subsequent applications for membership, in 1961 and 1967, were both blocked by Pompidou's predecessor, President De Gaulle. Final talks had begun after De Gaulle's resignation, in 1969.

# The Commonwealth

The Commonwealth [1] is a free association of nations comprising Great Britain and (in 1976) 35 other sovereign states that were once colonies or dependent territories within the British Empire.

The origins of the association go back to Britain's relations with her colonies of European settlement. For these she established during the nineteenth century a system in which they would acquire independence by stages [4]. Crown government concentrated power in the governor and his council, which might be advisory or executive. Later there might also be a legislative council or assembly that lent itself to constitutional progress as the proportion of elected members grew in relation to the nominated members. Further advances would occur when the executive council, or government ministers, became responsible to the representative assembly, and when the indigenous council and assembly acquired powers of internal self-government over all but special and external matters. Finally these, too, would be won when full independence was granted.

Perhaps the first significant step in the transition from empire to commonwealth was a report by Lord Durham (1792–1840) [2], in 1839, stating that one of the causes of contemporary unrest in the Canadian provinces was the lack of harmony between the executive and the legislature. The remedy, according to the report, was to choose executive ministers from the majority group in the representative assembly.

## From colonies to dominions
There were limitations on such local government: the management of foreign trade and relations, the disposal of unoccupied public lands and the amendment of constitutions remained with the British government.

These limitations were gradually removed, but that on the conduct of foreign relations remained until the twentieth century (by which time the self-governing colonies – Canada, Australia, New Zealand, South Africa and Newfoundland – were known as "dominions"). The precise status of the dominions was undefined until a committee under Lord Balfour (1848–1930) produced a report (1926) which stated, "They are autonomous Communities within the British Empire, equal in status ... although united by a common allegiance to the Crown, and freely associated as members of the British Commonwealth of Nations."

In those colonies that were not primarily of European settlement, constitutional advance was very much slower. In the 1930s colonial rule in Africa and Asia was assumed to have a long future ahead of it. World War II, however, helped to stimulate nationalist pressures, especially in India, which had already acquired some international recognition as a state. The struggle for independence in India had produced a number of powerful leaders, such as Mahatma Gandhi [3], who acquired worldwide fame for their defiance of imperial authority, usually by non-violent resistance. In 1947 and 1948 independence was granted to India, Pakistan and Ceylon.

## Nkrumah's "self-government now"
The concept of gradual progress was destroyed after Malaya and the Gold Coast became independent in 1957. In the Gold Coast, the nationalist leader Kwame

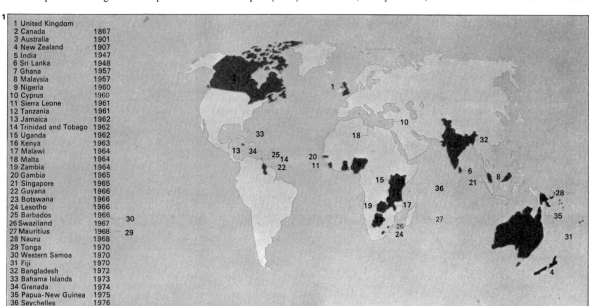

| 1 United Kingdom | |
|---|---|
| 2 Canada | 1867 |
| 3 Australia | 1901 |
| 4 New Zealand | 1907 |
| 5 India | 1947 |
| 6 Sri Lanka | 1948 |
| 7 Ghana | 1957 |
| 8 Malaysia | 1957 |
| 9 Nigeria | 1960 |
| 10 Cyprus | 1960 |
| 11 Sierra Leone | 1961 |
| 12 Tanzania | 1961 |
| 13 Jamaica | 1962 |
| 14 Trinidad and Tobago | 1962 |
| 15 Uganda | 1962 |
| 16 Kenya | 1963 |
| 17 Malawi | 1964 |
| 18 Malta | 1964 |
| 19 Zambia | 1964 |
| 20 Gambia | 1965 |
| 21 Singapore | 1965 |
| 22 Guyana | 1966 |
| 23 Botswana | 1966 |
| 24 Lesotho | 1966 |
| 25 Barbados | 1966 |
| 26 Swaziland | 1967 |
| 27 Mauritius | 1968 |
| 28 Nauru | 1968 |
| 29 Tonga | 1970 |
| 30 Western Samoa | 1970 |
| 31 Fiji | 1970 |
| 32 Bangladesh | 1972 |
| 33 Bahama Islands | 1973 |
| 34 Grenada | 1974 |
| 35 Papua-New Guinea | 1975 |
| 36 Seychelles | 1976 |

1 **A quarter of the world's land surface** is covered by the Commonwealth, which also embraces a huge number of languages and dialects as well as numerous religions. The feature common to all of the members is the historical accident of settlement, annexation or conquest by Britain; and British institutions and the English language also remain important elements in the modern association. Since 1965, there has been a permanent central secretariat, based in London. It organizes conferences and spreads information. But the Commonwealth has very little unity in international affairs. The dates of independence of each country are shown on the map.

2 **Lord Durham's report** in 1839 on the unrest in the Canadian provinces led to the introduction of responsible government in Canada and later in other colonies of settlement. This report opened the way for the development of independent parliamentary governments linked by a common allegiance to a single crown.

3 **The strong, moral leadership** of Mahatma Gandhi (1869–1948) lay behind much of the nationalistic agitation against the British in India after 1918. His asceticism, aura of holiness and his use of fasting and passive resistance often embarrassed the British Government and actively involved the masses in India in the campaign for independence.

Nkrumah [5], who became prime minister in 1952, refused to recognize any impediment to the early transfer of power, advocated positive action to cripple the forces of imperialism and popularized the slogan "self-government now". When the Gold Coast gained its independence, British Togoland joined it to form the new nation of Ghana. In 1960 Ghana became a republic, with Nkrumah as president. The "wind of change" speech by the British prime minister Harold Macmillan (1894– ) in 1960 reflected the new attitude of the British Government towards Africa.

The newly independent countries chose to remain in the Commonwealth, despite the fact that they lacked the ethnic and common historical origins of the older members. They believed that their participation in the Commonwealth would bring them economic and diplomatic benefits and enhance their international influence. But they did not feel the special attachment to the monarchy that the older members had felt, and in 1949 India was the first state allowed to retain its membership as a republic while accepting the British monarch merely as the symbol of the free association of the members.

All members participate in the Commonwealth system of consultation and co-operation that covers a multitude of activities at governmental level. Periodically the heads of government meet [8] in conferences.

## Expansion and the loosening of old bonds
Nevertheless, the old bonds of Commonwealth are not as strong as they used to be and much of the informal intimacy of earlier years has been lost as the association has expanded. Disillusionment with the Commonwealth was apparent among many members in the 1960s and 1970s – notably in Britain. The modern Commonwealth, however, continues to function as a flexible system of co-operation between states, enabling its member countries to confer with one another in an unusually frank, friendly and relaxed manner. As an association it represents the fulfilment both of the nationalist aspirations of colonial peoples and of a policy of constitutional evolution pursued by the imperial power.

**George V** was called "King of Great Britain, Ireland and the British Dominions beyond the Seas, and Emperor of India". His title illustrated the extent of his authority and also emphasized India's special position in the British Empire.

**4 The character of colonial government** varied in detail from one territory to another, but each was expected to follow much the same series of stages on the way to independence. And the advance, through responsible government, to dominion status by the old European colonies of settlement became the model. But in the final period of decolonization, the stages were not always as clearly defined as earlier.

**5 By campaigning strongly** for "self-government now" in the Gold Coast, Nkrumah (1909–72) helped destroy the concept of gradual transference of power in the restive African colonies.

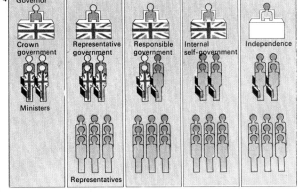

Governor

Crown government

Representative government

Responsible government

Internal self-government

Independence

Ministers

Representatives

**6 Conflict** – like this in Bangladesh – sometimes followed independence. National unity could be endangered and often parliamentary democracy was replaced by one-party rule and an autocratic president.

**7 Until colonial territories** in Africa and elsewhere became independent after World War II, the Commonwealth "family" – here assembled in 1926 – was a small, intimate group, all subscribing to British traditions and acknowledging one Crown.

**8 As membership of the Commonwealth** grew, the informality of heads of government meetings became more difficult to maintain. But the members still felt that the meetings were valuable for the discussion of problems and improvement of mutual understanding. When other capitals (here Singapore in 1971) began to offer to be host, this further emphasized that the modern Commonwealth was no longer "British" but a unique, worldwide association representing many races, creeds and cultures.

# The rise of fascism

Fascism developed in the years between World Wars I and II to become a major ideological and political force in many European countries, most notably in Italy and Germany. Expressed as an intense nationalism, often with strong social and collectivist overtones, it had the support of many different groups of people in countries that were suffering from, or seemed threatened by, a total breakdown of both their economy and their society.

## Fascist ideology

Although fascism shared many characteristics with reactionary nationalism and more conservative, authoritarian regimes, it had distinctive characteristics of its own. These were derived from its rejection of nineteenth century individualistic liberalism.

Fascist ideology embraced many thinkers, often distorting and misapplying their ideas. Indeed, fascism was never to formulate a clear ideology in the same way as Marxism, but remained open to a number of different interpretations, in which the component elements received varying emphasis. Among the most important contributors to fascist ideas were Friedrich Nietzsche (1844–1900), who stressed the need for dynamic "supermen"; Henri Bergson (1859–1941), who stressed instinct above reason; and Georges Sorel (1847–1922), who emphasized the moral value of action.

## Italian fascism and Mussolini

Italy emerged from World War I disappointed and frustrated by her war losses and the failure of the Versailles settlement to fulfil the treaty promises that had induced her to enter the war. Unemployment, strikes and violence [1] provided the background to the breakdown of parliamentary government. Right-wing groups, such as that led by Gabriele d'Annunzio (1863–1938), seized the port of Fiume on the Adriatic coast in 1919 in defiance of the Versailles settlement. In city and countryside riots, estate seizures by the peasants and countless sit-in strikes created a menacing and unpredictable revolutionary atmosphere.

In this situation Benito Mussolini (1883–1945) [Key], an ex-socialist school-teacher, organized anti-socialist *fascios* to combat left-wing groups by strong-arm methods. He received support from diverse conservative elements and by 1921 there were more than 800 branches of his "blackshirts", the *Fasci di combattimento*. Taking advantage of the disorganization of left-wing forces, he organized a "March on Rome" which ended with his installation as premier in October 1922.

Mussolini concentrated on liquidating and terrorizing opponents, establishing the Fascist Party in power and building up his personal position. Press, courts and unions were brought under his control and he established a concordat with the Roman Catholic Church. He inaugurated public works, such as the draining of the Pontine marshes, and mounted a drive for self-sufficiency for Italy. Increasing state intervention marked Mussolini's economic policy after 1925 as he tried to create a "corporate state" in which industrialists and workers co-operated for the good of the nation. Combined with his expansionist foreign policy, demonstrated both in the Abyssinian War and also his

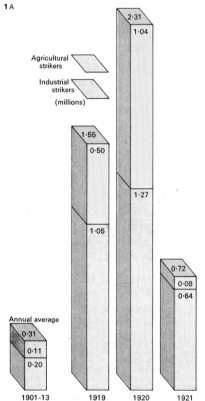

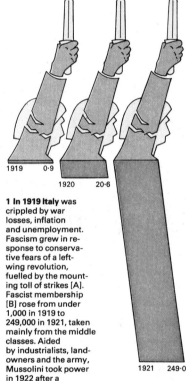

**1 In 1919 Italy was** crippled by war losses, inflation and unemployment. Fascism grew in response to conservative fears of a left-wing revolution, fuelled by the mounting toll of strikes [A]. Fascist membership [B] rose from under 1,000 in 1919 to 249,000 in 1921, taken mainly from the middle classes. Aided by industrialists, landowners and the army, Mussolini took power in 1922 after a threatened coup.

(totals in thousands)

**2 Field-Marshal Paul von Hindenburg** (1847–1934), a national hero of World War I, was President of the Weimar Republic from 1925. Under nationalist pressure, he made Hitler Chancellor in 1933.

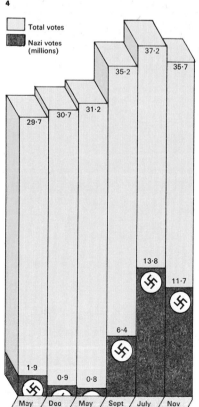

Total votes

Nazi votes (millions)

| May 1924 | Doo 1924 | May 1928 | Sept 1930 | July 1932 | Nov 1932 |
|---|---|---|---|---|---|
| 29·7 | 30·7 | 31·2 | 35·2 | 37·2 | 35·7 |
| 1·9 | 0·9 | 0·8 | 6·4 | 13·8 | 11·7 |

**4 The fluctuation in votes** for the Nazis reflected the economic fortunes of the Weimar Republic. In May 1924 the Nazis gained 1.9 million votes and 32 seats in the Reichstag. With the recovery of the Weimar Republic from its postwar difficulties and the inflation of 1923, the Nazi vote declined to its lowest point in 1928 when they held only 12 seats in the Reichstag. Under the impact of a renewed depression after 1929, and with the rise in unemployment and the polarization of the middle classes, the Nazi vote rose rapidly. By 1932 the Nazis were the largest party with 13.8 million votes. Although they lost votes, Hitler became Chancellor in January 1933.

**3 The Nazis** based much of their propaganda upon virulent anti-Semitism, in which the Jews were used as scapegoats for Germany's economic difficulties. The Nazis conducted boycotts of Jewish shops, attacked synagogues and assaulted individuals but were unable to adopt formal measures until Hitler's accession to power in 1933. Anti-Jewish laws promoted emigration and denied civil rights. Many Jews had left Germany or were in camps by 1939.

involvement in aiding Francisco Franco (1892–1975) in Spain, Mussolini's policies not only antagonized other European nations but also exhausted Italian resources.

## Hitler and German fascism

In Germany the Nazis (National Socialist Party) were founded in the disillusionment and economic chaos in the years following World War I. Joined by Adolf Hitler (1889–1945) [Key] in 1919, who expanded and transformed it, the party gained some seats in the Reichstag [4]. In 1923 Hitler tried, unsuccessfully, to overthrow the Bavarian government in a *putsch* in Munich, for which he was imprisoned.

Votes for the Nazi Party declined as the Weimar Republic recovered in the middle and late 1920s but the onset of the worst phase of the Depression after 1929 swelled party ranks with the young, the unemployed, and frightened middle-class and conservative elements. For Hitler and some of his followers, anti-Semitism [3] formed an important part of the programme, the Jews being cast as scapegoats for Germany's misfortunes

and as intruders in a purely Aryan Germany.

Support for the Nazis, however, seemed to have reached its peak towards the end of 1932 and the party was running into financial difficulties as funds from major industrialists dried up. In January 1933 Hitler was put into office through a coalition with the right-wing Nationalist Party, who hoped to control him. After the Reichstag fire [6], Hitler was able to assume dictatorial power. The rule of terror through the Gestapo gave the regime a more vicious character than Mussolini's in Italy. Like Mussolini's fascism, however, Nazism also offered an aggressive foreign policy and a solution to unemployment through public works and rearmament [5].

Fascist parties grew up in many other countries. In Spain [7], the Falange provided support for Franco, while in Eastern Europe the Romanian "Iron Guard" and the regime of Admiral Horthy in Hungary had strong fascist elements. In Western Europe the blackshirts of Oswald Mosley (1896– ) in Britain and the *Croix de Feu* in France [8] appeared, temporarily, to threaten the overthrow of democratic government.

**By 1934** Italy and Germany were ruled by fascist dictators. Mussolini (right) assumed power much earlier than Hitler (left), but the latter dominated international politics in the 1930s. The Rome-Berlin Axis was formed in 1936.

**5 Hitler aimed to satisfy public opinion** by cutting unemployment and creating a prosperous Germany. Public works, such as the building of the autobahn network, then the most extensive in the world, provided an advertisement for the regime in reply to the criticism of its domestic and foreign critics, and also served the purposes of the military. To increase vehicle building capacity, while also providing a cheap automobile for the population, the "people's car" or Volkswagen was launched in 1938. By the late 1930s, however, living standards had begun to stagnate as arms expenditure rose.

**6 Hitler's rise to power** was only half completed with his accession to the chancellorship. He awaited the opportunity to introduce emergency laws to strengthen his position and this was offered when a young Dutchman, Marinus van der Lubbe, set fire to the Reichstag on 27 February 1933. The Nazis were suspected of starting the fire, but it appears they merely took advantage of it to promulgate emergency decrees, banning rival political organizations, imprisoning opponents and vesting power in Hitler and the Nazi Party. Although the Nazis failed to achieve a majority, they were supported by the Nationalists.

**7**
Aid to Spanish fascists 1936-9

Monetary aid (£millions)

Italian 80
German 43

Italian 50,000
Portuguese 20,000
German 10,000-16,000
Irish 600

= 1,000

**7 By 1936** both Italy and Germany were expanding their influence in international politics. The outbreak of civil war in Spain provided diplomatic and military advantages for both countries. Mussolini hoped to gain military bases in the western Mediterranean. By 1937 Italian war production was beginning to show signs of strain. Hitler hoped to sow dissension between Britain and France, while binding Italy closer to him. He used Spain as a training ground for his air force, including the "Condor Legion", a force of 6,500 men consisting mainly of air force units but with a few supporting ground units. From 1937 Spain became a mere side-show.

**8 Political instability in France** promoted anti-Semitism, particularly in magazines such as *Le Cahier Jaune*.

# Britain 1930–45

Between 1930 and 1945 Britain experienced the deepest economic depression in its history and the massive mobilization of resources required for total war. In 1929, when a Labour government was elected under Ramsay MacDonald (1866–1937), Britain was already suffering from depression in its staple heavy industries: coal mining, iron and steel, textiles and shipbuilding.

## Consequences of the Depression

The Labour government was pledged to tackle the problem of unemployment, which stood at more than one million insured workers [4]. No sooner was the government formed, however, than the Wall Street crash plunged the major western industrial economies into deeper depression. By 1931 the government was faced with more than two-and-a-half million unemployed and a heavy drain on its resources to meet the cost of unemployment benefits. The Labour government had little to offer as a solution to the economic depression. Radical voices, such as that of Oswald Mosley (1896– ), a junior member of the Labour government,

and Lloyd George (1863–1945), leader of the Liberals, offered solutions along the lines later advocated by John Maynard Keynes (1883–1946), but were ignored in the pursuit of orthodox economic policy. This dictated that the government should curtail its expenditure and raise business confidence in the hope that normal trading conditions would begin to reduce unemployment. The recommended cuts in expenditure included a reduction in unemployment benefit.

In 1931, the Labour cabinet was deeply divided over implementing the cuts. The government was forced to resign over the issue, but MacDonald and a group of Labour MPs joined with the Conservatives and Liberals to form a coalition, the National Government. A general election was then called, which led to a resounding victory for the new administration [1].

The National Government introduced cuts in government expenditure, especially in unemployment benefit and the pay of state employees such as teachers and civil servants. Gradually the coalition was converted into a Conservative administration which trium-

phed at the general election of 1935.

In spite of the absence of major economic initiatives from governments in office after 1931, the economic situation began to improve from 1933 onwards. Unemployment reached a peak of almost three million in the winter of 1932–3 and remained at more than a million until the outbreak of war in 1939, but it was falling from 1933–4. Revival was concentrated in a range of new industries such as electricity supply, motor vehicles [2], consumer durables and chemicals. These industries brought increased employment to the southeast and the Midlands, while the older industries of the "distressed" areas remained depressed and only slowly began to recover.

## Political unrest and social change

The rise in prosperity in some areas helps to explain the failure of the extremist parties to obtain greater support before the war. Oswald Mosley [8] formed the British Union of Fascists in 1932, after leaving the Labour Party and adopted the style of continental fascist parties. The party espoused radical

1 Unemployment was the major issue of the early 1930s. In October 1931 the National government, formed the previous August, sought a mandate from the electorate for its economic policies – designed to deal with the Depression. Under Ramsay MacDonald, the ex-Labour premier, the National government campaigned for a restoration of business confidence and reduced unemployment. In a mood of deep national crisis, the electorate swung heavily towards the National candidates. Only 46 Labour MPs were returned, compared with 554 National government MPs. Every Labour ex-cabinet minister lost his seat, except George Lansbury (1859–1940).

2 Mass production methods, pioneered in the United States, were adopted in Britain during the interwar years. They brought the first cheap motor vehicles within the reach of the middle classes. By 1939 there were nearly two million motor vehicles in Britain and the "motoring revolution" had begun. Car production for the home market increased each year up to the war, with the exception of 1932.

4 The thirties witnessed a rapid growth in commercial air transport and routes were set up across the world. Imperial Airways, a government-subsidized amalgamation of several privately-owned companies, was established in 1924. One of its main aims was to routes throughout the empire. Airmail was as important as passenger services; by 1938 Imperial Airways carried all first-class mail to the empire.

IMPERIAL AIRWAYS

3 The communist-led National Unemployed Workers' Movement organized several | "hunger" marches on London in the thirties to protest about the plight of | the unemployed. The marches however, had little effect on government policy.

5 Private house building expanded greatly in the 1930s, and was a principal factor in the economic recovery during the last half of the decade. Despite government cuts in building programmes, private investment in housing boomed, especially in the thriving regions of the Midlands and the south-east. Nearly three million houses were built between 1930 and 1939. This expansion in building led to a boom in other industries such as electrical and household goods.

economic ideas but earned a reputation for violence and anti-semitism that cut it off from mass support.

The thirties witnessed the rise of new social patterns, with an enormous growth of suburban living, a housing boom [5], slum clearance, and ameliorative social legislation. Opportunities for leisure activities, such as the cinema [6] and dance halls, expanded and provided cheap entertainment. Another influential and inexpensive source of entertainment was the radio. The BBC broadcast hours of popular music daily and did much to enhance the reputations of some of the great dance bands of the 1930s. The rise of the football pools, with their lure of instant wealth, was another social phenomenon of the times.

There was a profound distrust and loathing of war in the thirties. Peace movements flourished and the governments of Baldwin and Neville Chamberlain (1869–1940) pursued a policy of appeasing the dictators. But rising international tension led to gradual rearmament from the mid-1930s, helping to revive the economy.

The experiences of the Depression and thirties followed by total war helped to create a new mood in Britain. The Beveridge Report of 1942 advocated a high level of employment and the creation of a welfare state. Even before the end of the war, the Butler Education Act of 1944 made free secondary education available to all.

**Postwar optimism**

World War II witnessed an acceleration of many of the trends evident in British politics and society before 1939. The war further stimulated new industries as well as reviving the old ones, and led to widespread recognition of social problems such as poverty and unemployment. Widespread and vigorous debate about the nature of postwar British society paved the way for a Labour victory at the 1945 general election. The Labour government inherited considerable good will from the electorate. Demobilization caused far less resentment than it had in 1918 [10] and Labour's programme seemed to meet the demand for new policies and an avoidance of mass unemployment.

**Edward VIII** (1894–1972), came to the throne on 20 January 1936 with considerable popular support, accumulated during his years as Prince of Wales. Public interest in his life showed the widespread devotion to the monarchy even during the worst years of the Depression. But the king's continuing relationship with an American divorcee, Mrs Wallis Simpson (1896– ), precipitated a constitutional crisis following her second divorce, in October 1936. The king wanted to marry her, but the prime minister, Stanley Baldwin (1867–1947), advised that she was unacceptable as a queen. In spite of considerable popular support for Edward, he abdicated in December.

**6 The cinema** was one of the most important forms of cheap mass entertainment in the 1930s. By 1939 there were 5,000 cinemas in Britain and more than 20 million cinema tickets were sold each week.

**7 Rising living standards** for those in work as well as a more widespread introduction of paid holidays contributed to a growth in holiday-making. The first holiday camps were opened in 1937.

**8 Oswald Mosley's** British Union of Fascists held many demonstrations and marches in the years before the war. Their use of uniforms and violent methods aroused widespread hostility, as did, more particularly, their anti-semitism. In 1936 the Public Order Act was passed forbidding the use of uniforms and strengthening police powers against political demonstrations and mass meetings.

**10 The immense war effort** in Britain put eight million people into uniform in World War II. Over 300,000 members of the armed forces and, on the home front, about 60,000 civilians lost their lives in the conflict. In contrast with 1919, demobilization went relatively smoothly, although in the Far and Middle East, British troops often became involved in local police-keeping and occupation duties, such as in Cyprus, that continued for some time after 1945.

**9 Britain was slow to rearm in the thirties.** Limited rearmament was undertaken from 1934, mainly in the airforce and navy, although German expenditure on arms was sometimes exaggerated. The government delayed thoroughgoing rearmament until after 1938 on the assumption that public opinion, as manifested in the Peace Ballot (a house-to-house poll) and by-election results, would not stand for sterner measures.

# Causes of World War II

The inter-war years in Europe saw the rise of fascist dictators [Key] in Italy and Germany. Their nationalistic and expansionist policies increasingly undermined the credibility of diplomatic negotiation.

## The rise of the dictators

World War I had left a bitter legacy in the crippling reparations and arbitrary divisions of territory that were features of the Treaty of Versailles (1919). Its effects were influential in the rise to power of Benito Mussolini (1883–1945) and Adolf Hitler (1889–1945). Italy had suffered losses in World War I and disappointments in the peace settlement at Versailles, and Mussolini owed a large part of his support to a policy of militant nationalism which was bound to create tensions in the postwar world [6]. Hitler also gained support from a policy of extreme nationalism that was determined to reverse the penal aspects of the Versailles Treaty and unify the German-speaking peoples in eastern Europe territorially [4].

The isolationism of the United States meant that the major initiative for peace lay with France and Britain as the two strongest European powers. Both nations were fearful of renewed war. They felt that war in 1914 had arisen out of the diplomatic system's inability to cope with international crises, so they believed that they must negotiate with the dictators.

During the 1920s faith was placed in the League of Nations and the pursuit of policies of disarmament – policies that foundered on mutual distrust among the great European powers. By the early 1930's it was increasingly clear that the League of Nations was unlikely to act as a guarantor of peace. Japan's invasion of Manchuria and then, more seriously, the Abyssinian crisis (1935–6) and the Spanish Civil War (1936–9) were patent indications that the League was incapable of restricting international aggression by powerful states.

## A policy of appeasement

For much of the 1930s, statesmen in both France and Britain believed that Hitler's policies were designed solely to satisfy Germany's legitimate demands for revision of the Versailles settlement. In spite of Germany's reoccupation of the Rhineland in 1936 [2] and virtual control of Austria [1], Britain in particular maintained the hope that war could be averted by concession. The efforts of both Stanley Baldwin (1867–1947) and Neville Chamberlain (1869–1940) to negotiate with Hitler were supported in large part by a populace afraid of another war and resentful of expenditure on armaments in a period of economic depression. Left-wing forces in Britain were convinced that policies of disarmament must be pursued to lessen the risk of war. Chamberlain was operating from a position of weakness when Hitler was busy rearming [3]. France was also beset by weakness; internal political divisions prevented a firm foreign policy and the country's losses in World War I inclined it to follow a defensive policy, enshrined in the construction of the Maginot Line.

Although Hitler's long-term aims cannot be determined with certainty, he exploited the confusion and weakness of the Western European powers to reverse the Versailles Treaty and further his plans for conquest in

**1 Chancellor Dollfuss of Austria** was murdered in 1934, on Hitler's orders, as the first stage of Germany's Austrian annexation. Virtual control was achieved in 1936; the take-over came in 1938.

**2 The Versailles Treaty** had excluded German forces from the Rhineland. In March 1936 German troops reoccupied it in defiance of France and Britain; neither was prepared to risk war to prevent this.

**3 Expenditure on defence** increased five-fold in Hitler's Germany between 1933 and 1938. Spending reached a peak in the latter stages of World War II. Germany started rearming immediately after Hitler came to power, but this drive became dominant only after 1936. Then the adoption of a four-year plan for rearmament directed more of the German economy to war than was the case in any other European country.

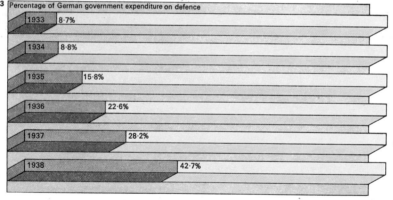

Percentage of German government expenditure on defence

| Year | Percentage |
|------|-----------|
| 1933 | 8.7% |
| 1934 | 8.8% |
| 1935 | 15.8% |
| 1936 | 22.6% |
| 1937 | 28.2% |
| 1938 | 42.7% |

**4 Hitler's *Mein Kampf*** was written while he was in prison following his abortive "Beer Hall" revolt in 1923. It contained a demand for *lebensraum* (living space) for the German peoples in the east. Expansion into eastern Europe and the USSR had long been a part of right-wing German thinking and Hitler adopted it as a major feature of his political policy. Its true place in his plans is much debated, but his conquests in eastern Europe by diplomacy and ultimately by war, backed by propaganda like this poster, fulfilled his professed policy.

**5 Germany's aim of absorbing** German-speaking parts of Czechoslovakia – the Sudetenland – almost plunged Europe into war. At Munich in 1938 Britain and France virtually sacrificed Czech industry and defence in an attempt to appease the Germans.

Key:
- Czechoslovakia before Munich
- Ceded to Germany at Munich
- To Poland September 1938
- To Hungary October 1938

the east at a later date. The reoccupation of the Rhineland was followed by the Austrian *Anschluss* and demands for the cession of the German-speaking Sudetenland from Czechoslovakia [5]. After threatening war, Hitler was placated by an agreement in 1938 that virtually dismembered Czechoslovakia in return for promises not to occupy the non-German-speaking areas of the country. Chamberlain's surrender was hailed as a triumph that had avoided war. But the occupation of Prague in March 1939 broke the illusion upon which appeasement had been based – that Hitler's demands were limited and had been satisfied.

### The influence of peripheral powers

Resistance to Hitler had been confused by suspicion of the Soviet Union's intentions. Coming out of isolation in the mid-1930s, the Soviet Union was concerned to prevent an alliance of Western European states against her, but became increasingly fearful of the rise of fascism in Germany with its implied threat to herself. The USSR sought to bring the Western powers into an anti-fascist alliance, but was frustrated by the faith in appeasement and widespread mistrust of the USSR in conservative circles. The actions of Britain and France over Czechoslovakia encouraged the USSR to form a non-aggression pact with Germany in 1939.

In the Far East, the rise of a militantly aggressive Japan provided an additional strain upon the fragile peace [7]. Japan's occupation of Manchuria (1931–2) and its war with China from the mid-thirties illustrated the weakness of the League and increased Japanese self-confidence and territorial ambitions.

Britain's guarantees in 1939 to Poland and Romania were a last attempt to restrain Hitler's actions. But he had agreed with the USSR to dismember Poland on the pretext of annexing the "Polish Corridor" [9]. Hitler probably expected Britain and France to back down once again as they had over Munich. Instead they presented Hitler with demands to withdraw. When the British ultimatum expired on 3 September 1939, Britain declared war on Germany, and France followed suit a few hours later.

**Hitler riding into Vienna** at the head of German troops symbolizes the domination of Europe by the dictators. While Mussolini was backing Hitler in the west, Japanese economic expansion threatened the stability of the Far East.

**7 Matsuoka** [left] the Japanese foreign minister from 1940 to 1941, was largely responsible for Japan's Tripartite Pact with Germany and Italy. Japan had already joined Germany in an Anti-Comintern Pact in 1936. Throughout the 1930s Japan pursued an aggressive foreign policy: in 1931 she had taken Manchuria, increasing tension in the Far East where the League of Nations was virtually powerless. In 1937 Japan went to war with China, seizing a large area of the Chinese mainland. Europe and America failed to resolve or control the conflict, encouraging Japan to further aggression.

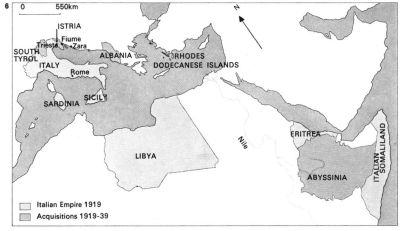

6
0    550km
ISTRIA
Fiume
Trieste  Zara
SOUTH
TYROL    ALBANIA    RHODES
ITALY    DODECANESE ISLANDS
Rome
SARDINIA   SICILY
LIBYA
Nile
ERITREA
ABYSSINIA
ITALIAN SOMALILAND

☐ Italian Empire 1919
▨ Acquisitions 1919-39

**6 Mussolini's main aim** from the time of his appointment in 1922 was to increase Italy's prestige and to consolidate her "Great Power" status by foreign acquisition and aggressive diplomacy. After 1922 Italy tightened her grip on Fiume, the South Tyrol and the Dodecanese Islands. Protests and sanctions from the League of Nations did not prevent war with Abyssinia in 1935 and the country's rapid annexation. Italy also intervened in Spain in 1936, leading her to a closer *entente* with Germany, which was formalized in 1939 by the "Pact of Steel".

**8 The appeasement policy** of Britain and France arose out of fear of renewed war and belief that the dictators' demands could be met by negotiation and concession. But concern grew that such "weakness" just provoked more demands.

**9 German troops symbolically destroyed** the Polish frontier when they invaded Poland in August 1939. Polish access to the Baltic had been guaranteed by Britain and France, who therefore declared war on Germany on 3 September.

# World War II

On 1 September 1939, German troops invaded Poland. Britain and France were pledged to support Poland and declared war on Germany two days later. Using revolutionary *Blitzkrieg* ("lightning attack") tactics the Germans defeated the outdated Polish army in 18 days and the country was partitioned between Germany and the Soviet Union, with whom Germany had just signed a non-aggression pact. A British army crossed to France but did not attack, and a "phoney war" lasted until the spring.

## German and Japanese victories

Germany overran Norway and Denmark in April 1940 and then on 10 May invaded Holland, Belgium and Luxembourg, which had been neutral. As the Allied armies swung forwards to meet them German tanks burst through the "impassable" Ardennes and reached the English Channel. The Allied army to their north was forced back into the Dunkirk region, and 338,226 British and French troops escaped to England by sea between 29 May and 3 June. Most of France, except for the southeast under the puppet Vichy regime of Henri Pétain (1856–1951), was occupied by the Germans.

Germany's leader, Adolf Hitler (1889–1945), expected Britain to make peace, but she fought on defiantly under the leadership of Winston Churchill (1874–1965). The *Luftwaffe* (air force) of Hermann Goering (1893–1946) then attempted to destroy the Royal Air Force (RAF) so that an invasion of England could be launched. But the Germans were defeated in the Battle of Britain fought between August and October 1940.

Taking advantage of the French Atlantic ports, German submarines intensified their attacks on British sea routes and in the next two years came near to strangling Britain [7].

Italy entered the war in June 1940 but suffered serious defeats in Greece and Libya. Germany sent forces under General Erwin Rommel (1891–1944) to help the Italians in North Africa and swiftly overran Yugoslavia, Greece and Crete in April and May 1941.

On 22 June 1941, in breach of the earlier pact, German troops swept into the Soviet Union [4], achieving total surprise. After five months they were just 30km (19 miles) from Moscow but were halted by bitter winter weather and stubborn Russian resistance. On 7 December 1941, in the second major onslaught of the war, Japan launched a surprise attack on the US fleet at Pearl Harbor.

The first half of 1942 saw the Axis forces (Germany, Italy, Japan and minor allies) at the height of their powers. In the Pacific the Japanese captured the Dutch East Indies, Malaya, Burma, the Philippines and many Pacific islands [5]. In the Soviet Union a German offensive advanced on Stalingrad and the Caucasus. In North Africa the British had been driven back to the borders of Egypt.

## The turn of the tide

A series of crucial battles later in 1942 and in 1943 gave the initiative to the Allies. In the Pacific, Japanese naval power was shattered at the Battle of Midway on 4–7 June 1942; and on 7 August US marines landed in Guadalcanal in the first of the amphibious assaults by which US naval power under Admiral Chester Nimitz (1885–1966) pushed back the Japanese. In bitter weather

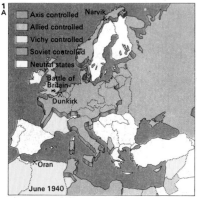

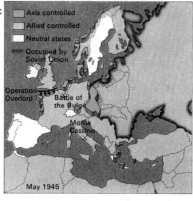

1 **The main theatre of war** was in Europe, as it was in World War I. [A] By June 1940 the Axis powers controlled almost the whole of Western Europe and Germany then broadened the conflict by attacking the Soviet Union a year later. [B] Axis conquests reached their peak in November 1942. [C] By May 1945 Russian counter-offensives and Allied landings in France and Italy had defeated Germany.

2 **Increasingly sophisticated weapons** appeared as the war progressed. [A] Mastery of tank warfare gave the Germans their initial successes. [B] Heavy bombers carried death and destruction deep into the German homeland but failed to break civilian morale. [C] The Allies then had to invent and perfect the techniques of amphibious warfare in order to invade "Fortress Europe".

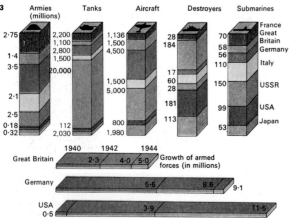

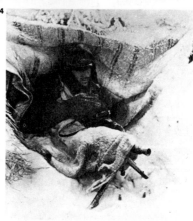
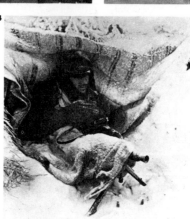

3 **This comparison of military power** at the outbreak of war shows that, although Germany had more aircraft in 1939, France and Britain together were in fact stronger in men and equipment. The vast size of the Soviet forces shows how advantageous the Stalin-Hitler pact was to Germany. Manpower was needed on a a massive scale and the lower half of the diagram shows the growth in armed forces, which was particularly appreciable in the United States.

| | Armies (millions) | Tanks | Aircraft | Destroyers | Submarines | |
|---|---|---|---|---|---|---|
| | 2·75 | 2,200 | 1,136 | 28 | 70 | France |
| | 1·4 | 1,100 | 1,500 | 184 | 58 | Great Britain |
| | 3·5 | 2,800 | 4,500 | 56 | 56 | Germany |
| | | 1,500 | | 110 | | Italy |
| | 20,000 | | 17 | | | |
| | 2·1 | 1,500 | 60 | 150 | | USSR |
| | 2·5 | 5,000 | 28 | 181 | 99 | USA |
| | 0·18 | 800 | | | | |
| | 0·32 | 112 | 800 | 99 | | Japan |
| | | 2,030 | 1,980 | 113 | 53 | |

| | 1940 | 1942 | 1944 | |
|---|---|---|---|---|
| Great Britain | 2·3 | 4·0 | 5·0 | Growth of armed forces (in millions) |
| Germany | | 5·6 | 8·6 | 9·1 |
| USA | 0·5 | 3·9 | 11·5 | |

4 **The turning-point of the war in Europe** came when Hitler attacked the Soviet Union in 1941 and failed to deliver a swift knock-out blow. The key battle took place at Stalingrad where, after weeks of frozen siege, the German 6th Army was forced to surrender. Germany was committed to a war on two fronts, with a possible counter-attack from Britain in the west and a war of attrition against the vast Russian reserves available in the east.

in the Soviet Union 110,000 men of the original German army of 270,000, fighting at Stalingrad, surrendered on 31 January 1943. The remaining 160,000 men had been killed. In North Africa the victory of General Bernard Montgomery (1887–1976) at El Alamein in October 1942, and an Allied landing in Algeria, forced the Axis troops back into Tunisia where 250,000 surrendered on 12 May 1943. In the Atlantic, Allied sonar and radar, more escorts and long-range aircraft led to increased U-boat losses.

### The beginning of the end
The last major German offensive in the Soviet Union was halted at Kursk in July 1943 and the Red Army pushed forward during the autumn and winter. The Allies under Field-Marshal Harold Alexander (1891–1969) invaded Sicily on 10 July 1943 and landed in Italy on 3 September. The RAF had made its first "1,000-bomber" raid on Germany in May 1942 and, with the arrival of the United States Army Air Force in mid-1943, massive day and night raids were mounted for the rest of the war.

On D-Day, 6 June 1944, Allied forces under General Dwight Eisenhower (1890–1969) landed in Normandy and crossed France and the Low Countries to reach the Rhine by November. In Italy, Rome had been captured on 4 June, while a Soviet offensive begun in the same month drove the Germans out of the Soviet Union and swept into Poland and the Baltic states. In the Pacific, American forces destroyed the remnants of the Japanese fleet at the battles of the Philippine Sea and Leyte Gulf, and invaded the Philippines in October 1944. In Burma, the British defeated a Japanese attempt to invade India and counter-attacked successfully.

The Allies crossed the Rhine in March 1944 and drove deep into Germany. A Soviet assault under Marshal Georgi Zhukov (1896–1974) began in January 1945 and reached Berlin in April. Hitler committed suicide and on 4 May Germany surrendered.

On 6 August US forces dropped the first atomic bomb on Hiroshima, Japan [8]. A second bomb on Nagasaki forced Japan to surrender on 14 August 1945.

KEY

| 1914-18 | 17 | total dead (millions) |
| 1939-45 | 37 | 45 |

Germany 7
Japan 2·6
Italy 0·8
35
12
3·3
USSR 100
75
Yugo-slavia 12·8
France 3·5
UK 0·62
USA
2·5
3·26
3
4

1939-45 casualties: major powers

Axis
Allies
Civilian = 100,000
Military = 100,000

**World War II was the most destructive** and wide-ranging war in history: the dead may have totalled 45 million. Military casualties were only slightly higher than in World War I, but massive bombing and German policies against civilians in the occupied territories meant that civilian deaths were far higher.

**5 The Japanese expanded** into the Pacific in order to secure the oil and minerals of southern Asia and then build a defensive perimeter against Allied counter-attacks.

Japanese possessions 1930
Territory gained by Dec 1941
Territory gained in 1942
Farthest extent of Japanese power
Japanese offensive bases
Japanese sea victory
US sea victory
Oil
Iron ore
Rubber
Tin

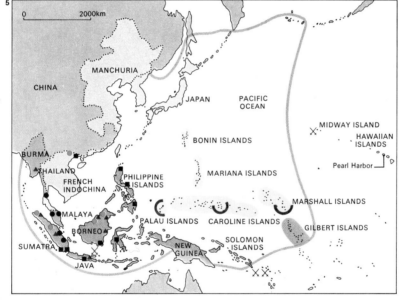

0    2000km

MANCHURIA
CHINA
JAPAN
PACIFIC OCEAN
MIDWAY ISLAND
HAWAIIAN ISLANDS
Pearl Harbor
BONIN ISLANDS
BURMA
THAILAND
FRENCH INDOCHINA
PHILIPPINE ISLANDS
MARIANA ISLANDS
MARSHALL ISLANDS
MALAYA
BORNEO
PALAU ISLANDS
CAROLINE ISLANDS
GILBERT ISLANDS
SUMATRA
JAVA
NEW GUINEA
SOLOMON ISLANDS

**6 The Allied counter-offensive** in the Pacific depended largely on a unique naval campaign in which carrier-borne aircraft played a decisive role. Quickly mastering this new type of warfare, the US Navy was able to destroy the Japanese fleet, bypass enemy-held islands and cut off Japan from its vital supplies. Major land campaigns took place only in Burma and the Philippines.

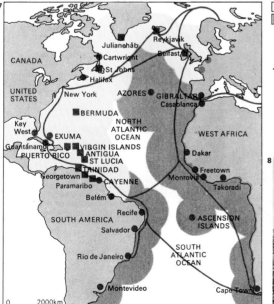

Allied air cover
Sept 1939—May 1945
Added 1942—May 1945
US air bases
Sept 1939—May 1945
Added 1942—May 1945
U-boat bases
Allied convoy routes

Reykjavik
Julianehåb
Belfast
Cartwright
St John's
Halifax
CANADA
UNITED STATES
New York
AZORES
GIBRALTAR
Casablanca
BERMUDA
Key West
NORTH ATLANTIC OCEAN
WEST AFRICA
EXUMA
Dakar
Guantánamo
VIRGIN ISLANDS
PUERTO RICO
ANTIGUA
ST LUCIA
TRINIDAD
Freetown
Georgetown
CAYENNE
Monrovia
Paramaribo
Takoradi
Belém
SOUTH AMERICA
Recife
ASCENSION ISLANDS
Salvador
Rio de Janeiro
SOUTH ATLANTIC OCEAN
Montevideo
Cape Town

0    2000km

**7 The Battle of the Atlantic** was a crucial one for Britain once the threat of a German invasion had been removed. The German U-boats hoped to starve Britain into submission, thus eliminating the possibility of a counter-attack in the west. In 1941–2 the U-boats almost succeeded in their aim, and it was not until anti-submarine measures had been intensified and improved that the U-boats were eventually mastered.

**8 Hiroshima was devastated** by the first atomic bomb. By later standards this was a very small bomb of less than one kilotonne, but it was enough to obliterate an entire city and kill more than 78,500 people in the space of one minute. A new era of warfare threatening total annihilation had been unleashed on mankind.

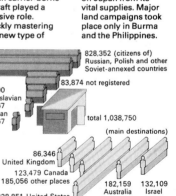

828,352 (citizens of) Russian, Polish and other Soviet-annexed countries
83,874 not registered
82,090 Yugoslavian
22,467 German
21,967 other
total 1,038,750
(main destinations)
86,346 United Kingdom
123,479 Canada
185,056 other places
328,851 United States
182,159 Australia
132,109 Israel

**9 By the end of the war** more than a million displaced persons were living in refugee camps throughout Europe. The majority were Soviet citizens or citizens of countries annexed by the USSR. The diagram shows where the east European refugees came from and where the International Refugee Organization succeeded in settling them.

# World War II: Britain's role

Britain's involvement in World War II was global. Though its principal areas of concern were Europe, North Africa and the Far East, the Royal Air Force flew missions on the Russian front and Royal Navy ships fought engagements off South America. And where Britain itself was not heavily involved – notably in the Pacific theatre – Australians and New Zealanders fought alongside Britain's American allies.

## Early campaigns

True to the British tradition of losing every battle except the last, the war opened disastrously. Hitler's *Blitzkrieg* through Poland, the Low Countries and into France [1] wrecked the British Expeditionary Force of ten divisions: by what seemed a miracle at the time, all but about 25,000 to 30,000 men got back to Britain but the BEF left behind all its heavy equipment.

With the Battle of France lost, the Battle of Britain opened on 10 July 1940 with Goering's Luftwaffe directing its efforts against convoys in the Straits of Dover. The convoys had to be stopped. Phase two, which began on "Eagle Day", 13 August, was aimed at RAF fighter bases in Kent. On 7 September, having lost 225 aircraft to the RAFs 185 in just eight days, the Luftwaffe turned aside to attack London. On 15 September – "Battle of Britain Day" – it lost between 56 and 60 aircraft to the RAF's 26. Chastened, Goering switched to night attacks against English cities, and Operation Sea Lion, the invasion of Britain, was first postponed and finally abandoned altogether after the invasion of Russia. The blitz, during which some 30,000 people were killed, continued until mid-April 1941.

## The dark days

A consequence of the fall of France was that the German navy was able to operate U-boats from France's west coast. In the first year of the war the U-boats never numbered more than 60, but they sank nearly a million tonnes of merchant shipping. The Battle of the Atlantic reached its peak in early 1941, but by the summer of 1943, the convoy system and American involvement prevailed.

In the Balkans Hitler's seven-week campaign through Yugoslavia and Greece ended with the British being ejected from Crete [2] in May 1941.

Germany's assault on Russia on 22 June 1941 [4] offered Britain a breathing-space. Britain could do little to help Russia beyond offering supplies: and the route to Murmansk and Archangel was, in the winter, the worst sea-route in the world.

While the Battle of the Atlantic and of the Russian convoys was under way, Britain was losing in the Far East. The Japanese attack on the US base at Pearl Harbour on 7 December 1941 was followed by the ignominious fall of Singapore [5], the loss of the battlecruiser *Repulse* and the battleship *Prince of Wales*, and a threat to India. The Japanese were within 200 miles of Australia: Australia and New Zealand, with most of their troops in North Africa, had to turn to the United States for protection.

## Towards final victory

The tide began to turn in 1942. In North Africa, after a see-saw series of battles in which the Italians and Erwin Rommel's

**1 The Allies and Germany** faced each other in the West at the outbreak of war more or less evenly matched in numbers. Britain and France had 122 divisions against Germany's 136, and 3,254 armoured vehicles against 2,574. But the Allies still pursued outmoded ideas of positional warfare, and made poor use of their armoured divisions. German armour was used to optimum advantage and coupled with air power to form the spearhead of the *Blitzkrieg*. This was designed to burst through and surround the enemy rather than fight head-on battles. As a result Paris fell in only four weeks.

**3 The arrival of Erwin Rommel** (1891–1944) and his Afrika Korps in February 1941 rescued his Italian partners from being completely overrun by British and Commonwealth forces in North Africa. Twice Rommel reached the frontiers of Egypt, engendering Allied nightmares of an Axis victory that, together with an advance in the Caucasus, could have completed a successful pincer movement.

**2 German paratroops,** here entering a JU52 transport aircraft, proved decisive in the capture of Crete, the final phase of Hitler's Balkan campaign. Bernard Freyberg (1889–1963), commander of the New Zealand Division, was in charge of all the forces on the island. Using 1,390 aircraft, the Germans forced the British to withdraw on 27 May, after three weeks' stubborn resistance.

**4 Hitler's invasion of the Soviet Union** began brilliantly with the German armies using tactics that had been perfected in Poland and France. Deep-thrusting columns destroyed more than a million enemy troops, but stiffening Soviet resistance and the onset of merciless winter conditions prevented the Germans from achieving the swift victory they needed. Despite some further successes in 1942, the Germans were catastrophically defeated at Stalingrad where they lost 300,000 men. Thereafter they could not hope to match the Soviet Union's apparently inexhaustible manpower and were steadily pushed back.

**5 The Japanese captured 85,000 men** at Singapore in February 1942: it was the largest surrender in the history of the British Army. Complacency about the Japanese threat had led Britain to neglect already inadequate defences, but even so British and Commonwealth troops outnumbered the Japanese who swept through Malaya and Burma. The Japanese relied on their mastery of jungle warfare to outflank British troops, who had virtually no jungle training. Singapore was approached and attacked from its lightly defended landward side and fell in a matter of days.

Afrika Korps [3] got to within 60 miles of Alexandria, and Australian and British units distinguished themselves by stubborn resistance in the isolated pocket of Tobruk. Montgomery won the Battle of El Alamein [6]. The battle opened on 23·October; on 4 November Rommel's Afrika Korps began to retreat; four days later Anglo-American forces landed in French North Africa. With victory in North Africa in the spring of 1943, Italy became the next objective. Sicily was invaded in July 1943 and mainland Italy – by the British 5th Army at Salerno – in September. American insistence that the Pacific and Burma campaigns be given priority in late 1943 meant, however, that the Italian campaign was drawn out. Of the Commonwealth troops who had fought in Africa, the New Zealanders went on to fight in Italy, notably at Monte Cassino [7] and the Australians returned home to help push the Japanese out of the Pacific.

The Mediterranean campaign ended effectively with the capture of Rome on 4 June 1944, although the German resistance in Italy did not end until May 1945.

The invasion of Normandy began on 6 June 1944, British troops landing on the coast near Caen and Bayeux and Americans farther west. After an initial period of close fighting in France, the Allies broke out and swept towards the Rhine. An attempt to speed matters by an airborne landing at Arnhem in The Netherlands [8] failed, but in the spring of 1945 renewed offensives resulted in Germany's surrender on 7 May.

In the Far East Slim's [9] "forgotten" 14th Army had been confronting the Japanese in Burma while Americans, Australians and New Zealanders island-hopped towards Japan following the Battle of Midway, an American carrier-fleet victory that ranked with Stalingrad in strategic importance. Two atomic bombs, on Hiroshima and Nagasaki, ended the war against Japan.

Britain lost far fewer men in World War II than in World War I – 300,000 dead against 750,000. Civilian casualties were higher: 60,000 against 1,500. The legacy of the war was an enormous economic debt – £4,198 million – the loss of an empire and, in compensation, an industrial leap forward.

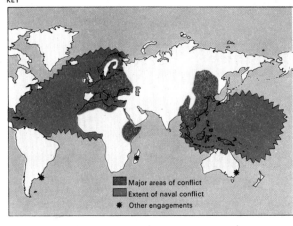

KEY

Major areas of conflict
Extent of naval conflict
✳ Other engagements

**World War II began in Europe,** but developed into a global conflict with campaigns in Africa, Asia and throughout the Pacific and Atlantic Oceans. Italy proved a weak member of the Axis in 1940, but Germany and Japan enjoyed a series of victories in the first three years. Thereafter, Allied superiority in potential manpower and industrial capacity steadily grew. More than any previous conflict, this was a war of technology, with developments in tanks, aircraft, submarines, radar – and eventually the atomic bomb – helping to influence strategic and tactical thinking.

**6 The turning-point in North Africa** came in July 1942 when the overstretched Afrika Korps failed to break through British 8th Army positions around El Alamein. Three months later, substantial Allied reinforcements enabled the new commander, Montgomery, to begin an offensive that secured North Africa.

**7 The ruins of Monte Cassino monastery** in Italy saw some of the most savage fighting of the war. The Allies believed that the Germans had turned the monastery into a strongpoint: their decision to bomb it not only provoked a controversy, it defeated its own end — the rubble was easier to defend than the intact monastery.

**8 British paratroops** experienced nine days of bitter street fighting – and final failure – at Arnhem in September 1944 when, with American and Polish forces, they attempted to capture 17 canal crossings and major bridges in Holland. Of the 35,000 troops involved, more than 17,000 became casualties. Four of the five major bridges were taken; the bridge at Arnhem was not. The plan devised by Montgomery – dashing, and contrary to his usual style – might have shortened the war had it worked.

**9 Lieutenant-General William Joseph Slim** (1891–1970) commanded the 14th British Army in Burma. In June 1944, he defeated a Japanese attempt to invade India at Kohima and Imphal, and then successfully went on to liberate the country.

**10 The Japanese in New Guinea** suffered their first major setback on land in September 1942 when Australian forces defeated an attempt to capture Port Moresby. After savage fighting in atrocious conditions, the Australians successfully counter-attacked. Throughout 1943 and early 1944, a series of small-scale but brilliant combined operations were mounted as part of a wider Allied offensive in the southwestern Pacific. These isolated and neutralized a whole Japanese army.

# The home front in World War II

World War II has often, and accurately, been described as "The People's War". No previous conflict in history had so directly involved the civilian population of the combatant countries or caused them so much privation and death.

## Civilian involvement in war

Even before war had been declared civilians had become involved through conscription, introduced in Germany in 1934, in Great Britain in June 1939, and in the United States on a selective "unlucky dip" basis in 1940. Once the war began even those civilians who escaped being called up into the armed forces found themselves in varying degrees directed into home defence (Local Defence Volunteers, later the Home Guard) [2] or civil defence or into essential work in factories [8] and vital services such as transport. In every combatant country (except the United States, which could meet almost all the demands made upon it) the share of the national resources allocated to civilians was by the end of the war sharply reduced to give priority to the fighting men.

Although they vastly outnumbered the soldiers, the civilians were in far less danger. Even in Germany casualties among civilians, including those caught up in military operations, were estimated at no more than 700,000 compared with 3,500,000 servicemen who died. The figures for Britain were 62,000 against 326,000 and for Japan 260,000 civilians compared with 1,200,000 servicemen; the United States had virtually no civilian casualties. But the civilian's life was far more at risk than in any previous war. Although each country claimed at first to be directing its bombers against only military objectives, such restraints were soon abandoned [11]. But bombs were not the main cause of civilian deaths. Under German occupation, far more deaths were caused by disease, famine and mass murder.

## Civilian daily life

Even within occupied Europe daily life varied enormously between different countries. In Denmark, Hitler's "model protectorate", the standard of living was far higher than in Britain. In France, if one had access to

the black market, it was also possible to live reasonably well. But in Holland by the winter of 1944–5 people were living on tulip bulbs and in the Channel Islands only the arrival of Red Cross parcels prevented starvation. All the occupied countries shared some shortages and discomforts. Fuel, both for heating and transport, was scarce [5]. Everyone's life was encompassed by curfews, permits and the fear of being rounded up as a suspect or forced-labour "volunteer".

In the countries still under arms the civilian population was encouraged to believe that a vast gulf separated them from their counterparts in enemy lands. Civilian experience in Germany probably had more in common with life in wartime Britain than in any other country. Both suffered the upheaval of evacuation [Key] and of long nights in shelters.

Almost all necessities were either rationed or hard to find and although the German system of control was more complicated and less efficient than the British there were many similarities between them. Household textiles and clothes, for example,

**1 Saucepans were collected** for aluminium for making aircraft after a British Government appeal in 1940.

**2 Britain's Local Defence Volunteers** were formed in May 1940. Here two railway men are briefed.

**3 "Dig for Victory"** was an early wartime slogan thought up to promote the campaign for home-grown food.

**4 Air raids on London** – the Blitz – began on 7 September, 1940, and lasted until mid-1941. In the opening phase the capital was bombed on 57 consecutive nights. In the first four months, 13,339 people were killed and 17,937 injured.

**5 Refugees flooded on to the roads** of Europe as the German armies advanced. This Frenchman's horsedrawn vehicle laden with goods was one way of overcoming the petrol shortage; bicycle taxis were also common.

**6 Nazi military bands** like this one, photographed in the Place de l'Opéra in Paris in June 1941, often played in public in the occupied countries. Ostensibly a goodwill gesture, they were also a symbol of German strength.

were rationed on a points system in Germany in 1940 and in 1941 the same system was used in Britain. To find consumer goods of any kind, from babies' prams to furniture, necessitated a long search and in both countries as coal was diverted to the war factories people struggled in winter to keep warm.

Food rationing made the deepest impact on most people and here, as in other spheres, the Germans probably suffered most. The same basic items were rationed in both countries: meat, butter, fats, bacon, cheese, sugar, jam, milk and eggs. But in Germany one also had to part with coupons for bread and potatoes, both plentiful in Britain [3], and there were no "lend lease" supplies from America to help fill empty stomachs.

American soldiers arriving in Europe readily admitted that "back home they don't know there's a war on". Even in the United States there was, in theory, some rationing – of many canned goods, sugar and coffee – but in practice there was no real shortage of any type of goods. The Japanese fuel shortage prevented their indulging in the constant ritual bathing demanded by tradition. Japan

also suffered a near-breakdown in the railway and island-ferry transport systems, and by 1945 food supplies had shrunk to no more than 1,300 calories a day, less than half the normal minimum.

### A new prosperity

If the war years brought unprecedented hardship to civilians they also brought many benefits. In both Germany and Britain, due to the fairer sharing out of food supplies and full employment, poorer families lived better than they had ever done before. Everywhere, rigid price controls kept the rise in prices within limits; by 1945 the cost of living was only a third higher than before the war.

For factory worker and farmer alike, in every combatant country, these were boom years. The new prosperity masked deeper long-term changes. The drift from country to city was accelerated; there was increased pressure for urban amenities to be extended to the countryside; it was demonstrated that full employment was not an impossible dream and everywhere people demanded a fairer social order after the war.

**Evacuation** was carried out by the British Government at the beginning of the war because of the fear of massive air-raids. Nearly 1,300,000 people, mainly children, left the cities.

**7 War savings were encouraged** by all countries to stop inflation. This US Victory Bond was designed by Walt Disney.

**8 The mobilization of women** was greatest in the USSR. Here ammunition is stacked to repel the Leningrad siege.

**9 The destruction of Hiroshima** on the morning of 6 August 1945 was the horrific culmination of the war in the Pacific.

**10 Propaganda was used by both sides,** both offensively and defensively. This German poster warns against careless talk.

**11 Allied bombing** devastated the non-military city of Dresden. These are the ruins of the church of St Sophia.

**12 "Traitor" warns this German poster.** German propaganda techniques were generally more sophisticated than the Allies'.

# The division of Europe

The cold war is usually thought of as a global struggle between the two Great Powers that had emerged by the end of World War II. These two powers, the Soviet Union and the United States, were initially by no means equal; the United States was far superior in terms of economic capacity, air power, and in the fact that she possessed nuclear weapons before the Soviet Union. However, the Soviet Union had an important advantage – the ability to threaten Western Europe with the might of her army. It was because of this Soviet threat that the United States was obliged to come to the rescue and defence of the Western European countries.

## East-West misunderstandings

This is the traditional view of the origins of the cold war and it derives from an interpretation whereby Stalin's Russia overran eastern Europe between 1945 and 1947 and seemed to threaten Western Europe too. Against this a different view has been suggested by some historians. They say that the USSR which had in the past been invaded many times from the West, was still

afraid of her titular allies at the end of World War II. In this view, the Stalinist takeover of Eastern Europe was a defensive reaction to possible attack.

These views are contentious, but it is fairly clear that mutual misunderstanding between the Soviet Union and America played a large part in bringing about the division of Europe [5]. When Churchill (1874–1965), Roosevelt (1882–1945) and Stalin (1879–1953) met at Yalta in 1945 [Key], Soviet suspicion of the Western timing of a Second Front gave way to Western suspicions over Soviet intentions in the East – particularly towards Poland. Thereafter the powers failed, through a series of increasingly acrimonious conferences, to reach agreement on Germany. The process of division inevitably took over.

## The division of Germany

At first the American forces had not intended to stay long in Germany. They did not expect the Soviet troops to remain either. The victorious powers were supposed to supervise German reconstruction only until they could

all agree on its future as a united country. All four – through their foreign ministers, Ernest Bevin (1881–1951), Georges Bidault (1899– ), Vyacheslav Molotov (1890– ) and Secretary of State George Marshall (1880–1959) [4] – administered Berlin equally. But the picture changed, partly because of Soviet dominance in Eastern Europe and in the Soviet zone of Germany, which was rapidly organized as part of the Soviet system. Also important was the Soviet reparations policy, which seemed to threaten the economic ruin of the West by leading to the total collapse of any German economy [2]. Between 1946 and 1948 it became clear that a German economic revival was necessary for Western Europe's recovery.

At first the United States had hoped to include Eastern as well as Western European countries, and certainly the whole of Germany, in a vast programme for European recovery based on American aid. This plan, the European Recovery Programme, or "Marshall Plan" of 1947, was rejected by the Soviet Union but was still applied to the western zones of Germany. Applying it there

**1 US and Soviet troops** met at Torgau, Germany, on 25 April 1945. But already Russian resentment over delay in the Second Front, and US distrust of Soviet motives, heralded the cold war.

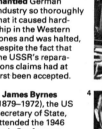

**2 The Russians dismantled** German industry so thoroughly that it caused hardship in the Western zones and was halted, despite the fact that the USSR's reparations claims had at first been accepted.

**3 James Byrnes** (1879–1972), the US Secretary of State, attended the 1946 Paris Conference which was to draft peace treaties with Italy, Romania, Finland, Bulgaria and Hungary. Achieving only part of its aim, the conference also showed up disagreements over Germany.

**4 Marshall, Bevin, Bidault and Molotov** made a futile attempt to agree on the German question, in 1947.

**5 From the Western point of view [A]** it appeared that a vast Soviet army had taken over Eastern Europe, reduced it to Stalinist rule and was poised ready for a westward advance. From the East [B], the superior economic power of the Western world backed by American nuclear weapons seemed ready to disrupt the defensive system that the USSR was trying to create. Each seemed to be threatening the other and so the cold war escalated.

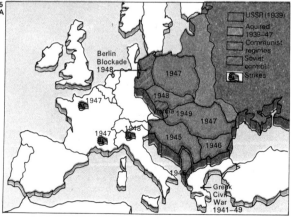

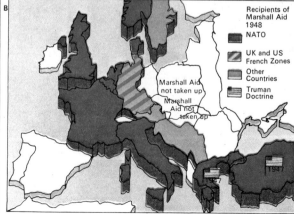

meant the introduction of a separate and reformed West German currency.

After the currency reform in West Germany the USSR began the blockade of Berlin. The blockade [6] lasted for nearly a year, from 1948 to 1949, and was a turning-point in the history of Europe. It came when the division of Europe was complete – for in February 1948 the Soviet Union had completed its take-over of the eastern countries by a coup against Czechoslovakia.

### The birth of NATO

It was against this background that the decision was taken to form NATO (North Atlantic Treaty Organization) [8, 9] – a long-term alliance by which the United States was pledged to the defence of Western Europe. The original (1949) members of NATO were the USA and Canada and the principal nations of Western Europe [10]. Greece and Turkey joined in 1951 and West Germany in 1955. Meanwhile West European countries began to recover and to co-operate. They had already sketched some form of co-operation in defence (in the West European Union

before NATO was founded) but equally important was the Organization for European Economic Co-operation (OEEC), formed in 1948, in which the United States supported the West European countries in creating a system of mutual prosperity. And from 1949 onwards the Europeans began to pool their resources in a system of co-operation that was eventually to form the European Economic Community.

In the east the Stalinist system of almost total control exercised through the Cominform was challenged only by Yugoslavia, although later a more co-operative pattern was established after 1949 through the Council for Mutual Economic Assistance (or COMECON). But the early contrast between Western co-operation and the Eastern dictatorship reinforced the division of Europe and the rigidity of the cold war.

Before this, in 1950, the Korean War had broken out and seemed to confirm the necessity of NATO. As a result, by 1955 West Germany was invited to join. When she did so, it meant that Germany could not be united, and the division of Europe was complete.

KEY

**The three leaders of the Grand Alliance,** Churchill [left], Roosevelt [centre] and Stalin, met at Yalta in February 1945. France was not invited. It has often been argued that Europe was divided into two blocs at this meeting, but the "Big Three" agreed on little beyond the final arrangements necessary for temporarily dividing Germany.

**6 The Berlin blockade** was the first great confrontation of the cold war. It arose from restrictions imposed by the Russians on Western access to Berlin. For months the city was maintained by an airlift. However, the outcome depended as much on the refusal of West Berliners to accept Soviet economic help in return for political surrender. The blockade divided Berlin and completed the division of Germany.

**7 The Allied Control Council** (shown here in 1948) governed Germany from 1945 to 1948. It did not establish a central government for the whole country, but served to resolve disagreements arising through the separate governments of the different zones. When the three Western powers decided to introduce a new currency in West Germany, the Russians walked out and the Council came to an end.

**8 The foreign ministers** of NATO countries gathered in Washington to sign the NATO Treaty before the Berlin blockade was over. Events in Europe had seemed to confirm the aggressive intentions of the USSR and the need for a firm Western response. Also, the economic recovery of Western Europe depended on a security guarantee. By committing the US to a long-term defence arrangement, NATO superseded European attempts to ensure security.

**9 NATO was formed to offset** the Soviet military presence in Europe. The forces committed to NATO were too weak to be anything but a stop-gap in the case of an emergency until, that was, the full resources of all the signatories could be mustered. In 1955 West Germany became a fully independent state and a member of NATO. In May of that year, partly in response to that event, the Soviet Union set up the equivalent defence organization of the Warsaw Pact.

NATO membership 1955

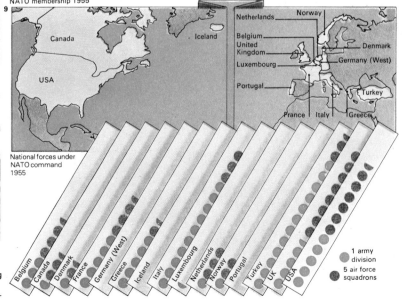

National forces under NATO command 1955

1 army division

5 air force squadrons

**10 By 1955 West Germany** had made an amazing recovery. At Paris in 1954 the powers met to determine the extent of her entry into the European community. Konrad Adenauer (1876–1967), seen here with other leaders, had worked for this since becoming Federal Chancellor of West Germany in 1949.

After six years of war Britain's return to peacetime conditions needed a prolonged period of adjustment. Despite the remarkably united and disciplined war effort, the country's economy had been overstrained, and Britain was not in a position to shoulder properly the burdens of occupying its zone of Western Germany while also playing its part in achieving some kind of peace settlement in the East as well as in the West.

## Labour victory and the Welfare State

Although Britain still ranked as one of the "Big Three" powers when the war ended, along with the United States and the Soviet Union, it soon became clear that it was no longer in the super-power league. At the 1945 general election, the bulk of the electorate showed that it was more interested in the approach to peacetime reconstruction offered by the Labour Party than in the continuation of Britain's role in big-power politics which it associated with Winston Churchill (1874–1965), linked as that would have been with a period of Conservative rule. A landslide victory for Labour deprived the

country of the world figure who had been – not just for the British but for millions elsewhere – the personification of resistance to Nazism and Fascism. Clement Attlee (1883–1967) became prime minister.

Ernest Bevin (1881–1951) as Foreign Secretary supplied something of Churchill's bulldog quality in the negotiations that began to shape the peacetime settlement. At the same time he and others undertook the vast work of decolonization, starting with the granting of independence to India and Pakistan in 1947.

Domestic changes were almost as dramatic as those taking place outside Britain. The government's brand of socialism stressed nationalization of various sectors of the economy as the way forward, while greatly extending the state health and medical services and education, creating a "Welfare State" [4]. The Bank of England was nationalized in 1946 and in 1947 the railways and the coal mines were also taken under state control. The steel industry was also nationalized, in 1947, after a constitutional crisis brought on by Conservative opposition

in the House of Lords, whose power to delay bills was subsequently reduced. What affected people most directly was the massive reorganization of the Health Services [2], accomplished by Aneurin Bevan (1897–1960), in order to provide medical and hospital treatment and prescriptions and also dental and other services "free", or at minimal rates.

The government had inherited a wartime economy. It continued rationing (not completely ended until 1954) and also policies of heavy taxation and wage restraint. Despite a large increase in exports, the country (or rather the sterling area as a whole) had an almost chronic deficit with the United States, which forced a devaluation of the pound from $4.03 to $2.80 in September 1949.

## Conservative rule

Long-drawn-out opposition by the British Medical Association to the Health Service reforms, and bitter wrangling in Parliament over steel, indicated that Labour's popularity was waning. At the 1950 election Labour was returned to power with a reduced majority,

**1 A landslide victory brought Labour** to power in 1945 with 393 seats against the 213 won by the Conservatives and their allies. The Conservatives and most foreign observers had assumed that Churchill, with his great wartime prestige, would carry them to victory. But the electorate was moved by Labour's promises of employment, housing and welfare and the proposals for nationalization of basic industries and state planning of the massive reconstruction that lay ahead. Years of wartime organization had left the people with a collectivist legacy that gave a strong appeal to Labour's socialist programme.

**2 The centrepiece of the new Welfare State** was the National Health Service, whose creation was the work of Aneurin Bevan. For the first time medical attention, prescriptions and many other services, generally became free or available on low charges. Some 3,000 hospitals were taken over under the scheme. While the hospital consultants welcomed the proposal, most of the doctors, organized by the British Medical Association, were bitterly opposed to it, as depicted in this contemporary cartoon. Bevan fought a long battle with the doctors, who saw in the scheme threats to their independence; but when the service began over 90 per cent of the doctors enrolled.

**3 Rationing in the postwar period** was more severe than in wartime. Until its defeat in 1951, the Labour government pursued an unpopular programme of austerity to rebuild the economy and finance government expenditure. Abroad things were serious; in The Netherlands and the British zone in Germany there was near famine and there was a lack of raw materials all over the world. But ironically a higher percentage of each age group in the London area in 1946 was classed as of "excellent nutrition" than in 1938, and this was true of the country as a whole. Rationing began to be reduced after 1948; in 1949 clothing and furniture were freed. Meat was the last item to disappear from the ration books, and that took place in 1954.

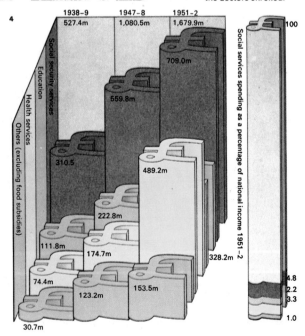

**4 Figures for spending on the social services** illustrate the economic reality behind the creation of the Welfare State. In 1938, the last full budgetary year before the war, social service spending was around £345 million or 37.6 per cent of total government expenditure; by 1950 this proportion had risen to 46.1 per cent. In 1955, R. A. Butler pointed out that during his period as Chancellor of the Exchequer, social service spending had increased by 40 per cent while the national income had increased by only 25 per cent. But government expenditure on defence remained high. The limited rearmament undertaken at the time of the Korean War (1950–53) deeply divided the Labour Party.

and at the following election in October 1951 the Conservatives under Churchill won a majority of 26. With this they denationalized the steel industry in 1953 (it was later re-nationalized by Labour in 1967).

The Chancellor of the Exchequer, Richard Butler (1902– ), introduced a series of measures designed to improve the balance of payments and to increase domestic consumption. In the 1955 election the Conservatives were returned with an increased majority. The party was now led by Anthony Eden (1897–1977) who had taken over the leadership after Churchill had resigned through ill health.

In addition to maintaining an independent nuclear deterrent [8] and continuing national service (until 1958), the government favoured British influence and defence commitments overseas on a scale that the economy could no longer support. The failure in 1956 of the Suez operation against Egypt, when the collusion of Britain and France with Israel was opposed by America, made it clear that Britain could no longer continue the stance of a world power.

Meanwhile, thanks in part to vast infusions of dollars through US loans and Marshall Aid, the economy had a run of good years. The standard of living rose, and the working classes, like most of the population, had "never had it so good". These words of Harold Macmillan (1894– ) [9], who became prime minister following Anthony Eden's resignation in 1957, can serve as a motto for this final phase of the 13 years of Conservative rule (1951–64).

### Loss of confidence
In the early years of the 1960s the economy took a downward turn, however, and successive pay policies introduced by the Conservatives failed. Britain's application for membership of the European Economic Community was vetoed by France in 1963, and the Beeching report proposing a one-third reduction in railway services also undermined Macmillan's popularity. Sir Alec Douglas-Home (1903– ), who took over the premiership after Macmillan had resigned because of illness in 1963, could not restore confidence.

**The Festival of Britain** in 1951 was conceived as marking a new era of reconstruction following the destruction of World War II. Opened by George VI (r. 1936–52) on 3 May, it attracted 8.5 million visitors to the Festival Hall and other sights on the south bank of the River Thames.

**5 The 1950 election** had returned Labour to power with a majority of only five. In 1951 under increasing pressure, the government resigned and an election gave the Conservative Party a majority of 26. The Conservatives presented an attractive alternative after the prolonged austerity of the preceding years.

**6 The coronation of Queen Elizabeth II** (1952– ) in June 1953 was taken by many to symbolize a new "Elizabethan Age" with the promise of great prospects for Britain in the postwar world. The event was televised worldwide and thousands of cheering spectators lined the streets to watch the colourful procession.

**7 A new youth culture** emerged in the 1950s, alongside the beginnings of rock 'n' roll music, which presaged predominant youth cultures of the 1960s. Like the music, the new style was aggressive and uncompromisingly youthful and reflected the new affluence of the postwar period. Styles included those worn by "Teddy Boys", who affected Edwardian-style suits, string ties, and duck's-tail haircuts.

**8 Ban-the-bomb demonstrations** were frequent after the CND (Campaign for Nuclear Disarmament) was founded in 1958. Many public figures shared this widespread concern.

**9 Harold Macmillan** (left) was prime minister for six years from 1957–63 until he retired from the Conservative leadership because of ill health. During that time the country had a period of prosperous and efficient government, although the economic problems that dominated British politics in the 1960s became evident during the final years of his term of office.

# Britain since 1945:2

The British general election of 1964 initiated a period of Labour rule broken only by nearly four years of Conservative government under Edward Heath (1970–4). The period as a whole was one of increasing economic difficulty for Britain. It failed to maintain its competitive position against trade rivals despite its entry in 1973 into the European Economic Community (Common Market), an action that was reaffirmed after a referendum in 1975 [8]. Only on the "invisible" side of its trading account (banking, brokerage, insurance and other services) did Britain maintain its position, thereby alleviating the effects of the frequent deficits in its balance of payments.

## Trade union militancy

Trade imbalances were offset by loans that became ever more massive, despite a few better years when repayments were made, notably during the period 1967–70. Among reasons for the weakness of trade were the increasing productivity of competitors, and their greater ability to adopt new methods and machinery both for older industries and for the new high-technology enterprises. In contrast, British management found it difficult to secure the co-operation of trade unions in introducing modern plant and reducing labour costs. This failure was coupled with successful union pressure for increased wages and reduced hours of work, backed by go-slows and strikes.

In Parliament the Labour Party was increasingly polarized between left-wing socialists of the Tribune Group and some Marxist-oriented MPs on the one hand, and those who pursued a moderate social-democratic line on the other.

Among the latter were Harold Wilson [1], prime minister 1964–70 and 1974–6, and James Callaghan, who followed him as prime minister. Wilson coped skilfully with the divisions in his party but at the cost of compromising over some important issues to the point where governmental authority was eroded. The continuing high cost of defence, together with growing education, health and pensions services, imposed burdens which the weakening position of the country in productivity and trade made it difficult to meet. This weakness was reflected in the tendency of inflation, which had been chronic but manageable (three to five per cent), to increase to, at times, more than 20 per cent. As a result, sterling weakened against other currencies [4].

## Devaluation of sterling

Labour's fine ideals in 1964 of modernizing Britain and moving it steadily towards socialism, were soon obscured by the fight to "save the pound". Desperate efforts were made to maintain the exchange rate of the pound at $US2.80 by large-scale borrowing from abroad – but to no avail. A seamen's strike in 1966 hastened the loss of confidence in sterling and the pound was devalued to $2.40 in November 1967. Attempts were made to bolster sterling by an incomes policy that restricted wage increases to certain ceilings or percentages. But the Labour programme for pursuing this objective, formulated in the White Paper, "In Place of Strife", failed in 1969 in the face of union militancy and left-wing opposition.

The Conservative government from

**1 Harold Wilson** (1916– ) became prime minister of a Labour government with a majority of only four in 1964. He consolidated his party's position at a further election in 1966. The youngest MP to attain cabinet rank in the first post-war government (at the Board of Trade), he took over the party leadership after the death of Hugh Gaitskell in 1963. Although his flexibility enabled him to hold together the left and right wings of his party, his hopes of modernizing the British economy and the trade union system were dashed first by the weakness of sterling and secondly by union opposition to sweeping changes.

**2 Holland Park Comprehensive** made news as a large purpose-built (1958) school in a fashionable part of London to which some public figures sent their children. With its sixth form block, ten science laboratories, ten art studios, seven workshops and three gymnasiums, it summed up the aspirations of a new-style education system based on the principle of giving all children, no matter what their background or means, equal opportunity. As some academic standards slipped, however, Labour's policy of replacing grammar, secondary modern and grant-aided schools by comprehensives provoked increasingly fierce controversy.

**3 Mick Jagger and the Rolling Stones,** seen here at a 1969 concert in Hyde Park, London, were the most aggressive, irreverent, anti-establishment rock group to appear in the entertainment world of the 1960s. Their appeal was less broadly based than that of the Beatles, whose popularity with virtually all age groups helped to break down some of the traditional barriers of class and accent in Britain. The driving music of the Rolling Stones was directed more frankly at youthful rebellion. It chimed in with trends of the times, reflected in the increasingly open treatment of sex and violence in films and on television, and the use of drugs as stimulants on a scale previously unknown.

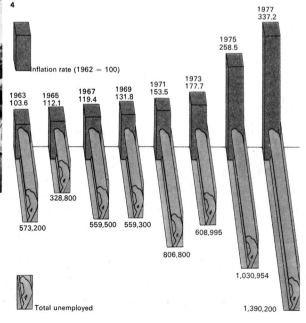

Inflation rate (1962 = 100)

| Year | Value | Total unemployed |
|---|---|---|
| 1963 | 103.6 | 573,200 |
| 1965 | 112.1 | 328,800 |
| 1967 | 119.4 | 559,500 |
| 1969 | 131.8 | 559,300 |
| 1971 | 153.5 | 806,800 |
| 1973 | 177.7 | 608,995 |
| 1975 | 258.5 | 1,030,954 |
| 1977 | 337.2 | 1,390,200 |

**4 Inflation** had been at the rate of 3% to 4% from 1945 until 1964, fuelled by the steady increase of government spending and the outpacing of production increases by wage rises. The rate of inflation jumped when the 14.3% devaluation of the pound in 1967 put up the prices of imported goods. From 1973 onwards, price rises imposed by the Organization of Petroleum Exporting Countries (OPEC) doubled the price of oil. Soaring costs and wages in 1975 brought inflation to 20%. Government efforts to hold down spending, together with some company failures, led to a rise in the number of unemployed to more than 1 million, the worst level of unemployment since the 1930s.

1970–4 fared no better in attempting to control inflation, and in fact worsened the position by dismantling some of Labour's controls, only to return to an incomes policy. Obdurate union resistance to pay restraints was exacerbated by the Industrial Relations Act, which established three-phase statutory wage and price controls. A coal-miners' strike [6] early in 1972, involving power-cuts when the miners obstructed coal deliveries to the generating stations, led to the treatment of the miners as a "special case". The 25 per cent pay rise they received breached the incomes policy. The Government attempted to counteract an overtime ban by the miners the following winter by introducing an emergency three-day working week to save fuel. But when in 1974 it sought a mandate for a firm line against union pressure for higher wages, a general election resulted in the return of Labour to power without an over-all majority.

Despite hopes of future prosperity through the development of North Sea gas and oil resources, the pound continued to sink, impelling a return to an incomes policy

under the chancellorship of Denis Healey. To restrain a rising rate of unemployment [4], the government was forced to back some ailing firms with public money [7].

**Political and social strains**

Economic weakness aggravated political problems. Proposals were made for devolution of some powers to local assemblies in response to demands for greater autonomy and even independence by parties in Scotland and Wales. In Northern Ireland, terrorist activity by the Irish Republican Army (IRA) and counter-terrorism by Protestant extremists led in 1972 to direct rule from Westminster, supported by large-scale and continuing army operations.

Socially, the strains of a further influx of Commonwealth migrants [5], major changes in patterns of education [2] and a shift in economic power from the older to the younger generation met with mixed success during the period after 1964. Pop music groups such as the Beatles and the Rolling Stones [3] were associated with a new image of London as the "swinging" capital [Key].

**Carnaby Street**, with its boutiques and shops specializing in fashionable clothes, colourful posters and the latest pop records, became a symbol for the new "swinging" London of the 1960s. Together with King's Road, Chelsea, it provided, a visual idea of a city that had cast off the imperial trappings of the past. London was now the capital of the youth orientated societies of the affluent Western countries, a youth whose tastes and demands needed up-to-the-minute satisfaction. One of the most popular of Carnaby Street's emblems was the Union Jack itself, converted from the national flag to almost anything, from a lively T-shirt to a plastic shopping bag.

**5 Immigrants from the West Indies** and Asia provided staff for medical, transport and postal services and for certain industries, notably textiles, after World War II. But their rising numbers and limited prospects brought social strains while problems of housing and education led to government measures to regulate their entry during the 1960s. The entry restrictions were partially waived to accommodate Asians holding British passports expelled from Uganda in 1972. Community services and immigration liaison offices were set up in several cities to help with their integration and improve race relations.

**6 Striking miners in 1972** supported wage claims of up to 47% made by the National Union of Miners at a time when the Conservative Government was hoping to bring inflation down from 6% to 5%. Rejecting increases of between 7% and 8%, miners picketed generating stations until power shortages forced the government to set up an inquiry. The strike, from 9 January to 28 February, ended with acceptance of increases averaging 25% recommended by a court of inquiry. Further miners' claims in 1973, were resisted by the Government, but its handling of the economy led to defeat in the 1974 election.

**7 Rolls-Royce engine manufacture** was threatened in 1971 when the company's financial problems forced it to seek assistance from a Conservative government pledged to leave "lame duck" industries to their fate. The government had to take over those parts of the company essential to defence. A similar crisis in 1975 in the American-based Chrysler company obliged the Labour government to inject £162.5 million to save the jobs of car plant workers.

**8 A last-ditch fight** against Britain's entry into the EEC was defeated when a referendum in 1975 produced a 67% vote in favour of continued membership of the Community. A large section of the Labour Party, particularly the left-wing Tribune Group, had opposed Britain's joining in 1973.

**9 Arabs shopping in London** became a new feature of life in the capital during the 1970s, reflecting rising incomes in the oil states of the Middle East, particularly Saudi Arabia and Kuwait. At the same time sterling balances held by the oil states became a key factor in Britain's management of her currency reserves. Arab investors in the UK tended to favour buying real estate, such as the Dorchester Hotel, rather than shares in British industry.

# The Soviet Union since 1945

The USSR at the end of World War II had lost more than 20 million of her citizens and four and a half million homes. Some 65,000km (40,000 miles) of railway track were laid waste, thousands of industrial and agricultural machines crippled and livestock vastly depleted. Reconstruction was a formidable task. Joseph Stalin (1879–1953) reintroduced five-year planning, and soon he declared many ambitious targets over-fulfilled.

## Costly progress

By the time of Stalin's death the Soviet Union had acquired nuclear weapons and had far surpassed prewar production in iron, steel, coal, oil and electricity. It achieved these targets at the cost of great sacrifices by its own people and those of Eastern Europe, whose resources were in effect put at Moscow's disposal after 1945.

Life was hardest in the countryside where under-investment, low prices for compulsory deliveries, high taxes on private plots and doctrinaire administrative measures hampered production. By 1953 agricultural output per capita was below that of 1928.

The onset of the cold war together with Stalin's attempts to contain the effect of Tito's independent line in Yugoslavia increased tension within the USSR. Stalin's "personality cult" reached its peak in the postwar era when purges were revived. Stalin's paranoia towards the end of his life and the sense of fear and suspicion he created around him were publicly expressed in January 1953 when he unjustly accused nine eminent doctors, most of them Jewish, of having murdered the deputy premier, Andrei Zhdanov (1896–1948). In his last days not even Stalin's closest intimates and advisers were safe from his secret police.

## Collective leadership

After Stalin's death on 5 March 1953 [1], "collective leadership" was proclaimed and accordingly the new Premier – Georgi M. Malenkov (1902–  ) – relinquished the position of senior Party Secretary ten days after assuming it. Soon the Kremlin doctors were released, their "plot" having been exposed as a fabrication. Curbs on secret-police power were dramatized by the secret trial and execution of Lavrenti Beria (1899–1953), the reorganization of his ministry and the progressive release from labour camps of an estimated 10–12 million people.

There were serious rivalries between Stalin's successors. Premier Malenkov and First Secretary Nikita S. Khrushchev (1894–1971) [2] disagreed over economic priorities and the implications of nuclear warfare, but while Khrushchev exploited their differences to engineer the removal of Malenkov from the premiership in February 1955, he subsequently endorsed many of Malenkov's proposals.

The trend towards relaxing domestic and foreign policies alarmed Foreign Minister Vyacheslav Molotov (1890–  ), especially after the 20th Communist Party Congress in February 1956 at which Khrushchev denounced Stalin and envisaged different roads to socialism. The subsequent turmoil in Poland and Hungary confirmed Molotov's fears. He spearheaded a revolt, culminating in the Party Presidium's vote for Khrushchev's dismissal in June 1957. However, in the Central Committee meeting that

**1 Stalin's funeral,** on 9 March 1953, drew crowds of Russians to Red Square in Moscow. Not everyone mourned. Some grieved for the man who had transformed their country into a powerful state, but others counted the cost. Without abandoning police control or strict censorship, Stalin's successors eradicated the "personality cult" and the rule of terror. Stalin's body was removed from the Lenin Mausoleum in 1961.

**2 Nikita Khrushchev** joined the Communist Party in 1918 and became a loyal executor of Stalin's policies. As First Secretary in the Ukraine in 1938, he administered the purges with fervour. Later, as the Party chief, he dismantled the cruder forms of terror and moved fitfully towards *détente*. His caprices and bombast infuriated all, yet his consignment to oblivion in 1964 was widely regretted.

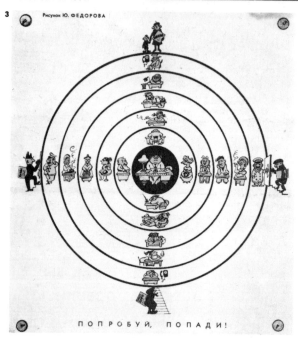

**3 This Soviet cartoon** satirizes the inadequacy of curbs on bureaucracy. Attacks on officialdom are tolerated, but criticism of higher officials and Party policy is banned.

**4 Output of Soviet agriculture** has been disappointing since collectivization. Price incentives and doubling of investment in the 1960s raised productivity. Today, with over 500 million acres under cultivation and a quarter of the workforce engaged in farming, Soviet agriculture is still unable to meet the population's demands for a better diet.

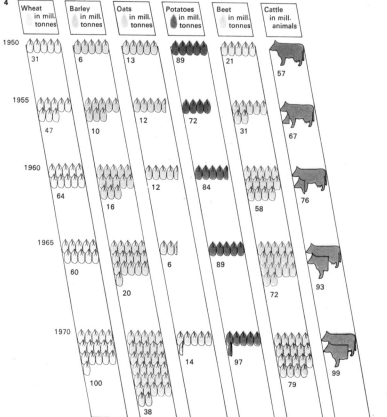

followed, Khrushchev's opponents were themselves defeated. Nikolai Bulganin (1895–1975) remained, but lost the premiership within a year to Khrushchev himself.

Khrushchev's elevation meant improved material conditions. He cut the working week, reduced wage differentials, diminished the stringency of Stalin's Draconian labour laws and gave greater priority to consumer needs. But over-centralized, often incompetent planning plagued economic development. Notwithstanding industrial performance [7] and the Sputniks and other space triumphs after 1957 [Key], agricultural production [4] remained disappointing despite increased investment. Khrushchev's failure aroused resentment and, in October 1964, he was dismissed.

## A decade of stable government
Despite policy disagreements, the post-Khrushchev leadership has been remarkably stable. Leonid Ilyich Brezhnev (1906– ), First Secretary of the Central Committee, Alexei Kosygin (1904– ), Chairman of the Council of Ministers, and Nikolai Vik-torovitch Podgorny (1903– ), President, having held office for well over a decade. The USSR has advanced militarily to achieve virtual strategic parity with the USA, while the rift with China, begun under Khrushchev, has widened. Economic progress has been less spectacular. Central planners have resisted complete decentralization, but they have permitted some degree of autonomy. In agriculture massive investment and concessions such as the relaxation of restrictions on private plots have helped to boost production, although major problems remain, despite military and space successes.

Yet there are signs of strain and nonconformity in the monolithic society of the USSR. Alcoholism is one problem, dissidence another. Outspoken intellectuals and writers, such as Sinyavsky and Daniel, along with protesters at political events such as the Soviet intervention in Czechoslovakia in 1968, suffer a harsh official response. But administrative measures have failed to silence the nonconformists or stem the clandestine circulation of *samizdat* (illegal typescripts).

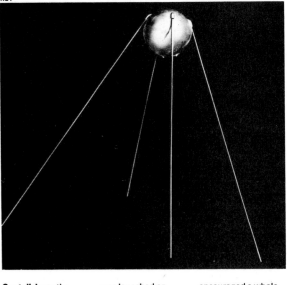

**Sputnik I** was the world's first artificial satellite. It was launched on 4 October 1957. This success encouraged a whole series of pioneering space ventures.

**5 Richard Nixon and Leonid Brezhnev** celebrated signing the first agreement on Strategic Arms Limitation (SALT) in 1972. It was designed to stabilize the Soviet-American nuclear relationship and reduce risks of war. Like agreements on trade and agriculture signed during the Nixon-Brezhnev summits, SALT has been hampered by suspicions following President Nixon's resignation from the US presidency.

**6 Gosudarstveni Universalni Magasin** – GUM – is Moscow's biggest department store, selling anything from luxury fur coats to simple hairpins. Queues abound, but, as in shops elsewhere in the USSR, GUM is better stocked than before, reflecting a rise in general living standards.

**7 Soviet industrial development** since the war has been impressive, even allowing for statistical exaggerations. In that period output increased tenfold, more than doubling during the 1960s after reforms which gave more scope to individual initiative. Expansion of heavy industry is still stressed, but consumer production is growing in importance. Productivity per man however is still lower than in the West, hence the Soviet interest in Western technology.

**8 International football matches** draw great crowds in Moscow. Sport receives generous official encouragement, as part of the view that physical accomplishment makes for healthy, contented citizens and international prestige.

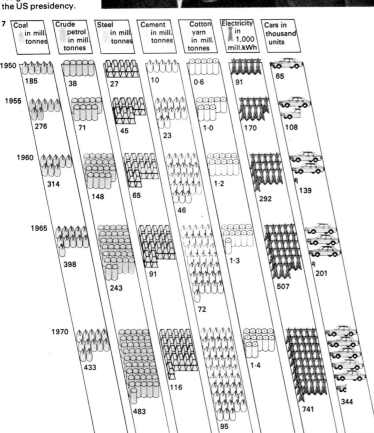

| | Coal in mill. tonnes | Crude petrol in mill. tonnes | Steel in mill. tonnes | Cement in mill. tonnes | Cotton yarn in mill. tonnes | Electricity in 1,000 mill. kWh | Cars in thousand units |
|---|---|---|---|---|---|---|---|
| 1950 | 185 | 38 | 27 | 10 | 0·6 | 91 | 65 |
| 1955 | 276 | 71 | 45 | 23 | 1·0 | 170 | 108 |
| 1960 | 314 | 148 | 65 | 46 | 1·2 | 292 | 139 |
| 1965 | 398 | 243 | 91 | 72 | 1·3 | 507 | 201 |
| 1970 | 433 | 483 | 116 | 95 | 1·4 | 741 | 344 |

# Eastern Europe since 1949

A successful coup made Czechoslovakia a communist country in February 1948 and extended the area of intensive Russian influence in Eastern Europe. Each country under communist control became a "people's democracy" – a one-party dictatorship closely modelled on that in the Soviet Union. The characteristic features of these regimes were: strict censorship of the press and control of all aspects of culture and religion; central economic planning; rapid and forced industrialization; at least partial collectivization of agriculture and in foreign policy submission to the line laid down in Moscow. Soviet control of Eastern Europe was guaranteed by the presence of Soviet troops in most of the satellite countries and numerous Soviet advisers and instructors.

After the defection of Yugoslavia (always the most independent of the satellite countries) from the Soviet bloc in 1948, purges took place in Albania, Bulgaria, Czechoslovakia, Hungary, Poland and Romania. These purges often culminated in show trials of officials accused of being sympathetic to the idea of the "separate roads to socialism"

advocated in Yugoslavia [3]. Non-communists, too, especially members of the Churches, were subjected to persecution and harassment during that period [2].

## Hungary – to encourage the others
After Stalin's death some of the most unpopular features of his policy towards Eastern Europe were modified by his successors, and East European leaders were allowed some degree of autonomy in their domestic policies. But in October 1956 Hungary openly revolted against its communist regime and repudiated its Soviet alliance [4]. At the same time in Poland the leadership of the party was restored to Wladyslaw Gomulka (1905– ), who had been dismissed and imprisoned in 1948 for the alleged adoption of an independent line. After a show of indecision, Soviet tanks were used to crush the Hungarian uprising, but the Soviet Union stopped short of more permanent intervention in Poland. This was a sensible decision. Within a year Gomulka cancelled the liberal concessions that had been wrung from the regime by the intelligentsia in

the autumn of 1956. However Poland kept its private agriculture while other East European countries went ahead with plans for full collectivization in the late 1950s.

No action was undertaken against Albania, which defected from the Soviet bloc in 1960 and promptly took China's side in the great Sino-Soviet quarrel that was just beginning. Romania opted for a more independent foreign policy in 1964, having for several years strenuously opposed Soviet plans for economic integration within Eastern Europe. But domestically both Albania and Romania remained one-party dictatorships.

## The 1968 invasion of Czechoslovakia
Czechoslovakia, which had been the Soviet Union's model satellite for 20 years, provoked the most serious crisis in postwar Eastern Europe in 1968. Alexander Dubcek (1921– ), who had become party leader and president in that year [Key], embarked on a course of energetic liberalization, of which the Soviet and some other East European leaders publicly disapproved. Censorship was relaxed, and a higher degree of local

1 COMECON, the Council for Mutual Economic Assistance (which includes Cuba and Mongolia), was founded in 1949 as Stalin's answer to the Marshall Plan in Western Europe. Revitalized in 1958 by Nikita Khrushchev, the Soviet leader, to consolidate Soviet economic control of Eastern Europe, COMECON has now embarked on a policy of integration adopted at Bucharest in 1971 and further elaborated at Budapest in June 1975. In 1973 COMECON with 366 million people accounted for only 12% of world trade (the EEC, by comparison, with a population of 253 million, accounted for 40%). However, its trade with the West and the EEC in particular, is growing fast, with an increasing proportion generated by "joint ventures" between partners from Eastern and Western Europe. Higher costs of Western imports are now provoking more inter-COMECON joint ventures and greater investment in Soviet projects for the exploitation of natural resources. However, Eastern Europe still needs the West for its advanced technology. Yugoslavia, an observer in COMECON, conducts over 70% of its trade with the non-communist world, and Romania deals direct with the EEC. Albania trades with both East and West. To make a direct connection between the presence of Soviet troops and a country's trading pattern seems dubious.

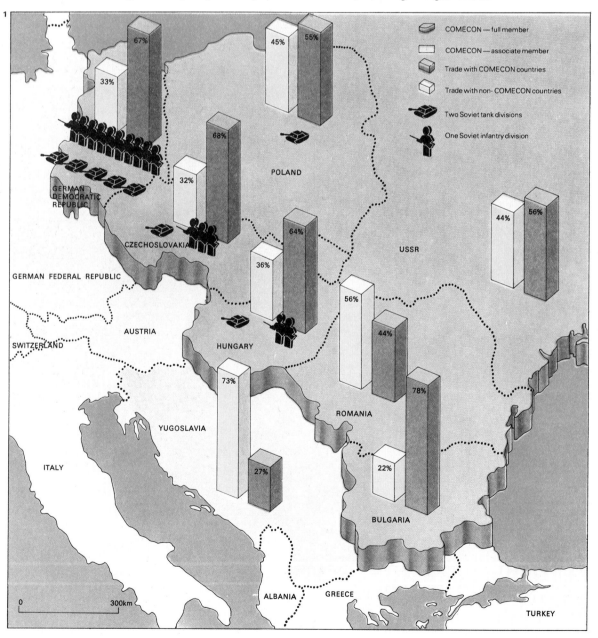

COMECON — full member
COMECON — associate member
Trade with COMECON countries
Trade with non-COMECON countries
Two Soviet tank divisions
One Soviet infantry division

autonomy was granted to the national minorities. In economic planning a move was made to reduce the high level of centralization, prices were allowed a closer relationship to market forces, and individual enterprises were given greater freedom. When Dubcek refused to bow to pressure from his allies, Warsaw Pact troops from the Soviet Union, Poland, East Germany, Hungary and Bulgaria marched in on 21 August 1968 [5]. Czechoslovak leaders were arrested and taken to Moscow, but when no replacements of any stature could be found they were allowed to stay in nominal power for a few months before being finally replaced in 1969.

Although Czechoslovakia's experiment was brutally suppressed, Hungary, under its leader Janos Kadar (1912– ), was allowed to carry out a relatively successful series of reforms. Kadar's popular shift towards the consumer goods sector, was emulated elsewhere in Eastern Europe. Poland's new leader, Edward Gierek (1913– ), who had replaced Gomulka after workers' riots in December 1970, made "Kadarization" one of the basic tenets of his policy. East Ger-

many, too, embarked on its own version of "consumer revolution" in 1971 after the dismissal of its conservative leader, Walter Ulbricht (1893–1973).

## The Soviet bloc closes ranks
Although agreements were reached which lowered some barriers between West Germany on one side and the Soviet Union, Poland and East Germany on the other in the 1970–72 period, there was a new ideological tightening up throughout Eastern Europe. This was due partly to Soviet fear of creeping liberalization and partly to a "backlash" among industrial workers and party officials against the material gains achieved from reform by the professional and managerial classes. New economic predicaments also helped the Soviet Union to turn COMECON's [1] focus eastwards once more. Western inflation had in the mid-1970s made imports from the West suddenly much more expensive; at the same time the Soviet Union raised the prices of oil and the other raw materials of which it holds a virtual monopoly of supply to Eastern Europe.

**Alexander Dubcek** (front, second right) kept in uneasy step with other Eastern European leaders at their meeting in Bratislava on 3 August 1968. Less than three weeks later, Warsaw Pact troops invaded Czechoslovakia. The pact was concluded between the Soviet Union and her satellites in May 1955. It forms the cornerstone of Soviet policy in Eastern Europe, bolstered by the presence there of 31 Soviet divisions.

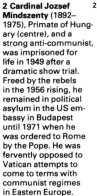

**2 Cardinal Jozsef Mindszenty** (1892–1975), Primate of Hungary (centre), and a strong anti-communist, was imprisoned for life in 1949 after a dramatic show trial. Freed by the rebels in the 1956 rising, he remained in political asylum in the US embassy in Budapest until 1971 when he was ordered to Rome by the Pope. He was fervently opposed to Vatican attempts to come to terms with communist regimes in Eastern Europe.

**3 Nikita Khrushchev** (1894–1971) [right], Malenkov's successor as Soviet leader, went to Yugoslavia in May 1955 to repair the rift caused by Yugoslavia's assertion of independence in 1948. Khrushchev blamed the quarrel on Beria, the ex-chief of Russian police, executed in 1953. Josip Broz Tito (1892– ) [left], the Yugoslav leader, insisted on formal Soviet recognition of Yugoslavia's ideological autonomy.

**4 Stalin's statue** was torn down in Budapest on 2 November 1956, a dramatic moment in the uprising against Soviet domination and the brutal Hungarian regime. Within two days 150,000 Soviet troops and 2,500 tanks were "pacifying" Hungary. The executions that followed the uprising soon gave way to the intelligent government of Janos Kadar. His policy combined better living standards with wider ideological freedom.

**5 The Warsaw Pact troops** who invaded Czechoslovakia in August 1968 met with no military resistance. However, the many spontaneous acts of obstruction such as raising roadblocks and setting fire to Soviet tanks were humiliating for the Soviet leaders who claimed that the intervention had been requested by Czechoslovak leaders. But supporters of the invasion were, in reality, few and had little encouragement.

**6 Communism went on show** in 1973 with the World Festival of Youth and Students, the largest propaganda rally since 1945. Held in East Berlin, it was a spectacular expression of East Germany's sense of achievement in the year of her worldwide recognition. However, despite the evidence of such displays, youth in Eastern Europe is also interested in Western culture and ideas and often dubious of Soviet bloc ideology and politics.

**7 The Berlin Wall** was built on 13 August 1961 to stop the continual exodus of large numbers of East Germans to the West. Between 1949, when Germany was divided, and 1961, more than 2,700,000 people escaped into West Berlin. Many East Germans still attempt to reach the West despite the dangers. However, this may change; East Germany now has higher living standards than any other communist nation and is the world's seventh largest industrial power.

# China: the People's Republic

The Chinese People's Republic was established on 1 October 1949 [Key] by a mandate from a constituent assembly convened under the aegis of the Chinese Communist Party (CCP). The immediate task of the new government was to rehabilitate the war-ravaged economy inherited from Chiang Kai-shek's Nationalist administration after its forced withdrawal to the offshore province of Taiwan. A gradualist policy was adopted, characterized by the creation of a coalition of the various elements in Chinese society and the avoidance of violent class struggle. The communists did not baulk at suppressing their most intractable class enemies, but they were preoccupied with carrying out measures to ensure economic survival.

## Major reforms of the 1950s

Mass support gave the new government the authority to take steps to conquer hyperinflation [1]. Land reform affecting over 80 per cent of the population was completed by early 1953. As a result the government gained control over surplus agricultural production; it also won the peasant backing it needed to weaken social institutions based on a kinship system dominated by elders [2]. This made it easier to set up new communist institutions in place of the old system. Another major reform was the implementation of the 1950 Marriage Law which greatly improved the status of women.

From 1953–7 China underwent a transition to socialism as commerce and industry were nationalized and agricultural institutions transformed. These changes were not accomplished without dissent but, as a 1957 rectification campaign showed, the power of the enlarged party machine considerably exceeded that of its critics. Meanwhile in foreign affairs China was aligned with the USSR, whose aid was crucial to industrialization during the first five-year plan (1953–7) and bitterly opposed to the United States, her major adversary in the Korean War (1950–53), proponent of the policy of "containment" and supporter of Taiwan.

Hoping to expand production rapidly by amalgamating collective farms into communes [3] and by adopting a backyard approach to industrialization [4], China began the Great Leap Forward in 1958 marking the implementation of a Chinese strategy of economic development and the rejection of the Soviet strategy employed in the preceding five years. As a result, an ideological dispute between China and the USSR gathered momentum, leading to a withdrawal of Soviet technicians and their blueprints in 1960. In the event the Great Leap Forward failed, owing to dissent, bad weather and an underestimation of the problems [5]. The outcome was an economic crisis and a forced retreat from Maoist principles.

## The Cultural Revolution

The retreat was only temporary. Once economic recovery had been achieved in 1963 Mao Tse-tung (1893–1976), who had given up his post as head of state in 1959 to be replaced by Liu Shao-chi (1898–1974), resumed his efforts to realize socialism in China [6]. By now the ideological split between the USSR and China was being reflected within the CCP and the specifically Maoist attempts at running the economy had been openly criticized. Mao Tse-tung coun-

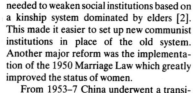

1 Queues outside banks in 1948 marked a collapse of confidence in China's currency and in the ability of the Nationalists to manage the economy. Inflation set off by the irresponsible issue of bank-notes was a problem during the Japanese war and it accelerated between 1945 and 1948 when the Shanghai price index rose 135,742 times, causing a hyperinflation. This the communist government inherited.

2 Burning of land title deeds and the public condemnation of landlords were common during the nationwide land reform campaign conducted by the Chinese government between mid-1950 and early 1953. The political and social impact of this campaign was as important as its economic effect. Socially, the destruction of the old system was underlined by the public humiliation of landlords and the venting of grievances by peasants led by communist cadres. Politically, the richer classes were isolated; economically, land redistribution among 300 million peasants stimulated their willingness to increase production.

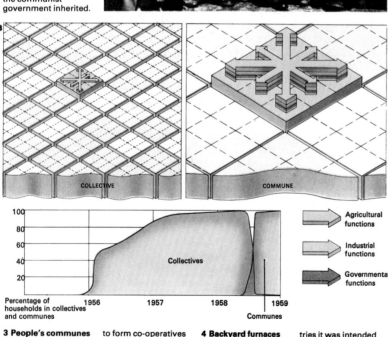

COLLECTIVE

COMMUNE

100
80
60
40
20

Collectives

1956    1957    1958    1959

Agricultural functions

Industrial functions

Governmental functions

Percentage of households in collectives and communes

Communes

3 People's communes were introduced in the summer of 1958. This was to be the culmination of the socialist transformation of agriculture. In 1953–4 peasant households had been organized into mutual aid teams. In 1955 these merged to form co-operatives which, in turn, were merged into collectives in 1956–7. About eight times larger than the collectives, communes were also units of government co-ordinating planning in agriculture, industry, defence and education.

4 Backyard furnaces and foundries epitomized the Great Leap Forward, a drive launched in February 1958 to accelerate expansion of the Chinese economy. By mobilizing underemployed rural labour in small, labour-intensive industries it was intended to complement the production of urban-based, capital-intensive industries at little extra cost to investment funds. Called "walking on two legs", this strategy of economic development was widely promoted.

tered by launching a campaign to reverse a deteriorating ideological situation and a weakening in his personal influence. The campaign, the Cultural Revolution, aimed on the one hand at purging the CCP and on the other at ridding China of aspects of traditional culture incompatible with socialism. Party members were ousted and the state structure usurped by revolutionary committees in circumstances that sometimes led to violence. The key to Mao Tse-tung's success was his ability to mobilize support, especially from the young people, [7], coupled with the loyalty of the armed forces.

During the Cultural Revolution Mao Tsetung presided over the rebuilding of the CCP and the mass organizations, a restoration of the state system, a restructuring of the education system and a reassessment of Chinese culture. The spilling over of the excesses of the Cultural Revolution into foreign affairs damaged China's international position for a while. Some 45 divisions of Soviet forces were deployed along the frontier, giving rise to armed clashes in 1969 [8]. China's foreign relations now became marked by alignment with the Third World, friendship with the medium-sized developed countries, trade and diplomacy with Japan and the USA and continuing confrontation with the USSR.

## Admission to the United Nations

The success of China's new foreign policy was characterized by her admission to UN membership in 1971 and by a visit by the American president, Richard Nixon (1913– ), in 1972 [9]. The eclipse of Lin Piao (1907–71), the defence minister and Mao's heir apparent, who was reported killed during a flight to the USSR in 1971, suggests that an accommodation with capitalism at the expense of a reconciliation with the Soviet bloc was not unanimously approved. Nevertheless, China moved to the Fourth National People's Congress in January 1975 (the first for a decade), a new constitution and, for the first time since 1966, a fully manned state structure. Mao died in 1976 and was succeeded by Hua Kuo-feng. In the disturbances that followed, Mao's widow and some other prominent politicians were arrested and accused of treason.

**Mao Tse-tung,** as Chairman of the Chinese Communist Party and chairman elect of the government, stood in Tien An Men Square in Peking to proclaim the establishment of the People's Republic of China on 1 October 1949.

**5 During the Great Leap Forward** agricultural and industrial output dropped. Inadequate planning and accounting led to miscalculation of potential yields and failure to meet the targets set. Lack of experience and disorganization meant that many communes were ill-equipped and badly run. The worst weather for a century in 1959–60 led to economic crisis and the policies of the Great Leap Forward were shelved.

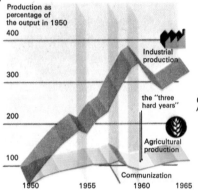

5
Production as percentage of the output in 1950

400 — Industrial production

300

the "three hard years"

200 — Agricultural production

100 — Communization

1950   1955   1960   1965

**6 Exemplary production units** singled out by Mao Tse-tung in 1964 were the Tachai agricultural brigade in Hsiyang county, Shansi province, and the Taching oilfield in Heilungkiang province. In Tachai [A] peasants transformed a poor environment and increased grain output without state aid or material incentives. In Taching [B] workers created a prototype agro-industrial community developed without foreign aid by reliance on their own technological innovations. Both show the importance attached to self-reliance, hard work and persistence in Chinese economic development after 1960. Then, as a result of frequent ideological differences, the Soviet Union withdrew her many technicians and cancelled all her aid programmes to the Chinese People's Republic.

6
A

B

**7 The Little Red Book** of quotations from Mao Tse-tung became the "bible" of the Cultural Revolution of 1966–8. It was studied on a nationwide basis as a pocket guide for action in any set of circumstances. But it was put to most use in the hands of young people, particularly Red Guards recruited from middle schools, universities and factories. As "successors to the revolution", they formed a main force in the campaign by Mao Tse-tung and his supporters against Liu Shao-ch'i, then head of state, and aspects of traditional culture standing in the way of Maoist policies.

**8 Border clashes** between Chinese and Soviet forces on the Ussuri River frontier in Heilungkiang in March 1969 showed the extent to which Sino-Soviet relations had deteriorated in the course of the ideological disputes of the late 1950s. After the worst fighting over Chenpao or Damansky island, China claimed that the Soviet Union had provoked 4,189 incidents.

7

8
👤 10 military divisions

※ Border incidents in 1969

USSR
• Novosibirsk
Chenpao
HEILUNGKIANG
Vladivostok
MONGOLIA
Peking •
KOREA
CHINA

9

**9 The visit of Richard Nixon,** the US president, in 1972 marked a new era in China's foreign relations. Less hostile Sino-US attitudes had indirectly contributed to the admission of the People's Republic of China to the UN in 1971. It also led to better relations between China and Japan and increasing diplomatic isolation of the Nationalist government of Chiang Kai-shek in Taiwan.

121

# Decolonization

Decolonization has been one of the greatest transforming processes in the world since 1945. A new word in the political vocabulary, it has achieved widespread usage and currency only since the middle 1950s as far-flung colonies have gradually achieved independence from their rulers.

## Processes of decolonization

The term decolonization covers a wide range of processes by which power is transferred from the departing colonial authority to the newly independent nation. To date, transfer has usually been peaceful and by agreement – for example from Britain to Ceylon (now called Sri Lanka) in 1948, Ghana in 1957 and Jamaica in 1962. In a few but important instances, strife has been an integral part of the process of decolonization but was not directly connected with the issue of independence – the Mau Mau emergency in Kenya, the *enosis* dispute in Cyprus, and British confrontation with Indonesia over the creation of the Malaysian Federation. In some of the best-known examples of decolonization, independence has been wrung by force from

a reluctant colonial power – from The Netherlands in Indonesia in 1949, and from France in North Vietnam in 1954 and in Algeria in 1962 [6]. In the Congo in 1960, the Belgians granted independence to a territory that was wholly unprepared for it, and bloody chaos ensued [5]. But there can be two-way effects of decolonization – as in Portugal in 1974 when internal dissent and colonial unrest resulted in a revolution that hastened the independence of its colonies in 1975.

The process of decolonization, and the consequent emergence of new states, has resulted in major changes to the political map of the world [1]. In 1914 there were only eight sovereign states in the whole of Asia and Africa, and of these only Japan was regarded as a power of real account in world affairs; almost everywhere else throughout those continents the rule of dominating influence of the West Europeans, the Russians or the Americans prevailed. Only since World War II has the great retreat from and dismantling of the overseas empires of the West Europeans come about, first in Asia in the late 1940s, and then only slightly in North

Africa in the early 1950s. After that, decolonization gathered pace, was in full flood between 1955 and 1965 [3], and eventually reached the Pacific and parts of the world that were once remote.

## The quickening pace

Most of the principal overseas empires of the West European powers were already dissolving when the fifteenth session of the UN General Assembly began in September 1960 and an Anti-Colonialist Charter drawn up by 43 African and Asian countries was adopted without dissent. The British Empire was moving into a state of more or less voluntary liquidation: India [Key], Pakistan, Burma, Ceylon, Ghana, Malaya, Cyprus and Nigeria [4] had become independent. "Empire-into-Commonwealth" was an accomplished but continuing fact, although the wider problem of the role of the white man remained unresolved in the apartheid regime of South Africa and in Rhodesia. In his forthright "wind of change" speech to the South African Parliament in February 1960, the British prime minister, Harold

**1 In 1926** there were more than 80 separate colonies and dependencies [A]. These comprised over 33% of the population and land area of the world. Seven West European countries (Britain, France, The Netherlands, Belgium, Portugal, Spain and Italy), whose total home population was about 200 million, controlled about 700 million people in overseas colonies. The British and French empires were by far the largest. Most of the new states of the post-1945 world [B] have come from these two empires. While the British Empire was truly worldwide, the French was predominantly in Africa and Indochina.

**2 The election of U Thant** of Burma as UN Secretary-General, after the death of Dag Hammarskjöld in the Congo in 1961, symbolized the growing number of voices and votes of new and non-aligned states in UN affairs, especially of Asian and African members. UN membership is valued by all newly independent states as an important symbol of their status.

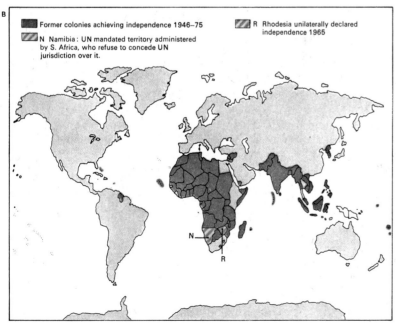

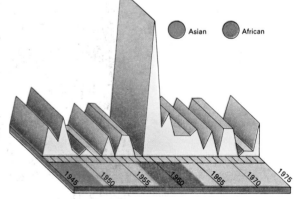

**3 Decolonization had three main phases.** First, from 1944 to 1949, it occurred in the southern flanks of Asia – Lebanon, Syria and Israel; then India, Pakistan, Burma, Ceylon; and the Philippines and Indonesia. From 1950 to 1956 little decolonization took place. Libya, Morocco and Tunisia became independent peaceably, and Algerians began the war for independence that ended in 1961. From 1956 to 1963 African decolonization got rapidly under way, with the Sudan in 1956, Ghana in 1957 and Guinea in 1958. In 1960 all of the French African colonies became independent, plus Nigeria and Belgian Congo.

Macmillan (1894– ), had rightly predicted that the rate of decolonization was quickening. In the same year France's colonial presence was to shrink considerably in Africa and soon to disappear completely. So, too, was that of Belgium from the Congo. Of the West European powers, only Portugal continued to insist that its mission in its territories overseas was permanent, although the revolution of 1974 brought a sudden change of attitude.

### Adjustment after decolonization

The whole period of decolonization, now virtually over, has created acute problems of adjustment for both former rulers and ruled. Some ex-imperial powers – notably Britain – have found the transition to lesser power status and a lower world standing acutely uncomfortable. Only since her decision to stay in the EEC, and with the Commonwealth discussions on world economic issues in June 1975, has Britain begun to find a new role as intermediary and honest broker between rich and poor, developed and developing countries. Most other colonial powers have domestic difficulties over decolonization.

The new states themselves have had to evolve political systems appropriate to their new situation and not necessarily those bequeathed by the outgoing authority [7]. Thus the abandonment of parliamentary constitutions in favour of one-party systems; the rejection of Russo-American models of development through industrialization in favour of the Chinese model of concentration on agriculture and self-sufficiency; and the adoption of a foreign policy independent of the decolonizing power can all be seen as a continuing the process of decolonization.

But if colonialism is almost dead "neo-colonialism" is alive. The United States, historically the greatest advocate of anti-colonialism, is also the country most often charged with "neo-colonialism". It may take the form of economic control through multi-national corporations, military influence through arms aid and advisers, or even political "destabilization" as practised against the Marxist regime of President Allende in Chile. The Soviet Union is accused in similar terms, chiefly by China.

**KEY**

**The inauguration of Earl Mountbatten** as Viceroy of India in 1947 prefaced her independence from Britain later in the same year. This event symbolized the advent of the age of decolonization, carried out with a formal transfer of power.

**4 Nigeria achieved independence** peaceably from Britain in 1960. Power was handed over to a working federal parliament and government. But six years later, Nigeria suffered two military coups in one year and a bloody, but unsuccessful, attempt to create a new secessionist state of Biafra.

**5 The Belgians' abrupt departure** in 1960 from the Congo (now called Zaïre) led to bitter civil war, much bloodshed and to the attempted, but ultimately unsuccessful, secession of the copper-rich province of Katanga. The introduction of a UN peace-keeping force caused great controversy.

**6 Algeria is one of the few countries** since 1945 to have won independence by means of a successful war against France. This lasted from 1954 until 1962. De Gaulle, who had returned to power backed by the slogan "Algérie Française", conceded independence in July 1962. Algeria then began to play an active part in Arab League affairs and later on, as an oil-producing country with limited reserves, within OPEC. A number of important Afro-Asian and non-aligned conferences have been held in Algiers, especially the short-lived Afro-Asian meeting of October 1965 and the 1973 summit.

**7 Most independence day ceremonies** for the newly independent states may at first seem to involve only changes of personnel, who in style and outlook often resemble their predecessors. They may even wear wigs and carry maces. But parliaments, British or French style, are not always resilient institutions and often give way to military rule. For most of these new-state societies their sense of community goes deeper than their constitutionalism. Almost all Third World societies are pluralistic, with deep economic and racial differences which stand in the way of political stability and sustained economic progress.

# Australia since 1918

Australia lost nearly 60,000 men killed during World War I. This gave authority to its representation at the Paris Peace Conference, where the prime minister, William Morris Hughes (1862–1952) [1], successfully defended the "White Australia" policy (a government policy that restricted the entry of non-Europeans into the country) and obtained for Australia a "C" class League of Nations mandate over the former German colony in northeastern New Guinea. The territory became a United Nations trusteeship after World War II, was administered jointly with Australia's colony of Papua, and both became independent as the joint state of Papua New Guinea in 1975.

## Economic and political changes

Manufacturing industry in Australia, stimulated by World War I, received continuing protection through tariffs supported by a trade union movement that was growing in strength, ideology and militancy. But tariffs did not help the farmers. In 1922, the new Australian Country Party (whose basic policy is aimed at increasing the effectiveness of primary industries) won enough seats to depose Hughes and join the Nationalists in government. With two short exceptions, such coalitions with the Nationalists — later renamed (with a Labor rump) the United Australia Party, and later again the Liberal Party — have held office for 30 of the 44 years to 1977. Labor (which is committed to "democratic socialization of industry, production, distribution and exchange") came into office for one three-year term during the economic depression [2] and not again until 1941.

The wage-price spiral of the 1920s restricted the opportunities for industrial exports [3], so that the economy continued to be dependent on rural exports vulnerable to world price fluctuations. Government appeals to Britain for "men, money and markets" were partly satisfied by migrant settlers [4], preferred access to the London capital market and imperial trade preferences that were rationalized at a conference in Ottawa in 1932.

At the 1926 Imperial Conference, the British dominions, including Australia, were declared to be a state of equal status with Britain, and this was formalized in the Statute of Westminster, 1931.

## Foreign policy expedients

Since early in the century, Australians and their governments had feared attack or absorption by an Asian power, especially Japan. Allied to Britain from 1902 until 1921, Japan had been a helpful if slightly ambiguous partner during World War I. Its expansion into Manchuria in 1931 fed Australian fears. But Japan had also become a major new export market for Australia [9], which thus encouraged rather than opposed Japan's aggression.

Australia's attitudes to foreign affairs during the 1930s tended to copy those of Britain: sanctions against, then appeasement of, Italy; eyes averted from Japanese aggression in China; and appeasement of Germany until 1939.

Australia entered the war against Germany one-and-a-quarter hours after Britain, and sent forces to the Middle East, Greece, the United Kingdom and South-East Asia.

1 W. M. ("Billy") Hughes was born in London, but went to Australia at the age of 20. He became involved in union politics and served as prime minister from 1915 to 1923 as leader of a Nationalist Government. He was a notable wartime leader and an astringent and turbulent politician, but failed to win support for his policy of conscription for war service overseas. He was expelled from the Labor Party and founded the United Australia Party.

2 The world depression of 1929–33 seriously affected Australia, whose economy was almost entirely dependent on exports of primary products, and on British loans for industrial development. The Labor Government had to accept the orthodox economies of the day, such as wage restraint, public spending cuts and high unemployment. The economy did not recover fully until the late 1930s. This linocut was produced in 1933 by the group of Workers' Artists.

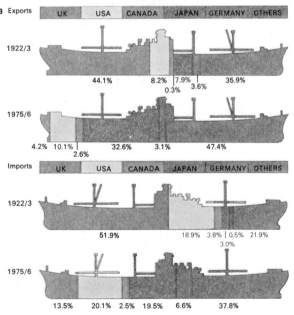

3 Exports

| | UK | USA | CANADA | JAPAN | GERMANY | OTHERS |
|---|---|---|---|---|---|---|

1922/3: 44.1% — 8.2% — 0.3% — 7.9% — 3.6% — 35.9%

1975/6: 4.2% — 10.1% — 2.6% — 32.6% — 3.1% — 47.4%

Imports

| | UK | USA | CANADA | JAPAN | GERMANY | OTHERS |
|---|---|---|---|---|---|---|

1922/3: 51.9% — 18.9% — 3.8% — 3.0% — 0.5% — 21.9%

1975/6: 13.5% — 20.1% — 2.5% — 19.5% — 6.6% — 37.8%

3 The traditional pattern of Australian trade, based on the export of wool, wheat, meat and minerals, and the import of consumer durables and industrial goods, began to change in the 1940s. There was also a shift away from the old markets and in particular from Britain, which had dominated trade earlier in the century. The main new markets were in Asia, and especially Japan, which in 1966 became Australia's largest customer. Britain's entry into the EEC in 1973 seriously affected the Australian export industries, especially that of dried and canned fruits, and dairy products.

4 Immigrants and their descendants make up Australia's white population. Some 80,000 British ex-servicemen and their dependants went to settle after World War I and were given assisted passages. After World War II, another scheme of assistance took refugees from most of Europe and from the Middle Eastern states. The assistance was cut in 1974. Race as a factor in immigration selection was formally dropped in 1973.

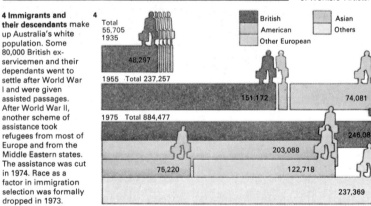

4

| British | American | Other European | Asian | Others |
|---|---|---|---|---|

Total 55,705 1935: 48,297

1955 Total 237,257: 151,172 — 74,081

1975 Total 884,477: 203,088 — 75,220 — 122,718 — 246,082 — 237,369

5 Australia's mineral resources are among the world's greatest. Although mining began in the 19th century, its expansion since World War II has been fundamental to the country's economic growth. Most of the extractive industries are concentrated in Victoria and New South Wales. Many valuable minerals are found in Australia, including gold, silver, platinum, uranium, lead and copper, as well as iron ore and coal, which is here being exploited in an open-cast mine.

Australians played an important part in helping to clear North Africa of Axis forces; in providing aircrews for the RAF in Britain and Europe; in naval actions in many theatres; and in stopping the Japanese southward thrust in New Guinea. The nation was an essential granary and major supplier for Britain and for American forces.

Industry grew rapidly during the war. So did the power of the central government, which assumed sole control over income taxation. After the war, restricted imports (for a period), a high rate of investment, and overseas demand for primary products during and after the Korean War brought boom conditions. Rising living standards continued until the early 1970s, stimulated by discoveries of massive mineral deposits [5].

### Postwar realignment

A conservative Liberal-Country parties government under Sir Robert Menzies (1894–1978) [7] was elected in late 1949, and remained in office for 23 years. During that time, Australia initiated the Colombo Plan for economic and technical co-operation in South and South-East Asia and became an ally of the United States under various security arrangements, including ANZUS (Australia, New Zealand, United States) and SEATO (South-East Asia Treaty Organization). It saw the need to encourage both Britain and the United States to remain committed to the security of South-East Asia, and sent forces to Malaya to help combat communist terrorists, and after the 1963 Indonesian "confrontation". Troops were also sent to Vietnam to fight under American command there [8].

By 1966 Japan had become Australia's most important customer, notably for minerals, the two economies becoming to a degree interdependent. The Labor Government of Gough Whitlam sought to weaken ties with the United States, and spent massively on education and a national health service. But it was hard hit by the recession of 1974, and Whitlam was removed from office in 1975. A conservative government was elected to cope with unemployment and inflation, which had begun to affect the Australian easy way of life [10].

**KEY**

**Sydney Opera House** was opened in 1973 and has come to represent the growing cultural identity of Australia in the modern age. Designed by the Danish architect Joern Utzon (1918– ) in response to a competition in 1956, its cost increased far above original estimates because of engineering problems caused by its revolutionary design. Extra money to pay for the building was raised by lotteries. The final cost was more than A$100 million.

**6 Isaac Isaacs** (1855–1948) was the first Australian-born governor-general of the country on his appointment in 1931. The governor-general has been the representative of the Crown in Australia since Federation in 1901, and he normally takes a purely nominal constitutional role in the country's politics. The office became controversial in 1975 when the incumbent John Kerr (1914–    ) dismissed the Labor prime minister Gough Whitlam (1916–    ), although he had a working majority in Parliament. In the ensuing election it was claimed that the action was undemocratic, and led to demands for the abolition of the office of governor-general. But Labor was defeated at the polls.

**7 Robert Menzies**, seen here on his appointment as Warden of the Cinque Ports in England in 1965 (the first Australian to receive that honour) was Australian prime minister for a record 18 years. His second term of office (1949–65) was a period of growing national development and prosperity coupled with limited involvement in wars in Asia. Emotionally committed to ties with Britain and the Crown, he saw the USA as Australia's ultimate protection and international communism as the main threat. He encouraged overseas investment in Australian industry, stimulated an expansion of university education and the growth of Canberra as an effective and attractive capital of the nation.

**8 Australia's defence links** with the USA prompted Menzies to respond to American and South Vietnamese appeals to help defend South Vietnam against communist insurgents and North Vietnamese attacks. A number of training advisers were sent in 1962 and 1964 and the first infantry battalion went in 1965, to be followed by two more battalions, supporting arms and services, air force and naval elements, under overall US command. The main Australian ground operations were in Phuoc Tuy province. Initially there was little opposition to the war, but as it dragged on, the issue of conscription became controversial and divided the nation.

**9 Port Hedland**, north Western Australia, is a centre for iron-ore export. In 1971, about 25 million tonnes of iron ore was exported to Japan. Many of the Australian extractive industries are financed by Japanese investment. But imports of Japanese manufactured goods are still low, and Australian investment in Japanese industry is still more substantial than the Japanese contribution to Australian industry.

**10 Australia's open spaces**, long hours of sunshine and high standard of living mean that life is healthy and often out-of-doors. The typical home is a bungalow on a quarter-acre plot of land, with a barbecue (shown here) in the back garden. Rising costs of beef and lamb may eventually limit the Australians' propensity for meat-eating, but in the late 1970s their calorie consumption was among the highest in the world. Sport, including skiing in the winter and swimming or cricket in the summer, is important to many Australians.

# New Zealand since 1918

New Zealand in 1918 was still virtually an outpost of Great Britain. Although it had been an independent, self-governing Dominion since 1907, its economy depended entirely on the British market for agricultural exports, its defence policy relied on British naval protection, and its self-awareness was European if not exclusively British in character. Half a century later the Pacific Basin had become a focus of its economic, strategic and cultural attention.

## The aftermath of World War I

The prosperity of the World War I years, when Britain bought all the wool, meat, cheese and butter that New Zealand could produce, continued for a brief period into the peace. Confident that "you couldn't go wrong farming", New Zealanders indulged in a bout of land speculation helped along by £23 million of government loans to ex-servicemen.

When export prices collapsed in 1921, so did the land boom. Many farmers, unable to meet mortgage repayments, sold out at giveaway prices; others left their farms derelict. Despite the reality of rural poverty, there was a positive outcome. The universal shortage of credit, and the unpreparedness of the government to meet the economic downturn, drove farmers to co-operate in the setting-up of marketing-boards, for meat in 1922, for dairy products in 1923.

Townsmen were even worse hit by the slump. The economy deteriorated further in the early 1930s, with the onset of worldwide depression. Unemployment became an epidemic; wages were savagely forced down, while diminished government revenue resulted in heavy cuts in public spending. Public discontent was expressed in riots in Auckland and Wellington [1].

## The economy and the Labour Party

The political consequences were no less dramatic. In the 1935 general election, the Labour Party assumed office for the first time. Elected mainly on the votes of small farmers and town workers, Labour announced, and in large measure carried through, an extensive welfare programme [2]; higher wages and shorter hours for the town worker, pensions and benefits for the old, the widowed and the disabled, and a state rental housing scheme of subsidized accommodation [3]. Farmers were guaranteed a minimum price for however much they produced.

The first Labour government held office for 14 years. On the whole they were good years for the government and the economy. The world began to emerge from the Depression after 1935, and when another downturn threatened in 1938-9, World War II boosted demand for food exports. The war also fostered the extension of government economic controls.

In 1949 Labour lost power to the more free-enterprise inclined National Party, led by Sidney Holland (1893–1961). Since then, the two parties have alternated in office. National, led by Holland, Keith Holyoake (1904– ), John Marshall (1912– ), and Robert Muldoon (1921– ), have held office in 1949–57, 1960–72, and since 1975. Labour, under Walter Nash (1882–1968), Norman Kirk (1923–74) and Wallace Rowling (1927– ) have been in

**1 The army and navy** had to be called in when violence broke out in New Zealand cities during 1932, the low point of the Depression. Registered unemployment was 80,000 in a population of 1,500,000.

**2 Labour's social security system**, set up in 1938, included a medical and hospital service. All were guaranteed treatment, irrespective of ability to pay. The local branch of the British Medical Association objected to the scheme and *New Zealand Herald* cartoonist Minhinnick made this comment on Labour's answer. Principals are Prime Minister Michael Savage and Minister of Finance Walter Nash.

**3 Since March 1937,** when the state housing scheme came into effect, New Zealand has built more than 77,000 state houses or flats, to standards shown by these, which were built in 1938 in Wellington. The houses are allocated on a basis of need, formerly measured by income but since 1973 by a more complicated points system. The state also offers low-cost mortgages to young couples.

**4 A "friendly invasion"** by the United States Marines occurred after the long-standing New Zealand nightmare of a Japanese invasion seemed about to be realized in 1941. With the New Zealand Division serving in North Africa, only a handful of badly equipped reservists were available to repel an invasion. But the Battle of the Coral Sea on 7-8 May 1942 stopped the Japanese advance. The Americans, some of whom are seen here with a Maori girl at Rotorua, North Island, retained training camps in New Zealand until the end of 1944.

power in 1957–60, and 1972–5. Both parties are committed to full employment, high state spending and export promotion. Both recognize that welfare services are becoming increasingly expensive and difficult to finance out of general revenue. Both are aware of the social problems brought to inner city areas by an increasing Maori population, and by the immigration of Pacific Islanders. For both, the dominant economic problems have been to encourage local industry without over-protecting it, and to restrain the country's propensity to spend more on imports than it makes from the agricultural products that earn more than 80 per cent of its export income.

### Fewer ties with Britain
World War II also brought home the lesson that New Zealand's defence could no longer be based on British protection. In 1939 as in 1914, New Zealand prepared for a faraway war. A division was sent to the Middle East, naval and air force units and men were dispatched to Europe. The home economy was dominated by the "Food for Britain" slogan.

But the entry of Japan in 1941 posed a threat to the homeland. As the Japanese advanced southwards, New Zealand had to rely entirely on the power of the United States [4]. In 1951 New Zealand joined ANZUS, the defensive alliance with Australia and the United States. It sent small forces to Korea in 1950 and to support the Americans and Australians in Vietnam in 1965.

Pacific interest and commitment has been a continuing feature of the postwar period. In the early 1950s New Zealand started to co-operate with the Colombo Plan in supplying various forms of aid, chiefly agricultural, to South Asia. New Zealand troops served in the Malayan emergency of the 1950s and co-operation with Malaysia and Singapore continues through the Five Power Defence Arrangements (1971).

Since Britain entered the EEC in 1973 the need to diversify both markets and products has been starkly apparent. By 1976, although Britain was still New Zealand's largest single customer, almost half the trade was with the Pacific Basin, and the proportion was increasing [6,7].

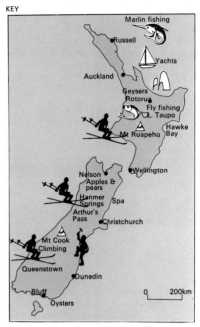

KEY

**New Zealand's tourist attractions**, some of which are shown here, often have a dual economic value. Thermal regions, for example, not only attract tourists but also power geothermal electricity stations; total fish exports totalled more than $19 million in 1974; and even deer, culled as a pest and for sport, contribute to overseas income – venison worth nearly $7 million was exported in 1974. En route to becoming one of the world's main primary producers, as well as a Pacific playground, New Zealand followed a path similar in some respects to that of the United States in its frontier stage. But isolation and a small population have strongly influenced its development.

**5 Rugby** (here the Maori All Blacks play the Lions in 1950) has been called the religion of New Zealand. The All Blacks who toured Britain in 1905 lost only one game to Wales. New Zealanders still dispute the deciding try.

**6 Kinleith pulp and paper mill** produces 200 million tonnes of paper and 130 million tonnes of pulp each year. It is one of six such plants. Japan is the largest customer, taking almost half the output.

**7 New Zealand milk powder unloaded in Brazil** exemplifies the useful outlet that Latin America has become in recent years for dairy products and some meat. Intensive efforts by New Zealand to find new export markets such as these began even before Britain joined the EEC in 1973. Of NZ's 1967-8 dairy exports (476,000 tonnes), 301,500 went to the UK. In 1975-6 the totals were 458,000 and 149,000.

**8 Air New Zealand,** a development of Tasman Empire Airways Ltd, flies DC-10 aircraft on profitable routes to Los Angeles, Hong Kong and Singapore, but a third of its annual 3 million passenger kilometres (nearly 2 million passenger miles) is still flown across the Tasman Sea. The 1,200-mile flight is made by tourists, businessmen and migrant workers.

**9 Kiri Te Kanawa** (1948—  ) is, with Inia Te Wiata (1915–71) and Donald McIntyre (1934—  ), one of several New Zealand opera singers who have acquired an international reputation since the war. She is under contract to the Royal Opera House and has sung at the Paris Opera and the Metropolitan Opera, New York.

# Southern Africa since 1910

When World War I broke out in 1914 Rhodesian police immediately occupied the Caprivi Strip in German South West Africa and Union forces immediately destroyed German coastal wireless stations. A pro-German rebellion in Transvaal was speedily crushed. On 9 July 1915 German South West Africa surrendered to Louis Botha (1862–1919). On 4 September 1916 Jan Christiaan Smuts (1870–1950) [3] took Dar es Salaam and most of German East Africa, operations which ended only in 1918.

## Wealth and prosperity

In 1918 the Union of South Africa was the lodestone for all southern Africa, importing labour even from Mozambique. In gold [5] and diamonds [2] it had a wealth unique in Africa, and an era of prosperity seemed ahead. The collapse of the postwar boom impoverished White urban workers and Afrikaner farmers, and in 1924 brought to power a coalition of Nationalists and the Labour Party. In 1923 Rhodesian settlers obtained self-government, following a referendum in the previous year rejecting

union with South Africa. In general a new African élite was emerging, teachers, preachers, clerks, some traders and some farmers. In the Union of South Africa the African National Congress was founded in 1913, with parallel organizations in Southern Rhodesia in 1934, Nyasaland in 1943, and Northern Rhodesia in 1949. The pass laws restricting the free movement of Africans and refusal to recognize their trade unions were bitterly felt African grievances.

Smuts, prime minister of South Africa 1919–24 and 1939–48, played a major role in World War II on the side of the Allies, thereby losing the support of the neutrals within South Africa. The French African territories were promised independence in 1944, and the independence of Burma, Ceylon, India and Pakistan taught their own lesson. Following Smuts's defeat at the polls in 1948, government attitudes towards race became more aggressive. The word apartheid, coined in 1929 to express separate white and African development, now took on a new meaning with the installation of Daniel Malan (1874–1959) as prime minister

(1948–54) and leader of the Nationalist Party, which has remained in power since 1948. "Race" meant Afrikaner dominance, and the expansion of the economy after 1948 gave apartheid a specious seal of success. White South Africans enjoyed one of the highest standards of living in the world but the average monthly wage for a White was thirteen times that for a Black.

## International tensions and UDI

In 1953 a Federation of Central Africa – Northern and Southern Rhodesia and Nyasaland – was brought into being by Britain in spite of considerable African opposition. That opposition brought the Federation to an end in 1963. Meanwhile the Union, under Hendrik Verwoerd (1901–66) as minister for native affairs, and then prime minister 1958–66, sought a solution to African antagonism by creating Bantustans, where Africans could eventually develop autonomous African states. At Cape Town on 3 February 1960 the British prime minister Harold MacMillan (1894– ) made his "wind of change" speech, in

1 **The fibre-producing sisal plant** was originally a native of South America, but was smuggled into German East Africa in 1891. Only 41 plants survived the journey and from these all the sisal plantations of eastern and southern Africa, an important export crop, descend.

2 **Diamonds** were first discovered in South Africa near the Orange River in 1867, but these workings were soon surpassed in wealth by the dry diggings at Kimberley – the Great Hole – In 1871. The mines in South Africa and Namibia (shown here) are the wealthiest in the world, with an annual output of more than £60 million in value.

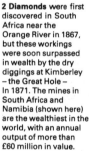

3 **Jan Christiaan Smuts** is one of the major political figures in the history of South Africa. He helped to formulate the 1910 constitution and was prime minister twice. He played leading roles in the League of Nations and the United Nations.

4 **Fort Hare University** was the first college to be opened to non-Whites (in 1916), and in 1969 it was restricted to members of the Xhosa tribe only. Other similar universities are those of Zululand, for Zulus only, the North, for Tsonga, Sotho and

Venda only, one for Coloureds in Cape Town, and one for Indians in Durban. In addition South Africa has nine universities for Whites only. In 1972, 2.1 per cent of the White population and 0.2 per cent of the non-Whites managed to achieve university education.

5 **Gold is the basis of South Africa's wealth.** The precious metal was mined in Rhodesia from earliest times and its discovery at Witwatersrand in 1886 produced one of the world's great gold rushes. That goldfield, located in the Transvaal province of South

Africa, is still the world's richest. By 1910, gold amounted to 59% of South Africa's exports. It has attracted enormous foreign investments and has encouraged the development of the railways as well as a number of manufacturing industries.

which he condemned apartheid and demanded that legitimate African aspirations to be recognized. On 21 March the Pan-African Congress demonstrated at Sharpeville, and a massacre ensued [7]

On 31 May 1961 the Republic of South Africa came into being, having withdrawn from the British Commonwealth. The Republic was also expelled from many international organizations that found South African presence distasteful. Despite strenuous diplomatic efforts, South Africa remained almost friendless: racial discrimination, police brutality, imprisonment without trial – all brought their consequences. In 1964 Northern Rhodesia and Nyasaland became independent as Zambia [6] and Malawi, while the white government in Rhodesia (formerly Southern Rhodesia) moved away from its previous attempts to provide for limited African political involvement. On 11 November 1965, having been refused independence without majority rule by Britain, Rhodesian prime minister Ian Smith (1919–    ) unilaterally declared independence (UDI). Britain declined to use force but joined with United Nations in sanctions [8], which have largely been evaded by South African aid. In the early 1970s guerrilla operations, at first scattered, escalated and posed a serious threat to the white regime. Britain continued to make efforts to conciliate the parties.

## Developments among the smaller states

Britain gave independence to Basutoland and Bechuanaland as Lesotho and Botswana in 1966, and to Swaziland in 1968. Both Lesotho and Swaziland are heavily dependent upon the Republic. In 1976 the Republic purported to grant independence to Transkei, but under conditions such that no other country accorded it sovereign recognition. In 1967 the UN General Assembly had declared the continuation of the South African mandate over South West Africa unlawful, and had appointed an administrative council for it as Namibia. This action was ignored by the Republic, which gave it a parliament elected on a slender franchise together with the promise of independence at the end of 1977.

The Houses of Parliament, Cape Town, are the legislative centre of South Africa; the administrative capital is Pretoria. Cape Colony first enjoyed self-government under the constitution of 1872; this was superseded by the British South Africa Act, 1909, which established the Union of South Africa in 1910. The policy of apartheid made important changes to the constitution. Originally there was no restriction of race or colour for voters, but in 1956 the clauses of the South Africa Act protecting Coloured voters were abrogated and parliament has since been elected by Whites only.

6 Kenneth Kaunda (1924–    ), president of Zambia since that country's independence in 1964, was originally a schoolmaster. He became a district secretary of the African National Congress in 1950 and was twice gaoled for his political activities. Later he became prime minister of Northern Rhodesia. His book, *Humanism in Zambia and its Implementation* (1967), explains the theoretical and practical aspects of his moderate socialist policy.

7 The Sharpeville massacre, in March 1960, happened when the police opened fire on a demonstration against the discriminatory laws passed by the government, killing 67 and wounding 186 African demonstrators. The racial policies of the Afrikaner Nationalist Party, in power since 1948, stimulated African unrest. From 1952 onwards the African National Congress organized agitation against the legislation aimed at non-Whites.

8 Escorted convoys between Rhodesia and South Africa were organized because of guerrilla attacks by African nationalists, whose operations by 1976 were seriously threatening the security of the white regime in Rhodesia. Apart from being Rhodesia's only land link for trade, South Africa has played an important role in supporting the white regime while seeking a majority Rhodesian government with which it could co-operate.

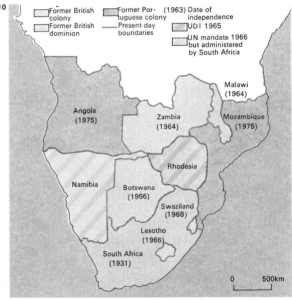

KEY

Former British colony
Former British dominion
Former Portuguese colony
Present-day boundaries
(1963) Date of independence
UDI 1965
UN mandate 1966 but administered by South Africa

Malawi (1964)
Angola (1975)
Zambia (1964)
Mozambique (1975)
Rhodesia
Namibia
Botswana (1966)
Swaziland (1968)
Lesotho (1966)
South Africa (1931)

0    500km

9 Rioting erupted in June 1976 at Soweto, a black township on the outskirts of Johannesburg, when thousands of black youths protested against teaching in Afrikaans as well as English in Bantu schools. Savagely repressed with 176 killed and 1,222 wounded, the unrest spread into an unprecedented wave of defiance that forced some reforms in townships and the rescinding of the language order. The riots showed a new African militancy.

10 Although most countries achieved independence peacefully in southern Africa, there remain a number of points of conflict within the current political map. In Rhodesia (Zimbabwe) UDI was only a culmination of the growing disagreements with Britain's resolve to transfer power to a majority government. Since then a number of diplomatic moves have failed and the conflict is increasingly moving towards the battlefield. South Africa claimed to have made Transkei independent in 1976, but this has not received international recognition. Guerrilla warfare is also being waged in South West Africa (Namibia) where the UN's decision to end South Africa's mandate, in 1966, was disregarded, although independence has been promised for 1977.

129

# Non-alignment and the Third World

In Europe, Asia and North Africa in the early 1950s, the term "neutralist" was applied to countries that were outside the alliance systems of the Great Powers and wished to remain dissociated from the cold war struggle between the United States and the Soviet Union. Leaders such as Jawaharlal Nehru (1889–1964) of India, Gamal Abdel Nasser (1918–70) of Egypt and Josip Broz Tito (1892–  ) of Yugoslavia [Key] denied the need to enter alliances, to acquire nuclear weapons [3] or to allow foreign military bases to be set up in their respective countries.

## Motives for non-alignment

A neutralist stance had been adopted by the United States itself during the nineteenth century. But the violation of the neutrality of several European countries in two world wars and the global scope of the power struggle that began after World War II led to a belief, particularly in the United States [5], that neutralism was a wishful attitude which failed to recognize that effective protection against "international communism" could be obtained only within the shelter of an alliance

of the "Free World". However, for leaders of the militarily weak new nations of Africa and Asia a neutralist stance had three compelling advantages. It allowed them to assert an independence that would have been compromised by their military dependence on one of the Great Powers. It enabled them, by skilful diplomacy, to draw on aid from both the Western and Soviet blocs. And it gave them an opportunity to attempt objective moral leadership at a time when both power blocs were taking up rigid attitudes.

The neutralist, or "non-aligned" nations as they more accurately called themselves, emerged as a coherent force in world politics with the organization of the Bandung Conference in April 1955 in Indonesia, a country that played a leading role in the movement against colonialism [2]. The conference was dominated by Premier Chou En-lai (1898–1976) of China whose moderate attitudes at the conference did much to diminish Asian tensions. Further conferences were held in Belgrade in September 1961 [4]; Cairo, October 1964; Lusaka, September 1970; and Algiers, September 1973 [9]. The

conferences steadily increased in the numbers of those attending and in importance.

The political label "Afro-Asian bloc" first gained general currency at Bandung. The more current term "Third World" or *Le Tiers Monde* [1], was coined in France in the mid-1950s to denote decolonized areas that wished to avoid conscription into American alliances or overseas base agreements. (They were collectively designated by some American strategists, including the later United States Secretary of State Henry Kissinger [1923–  ], as "the grey areas".) The voting power of this bloc at the United Nations made it a force that none of the Great Powers could afford to ignore.

## Developments in the 1960s

Events of the later 1950s and 1960s led to significant shifts in the over-simplified tripartite division of the world into communist, Western and non-aligned blocs. The credibility of India's neutralist stance was reduced by her call for Western aid during her clash with China in 1962. Egypt became heavily dependent on Soviet military aid after the

**1 Membership of the Third World** has grown with the spread of decolonization and now includes substantial parts of Latin America. China's leaders also claim membership. "Third World" is a general political label applied to newly independent, ex-colonial, poor or developing nations and peoples.

80 members
56 members
47 members
25 members

1961 Belgrade   1964 Cairo   1970 Lusaka   1973 Algiers
Attendance of Third World countries at Non-Aligned conferences

**2 Demonstrations in Indonesia** in the early 1960s against the establishment of Malaysia marked a phase of intense anti-colonialism under the feverish leadership of Achmad Sukarno (1901–70), who took Indonesia out of the UN in 1965 and proposed a rival organization of New Emerging Forces.

**3 The mushroom cloud** of China's first nuclear explosion in October 1964 while the Cairo non-aligned summit was meeting also marked the first entry to the "nuclear club" of a member of the Afro-Asian bloc. Nuclear testing, the spread of nuclear weapons and the possibility of nuclear blackmail by the Great Powers have been central and recurrent worries of non-aligned nations.

**4 The first large meeting** of the non-aligned nations at Belgrade in September 1961 drew representatives from 25 countries. Earlier, a number of smaller meetings had been called between Tito, Nehru, Nasser and some other leaders. Non-aligned nations had also conferred in some larger forums, in particular at the UN General Assembly late in 1960. The 1961 conference and subsequent meetings had to resolve frequent controversy about the admission of new members and whether they were genuinely non-aligned. But the number of nations attending grew steadily and the conferences provided the opportunity for broad discussions of topical world issues.

Arab-Israeli war of 1967 and, in the same year, the failure of a communist coup in Indonesia turned that country towards a more Western alignment. At the same time, Sino-Soviet tensions and dwindling of the cold war led to more subtle and complex international groupings [10].

### Third World economic policies

In the mid-1970s relations between the Great Powers became less hostile, and Third World opposition to alliances and pressure against colonialism were subsidiary to economic concerns, particularly the wish to see the emergence of a new international economic order. Non-alignment continued to be a predominantly Afro-Asian movement, but it was the Arab and Latin American members who did most to infuse the non-aligned movement with new vitality.

The Arab nations led the way by seizing the initiative after November 1973 when OPEC, the Organization of Petroleum Exporting Countries, unilaterally quadrupled the price of oil and dealt a major blow to the existing worldwide distribution of

wealth. The Latin Americans broadened the argument from oil to natural resources in mid-1975 when Cuba [7] proposed that all countries wishing to protect their natural resources should join the non-aligned. The most important issue on the agenda at the Lima conference of foreign ministers of non-aligned states in August 1975 – the statute on foreign investment, multinational companies and technology – was modelled closely on regulations established in the Andean Pact, Latin America's economic integration movement launched in 1968.

These moves were aimed at retaining control of national development and strategic resources. Foreign investment was viewed as acceptable only as long as it contributed to national goals. The non-aligned movement grew from being a negative reaction to the cold war into a positive policy to protect national resources and control foreign investment.

Non-aligned leaders intended to ensure that in future the rich, industrialized nations would no longer find it easy to negotiate with weak producers' associations.

**Tito, Nehru and Nasser** (pictured left to right at the Belgrade Conference, 1961) worked together as leaders and promoters of non-alignment from the mid-1950s. Nehru, spokesman for newly independent India, advanced non-alignment as a positive moral force and advocated non-nuclear "areas of peace". Tito represented independent Marxism resisting the pressures of Stalinist Russia. Nasser, leader of the new nationalist government in Egypt and of the larger Arab world, successfully played off cold war competitors with rival aid bids and rid Egypt of British military bases.

**5 John Foster Dulles** (1888–1959), US Secretary of State from 1953–9, was an unrelenting opponent of communism and the chief advocate of American strategy to contain China and the USSR by military alliances. Announcing in June 1956 that 42 nations were allied with the US, he achieved some notoriety when he said that "except in very exceptional circumstances, neutrality is an immoral and shortsighted conception".

**6 Nuclear-free zones** and zones of peace or neutrality are being proposed, debated and actively promoted in South-East Asia, southern Asia, the Indian Ocean and parts of Africa. A lead was given in 1967 by Mexico and some other nations when the Treaty for the Prohibition of Nuclear Weapons in Latin America (the Treaty of Tlatelolco) was signed. Most other zones have yet to be ratified.

KEY

Official nuclear-free zone
Nuclear-free zone proposed by Pakistan
Nuclear-free zone proposed by India
Proposed neutral zone
Proposed Australian zone of peace

**7 Strident anti-US attitudes** emerged in Cuba after Fidel Castro (1927–  ) came to power early in 1959. A large Cuban delegation attended a turbulent 15th session of the UN General Assembly in September 1960. Cuba's role as a small nation defying a neighbouring superpower was further dramatized by an abortive US-backed invasion by Cuban exiles at the Bay of Pigs in April 1961 and a Soviet attempt to arm Cuba with nuclear missiles in 1962. Cuba has campaigned to make Havana a Third World capital linking Afro-Asia and Latin America.

**8 OPEC,** the Organization of Petroleum Exporting Countries, meeting at Geneva in January 1974, represented the most powerful cartel in the world – a position gained through the importance of oil in the world economy.

**9 A World Food Conference** sponsored by the UN in Rome in November 1974 and attended by 1,250 delegates from some 130 nations originated with the 1973 Algiers conference of non-aligned countries. The idea was adopted by Henry Kissinger, US Secretary of State, with Western backing.

**10 Commonwealth prime ministers,** seen at Kingston, Jamaica, in 1975, make up an international grouping that includes aligned and non-aligned, nuclear and non-nuclear, rich and poor nations. This voluntary association of former members of the British Empire engages in continuous consultation.

# Latin America in the 20th century

The history of Latin America in the twentieth century is, above all, the story of attempts to break out of the economic, political and social patterns of the nineteenth century and of the resistance such attempts have encountered. Developments in Latin America have been increasingly affected by outside influences. The great Depression brought a collapse of world prices for Latin American exports and two world wars further stimulated industrialization and modernization by cutting the region off from traditional markets and sources of capital goods. There has been a rapid growth of the major cities such as Buenos Aires, Mexico City and São Paulo, swollen, in some instances, by immigration.

## Dictatorships and the military in politics

Industrialization and modernization did not themselves bring fundamental political and social change to Latin America. Trade and industry were dominated by foreign enterprises, increasingly those of the United States. Nor did the growing middle classes in Latin America play the social role of their counterparts in the United States or Western Europe, and middle-class political parties seldom carried out essential reforms when they gained office. This situation encouraged the emergence of a new kind of dictator – one who sought the support of the urban workers. Such a dictator was General Juan Perón (1895–1974) of Argentina [3].

The military has remained a significant element in Latin American politics. Military intervention was given a considerable impetus from 1929 by the Depression which caused political convulsions in most Latin American countries. It was later encouraged by the cold war. Often faced by weak and ineffective civilian governments, the military has tended to regard itself as the true guardian of the national interest. Nationalism has always been strong in the Latin American military, and – although the latter has generally been conservative and, in recent decades, strongly anti-communist – this has sometimes been allied with radicalism, especially among younger army officers. As early as the 1920s a military president, Colonel Carlos Ibáñez (1877–1966) [2], carried out a programme of social reform in Chile. The most far-reaching

of such programmes, however, has been that of the Peruvian military government which seized power in 1968. It began with the expropriation of a prominent United States-owned oil company and continued with the United States' interests as prime targets of Peruvian nationalism.

## Antipathy towards the United States

Latin American nationalism has for a long time been directed mainly at the United States, which is by far the most important foreign presence in the region [Key]. The United States has usually exerted its influence in favour of stability and the status quo and against revolutionary changes which would threaten her interests. Fear of communism has often led her to support Latin American dictatorships. When, in 1961, President John F. Kennedy (1917–63) began the Alliance for Progress – an ambitious programme of economic and social development in Latin America involving substantial reforms and the promotion of democracy – it met with apathy and resistance. Latin Americans have since denounced "aid" as

1 **The ideology of the Mexican** revolution is symbolized in these huge murals by Rivera, Orozco and Siqueiros. The revolution was nationalist and the murals are a vivid expression of cultural nationalism. They depict great violence: the oppression of the Indians by the Spanish conquerors and the furious reaction of the Mexican peasants and workers. The Indians and their leaders are idealized in these murals, the oppressors grotesquely caricatured. In this picture Marx is exhorting the workers, while the Church and the capitalists are engrossed in wealth.

2 **Colonel Carlos Ibáñez** became President of Chile in 1927 and pursued policies combining nationalism and social reform. But they were undermined by the great Depression and he resigned.

3 **General Juan Perón** was President of Argentina from 1946–55. Assisted by his wife, Eva, he won over the urban masses with social benefits. After Eva's death in 1952 his position deteriorated and he was eventually overthrown by the military. The *peronistas* remained a key element in Argentine politics. Perón was recalled to power in 1973 but he died in the following year.

4 **Fidel Castro**, the charismatic leader of revolutionary Cuba, seen here addressing one of the countless gatherings at which he explains his policies, is probably the most widely known Latin American figure since Simón Bolívar. Although "Castroism" has not spread to other parts of the continent, Castro's success in defying the dominance of the US in the area has profoundly affected the latter's policies and prestige in Latin America.

5 **Salvador Allende** became the first freely elected Marxist head of state when he won the Chilean presidential election in 1970. Although faced with Congressional opposition and US hostility he embarked upon an ambitious socialist programme. Both his supporters and his opponents resorted to unconstitutional tactics. Economic chaos and violence culminated in his overthrow by a military coup and his violent death in 1973.

increasing their dependence upon the United States and serving the latter's interests more than their own.

Despite United States influence and the durability of traditional social structures there have been three authentic revolutions in Latin America during the twentieth century: in Mexico (1910), Bolivia (1952) and Cuba (1959). The Mexican revolution [1] brought about a new system of government, a sizeable redistribution of land and an improvement in the status of the Indians. It also asserted Mexican nationalism by taking over the foreign-owned oil industry in 1938. The Bolivian revolution, although less far-reaching, destroyed the privileges of the great landowners, nationalized the tin mines (Bolivia's main source of foreign exchange) and also raised the status of the Indians. The Cuban revolution has been the most radical, leading to the creation of an avowedly Marxist state aligned with the Soviet Union under the leadership of Fidel Castro (1927– ) [4].

The Cuban example has not been followed elsewhere in Latin America, although there has been a marked increase in urban guerrilla violence in some countries, notably Argentina. The victory of Salvador Allende (1908–73) [5] in the Chilean elections of 1970 – even though he was ousted and killed three years later – was significant.

## Third World co-operation

Meanwhile, the countries of Latin America have come to identify themselves with the developing countries of Asia and Africa [6] and to co-operate with them in endeavouring to obtain better trading terms from the richer industrialized nations. They have also tried to co-operate more closely with each other and to increase their trade outside the Western Hemisphere in order to lessen dependence upon the United States.

Brazil [7], traditionally more friendly towards the United States than the Spanish American countries, has for a long time entertained ambitions to be a great power. With its considerable economic progress from the mid-1960s onwards (under a military government), Brazil no longer sees itself as a developing nation. It could fulfil its ambitions by the end of this century.

The **Pan-American Union building** in Washington, DC, is the headquarters of the Organization of American States (OAS) which links Latin America with the United States.

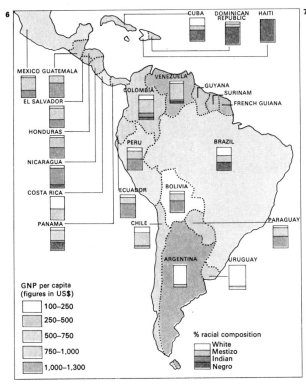

**GNP per capita** (figures in US$)
- 100–250
- 250–500
- 500–750
- 750–1,000
- 1,000–1,300

% racial composition
- White
- Mestizo
- Indian
- Negro

**6 The identification of Latin America** with the Third World of developing countries is illustrated by this map showing the average per capita income and racial composition of each country. The gap between rich and poor is often extreme.

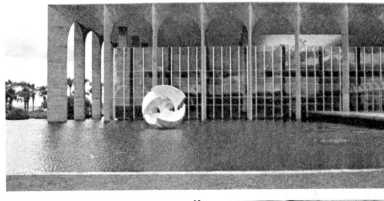

**7 The Ministry of Foreign Affairs** building is in Brasília, the new capital of Brazil. Brasília symbolizes Brazil's ambition to become a power and to exploit the hitherto largely untapped wealth of the country's interior.

**8 Shanty towns,** such as this one in Rio de Janeiro, demonstrate the glaring disparity between rich and poor in Latin America, as well as the population drift into the burgeoning cities from the stagnant countryside areas.

**9 The Transamazonian highway** in Brazil exemplifies modernization in Latin America. When complete, the network of roads is designed to integrate the vast, unpopulated but richly endowed Amazon basin with the more developed coastal regions of Brazil.

**10 General Alvarado** (1910– ), head of the Government of Peru, has pursued a policy of revolutionary nationalism since 1968, and actively fostered co-operation among Third World countries. In 1975 a conference of non-aligned nations was held in Lima.

# Evolution of the Western democracies

World War II left Europe divided into two political camps. Except for Greece, where a communist-led revolt was raging, Eastern Europe was under Soviet occupation, including East Germany – although the Western Allies held part of Berlin. The first task was to put the war-torn countries of Europe on their feet. This was done by the USA through the multi-billion-dollar European Recovery Programme [3], also called Marshall Aid after its initiator, Secretary of State George Marshall (1880–1959) [2].

## Breach with the Soviet Union

The Marshall Plan was designed to redevelop industries throughout Europe on an aid-sharing basis through the Organization for European Economic Co-operation (OEEC). The Soviet Union was invited to join in but refused in July 1947, while vetoing the participation of other countries within its sphere of influence. These included Czechoslovakia, which, had just been incorporated in the Soviet bloc by the coup of 20–25 February 1948.

In addition to having complete power over East Germany, the Soviet government wished to exact heavy reparations from West Germany through the arrangements for Four-Power control. This meant continued dismantling of factories, thus preventing the recovery of West Germany that the other powers held to be vital for the economic recovery of Europe. By 1948 the breach between the Soviet Union and its former, Western allies was complete.

The Americans and British introduced a currency reform into West Germany that had striking success in bringing goods once more into the shops and restarting the wheels of industry. But when they extended the reform to their occupation zones in West Berlin the Russians imposed a blockade (June 1948). This was beaten by the organization of a gigantic airlift and the Russians called off the blockade in May 1949. Meanwhile the Western Allies effected the transition of West Germany to independent status as the German Federal Republic in May 1949.

A strong wave of idealism, strengthened by Churchill's call for a United States of Europe (Zürich 1947), brought into being the Council of Europe (1949), comprising most countries outside the Soviet bloc. But it disappointed many of its promoters because the British kept it a loose intergovernmental body with no real powers.

## Steps to unity

Britain, with its predominant position in Western Europe in the immediate postwar years, had similarly been able to thwart American hopes that the OEEC could become a supranational body. Promoters of West European unity led by Jean Monnet (1888–1979) accordingly took another initiative. With the aid of Robert Schuman (1886–1963), the French Foreign Minister [4], supported by West Germany and Italy, they set out to bring together their countries and others in a supranational organization to administer their coal and steel industries jointly [5]. In May 1950 the Schuman Plan was launched, which led to the setting up in 1951 of the Coal and Steel Community of France, West Germany, Italy, Belgium, The Netherlands and Luxembourg. This act of statesmanship was made possible by the displacing of wartime resentments, through

1 **General de Gaulle's entry into Paris** at the head of Free French forces on 26 August 1944 marked the beginning of the end of World War II in the west. But the German armies resisted until May 1945. As Russian forces fought their way across eastern Europe and the Western Allies advanced through Italy and across the Rhine, the postwar political division of Europe began to take shape.

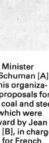

2 **US Secretary of State Marshall** [left], seen with the British Foreign Secretary, Ernest Bevin (1881–1951), initiated the aid scheme named after him in 1947–9 to restore a weakened Europe that might otherwise follow the path of communism.

3 **The European recovery programme,** set up to administer Marshall Aid, disbursed $13,150 million between 1948 and 1952 in addition to the $9,500 million already granted for Western Europe since the end of the war and $500 million worth of private food parcels. By mid-1951 industrial production was 42% higher than the prewar level, while agricultural output was 10% higher. Trade had more than doubled while in the early 1950s coal and steel production made massive advances.

4 **Two Frenchmen initiated the scheme** for the European Coal and Steel Community of France, West Germany, Italy, The Netherlands, Belgium and Luxembourg, established by the Treaty of Paris in 1951. Foreign Minister Robert Schuman [A] based this organization on proposals for pooling coal and steel output which were put forward by Jean Monnet [B], in charge of plans for French modernization.

5 **Coal seams cross frontiers** in northern Europe and the ECSC countries saw that they could build up an efficient coal and steel industry only by devising a supranational system. In this way the coal and coke of the Ruhr could supply the steel industry of Lorraine while the Benelux countries (Belgium, Luxembourg, The Netherlands) and Italy could enjoy similar advantages. By combining these industries (vital for armaments) the risk of another war was reduced.

personal and political reconciliations [Key].

Belgium, The Netherlands and Luxembourg had set up a customs union (Benelux) at the end of the war. This served as a pilot scheme when these countries took the lead in a further step towards the unity of Western Europe, with the creation [6] of the European Economic Community and European Atomic Community. The immediate objectives of the EEC were to create conditions of fair trade first for manufactured goods then, by the Common Agricultural Policy, for agricultural products.

Although the EEC Commission, with powers of initiative and supervision, is a supranational body, main decision-making is in the hands of a Council of Ministers of member states. Attempts to increase the powers of the Commission as a decision-making body were thwarted by General de Gaulle [1] as President of France, and the Council continued as an inter-governmental body with every minister retaining the individual right of veto.

De Gaulle's position was particularly strong after he returned to power in 1958,

settled France's colonial problem in Algeria and initiated the French Fifth Republic, whose constitution gave large powers to the president. He asserted the right of France to leadership of "European Europe" in opposition to American influence. In pursuit of this policy he blocked moves for America's close ally, Britain, to join the EEC. In 1966, he took France out of the military committee of the North Atlantic Treaty Organization. West Germany joined NATO in 1955.

## Expansion of the EEC

After de Gaulle resigned in 1969, France's veto on British entry to the European Community was soon removed [7]. Denmark and Eire joined at the same time, in 1973. The countries of the European Free Trade Association [8], an industrial customs union that Britain had set up as a rival to the EEC in 1956, were given favoured relations with the Community. An EEC system of associated states that had begun with the ex-French colonies, was extended to a large number of African and Caribbean states by the Lomé Convention of 1975.

**Reconciliation of France and Germany** laid the foundation for a new political and economic structure within which the countries of Western Europe could be integrated. After more than 80 years of suspicion, tension and conflict, including three major wars, the two countries joined forces in the Schuman Plan (1950) leading to the European Coal and Steel Community. In January 1963 the West German Chancellor, Konrad Adenauer (1876–1967), and the French President, Charles de Gaulle (1890–1970) [left and right respectively], met to sign the Franco-German Treaty of Friendship.

**6 The signing of the Treaty of Rome** in March 1957 set up the European Economic Community after intensive negotiations under the chairmanship of Paul-Henri Spaak of Belgium (1899–1972). Six member states established a common market for industrial and later for agricultural products, along with schemes to "harmonize" regulations affecting, for instance, working conditions to ensure fair competition.

**7 Consultations in May 1971** between Edward Heath (1916–    ), Prime Minister of Britain [left], and Georges Pompidou (1911–74), President of France, cleared the way for Britain's entry to the EEC, a step that successive British governments had tried to take since 1961. De Gaulle twice vetoed British entry but a changed French attitude enabled Britain, Denmark and Eire to become full EEC members in 1973.

**8 The European Free Trade Association** was set up under the leadership of Britain before she entered the EEC to offset advantages the "Six" were gaining. EFTA, a customs union for industrial goods, facilitated trade between its member-states, although trade growth was faster within the more powerful EEC. Some countries, such as Greece, were associated with the EEC pending full membership. EFTA continued after Britain entered the EEC, with special trading links to the EEC.

**9 Riots in Paris in 1968** were led by students who, in both France and Germany, sought reforms of higher education and had other political aims. Sit-ins and growing violence developed into a general strike in France. De Gaulle's regime recovered after the army pledged support but was badly shaken. Promises of far-reaching educational reforms and generous wage settlements ended the strikes and unrest, although De Gaulle himself did not long remain in office as president.

**10 Arab representatives** appeared unexpectedly at the first summit meeting of the enlarged EEC at Copenhagen in 1973. The summit closely followed the October Arab-Israeli war and consequent oil embargo. A steep increase in oil prices indicated a fundamental change in the relative positions of oil-producing and industrial nations, particularly affecting Europe. The Arabs arrived in Copenhagen in search of support against Israel.

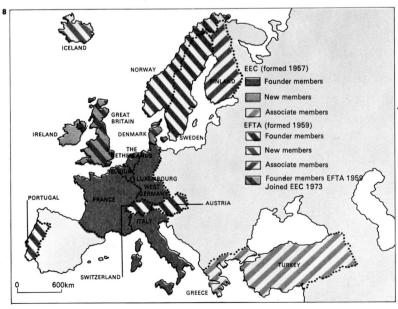

ICELAND
NORWAY
FINLAND
GREAT BRITAIN
IRELAND
DENMARK
SWEDEN
THE NETHERLANDS
BELGIUM
LUXEMBOURG
WEST GERMANY
AUSTRIA
PORTUGAL
FRANCE
ITALY
SWITZERLAND
GREECE
TURKEY

EEC (formed 1957)
Founder members
New members
Associate members
EFTA (formed 1959)
Founder members
New members
Associate members
Founder members EFTA 1959 Joined EEC 1973

0    600km

# Scotland in the 20th century

Two main political developments have occurred in Scotland in the twentieth century. One was the rise to power of the Labour Party, which was presaged by events in the nineteenth century and led by figures such as Keir Hardie (1856–1915). The other was the rise of the Scottish National Party (SNP) and the spread of Scottish nationalism, which has grown in response to economic and political developments both inside and outside Scotland during this century.

## Nationalism and political changes

The displacement of the Liberal Party by the Labour Party in Scotland began before World War I with the work of Keir Hardie and several small socialist groups of which the Independent Labour Party (ILP) was the most important. The breakthrough came during and after the war, partly as a result of the great bitterness in labour relations on Clydeside [1, 2]. Shipyard and munitions workers there reacted angrily to the sweeping actions of the wartime coalition government, to wage controls and to the "dilution" of labour, as well as to alleged profiteering by manufacturers. In 1906 there were only two Scottish Labour MPs; by 1923 there were 35, and they were the largest party in Scotland – a position they have generally maintained since World War II even when the rest of Britain was returning to a Conservative administration.

The SNP, founded in 1928 as the National Party, sought Home Rule at first rather than independence. Ridden with factions and weak in membership, it made little impact until after 1962. Thereafter it grew fast, and Winifred Ewing's (1929– ) victory at the Hamilton by-election in 1967 [Key], followed by the discovery of oil in the North Sea [10], increased support for the party [9] and made the prospect of an independent Scotland seem economically attractive. By 1974 the SNP had the allegiance of nearly a third of Scottish voters, 11 MPs, and a chance to displace Labour as the largest single political party in Scotland.

Both the Liberal and Labour parties have historically had a commitment to forms of Home Rule; the Liberals introduced unsuccessful bills in 1913 and 1914, and the ILP put it high on their programme, although a private member's bill in 1927 failed. Even the signing of almost two million names to a national "covenant" calling for a Scottish parliament within the framework of the United Kingdom in 1950 failed to move postwar governments to renewed action.

The success of the SNP produced new devolution proposals in the 1970s, but the failure of the Labour administration in 1977 to push through its original bill setting up a Scottish assembly with limited powers left the future fluid and uncertain.

## Economic problems

Dissatisfaction with the Union can be related to the economic weaknesses of modern Scotland. In 1913 national income per head was probably only five per cent or less below the British average. Both in absolute and relative terms it had grown rapidly in the previous century with the differential between Scotland and England constantly narrowing. In the interwar years, however, severe depression in the heavy industries that dominated the Scottish economy (there were

1 **Women were introduced** with other unskilled workers (dilution) to maintain the workforce numbers in the vital heavy industries of the Clyde during World War I as more and more men joined up. But dilution, with government attempts to direct labour, held down wages at a time of inflation, rising profits and rent increases, and placed a great strain on labour relations. Clydeside in particular was the scene of strikes and unrest.

2 **Industrial unrest reached a peak** in Glasgow shortly after World War I. In January 1919, munitions workers, threatened with unemployment, called a strike and a red flag was raised above the town hall in support of demands for a 40-hour week. The Lord Provost asked the demonstrators to return in two days for his answer; when they did so, the police attempted to clear the meeting and a riot ensued in which the strike leaders, including Emanuel Shinwell (1884– ), a later minister, were arrested. The next day, tanks and troops were called in, but the strike had already collapsed.

3 **John Wheatley** (right) (1869–1930), a self-educated miner, was influential in bringing the Catholic vote to the Labour Party in Scotland despite the initial opposition of the clergy. Later, as minister of health in the first Labour Government in 1923, he introduced the first really effective Housing Act, designed to deal with the housing shortage. It increased rent subsidies and government finance to assist local authorities to build more council houses.

4 **Scottish and UK levels of unemployment** differed only marginally until the outbreak of World War I. But the greater dependence of Scotland on heavy industry meant that the impact of the depression was intensified and unemployment rose to exceed significantly the UK rate. This high rate of unemployment has tended to persist, despite efforts to diversify the Scottish economy.

| 1939 | 1959 | 1976 |
| --- | --- | --- |
| | | 4.4% |
| 7% | | |
| | 2.3% | |
| | | 5.8% |

Scotland 12.9%

16.3% United Kingdom

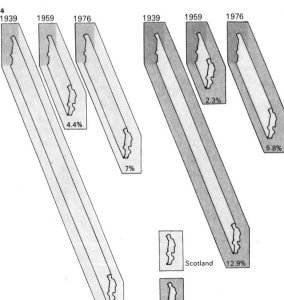

5 **Scottish military bases** in the two World Wars were important as part of the British defences. In World War I, the Grand Fleet found safe anchorage in Scapa Flow in the Orkney Islands (shown here). The German High Seas Fleet was interned, and scuttled itself there in 1919. In World War II Scapa was again a naval base and the fortifications against submarine and air attack strengthened. In 1956 the base was abandoned and an important source of employment was lost to the region.

nearly 400,000 unemployed in 1932) caused the gap to widen to ten per cent and more [4]. Between 1921 and 1931 so many Scots emigrated that the population actually fell.

Since 1940 the economy has performed better, but well-paid employment has often been hard to come by for the Scot who stayed at home. Government regional policies aimed at producing new industries (such as motor vehicles at Linwood and Bathgate) have not cured the problems in the old industrial centres such as Clydeside and Dundee. As a result of the discovery and exploitation of North Sea oil in the 1970s, the gap between Scottish and English earnings is narrower again now than at any time since before World War I, but the prosperity is mainly in the north and rests only on this fragile base.

Although the modern Scot is much better off than his nineteenth-century predecessor, the annual rate of economic growth has not been as high as it was in the late nineteenth century. One consequence is that resources have never been sufficient to remove the stain of urban deprivation. Glasgow still has some of the worst slums in northern Europe, some of them now in modern council-built tenements.

## Modern Scotland

The nature of the modern state has also added to Scottish frustrations. Since 1945 more Scottish firms have been directed by private capital operating from England, Europe and America, or have been nationalized and run by civil servants answerable to London. Despite the high calibre of the Scottish Office in Edinburgh, there has been a sense in which for the first time since Union in 1707 the Scots have begun to feel no longer in command of their own country.

Nevertheless modern Scotland is not completely introverted. The fame of John Logie Baird (1888–1946), the inventor of television, and of Alexander Fleming (1881–1955), the discoverer of modern antibiotics, is worldwide. In other fields the Edinburgh Festival (founded in 1947) has an international reputation; and the successful tourist trade has become an important earner of foreign currency.

**Winifred Ewing's** extraordinary victory at Hamilton in 1967 crowned nearly 40 years of struggle

out of obscurity by the SNP. Although she later lost the seat, in 1970, by 1974 the SNP

had gained the allegiance of almost a third of the Scottish voters and had 11 MPs at Westminster.

**6 Cumbernauld** is one of Scotland's most successful postwar towns. Designed in 1956 as an overspill town from Glasgow, it was intended to relieve some of the worst housing conditions and overcrowding in the city. Since then it has successfully attracted light industry and skilled workers, but Glasgow has been left with older, often declining, firms and fewer skills among its workforce.

**8 Hydroelectric power in the Highlands** was first systematically developed in 1943. Among the most spectacular and successful schemes that were undertaken was this one on the River Awe, in Argyllshire.

**9 In the late 1960s** the Scottish National Party came to the fore in Scotland and united the disparate voices of Scottish discontent through a straight appeal to national self-interest, to "Put Scotland First".

**7 The Scottish fishing industry,** prosperous before 1914, was badly hit by

foreign competition in the interwar years and has had mixed prosperity since.

Over-fishing by foreign vessels close to the limits has also reduced the catch.

**10 The discovery of North Sea oil** transformed British and Scottish politics in the 1970s. The SNP claimed the oil for Scotland, but the UK government, hard pressed by balance of payments problems and worried about British energy supplies, would not contemplate devolving control over it. Eighty per cent of the oil reserves are located off the Orkney and Shetland Isles, ironically areas that do not always consider themselves as being part of Scotland.

# Wales in the 20th century

World War I introduced a number of crucial changes in the nature of the Welsh economy. In rural society the most significant change occurred in the pattern of land ownership. The massive estates that had dominated the countryside since Tudor times were put up for sale and bought by freehold farmers. In 1887, only ten per cent of the total cultivated surface of Wales was owned by peasant proprietors. By 1970, 61 per cent was in their hands.

## Short-lived prosperity

Landlords had been prompted to sell by the boom years of World War I. But this prosperity proved both artificial and fleeting. The repeal of the Corn Production Act of 1917 meant that Welsh farmers no longer had an incentive to cultivate land. The development of motorized transport made milk production the most lucrative alternative. Mechanization, however, reduced the number of farm hands required, and they were forced to find alternative jobs either in the industrial south or in England.

Economic prosperity in industrial communities during the war years was no less artificial than in rural areas. Once the wartime demand for coal and steel contracted in 1923, the Welsh export market suffered a sharp decline. As oil became increasingly used by the navy, coal-mining areas were rapidly caught up in a deepening industrial recession. Reflecting the decline in the coal industry in South Wales, the number of miners employed fell from 265,000 in 1920 to 138,560 in 1933. South Wales had produced a record 57 million tonnes of coal in 1913. Yet on the eve of the nationalization of the coal industry in 1947 only a dozen mines remained in production. The decline of the iron, steel, tinplate and slate industries was no less disquieting. Stiff competition from foreign steelmakers with updated plant led to the closure of the Cyfarthfa and Dowlais ironworks, and unemployment descended "like the ashes of Vesuvius" on the industrial towns of South Wales.

By 1932, one-fifth of the working population of Wales was unemployed [4]. Shortages and restrictions created a bleak, disillusioned society which remained constantly under the strain of poverty and hardship [3]. For many, migration was the only outlet: the Rhondda Valley lost a fifth of its population between 1921 and 1939 [2] and a thousand people left Merthyr annually.

## State assistance

In 1932 to meet the emergency South Wales was declared a "special area" by the government and a campaign was launched to modernize the traditional industries and to develop alternative industries. The most decisive development occurred when Richard Thomas and Company were persuaded in 1935 to open a strip mill at Ebbw Vale. Post-1945 developments were even more crucial. The contraction of the coal industry was offset by a huge expansion in steel production, particularly in the new plants established at Port Talbot [Key] and Llanwern. New tinplate works were established as old mills closed.

World War I also saw in sweeping political changes in Wales. With the decline of Nonconformity and the large estates, Liberalism lost its hold on the affections of

**1 A World War I recruiting drive** in Cardiff used children to win volunteers. Enthusiasm for the war remained high even after conscription was introduced in 1916, and more than 280,000 Welshmen served in the forces. Pacifists such as Keir Hardie (1856–1915), MP for Merthyr, were in a minority.

**2 A decline in the Welsh population** during the 1920s and 1930s reversed a growth trend that had been steady since the census of 1801. During the Depression years Wales lost all its natural population increase and a further 191,000 people, many of them to southeast England and the Midlands.

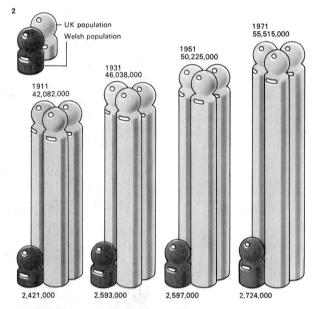

UK population
Welsh population

1911 42,082,000
1931 46,038,000
1951 50,225,000
1971 55,515,000

2,421,000
2,593,000
2,597,000
2,724,000

**3 Soup kitchens** such as this became an important means of supplementing the diet of many miners' families in South Wales during the Depression years when whole areas were progressively impoverished through unemployment. Malnutrition was common during periods of industrial action and unemployment, when long-term idleness created severe domestic problems. Fortunately, working-class communities were bound together by selfless effort, collective spirit and genuine compassion. These traditional values helped to alleviate the harsh social problems of the time. The Welsh poet Idris Davies wrote: "No manna fell on these communities and self-help was the only answer".

**4 Miners from the Rhondda Valley** and other Welsh mining areas marched to London to join a hunger demonstration by 200,000 people, from all parts of Britain, in Hyde Park on 8 November 1936. Many of the Welsh marchers had to sing on the streets for pennies to buy themselves food. The suffering and humiliation of the Depression years left deep scars on the hearts and minds of working-class people in Wales. Their sense of injustice led to a strengthened trade union movement and increased willingness among industrial workers to force action by demonstrations and strikes. In 1932 Welsh unemployment reached a quarter of a million.

the Welsh people. By contrast, the Labour Party emerged as the dominant political party in South Wales during the interwar years [5]. After 1945, socialism penetrated North Wales, and when the Labour Party won 32 seats out of 36 in the general election of 1966 it reached the peak of its dominance.

## Welsh nationalism

*Plaid Cymru* (the Welsh Nationalist Party) was slower to achieve parliamentary success [6]. From the 1960s onwards, however, it extended its membership in both rural and industrial areas. In 1974 three Plaid members were elected to Parliament and the party has since established itself as the major rival to the Labour Party in Wales.

In 1964, the Labour Government established a Welsh Office in Cardiff, but because this body was granted little executive authority it scarcely began to fulfil the demands of the devolutionists, who called for the setting up of a representative assembly within Wales. The Kilbrandon Commission, established in 1968–9, came out in favour of a large measure of devolution for Wales.

Depression, unemployment and depopulation in the 1920s and 1930s all affected Welsh language and culture in general. Since Tudor times the Welsh language had been relegated to an inferior status in matters of law and administration. In the twentieth century the influx of English speakers into the coalfields, the anglicization of the education system, the decline of Welsh Nonconformity and the rise of broadcasting and tourism all influenced a startling drop in the number of Welsh speakers. From 54.4 per cent in 1891, the percentage of Welsh people who could speak Welsh dropped to 36.8 in 1931 and 21.0 in 1971.

Valiant efforts have been made to arrest this decline [7]. *Urdd Gobaith Cymru* (the Welsh League of Youth), founded in 1922, fosters the language by inviting children to camps, sporting events and eisteddfodau; a growing number of schools teach in the vernacular at both primary and secondary level; and Welsh authors and publishers receive substantial grants. The Welsh Language Act (1967) has granted – in principle at least – Welsh equal validity with English.

**The Port Talbot steelworks** at West Glamorgan became a major factor in the Welsh economy after the massive Abbey Works and hot strip mill was built there in 1947, modernizing the existing plant. In the wake of the dramatic collapse of the coal industry, the expansion of steel production has brought changes in the industrial and social structure of Wales that are as far-reaching in many ways as the transformation that occurred during the first Industrial Revolution.

**5 Aneurin Bevan** (1897-1960), son of a Tredegar miner, entered Parliament in 1929 as Labour member for Ebbw Vale. He rapidly became the most stimulating socialist thinker of his day. A colourful personality and a brilliant spontaneous debater, he preached the gospel of democratic socialism with wit and passion. After editing the socialist *Tribune* (1942-5), he became Minister of Health and principal architect of the National Health scheme. Later, in opposition, he led a left-wing Labour group critical of the rearmament policies of the 1950s. Hugh Gaitskell defeated him for the party leadership in 1955.

**6 Saunders Lewis** (1893-    ), Welsh author, has been an inspiration to the nationalist movement as one of the founders, and later as president, of Plaid Cymru from 1925. The party, fired by Ireland's success in winning independence, made slow headway until after World War II. But its activities, at times explosive, were a major factor in achieving formal recognition for the Welsh language in schools and in such sensitive areas as broadcasting, which is now carried in two languages. The growing strength of the party at the polls has been accompanied by moves towards greater political autonomy.

**7 Civil disobedience** has been a tactic of *Cymdeithas yr Iaith Gymraeg* (the Welsh Language Society) since 1969. In 1971 members interrupted a High Court case in London to publicize their cause. The society, founded in 1962, aims to secure for the Welsh language equal status with English.

**8 A new structure of local government** administration was established for Wales in April 1974, dismantling a framework of shires that had lasted for more than 400 years. The 13 Welsh counties set up by the Tudors under the Act of Union in 1536 were abolished and in their place emerged eight units based broadly on ancient medieval divisions.

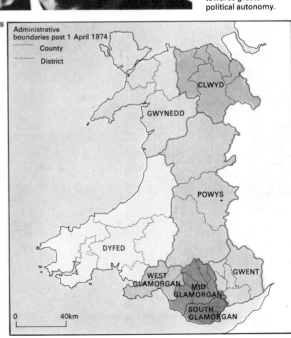

Administrative boundaries post 1 April 1974
County
District

CLWYD
GWYNEDD
POWYS
DYFED
GWENT
WEST GLAMORGAN
MID GLAMORGAN
SOUTH GLAMORGAN

0    40km

# USA: the affluent society

The pervasive theme of American society since the end of World War II has been growth, bringing prosperity, innovation and, not least, growing pains. This growth has been most evident in the number of people living in the United States [1]. The population at the time of the 1940 census was 131 million; by 1970 the population was 203 million, an increase of 72 million. The population explosion had been fed more by the baby boom after the end of World War II, by the "second generation" baby boom of the late 1960s, and by people living longer, than by continued immigration from Europe. By 1972 the rate of immigration was about one-sixth what it had been before World War I and less than six per cent of the country's population was foreign born.

The increase in population has meant a vast expansion in the size of conurbations, although typically the city centres themselves have lost population. Those who remain in older urban areas are often black [6]. Among large American cities nine have populations that are 40 per cent or more black, including Washington, DC, which is more than two-thirds black. The growth in population has been greatest in the so-called "Rim States" along the American coast, from Florida through to Texas and California. In 1940 California had less than half the population of New York; by 1970 it had become the largest state in the Union.

## The rise of the bureaucratic leviathan

The population explosion has been mirrored by an enormous growth in government. The number of public employees has trebled since the 1930s and more than doubled since 1945, and now constitutes nearly 20 per cent of the total workforce. The expansion of the American military is shown by the fact that there were 28 million ex-servicemen in America in 1975.

The growth in government is reflected in the creation of three new cabinet departments (Health, Education and Welfare; Housing and Urban Development; and Transportation), a response to the federal government's commitment to expand its capabilities for looking after its citizens, and mobilizing national resources.

Superficially, party politics has changed less than society as a whole. The presidency is contested by candidates of the Democratic and Republican parties, as it was a century ago. But the voting has been very unstable. Throughout most of the period, the Democratic Party has controlled both houses of the United States Congress [3]. Moreover, although the country claims to have a two-party system, in three postwar elections the president elect took less than half the vote, because of divisions within the two parties.

## Expanding economy and prosperity

The American government has been able to expand activities at home and abroad because of the continuing growth of the nation's economy. In 1950 the gross national product was $284,000 million; by 1971 it had increased almost fourfold to $1,050,000 million. The growth in total national resources meant that, even without raising tax rates, the flow of money into the federal treasury increased massively. The amount of money left in the pockets of individual consumers also increased, although by a lesser

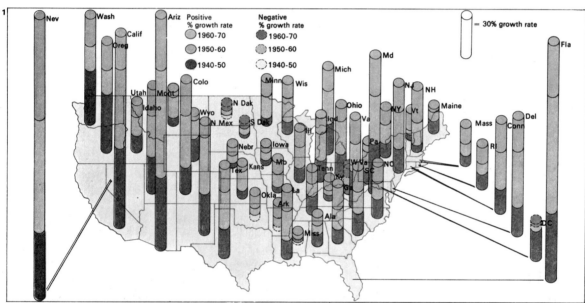

1 **Rapid population growth** in America after the war was due more to a marked increase in the birth-rate and life expectancy than to immigration; since 1945 total population has increased by over 50%. This in itself did not greatly affect population distribution across the continent. But there has been a significant movement of people to new centres of growth, north and south mixing in this internal migration. Florida and California, for example, were centres for this migration, as the diagram indicates. America's manpower and wealth provided the means of a world-wide "defence" effort postwar, but Vietnam showed that these alone are not enough.

2 **Postwar presidents** have been almost equally divided in party terms, Eisenhower [B], Nixon [E] and Ford [F] being Republicans, and Truman [A], Kennedy [C], Johnson [D] and Carter [G], Democrats. But all gave priority to foreign affairs. Truman found this compensated for domestic policy set-backs, but Johnson lost by his foreign policy the support that his domestic war on poverty had gained. Nixon found that his success abroad could not bury the Watergate affair. Of these men John F. Kennedy, the Harvard-educated son of a millionaire, came from the east coast; the others were all brought up in small towns, or came from unsophisticated farming regions.

rate, because a portion of the increase went to looking after the increased number of children and elderly and to employ the larger number of Americans of working age. The family income of Americans has risen steadily, even when allowance is made for the effects of creeping inflation. The real income of the average American family doubled from 1947 to 1971, when it exceeded $10,000 a year.

Higher earnings meant Americans could afford to buy more of everything. The great postwar housing boom caused a drop in the proportion of Americans living in substandard houses from nearly two in five in 1945 (many living in old farmhouses) to one in 20 in the early 1970s. The number of cars sold more than doubled from prewar years, totalling more than 8.5 million in 1970 [5]. Americans have also been investing more money in education. The proportion of young people receiving a high-school diploma (a secondary school leaving certificate) increased from one-half to three-quarters.

One of the biggest changes in American society in the postwar era occurred through the courts and the statute books, with the integration of blacks as full citizens in American society. A series of United States Supreme Court decisions culminated in 1954 in the declaration that segregation was unconstitutional. This led to major changes in education patterns throughout the country as subsequent court orders enjoined increasingly stringent methods of assuring a balance of blacks and whites in the schools.

**The raising of black consciousness**
In the 1960s blacks began to turn to the streets, protesting peacefully under leaders such as Martin Luther King (1929–68) [4], or rioting as an expression of frustration, as in the Watts area of Los Angeles, in Detroit, Newark and even in Washington, DC. Black family income, reflecting generations of discrimination, does not yet equal that of whites. Nonetheless it has been rising, both in absolute terms and as a proportion of white income, as more blacks receive better education and as the federal government enforces stricter practices for equal opportunity in most areas of employment.

**The supermarket,** with its variety and abundance of goods, symbolizes the affluence of postwar America. In the decade following World War II this wealth was highlighted by the austerity of a Europe recovering from conflict.

**3 Political control**
Congress

Presidency

1945 47 49 51 53 55 57 59 61 63 65 67 69 71 73 75

Truman    Eisenhower    Kennedy Johnson    Nixon    Ford Carter
49    53    57    61    65    69    73    77

☐ Democrat controlled    ☐ Republican controlled

**3 Since 1944 Republican presidents** have generally faced a Congress held, almost continuously, by the Democrats. However, internal Democratic divisions have reduced the potential for conflict.

**4 Martin Luther King** organized the Montgomery, Alabama, bus boycott of 1955–6, the first great civil rights protest in the south. This nationwide spokesman for the black community was murdered in 1968.

**5**

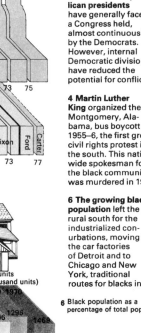

Televisions
1950 1960 1970

Automobiles
1950 1960 1970

Washing machines
1950 1960 1970

New housing units started (in thousand units)
1950 1960 1970
1396 1295 1469

3364
4273 4094

4851
5708
6666 6675 6547

7464

Sales in thousands of units

**6 The growing black population** left the rural south for the industrialized conurbations, moving to the car factories of Detroit and to Chicago and New York, traditional routes for blacks in search of work, and also to new growth areas such as Los Angeles and Houston. This influx provoked an outflow of white residents to the suburbs. The whites were partly attracted by suburban life and partly fearful of the urban ghettos. As a result of this movement, America's most important cities today often contain its greatest social, political and economic problems, generated by years of racial antagonism.

**6** Black population as a percentage of total population

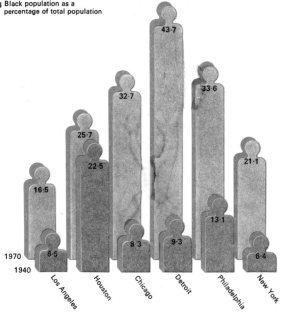

43·7
32·7    33·6
25·7
22·5    21·1
16·5    13·1
8·3    9·3
6·5    6·4

1970
1940

Los Angeles    Houston    Chicago    Detroit    Philadelphia    New York

**5 The consumer goods boom** in postwar USA began a "democracy of consumption": new homes, cars, washing machines and televisions became virtually the birthright of most Americans. Typical was the demand for television sets, first for black-and-white sets in the 1950s and later for colour sets, as technological advance made black-and-white television obsolescent. The boom in house construction brought mass production to the building industry, with economies of scale and standardization of product. A record of building well over a million houses a year meant that by the mid-1970s the number of homes built in the postwar era would have been able to provide a new house for almost every US family in 1939. Consumer durables also generated further costs – most notably the motor car. It consumed tracts of land for highways in and around cities and oil to fuel engines. Until the oil crisis of the 1970s resources to maintain this boom seemed boundless.

# 20th-century sociology and its influence

In the years following the end of World War II, sociology began to change from a theoretical system to a practical tool that could be used by government and industry. But it did not lose sight of its origins. It had begun from a desire to explain – and to counteract – the forces in industrialization that divided people, both economically and socially. Modern sociologists have continued to concentrate on ways of reducing inequalities and of increasing social integration.

## The "good society"

The insecurity and disruption of the 1930s and 1940s had served to increase the concern of sociologists with the "good society". The good society was seen by some theorists as involving a high level of integration and stability, a common core of values and an emphasis on community. One school of thought that echoed these themes was that of structural functionalism which developed a picture of society as a self-regulating organism, in which all the various elements (institutions) perform necessary functions. Functionalism originated with Emile Durk-

heim and was developed in America by Talcott Parsons (1902–   ) and Robert Merton. Bronislaw Malinowski and Alfred Radcliffe-Brown founded British social anthropology with their studies in New Guinea, Africa and elsewhere of small-scale "primitive" cultures. The accessibility of the constituent elements of these small societies make an exhaustive study seem possible.

The conservative tenor of structural functionalism is apparent in its concentration on moral integration, in its emphasis upon existing social institutions and in its tendency to identify their functions with the interests of the more powerful groups in society.

## Sociology and "social engineering"

Functionalism provided a theoretical basis for the widespread use of sociologists as "social engineers", dealing with particular problems for industry or government. A variety of different policies was drawn from functionalist analyses – while some, for example, stressed the need for different social levels, others advocated integration. Busing and comprehensive schooling are

government policies adopted to promote integration and equality by bringing together privileged and underprivileged children at school [9]. Delinquency is another problem for which governments have increasingly employed sociologists. Functionalist analysis underlay the 1958 "Mobilization for Youth" programme in the United States, which hoped to narrow the gap between the goals desired by, and the actual opportunities offered to, the underprivileged – a gap that the originators of the programme believed to be a cause of delinquency [5]. In their postwar major rehousing and urban renewal schemes, governments of many industrialized nations have employed sociologists in planning and design [4] in an attempt to provide a solution to the concentration of social problems that seemed inherent in prewar slums everywhere.

The pioneering experiments at the Western Electric Company into the productivity and working conditions found in their factories in 1927 showed the great importance of "human factors" in raising productivity levels. The value of those findings led to

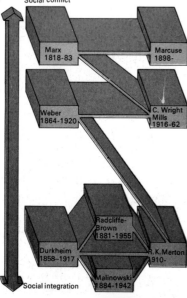

**1 Sociological thought in the 20th century** is, in many respects, as divided as that of the 19th century when many of its current disagreements began. There is no one sociological theory, but instead a number of different theories, some complementary and some conflicting. One of the most fundamental of these concerns the model of society with which the sociologist starts out. Some, such as Talcott Parsons, define society as a harmonious, self-regulating system. Others, like Marcuse, argue that society is not as harmonious as it may sometimes appear, but is deeply divided by economic inequalities which lead to both conflict and violent unrest.

Social conflict

Marx 1818-83 | Marcuse 1898-

Weber 1864-1920 | C. Wright Mills 1916-62

Radcliffe-Brown 1881-1955

Durkheim 1858-1917 | R.K.Merton 1910-

Malinowski 1884-1942

Social integration

**2 The "nuclear family"** – consisting of parents and their children only – appears to fulfil the basic function of caring for children and socializing them. Whereas functionalists see it as an essential unit, other sociologists and social psychologists such as R. D. Laing attack it for being so tightly integrated that it may breed neurosis and repression, a point taken up strongly by the Women's Liberation Movement.

**3 The Israeli kibbutz**, one of the experiments in group living in Western society, demonstrates that, contrary to early functionalist thinking, the nuclear family is not the only possible structure that can care for children. In theory, children on the kibbutz are raised collectively, although some sociologists have pointed out that a strong sense of the family unit remains despite the communal features.

**4 Governments have increasingly employed** sociologists to assist in social planning. Postwar prosperity and recognition that slums were a focus of social problems, led to large-scale rehousing schemes. In many cases, however, "improvements" were carried out with little thought of what effect they would have on the people rehoused. Established communities with strong, supportive social systems were broken up in the move to well-designed but socially anonymous new towns. Various measures, from the way houses were grouped in small units to the siting of shops (shown here is the Postgate shopping centre, Scotland), have been tried to re-create a community feeling.

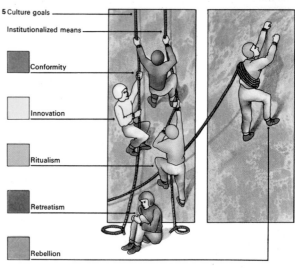

5 Culture goals
Institutionalized means

Conformity
Innovation
Ritualism
Retreatism
Rebellion

**5 Individual adjustment** within a structure of socially defined goals and means is shown on this diagram by Merton. With this model it is possible to analyse the behaviour of the delinquent (who may pursue a socially acceptable goal, but who does not follow morally prescribed means of attaining it) and of rebels who seek to change goals and means in society.

the large-scale employment of sociologists by management to work in such areas as marketing and industrial relations.

**The legacy of Karl Marx**

Structural functionalism was paralleled by Marxist theory. Whereas the structural functionalists stressed the notions of integration and co-operation, those inspired by Marx saw society as composed of conflicting classes divided by their differing economic positions.

Influenced by Marx, C. Wright Mills in his book *The Power Elite* pointed to a three-fold power concentration – the corporations, the military and the political – whose interests and actions were closely related [6]. But he argued that the power basis of this alliance could not be explained simply in Marxist, economic terms but required a wider analysis of social organization. Marxist analysis greatly influenced the Black Power movement, whose leaders were disillusioned with the philosophy of integration advocated by the Civil Rights movement, and who questioned whether integration was possible or even desirable. Following the race riots

across the United States in 1968, black and white politicians and sociologists argued for increased aid and social legislation for the ghettos, proposals rejected by the Black Power movement as mere palliatives.

The Vietnam War and the rise of student protest also brought to the fore a well-developed but previously uninfluential school of sociology – the Frankfurt School. It emphasized the control of knowledge through the mass media. The media were seen to be the new opiate of the masses, in part explaining popular acceptance of what is, according to Marxists, an oppressive economic state.

The development of this theme by Herbert Marcuse [7] rose to prominence in the theoretical base of the growing student protest movement [10]. According to Marcuse, students along with marginal and dispossessed groups are the contemporary revolutionary agents, precisely because they are outside the hypnotic culture of consumer society. However, the complex and incisive work of the Frankfurt School has, as yet, had little influence.

**The 20th century has been characterized** for many by a widening gap between living standards and expectations (developed, for example, through advertising). Sociologists have viewed this gap in different ways. Some have seen it as a cause of unrest and social problems; others have attributed the apathy of the underprivileged towards improving their situation to the use of advertising and the creation of a "consumer dreamworld". This gap has also contributed to the use of sociology by governments who have increasingly intervened to reduce inequalities. In the commercial field, sociologists have developed techniques to maintain and exploit the gap.

**6 The basis of power in American society**, according to C. Wright Mills, greatly depends on the common social background of the political, military and business leaders. Educated similarly, attending the same social events, yet careful to maintain a popular image – here President Eisenhower opens the 1960 baseball season – they sustain a common outlook that obviates the need for a conscious conspiracy to preserve their rule.

**7 Herbert Marcuse** (1898– ), Professor of Sociology at Berkeley University, shown here in discussion with students, provided a stimulating critique of modern society. His analysis of modern democracy as characterized by "repressive liberalism", in that freedom to disagree is more apparent than real, gave rise to a new approach to the study of social institutions. In the achievement of a truly liberated society, Marcuse allotted a central role to students. His work constitutes an important strand in the ideology of the student movement of the 1960s. Many of those involved in the student unrest of 1968 acknowledged Marcuse as their mentor.

**8 Social science research** has undergone a rapid expansion since the mid-1950s, as this diagram of US Federal support shows. But institutions like the Ford Foundation have provided the largest proportion of money in this area. The methods and findings of sociology have been applied to a wide variety of public and private fields, from military strategy to housing, and from marketing to industrial relations.

**8** Federal spending on social science research in the USA (in $ million)

1970 216m
1966 166m
1962 63m
1958 31m

**9 The policy of busing** black, underprivileged children to white schools encompasses two key sociological ideas. The first is the belief that educational achievement is as much a matter of environment as of heredity (emphasizing the need to equalize opportunities in the classroom). The second is that of racial integration. Public discontent with this policy, typified in the Boston busing "war" shown here, points to the limitations of such attempts at social engineering.

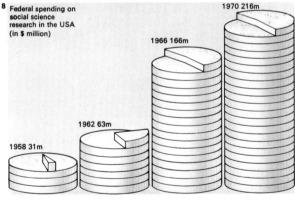

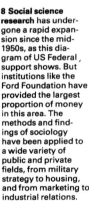

**10 Social science students** figured prominently in demonstrations against American involvement in Vietnam, such as this at Fort Dix, New Jersey, in 1970. Reaction to the war in Vietnam illustrates the paradox of sociology's influence on 20th-century political affairs. On the one hand sociology is charged with inciting conflict and change; on the other, it is accused of assisting in the maintenance of the existing social system. The involvement of radical social science students in opposing the war was more than equalled by the time, effort and particularly money spent on social scientific research designed to make the war more efficient.

# The wars of Indochina

In the brief interlude between the Japanese surrender at the end of World War II and the arrival of Allied troops to enforce it in French Indochina, the communist-dominated Viet Minh movement [Key] seized power in Vietnam and proclaimed the country's independence on 2 September 1945. With British support, however, the French returned to Vietnam and as a result the Viet Minh were forced to try to negotiate independence. But their hopes were dashed at the Fontainebleau Conference [2] in 1946 and fighting broke out towards the end of that year [6].

### The Geneva Agreements
In spite of heavy American financial support, the French were unable to defeat the Viet Minh backed by China and the Soviet Union and growing war weariness at home compelled them to seek a negotiated settlement. An international conference convened in Geneva in 1954 met in the shadow of the Viet Minh victory at Dien Bien Phu [4]. Vietnam was temporarily partitioned, and reunification elections were to be held in 1956.

After Geneva the communist regime in North Vietnam concentrated upon socialist reconstruction and instructed its followers in the south to restrict their activities to the political sphere. An anti-communist regime in the south had supported peaceful decolonization and did not sign the Geneva Agreements. By 1956, under the leadership of Ngo Dinh Diem (1901–63) [5], it had consolidated its authority, with American support, and felt strong enough to block reunification elections on the northern regime's terms and to move against communist supporters in the south. In January 1959, faced with the near destruction of its apparatus in the south, the Communist Party's central committee in Hanoi gave the order for armed struggle to begin.

By the autumn of 1961 President John F. Kennedy (1917–63) felt obliged to send large numbers of military advisers to South Vietnam. These did not turn the tide of insurgency and on 8 February 1965 President Lyndon B. Johnson (1908–73) ordered American bombing of North Vietnam to deter the movement of manpower and weaponry to the south. But the war on the ground [9] continued and the United States was forced to commit further aid and growing numbers of its own troops to the fighting from April 1965 onwards [8].

### American withdrawal
In January 1968 the communists, who now included large numbers of North Vietnamese regular soldiers, launched the Tet or New Year offensive through South Vietnam. After some intensive fighting, it was beaten back, but it weakened America's will to fight. President Johnson announced, on 31 March, a cutback in the bombing of North Vietnam and his own withdrawal from the forthcoming presidential election campaign.

His successor, President Richard M. Nixon (1913– ), pinned his hopes upon "Vietnamization". Although the United States continued to provide air and sea support for the South Vietnamese forces, US combat troops were gradually withdrawn.

Meanwhile, negotiations between the Americans and the North Vietnamese had begun in Paris in May 1968 and after the stalemate of a second major communist

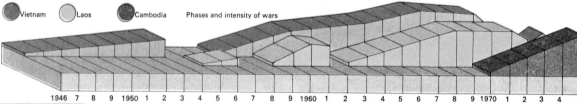

**1 The intensity of war in Indochina** increased over a 30-year period, spreading from Vietnam alone to Laos and finally to Cambodia, although fighting was on a smaller scale in those countries.

Vietnam  Laos  Cambodia  Phases and intensity of wars

1946 7 8 9 1950 1 2 3 4 5 6 7 8 9 1960 1 2 3 4 5 6 7 8 9 1970 1 2 3 4 5

**2 At the Fontaine-bleau Conference** in July 1946 Ho Chi Minh insisted on the unity of Vietnam, which the French had divided into the colony of Cochin China in the south, Tonkin in the north and Annam in the centre. The conference broke down when France made Cochin China a separate republic.

**4 The raising of the Viet Minh flag** on the French command post at Dien Bien Phu on 7 May 1954 marked the greatest military setback ever suffered by a European colonial power at the hands of local forces. This French fortress in north-west Vietnam fell to General Vo Nguyen Giap (1912– ) after a 55-day siege.

**3 Catholic influence** (shown in this classroom and chapel at an orphanage in An Loc) was important in the educational system introduced to Vietnam by the French and was a factor in the anti-communism of many in the south. In 1939 about 1.6 million Vietnamese (about 8% of the population) were Catholic.

**5 Ngo Dinh Diem** a Roman Catholic, was bitterly opposed to both French colonialism and communism. These traits initially won him US support when he became prime minister of South Vietnam in 1954. Gradually, however, nepotism and his authoritarian rule alienated the US. In 1963 the administration of President Kennedy connived at a coup by dissident South Vietnamese generals. Diem was assassinated in November 1963.

offensive in March – May 1972 and renewed American bombing raids upon Hanoi in December of that year, a peace agreement was signed on 27 January 1973.

Communist armed forces from North Vietnam were not obliged by the agreement to withdraw from the south [7] and further fighting began almost immediately as both sides jockeyed for position. The final collapse of the South Vietnamese goverment to communist forces [10] came on 30 April 1975.

### Laos and Cambodia

Laotian nationalism split, in 1949, into pro-communist (Pathet Lao) and anti-communist sections and it was to the latter that the French conceded independence in 1953. With the United States striving to preserve an anti-communist government and the Viet Minh supporting the Pathet Lao, a full-scale civil war developed in 1960 and an international conference at Geneva in 1961–2 only temporarily defused the crisis. United States' bombing of North Vietnamese and Pathet Lao positions in Laos, controlling supply routes to South Vietnam, increased steadily

after 1964. The January 1973 ceasefire in Vietnam was followed by one in Laos on 22 February and by mid-1975 the Pathet Lao had virtually taken over the country.

Cambodia also obtained its independence from France in 1953. Under its ruler, Prince Norodom Sihanouk (1922– ), it managed to maintain a position of neutrality in the Indochina conflict for some years, but with the escalation of the war in Vietnam was forced to act as the main supply route for arms to the communists and to grant them virtual freedom of action in border areas. On 18 March 1970 Sihanouk was overthrown by a right-wing coup and Cambodia was plunged not only into its own civil war, but also into the wider Indochina conflict [1]. While America and South Vietnam attacked the communists in Cambodia, Sihanouk proclaimed a government-in-exile in Peking and allied himself with the left-wing Khmer Rouge rebels who had taken up arms against his own regime in 1967. The American bombing of Cambodia ended in August 1973 and the "Red Khmers" took the capital, Phnom Penh, on 18 April 1975.

**Ho Chi Minh** (1890–1969), principal figure in the Viet Minh struggle against the French and leader of North Vietnam after 1954, was born Nguyen That Thanh in north-central Vietnam. He left Vietnam in 1911 and was converted to communism in France after World War I. As a Comintern agent he founded the Indochinese Communist Party in 1930 but did not return to Vietnam from France until 1941, when he set up the Viet Minh front. In 1944 he organized the Viet Minh seizure of power in August 1945. Ho Chi Minh, whose adopted name means "he who enlightens", is shown (right) with the premier of Vietnam, Pham Van Dong (1902– ).

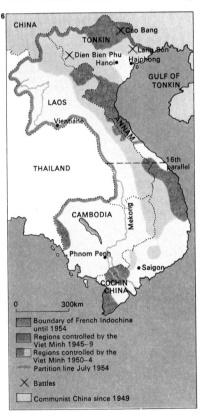

**6 The war in Indochina** between the Viet Minh and the French leading to the Geneva Agreements of July 1954 had two main phases. A French defeat at Cao Bang and the subsequent loss of Lang Son in October 1950 marked the onset of a more aggressive strategy by the Viet Minh, supported by aid from the newly established Chinese People's Republic. A French recovery followed, but only temporarily.

**7 The ceasefire position early in 1973** left the main prizes of the long Indochina war still to be won. Communist forces held key border areas in South Vietnam, Laos and Cambodia along the Ho Chi Minh Trail carrying military supplies from North Vietnam. The peace agreement, designed chiefly to allow US withdrawal, called for a political settlement but both sides prepared for a military solution.

Boundary of French Indochina until 1954
Regions controlled by the Viet Minh 1945–9
Regions controlled by the Viet Minh 1950–4
Partition line July 1954
X Battles
Communist China since 1949

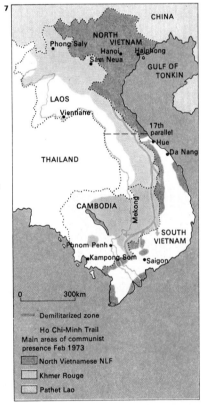

Demilitarized zone
Ho Chi-Minh Trail
Main areas of communist presence Feb 1973
North Vietnamese NLF
Khmer Rouge
Pathet Lao

US military aid in dollars (thousands of millions)

US combined forces (totals in thousands)

**8 US military aid to South Vietnam** rose to a peak in 1968 when American combat troops totalled 545,000. Actual (incremental) US war expenditure that year was $23,000 million with $1,000 million more in aid. Spending fell as this effort produced only stalemate.

**9 An American patrol in rough country** epitomizes the problem faced by the US in Vietnam where sophisticated technology failed to win the war on the ground. Alongside the fighting an ultimately more important struggle for the allegiance of Vietnam's mainly peasant population was being won by the communists at village level.

**10 As Saigon fell** American helicopters evacuated their allies on 29 April 1975.

# Ireland since Partition

By July 1921, the British government was at last ready to recognize Irish nationalism, and the credentials of Eamon de Valera [5] as spokesman for the Irish people. On 6 December the Irish delegates, led by Arthur Griffith (1872–1922) and Michael Collins (1890–1922), returned to Dublin with an agreement for a new Irish Dominion, within the Commonwealth, with the six counties of Northern Ireland separate [Key].

The Treaty embodying the terms was passed by the Dail on 7 January 1922, by only 64 votes to 57. Opponents included de Valera, who called it a betrayal. This rhetoric was soon to be backed with arms. The majority, however, led by Griffith, Collins, William Cosgrave [1] and Kevin O'Higgins [3], claimed that they had won the freedom to achieve their ultimate goals.

## From Civil War to World War II

By the time the Civil War ended in victory for the pro-Treaty party in May 1923, Griffith was dead and Collins, his successor, had been murdered. Cosgrave became leader of the new state through its formative years.

Anti-Treaty politicians continued to boycott Parliament until 1927. In December 1925, hopes in Dublin of incorporating Northern Ireland in the Free State were dashed when the Boundary Commission failed.

O'Higgins was assassinated in 1927. The ensuing tough, anti-terrorist legislation finally persuaded de Valera, who had formed the Fianna Fail Party a year earlier, to take his seat in Parliament. In 1932, with Labour support, his party won power. By then much had been gained internationally. Inside the developing Commonwealth, the Irish pursued full sovereign status for the dominions, and played a full part in the Imperial Conferences of 1926 and 1930, and in the preparation of the 1931 Statute of Westminster. At Geneva, where the Free State joined the League of Nations in 1923, the cause of small states was championed, and non-permanent membership of the League Council gained in 1930. De Valera did not like some of the commitments to Britain that he inherited, and Anglo-Irish relations for the next six years were marked by economic and constitutional disputes. Dur-

ing those years, de Valera gained an overall majority, unilaterally cancelled some of the Treaty terms, re-defined Irish nationality and, in 1937, adopted a new constitution, changing the country's name to Eire.

Differences with Britain were resolved in 1938, bringing much-needed financial and trade agreements – and Irish control of three naval installations. It was this that enabled de Valera to keep his country neutral in World War II. Neutrality was favoured by most Irishmen, although many volunteered to serve in the British forces.

## Inflation and austerity

In 1948, electoral discontent brought to power a coalition government, led by John Costello (1891–1976) of Fine Gael (Cosgrave's former party). This administration lasted until 1951, during which time Eire withdrew from the Commonwealth and declared itself a republic (1949). Following the collapse of the coalition, de Valera headed a minority administration for three years, until Costello was again returned. But inflation and Costello's austerity programme

1 **William Cosgrave** (1880–1965), minister for local government in the first Dail, showed wisdom and steadiness when he unexpectedly became president in 1922. After defeat, he was leader of the opposition (1932–44).

2 **The Shannon hydro-electric scheme,** constructed between 1925 and 1929, was the first major venture by the new Irish government. The scheme provided countrywide electrification over a national grid devised in 1927. It set a pattern for state aid that was extended into many areas in need of development capital. It was agriculture, however, rather than heavy industry, to which money was diverted, notably towards the new beet sugar and the turf-processing sectors.

3 **Kevin O'Higgins** (1892-1927) was the dominant figure in the first Irish government, establishing law and order and serving in many cabinet posts and from 1923 as vice-president until he was assassinated.

4 **Harland and Wolff shipyards,** Belfast, founded in 1863, are Northern Ireland's main employers and exporters. Business has declined during the 20th century but the firm is still a barometer of the economy.

5 **Eamon de Valera** (1882–1975) resigned the presidency of Ireland when he was out-voted by pro-Treaty colleagues in January 1922. He was gaoled in 1923 for fighting against the government in the Civil War (1922–3) but broke with the IRA and became the dominant figure in Irish politics after reorganizing the Republican Party as Fianna Fail. The architect of Eire, he was a political leader from 1927 to 1973. Born in New York of a Spanish father and Irish mother, he went to Ireland as a child.

contributed to disenchantment at the polls, and de Valera's Fianna Fail were voted back in 1957 to begin 16 years of rule.

De Valera himself retired to become president in 1959, handing over to Sean Lemass (1899–1971), who was prime minister until 1966 when Jack Lynch [9] succeeded him. Lemass made new contacts with the Northern Ireland government in 1965, when he went to Belfast for talks with the Ulster premier, Captain Terence O'Neill (1914–    ), but it was Lynch who had to respond to armed conflict in the north.

In March 1973, only three months after taking Eire into the European Economic Community, Lynch's government was defeated at the polls by another combination of Fine Gael and Labour, led by William Cosgrave's son Liam.

### The troubles of Northern Ireland

Northern Ireland had been a state, albeit subordinate to Westminster, since 1920. The first prime minister, James Craig (1871–1940), had hoped for unity between conflicting factions, but the Catholic minority stood aloof from the moulding of the state. As a result, the civil service, police, judiciary and educational system were very much tailored to Protestant needs.

Postwar Northern Ireland was transformed by the Welfare State. Social benefits so far outstripped those of Eire that the Catholics in Northern Ireland were at last ready to identify themselves with the state, but only on the basis of equal citizenship. Demands for equality were backed by the short-lived People's Democracy, and later by the Social Democratic and Labour Party of Gerry Fitt (1926–    ) and John Hume (1937–    ), the Alliance Party, and even by moderate Ulster Unionists.

When the civil rights movement [7] met Protestant resistance, violence erupted, enabling the Irish Republican Army (IRA) to revive the issue of nationalism. Fighting between Catholic and Protestant extremists brought British troops into the streets from 1969 [10], internment without trial (1971), and the end of the Northern Ireland Parliament at Stormont, scrapped in favour of direct rule from Westminster (1972).

Northern Ireland

Irish Free State
Est. Dec 1922 (Eire)

Counties with
most incidents 1920–21

Martial law declared 1921

0    100km

**Britain's partition of Ireland** (1920) with a limited form of self-government for both north and south was accepted by the six counties of Ulster in 1921, when a parliament was established at Belfast. Southern Ireland used the 1920 Act to elect the Dail Eireann (outlawed since December 1919), but went on struggling for full independence. IRA (Irish Republican Army) forces were pitted against the British army, the Royal Irish Constabulary (supported by former soldiers nick-named "Black and Tans") and Auxiliaries whose reprisals upset liberal opinion in Britain, encouraging Lloyd George's government to seek a settlement. A truce was established on 11 July 1921, and four months later negotiations began in earnest.

**6 A modern Dominican church** at Athy, Co Kildare, reflects the continuing importance of Catholicism in Irish life. In the republic in 1971, Roman Catholics made up 93.9% of the population, showing 2,795,666 adherents, as against 119,437 Protestants (4%) and 63,145 (2.1%) others. In Northern Ireland the groupings were: Protestant 811,272 (53.9%), Roman Catholic 477,919 (31.1%) and others 230,449 (15%). The strong contrast does not need underlining.

**7 Demonstrations in 1968** by the Civil Rights Association sought reforms in Northern Ireland's system of police, local government and housing to remove widespread discrimination in favour of Protestants. Predominantly Catholic, the movement was identified as a republican front by Protestant Unionists. Extremists under Ian Paisley (1926–    ) stirred anti-Catholic feeling and despite some reforms community distrust grew. After the disbanding of Stormont, Brian Faulkner (1921–77) failed in his efforts to rule with a Catholic-Protestant executive, established temporarily in 1974.

**8 Guinness's brewery in Dublin** is among the growth industries that have enabled the Irish Republic to reduce unemployment and emigration, two chronic features of the economy for more than a century.

**9 Jack Lynch** (1917–    ), was premier of the Irish Republic from 1966 to 1973, and re-elected in 1977. He was faced with the developing troubles in the north and the activities of the IRA, not only there but also in the south, which compromised his position in 1973.

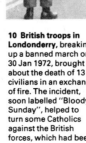

**10 British troops in Londonderry**, breaking up a banned march on 30 Jan 1972, brought about the death of 13 civilians in an exchange of fire. The incident, soon labelled "Bloody Sunday", helped to turn some Catholics against the British forces, which had been sent to Ulster in August 1969 to separate Protestants and Catholics after violence had erupted in Derry and Belfast. The revived IRA split into feuding wings — militarily active Provisionals and more politically oriented Officials. Posing as defenders of the Catholic community, the "Provos" renewed the fight for union with the south, attacking both British forces and the whole Protestant community. Protestant paramilitary groups retaliated and sectarian strife brought 1,600 deaths by January 1977, together with widespread injuries and property damage from bombs. A peace movement, founded in 1976 by Betty Williams, Mairead Corrigan and Ciaran McKeown, offered hopes of reconciliation, and strengthened the concern for a peaceful settlement.

# The question of Israel

Zionism, the movement by Jews to set up a state in their ancient homestead of Palestine emerged late in the nineteenth century as a form of the nationalism then sweeping Europe. It represented an attempt to channel the Jewish sense of corporate existence into a secure political entity that would provide an answer to continuing persecution. Among Arabs at about the same time the nationalist concept began to fertilize a deep-rooted sense of separate identity lying dormant under Ottoman rule.

## Origins of the conflict

Zionism and Arab separatism clashed from the beginning. In 1882 the first modern Jewish agricultural settlement was founded in Palestine, where Jews had been a minority for centuries. Muslim and Christian notables of Jerusalem urged the Ottoman administration to prevent further immigration. Nonetheless, the Zionist movement grew slowly and the Jewish population of Palestine gradually increased.

During World War I the defeat of the Turks was a vital military objective for the Allies. Britain secured the assistance of Hussein Ibn Ali (1854–1931), ruler of the Hejaz and guardian of Mecca, by pledging in vague terms to help Arab independence.

On 2 November 1917, Zionist hopes also seemed near fulfilment when the British foreign secretary, Arthur Balfour (1848–1930), declared: "His Majesty's government view with favour the establishment in Palestine of a national home for the Jewish people . . .". But meanwhile, in 1916, the Allies had agreed secretly to a postwar Middle East division of spoils that paid no immediate heed to Zionist hopes and reduced the Arab state to a Franco-British puppet. At the San Remo Conference in 1920 Palestine, which had been under direct British military rule since 1918, came under British mandate.

Over the next 25 years the situation in Palestine steadily worsened. The Jewish population increased [1] and so did Arab violence against the Jews, erupting in riots in 1921 and 1929. With the advent of racist persecution in Nazi Germany during the 1930s the Zionists felt that increased immigration was desperately necessary. On the other hand, new and more extremist Arab Palestinian leaders advocated halting immigration by force. Britain finally crushed an Arab revolt of 1936–9 [3], but its 1939 White Paper restricting Jewish immigration was a political victory for the Arabs.

During World War II, under the stress of Nazism, Zionism became a mass movement, lobbying the US government and public for support. After 1945 American Zionists shipped money and arms to the Haganah, a semi-underground Jewish army, and to more extremist guerrillas. In the face of British refusal to increase immigration, Jewish guerrilla violence and British counter-violence intensified. Finally Britain referred the problem to the UN, which in August 1947 recommended partition.

## The birth of Israel

The British left on 14 May 1948; that same day the state of Israel was proclaimed [Key] and the armies of five Arab states attacked it. But armistices in 1949 left Israel holding most of the territory it had been granted,

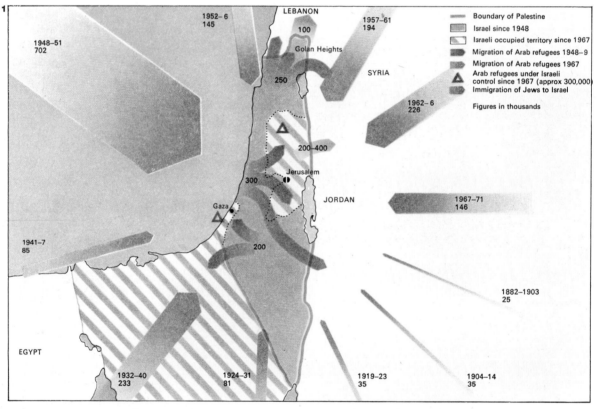

**1 Migration to Palestine** began in the late 19th century as groups of Jews sought freedom from persecution and re-affirmation of Jewish dignity through establishing settlements there. After the foundation of the World Zionist Organization by Theodor Herzl (1860–1904) in 1897, more Jews arrived buying land for collectives. During the Mandate, immigration fluctuated. Up to 1948 most arrivals were from Europe. After this, many Jews living in Arab countries migrated or fled to Israel. The Palestinians left their homes in two waves, the majority (more than half a million) in 1948 and a second group of between 200,000 and 400,000 during the war in 1967. Most were herded into UN refugee camps, only Jordan granting them citizenship. After 1967, 300,000 of them lived in refugee camps run by Israel.

Boundary of Palestine
Israel since 1948
Israeli occupied territory since 1967
Migration of Arab refugees 1948–9
Migration of Arab refugees 1967
Arab refugees under Israeli control since 1967 (approx 300,000)
Immigration of Jews to Israel

Figures in thousands

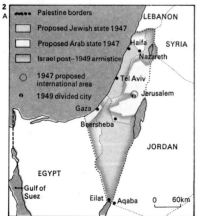

Palestine borders
Proposed Jewish state 1947
Proposed Arab state 1947
Israel post-1949 armistice
1947 proposed international area
1949 divided city

Ceasefire lines June 1967
Israeli occupied territories after June 1967

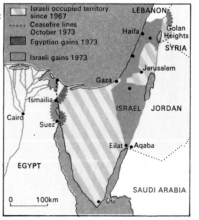

Israeli occupied territory since 1967
Ceasefire lines October 1973
Egyptian gains 1973
Israeli gains 1973

**2 Israel's borders** at the time of the 1949 armistice were wider than envisaged in the 1947 UN partition plan [A]. Arab Palestine had been largely incorporated into Jordan. After the 1967 war, Israel occupied East Jerusalem, the West Bank, the Golan Heights and the whole of Sinai [B]. The war of October 1973 and subsequent disengagement agreements returned some of the Golan to Syria and the Suez Canal and part of Sinai to Egypt [C].

together with some of the territory allotted for an Arab Palestinian state [2]. In the absence of this state, Jordan acquired the West Bank and Egypt the Gaza Strip. About 600,000 Palestinian Arabs lost their homes.

Israel was left surrounded by hostile neighbours and Arab humiliation and defeat demanded redress. Open war broke out on three further occasions. In 1956, with its shipping blocked by Egypt, Israel joined in an Anglo-French conspiracy to recapture the nationalized Suez Canal. In a lightning attack the Israelis occupied the Sinai Peninsula on the east bank of the Suez Canal. Pressure by the US and USSR forced Israel to withdraw from Sinai but a UN force was established in the Gaza Strip to act as a buffer.

When Egypt ordered the departure of the UN force in 1967 and on 22 May closed the Strait of Tiran, the Israelis seized the initiative on 5 June by a pre-emptive strike on the airfields of Egypt, Jordan, Syria and Iraq. After six days of fighting Israel held all Jerusalem [5] as well as the Suez Canal; the Jordanian army had been forced across the Jordan and the Syrian Golan Heights were

occupied. This time Israel did not withdraw.

The lesson of the first strike was not lost on the deeply humiliated Arabs. On 6 October 1973 the forces of Egypt and Syria attacked simultaneously, Egyptian troops crossing the canal while Syrian troops advanced over the Golan plain. At the end of 16 days Egypt and Syria had gained a little territory and a great deal of prestige.

### Distant hopes of peace

Stagnating in camps, the exiled Palestinians meanwhile had formed desperate guerrilla groups, which eventually united in 1969 under the umbrella of the Palestinian Liberation Organization. In October 1974 the PLO was recognized by all Arab countries as the sole representative of the Palestinians [6].

The realities of the Arab-Israel conflict have often been blurred by its being a focus of superpower rivalry, with the US supplying Israel and USSR arming the Arabs. In 1975, however, Egypt and Israel arrived at an interim peace agreement in which there were seeds of hope. Irreconcilable nationalist aims remain the core of the problem.

**David Ben-Gurion** (1886–1973), first prime minister of Israel, proclaimed the establishment of the Jewish state in the Museum of Modern Art in Tel Aviv on 14 May 1948, the day on which the last British high commissioner departed.

**3 Arab revolts broke out in April 1936** against British rule in Palestine, partly as a result of declining prosperity but mainly because of mounting Jewish immigration. Spontaneous and horrifying attacks on Jews occurred throughout the country. At the same time Arab leaders called a six-month general strike in an effort to force the British to suspend Jewish immi- gration. At first directed against the Jews, the revolt later became anti- British, and eventu- ally armed bands of unemployed also attacked Arabs who opposed them. The unrest ended in 1939.

**4 Martial law was imposed in Tel Aviv** in 1945. Jews saw the immigration limits in Britain's White Paper of 1939 as a betrayal, and reaction was muted only by the outbreak of war. Ben-Gurion said: "We shall fight with Britain as if there was no White Paper and we shall fight the White Paper as if there was no war". An unofficial Jewish army, the Haganah, had existed since the 1920s and in 1937 a more extreme group formed the Irgun (or Etzel). Allied in September 1945, these groups set out to change British policy by increas- ingly violent attacks on British troops. British military reaction was viewed as counter-violence.

**5 Jerusalem, a city sacred to Judaism,** Christianity and Is- lam, was visualized in all external par- tition plans for Palestine as an inter- national city. In the 1948–9 war it was divided, with the east and Old City held by Jordan and the west by Israel. During the Six Day War of 1967 the city was forcibly reunited by the Israelis. New buildings encircling the whole city (in the distance here) are evidence of Israel's determination to retain control in its own hands.

**6 Arab opposition to Israel** has taken dif- ferent forms. Under Anwar Sadat (1918–   ) [A] Egypt, the main combatant, adopted a new and much-criticized course in 1975 by con- cluding an interim peace agreement with Israel. From a rigidly Islamic standpoint that re- jected the idea of any part of the Islamic world under non- Muslim rule, Saudi Arabia used its enormous oil wealth [B] to help "front- line" Arab states like Syria maintain a bellicose attitude. While the PLO [C] aimed politically at a "secular democratic state" in the whole of Palestine, its militant extremist wings [D] captured world headlines with violent attacks inside and outside Israel.

# The United Nations and its agencies

The name "United Nations" was devised by United Sates President Franklin D. Roosevelt (1882–1945) and was first used in the Declaration by the United Nations of 1 January 1942, when representatives of 26 nations pledged their governments to continue fighting together against the Axis powers. The new United Nations (UN) was effectively a drastically reorganized and updated version of the League of Nations.

The charter of the UN was drawn up by the representatives of 50 countries at the United Nations Conference on International Organization, which met at San Francisco from 25 April to 26 June 1945. The charter was signed on 26 June 1945 and the UN began officially on 24 October 1945 [1].

## Peace and security
In theory, UN membership is open to all peace-loving states that accept the obligations of the charter. In fact, the principle of universality has been accepted, so that apart from Switzerland (with its rigid neutrality) all independent nations have joined or are doing so. By 1976 there were 144 members.

The UN is not a world government or suprastate. All member states are sovereign and equal. The charter provides that the UN shall not intervene in the internal affairs of any country, except when it is acting to maintain or restore international peace.

In the Security Council the five permanent members (France, UK, USA, USSR and the People's Republic of China) each have a veto. But conflicting outlooks – particularly the ideological cold war between the USSR and the West – have meant that one or other of the Great Powers has been able to frustrate the General Assembly's wishes, although the Uniting for Peace Resolution of 1950 gave the Assembly authority to recommend enforcement action over a veto.

The UN has been involved in more than 100 situations where peace has been at risk [2, 5]. For example, the Security Council played an important part in solving the dispute between The Netherlands and Indonesia over the latter's independence in 1949; it prevented a threatening situation from escalating into outright hostilities when foreign troops intervened in the Lebanon and

Jordan in 1958; it contributed towards the peaceful transition of colonies to independence through organizing plebiscites and referenda, and on numerous occasions the secretary-general of the UN [4] has used quiet diplomacy to prevent conflicts over issues that could have become explosive.

The preamble to the UN charter determines to "reaffirm faith in fundamental human rights, in the dignity and worth of the human person, in the equal rights of men and women". Major steps to this end have been the 1946 Convention on the Political Rights of Women, the 1948 Universal Declaration of Human Rights, the 1951 Convention on Genocide and the 1965 Convention on the Elimination of Racial Discrimination.

## Economic and social work
More than 80 per cent of the UN's funds are devoted to helping poorer countries develop their own human and economic resources [9].

Under the supervision of the Economic and Social Council, there are seven functional commissions that make studies, issue reports or draft international treaties relating

**1 Joseph Paul Boncour** (1873–1972) signs the United Nations Charter for France at the first meeting of the organization in San Francisco in 1945. Since the first 50 members appended their signatures to the charter the membership has grown to almost treble that original number. As they have joined, the very many emergent nations have gradually weakened the Great Powers' 20-year domination of the UN.

**2 UN troops cross the Han River** in Korea as they move to meet the North Korean invaders of South Korea in 1950. It was the UN's first military intervention in a war – but almost by default. The USSR, at that time boycotting the Security Council, was unable to veto a recommendation that the UN should go to the aid of South Korea. Sixteen nations responded to the call to arms, but in the event it was overwhelmingly the US that provided the men, equipment and overall command to drive the North Koreans back across the dividing line of the 38th Parallel.

**3 The "political" aspect of the UN** is dominated by the General Assembly and the Security Council, but apart from these there are four other bodies. The Economic and Social Council (ECOSOC), under the supervision of the General Assembly, co-ordinates the UN's economic and social work and that of 14 of its specialized agencies. The Trusteeship Council was established to supervise the affairs of 11 trusteeship territories, of which all but one (the Pacific Islands) have now achieved independence. The International Court of Justice is the principal judicial organ and all UN members are parties to its statutes and can refer cases to it. It consists of 15 judges elected by the General Assembly and Security Council voting independently. The judges serve an initial term of nine years. Lastly, the Secretariat services all the other organs and administers the programmes and policies laid down by them.

1 UNCTAD Conference on Trade and Development
2 UNIDO Industrial Development Organization
3 UNITAR Institute for Training and Research
4 UNHCR High Commission for Refugees
5 UN Capital Development Fund
6 UNDP Development Programme
7 Trade and Development Board
8 UNICEF Children's Fund
9 UN-FAO World Food Programme

General Assembly
Secretariat
Trusteeship Council
Security Council
International Court of Justice
Economic and Social Council
IAEA Atomic Energy Agency

IMF Monetary Fund
WHO World Health Org.
FAO Food and Agricultural Org.
ILO International Labour Org.
IDA Development Assoc.
UNESCO Education, Scientific and Cultural Org.
IBRD Bank of Reconstruction and Development
IFC Finance Corp.
ICAO Civil Aviation Org.
Universal Postal Union
ITU Telecommunications Union
WMO World Meteorological Org.
IMCO Maritime Consultative Organization
GATT General Agreement on Tariffs and Trade

**4 The chief administrator of the UN** is the secretary-general, a man proposed by the Security Council and elected by the Assembly. Since 1946 there have been four; Trygve Lie (1896–1968) [A] of Norway, (1946–53); Dag Hammarskjöld (1905–61) [B] of Sweden, whose term ended tragically in an air crash in N. Rhodesia; the Burmese, U Thant (1909–74) [C], who retired in 1971; and Kurt Waldheim (1918– ) [D] of Austria.

to subjects such as human rights and control of narcotic drugs. There are also five regional economic commissions – one each for Africa, Western Asia, Asia and the Pacific, Europe and Latin America. Increased stress on direct operational field activities is reflected in the stepped-up pace of the United Nations Development Programme, a voluntarily financed operation carried out by the UN and 15 related agencies.

## The emergence of a new majority
Until the 1960s the balance of power within the UN General Assembly lay with the Western Alliance, partly because of the composition of the Security Council, but as colonial territories acquired independence in the 1960s so new states with traditions and interests very different from those of the US and the European liberal democracies joined the UN. The influence of these new states became manifest in the General Assembly, where an increasing emphasis was placed on the evils of colonialism and apartheid and on the need for economic development. The numerical majority of present members are

from Africa, Asia, Latin America and the Middle East. By 1970 it was apparent that the balance of power in the Assembly had positively shifted to a non-aligned group, which did not necessarily support either side in the East/West ideological battle [7]. The states of the Western Alliance found themselves in a minority as resolutions favouring the non-aligned group was passed, often with Eastern European backing.

The full effects of this change, however, were not felt until 1974, when the special session of the Assembly adopted a declaration and a programme of action on the establishment of a new international economic order. In the declaration, UN members solemnly proclaimed their determination to work urgently for "the establishment of a new international economic order based on equity, sovereign equality, interdependence, common interest and co-operation among all States, irrespective of their economic and social systems, which shall ensure steadily accelerating economic and social development in peace and justice for present and future generations".

The "Parliament of the World", the UN General Assembly, has its permanent home in Manhattan, New York. It can discuss and make recommendations on any subject mentioned in the UN charter except when the Security Council is discussing it, but it has no power of enforcement. It elects members to the other UN agencies, appoints the secretary-general and fixes and allocates the budget.

**5 Potential "powder keg" situations** throughout the world have seen the presence of UN peace-keeping forces since the organization moved to back South Korea when it was invaded in 1950. They have been used to separate forces in the Middle East, to control armed conflict, and keep internal order in the Congo after its independence (1960–64) and in Cyprus, (1964 onwards) where clashes between Greek and Turkish communities erupted into an invasion of the island by Turkey in the course of 1974. Non-combatant observers have been in Indonesia, Korea, Lebanon, Jammu and Kashmir, West Iran and the Yemen.

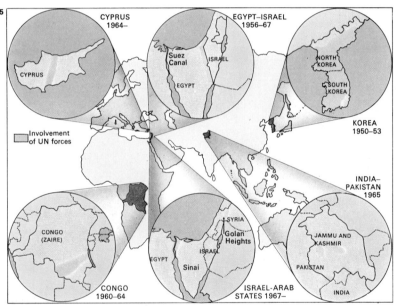

CYPRUS 1964–
EGYPT–ISRAEL 1956–67
Suez Canal
ISRAEL
EGYPT
NORTH KOREA
SOUTH KOREA
KOREA 1950–53

Involvement of UN forces

CONGO (ZAIRE)
CONGO 1960–64
SYRIA
Golan Heights
ISRAEL
EGYPT
Sinai
ISRAEL-ARAB STATES 1967–
JAMMU AND KASHMIR
PAKISTAN
INDIA
INDIA–PAKISTAN 1965

**6 The giant monuments of Abu Simbel** were saved from the waters of Lake Nasser by UN agencies, in particular by UNESCO. As yet the UN's cultural work, like its exercises in international diplomacy, has been less impressive than its continuing battle against disease and famine through the work of the World Health Organization and the Food and Agriculture Organization.

**7 The UN membership** consists of sovereign states that accept the obligations contained in the UN Charter. From time to time non-self-governing territories have been allowed to put their case to the committees of the Assembly but a precedent was set in 1975 when the head of the Palestine Liberation Organization, Yasser Arafat, was allowed to address the Assembly.

**8 After the Arab-Israeli War resumed** in October 1973 two ceasefire resolutions sponsored by the Soviet Union and the US were adopted by the Security Council. But the fighting continued and it was the eight non-aligned members of the Security Council who then proposed the dispatch of this non-combatant observer force, whose function was to supervise the ceasefire conditions.

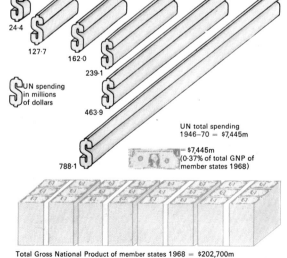

1946 24·4
1950 127·7
1955 162·0
1960 239·1
1965 463·9
1970 788·1

UN spending in millions of dollars

UN total spending 1946–70 = $7,445m

= $7,445m (0·37% of total GNP of member states 1968)

Total Gross National Product of member states 1968 = $202,700m

**9 UN members contribute** according to their yearly product, the USA paying most. The total UN expenditure since 1946 is only a fraction of the annual wealth produced by its members.

# The world's monetary system

The establishment of a new and more stable international monetary system was one of the most important tasks for world leaders as World War II drew to a close. At the Bretton Woods Conference in 1944 negotiators had bitter memories of the 1930s when the breakdown of the gold standard [1] as a semi-automatic system of adjusting imbalances in trade and payments between nations was followed by a period of unstable exchange rates, restrictive trade practices and deep economic slump in most major countries. It was the aim of the conference to devise a monetary system that would encourage international co-operation and end instability.

## The Bretton Woods system
The essential features of the new system were: stable, or fixed, exchange rates; the creation of a new central organization, the International Monetary Fund (IMF), to oversee the new arrangements and assist countries in balance-of-payments difficulties [Key, 2]; and assistance, through the newly established World Bank (International Bank for Reconstruction and Development), to

poor countries. Stable exchange rates required each IMF member to report to the Fund the value of its currency (in terms of gold). Since all currencies were thus "priced" in terms of a single denominator, gold, this also established rates of exchange between them. These rates were to be regarded as essentially fixed and a major change in the value of a currency was permitted only when a country was suffering from "fundamental disequilibrium" in its balance of payments. To correct a "fundamental" surplus (exports greater than imports) a country would revalue (making its exports more expensive and its imports cheaper); to adjust a deficit it would devalue.

The US dollar, and to a lesser degree the British pound sterling, came to play a central role in the new system. Sterling had long had an important position as a major trading or "hard" currency [4]. The dollar's pre-eminence was largely a postwar phenomenon and reflected the economic and political strength of the United States in a world in which most other leading countries were still ravaged by the results of the war. Together

with the fact that the US Treasury undertook to convert foreign holdings of dollars into gold at a fixed price of $35 per ounce (thus making the dollar "as good as gold") this prompted other countries to accumulate holdings of dollar balances on which they could earn interest. The dollar and sterling thus acted as key "reserve currencies", supplementing gold. The Bretton Woods system became fully operational only in 1958 when, after a prolonged period of postwar reconstruction, all major currencies became freely convertible one for another.

## Pressure on sterling
The crucial requirement for the smooth functioning of the Bretton Woods system was the willingness of countries to hold the two reserve currencies. In general they did so until 1964, after which a series of currency crises progressively undermined the fixed exchange rate system. Pressure centred initially on sterling. International confidence was eroded by Britain's chronic economic problems at home and overseas. There was heavy selling of sterling by international

1 **Under the gold standard** imbalances in trade are settled by transfers of gold between countries. If the value of exports and imports balances [A] a country neither loses nor gains gold. The value of money circulating in a country is directly tied to its stock of gold [B]. When a deficit arises because imports are greater than exports [C] an outflow of gold takes place to settle the difference [D]. This reduces the volume of money at home, depressing wages and prices [E]. Goods for export are cheaper, more are sold, and equilibrium is restored with a smaller gold stock [F].

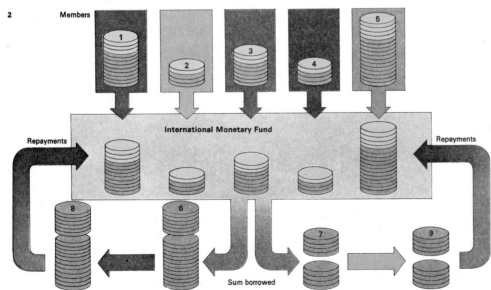

2 **The resources** of the International Monetary Fund come from quotas subscribed by its members [1–5], 25% in gold [yellow] and the rest in their own currency. Any member in balance-of-payments difficulties can borrow from the Fund the currency of other members up to a top limit of 200% of its own quota. Country 1 is borrowing 150% [6] while country 2 draws the full 200% [7]. So that appropriate balance of currencies is maintained repayments [8, 9] must be made within five years in the currencies of members whose money has been borrowed from the Fund.

Members

International Monetary Fund

Repayments

Repayments

Sum borrowed

3 **The flow of world money** is very fast indeed. The foreign exchange rooms of bankers such as Samuel Montagu turn over millions of pounds a day.

holders on many occasions, facilitated by the gradual build-up of large quantities of easily transferable or "hot" money in the Eurodollar market [8]. Selling could be stemmed only at the cost of the Bank of England's running down its own holdings of foreign currency in order to buy up sterling in the exchange markets and thus prevent the exchange rate falling below its agreed value. Even the provision of additional funds to the Bank of England by other central banks and by the IMF (through loans and by boosting total world reserves through the creation of a new reserve asset, the Special Drawing Right [7]) could not succeed in saving sterling, and in November 1967 the pound was devalued by 14.3 per cent.

The crisis of confidence soon spread to the dollar, took the form of persistent demand by holders of dollars for their conversion into gold and resulted in a serious drain on US gold reserves. In August 1971 President Nixon took steps to check this out-flow and shocked the world by announcing the ending of the longstanding US commit-ment to sell gold for dollars. President Nixon's surprise package prompted new international negotiations and resulted in the Smithsonian Agreement of December 1971. This provided for a substantial revaluation of all major currencies against the dollar and was intended to produce a more realistic dollar exchange rate.

## Floating exchange rates
The Smithsonian Agreement failed to restore confidence [6] and renewed pressure against sterling early in 1972 culminated in a decision in June to allow the pound to "float" and find its own value in the foreign exchange markets. Early in 1973 Italy, Switzerland, Japan and eventually all the major European currencies had to follow suit and allow their currencies to float against the dollar.

This system of generalized floating [5] still prevails. The authorities, however, do not let the markets freely determine the rate, but intervene occasionally to serve national interests. Despite repeated attempts, both within the IMF and outside to reach agree-ment on a more stable monetary system, negotiations remain deadlocked.

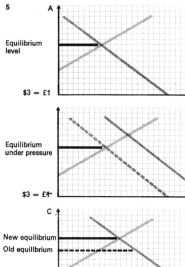

**The International Monetary Fund** has its headquarters in Washington. Set up in 1945 to stabilize exchange rates and help finance world trade, it draws its membership from all the major non-communist coun-tries of the world.

**4 World currencies** can be roughly split into "hard" or "soft", but in some areas these categories are changing, notably as a result of oil revenues. Hard cur-rencies were once those convertible at a fixed rate and much used for trade. Soft currencies included those in limited use or not convert-ible. With the break-down of fixed rates the terms now have a more general meaning of strong and weak currencies.

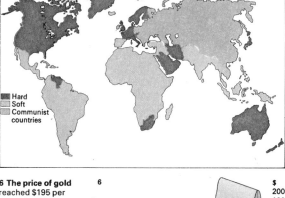

Hard
Soft
Communist countries

**6 The price of gold** reached $195 per ounce in 1974 compared with the fixed price of $35 maintained until 1968. Investors turned to gold as confidence in the dol-lar weakened, but it revived again in 1975.

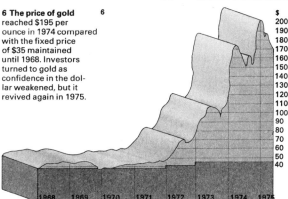

| | | | | | | | $ |
|---|---|---|---|---|---|---|---|
| | | | | | | | 200 |
| | | | | | | | 190 |
| | | | | | | | 180 |
| | | | | | | | 170 |
| | | | | | | | 160 |
| | | | | | | | 150 |
| | | | | | | | 140 |
| | | | | | | | 130 |
| | | | | | | | 120 |
| | | | | | | | 110 |
| | | | | | | | 100 |
| | | | | | | | 90 |
| | | | | | | | 80 |
| | | | | | | | 70 |
| | | | | | | | 60 |
| | | | | | | | 50 |
| | | | | | | | 40 |

1968  1969  1970  1971  1972  1973  1974  1975

**7 Special Drawing Rights** (SDRs), intro-duced in 1970, were created by IMF to increase the volume of resources for fi-nancing world trade. They have two main advantages. First, they are a stable, internationally ac-ceptable form of exchange. Second, they enable the IMF to make transferable loans to those countries that need additional foreign reserves to finance trade deficits. In this way they act as a convenient international system of debits and credits.

Total reserves $222,132 million (1974)

Foreign exchange $156,628 million
Special drawing rights $10,977 million
IMF reserves $10,829 million
Gold reserves $43,698 million

**5**

A
Equilibrium level
$3 = £1

Equilibrium under pressure
$3 = £1

C
New equilibrium
Old equilibrium
$4 = £1

**5 A floating rate of exchange** finds its level according to supply and demand in the world's money markets at any given point in time. Assum-ing that a home cur-rency is $ and the foreign currency £, the exchange rate settles at a level that will equate demand [red] and supply [blue] [A]. If demand for imports increases, in the absence of coun-tervailing measures, demand for foreign currency will exceed supply at the old ex-change rate [B]. The price of foreign cur-rency therefore rises or, in other words, the exchange rate of the home currency depreciates [C]. The world has had a sys-tem of floating or fluctuating exchange rates since 1972.

**8 A Eurodollar** is created when a dollar passes to a holder outside the United States and, instead of being converted to another currency or deposited within the United States, it is deposited with a bank outside the United States. There are other "Euro" currencies, such as Euroster-ling. The term signi-fies that the currency concerned is depos-ited outside its coun-try of origin. Once a European bank [A] has received a Euro-currency deposit from, for instance, a French exporter it can lend it in turn to other banks in need of funds [B, C, D] and it may fin-ally be borrowed by a British business-man who wants to finance investment. The Eurocurrency market emerged in the late 1950s and constitutes a vast international pool of highly mobile money sometimes used for currency speculation. Latest estimates put its size at $200,000 million.

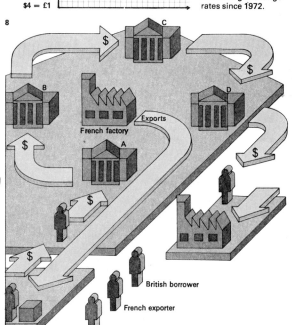

French factory
Exports
British borrower
French exporter
US importer

# Underdevelopment and the world economy

The decades following World War II have been characterized by a marked division between a small group of mostly industrialized nations where general living standards and prosperity have risen quite rapidly, and the overwhelming majority of nations where poverty remains acute [Key, 1]. In the former group are found the highly industrialized countries of North America, Australia and New Zealand, and most of Europe and Japan, and in the latter the extensive regions of underdevelopment in South America, Asia and Africa, although Brazil has shown a very marked rise in gross national product (GNP) in this period.

## Patterns of trade
Simultaneously with this steadily widening gap in material standards, dozens of new nations have been created in the process of decolonization. But self-government has not brought economic freedom. The pattern of trade established during the colonial period means that the new nations are still frequently dependent on the old metropolitan countries. Their economic role remains largely one of supplying agricultural goods and industrial raw materials [3], serving as markets for the surplus manufactures of the industrialized nations and acting as a reservoir of cheap labour. Finally, much of the trade and industry of the ex-colonies is in the hands of international companies based in the rich countries and whose profits do not accrue where they are created.

As a consequence of these traditional ties, the less developed countries have also suffered the booms and recessions of the industrialized world. There have been sharp swings in demand for the primary products sold by the poorer nations leading to violent fluctuations in commodity prices and therefore in their foreign earnings [2]. This (together with the inevitable unpredictability of agricultural production) makes planning a development programme almost impossible because unpredictable export earnings force planners to curb necessary imports of machinery and capital equipment.

Although the rich countries provide some overseas aid [6], the flow of funds is inadequate and few of the less developed countries

have what economists call "self-sustained growth" – that is, profit levels are not high enough to finance expansion on the scale desired. Indeed there is much argument about whether the conditions that led to industrialization and economic take-off throughout the 1800s in western Europe and North America still exist and whether it is even feasible for the less developed countries to copy the industrialized West.

## The developing nations and cartels
If the governments of the Third World nations are to eradicate poverty and maintain social and political stability it would nevertheless seem that they have no alternative but to take their peoples down the road to industrialization [4] in the hope of finding a formula for self-sustained economic growth. This means mechanizing industry and agriculture and has led to demands that the existing industrialized nations should provide the requisite funds. For example, it has been suggested that they should lower the present customs duties and quotas they impose on some of the industrialized goods

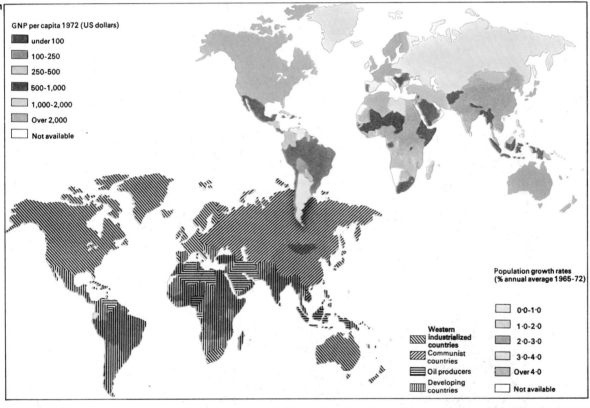

1 GNP per capita 1972 (US dollars)
- under 100
- 100-250
- 250-500
- 500-1,000
- 1,000-2,000
- Over 2,000
- Not available

Population growth rates (% annual average 1965-72)
- 0·0-1·0
- 1·0-2·0
- 2·0-3·0
- 3·0-4·0
- Over 4·0
- Not available

Western industrialized countries
Communist countries
Oil producers
Developing countries

1 Some 600 million people live in countries which in 1970 had per capita incomes of between $2,000 and $3,000 a year; another 2,000 million live in countries where per capita income is estimated at less than $200. In countries where small labour-intensive land-holdings predominate rural population increase is often stimulated beyond the ability of the land to support it, encouraging migration to the towns where the urban labour market cannot support it either. Indeed the poorest countries are usually those in which the population growth rate is highest: there were over 538 million people in India by 1970 and the numbers have been swelling at the rate of 2.3% a year. Mexico's annual rate of increase in the 1960s was 3.5%. By contrast population in many western European countries is rising by less than 1% per annum.

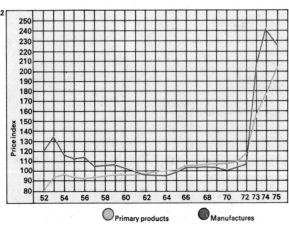

2 World export prices between 1950 (the peak of the commodity boom of the Korean War) and 1970 moved first of all in favour of the products of the less developed countries but after a period of relative strength this advantage was lost. Some economists blame the weak economic performance of the less developed countries on a marked deterioration in their "terms of trade" – the fall in the price they get for exports relative to the cost of their imports.

Primary products
Manufactures

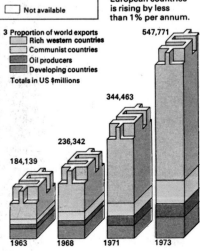

3 Export figures for the 1960s and early 1970s show that developing countries accounted for a relatively small proportion of world trade. This began to change in 1974, but only as a result of higher oil prices. The exports of most developing countries are still agricultural products like coffee or sugar and raw materials for industry like rubber or tin. Only about 25% of their exports – frequently textiles – are manufactured goods.

3 Proportion of world exports
- Rich western countries
- Communist countries
- Oil producers
- Developing countries
Totals in US $millions

184,139   236,342   344,463   547,771
1963      1968      1971      1973

they import from the Third World – such as textiles – which at present often encounter high tariffs because they compete with the industries of the industrialized nations. For these reasons political tensions have been increasing between rich and poor countries.

Some less developed countries have also attempted to achieve higher prices for their primary products by banding together in associations. One of the most successful of these has been the Organization of Petroleum Exporting Countries (OPEC). Because of its near monopoly in the export of oil, OPEC succeeded in getting a fivefold increase in the oil price during 1973 and 1974. Other groups of commodity producers have not been as successful and higher oil prices and the resultant higher price of manufactured goods have hurt developing countries, such as India, which do not possess oil. In spite of this, the example set by OPEC has proved an inspiration for other producers of raw materials, although many economists argue that such associations, or "cartels" as they are called, cannot last for long because supply and demand will eventually drive

the price back down to a sustainable level.

The desire of developing nations for changes in the world trading system has also led to political initiatives such as the United Nations special conference on raw materials in 1974 which adopted a programme for a "New International Economic Order". A resolution to this effect was approved by most countries despite opposition from many of the richer nations. However, it is generally recognized that a new economic order can be established only if the industrial countries are prepared to meet a far-reaching list of demands from the Third World nations.

**Future prospects**
The success of OPEC, the possible growth of more such cartels and the fear of political upheaval in the Third World should existing levels of poverty persist have produced statements of willingness on the part of the industrialized group to make at least some concessions. But despite growing concern about Third World problems and sincere efforts by certain countries, the general level of aid has been dropping since the 1960s [6].

Undernourishment, disease and bad housing loom over / 80% of the world's 4,000 million people, in stark / contrast to the affluence of a few nations.

**4 Factories set up** by many developing countries reflected a belief that poverty could be eliminated by rapid industrialization. But this proved to be over-ambitious and led to many problems. There was a lack of skilled manpower and the industrial programmes did not help the rural poor, although they attracted unskilled men to the cities where work was not available for the large numbers seeking it.

**5 Rice-planting in India** and elsewhere in the 1960s raised the hopes that some less developed countries could become more self-sufficient in food by a "Green Revolution". This was the introduction of new, high-yielding rice and wheat plants which could greatly increase harvests. Although modestly successful in some areas, the costs involved have proved formidable for peasants borrowing at high local interest rates.

**6 The rich countries provide foreign aid** both in goods and in funds. Here [A] a US helicopter lands supplies. But aid is inadequate when set against the real food shortages and lack of jobs. Some 80% of the money invested in developing nations comes from their own limited resources. Official development assistance from 17 of the world's richest nations [B] in 1974 was just 0.33% of their combined GNP, much less than the figure of 0.53% that was given in 1960.

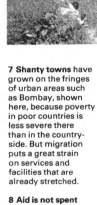

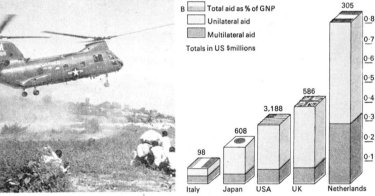

B ▨ Total aid as % of GNP
☐ Unilateral aid
▨ Multilateral aid

Totals in US $millions

| | | | | | |
|---|---|---|---|---|---|
| 98 | 608 | 3,188 | 586 | 305 | |
| Italy | Japan | USA | UK | Netherlands | |

**7 Shanty towns** have grown on the fringes of urban areas such as Bombay, shown here, because poverty in poor countries is less severe there than in the countryside. But migration puts a great strain on services and facilities that are already stretched.

**8 Aid is not spent on welfare alone.** Some of it is committed to prestige projects such as the Organization for African Unity building in Addis Ababa.

# Modern Christianity and the New Beliefs

Developments in the life of the Christian Churches during the latter half of the twentieth century have been faster and more far-reaching than at any stage since the Protestant Reformation of the sixteenth century. The main features have been the ecumenical movement (for the reunion of the Churches), the Churches' deeper commitment to the service of the secular world and the cause of world justice, and the dialogue with "unbelief", notably Marxism. Two outstanding events have been the foundation of the World Council of Churches, to which the Roman Catholic Church does not belong, and the Second Vatican Council (1962–5).

## The work of the World Council

The World Council of Churches [1], formed in 1948, today includes 271 Churches working in 90 countries. It is neither a church nor a union of churches, but a forum for the joint study of theology and ecumenism and of Christian insights into the socio-economic and political problems of society; it also organizes relief and other social services for the deprived regions of the world. The principal Churches represented are Anglican, Baptist, Congregationalist, Lutheran, Methodist, Moravian, Old Catholic, Orthodox, Presbyterian and Reformed; the Society of Friends is also a member.

There has not yet been a fusion of major Churches on a global basis, but there have been hundreds of unions of Christian groupings on a local level.

At first the Roman Catholic Church, although sympathetic, stood apart from the World Council, but soon it began to send observers to World Council meetings and eventually to have permanent links with it in the fields of social theology and action. A new ecumenical climate, fostered by Pope Pius XII (pontificate 1939–58) on the Roman Catholic side, received dramatic impetus from the pontificate of Pope John XXIII (1958–63) and the visit to Pope Paul VI (1897–1978) in 1966 by the Archbishop of Canterbury, Dr Michael Ramsey. The joint theological commission they set up has already reached a degree of unanimity over, for instance, the central doctrine of the Eucharist, for which few Christians would have dared to hope a decade before. Two of the major hurdles yet to be surmounted are the questions of the teaching authority in the Church and the position of the Papacy.

## Effects of the Second Vatican Council

The Second Vatican Council of the Roman Catholic Church [2], summoned by Pope John, attended by observers from other Churches and completed under Pope Paul, to some extent narrowed the theological gaps among the Churches in regard to revelation (the Bible and tradition), authority (the collegial authority of the bishops), the nature of the Church and the recognition that all Christians are united in Christ by baptism. The Council opened many doors to dialogue between Christianity and the great non-Christian religions, and also between Christians and unbelievers. The Church's commitment to the service of the world was reinforced by Pope Paul's many journeys overseas, especially his visits to the United Nations Organization and to the developing countries of the Far East and Latin America. His first visit to Jerusalem, where he met the

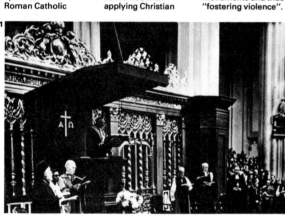

**1 The World Council of Churches** held its first General Assembly in Amsterdam in 1948. The WCC includes the main Christian Churches apart from the Roman Catholic Church. It is not an amalgamation of Churches but a forum for theological discussion intended to lead to ultimate Christian reunion. It is also concerned with applying Christian teaching to the problems of world justice. It gives aid to development projects in deprived regions but has been criticized for helping freedom fighter movements and thus "fostering violence".

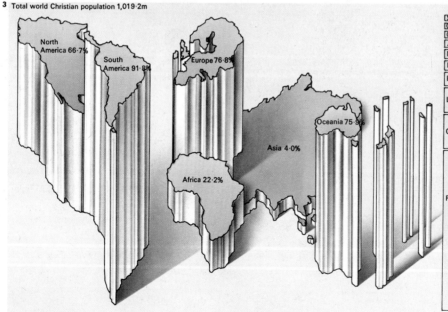

**2 The Second Vatican Council** was opened in 1962 in St Peter's, Rome, by Pope John. It brought together nearly 3,000 bishops and other Roman Catholic Church leaders whose purpose was to renew the spirit of the Church from within. The Council, in its theological statements, narrowed the gap between itself and the other Christian communions. It committed itself to being "The Church of the Poor", and opened the way to dialogue with non-Christian religions and also with the communists, thus ending the postwar period of direct confrontation with the communist powers.

**3 The distribution of** the world's Christians is historically determined. Through the Roman Empire Christianity spread throughout Europe, to be transmitted worldwide by European emigration and by colonial and missionary activity. The Catholic Church still has by far the largest Christian congregation, claiming almost 60 per cent of the estimated total world Christian population. World Christianity divides into three main streams: the Catholic (Orthodox, Anglican and Roman), the Protestant (Calvinist and Lutheran) and Free Church (Congregationalist, Baptist and Methodist). Map figures show the estimated percentage of Christians within the population of each continent.

**3 Total world Christian population 1,019·2m**

North America 66·7%
South America 91·8%
Europe 76·8%
Oceania 75·9%
Asia 4·0%
Africa 22·2%

| | |
|---|---|
| Seventh Day Adventists | 0·37% |
| Congregationalists | 0·58% |
| Others | 2·7% |
| Anglicans | 3·9% |
| Methodists | 4·0% |
| Presbyterian and Reformed | 5·15% |
| Baptists | 5·8% |
| Lutherans | 7·5% |
| Orthodox and Eastern | 11·9% |
| Roman Catholics | 57·0% |

Orthodox Ecumenical Patriarch Athenagoras in 1964 [Key], was seen as the first great step towards healing the breach, nearly a thousand years old, between Rome and the Orthodox Churches of the East. Pope Paul's pontificate is also notable for a series of conversations with the communist powers.

**Revolt against tradition**
The 1960s was a period of intense interest in the concept of the "Death of God" theology identified with Protestant thinkers such as Paul Tillich (1886–1965) [4] and Dietrich Bonhoeffer (1906–45) ("religionless Christianity"), and popularized in *Honest to God* (1963) by an Anglican bishop, Dr John Robinson. Broadly speaking this line of thought rejected the traditional "analogous" way of talking about God. He was not "a person" somewhere "out there" but the transcendent "ground of being", and manifested to the world in the life of Christ.

Eventually the "Death of God" theology faded and was replaced by the more positive concept of the "Theology of Hope", which owes much to the thought of the Jesuit scientist Pierre Teilhard de Chardin (1881–1955). It has been called a "this world" theology, which in Latin America has provoked what is now called the "theology of liberation" [7].

One of its first practical exponents was the Colombian priest Camilo Torres who, despairing of converting the rich oppressors of the poor, joined the local guerrillas in 1965, was soon afterwards killed by the police and became known as the Christian counterpart of Che Guevara (1928–67). The corresponding witness of the Anglican Church has been most notable in South Africa [8], beginning with the championship of the African people by Father, now Bishop, Trevor Huddleston (1913–  ).

Finally, the last generation has witnessed the rise of movements in the Christian communions that lay less stress on intellectual religious experience and more on emotional fervour and "discernment". A convert-making revivalism in the 1950s and 1960s, such as that of the American evangelist Billy Graham (1918–  ), has been succeeded by what is known as "Pentecostalism" or "Charismatic Renewal" [9].

**The meeting in Jerusalem** in 1964 between Pope Paul VI and the Orthodox Ecumenical Patriarch Athenagoras was the first of its kind since the Eastern Church broke away from the Papacy nearly 1,000 years ago.

**4 Paul Tillich,** the great German Protestant theologian, rejected traditional ideas of God and called Him instead "the ground of our being", a theme taken up by Bishop John Robinson.

**5 Rudolf Bultmann** (1884–  ), another prominent German theologian, became famous for demythologizing the New Testament, stressing Christ as a spiritual rather than an historical figure.

**6 A freedom march** of black demonstrators in Dallas, Texas, is led by a white priest. One of the Church's most obvious contributions to the new social order in the postwar period has been its active opposition to all forms of discrimination and its struggle to defend the rights of the black people of North America and oppressed peoples in various parts of the African continent.

**8 Students in Cape Town** demonstrated outside the cathedral in 1972. The meeting was called to support the principle of racial equality in education. The students obtained the permission of the Anglican dean to hold their meeting on Church property because street demonstrations were banned, but this did not protect them from brutal intervention by the local police.

**7 Archbishop Helder Camara** of Recife, Brazil, is one of the religious leaders of the battle for social revolution in Latin America. The Archbishop's methods have remained non-voilent, unlike those of Father Camilo Torres, the priest turned guerrilla. The Church's struggle for the underprivileged in the sub-continent has taken many forms: the constitutional struggle through the Christian Democrat parties and the dialogue between Christians and Marxists, social action via the Church's co-operatives and credit union, housing and educational programmes and the proclamation of the theology of liberation. Many priests in Latin America have suffered heavily for their actions.

**9 The Children of Jesus,** swooning in ecstasy, are one of many spontaneous prayer groups seeking knowledge of God and Christ through emotional experience as distinct from reasoned theology. Some of the movements appear to be extremist and grounded in emotional instability. Others, such as the Pentecostalists, who talk about "Charismatic Renewal", are a more convincing blend of quasi-mysticism and "service of the brethren".

157

# Europe from confrontation to détente

Between 1955 and 1975 Europe moved from the cold war to the beginnings of co-operation. In a military sense the confrontation continued because the countries of both the North Atlantic Treaty Organization (NATO) and the Warsaw Pact built up their armed strength and deployed nuclear weapons [1]. But gradually the confrontation came to be accepted as a guarantor of stability in the relations between the Eastern and Western powers.

## The meaning of détente

Détente, however, took many years to develop. Originally, it appeared that there were two reasons for optimism. The first was the denunciation of Stalin's methods by Nikita Khrushchev (1894–1971) in 1956. De-Stalinization seemed to promise greater liberalism in Eastern Europe and an improvement in East-West relations. The agreement on a neutral and independent Austria through the Austrian State Treaty appeared to confirm this [Key].

The second ground for hope lay, paradoxically, in German rearmament.

When West Germany joined NATO in 1955, the Soviet response was to organize its allies, including East Germany, in the Warsaw Pact. While this reaction appeared threatening, the Soviet Government clearly expected that each superpower would now recognize the final division of Germany and that this would provide the basis for peaceful co-existence. Both hopes were speedily disappointed. When Soviet control in Hungary was threatened [2], Soviet tanks soon demonstrated the limits of the new liberalism. At the same time the Western powers refused to recognize East Germany. In response, Khruschev tried to make them do so by creating a series of crises over Berlin [3]. These crises, which continued from 1958 to the building of the Berlin Wall in 1961, appeared at times to threaten a third world war and helped to accelerate the arms race.

## The fear of nuclear war

From 1957 onwards, nuclear missiles were introduced into the arms race (and tactical nuclear weapons into Europe). Crises between the superpowers became increasingly

dangerous and it was the most intense of these crises, over the emplacement of Soviet missiles in Cuba in 1962 [5, 7], which induced the superpowers to reconsider their relations and move towards détente.

At their level the two superpowers agreed – tacitly at least – to respect each other's spheres of influence and this implied an acceptance of the alliances as they stood. But at the European level there were certain attempts to change the existing system. In Eastern Europe such attempts arose from a desire to win greater independence from the Soviet Union. In Western Europe they arose from a sense of growing economic power and partly from a wish to see greater liberalization in the East. The most articulate spokesman of this Western European approach was President Charles de Gaulle (1890–1970) [9], who went so far as to take France out of military commitments to NATO (but not the alliance) in 1966 in an attempt to create a more flexible political system in Europe.

However, from 1963 onwards the two superpowers developed an increasingly close understanding, based on the attempt not only

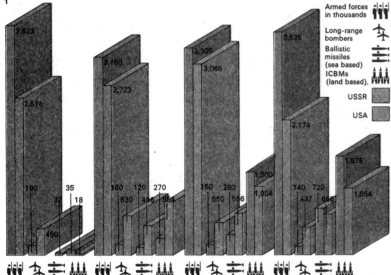

1 The USSR maintains a much larger army than the US, and now has a greater number of land and sea-based strategic missiles, although the number of nuclear warheads held by each side is uncertain.

Armed forces in thousands
Long-range bombers
Ballistic missiles (sea based)
ICBMs (land based).
USSR
USA

2 In 1956 there was a popular revolt against communism in Hungary. The rebel government, headed by Imre Nagy (1895–1958), demanded that the Russian troops leave. Instead, more tanks arrived in

November and during the next two weeks thousands of "freedom fighters" were killed by Soviet troops. Despite de-Stalinization in Russia, the Hungarians were not allowed to break up the Eastern bloc.

3 Instead of leading to better relations, the scaling down of the policies of Joseph Stalin (often referred to as de-Stalinization) and peaceful co-existence proved to be but a prelude to crisis. Through pressure on Berlin, Nikita Khrushchev tried to force the West to acknowledge the division of Germany. But the two superpowers also tried to manage the crisis through a common understanding. Although at this 1959 meeting Eisenhower and Khrushchev [left] failed to resolve the crisis it set a precedent for later consultations and suggested that the powers recognized that their interest in avoiding war was more important than victory from a conflict.

4 A new crisis arose when an American intelligence aircraft was shot down in Russia in May 1960. The pilot, Gary Powers, was captured. At the Paris conference in May Khrushchev demanded that Eisenhower apologize for the incident; when the US President refused, Khrushchev left the conference, which then broke up. He also withdrew his offer to Eisenhower to visit the Soviet Union. Eisenhower had previously accepted responsibility for the incident.

5 The relationship between President Kennedy and Khrushchev fluctuated over the years 1961–3. They first met in Vienna in 1961 to discuss the future of Berlin. Khrushchev demanded an end to

the military occupation but Kennedy did not agree with him. It was not until they reached the brink of war over Cuba that the Soviet premier began to respect the young, inexperienced Kennedy.

to avoid nuclear war but also to control the arms race that might produce it. Their agreements began in 1963 with the renunciation of nuclear tests in the atmosphere or space; they continued through the attempt to halt the spread of nuclear weapons (which might have made other conflicts more dangerous) in the non-proliferation treaty of 1968, and they culminated in a whole series of talks and agreements designed to control the dangerous new weaponry that each was capable of developing – the Strategic Arms Limitation Talks (SALT) [8].

This understanding on controlling the arms race also helped to provide the basis for other agreements, most notably the Berlin Agreement of 1972, that reduced conflict; in addition a series of economic agreements designed to create a positive interest in détente were reached.

### Problems in Eastern Europe
But this process of increased understanding was not smooth. The period of relative Soviet tolerance ended in 1968 when the Soviet Union and members of the Warsaw Pact invaded Czechoslovakia to destroy the programme for democratic government of Alexander Dubcek (1921– ).

Thereafter it was the West German Chancellor, Willy Brandt (1913– ) [10], who restored European détente at about the same time as the two superpowers began the SALT talks. Brandt's *Ostpolitik* established political and economic agreements between West Germany, the Soviet Union and Poland, and subsequently East Germany. It was this last agreement that led to the recognition of East Germany by all the Western powers. Since his *Ostpolitik* was also instrumental in bringing about the Berlin Agreement, it laid to rest two of the major causes of tension of the entire cold war.

Détente was by then firmly established, and became the basis of US foreign policy under Henry Kissinger (1923– ). At the same time the Conference on Security and Co-operation in Europe, culminating at Helsinki in 1975, established the guidelines for agreement over a range of issues. It was still unclear how far détente could lead to real co-operation, but the foundations had been laid.

**The independence of Austria** was restored by treaty in 1955, as the Allies had agreed it would be after Stalin's death. The Soviet Foreign Minister, Molotov (1890– ) is seen here signing the treaty in Vienna. However, the Warsaw Pact had been set up the day before, enabling Soviet troops to remain in neighbouring Hungary. Whether this was to be the beginning of the end of the cold war was not known. Until an agreement on Germany was reached, the outcome was uncertain.

**6 By 1961 the refugee flood** from East Berlin threatened East Germany itself. The Soviet Government hesitated to start a new crisis by sealing the city off, but finally began the wall in August.

**7 In October 1962 the US discovered** that Russia had set up missile bases in Cuba, installed by Khrushchev as a counterbalance to US superiority. President Kennedy demanded at the Security Council the removal of the missiles and isolated Cuba with naval forces. Khrushchev offerred to withdraw if he was allowed Turkish bases. This resulted in stalemate which saw the USSR back down after a week.

**8 Nuclear arms : US-USSR agreements**

Sept 1975 European security conference

Dec 1970 Banning from the sea-bed

Nov 1969 SALT

July 1968 Non-proliferation

Jan 1967 No nuclear arms in space

August 1963 Limited test ban
June 1963 Hot Line Agreement

**8 After the Cuban crisis,** East and West tried to come to agreement on control of the arms race and on forms of co-operation which gave each side an interest in maintaining détente. They substituted agreement for threat.

**9 Charles de Gaulle wanted the European** powers to develop their own interests irrespective of the superpowers. He found a natural ally in Romania, which was trying to establish its independence from the Soviet bloc.

**10 Willy Brandt** was German Chancellor from 1969–74 when he harmonized the attitudes of détente that developed in Europe during the 1960s. He established a new relationship with the USSR and improved relations with the East European countries. His record as an opponent of Nazism and his willingness to offer amends for German atrocities won him trust abroad. His *Ostpolitik* led to Western recognition of East Germany and ended the postwar German problem.

# 1825-1850 Liberalism and nationalism

## Principal events

**The spread of industrialism from England to north Europe brought the rise of a solid middle class advocating liberal and nationalist ideas, as well as a new urban radicalism focused by regular economic booms and slumps. In spite of attempts to suppress them, these ideas spread throughout Europe, culminating in the nationalist and radical revolts of 1848. At the time this was a failure but the ideals of 1848 would be realized later as Italy and Germany achieved unification and the old empires collapsed.**

**The United States expanded vigorously westwards, her population and industry increasing, while European colonialism was most active in Asia. The impact of British culture was felt in India for the first time and the process of penetration of China began in earnest with the end of the Opium Wars which forced China to open her ports to foreign trade.**

### 1825-28

Following a liberal **Decembrist revolt**, 1825, **Nicholas I**, *r.* 1825-55, introduced repressive measures. **Charles X**, *r.* 1824-30, alienated bourgeois support in France by restoring to nobles land lost in the Revolution. **The British in India** ended their titular subservience to Mogul rule, 1827. **The Javanese rebelled** against Dutch rule but were put down.

### 1828-1830

**Lord Bentinck**, 1774-1839, built new canals and roads in India and prohibited the customs of suttee and thuggee. **Turkey recognized Greece's independence** after British and Russian intervention, 1829. **Uruguay** was established as an independent buffer state between Argentina and Brazil, 1828. **The Workingmen's Party** was established in the US, pledged to social reform. **Charles X** faced rising opposition in France after 1825.

### 1830-33

**The French liberal opposition** expelled Charles X, replacing him with **Louis-Philippe**, pledged to rule with middle-class support, 1830. This sparked off a liberal and nationalist revolt in Belgium, which became independent of the Netherlands. **Nationalist risings** in Italy and Germany were unsuccessful. **The French** established their authority in Algiers, 1830. **The Young Italy** group was launched by **Giuseppe Mazzini**, 1805-72, in Italy in 1831.

### 1833-5

**Slavery** was abolished throughout the British Empire, 1833. **The German customs union**, completed in 1834, became the focus of German nationalism. **Regional opposition** to the liberal Spanish regime led to the **Carlist Wars**, 1834-9, in support of **Don Carlos**. **Louis-Philippe** renounced his radical support and introduced strict censorship, 1835. **British trade with China** increased after the East India Company's monopoly ended.

## National events

**The social problems that came with industrialization reached their peak in the 1840s, manifesting themselves in the Chartist movement. Parliamentary reform in 1832 recognized the new importance of the industrial towns and was followed by a series of attempts to regulate conditions of work.**

**The first public railway** between Stockton and Darlington was opened, 1825, leading to a boom in competitive railway building after 1830.

**The growth of an Irish nationalist movement** brought the repeal of anti-Catholic laws, 1829. **The "new" police force** was set up in London in 1829.

**The Reform Act**, 1832, introduced new industrial constituencies. The supremacy of the landowners was nevertheless maintained in Parliament.

**The Poor Law Amendment Act**, 1834, set up workhouses for the poor. **The Tolpuddle Martyrs** were transported, 1834, for trades-union activity.

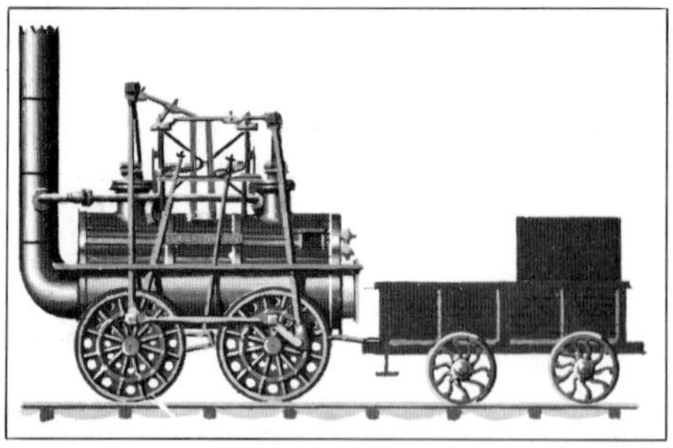

Stephenson's *Locomotion*, 1825

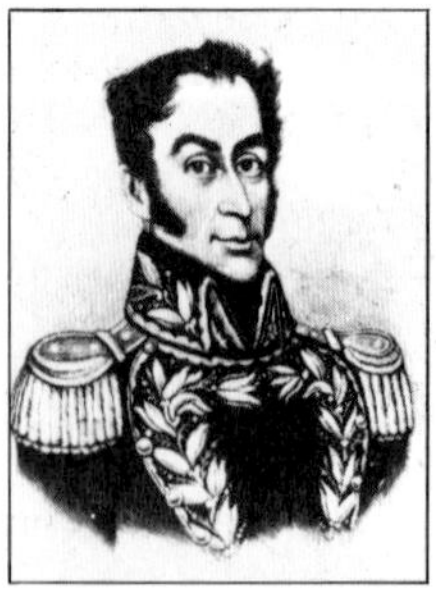

Simon Bolivar

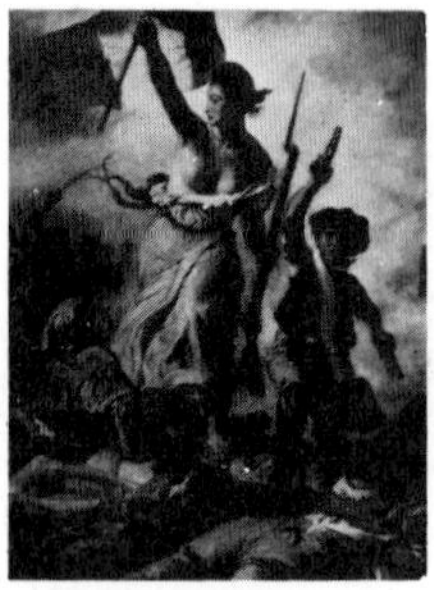

Delacroix: "1830 Revolution"

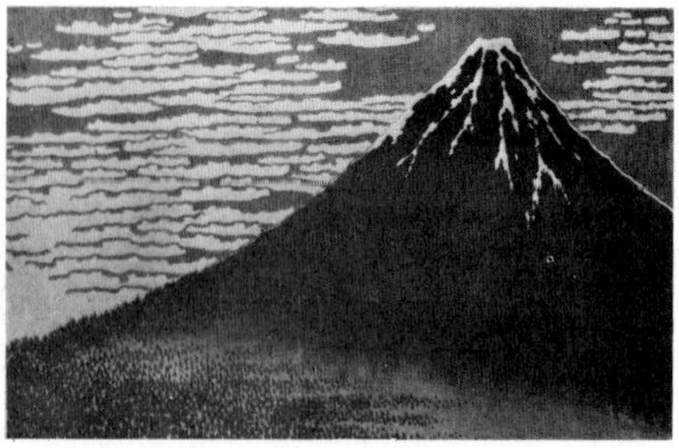

"View of Mount Fuji" by Hokusai

## Religion and philosophy

**Several European thinkers, principally in France, advocated the application of the observational, or "positive", methods used in the natural sciences to the study of social phenomena.**

**The growth of the industrial system stimulated new and radical thought. Saint-Simon and, after him, Comte, argued that industrial society should be governed by a new "priesthood" trained in the positivist method, while the existing forms of social organization were criticized by utopian thinkers who looked forward to ideal societies free from inequality and injustice.**

**Marx and Engels, who were influenced by French utopianism as well as German idealism and British political economy argued that in order to end the inequality and injustice of existing society there must be a working-class revolution.**

**A number of Adventist sects prophesying the return of Christ emerged during these years, especially in the USA.**

**Henri de Saint-Simon**, 1760-1825, in *New Christianity*, 1825, sought to combine the ideals of Christianity with science and a belief in industrialism to form a new religion of socialism based on a science of society. He advocated management of society by experts in the new social science, to aid welfare and progress. His theories were further developed by his one-time secretary, **Auguste Comte**, 1798-1857.

**François Guizot**, 1787-1874, published his *History of Civilisation in France*, 1829, a study of social institutions using empirical data and a historical approach. **James Mill**, 1773-1836, in his *Analysis of the Human Mind*, 1829, developed Bentham's pleasure-pain doctrine in the field of psychology. **John Darby**, 1800-82, set up the **Plymouth Brethren** sect in Ireland, 1830, emphasizing the second coming of Jesus Christ.

**Mormonism** was founded in New York State by Joseph Smith, 1805-44, in 1830 and based on the *Book of Mormon*. Opposition to their enclosed community life caused them to settle in Utah, 1847. **Modern Adventism** was founded in the USA by **William Miller**, 1781-1849, who began in 1831 to prophesy the imminent end of the world. The failure of his predictions produced many breakaway sects, including the **Seventh Day Adventists.**

**The Oxford Movement** within Anglicanism began, 1833, under the leadership of **John Keble**, 1792-1866, and Cardinal **John Newman**, 1801-90. They sought to revive the ideals of the medieval Church and reintroduced elaborate rituals. **Félicité Lamennais**, 1782-1854, a French Catholic priest, argued in *Thoughts of a Believer*, 1834, for the separation of Church and state and attacked the papacy for its interference in politics.

## Literature

**While Romanticism spread to Russia with Lermontov and Gogol, its brooding introversion began to break down in Western Europe and the political implications of its rebellion were explored. The Jung Deutschland group insisted on the political role of literature and in France the realistic depiction of the past or of contemporary society became important new themes. The social and nationalist commitment of writers found expression in the revolutions of 1848, in which authors such as Hugo and Lamartine played an important role.**

**In England novelists explored social relationships. Dickens concentrated on the evil results of industrialization with a wealth of characterization equalled only by Balzac.**

**James Fenimore Cooper**, 1789-1851, gained international fame with his historical novel *The last of the Mohicans*, 1826, in which he portrayed the American Indians. *I Promessi Sposi*, 1825-27, by the Italian **Alessandro Manzoni**, 1785-1873, is a love story set in 17th century Italy with delicate Christian idealism.

**The Cenacle group** of poets was set up in Paris, 1827, by **Victor Hugo**, 1802-1885, and **Sainte-Beuve**, 1804-1869. Hugo's *Odes et Ballades*, 1826, celebrated the theme of liberty. The romantic poetry of **Alfred de Musset**, 1810-57, and the stoical pessimism of **Alfred de Vigny**, 1797-1863, reflected French disillusionment in the post-Napoleonic era.

**Social realism** in the French novel began with the work of **Stendhal (Henri Beyle)**, 1783-1842. A soldier and critic, he wrote *Le Rouge et Le Noir*, 1830. **George Sand**, 1804-76, produced idealized novels of peasant life, such as *Mauprat*, 1837, and **Prosper Merimée**, 1803-70, brought archaeological exactness to the romantic novel.

**The first great modern Russian** writer, **Alexander Pushkin**, 1799-1837, broke down the archaic stiffness of the written style, and introduced realistic language. He used peasant folk songs in the poem *The Dead Princess*, 1834, and medieval history as the source for the novel *Eugene Onegin*, 1823-31, and the tragic drama *Boris Godunov*.

## Art and architecture

**Naturalism in painting – the devotion to truth to nature – received a special impetus from work in Britian where scientific advances and the Industrial Revolution affected art.**

**British landscapists such as John Constable studied natural effects in a scientific manner rather than composing classical panoramas, and French artists emulated his innovations.**

**The interest in history and in different historical styles continued throughout Europe and America. A large number of paintings of historical scenes were produced but it is in architecture that the range of interest in different styles was clearest. Italian models remained a source for the style of secular public buildings but the Gothic revival received a new impetus.**

**England's new wealthy middle classes began to impose their taste on painting and architecture, while rapid urbanization generated the need for new solutions in town planning.**

**The American ornithologist** and painter **John James Audubon**, 1785-1851, published *The Birds of America*, from original drawings in England between 1827 and 1838. **Italian Renaissance architecture** inspired the Travellers' Club, London, by **Charles Barry**, 1795-1860, an example of the neo-Renaissance style. **In France oil paints** were sold in tubes for the first time *c.* 1830, which made painting out of doors much easier.

**A craze in France for things English** known as *anglomanie* developed in the post-Napoleonic era. Watercolour painting became popular in Paris where **Richard Parkes Bonington**, 1802-28, worked after 1820. British oil painting techniques were studied by French artists, especially after the exhibition of Constable's work in the Paris Salon of 1824, and **Delacroix** illustrated Byron's poem in his "The Execution of Doge Marino Faliero"

**The School of Architecture, Berlin**, 1832-5, by **Karl Friedrich Schinkel** was based on strict units of measurement and the design used iron frame structures. It had vestiges of classical detail but came close to a "modern", simple and functional style. **English industrial towns** such as Manchester developed the back-to-back house as a solution to the housing needs generated by the Industrial Revolution.

**In England**, the taste and buying power of the new, wealthy middle classes resulted in an increasing demand for genre and small-scale historical or romantic scenes with emphasis on narrative, as in "Giving a Bite", 1834, by **William Mulready**, 1786-1863. **Japanese colour printing** reached its height in "The Thirty-six views of Mount Fuji", 1834-5, by **Hokusai** and the poetic "Views of Kyoto", 1834, by **Ando Hiroshige**, 1797-1858.

## Music

**Romanticism evolved further in Europe, where composers came to consider music a kind of poetry that penetrated to the heart, ennobling the soul and stimulating the imagination. It was at times extravagant and replete with epic works and cult figures, stimulating growth in orchestration techniques and producing such new forms as the symphonic poem.**

**Paganini**, arrived in Vienna in 1828 and set out to refute rumours that he had been in prison between 1801 and 1804.

**The mouth organ**, the Chinese sheng, came to Vienna in 1829. **Felix Mendelssohn**, 1809-47, revived Bach's music in 1829 after a century of eclipse, giving it the status it enjoys today.

**Hector Berlioz**, 1803-69, made inspired use of the orchestra to express the extra-musical allusions of programme music, as in his *Symphonie fantastique*, 1830, with its elaborate story line.

**Frederic Chopin**, 1810-49, a Polish exile working mostly in Paris from 1831, wrote dazzling short pieces for piano in such forms as nocturne, mazurka and polonaise, often based on dances.

## Science and technology

**The railway system which now grew up in Britain, providing cheap transport for labour and raw materials, proved a vital precondition for the expansion of any industrial society. The process of industrialization, however, brought more and more people into the cities and led to a severe worsening of the conditions of working people. In Bristol, England, the death rate doubled between 1831 and 1841, though advances in medicine and public health began to improve matters from 1840 onwards. The discovery of asepsis was particularly important in lowering the child mortality rate.**

**In pure science the discovery of alternative geometries to that of Euclid prompted new enquiries into formerly accepted theories, clearing the way for Mach and Einstein.**

**The discovery of Brownian motion finally established the existence of unobservable particles, in this case molecules; an important step towards the eventual acceptance of atomic theory.**

**The first public steam railway** opened in 1825 between Stockton and Darlington in England. The first train was drawn by *Locomotion No. 1*, built by the British engineer **George Stephenson**, 1781-1848. **Robert Brown**, 1773-1858, a British botanist, observed the random motion of particles, **Brownian motion**, in 1827, thus proving that molecules existed. **Ohm's law**, relating current, voltage and resistance, was laid down in 1827 by German physicist **Georg Ohm**, 1787-1854.

**The polarimeter**, which analyses the passage of polarized light through matter, was developed in 1828, by British physicist **William Nicol**, 1768-1851. **Embryology** was founded, 1828, by the German biologist **Karl Baer**, 1792-1876. He studied germ layers and the growth and development of the embryo. **Organic chemistry** began with the synthesis of urea by German chemist **Friedrich Wöhler**, 1800-82, in 1828. He showed that organic substances do not always come from living things.

**Non-Euclidean geometry**, was developed *c.* 1829-30 by **Nikolai Lobachevski**, 1793-1856. **Screw threads** were standardized, 1830, by the Briton **Joseph Whitworth**, 1803-87, making mass production of screws viable. ***Principles of Geology***, 1833, by **Charles Lyell**, 1797-1875, showed rocks evolve slowly. **Electromagnetic induction** was discovered, 1831, by a British physicist, **Michael Faraday**, 1791-1867. This discovery led to the electric generator.

**Karl Gauss**, 1777-1855, a German mathematician, devised a set of units for magnetism, presented in 1833. **Charles Babbage**, 1791-1871, a British mathematician, developed the principles of the mechanical computer in the 1830s. **The *Royal William*,** a Canadian vessel, was the first steamship to cross the Atlantic wholly under its own power, 1833. With the building of the ***Great Western***, in 1838, by **I. K. Brunel**, 1806-59, transatlantic services became regular.

## 1835-7

**The Boers of South Africa** began the **Great Trek**, 1835, to find new territory free from British rule. British attempts to unite her colonies of **Upper and Lower Canada** led to revolt, 1837. **Victoria**, *r.* 1837-1901, succeeded to the British throne. **Britain** attempted to intervene in Persia, 1834-8, to forestall Russian influence, but was repelled by **Muhammed Shah**, *r.* 1835-48.

## 1837-40

**A working-class radical Chartist movement** developed in England, stimulated by European economic depression. China seized opium imports from India, provoking the **Opium Wars** with Britain, 1839. **British industrialists'** attempts to introduce free trade led to the foundation of the **Anti-Corn Law League**, 1839. **Ieyoshi**, *r.* 1838-53, the Japanese shōgun, opposed mounting pressure for Occidental trade.

## 1840-44

Britain annexed **Natal**, 1843. **Upper and Lower Canada** were united in 1840 and given responsible government. **The Straits Convention**, 1841, between Russia, Britain, France, Austria and Prussia, closed the Dardanelles and Bosphorus to foreign shipping. **Frederick William IV** of Prussia, *r.* 1840-61, encouraged German nationalism. **The Treaty of Nanking**, 1842, opened Chinese ports to British trade.

## 1844-5

**The persecution of Christians** in Confucianist French Indo-china led to French military involvement, 1840-50. **Sanitary reform** and slum clearance was introduced in England in the 1840s. **The Anglo-Sikh** wars broke out in India, 1845-9. **Texas was annexed** by the United States in 1845. **Utopian socialism** became popular in France among intellectuals and the working classes.

## 1845-8

**A potato famine** in Ireland resulted in mass emigration to the United States, 1846-8. **The US invaded Mexico** and occupied the capital in 1847, defeating Mexico after conflict over Texas, 1846-8. **Liberal hopes** in Prussia were raised when the **Landtag** was called, 1847, by the king, who asked for funds to build railways. The accession of the liberal **Pope Pius IX**, *r.* 1846-78, raised nationalist hopes in Italy.

## 1848-50

**Britain annexed the Punjab** and won Sikh loyalty, 1845-8. **An outburst of urban radicalism** brought the expulsion of **Louis-Philippe** in France and the establishment of a republic, 1848. **Metternich** resigned in Austria. **Hungary** declared herself independent and German and Italian nationalist movements emerged. By 1849 Austria had defeated the Italian revolt and racial disputes split Hungary. **The gold rush in California** opened up the West, 1848-50.

---

**The abolition of slavery** in the colonies led to increases in the price of their products. **A great railway building boom** began, 1836.

**The radical Chartist movement** grew up in the North with six demands including universal suffrage. **The penny post** was introduced.

**The Anti-Corn Law League** led by the industrialists **Cobden**, 1804-65, and **Bright**, 1811-89, became the focus of extra-Parliamentary agitation.

**Robert Peel**, 1788-1850, gave the Bank of England a monopoly on printing money, 1844, and established its authority over other banks.

**The Corn Laws** were repealed, 1846. Competition from food imports led to **agricultural improvements**.

**The Public Health Act**, 1848, attempted to introduce regular sewerage and clean water. The first attacks on slums began.

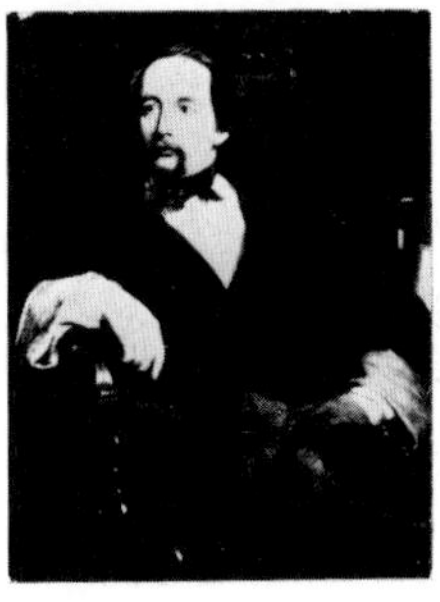

Charles Dickens

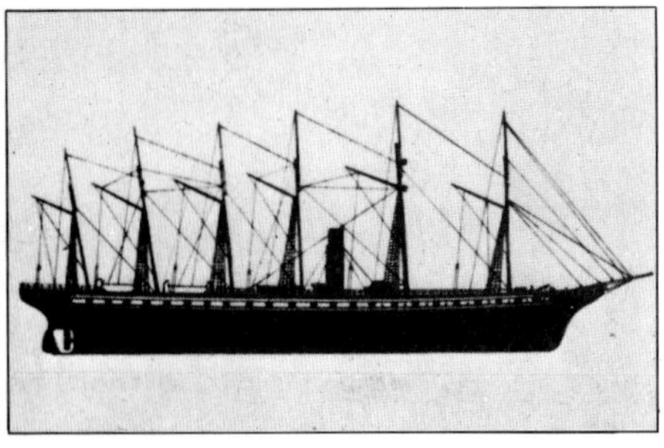

Brunel's *Great Britain*

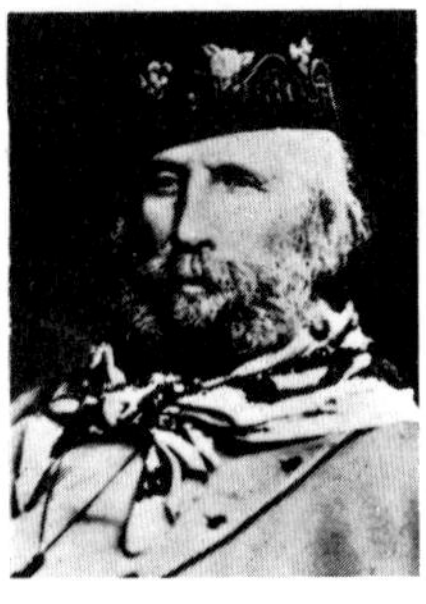

Giuseppe Garibaldi

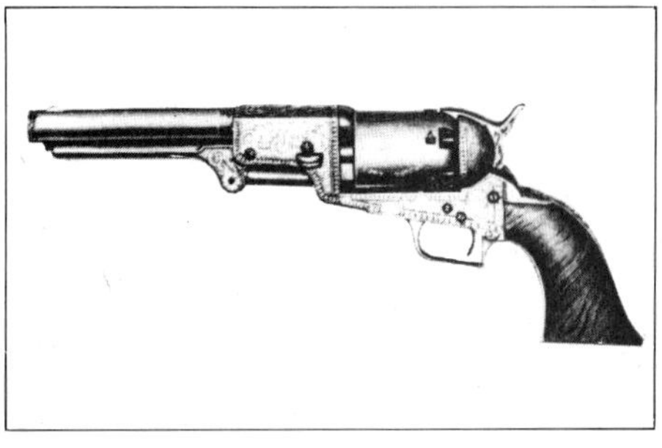

Colt Dragoon revolver, 1848

---

**Probability theory** and statistical methods applied to social phenomena by the Belgian **Adolphe Quetelet**, 1796-1874, led to the discovery that the frequency of suicide in a society was constant and therefore predictable. **Ralph Emerson**, 1803-82, an American Unitarian, developed in *Nature*, 1836, a belief called **Transcendentalism**, proposing that spiritual exploration of one's soul in communion with nature led to the highest wisdom.

**The terms "sociology"** and **"positivism"** were coined by the Frenchman **Auguste Comte**, 1798-1857. His *Course of Positive Philosophy*, 1830-42, argued for the use of positivist methods in social studies. He stated that man's thought had passed through the theological and metaphysical stages and reached the positivist stage. He divided sociology into statics, the study of the interdependence of social institutions, and dynamics, the study of change.

**Ludwig Feuerbach**, 1804-72, in *The Essence of Christianity*, 1841, advocated a humanistic atheism. His critique of Hegel and his claim that God is nothing other than a projection of human nature influenced Marx. **Sören Kierkegaard**, 1813-55, a Danish religious philosopher, published *Either/Or*, 1843. Regarded as the founder of existentialism, he argued against rationalism and emphasized the need to make choices between ethical or aesthetic alternatives.

**The Babi movement**, which developed into the **Bahai** religion, was founded in Persia, 1844, by **Ali Muhammed**, 1819-50. It drew inspiration from diverse sources and emphasized the unity of mankind. **Alexis de Tocqueville**, 1805-59, the first sociologist to examine the impact of democracy on non-political institutions, held that democratic emphasis on equality might suppress individuality and lead to total conformity – a tyranny of the majority.

**Pierre Proudhon**, 1809-65, a French philosopher, held that "property is theft". His book *The Philosophy of Misery*, 1846, formulated anarchism as a political theory. Together with his fellow Frenchmen **Louis Blanc**, 1811-82, and **Louis Blanqui**, 1805-81, he called for an end to the capitalistic exploitation of labour and for a revolutionary change in the existing social and economic orders. These men participated in the revolt of 1848.

**The Christadelphians**, a pacifistic millenial adventist sect, was founded in 1848 in the US by **John Thomas**, 1805-71. **Karl Marx**, 1818-83, and **Friedrich Engels**, 1820-95, wrote the *Communist Manifesto*, 1848, predicting the revolutionary overthrow of capitalism and its replacement by socialism. Marx saw history as a class struggle for ownership of society's material resources.

---

**Heinrich Heine**, 1797-1856, a German poet and a member of the **Jung Deutschland** group which described romantic idealism and wanted all literature to have a political role, wrote *Die Romantische Schule* in Paris, 1836. **Giacomo Leopardi**, 1798-1837, used the romantic theme of man's helplessness in the face of nature, in *La Ginestra*, 1836.

**The prolific French novelist Honoré de Balzac**, 1799-1850, wrote over 90 interconnecting novels and stories, 1829-43, set in Paris and the provinces in the 1820s, which he called *La Comédie Humaine*.

**Mikhail Lermontov**, 1814-41, stands at the beginning of Russia's golden age of prose. Pushkin's successor as poet, playwright and novelist, he was directly influenced by Western literature, especially the work and the flamboyant romanticism of Lord Byron. His novel, *A Hero of Our Times*, on the tragic theme of a man without a purpose, appeared in 1840.

**The fantastical** and tormented aspects of Russian fiction stem from **Nikolai Gogol**, 1809-52. His novel *Dead Souls*, 1842, a moral satire on bureaucracy, centred on the career of a man who deals in dead serfs. **Adam Mickiewicz**, 1798-1855, Poland's national poet, used themes of Lithuanian folklore in his vibrant epic works.

**Powerful imagination** and insight marked the works of the English novelists the **Brontë sisters. Emily**, 1818-48, wrote *Wuthering Heights*, 1847, an account of ferocious passions set against a raw elemental background. *Jane Eyre* by **Charlotte**, 1816-55, was published in the same year and *The Tenant of Wildfell Hall* by **Ann**, 1820-49 in 1848.

**The English social novelist Charles Dickens**, 1812-70, published one of his greatest novels, *Dombey and Son*, 1846-8, dealing with the Victorian family. **W. M. Thackeray**, 1811-63, wrote his caustic attack on the false face of polite society, *Vanity Fair*, 1847-8, a satirical novel which is set on the eve of the Napoleonic wars.

---

**American primitive painting** continued in the work of the Quaker painter **Edward Hicks**, 1780-1849, whose naive landscape with animals, "The Peaceable Kingdom", uses simple forms, flat colours and two dimensions. **French romantic sculpture** stressed dramatic movement and fleeting gestures, poses and expressions and was epitomized by the "Marseillaise" on the Arc de Triomphe, 1833-6, by **Francois Rude**, 1784-1855.

**The Hudson River School** of American landscape painters produced picturesque and romantic views of the eastern states, exemplified by **Thomas Cole**, 1801-48 and **Asher Durand**, 1796-1886. **An increased range** of oil colours was introduced, including mauves, violets, bright greens and intense yellows.

**The Gothic Revival** in Europe which had begun *c.* 1750 and was based on serious investigation of medieval sources, prompted the decision to build the **Houses of Parliament**, London, 1836-68, in a Gothic style, and the similar exploration of national Gothic styles in the rest of Europe. **Political cartoons** reached a high level of sophistication in England in the work of **George Cruikshank**, 1792-1878, and in France with **Honoré Daumier**.

**Joseph Turner**, 1775-1851, in England was one of the first painters to celebrate contemporary technology. His "Rain, Steam and Speed", 1844, proclaims the power of the machine in a diffuse, misty style suggesting the speed of the train. **The Barbizon School** of French landscapists, including **Jean François Millet**, 1814-75, settled near Fontainebleau. **John Ruskin**, 1819-1900, emphasized truth to nature in "Modern Painters"

**Photography** (daguerreotypes) and the style of early photographic portraits, where the subject had to maintain a still pose during the long exposure period, influenced such painters as **Ingres**, particularly in his portrait of "La Comtesse d'Haussonville", 1845. **Historical architecture** spread in the US, as in Europe. The picturesque, Neo-Norman Smithsonian Institute in Washington, 1846, was built by **James Renwick, Jr**, 1818-85.

**The Pre-Raphaelite Brotherhood** was founded in England, 1848. Its painters sought a return to the purity and moral seriousness of 15th-century Italian art and rejected contemporary academic styles. Their work was characterized by great detail and the use of brilliant colours on a white ground, as in "The Awakening Conscience", 1852, by **William Holman Hunt**, 1827-1910, and "Christ in the House of his Parents", 1849, by **John Everett Millais**, 1829-96.

---

**Robert Schumann**, 1810-56, was an arch-Romantic, especially in his evocative piano music like *Carnaval*, 1834-5. He founded the *avant-garde* publication *Neue Zeitschrift für Musik* in 1834.

**Mikhail Glinka**, 1804-57, in such works as *A Life for the Tsar*, 1836, heralded the rise of a Russian national school, using folk music and inspired by the Napoleonic Wars.

**Vienna**, in Ferdinand I's reign, 1835-48, was the centre of popular dance music, exporting the Viennese waltz and works of the older **Johann Strauss**, 1804-49, to the rest of Europe.

**Brass bands**, especially in Germany, produced a popular music of their own. The cornet provided a high voice, and became a virtuoso solo instrument.

**Franz Liszt**, 1811-86, a great piano virtuoso who toured the capitals of Europe, supported the work of young musicians at the court of Weimar, 1848-61.

**The symphonic poem** or tone poem was established by Liszt while at Weimar, the first appearing in 1848-9. The form expressed a poem, story or idea in terms of orchestral music.

---

**The electric telegraph**, was patented in Britain by **Charles Wheatstone**, 1802-75, in 1837. **The Colt pistol**, the first repeating firearm, was patented, 1835-6. **Robert Brown**, 1773-1858, first discovered and named the nucleus of a living cell.

**The Morse code** was invented, 1837, by **Samuel Morse**. **Stellar parallax** was detected in 1838 by **Friedrich Bessel**, 1784-1846, showing that the stars lie at immense distances from the Earth. **Vulcanization**, was discovered in 1839 by the American inventor **Charles Goodyear**, 1800-60. **Theodor Schwann**, 1810-82, and **Matthias Schleiden**, 1804-81, both German biologists, in 1839 first described the anatomy of animal and plant cells and the parts they play

**Jean-Louis Agassiz**, 1807-73, a Swiss naturalist, studied glaciers and showed, 1840, that an Ice Age had once occurred, producing glacial action that had helped to shape the land masses. **Anaesthesia** had its beginnings in 1842, when American surgeon **Crawford Long**, 1815-78, operated on an etherized patient. **The *Great Britain***, the first iron-hulled steamer powered by a screw propeller, crossed the Atlantic in 1843. **Artificial fertilizer** was first prepared *c.* 1840.

**Nitroglycerine** was discovered 1846 by the Italian chemist **Ascanio Sobrero**. **Neptune** was discovered, 1846, by the German astronomer, **Johann Galle**, 1812-1910.

**The mechanical equivalent of heat** was first measured and the principle of the conservation of energy put forward by **Julius von Mayer**, 1814-78, a German physicist, in 1842. The British physicist **James Joule**, 1818-89, and the German **Hermann Helmholtz**, 1821-94, established both more thoroughly *c.* 1847. **The rotary printing press** was invented in 1847 by the American **Richard Hoe**, 1812-86.

**Asepsis** was demanded, 1847, by **Ignaz Semmelweiss**, 1818-65, a Hungarian physician. He showed that childbed fever could be prevented if hospital doctors cleaned their hands regularly. **The St. Lawrence Seaway** was first opened in 1848. **Reinforced concrete** was invented, 1849, by a French engineer, **Joseph Monier**, 1823-1906. **A telegraphic cable connection** across the English Channel was laid in 1850.

# 1850-1875 Darwin and Marx

## Principal events

**The development of ruthlessly pragmatic political planning epitomized by the ministry of Bismarck in Prussia brought about the national unification of Italy and Germany, where the idealism of the 1848 revolutions had failed. Industrial expansion went hand in hand with cynical foreign policies which, with the death of liberal ideals, contributed to the growth of international tensions.**

**British imperial power was at its peak after the defeat of the Indian mutiny. Britain's economic supremacy, backed up by military strength, made her unchallengeable throughout the world.**

**The victory of the North in the American Civil War ended slavery and prepared the way for American industrial and political expansion, while the European powers extended their domination in South-East Asia and Japan set out to transform herself into a modern industrial society.**

### 1850-3

**Napoleon III**, *r.* 1852-70, restored the French Empire after the upheavals of 1848.
**The rights of national minorities** were suppressed in the Austro-Hungarian Empire.
**California** became a free state in 1850 and a compromise was reached on slavery in the United States in 1850.
**The vastly destructive Taiping Rebellion** broke out in China in 1850.
**The English in India** subdued Burma, 1852-3.

### 1853-5

**Russia's defeat** in the Crimean War, 1854-6, checked her ambitions in eastern Europe.
**The New York-Chicago rail** link was completed, 1853.
**The discovery by David Livingstone**, 1813-73, of the Victoria Falls, 1855, sparked off European exploration of the African interior.
**Europe** experienced an economic boom, 1852-6.
**Camillo Cavour**, 1810-61, began the industrialization of Piedmont in northern Italy.

### 1855-8

**After the Crimean War**, the Black Sea was declared neutral and the virtual independence of Serbia recognized by the major European powers, 1856.
**The Indian Mutiny**, a series of mutinies by Sepoy troops and scattered popular uprisings against British rule, was ruthlessly suppressed, 1857-8.
**John Brown**, 1800-59, militantly pursued the anti-slavery cause in the southern USA.
**China** was finally opened up by the treaties of Tientsin, 1858.

### 1858-60

**By the Government of India Act**, 1858, British rule in India was transferred to the Crown. Administrative reforms and the building of railways with British investment followed.
**Piedmont** drove the Austrians from northern Italy with French assistance, 1859.
**British troops** raided Peking, 1860.
**The Suez Canal** construction was begun by de Lesseps, 1805-94.
**Russia** expanded at China's expense, 1858-60.

## National events

**The rising prosperity of the mid-Victorian system, based on a rapid expansion of population, industry and trade, resulted in higher wages and the birth of a strong labour movement. Electoral reform and governmental interest in social and economic planning changed the face of British politics.**

**The Great Exhibition**, 1851, symbolized growing prosperity.

**Lord Palmerston**, 1784-1865, became prime minister in 1855.
**The Northcote-Trevelyan Report**, 1854, introduced Civil Service reform.

**Palmerston's first ministry**, 1855-8, reflected Britain's confidence in international politics and stability at home.

**William Gladstone**, 1809-98, signed a commercial treaty with France, 1860, hoping that her trade would lead to international harmony.

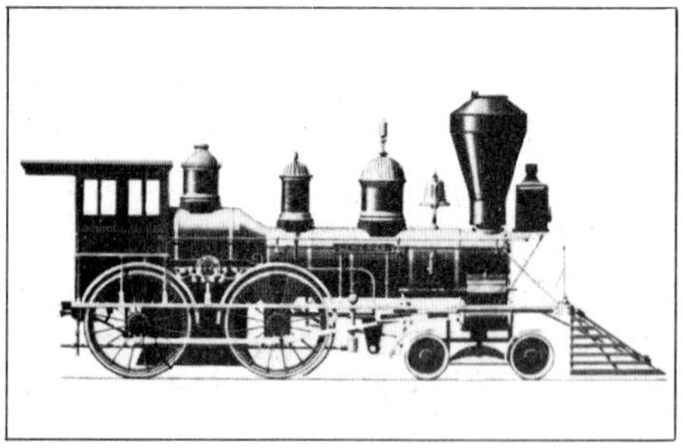

Western and Atlantic Railroad: the *General*, 1885

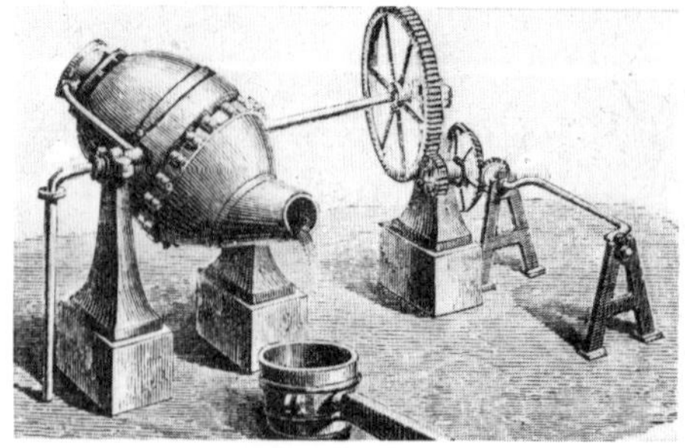

Bessemer steel producing process

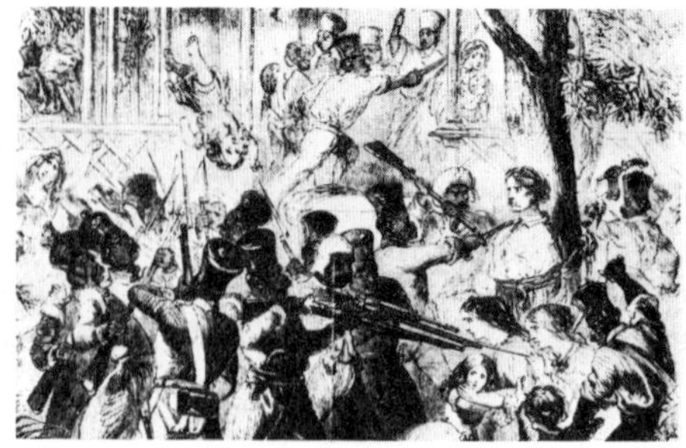

Indian Mutiny: massacre at Delhi

## Religion and philosophy

**The spread of industrialization provoked a major reassessment of moral, social and political thought. Many Christians campaigned to relieve the worst aspects of urban poverty and sociology developed tools to describe the changes in social relationships, while many political and moral philosophies grew up which rejected urbanization and capitalism, laying stress on personal withdrawal or social revolution. The latter was advocated in particular by Karl Marx whose work provided a radical attack on capitalist economics and stated that the victory of the proletariat over the bourgeoisie was an historical inevitability.**

**Darwin's theory of evolution proved as influential as the ideas of Marx, challenging many of the basic tenets of Christian belief and forcing the importance of scientific thought to the fore. Many attempts were made to apply his ideas to the political and cultural fields.**

**The Taiping Rebellion** in China, 1850, under the leadership of **Hung Hsiu-Chuan**, 1814-64, was a radical religious movement influenced by Protestant Christian teaching which demanded the communalization of property, equal redistribution of land and equality between men and women.
**T. B. Macaulay**, 1800-59, an English historian, published a *History of England* between 1848 and 1861, stressing the victory of liberalism since 1688.

**Frederick Denison Maurice**, 1805-72, the major theologian of 19th-century Anglicanism, published his *Theological Essays*, 1853. He helped to found the **Christian Socialist movement** in England, which tried to apply Christian ideals in an industrial society, and joined the co-operative movement.
**Henry Thoreau**, 1817-62, an American, described his attempt to practise **Transcendentalism** by living a simple life in the midst of nature, in *Walden*, 1854.

**Frederic Le Play**, 1806-82, a French sociologist, developed a technique of collating field data that influenced methods of statistical sampling in *European Workers*, 1855. He defined three basic family types, related to general social conditions.
**Hippolyte Taine**, 1828-93, a French historian, argued in *The French Philosophers* for the use of a scientific (positivist) method in the study of culture, 1857. He had a great influence on later 19th-century thought.

**Charles Darwin**, 1809-82, published *Origin of Species*, 1859, arousing opposition from the English Church because he contradicted Genesis and seemed to render the role of God in the creation superfluous. By implying that man stood at the pinnacle of evolutionary development, Darwin's theory reinforced contemporary ideas of the inevitability of social progress. After defeat in the debate, the Church ceased to intervene in science.

## Literature

**As the realist novel produced the powerful and candid tragedy of *Madame Bovary* by Flaubert, new literary styles were also emerging in French poetry. Baudelaire's attempt to explore his inner self would lead to the symbolist movement to which reality beyond the poet's own imagination was irrelevant.**

**In Russia, Dostoevsky and Tolstoy were writing and the moral, psychological and political issues they explored recurred in the literature of the English Victorian novelists from Charles Dickens to George Eliot.**

**American literature reached maturity with the poetry of Whitman – a distinct contrast with contemporary European styles – and the strong prose of Melville's epic novel *Moby Dick*.**

**The Victorian Alfred Lord Tennyson**, 1809-92, showed in his elegiac poem *In Memoriam*, 1850, verbal grace and awareness of the moral dilemmas of the age.
**The American novelist, Nathaniel Hawthorne**, 1806-64, wrote *The Scarlet Letter*, 1850, and **Herman Melville** produced his allegorical *Moby Dick*, 1851, with an American delight in vigorous prose.

**The fantastic** and dream-inspired poems of *Les Chimeres*, 1854, by **Gérard de Nerval**, 1808-55, would influence later symbolists.
The *Poems* of **Matthew Arnold**, 1822-88 were an intellectual expression of Victorian unease, as was the poetry of **Robert Browning**, 1812-89, whose dramatic monologues are full of human insight.

**Walt Whitman**, 1819-92, published his autobiographical *Leaves of Grass* in 1855.
**Modern poetry** began with *Les Fleurs du Mal*, 1857, by the Frenchman **Charles Baudelaire**, 1821-67.
**Theophile Gautier**, 1811-72, proclaimed the concept of art for art's sake, 1857.
**Gustave Flaubert**, 1821-80, published *Madame Bovary*, 1856.

**Adalbert Stifter**, 1805-68, wrote of the harmony of man and nature in *Der Nachsommer*.
**Ivan Goncharov**, 1812-91 wrote *Oblomov*, 1859, mocking the bankruptcy of intellectualism.

## Art and architecture

**The reaction against academic precepts, which ruled the bulk of official painting in Europe, began in earnest and took the form of the assertion that the subject matter of everyday life was worthy of art.**

**The Impressionists broke new ground with their revolutionary techniques for representing light and colour, best seen in the works of Monet; while Realist painters like Courbet stated that art must have a social and political purpose. In the same period English art saw a distinct reaction against the aesthetics and values of industrial society with the work of the Pre-Raphaelites and the Arts and Crafts movement.**

**Town planning became a priority in the European capitals and the use of cast iron revolutionized municipal architecture.**

**Trading contact with the East and the Meiji restoration in Japan brought an interpenetration of Eastern and Western art.**

**Realism** reached its height in the works of **Gustave Courbet**, 1819-77, such as "The Stonebreakers", 1850.
**Jean Francois Millet**, 1814-75, created an ennobling picture of peasants in his canvas "The Sower", 1850.
**The Pre-Raphaelite Brotherhood**, were defended by **John Ruskin**, 1851.
**Prefabricated units of iron and glass** were used by **Joseph Paxton**, 1803-65, in the Crystal Palace, London, 1851.

**Honoré Daumier**, 1808-79, painted children in "La Ronde", 1855.

**Baron Haussmann**, 1809-91, introduced squares, parks and boulevards into Paris, 1851-68. His wide streets were designed to create impressive views and to ensure easy policing of the city centre.
**The New Building of the Louvre**, 1852-7, and the Paris Opera, 1861-74, illustrate the powerful Neo-Renaissance and Neo-Baroque forms which were key to the civic architecture of the Second Empire.

**Landscapes** by **Jean Baptiste Camille Corot**, 1796-1875, such as "The Valley", 1855-60, anticipated the Impressionists with their use of muted colours and soft outlines.
**The Arts and Crafts movement** in England led by **William Morris**, 1834-96, and **Philip Webb**, 1831-1915, originated in a dissatisfaction with manufactured goods and a respect for the medieval craftsman. It produced wallpapers, furniture, tapestries and carpets usually by hand.

## Music

**Romantic ideals were reinforced in 1858 by Darwin's theory of evolution through the survival of the fittest, and confirmed the common view that man verges on perfection. The odd conclusion that art, like life, evolves from lower forms to higher led to an increasing distinction between serious and popular music, a distinction that remains prevalent in the West even today.**

**Musical forms** still developed themes, much as the classics had done, but the work of composers such as **Liszt** gave music a mystical aura and set it apart from normal experience.

**Late Romantic composers**, such as **Richard Wagner**, 1813-83, and **Anton Bruckner**, 1824-96, aimed for grandeur by using large forces and a rubato (freer) beat to savour the sound.

**Use of rubato** tended to slow down performances and to produce rhythmic problems in large ensembles so that performances became dull and turgid.

**Grand opera** carried the Romantic ideal to a peak in the works of **Giuseppe Verdi**, 1813-1901, in such works as *Un Ballo in maschera*, 1859, evoked specific characters and moods.

## Science and technology

**Science and technology became more closely tied to the needs of industry in this period, especially in Germany where chemists produced dyes and explosives and in the United States where engineers enjoyed a high social status. The abolition of slavery in America and the rise of trade unionism in Europe both raised labour costs and so stimulated mechanization, while the Crimean War provided an incentive for the development of new and better kinds of steel.**

**While Darwin's theory of evolution, backed up by Mendel's researches into genetics, was the most popular scientific breakthrough, chemistry and astronomy both advanced dramatically with the development of spectroscopy in Germany and the application of the Doppler Effect. The former permitted many new elements to be discovered, while the latter, through the measurement of red-shift, produced more accurate estimates of the size of the known universe.**

**Entropy**, following from the second law of thermodynamics, was conceived, 1850, by the German **Rudolf Clausius**, 1822-88.
**The sewing machine** was developed, 1851, by **Isaac Singer**, 1811-75, an American.
**Physiology** advanced with the work, *c.* 1851, of the French scientist **Claude Bernard**, 1813-78.
**The rotation of the Earth** was demonstrated conclusively in 1851 by the French physicist **Jean Foucault**, 1819-68.

**Symbolic logic** was founded by **George Boole**, 1815-64, a British mathematician, with his *Laws of Thought*, 1854.
**Agriculture** gained a scientific basis with the publication in the 1840s and 1850s of work by the German **Justus von Liebig**, 1803-73, showing how plants use vital elements in cycles.

**The first synthetic plastic material**, later named celluloid, was patented in 1855 by the British chemist Alexander Parkes, 1813-90.
**Mauve**, the first artificial dye, was derived from aniline, 1856, by the British chemist **William Perkin**, 1838-1907. Production of the new synthetic substances stimulated the growth of modern organic chemistry.
**Steel** was produced cheaply in the converter patented in 1856 by the British metallurgist **Henry Bessemer**, 1813-98.

**The principles of molecular structure**, were discovered by **Friedrich Kekulé von Stradonitz**, 1829-96, in 1858.
**The theory of evolution** was put forward in 1858-9 by the British naturalists **Charles Darwin**, 1809-82, and **Alfred Wallace**, 1823-1913.
**The first oil well** was struck near Titusville, Pennsylvania, in 1858.
**Atomic weights and chemical formulae** were standardized by the Italian **Stanislao Cannizzaro**, 1826-1910, in 1858.

## 1860-3

**Abraham Lincoln**, 1809-65, was elected president of the US on an anti-slavery platform.
**The Confederate states** took Fort Sumter, 1861, and this sparked off the Civil War.
**Giuseppe Garibaldi**, 1807-82, liberated southern Italy from Neopolitan rule and gave it to Piedmont, uniting Italy, 1861.
**Alexander II** of Russia, *r.* 1855-81, emancipated the serfs in 1861.
**French troops** occupied Mexico City, 1863, and set up a puppet emperor, Archduke Maximilian.

## 1863-5

**An allied Western expedition** participated in a violent civil war in Japan, 1864.
**Rome** remained under papal rule as a virtual protectorate of France.
**The northern American states** defeated the South, 1865.
**Slavery** was abolished and Lincoln assassinated, 1865.
**Karl Marx**, 1818-83, presided over the First International in London 1864.
**Christianity** was spread in China by missionaries.

## 1865-8

**After the defeat of Austria** by Prussia in the war of 1866, the North German Confederation was set up.
**American objections** and opposition at home led to French withdrawal from Mexico, 1866.
**The Dominion of Canada** was established by the British North America Act, 1867.
**The Dual Monarchy of Austria-Hungary** was established, 1867 – an unpopular compromise on the nationalist question.

## 1868-70

**Napoleon III** instituted liberal reforms to quell the growing opposition, but his empire collapsed in the face of a Prussian invasion, 1870.
**By 1870 the railway systems of** France, England and Belgium were virtually complete, stimulating heavy industry.
**The victory of Mutsuhito**, *r.* 1868-1912, in Japan led to a policy of industrialization and an end to the shōguns.
**Negro suffrage** was enforced in the United States, 1870.

## 1870-3

**A revolutionary commune** set up in Paris, 1870-1, was ruthlessly suppressed. It rejected the authority of the French government after the surrender to Prussia.
**Prussia's seizure of Alsace-Lorraine** completed German unification and a German Empire was proclaimed under **Wilhelm I**, *r.* 1861-88.
**An American attempt** to open up Korea failed, 1871-3, but Britain forced the Treaty of Pangkor on Malaya.

## 1874-5

**The conservative Third Republic** was set up in France after the defeat of the Commune, in spite of repeated attempts to restore the monarchy.
**Britain** bought a decisive share in the **Suez Canal**, 1875, thus acquiring a quick route to India.
**French power** in Indochina, extended by Napoleon III, was confirmed, 1874.
**The revelation of corruption** in the Grant administration in the US resulted in financial panic and economic depression.

**The Companies Act,** 1862, introduced limited liability companies.
**The first underground railway** was built in London, 1860-3.

**The demand for electoral reform** among liberals and radicals was blocked by Palmerston's conservatism until his death in 1865.

**Benjamin Disraeli**, 1804-81, introduced household suffrage, 1867.
**The Trades Union Congress** was founded in 1868.

**Gladstone** became committed to disestablishing the Anglican Church in Ireland, where a nationalist movement was growing in strength, 1868-74.

**The Education Act**, 1870, made primary education open to all.
**Depression** after a financial crisis ended the peak of British economic supremacy.

**The Public Health Act** codified sanitary law and the Artisans' Dwelling Act tried to improve slum conditions, 1875.

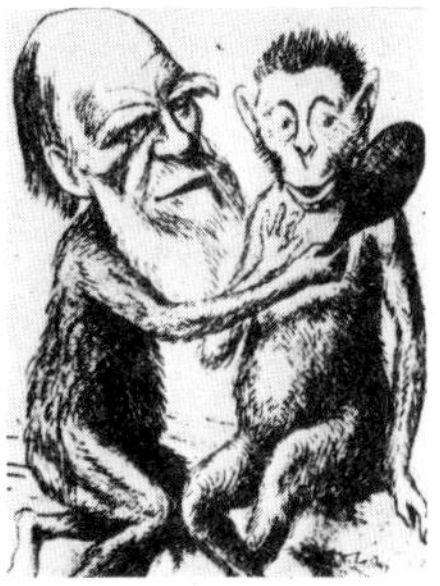

Charles Darwin lampooned

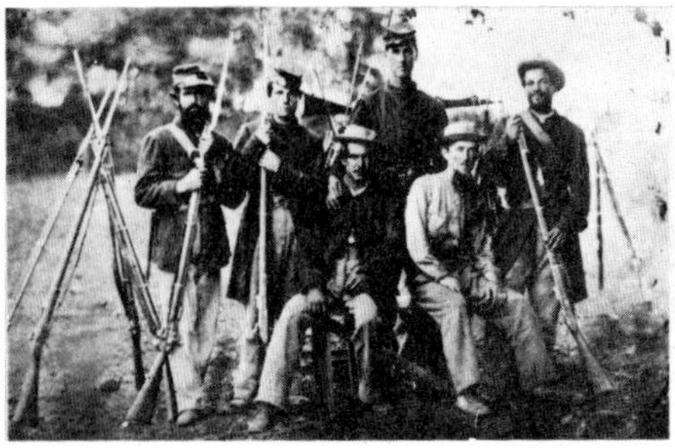

Confederates in the American Civil War

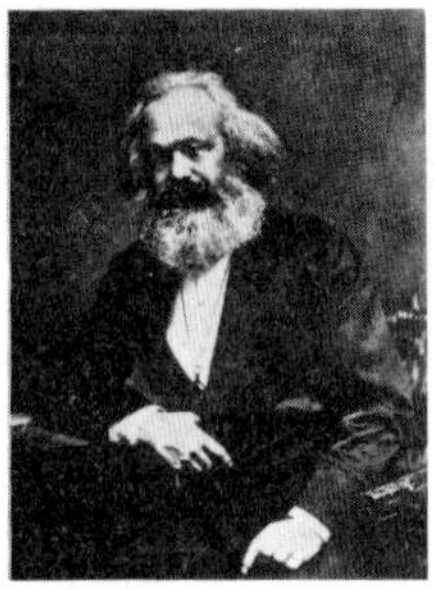

Karl Marx

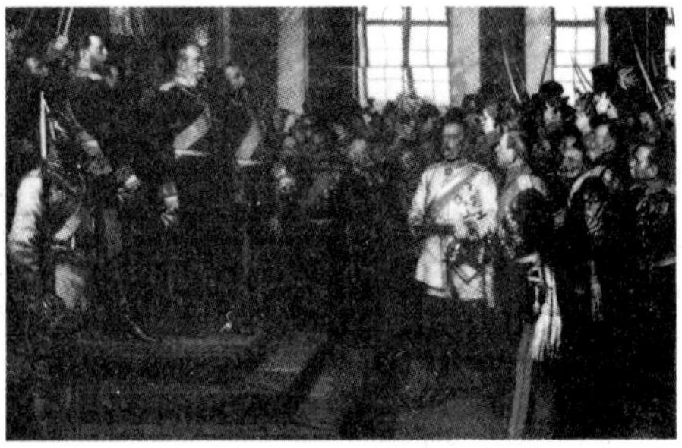

Wilhelm I of Prussia acclaimed German emperor

**Ferdinand Lassalle**, 1825-64, urged German workers to seek universal suffrage, 1862. His programme formed the basis of the German Social Democratic Party established in 1869 in opposition to the revolutionary Marxist International, and foreshadowed later social democratic and parliamentary movements.
**Ernest Renan**, 1823-92, wrote *The Life of Jesus*, 1863, in a positivist framework, stressing historical detail.

**John Stuart Mill**, 1806-73, an Englishman, attempted to create a political theory uniting the conditions of industrialism with basic tenets of human freedom. He argued in *Utilitarianism*, 1863, that what gives pleasure to man is good, while in *On Liberty*, 1859, he insisted that a man must be free to act as he wishes without disturbing the freedom of others. His political critique of English society brought him close to a socialist position.

**Karl Marx**, 1818-83, published Volume I of *Capital*, 1867, providing a theoretical analysis of the workings of capitalism. He argued that industrial profits were made by exploiting the workers, but claimed that capitalism would plunge into chaos through its inner contradictions.
**William Booth**, 1829-1912, shocked at the extent of poverty and degradation in London, began his Evangelical ministry in 1865 and later founded the **Salvation Army.**

**Papal infallibility** was asserted by the first Vatican Council, 1869-70, which ruled that the pope or an ecumenical council of bishops was immune from error when pronouncing on matters of faith or morals. The pope's increased prestige resulting from this ruling partly compensated for the loss of the Papal States to Italy.
**The classic statement** of the case for women's suffrage was presented by **J. S. Mill** in *The Subjection of Women*, 1869.

**Bakunin**, 1814-76, a Russian anarchist, stressed the need for violent revolution to overthrow the state and allow the essential goodness of man to develop. His rejection of centralization and subordination to authority in favour of the free spirit of revolt led to his expulsion from the Internationale, 1872, after conflicting with Marx.
**Johann von Döllinger**, the German theologian, 1799-1890, was excommunicated, 1871, for opposing the idea of infallibility.

**An upsurge of religious revivalism** associated with the Temperance Movement, which saw alcohol as the cause of working-class degradation, was started in America and Britain by **D. L. Moody**, 1837-99.
**Wilhelm Wundt**, 1832-1920, a German who published *Principles of Physiological Psychology*, 1873-4, established experimental psychology. He sought to investigate by introspection the immediate experiences of consciousness.

**An impressionistic realist style** based on detailed social observation was developed in France by the brothers **Edmond and Jules de Goncourt**, 1822-96 and 1830-70, in their *Journals*.
**The realist novel in Russia** produced a varied account of the conflicts in Russian society.

**The debate between Slavophiles and Westernizers** was described in *Fathers and Sons* by **Ivan Turgenev**, 1818-83, an ardent Westernizer.
**Count Leo Tolstoy**, 1828-1910, the greatest exponent of the Russian realist novel, dealt in his epic *War and Peace*, 1865-72, with the Napoleonic Wars, combining a panoramic vision with acute analysis of character.

**The Parnassians**, a group of French poets including **Charles Marie Leconte de Lisle**, 1818-94, and later **Paul Verlaine**, 1844-96, rejected the emotionalism and loose forms of the Romantics and wrote strictly disciplined, detached verse following **Theophile Gautier**. Their name derived from the journal *Le Parnasse Contemporain*, first published in 1866.

**The great novels of Fyodor Dostoevsky**, 1821-81, including *Crime and Punishment* 1866, *The Brothers Karamazov* 1879-80, and *The Idiot* 1868, study totalitarianism, the conflict between atheism and compassionate Christianity, and good and evil in man.
**The English novelist Charles Dickens** continued his prodigious output of social novels.

**George Eliot**, the pseudonym of Mary Anne Evans, 1819-80, described the conflicts within English provincial society in *Middlemarch*, 1871-2.
**The early French symbolist poets, Arthur Rimbaud**, 1854-91, and **Paul Verlaine**, 1844-96, aimed to devise a truly poetic visionary language; Rimbaud wrote *Une Saison en Enfer* in 1873.

**Jules Laforgue**, 1860-87, a symbolist, was one of the first French poets to use free verse.

**The Salon de Refusés** which exhibited some of the 4000 canvases rejected by the official Salon, was established in Paris in 1863. It included works by **Pissarro**, **Cezanne**, **Whistler**, and **Edouard Manet**, 1832-1883, whose "Déjeuner sur L'Herbe", of a naked woman enjoying a picnic with friends, created a sensation.
**Gustave Doré**, 1832-83, established his reputation with illustrations for Dante's *Inferno*, 1861

**Eugène-Emmanuel Viollet-le-Duc**, 1814-79, published his *Dictionary of French Architecture from the 11th to the 16th Centuries*, 1858-75.
**Japanese draughtsmanship**, flat expanses of colour and subject matter, strongly influenced the Impressionists and later Van Gogh and Gauguin. Their impact on Parisian artists can be seen in **Manet's** "Portrait of Emile Zola", 1868, and in **Whistler's** "Princess of the Land of Porcelain", 1864.

**Japanese prints** were being collected in Paris in the 1860s and were exhibited at the **Exposition Universelle**, 1867.
**The effects of light** out of doors on the surface of an object or figure was first captured and faithfully recorded by **Claude Monet**, 1840-1926, in his painting "Women in the Garden", 1866.

**Mural painting** in France was revived by **Pierre Puvis de Chavannes**, 1824-98, whose monumental style and subdued colours seen in "Ludus Pro Patria", 1865-9, inspired the Symbolists of the 1880s.

**Monet**'s painting "Impression, Sunrise", 1872, exhibited in 1874 with works by **Pierre Auguste Renoir**, 1841-1919, **Alfred Sisley**, 1839-99, **Edgar Degas**, 1834-1917, **Pissarro** and **Cézanne**, gave its name to the Impressionist movement with which these painters were associated. **Impressionism** abandoned traditional linear representation, aiming to capture the fleeting effects of light and colour by using small dashes and strokes of colour.

**The later Pre-Raphaelite style** in England, best represented by the work of **Edward Burne-Jones**, 1833-98, like the "Briar Rose" series, 1871-90, later influenced the Symbolist movement.
**London's first garden suburb**, Bedford Park at Turnham Green, was designed by the Victorian architect and associate of William Morris, **Richard Norman Shaw**, 1831-1912, in 1875.

**The opera *Faust*,** by Charles Francois Gounod, 1818–1893, was produced in London, Dublin and New York in 1863.

**Negro spirituals** emerged in the US as blacks took up the singing school tradition of colonial America, but mixed with it a rhythmic work-song style.

**Light opera** centred on Paris and Vienna, with the theatrical humour of **Jacques Offenbach**, 1819-80, and the lavish settings of the younger **Johann Strauss**, 1825-99.

**Wagner** revolutionized opera, using a continuously moving harmonic structure over which leitmotive (short themes) identified dramatic elements. He believed opera should combine all the arts.

**César Franck**, 1822-90, a Belgian working in the classical tradition, attracted little attention in his lifetime but influenced an important group of younger French composers.

**Johannes Brahms**, 1833-97, carried on Beethoven's tradition especially in the symphony. Brahms's classical control of the emotional impulses in his music gives it a rich dramatic quality.

**The open hearth process** for the production of steel was developed in France, following the invention of the regenerative furnace by **William Siemens**, 1823-83, and **Frederick Siemens**, 1826-1904.
**A submarine telegraphic cable** was laid across the Atlantic from Ireland to Newfoundland, 1858-66.
**Colloids** were distinguished in 1861 by the British chemist **Thomas Graham**, 1805-69. He also discovered **osmosis**.

**The first underground railway** opened in London in 1863.
**The Massachusetts Institute of Technology** was founded, 1865.

**Dynamite** was invented in 1866 by the Swedish inventor **Alfred Nobel**, 1833-96, who founded the Nobel Prize.
**Antiseptic surgery** was introduced by the British physician Lord Lister, 1827-1912, by 1867. Following Pasteur's research into the nature of disease, he used carbolic acid to disinfect the operating theatre.
**Genetics** was founded with the publication, 1865, of the experiments of the Austrian botanist **Gregor Mendel**, 1822-84.

**Bacteriology** was founded with the work of the French chemist **Louis Pasteur**, 1822-95, in the 1860s. Pasteur discovered that micro-organisms cause fermentation and disease, and used sterilization to kill bacteria.
**Light** was shown to be an electromagnetic radiation by the British physicist **James Clerk-Maxwell**, 1831-79. He predicted other such radiations.

**The Periodic table** of the elements was devised by the Russian chemist **Dmitry Mendelyev**, 1834-1907, in 1869.
**The typewriter** was developed commercially after the 1867 invention of American **Christopher Sholes**, 1819-90.
**The Challenger expedition** of 1872-6 founded oceanography.
**Intermolecular forces** were calculated by **Johannes van der Waals**, 1837-1923, in 1873. He accurately described the behaviour of real gases, using mathematical equations.

# 1875-1900 The age of imperialism

## Principal events

**Domination of the world outside the Americas lay with a few European states. Among them Britain was still the greatest imperial and industrial power but Germany now increasingly challenged this position. The US also grew in strength and by 1900 overtook Britain in the production of basic industrial materials.**

**The emergence of a group of fixed alliances in Europe served to polarize foreign affairs and the Balkans, in particular, presented an inflammatory arena for international conflict.**

**Improvements in communications, however, and the quest for new bases of economic and political power shifted the focus of rivalries between the states to Africa and Oceania. Britain greatly extended her empire but the other European states, the US and a newly modernized Japan also joined in the scramble. By 1899 all Asia was in the hands of Europe and China was in thrall to the West.**

### 1875-8

**Britain** bought the Khedive's Suez Canal shares, 1875, and annexed South Africa, 1877.
**The Slav nationalist forces** in the Balkans erupted against Turkey and the Bulgarian massacres, 1875, aroused a public outcry in Britain. Russia supported the insurgents, hoping to win new authority in the Balkans.
**The Satsuma rebellion**, 1877 led by conservative forces in Japan, failed to halt the tide of reform and new ideas.

### 1878-80

**After Russia's defeat of Turkey**, 1878, Britain and Austria-Hungary intervened to check Russian ambitions and the Powers met at the Congress of Berlin, 1878, to decide the future of the Balkans.
**Germany and Austria-Hungary** formed a Dual Alliance, 1879.
**In Afghanistan** Britain sought to secure her position in India against Russian expansion, 1878-80.
**Chile** began her successful war against Bolivia and Peru, 1879.

### 1880-3

**British imperial expansion** in Africa was checked by defeat in the Transvaal, 1881, but British occupation forces were installed in Egypt in 1882.
**Under Bismarck**, 1815-98, Germany aimed to build a solid European power structure, signing the **Three Emperors' Alliance** with Russia and Austria, 1881, and a similar alliance with Italy, 1882. At home, Bismarck introduced sickness benefits to help weaken the growing appeal of socialism, 1883.

### 1883-5

**Britain** consolidated her position on the Afghan border and in Egypt but was defeated by native forces in the Sudan, 1885.
**France** took Indochina, 1884.
**The Treaty of Berlin**, 1884, defined the rights of 14 European powers in Africa. This helped stop the scramble for colonies which could have led to a major war.
**Eastern Rumelia's union** with Bulgaria, 1885, provoked war with Serbia and Austria acted to save Serbia from invasion.

## National events

**Britain's economic supremacy was challenged by other powers. The extended franchise gave a more popular ring to politics and saw the foundation of an Independent Labour Party, 1893. The traditional parties changed the emphasis of their policies as imperialism and Ireland became the major political issues.**

**Legislation** in 1875 legalized peaceful picketing and freed trade disputes from the law of conspiracy.
**Victoria** took the title Empress of India in 1876.

**Charles Parnell**, 1846-91, mobilized the Irish nationalists and aimed to reform the Irish Land Law.

**The Irish problem** was accentuated by terrorism in Ireland.
**Textile output** in England began to decline after 1880.

**Virtual universal male suffrage**, led to an intensive party activity at the constituency level.

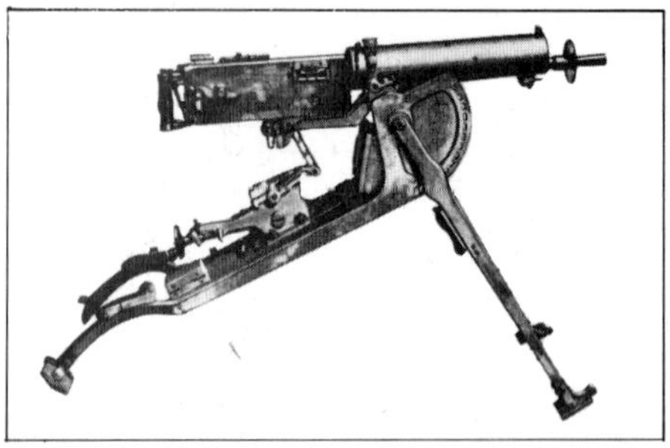

Maxim machine gun

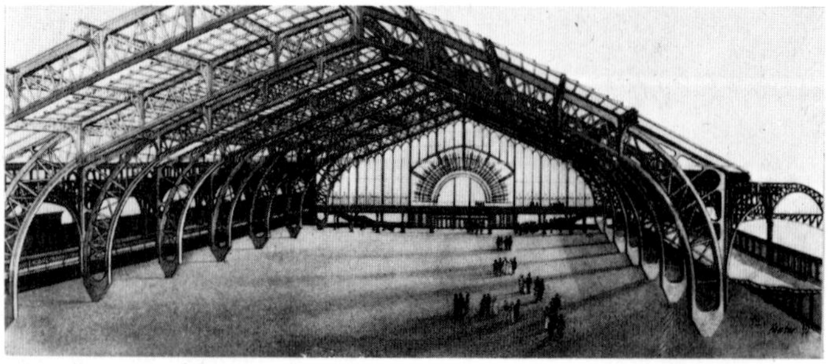

Paris Exhibition 1889: the Machine Hall

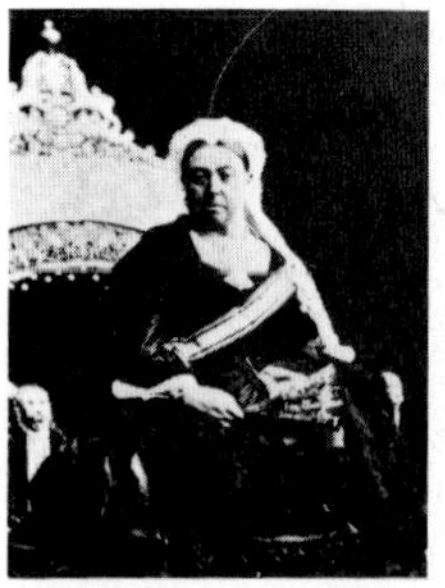

Queen Victoria

## Religion and philosophy

**Growing interest in the attempt to link social theory to biological evolutionism gave rise to more subtle sociological and anthropological studies in the English-speaking world. Drawing on the experience of colonial administration, men such as Tylor, Spencer and Frazer developed the notion of a natural progression between "primitive" and "advanced" societies. Meanwhile in Vienna, Freud began to formulate profoundly influential ideas on the subconscious and the nature of man.**

**In philosophy the absolute idealism of Hegel found its first supporters in England with Bradley, while in the United States pragmatic thinkers such as William James argued that the truth of an idea depends on its social function.**
**The ideology of anti-semitism grew up in the wake of heightened nationalist sentiment, while an evolutionary type of socialism grew more popular than its revolutionary counterpart.**

**Hinduism** witnessed the rise of various reform movements in the 19th century under the impact of Western thought. Most important was that led by **Ramakhrishna**, 1836-86, an extreme ascetic in the Vedanta tradition, who believed that all religions were essentially identical.
**The Theosophical Society**, which set out to foster the transmission of Eastern thought to the West, was founded in New York in 1875 by **Helen Blavatsky**, 1831-91.

**The Jehovah's Witnesses**, an evangelical movement believing in the second coming of Christ, were founded by **Charles Russell**, 1852-1916, in the United States.
**Christian Science** was founded in Boston by **Mary Baker Eddy**, 1821-1910, who rejected medicine and saw prayer as the only cure for illness.
**Heinrich von Treitschke**, 1834-96, fostered German nationalism in his *History of Germany in the 19th Century*, 1879-94.

**A theory of social evolution** was developed by the Englishman **Edward Tylor**, 1832-1917, in his *Anthropology*, 1881. Through studying primitive religion, he concluded that many existing social customs were "survivals" from earlier stages of development. Similar ideas were defended in America by **Lewis Morgan**, 1818-81, who developed the study of kinship systems.

In Russia, **Peter Kropotkin**, 1842-1921, was the leading theorist of the Anarchist movement. In *Words of a Rebel*, 1884, he emphasized non-violence and argued that co-operation rather than conflict was the basis of evolutionary progress.
**The Fabian Society**, founded in Britain, 1884, advocated a gradual evolution towards socialism.
**The Zionist Movement** held its first conference in Prussia in 1884 as anti-semitism grew.

## Literature

**The pessimistic application of theories of evolution is found in Zola's naturalistic novels which stressed the limitations on man's actions stemming from his inherited characteristics and the environment and portrayed the most sordid aspects of French lower-class life. English literature exchanged the exuberance of Dickens for the critical mood of Hardy.**

**Nationalism still acted as a vital cultural stimulus, creating a school of national regeneration in Spain in reaction to the political weakness highlighted by the war with Cuba, and in Italy celebrating unification. In both, writers turned to their national classics for models. The first self-conscious Latin American school grew up asserting independence from European traditions.**

**English literature after 1875** saw a reaction to the confidence of the high Victorian era, reflected in the decadent poetry of **Algernon Charles Swinburne**, 1837-1909. His sensual *Poems and Ballads* show traces of symbolist influences.
**Gerard Manley Hopkins**, 1844-89, described the tensions of his religious vision in lyrical, experimental poetry.

**Realism in the theatre** was pioneered by the Norwegian **Henrik Ibsen**, 1828-1906, who dramatized social issues using ordinary conversation, as in *A Doll's House*, 1879.
In England **G. B. Shaw**, 1856-1950, also attacked social complacency in plays enlivened by vivid characterization, satire and wit such as *Mrs. Warren's Profession* and *The Devil's Disciple*.

**Native American humour** was found in *The Adventures of Huckleberry Finn* by **Mark Twain**, 1835-1910.
**The meeting of the New World with the Old** was explored by **Henry James**, 1843-1916, in *Portrait of a Lady*, 1881. He probed subtleties of character, temperament and motive, as in *Washington Square*, and the dazzling *The Golden Bowl*.

**Naturalism in literature** was inaugurated in France by **Emile Zola**, 1840-1902, who explored deterministic notions of the relation between heredity and environment and the casualties of urban society in the novels *Les Rougon Macquart*, 1871-93.
**Guy de Maupassant**, 1850-93, followed him in his novels and short stories such as *Boule de Suif*.

## Art and architecture

**A self-conscious and revolutionary avant-garde emerged in European art at the end of the 19th century. In France Van Gogh, Gauguin and Cézanne, the major innovators of this time, developed their different styles out of their Impressionist origins. The symbolists rejected the Impressionist vision, turning instead to the past and to the exotic imagery of the later English Pre-Raphaelites in which Art Nouveau, an essentially decorative style and the first non-historical style to win wide acceptance, also had roots. Beginning in Belgium and England Art Nouveau owed its original character to a semi-abstract use of natural forms and had far-reaching effects in architecture and the applied arts.**

**Construction in metal became even more popular after the Paris exhibitions of 1878 and 1889, encouraged by the substitution of steel for iron, which also made possible the development of the skyscraper in the US.**

**A parallel to the Impressionist idea of forms dissolved in light** appeared in the work of the greatest 19th-century sculptor **Auguste Rodin**, 1840-1917, who produced his first free-standing figure, "Age of Bronze", in 1877.

**Ballet girls, working girls,** and cabaret artists were the subject matter for such works of **Edgar Degas**, as "Scènes de Ballet", 1879. He worked in a great variety of media and was influenced by the action photographs of dancers and racing horses taken by **Muybridge**.
**A Slavic revival in Russia** reached its peak in the '70s and '80s based on a careful documentation of national cultural history.

**Official painting in England** was represented by **Lawrence Alma-Tadema**, 1836-1912, and **Frederick Leighton**, 1830-96, who painted pseudo-classical scenes in a realistic though sentimental manner.
**A move from Impressionism** was evident in the works of **Paul Cézanne**, 1839-1906, who achieved an almost abstract quality in such paintings as "L'Estaque", *c.* 1882-5, with its emphasis on form, colour, planes and light.

**Neo-Impressionism** or **Pointillism** was developed by **Georges Seurat**, 1859-91, **Paul Signac** 1863-1935, and **Camille Pissarro**, 1830-1903. A reaction against the spontaneity of Impressionism, it created the optical effect of light by means of dots of colour which were fused by the eye into continuous tones.
**The Berlin Reichstag**, 1884-94, and the **Victor Emmanuele II** monument in Rome, 1885-1911, used antique forms to create a sense of civic grandeur.

## Music

**Romanticism began to decline as nationalism and impressionism became more important ideals in music. Meanwhile the future of American and European popular music was formed in the United States into the increasing appreciation of the rhythmic genius of Negro folk musicians and an awareness of the potential of the newly developed gramophone.**

**National qualities** appeared in serious music both out of patriotism, heard in **Bedřich Smetana's** Czech *Má Vlast*, 1874-5, and of exoticism, in **Emmanuel Chabrier's** *España*, 1883.

**Art songs** were composed all over Europe, after decades of domination by German lieder writers. The form was finely worked by French composers like **Henri Duparc**, 1848-1933.

**English light opera**, notably the deft, tuneful creations of **W. S. Gilbert**, 1836-1911, and **Arthur Sullivan**, 1842-1900, became a craze throughout Europe, the US and Australia.

**The origins of jazz and blues** are found in the work songs that united poor blacks as they toiled in fields, and in gospel songs that united them in church.

## Science and technology

**Germany now took the lead in the science-based industries as a result of the emphasis on science and technology in education and a political system that gave power to industry. She possessed a flourishing heavy industry, became the centre of early motor-car development and led the field in medicine, now a preventative as well as a curative science, with the discovery of antibodies and of new drugs. Koch's work on tuberculosis was the most important advance. As a result of these technical discoveries combined with the widespread building of new hospitals, mortality rates dropped throughout western Europe. Other technological achievements that would alter society were the inventions of the telephone and phonograph.**

**Classical physics failed to explain discoveries made in radioactivity and the problem posed by the Michelson-Morley experiment, and entered a time of uncertainty that would only be resolved by Einstein's theory of relativity.**

**The telephone was invented** in 1876 by the American inventor **Alexander Bell**, 1847-1922.
**Bacteria were identified** by methods of growing and staining cultures, developed from 1876 onwards by the German bacteriologist **Robert Koch**, 1843-1910. He found the bacteria that cause tuberculosis, anthrax and cholera.
**The phonograph was invented** in 1877 by the American inventor **Thomas Edison**, 1847-1931.

In 1879 **Edison** patented his incandescent light bulb. But in 1878 **Joseph Swan**, a British physicist, had patented the **first successful filament electric lamp**. In 1879-80 both Swan and Edison independently produced a practical light bulb.
**Piezoelectricity**, electricity produced by the compression of certain types of crystal, was discovered, 1880, by a Frenchman **Pierre Curie**, 1859-1906.

**The ether** was proved not to exist by the experiments of the American physicists **Albert Michelson**, 1852-1931, and **Edward Morley**, 1838-1923, from 1881. This result led to the **theory of relativity**.
**The electric tram** first ran in Berlin in 1881.
**Cell division** was described in 1882 by the German anatomist **Walther Flemming**, 1843-1905.
Following Koch's work, **Pasteur** used attenuated bacteria to confer immunity to anthrax, 1881, and against rabies, 1885.

**H. C. Maxim**, 1840-1916, invented the **Maxim machine gun** in England, 1884.
**The steam turbine** was made in 1884 by the British engineer **Charles Parsons**, 1854-1931.
**Motor transport** was founded in 1885 with the invention of the motor car by **Karl Benz**, 1844-1929, a German engineer. In the same year another German engineer, **Gottlieb Daimler**, 1834-1900, patented a gasoline engine which he used initially to power a motorcycle.

## 1885-8

**The Canadian Pacific Railway** was completed, 1885.
**All American Indians** were confined to reservations by 1887.
**The American Federation of Labor** was set up in 1886.
**Germany** signed a Reinsurance Treaty with Russia, 1887, to minimize the danger of war between them in the Balkans.
**Britain, Italy and Austria-Hungary** agreed to maintain the status quo in the Mediterranean and the Near East, 1887.

**Conservatives and Liberal Unionists** opposed Gladstone's Irish Home Rule Bill, 1886.
**"New unionism"** began to mobilize the working masses, 1888.

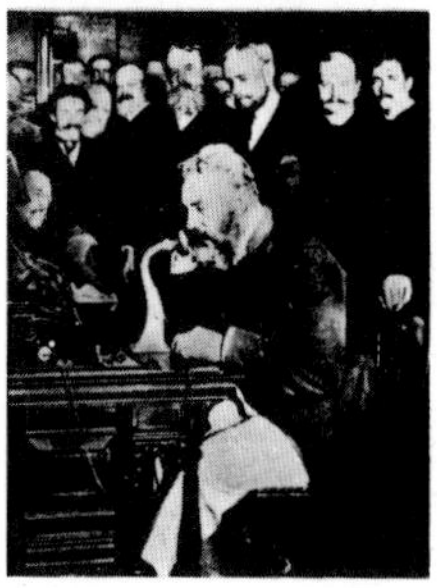

**Bell at his telephone, 1892**

**Friedrich Nietzsche**, 1844-1900, a German, vehemently rejected Christianity, science and conformist moralities in *Beyond Good and Evil*, 1886.
**Edouard Drumont**, 1844-1917, popularized anti-semitism in *La France Juive*, 1886.
**Ferdinand Tönnies**, 1855-1936, the German sociologist, published *Community and Association*, 1887, distinguishing "communities", involving moral consensus, from "associations", based on self-interest.

**Symbolist poetry** developed in France with the *Poésies*, 1887, of **Stéphane Mallarmé**, 1842-98. He sought for an ideal world, but one of the intellect and not the emotions. **Maurice Maeterlinck**, 1862-1949, in Belgium, wrote symbolist plays.
In Sweden **August Strindberg**, 1849-1912, wrote plays such as *Miss Julie* in a naturalist vein.

**Vincent van Gogh**, 1853-90, a painter obsessed with the problems of expression, painted tormented landscapes and portraits using heightened colour and a frenzied and turbulent style seen in "The Sower", 1888.
**Impressionist ideas** were taken to England by **Wilson Steer**, 1860-1942, and **Walter Sickert**, 1860-1942, who set up the **New English Art Club**, 1886, in protest against pseudo-classical styles.

**Russian music** gained its national qualities – lyricism, vitality and colourful orchestration – in the work of **Peter Tchaikovsky**, 1840-93 and **Nikolai Rimsky-Korsakov**, 1844-1908.

**Aluminium could be produced economically** from 1886 by the electrolytic process developed, almost at the same time, by an American chemist, **Charles Hall**, 1863-1914, and a French chemist, **Paul Héroult**, 1863-1914.
**Radio waves were produced** about 1887 by **Heinrich Hertz**, 1857-94, a German physicist.
**Edison** set up a **research laboratory** at West Orange, 1887, with teams of inventors working together systematically.

## 1888-90

**The partition of Africa** neared completion with Britain dominating the centre and south.
**In Japan, Emperor Meiji**, *r.* 1868-1912, granted a Western-style constitution.
In France the war minister **Georges Boulanger**, 1837-91, attempted to seize power.
**The US overtook Britain** in steel production by 1890.
**The Social-Democratic Party**, the most popular in Germany, was legalized, 1890.

**Intellectual socialist parties** began to develop in the 1880s.
**The Irish nationalists** were split by Parnell's divorce scandal, 1890.

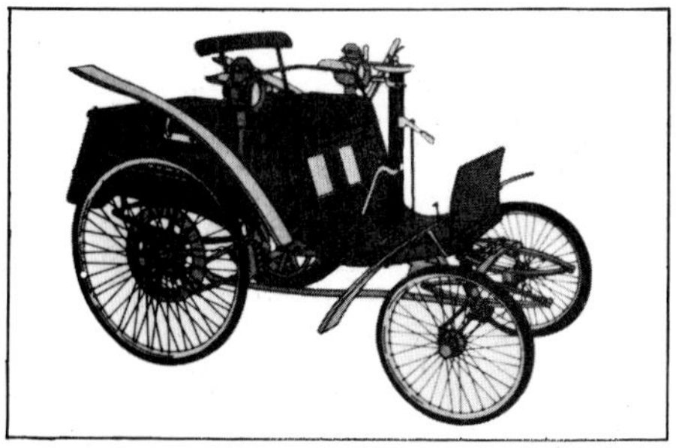

**Benz Velo motor car, 1896**

**James Frazer**, 1854-1941, a British anthropologist, surveyed a great range of beliefs and customs in *The Golden Bough*, 1890. He claimed that there was a natural progression from magical, through religious to scientific belief systems.

**Italian nationalist ideas** were voiced by **Giosuè Carducci**, 1835-1907. A scholar and anti-romantic, his *Odi Barbara* is a patriotic vision of Italy's glorious past and future destiny.
**Verismo**, Italian realism, was developed by **Giovanni Verga**, 1840-1922, whose novels combined a perceptive study of the Sicilian class structure with the personal cares of *Mastro Don Gesualdo*.

**Symbolist art** which developed after 1886 sought an escape from the present and appealed to the imagination and the senses. In France its chief exponents were **Gustave Moreau**, 1826-98, whose paintings have a rich, jewel-like quality, and **Odilon Redon**, 1840-1916, who used his fantastical imagination in the illustration of Baudelaire's *Fleurs du Mal*, 1890.
**The Eiffel Tower** was constructed in 1889, demonstrating contemporary engineering skills.

**Symphonic traditions** continued in Europe with vast works by **Anton Bruckner**, 1824-96, and **Gustav Mahler**, 1860-1911, who introduced folk elements.

**The pneumatic tyre** was invented in 1888 by the British vet **John Dunlop**, 1840-1921.
**Photographic film** and paper was developed, 1884-8, by **George Eastman**, 1854-1932, an American inventor. Eastman's work made the cinema, as well as still photography, a possibility.

## 1890-4

In Germany, **Kaiser Wilhelm II**, *r.* 1888-1918 dismissed Bismarck in 1890 and let the treaty with Russia lapse.
**The European alliance blocs** took shape. **The Triple Alliance** of Germany, Austria-Hungary and Italy was renewed in 1891. Russia and France made a **Dual Alliance**, 1891.
**Brazil** adopted a federal republican constitution, 1891.
**In the US**, the **Populist Party** grew out of agrarian protest at currency deflation.

**The Independent Labour Party** was founded, 1893.
**Gladstone's** Liberals returned to power but the Lords rejected their second **Home Rule Bill**.

**The Neoclassical school of economics** was established by the Englishman **Alfred Marshall**, 1842-1924, in his *Principles of Economics*, 1890. He united the "classical" view that prices are determined by costs with the "marginalist" view of **W. S. Jevons**, 1835-82, that prices depend on the interaction of supply and demand.
**K'ang Yü-wei**, 1858-1927, advocated social equality in China, and argued that Confucius had supported historical progress.

In his novels of English rural life such as *Tess of the D'Urbervilles*, 1891, **Thomas Hardy**, 1840-1928, expressed a pessimistic view of life in which man was swamped by cosmic ironies.
**The English Decadent movement** is epitomized by *The Picture of Dorian Gray*, 1891, by Oscar Wilde, 1854-1900, who was inspired by *A Rebours* by **J. K. Huysmans**.

**Art Nouveau**, an international decorative style using flat, flowing and tendril-like forms, was popularized in England by the graphics of **Aubrey Beardsley**, 1872-98, for the magazine *Studio*, from 1893, and the buildings of **Victor Horta**, 1861-1947, in Belgium.
**Gothic forms and wild extravagant decoration** characterized the buildings of the Spanish architect **Antoni Gaudi**, 1856-1926. His church of **Sagrada Familia** in Barcelona, from 1893, is related to Art Nouveau.

**National styles** developed in the works of composers like **Jean Sibelius**, 1865-1957, in Finland and **Isaac Albéniz**, 1860-1909, in Spain.

**Diphtheria antitoxin** was isolated in 1892 by the German biologist **Paul Ehrlich**, 1854-1915.

## 1894-6

**In the victorious war** against China, 1894-5, Japan gained Formosa and a free hand in Korea. The Powers' scramble for diplomatic and trading concessions in China began.
**Sergei Witte**, 1849-1915, reformed Russian finances and stimulated industrialization and eastward expansion, 1890s.
**The Dreyfus case**, 1894-9, revealed deep splits in French society between the liberal radicals and the Church and army.

**Joseph Chamberlain**, 1836-1914, began a policy of colonial expansion in southern Africa.
**The Land Act**, 1896, extended tenants' rights in Ireland.

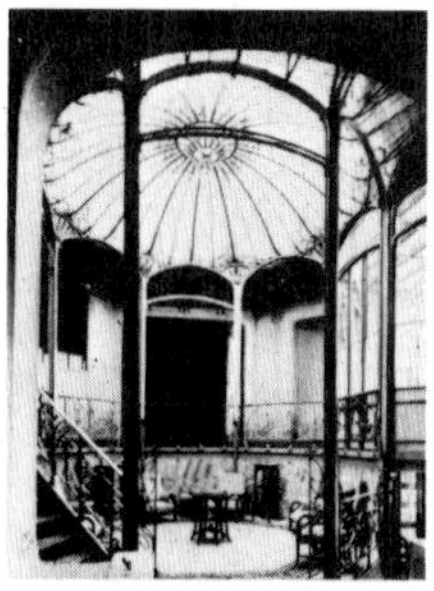

**Art nouveau: Horta interior**

**Herbert Spencer**, 1820-1903, constructed and popularized a **comprehensive evolutionary theory** which saw all things as progressing from simplicity to complexity. His sociology, based on an analogy between societies and organisms, used the idea of the survival of the fittest.
**F. H. Bradley**, 1846-1924, was an English proponent of Hegel. He argued that an idea's truth depended on its coherence with the set of ideas comprising the Absolute.

**Knut Hamsun**, 1859-1952, a Norwegian, condemned an over-emphasis on social issues.
**The stories and poems of Rudyard Kipling**, 1865-1936, examined the relationship between British and Indian culture.
**H. G. Wells** pioneered science fiction in *The Time Machine*.

**Synthetism**, a style characterized by the use of strong flat colours organized into well-defined areas, was developed by **Paul Gauguin**, 1848-1903, in his paintings executed in Tahiti. He influenced the **Nabis**, a group of French painters led by **Paul Serusier**, 1865-1927, who rejected the naturalism of the Impressionists.
**A large collection of Benin art**, the first African art well known in Europe, was brought back by a punitive expedition in 1897.

**Claude-Achille Debussy**, 1862-1918, brought Impressionism to music. His intricate tone colour and continuous form utilized exquisite harmony and a whole tone scale.

**The diesel engine was invented** by the German engineer **Rudolf Diesel**, 1858-1913, and demonstrated in 1896.
French inventors **Auguste Lumière**, 1862-1954, and his brother **Louis**, 1864-1948, developed good cine equipment. The first public showing of their films took place in 1895.
**X-rays** were discovered, 1895, by the German physicist **Wilhelm Röentgen**, 1845-1923.
**Radioactivity was discovered** in 1896, by the French physicist **Antoine Becquerel**, 1852-1908.

## 1896-8

**After the abortive Jameson raid**, 1895-6, Britain faced a crisis with the Boer republics.
**On the Nile**, Anglo-French tensions were relaxed after the conquest of the Sudan by **Lord Kitchener**, 1850-1916, and his meeting with the French at Fashoda, 1898.
**France** aimed to consolidate the Saharan empire with a sphere of influence in Morocco.
**Russia** threatened China, where the Powers gained territory and concessions, 1897-8.

**Victoria's Diamond Jubilee Year** 1897, marked the peak of British imperialist ambitions.
**Chamberlain** opposed home rule.

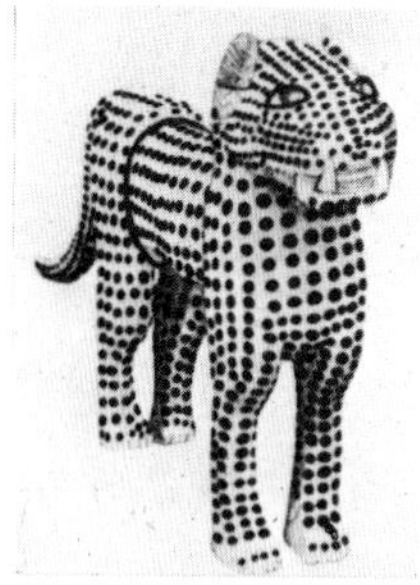

**Leopard from Benin**

**Philosophical pragmatism** was expounded by the American psychologist **William James**, 1842-1910, in *The Will to Believe*, 1897. He argued that a belief was true if its acceptance aided the solution of practical problems.
**Emile Durkheim**, 1858-1917, stirred French opinion with his sociological study *Suicide*, 1897, which attempted to link positivist social ideas with an interest in morality, which he saw as the basis of society.

The height of the **Modernismo** movement in South America was realized in *Prosas Profanas* by the Nicaraguan poet **Ruben Dario**, 1867-1916.
**The Generation of '98**, a group of Spanish intellectuals, set out to counteract Spanish apathy and revitalize Spanish culture. The group included the poet, philosopher and novelist **Miguel Unamuno**, 1864-1936.

**The Vienna Sezession**, set up to promote the Austrian form of Art Nouveau, 1897, was concerned mainly with interior design. **Gustav Klimt**, 1862-1918, was its leading exponent.
**The English Vernacular style** of domestic architecture pioneered by **C. A. Voysey**, 1857-1941, emphasized natural materials and solid construction and developed many of the designs which became part of a modern (non-historical) European style.

**The American John Sousa**, 1854-1932, wrote superb **marches** for marine bands, including *The Stars and Stripes Forever*, 1897.

**The theoretical basis for space travel** was provided in the work of **Konstantin Tsiolkovsky**, 1857-1935. In 1898 he proposed a liquid fuel rocket.
The Polish-French chemist **Marie Curie**, 1867-1934, working with her husband **Pierre**, discovered polonium and radium in 1898.
**The electron was discovered** in 1897 by the British physicist **J. J. Thomson**, 1856-1940.
**Malaria** was shown to be transmitted by the mosquito by the British physician **Ronald Ross**, 1857-1932, in 1897

## 1898-1900

**In China**, 1898, reactionary forces acted to stop the Westernizing **Hundred Days of Reform**, and an anti-foreign **"Boxer" rebellion**, 1900, brought disruption and resulted in foreign intervention and further impositions on Chinese sovereignty.
**Faced with depression** the US raised its tariff wall, 1897, and joined in expansion overseas, fighting Spain, 1898, over **Cuba** and securing **Puerto Rico** and the **Philippines**.

**Britain** was hard pressed in the **Boer War**, 1899-1902.
**The Labour Representation Committee** was founded in 1900.

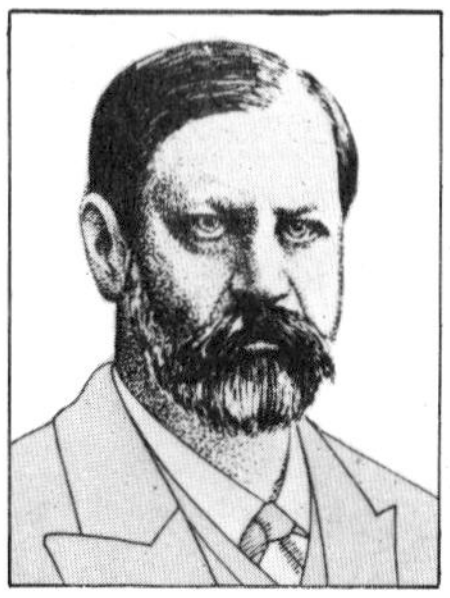

**Sigmund Freud**

**Sigmund Freud**, 1856-1939, elaborated the main tenets of psychoanalytic theory in *The Interpretation of Dreams*, 1900, developed in the course of clinical experience in Vienna. He divided the mind between the ego, id and superego, and argued that psychological disorders stemmed from the repression of sexual urges in early life. His emphasis on the subconscious influenced later irrationalism.
**H. S. Chamberlain**, 1855-1927, spread racialist ideas.

**Russian realist drama** reached its peak with the work of **Anton Chekhov**, 1860-1904, which had a huge effect on European drama, notably *Uncle Vanya* and *The Seagull*. Chekhov was also a masterly short story writer, able to convey pessimistic themes with a humorous twist.
**The Greek poet Cavafy**, 1863-1933, wrote about the ironies of man's existence.

**The sources of German Expressionism** can be seen in the works of the Norwegian painter **Edvard Munch**, 1863-1944, who concentrated on the expression of intense emotion in his "Frieze of Life" c. 1890-1900.
**The Chicago school of architecture** pioneered a modern American public style, creating the skyscraper. The Schlesinger-Mayer store by **Louis Sullivan**, 1856-1924, begun in 1899, rose to nine floors and had detailing suggestive of Art Nouveau.

**Ragtime** was played in the US in the 1890s by black pianists, notably by **Scott Joplin**, 1868-1917. The bright syncopation of the style overlaid European dance and march forms.

**Viruses were discovered**, 1898, by the Dutch scientist **Martinus Beijerinck**, 1851-1931, while investigating the cause of tobacco mosaic disease.
**Radioactivity** was found to include two different kinds of rays, alpha rays and beta rays, in 1899 by a British physicist, **Ernest Rutherford**, 1871-1937. In 1913 he used the rays to **penetrate the atom**.
**Aspirin** was first marketed as a small drug by **Bayer AG**, a German pharmaceutical firm, in 1899.

# 1900-1925 Europe plunges into war

## Principal events

**World War I, arising from political and economic competition among the European Powers, dominated the period. In it, Europe suffered great losses in manpower and economic strength, while the United States and Japan won new political prestige. The need for organization on an unprecedented scale brought social and political upheaval in many countries. The old empires disappeared, leaving many new nationally based states, an embittered and dismembered Germany and a communist Russia. Fear of socialism grew stronger and was linked with economic discontent to stimulate fascism in Italy.**

**The new location of power outside Europe and the rise of nationalism in India and China marked the transition from an international order based firmly on Europe to a world arena of politics, which would lead to widespread decolonization after World War II.**

### 1900-3

**The US Steel Corporation** integrated the industry, 1901.
**As France and Italy** made an entente in 1902, weakening Italy's links with Germany, **Britain** emerged successfully from the **Boer War** and formed an alliance with **Japan**. This countered the Russian presence in **Manchuria** and encouraged Japan's expansionist ambitions on the Asia mainland.
**The United States** extended its influence over **Panama**, 1903, winning canal-building rights.

### 1903-5

**The Entente Cordiale**, 1904, of France and Britain settled the two powers' outstanding colonial disputes, especially in Egypt.
**Japan** firmly established her military power, defeating Russia in 1905 in Manchuria.
**In defeat Russia was convulsed**, 1905-6, with a revolution against tsarist autocracy by the industrial and intellectual classes.
**Intervention by Wilhelm II**, *r.* 1888-1918, in Morocco, 1905, alarmed France which claimed supremacy there.

### 1905-8

**The Powers** met at Algeçiras in 1906 to settle the Moroccan question in favour of France.
**Tsarist rule** in Russia was re-imposed with only minor constitutional reforms.
**Russia and Japan reached agreement** over China in 1907.
**Britain, France and Spain** agreed to oppose German naval expansion in the Mediterranean.
**An Anglo-Russian Convention** covered Persia, Afghanistan and Tibet and brought Britain into Europe's power blocs.

### 1908-10

**Increasing Anglo-German competition** was expressed in a race to build warships.
**With Russian agreement**, Austria annexed Bosnia-Hercegovina in 1908.
**Nationalist unrest in Catalonia** disrupted Spain, 1909.
**The Powers** intervened to prevent a Serbo-Austrian war.
**India** secured constitutional reforms in 1909.
**The former Boer republics** helped form a new dominion, the **Union of South Africa**, 1910.

## National events

**The progressive forces of the new Liberalism, which stressed social reform, checked the Labour Party advance. But the Irish Question, constitutional crises and wartime pressure split the party. The power of the Lords was much reduced and Labour inherited the second party role, 1923.**

**The Education Act**, 1902, put the responsibility for education in the hands of local authorities.

**Joseph Chamberlain**, 1836-1914, campaigned for protective tariffs favouring imperial exports. The Tories split on **Free Trade.**

**Henry Campbell-Bannerman**, 1836-1908, led the Liberals in their 1905 election landslide, introducing social reforms, army and navy reorganization.

**A constitutional crisis** ensued after the Lord's rejected the **"Peoples' Budget"**, 1909, which provided for social expenditure financed from income tax.

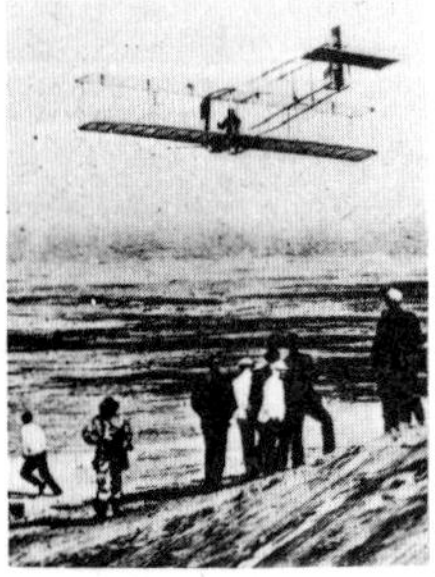

Wright Brother's flight

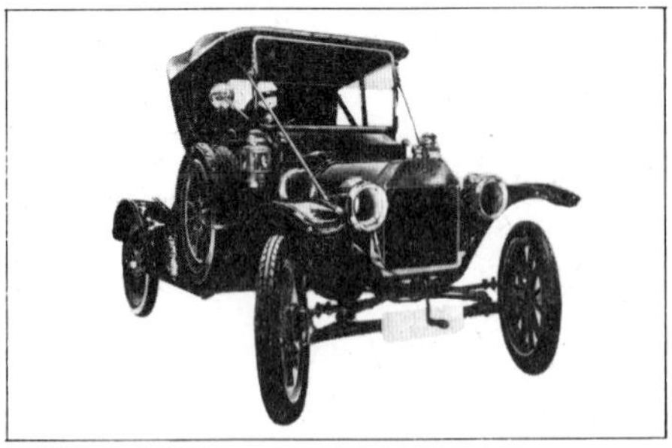

Model T Ford

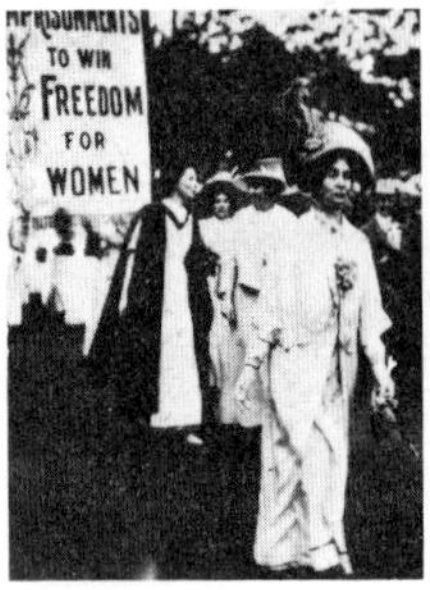


Suffragettes, 1911

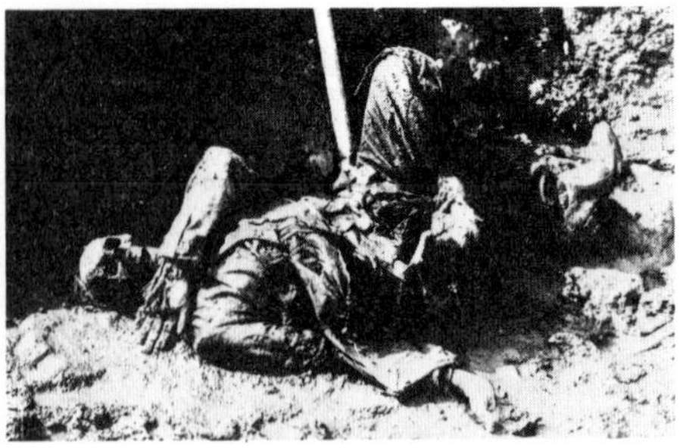

World War I: German skeleton in the trenches

## Religion and philosophy

**The philosophies of Bergson, Croce, Dilthey and Husserl, stressing intuition and immediate sympathy as the basic method of understanding, contributed to the development of a concept of the human sciences distinct from the natural sciences.**

**Under their influence Max Weber investigated the motives as well as the causes of human action, notably the effect of religion on man's supposedly "rational" economic behaviour. Russell and Wittgenstein, however, still took science and mathematics as the paradigm of knowledge in their work on the logical structure of language.**

**Psychoanalytic theory continued to explore the nature of the unconscious but two of Freud's colleagues, Adler and Jung, criticized his insistence on the sexual basis of neuroses.**

**The Russian Revolution accentuated the socialist split between violence and the peaceful battle for working-class rights.**

**The Pentecostal Movement** began in America *c.* 1902.
**Vilfredo Pareto**, 1848-1923, an Italian and a positivist wrote *The Socialist Systems*, 1902, a refutation of Marxist economics and sociology. He accepted the existence of class conflict but saw the process Marx described as a series of progressive revolutions as no more than the successive replacement of ruling elites by each other.

**Max Weber**, 1864-1920, a German historian and sociologist, was concerned to combat the influential Marxist school of historical materialism. He opposed a simplistic belief in economic determinism and stressed the causal role of ideas in history.
**In France, Maurice Barrès**, 1862-1923, and **Charles Maurras**, 1868-1952, argued influentially for cultural unity, the supremacy of the state and the primacy of the national interest.

**Henri Bergson**, 1859-1941, in *Creative Evolution*, 1907, stressed the importance of change through a creative life-force, in opposition to the static scientific view of nature. His view that intuition was superior to scientific or intellectual perception was echoed by **William Dilthey**, 1833-1911, in Germany, to support an ethical relativism.
**The Modernist Movement** in Catholicism was condemned by Pope Pius X in 1907.

**Georges Sorel**, 1847-1922, in *Reflections on Violence*, 1908, celebrated the use of violence and rejected all bourgeois values. He influenced Mussolini. The German historian **Friedrich Meinecke** (1862-1954) looked for a meaning within the historical process itself, but sought to avoid cultural relativism. His *Cosmopolitanism and the Nation State*, 1908, acknowledged the significance of the unification of Germany but regretted the death of the culture that preceded it.

## Literature

**The need for new forms of self-expression able to encompass a growing awareness of the unconscious gave rise to many strong and individualistic movements in European literature.**
**The surrealists evolved out of the symbolists, and their attempt to "trap" the subconscious in a spontaneous literary form broke down all restrictions of style.**

**In the English-speaking world a more formal school grew up with the modernist poets Pound and Eliot.**

**The German Expressionists were among the first to voice a lack of faith in society. Their prophecies were realized with World War I, the image of which haunted later writers.**

**Japan came into contact with Western realist and naturalist schools.**

**The Celtic literary Renaissance** was a cultural reflection of Irish independence. Ancient legends were revived by **W. B. Yeats** 1865-1939, **J. M. Synge**, 1871-1909, and **Sean O'Casey**, 1880-1964.
**James Joyce** was self-consciously Irish but hostile to the Celtic Renaissance.

**Impressionism**, a German literary style which set out to describe complex emotional states by using symbolic imagery, is used in *Stundenbuch*, 1905, by **Rainer Maria Rilke**, 1875-1926.
**Revolution** and man's capacity to withstand extremities dominate such novels of **Joseph Conrad**, 1857-1924, as *Nostromo*, 1904.

With the publication of *Kormichiye*, 1907, **Ivan Ivanovich**, 1866-1949, was acclaimed leader of the Russian Symbolist movement, which also included the poet **Alexander Blok**, 1880-1921.
**Stefan George**, 1868-1933, was influenced by Nietzsche in his desire to ennoble German culture with his esoteric poetry, such as *The Seventh Ring*, 1907.

**Modern Japanese fiction** began after 1905 with a powerful naturalist school including **Shimazaki Toson**, 1872-1943, and **Tayama Katai**. **Mori Ogai**, 1862-1922, reacted against their obsession with squalor in *Vita Sexualis*, 1909.
The American **Jack London**, 1876-1916, was stirred by social injustices to write popular tales and political tracts.

## Art and architecture

**Traditional forms and concepts of art were dramatically broken down between 1900 and 1925 as a variety of alternative aesthetic principles developed. In particular Cubism attempted to break away from the conventions of perspective that had ruled European art since the Renaissance, while Dadaism and Russian Constructivism aimed to destroy the distinction between art and life.**

**In architecture, too, definitive new styles emerged in the US and Europe with the publication of Frank Lloyd Wright's early designs and the establishment of the Bauhaus, both emphasizing assymetry and plain surfaces.**

**The cinema transformed the whole scope of the visual arts, developing from the early popular experiments of 1900 to the politically motivated films of Eisenstein in Russia (where the Revolution stimulated artistic innovation in many fields), the dramas of Griffith and the popular comedies of Chaplin.**

**A reaction in architecture** against the highly decorated surfaces of Art Nouveau produced the simple rectangular forms seen in the **Convalescent Home**, Vienna, 1903, by **Josef Hoffman**, 1870-1956. In France this trend is found in the garage, rue Ponthieu, Paris, 1905, by **Auguste Perret**, 1874-1954.
**The Intimiste painters Edouard Vuillard**, 1868-1940, and **Pierre Bonnard**, 1867-1947, used Impressionist techniques in domestic scenes after 1900.

**Cubism**, rejecting traditional methods of portraying reality began in 1907 with **Picasso's** "Demoiselles d'Avignon", 1907. Other Cubists include **Juan Gris**, 1887-1927, **Robert Delaunay**, 1885-1941, **Fernand Léger**, 1881-1955, and **Georges Braque**, 1882-1963.
In Paris **Pablo Picasso**, 1881-1973, began his Blue period, 1901-4, and his Rose period, 1905, producing lyrical, conventionally representational paintings.

**The Fauvist period** in painting, 1905-8, was characterized by the use of flat patterns and intense, unnatural colours. "Open Window, Collioure", 1905, by **Henri Matisse**, 1869-1954, is typical, as are the works from this period of **André Derain**, 1880-1954, **Maurice Vlaminck**, 1876-1958 and **Raoul Dufy**, 1877-1953.

In Germany the Expressionist painting of the **Die Brücke group** 1905-13, distorted reality to produce a personal view of the world, depicting intense and painful emotions after the style of **Edvard Munch**. They were chiefly represented by **Emil Nolde**, 1867-1956.
**The Italian Futurists** produced work and manifestos that extolled the technological energy of modern life, from 1909.

## Music

**The Romantic tradition lingered on into the early twentieth century. Popular music began to make its mark, and many serious composers sought a radical break with the past while others turned to folk music for their inspiration. The radicalism in the arts that followed World War I produced a variety of new musical techniques as well as altering aesthetic principles.**

**Richard Strauss**, 1864-1949, continued the romantic tradition with operas and tone poems in a grand Wagnerian style.

**Giacomo Puccini**, 1858-1924, brought Italian grand opera to a grand finale with such dramatic and melodic operas as *La Bohème*, 1896, *Tosca*, 1900, and *Madame Butterfly*, 1904.

**Blues** grew steadily more popular in the early 20th century in the United States. Their cross-rhythms and varying intonation brought great expression to the simple *aab* 12-bar form.

**New Orleans** became the cradle of **jazz** as ragtime bands, using instruments left over from the Civil War, took up improvisation and developed into small traditional jazz bands.

## Science and technology

**Einstein's theories of relativity and Planck's Quantum theory revealed a new picture of the ultimate workings of nature. Although Newton's theories still proved accurate enough for most predictions, Einstein held that there was no absolute motion, motion in respect of empty space. His relativity principle stated that motion must always appear as the relative motion of one object with respect to another. It related time, mass and length to velocity and mass to energy, and provided a theoretical basis for the development of nuclear physics.**

**Although World War I stimulated research and technology in Europe, the impetus for scientific advance shifted to America. The invention of the electronic valve which allowed the development of the radio transmitter to proceed, and the development of powered flight speeded up intercontinental communications and the introduction of mass-produced cars revolutionized private transport.**

**Blood groups** were first distinguished in *c.* 1900.
**Gamma rays** were discovered in radioactivity, 1900, by **Paul Villard**, 1860-1934.
**The quantum theory** that energy consists of indivisible units, was proposed by **Max Planck**, 1858-1947, in 1900.
**Guglielmo Marconi**, 1874-1937, was the first to transmit radio signals across the Atlantic, in 1901.
**The fingerprint** system was introduced in Britain, 1901.

**The first sustained flight** by a power-driven aeroplane was made by **Wilbur** and **Orville Wright** in the USA, 1903.
**Detroit** became the centre of the motor car industry, 1903.
**The first electronic valve** was made in 1904.
**The special theory of relativity** was published in 1905 by **Albert Einstein**, 1879-1955.

**Mass production** of cars began in the US with the Model T Ford in 1908.
**The third law of thermodynamics**, that absolute zero cannot be attained, was put forward in 1906.
**Emil Fischer** 1852-1919, showed in 1907 that proteins are composed of amino acids – a vital step in molecular biology.
**The first helicopter** flew, 1907.
**The cloud chamber**, used in detecting the paths of atomic particles, was perfected 1906 by **Charles Wilson**, 1869-1959.

**Ammonia** was synthesized in 1908, enabling Germany to produce the first high explosives.
**Chromosomes** were established as the carriers of heredity, 1909.
**Bakelite**, a synthetic polymer used for making electric plugs was invented in 1909. Its success stimulated the development of plastics.
**Combine harvesters** were common in the US by 1910.
**Louis Blériot** made his first flight in 1907 and crossed the English Channel, 1909.

## 1910-13
**In Mexico, Porfirio Diaz**, *r.* 1877-1911, was overthrown and the US intervened by occupying Vera Cruz.
**The Triple Entente powers** of France, Russia and Britain made military and naval agreements. After the 1911 Agadir incident when the Germans sent a gunboat to frighten the French, they countered German ambitions in Morocco.
**A nationalist republic** was set up in China in 1911 under **Sun Yat-sen**, 1866-1925.

## 1913-15
**Austria's Archduke** Franz Ferdinand, 1863-1914, was assassinated in June 1914 by Serbian nationalists, setting off events leading to world war.
**By 1915** Germany and Austria, with Turkey and Bulgaria, were fighting against the Entente allies, with Italy and Japan.
**Military operations** extended from the main "front" in France and Belgium to the Russian plains, the Balkans, the Middle East and the German colonies in Africa.

## 1915-18
**Germany** started a blockade of British shipping. The main naval battle at Jutland, 1916, was inconclusive. Germany's unrestricted submarine warfare (leading to the sinking of the ***Lusitania*** in 1915) provoked the US to enter the war, 1917.
**The strain of war** brought revolution to Russia in 1917. The tsar abdicated and **Bolshevik** forces led by **Lenin**, 1870-1924, won power and withdrew Russia from the war, after defeating the liberal government.

## 1918-20
**Britain, France and the US defeated Germany** in 1918. In the **Versailles Treaty**, 1919, inspired by the democratic ideals of **Woodrow Wilson**, 1856-1924, the US president, new ethnic Balkan states were established and Turkey was partitioned. **War guilt** and indemnity were assigned to Germany, where an abortive revolution disrupted the new republic, 1919.
**Wilson's League of Nations** was inaugurated in 1920 but without US participation.

## 1920-22
**In Russia**, reactionary forces with allied aid tried unsuccessfully to defeat the Bolsheviks.
**Germany**, struggling against economic chaos after the loss of the major industrial centres, secured Soviet friendship in the **Treaty of Rapallo**, 1922.
**Japan**, which had been granted Germany's rights in China by the Versailles Treaty, made peace with China, 1922.
**Benito Mussolini**, 1883-1945, established fascist power in Italy in 1922.

## 1922-5
**Germany** countered France's occupation of the Ruhr, 1923-5, with passive resistance and suffered massive inflation, which destroyed the economic strength of the middle classes.
**The Dawes plan**, 1924, eased the repayment schedule for German war reparations.
**Mustafa Kemal**, 1881-1938, president of the new Turkish republic, began modernization of Turkish society, 1923.
**The American economy** boomed until 1929.

---

**Herbert Asquith**, 1852-1928, secured passage of the **Parliament Act**, 1911, which limited the power of the Lords. **National insurance** was introduced.

**Industrial disorder**, suffragettes and Ulster opposition to **Irish Home Rule** inflamed society. The world crisis postponed civil war in Ireland.

**The 1916 Easter Rebellion** boosted the republican Sinn Fein in Ireland. **David Lloyd George**, 1863-1945, maximized the war effort.

**Women over 30** gained the vote in 1918 in recognition of the suffragette campaign, 1903-14, and the importance of the role played by women in the war effort.

**The 1920 Home Rule Act** partitioned Ireland. Republicans rejected the 1921 Free State settlement but met defeat in a civil war, 1919-21.

**Labour** became the official opposition in 1923 and in 1924 first exercised minority rule under **Ramsay MacDonald**, 1866-1937.

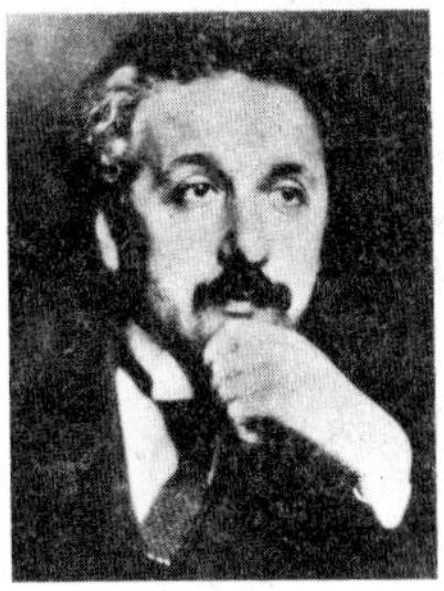

Albert Einstein

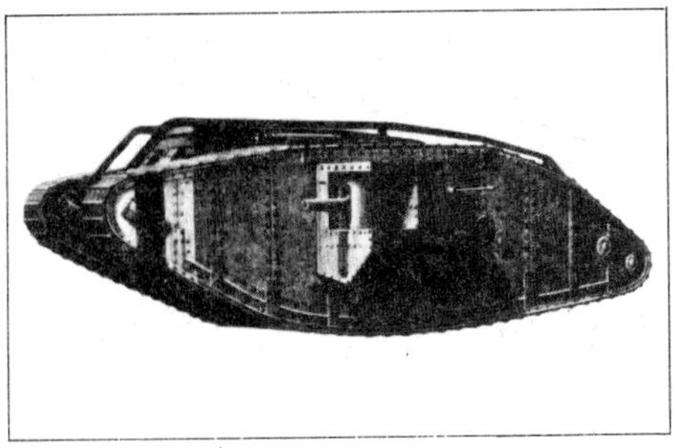

World War I tank

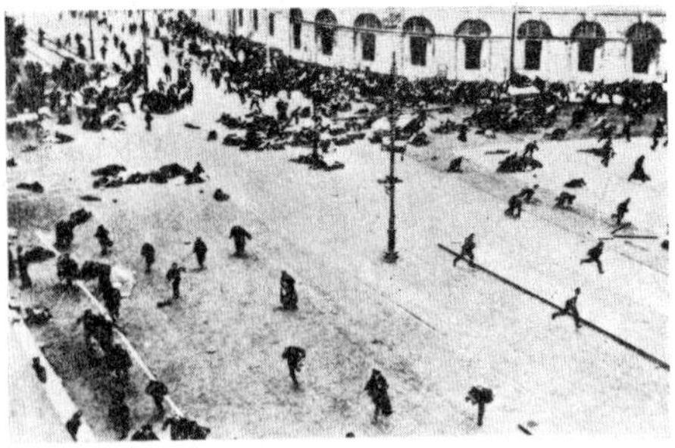

Russian Revolution: street scene in Petrograd, 1917

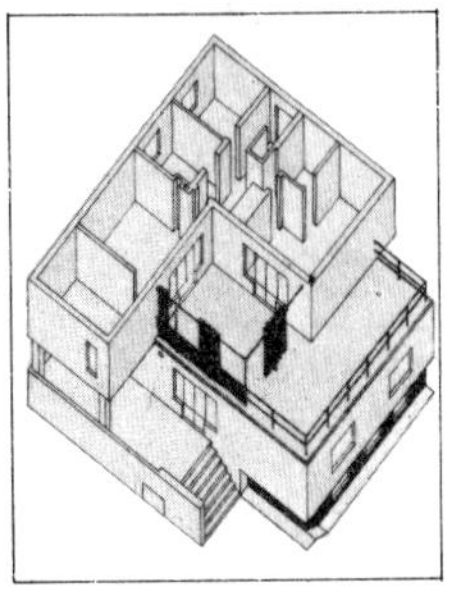

Bauhaus: house by Gropius

---

**Sophisticated physics** produced scientific theorists such as the Austrian **Ernst Mach**, 1838-1916, and the Frenchman **Henri Poincaré**, 1854-1912, who argued that unobservable entities like atoms should be regarded only as useful postulates about material nature.
**Phenomenology** was founded by the German philosopher **Edmund Husserl**, 1859-1938, who argued that true knowledge stemmed from the imaginative analysis of direct experience.

**Bertrand Russell**, 1872-1970, the English philosopher and mathematician, applied empiricist principles to language, which he claimed to be constructed solely from sensory ideas and logic. In *Principia Mathematica*, 1910-13, he attempted, with **A. N Whitehead**, 1861-1947, to derive mathematics from the axioms of logic.
**Opposition to the war** led **Rosa Luxemburg**, 1871-1919 to found the left-wing Spartacist party in Germany.

**V. I. Lenin**, 1870-1924, the Russian politician, argued in *The State and Revolution*, 1917, for a party of professional revolutionaries.
**Freud's** emphasis on the sexual basis of psychiatric disorders led to the defection of two of his followers, **Carl Jung**, 1875-1961, and **Alfred Adler**, 1870-1937. Jung developed a theory of the collective unconscious, while Adler tried to derive a psychology from man's tendency to strive for perfection.

**The British anthropologists Malinowski** 1884-1942 developed **functionalism** 1914-18 in anthropology, studying social phenomena in terms of their function within an integrated social structure, in opposition to evolutionist anthropology.
**Oswald Spengler**, 1880-1936, published *The Decline of the West*, 1918, claiming that Western civilization had ceased to be "creative" and had become concerned only with materialism.

The *Tractatus Logico-Philosophicus* of **Ludwig Wittgenstein**, 1889-1951, an Austrian living in London, was published in 1921; it argued that philosophy was an analytic, not a speculative, subject.
**Aimee Semple McPherson**, 1890-1944, built the Angelus Temple in Los Angeles in 1922 and preached the religion of the foursquare gospel.

The Hungarian **Gyorgy Lukacs**, 1885-1971, a Marxist influenced by Hegel's idealism, wrote of the role of creative awareness in the development or revolutionary consciousness, in *History and Class-consciousness*, 1923.
**Benedetto Croce**, 1866-1952, a historian who argued that the past could be understood only when seen in relation to current problems, became the spokesman for the opposition to Fascism in Italy after 1923.

---

**The German Expressionists** described visions of the collapse of society. **George Heym**, 1887-1912, prophesied a great war in *Umbra Vitae*, 1912, as did **George Trakl**, 1887-1914, in his poem *Sebastian im Traum*, 1914.
**Guillaume Apollinaire**, 1880-1918, dominated the surrealist and avant garde movements in Paris from 1913 until his death.

**Franz Kafka**, 1883-1924, described man's spiritual bereavement in symbolic terms in *The Trial*, 1914-15.
**Ezra Pound**, 1885-1972, worked on his *Cantos* from 1914 until his death. His allusive erudite style influenced many English poets.

**The "literary revolution"** in China in 1917, used the vernacular language in literature.
**The English war poets** voiced their horror of mass warfare. **Rupert Brooke**, 1887-1915, and **Wilfred Owen**, 1893-1918, died while on duty. **Robert Graves**, 1895-   , and **Siegfried Sassoon**, 1886-1967, also wrote about the period, both in prose and verse.

The Hindu writer **Rabindranath Tagore**, 1861-1941, translated the mystical *Gitanjali*.
**Mohammed Iqbal**, 1873-1938, wrote in Urdu and Persian and voiced a growing resentment against the West, in India.
**André Gide**, 1869-1951, kept his *Journals* from 1889-1949.
**Hermann Hesse**, 1877-1962, wrote *Demian*, 1919.

**T. S. Eliot**, 1888-1965, whose *The Waste Land*, 1922, is a dense and highly literary meditation on the situation of modern man.
**Luigi Pirandello**, 1867-1936, reflected the spiritual confusion of the post-war years in his play *Six Characters in Search of an Author*, 1921.

**The Stream-of-consciousness technique** was used by **Marcel Proust**, 1871-1922, to evoke the past in the long series of novels *A La Recherche du Temps Perdu*, 1913-27, and by **James Joyce**, 1882-1941, in *Ulysses*, 1922. This and *Finnegans Wake*, 1939, are highly experimental, original and questioning works.

---

**Analytical Cubism**, 1910-12, concentrated on pure form, excluding interest in colour. **Synthetic Cubism**, 1912-14, involved the construction of an image often by means of collage, such as the "Bottle of Anis del Mono", 1914, by **Juan Gris**.
**Dar Blaue Reiter** group of Expressionist painters, 1911-14, used colour and abstract forms to convey spiritual realities and included **Wassily Kandinsky**, 1866-1944, and **Paul Klee**, 1879-1940.

**Russian Constructivism**, 1913-mid-20s, was initiated by **Vladimir Tatlin**, 1885-1953, and exploited the concept of Synthetic Cubism. Its emphasis was on abstract structures made of a variety of materials. Tatlin's "Constructions", 1913-14, were made of wood, metal and glass.
**The first long feature films** included the Italian *Cabiria*, 1914, and *The Birth of a Nation*, 1915, directed by **D. W. Griffith**, 1875-1948, a drama about the American Civil War.

**The Dadaist movement** developed in Zurich in 1916 in the work of **Jean (Hans) Arp**, 1887-1966, and **Tristan Tzara**, 1896-1963. It was deliberately "anti-art" and aimed to outrage and scandalize a complacent society. Its chief exponent was **Marcel Duchamp**, 1887-1968, whose "Fountain", 1917, consisted of a urinal.
The films of **Charlie Chaplin**, 1889-1977, including *The Tramp*, 1915, won international acclaim.

**The de Stijl group** founded in Holland by **Theo van Doesburg**, 1883-1931, and **Piet Mondrian**, 1872-1944, developed their art and architecture based on spatial relationships. They used straight lines, right-angles and primary colours.
**The Bauhaus school** of architecture, design and craftsmanship was founded in Germany in 1919 by **Walter Gropius**, 1883–1969. It attempted to reconcile art and design with industrial techniques.

In France **Fernard Léger's** paintings reflected contemporary interest in machinery. His "Three Women", 1921, reduces figures to machine like forms and uses metallic colours.
**Frank Lloyd Wright**, 1869-1959, the greatest and most influential of American architects, designed the Imperial Hotel, Tokyo, 1919-22, using an entirely new anti-earthquake construction.

Architects in Europe such as **Walter Gropius, Mies van der Rohe**, 1886-1969, and **Le Corbusier**, 1887-1965, convinced of the need for streamlined, functional buildings, used the new media of concrete and glass to achieve a modern style epitomized in Gropius' design for the **Bauhaus**, 1925-6.
**The Russian Revolution** stimulated experimental cinema, led by **Sergei Eisenstein**, 1898-1948, whose *Battleship Potemkin*, 1925, preached socialism.

---

**The Ballets Russes** of **Sergei Diaghilev**, 1872-1929, commissioned major works, such as **Igor Stravinsky's** *Petrushka*, 1911, and **Maurice Ravel's** *Daphnis and Chloe*, 1912.

*The Rite of Spring*, 1913, by **Stravinsky**, 1882-1971, gave new emphasis to the role of rhythm in serious music, using irregular metre and highly varied motifs.

**Charles Ives**, 1874-1954, became the first truly original American composer, working in several keys and rhythms at once in many works, such as his *Concord Sonata*, 1909-15.

**Harmony reached a peak of complexity** with **Stravinsky**, who worked in several keys simultaneously, and then split asunder in the key-less music of **Arnold Schoenberg** and **Béla Bartók**.

**Bartók**, 1881-1945, created a style marked by extreme dissonance and elegant melody, particularly in his six quartets, 1907-39. He collected and studied Hungarian folk music.

**Twelve-note or serial music**, created in 1924 by **Schoenberg**, 1874-1951, was based on an arbitrarily ordered series or row using the 12 notes of the chromatic (half tone) scale.

---

**Electrical superconductivity** was discovered in 1911.
**Nuclear theory**, that the atom contains a central nucleus, was announced by **Lord Rutherford**, 1871-1937, in 1911, in England.
**Vitamins** were recognized as essential to health in 1906; their classification in 1911 stimulated dietary studies.
**Continental drift**, the theory that the continents shift, was first proposed in 1912.
**Cellophane** was first manufactured in 1912.

**The proton** was recognized as the nucleus of the hydrogen atom by Lord Rutherford, in 1913.
**Niels Bohr**, 1885-1962, showed, 1913, how changes in the electron orbits of the atom produce energy.
**The Geiger counter** was used to measure radioactivity, 1913.
**Atomic numbers** were determined by an X-ray method discovered in 1914.
**The life cycle of stars** was determined by work done in 1914.
**Stainless steel** was made in Germany from 1914.

**The general theory of relativity** was published by Einstein in 1915.
**Tractors**, introduced by Ford in 1915, used the diesel engine.
**World War I stimulated technological advance** on both sides, particularly in weaponry and transport. **The diesel engine** was used in tanks and the aircraft industry expanded.
German development of **synthetic rubber and of cellulose** as a substitute for cotton led the search for new artificial fabrics.
**Gas** was used as a weapon.

**The first transatlantic flight** was made, 1919, by the British aviators **Alcock and Brown**. The flight lasted almost 16½ hours.
**The first mass spectrograph** was developed in 1919.
**The first commercial aeroplane** service, between London and Paris, was set up 1919.

**Diesel locomotives and railcars** came into use *c.* 1920. The growing use of internal combustion engines led to a decline in the supremacy of coal as the major industrial fuel after 1910.
**Radio broadcasting** on a regular basis began in the United States in 1920.
**Insulin**, a hormone, was isolated in 1922 and first used in the treatment of diabetes.
**The teleprinter** was developed in 1921, greatly speeding the transmission of long-distance information.

**Radioactive tracers**, used for the determination of many biological reactions, were developed in 1923.
**Electrons** were shown to behave as waves as well as particles, in 1922-4. This discovery made possible the invention of the electron microscope, in 1932.
**External spiral galaxies** were found by Edwin Hubble, 1923.
**Clarence Birdseye** 1886-1956, experimented with quick-frozen foods commercially, 1924.

# 1925-50 From depression to recovery

## Principal events

**The legacy of mistrust and depression following World War I brought a worldwide economic crisis at the end of the 1920s. The stronger industrial powers survived with the aid of new economic and social policies but in Germany, where the obligation to pay war debts exacerbated the effects of national defeat, the Nazi regime took power whose militarist ambitions in Europe would help to precipitate World War II.**

**In the USSR a policy of forced industrialization was pursued under Stalin, destroying many of the ideals of the Revolution, while the basis for a communist China was laid after a long civil war. India won her independence, but only at the cost of partition.**

**World War II left Europe shattered and weak and Germany divided, with the capitalist and socialist blocs locked in a continuing, though ostensibly peaceful, struggle for power.**

### 1925-8

**Chiang Kai-shek**, 1887-1975, ousted the left-wing from the Kuomintang (nationalist party) in China. He captured Peking and unified the country, 1928, against Japanese expansion.
**Germany** joined the League of Nations, 1926, which hoped to bring peace by disarmament.
**Fascist rule in Italy** became increasingly authoritarian.
**Joseph Stalin**, 1879-1953, began forcible industrialization in Russia, 1928, after Lenin's death, 1924.

### 1928-30

**The Kellogg-Briand Pact** was signed by 23 powers in 1928 to outlaw war.
**The last allied forces** left the Rhineland, 1929.
**Leon Trotsky**, 1879-1940, was exiled from Russia, 1929.
**The Wall Street Crash**, 1929, led to business depression in America, causing economic recession throughout Europe and a rise in left-wing activity.
**Gandhi**, 1869-1948, began a civil disobedience campaign against British rule in India.

### 1930-33

**The Round Table Conferences on India** failed to satisfy nationalist demands, 1930-1.
**The Hoover moratorium** on war debts helped Europe to survive the depression, 1931, but the economic slump in Germany brought fighting between left- and right-wing groups.
**Japan occupied Manchuria**, 1931, after fears that trading contacts with China would be cut.
**A republic was set up in Spain**, 1931, dominated by liberals and socialists.

### 1933-5

**Japan** left the League of Nations, 1933, after condemnation of her action in Manchuria.
**Adolf Hitler**, 1889-1945, elected German chancellor, set up a Nazi dictatorship, 1933.
**Franklin D. Roosevelt**, 1882-1945, introduced a New Deal of social and economic reforms in the US to end the slump, 1933.
**Stalin** began a massive purge of Russian party officials, 1935.
**Civil war in China** between the left-wing and nationalists led to **the Long March**, 1934-5.

## National events

**Amidst economic depression, a national government was set up in 1931. It faced continuing social distress, imperial decay and major European commitments. After the upheaval of war, Labour's promise in 1945 of social transformation as outlined in the Beveridge report was realized.**

**The 1926 general strike** came in reaction to massive unemployment. Action by government and mainly middle-class volunteers left a legacy of bitterness.

**A second minority Labour government**, 1929-31, failed to cure the rising unemployment and economic depression owing to the financial crisis.

**Ramsay MacDonald** split the Labour Party in 1931 over economic measures. He joined the Conservatives in a **national government**, 1931-35.

Legislation in 1934 introduced an unpopular **means test** for those on national assistance. There were over two million unemployed.

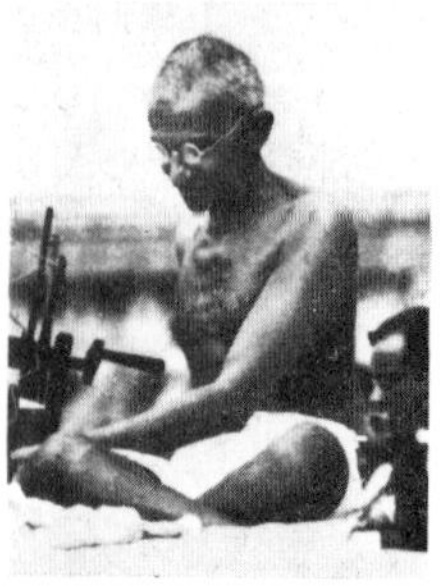

Gandhi in Calcutta, 1925

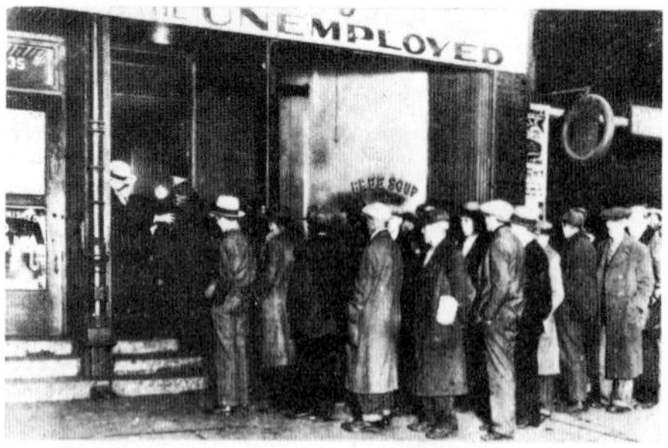


The Depression: soup kitchen in Chicago, 1930

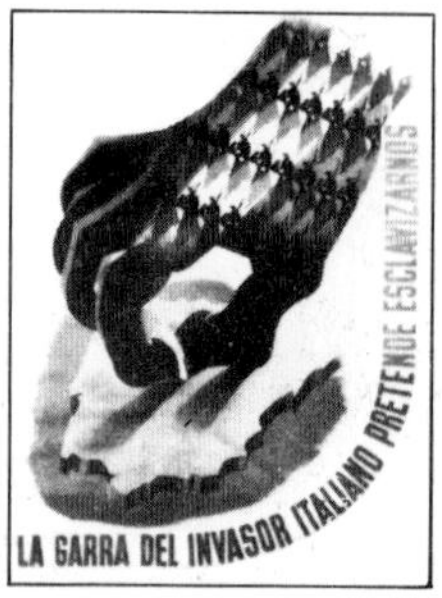


Spanish Civil War poster

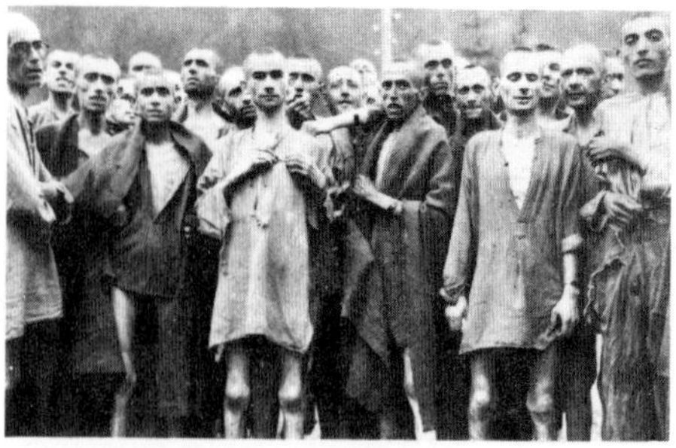

Victims of Hitler's concentration camps

## Religion and philosophy

**Political thought was dominated by conflict between the democratic ideal and its opponents on the left and right. Marxist political theory developed divergent trends as the Russian and Chinese revolutions took their course, but its influence in the West declined as supporters of liberalism rallied to oppose fascism, with its ideological roots in 19th century irrationalism. A new democratic philosophy, sustained by Keynes' economic theories of consumer prosperity, became linked with attempts to control political violence on a worldwide scale, marked by the founding of the United Nations.**

**The Christian Church came face to face with growing secularization in the industrialized countries and the need to find a new approach to the problems of an emergent Third World.**

**Philosophy remained split between those primarily studying human consciousness, and those who used a scientific model to understand reality.**

**The American J. B. Watson** 1878-1958, developed behaviourist psychology in *Behaviourism*, 1925, seeking to explain behaviour wholly in terms of responses to external stimuli.
In *Mein Kampf*, 1925-7, **Hitler** drew upon the ideas of **Gobineau**, 1816-82, who argued that the development of a civilization depends on racial superiority and purity, and requires military aggression. Hitler condemned democracy as based on invalid egalitarianism.

**Existentialism** was developed in Germany from Husserl's phenomenological ideas, by **Martin Heidegger**, 1889-1976, who was appointed professor of philosophy at Freiburg in 1928. He argued that authentic human existence consists in not being subordinated to the external world.
**The word apartheid** was first used to describe racial segregation in South Africa in 1929.

**J. M. Keynes**, 1883-1946, overthrew the neoclassical orthodoxy in economics with two books, *Treatise on Money*, 1930, and *The General Theory*, 1936. He stated that market forces which lowered wage rates would not cure economic depressions; production and investment would only increase if spending by consumers, business and government went up. His theory influenced the New Deal and economic planning in the West, until the 1970s.

**Leon Trotsky**, 1879-1940, a Russian Marxist, argued for permanent revolution in his *History of the Russian Revolution*, 1932-3. He claimed that socialism in Russia could not survive unless revolutions also took place in more advanced countries, and opposed Stalin's doctrine of socialism in one country.
**Gandhi** organized *satyagraha* (truth force) campaigns to foster Indian nationalism by non-violence and emphasized the values of village life.

## Literature

**The insistent excavation of personal experience which had begun with the Romantics and reached a peak with the stream-of-consciousness writings of Proust and Joyce found a new exponent in Virginia Woolf and the more consciously Freudian Surrealists. Much European writing of the interwar period, however, reflected a need to grasp social issues of the time. Some, such as Camus, accepted the fact of social commitment while admitting the ultimate meaninglessness of existence. Others like Brecht developed new artistic forms to embody their political vision with a lesser emphasis on the individual. In the Third World, too, where writers were inspired by the ideal of national independence, a new, more confident literature emerged.**

**A major writer** who met the requirements of socialist realism was **Mikhail Sholokhov**, 1905- in his *Tales from the Don*, 1925.
**The Bloomsbury Group** in London included the novelist **E. M. Forster**, 1879-1970, and **Virginia Woolf**, 1882-1941, who used a personal style of imagery in *To the Lighthouse*, 1927. Highly personal experience was used in the **English Realist novel**.

**D. H. Lawrence**, 1885-1930, challenged the taboos of class and sex in novels such as *Lady Chatterley's Lover*. **John Cowper Powys**, 1872-1963, studied man in his environment, while **Malcolm Lowry**, 1909-57, wrote of his devastating experiences in Mexico.
**A group of left-wing poets** in London in the 20s included **W. H. Auden** 1907-73, and **Stephen Spender**, 1909-

A forerunner of the **Theatre of the Absurd, Luigi Pirandello**, 1867-1936, explored the theme of mutual incomprehension.
**American writing** was richly varied, ranging from the southern novels of **William Faulkner**, 1897-1962, whose *Light in August* appeared, 1932 to *The Grapes of Wrath* by **John Steinbeck**, 1902-68, treating the hardship of the depression.

**"The Lost Generation"**, a group of Americans in Paris in the 1920s and 1930s, included **Scott Fitzgerald**, 1896-1940, whose *Tender is the Night* was an elegy for the American Dream; the masculine **Ernest Hemingway**, 1899-1961, **Gertrude Stein**, 1874-1946, an influential experimentalist; and the less typical **Henry Miller**, 1891- who shattered sexual taboos.

## Art and architecture

**In Europe before World War II there was increasing integration between art forms. Furniture design, painting and architecture were developed by the de Stijl and Bauhaus groups. Formal developments in painting also affected architecture. By 1932 the new International Style had come into existence. The first Surrealist manifesto in 1924, with its emphasis on exploration of the unconscious, represented the culmination of the avant-garde movement in art, which linked radical artistic and political ideas.**

**Many of the artistic movements of the postwar period found expression in the cinema, but the depression caused the collapse of the film industries of many European countries and introduced a period of Hollywood supremacy based on large studio organizations, which had the effect of suppressing much individual talent, and leading to the development of styles suited to a mass market.**

**Expressionist techniques** were used by **Chaim Soutine**, 1893-1943, in "Page Boy at Maxim's", 1927, and by **Marc Chagall**, 1889- , in "Russian Wedding", 1925.
**Expressionist cinema** was developed by **Fritz Lang**, 1890-1976, in his vision of the future *Metropolis*, 1926, while **Dali** explored surrealist cinema in *Le Chien Andalou*, 1928.
*The Jazz Singer*, 1927, was the first talking picture.

**Surrealism**, founded in Paris, explored the reality of the subconscious. Its leading exponent was **Salvador Dali**, 1904- , whose "Illuminated Pleasures", 1929, shows objects taken out of context and replaced in fantastic juxtapositions. Other important artists were **René Magritte**, 1898-1967, **Giorgio de Chirico**, 1888-1978, **Joan Miró**, 1893- , and **Max Ernst**, 1891-1976. **Ernst** and **André Masson**, 1896- , practised automatism, a free-brush style.

**The International Style** in architecture, 1932, recognized a new and independent style that had emerged in the twenties. This was typified in the Villa Savoye, 1928-31, by **Le Corbusier**, with its white rectangular exterior and horizontal windows. The individual style of the French painter **Georges Rouault**, 1871-1958, whose religious works achieve a stained glass quality, can be seen in his "Christ mocked by Soldiers", 1932.

**In Germany anti-Nazi artistic expressions** by artists such as **Otto Dix**, 1891-1969, **George Grosz**, 1893-1959, **Max Beckmann**, 1884-1950, and **Oskar Kokoschka**, 1886- resulted in either suppression or exile for the artists concerned.
**Socialist Realism** was officially adopted in the USSR under Stalin in 1934, using an explicit, academic style in order to convey clearly the message of the dignity of the working classes.

## Music

**Serious music split into several mutually exclusive schools, most of which could attract few listeners or performers in spite of the spread of the radio and gramophone. However, these did help to broaden the audience for popular music which, in various jazz forms and "musicals", flourished widely.**

**An English school**, including **Frederick Delius**, 1862-1934, **Gustav Holst**, 1874-1934, and **Vaughan Williams**, 1872-1958, produced pastoral music after **Edward Elgar**, 1857-1934.

**Louis Armstrong**, 1900-71, created a solo style in jazz with his innovative trumpet improvisations of 1925-30.
**Duke Ellington**, 1899-1974, began an orchestral style in jazz.

***Ionization***, 1931, by **Edgard Varèse**, 1885-1965, written solely for percussion instruments, showed that a piece of serious music could be constructed successfully using rhythm only.

**The Neoclassic movement** reinterpreted classical form in modern sound. Initiated by **Stravinsky**, the style attracted **Sergei Prokofiev**, 1891-1953, and **Paul Hindemith**, 1895-1963.

## Science and technology

**Economic depression and war hindered some areas of science while advancing others. In the West, steelmaking, engineering and agricultural production fell during the thirties, but falling prices stimulated consumer industries and aviation, radio, the car industry and artificial fibres continued to develop. The USSR, too, was industrializing fast.**

**With the rise of Hitler, many nuclear physicists fled to America, where their research ensured that Germany's supremacy in physics was lost and that the Nazis would not be the first to possess nuclear weapons.**

**World War II made great use of science, both to destroy and to save lives. Electronics, radar, nuclear technology, jet aviation and antibiotics were all products of the war.**

**In Britain important work was done in astronomy, exploring the implications of Einstein's theories to produce conflicting concepts of the origin of the universe.**

**Modern sound recording** began with the introduction of electric recording in 1925.
**Liquid fuel rockets** were first tested in America in 1926.
**The big bang theory** of the origin of the universe was first put forward in 1927, by **Abbé Lemaître**, 1894-1966.
**Wave mechanics**, was founded by **Erwin Schrödinger**, in 1928.
**The Heisenberg uncertainty principle**, that every observation has a degree of probability, was proposed in 1927.

**John Logie Baird** invented a high-speed mechanical scanning system, 1928, which led to the development of television.
***The anti-bacterial activity of Penicillium*** mould was discovered, 1928, by **Alexander Fleming**, 1881-1955, but it was not made stable enough for medical use until 1943.
**The distance of galaxies** was related to their speed of recession as measured by the red shift, 1929, by **Edwin Hubble** 1889-1953.

**The cyclotron** and other circular particle accelerators were developed from a working model made in America c. 1930.
**Wallace Carothers**, 1896-1937, invented **nylon** in 1931.
**Radio astronomy** began in 1931 with the detection of radio signals from outer space.
**Deuterium**, heavy hydrogen, was discovered in 1931.
**The first nuclear reaction** using an accelerator was activated in 1932.
**Neutrons** were discovered, 1932.

**Sky-scraper** building in the US was interrupted by the depression of the 1930s.
**The first radio-isotopes** were prepared by **Frédéric Joliot-Curie**, 1900-58, and his wife **Irène**, 1897-1956, in 1934.
Experiments made by **Robert Watson-Watt**, 1892-1973, after 1935 led to the invention of **radar**.
**The meson**, a sub-atomic particle, was predicted in 1935.

## 1935-7

**The governmental reforms** of 1935 in India again fell short of nationalist demands. **Mussolini invaded Abyssinia** in 1935 to satisfy fascist imperial ambitions. The League failed to intervene effectively. **Hitler** re-militarized the Rhineland, 1936, and Mussolini proclaimed the **Rome-Berlin axis**. **A right-wing coup** after the Popular Front won the elections led to civil war in Spain, 1936-9. **The Japanese** began their attack of China in 1937.

## 1937-40

**Germany annexed Austria**, 1938. Europe's powers met at **Munich**, 1938, to discuss German claims in Czechoslovakia, but failed to restrain Hitler. **German threats** to take Danzig in Poland resulted in Anglo-French intervention. **A European war** began in Sept 1939. **Francisco Franco**, 1892-1975, became dictator of Spain after defeating the republicans. **Germany took France** in 1940. **Japan** had conquered most of eastern China by 1939.

## 1940-43

**Germany** waged a lightning war in the West, but failed to invade or destroy Britain, which fought at sea and in the air, and opposed Italy in north Africa. **In June 1941 Germany invaded Russia** and drove the Red Army back to Moscow. **Japanese aggression** in the Pacific, culminating in the attack on **Pearl Harbor**, Hawaii, 1941, brought the US into the war. **Hitler** began the systematic genocide of the Jews, 1941.

## 1943-5

**In 1943 Russia stopped the Germans** at Stalingrad and Anglo-American forces took north Africa and invaded Italy. **Guerrilla action**, especially in Yugoslavia and France, weakened Nazi control. **The invasion of Normandy** by Britain and US in June 1944 opened a "second front" and Allied forces from east and west met on the Elbe in April 1945. **The Allies** agreed on Soviet and western spheres of influence at Yalta in 1945.

## 1945-7

**America dropped two atomic bombs** on Japan and ended the war in the Pacific, 1945. **The United Nations** was formed in 1945. **The Truman doctrine**, 1947, promised aid to non-communist countries, particularly Turkey and Greece. **Britain granted independence to India**, 1947, which divided through religious conflict. **The Chinese communists** were aided by Japan's defeat, controlling Manchuria by 1947.

## 1947-50

**The USSR** blockaded Berlin, 1948-9, to isolate it from the west. **Zionists** declared Israel's independence, 1948. **Indonesia** threw off Dutch rule. **Mao Tse-tung**, 1893-1976, set up the People's Republic of China, 1949. **The North Atlantic Treaty Organization** provided for mutual assistance against aggression among the Western powers. **The socialist coup** in Czechoslovakia, 1948, extended Soviet control of eastern Europe.

**Edward VIII**, *r.* 1936, abdicated to marry a divorcee. **A tariff war** and a revised constitution for **Eire** weakened Anglo-Irish relations.

**Neville Chamberlain**, 1869-1940, aimed to avoid war at Munich, 1938. He abandoned appeasement after Hitler took Prague in 1939.

**British troops** were repulsed in Europe. **Winston Churchill**, 1874-1965, led a coalition government, uniting Britain against German air attacks, 1940.

**With conscription** British military forces totalled 4.5 million in 1944. **Labour** won a landslide victory in 1945.

**Clement Attlee**, 1883-1967, led Labour's radical programme of strict economy combined with nationalization, welfare and decolonization, 1945-50.

**The National Health Service** came into operation in 1948, and rationing was relaxed. More curbs were imposed on the power of the Lords.

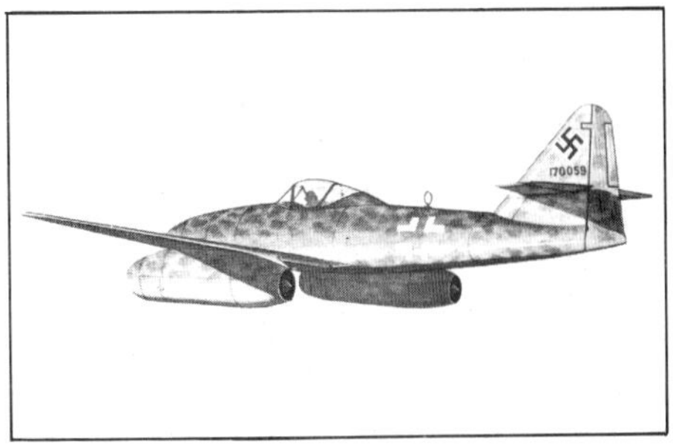


Messerschmitt-262

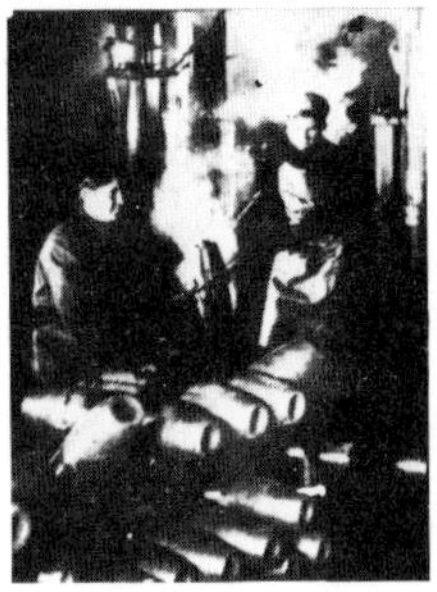

Women munitions workers

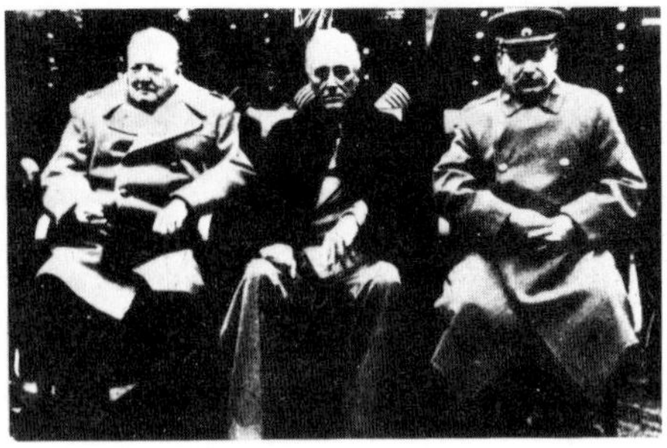

Churchill, Roosevelt and Stalin at Yalta

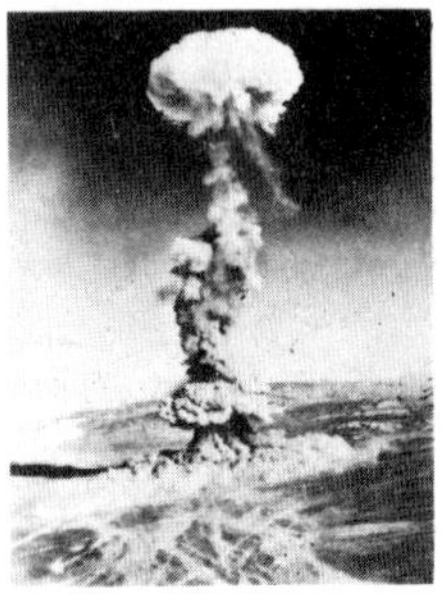

Nuclear bomb test

**The Vienna Circle**, a group of philosophers who met there, 1922-36, including **Moritz Schlick** 1882-1936 and **Rudolf Carnap**, formulated logical positivism, an empiricist philosophy of language according to which only statements that could be verified by observation were meaningful. **Pope Pius XI**, *r.*1922-39, condemned fascism and communism in 1937. He adopted a friendly attitude to Protestant liberalism, although opposing *laissez-faire* social policies.

**Mao Tse-tung**, 1893-1976, adapted Marxism-Leninism to Chinese conditions, and argued that the peasantry, as well as the industrial proletariat, could succeed in making a socialist revolution. Mao later maintained that socialism could only be reached by a permanent revolution to prevent the development of privilege. His studies in guerrilla warfare were important to his political success and influenced later Third World revolutionaries.

**Phenomenology** was developed in France by **Maurice Merleau-Ponty**, 1908-61, in *The Structure of Behaviour*, 1942. Closely associated with him was **Jean-Paul Sartre**, 1905- , who in *Being and Nothingness*, 1943, advanced the Existentialist claim that authentic existence requires the individual exercise of free choice between alternative possibilities, without reference to accepted social roles. **Oxfam** was founded, 1942, to combat Third World poverty.

**Karl Popper**, 1902- , an Austrian living in England, argued that scientific theories must be open to falsification, so that scientific progress required a community in which accepted ideas were subject to criticism. In *The Open Society and its Enemies*, 1944, he went on to attack the belief that there are general laws in history, which he saw as leading to totalitarian politics.

**T. Adorno**, 1903- , and **M. Horkheimer**, 1895- , of the **Frankfurt School of Sociology**, argued in *Dialectics of Enlightenment*, 1947, that true knowledge could only be achieved by a social revolution which would liberate man from the idea that nature is independent of, and external to, him. **Dietrich Bonhoeffer**, 1906-45, a German Protestant, argued that God is dead and sought a conception of Christianity relevant to a secular society.

**Martin Buber**, 1878-1965, a Jewish thinker influenced by the mysticism of the Hasidic tradition in Judaism, advocated a direct, personal relationship of man with God, and praised the new *kibbutzim* in Israel as almost ideal socialist communities, in *Paths to Utopia*, 1947. **The World Council of Churches** first met in 1948. **The welfare state** uniting private enterprise with state responsibility, took shape with the British National Health Service, 1948.

**Spanish folk traditions** and modern cruelty were studied by the dramatist **Federico Garcia Lorca**, 1898-1936. In Germany an aesthetic and idealist style was used by **Thomas Mann**, 1875-1955. His *Joseph and his Brothers*, 1933-43, explores the theme of exile. **A sense of cultural collapse** inspired **Robert Musil**, 1880-1942, to write *The Man Without Qualities*.

**Experimental epic theatre** was pioneered by the German Marxist **Bertold Brecht**, 1898-1956. **Many foreign writers** fought in the Spanish Civil War. **George Orwell**, 1903-50, described it in *Homage to Catalonia*, 1939. **Important English novelists**, dealing with traditional themes were **Graham Greene**, 1904- , **Aldous Huxley**, 1894-1963, and **Evelyn Waugh**, 1903-66.

**The *Makioka Sisters***, 1943-8, an account of a Japanese family by **Tanikaki Junichiro**, 1886-1965, owes much to Western realism. **Serious native American drama** was created by **Eugene O'Neill**, 1888-1953 and **Tennessee Williams**, 1911- , who explored the frustrations of urban society. The plays of **Arthur Miller**, 1915- , deal with individual moral and political responsibility.

**Salvatore Quasimodo**, 1901-68, opposed fascism in Italy in lyrical symbolist poetry. **The "negritude" movement**, calling for black cultural identity, was initiated by **Leopold Senghor**. **Latin American literature** flourished with the "poetry for simple people" of the Chilean **Pablo Neruda**, 1904-73, and the complex stories of the Argentinian **Jorge Luis Borges.**

**In *Deaths and Entrances*** 1946, the exuberant imagery of the Welsh poet **Dylan Thomas** 1914-53, is at its best. **Russia's history from 1900-30** was the subject of the humanistic novel *Doctor Zhivago*, by **Boris Pasternak**, 1890-1960. **Italy's** leading novelists, **Cesare Pavese**, 1908-50 and **Alberto Moravia**, 1907- , both condemned the estrangement of the modern age.

**Jean-Paul Sartre**, 1905- , gave existential philosophy a literary form in his war trilogy, *Les Chemins de la Liberté*, 1945-9. The existential dilemma also masks the feminist novels of **Simone de Beauvoir**, 1908- . **Albert Camus**, 1913-60, formulated his theories of **The Absurd** in his novels and essays, notably *The Outsider*, and *The Plague*, 1947.

**Ben Nicholson**, 1894- , one of Britain's leading abstract artists, achieved worldwide recognition in the Cubist and Abstract Art exhibition, New York, 1936. The rectangular, textured "White Relief", 1935, is typical of his style at this time. **Frank Lloyd Wright**, the American architect, produced outstanding buildings, including his famous **Falling Water**, Bear Run, Pa. 1936-7.

One of **Picasso's finest paintings**, "Guernica", 1937, was prompted by the destruction of this Basque town by German bombers during the Spanish Civil War. **Hollywood** won an international supremacy in film-making during the depression, using enormous casts in lavish productions such as *Gone with the Wind*, 1939.

**American artists** turned increasingly to the depiction of provincial life in a realistic style. "Nighthawks", 1942, by **Edward Hopper**, 1882-1967, records with formal precision the isolation of a city at night. **Hollywood cinema** escaped the limitations of its genres (westerns, gangster films and love stories) with *Citizen Kane*, 1941, directed by **Orson Welles**, 1915- , and *The Grapes of Wrath*, 1940, by **John Ford**, 1895-1973.

**Official war artists** in Britain such as **Graham Sutherland**, 1903- , and **John Piper**, 1903- , recorded the devastating effects of the bombings. **Mies van der Rohe**, in the US from 1938, designed during the war years the campus of the Illinois Institute of Technology, using cubic simplicity and perfect precision in details.

**Emaciated single figures** on wire frames characterized the work of the Swiss sculptor **Albert Giacometti**, 1901-66, such as "Man Pointing", 1947. The British sculptor, **Henry Moore**, 1898- , used his material to express natural forms in terms of stone or wood. "Three Standing Figures", 1947-8, is characteristic of his work. **Italian neo-realist cinema** relied on simple stories and untrained actors, as in *Rome, Open City*, 1945, by Roberto Rossellini, 1906-77.

**Abstract Expressionism** developed in the US after 1945, expressed in the drip paintings of **Jackson Pollock**, 1912-56, in the "black and white" paintings of **Willem de Kooning**, 1904- , and in the blurred expanses of rich colours in the work of **Mark Rothko**, 1903-70. The Unité d'Habitation, 1946-52, by **Le Corbusier**, a huge block of 337 two-storey apartments, was the first building to use rough cast concrete.

**Musical theatre** reached a peak of sophistication in the United States, with lavish shows and beautiful songs, notably by **George Gershwin**, 1898-1937 in *Porgy and Bess*, 1935.

**Serial music** developed further with the work of **Alban Berg**, 1885-1935, and **Anton Webern**, 1883-1945, eventually submitting all musical elements to mathematical procedures.

**Glen Miller**, 1904-44, leader of the US Army Air Force Band in Europe, entertained troops with his distinctive, "big band" saxophone sound.

**The swing era**, 1935-45, dominated the popular music interest in the US, featuring such big bands as **Benny Goodman's**, playing highly arranged jazz with an energetic beat.

**Be bop**, a complex form of jazz featuring virtuoso improvisation, emerged in 1945 as a reaction to the widely popular swing style. Its principal creator was **Charlie Parker**, 1920-55.

**Radio and gramophone** disseminated music to all developed countries, spreading new forms and styles so widely that national schools could no longer emerge.

**The first television service** was opened in Britain in 1936. **New industries** were developed to escape the depression. In Britain and the US, the new interest in consumer expenditure, combined with the completion of the electricity supply, led to the growth of consumer durable industries, while in Germany road-building was encouraged. **The citric acid cycle**, which occurs in bodily energy production, was found in 1937.

**The Graf Zeppelin** (LZ 130) was built in 1938, the largest airship to be made. It ran on a regular commercial transatlantic service. **The Volkswagen "Beetle"**, designed by **Porsche** to Hitler's requirements, was built 1938. **Nuclear fission**, developed as a source of energy in the US, was first achieved in 1939. **Einstein told the US president** of the possibility of making an **atomic bomb**, 1939, to pre-empt German research. **Food-dehydration** by vacuum-contact drying was developed.

**Plutonium**, the first artificial element, was made, 1940. **The first jet-powered aircraft** flew in 1941, using an engine made by **Frank Whittle**, 1907- . **The first nuclear reactor** was built in 1942 in Chicago. **Penicillin**, the first antibiotic, was produced on a large scale from *Penicillium* mould in 1943. The German development of the **V2 rocket-bomb**, 1942, provided the basis for future rocket development. The war also brought improvements in electronics and medical equipment.

**Large diameter pipelines** were introduced in the US, facilitating the distribution of oil, 1943. **DNA** was shown to carry hereditary characteristics, 1944. **The kidney machine** was developed in 1944. **IBM** produced a mechanical calculating machine, 1944. **DDT** was discovered in 1939 and introduced as an insecticide, 1944, as synthetic fertilizers became available, leading to an increase in agricultural yields.

**The first nuclear bombs** were made in the US in 1945 and tested at Alamogordo, New Mexico, in 1945. **Britain's first atomic power station** was built, 1947. **The sound barrier** was broken by the Bell XI rocket-propelled American aircraft, 1947. **Radiocarbon dating**, a method of accurately finding the ages of archaeological discoveries, was perfected in 1947.

**A Jaguar sports car**, capable of 193km/h (120mph) was put into production in 1948. **The "steady-state" theory** of the universe was proposed by **H. Bondi and T. Gold**, 1948. **The transistor** was invented in 1948. Its invention made possible the miniaturization of electronic equipment and, with micro-circuitry, the computer. **A United States step rocket** sent a vehicle to a height of more than 390km in 1949. **The World Health Organization** was set up in 1948.

# 1950-1979 The modern world

## Principal events

**The division of the world into two major power blocs after World War II was confused by a Sino-Soviet ideological split, and after a series of dangerous incidents between Russia and America in the 1950s and early 1960s the Cold War gave way to a period of official détente.**

**In spite of continuing imperialism by the major powers, whether militarily or by economic intervention, Third World liberation from European control has accelerated, changing the composition of the United Nations as the newly independent African and Asian states have joined and forcing industrialized countries to pay a higher price for raw materials.**

**Economic planning has become increasingly world-wide with the rise of development economics and the attempt to control currency exchange rates. In the 1970s serious inflation has spread to all the industrialized countries.**

### 1950-2

**War** between North and South Korea, which had its roots in the Communist triumph in China, produced UN intervention.
**The Arab League** powers formed a security pact and began a blockade of Israel, 1950.
**No agreement on Germany's future** was reached, but peace was made with Japan, 1951.
**The US** strengthened defence links with Japan and Formosa.
**Six European** powers joined a single **Coal and Steel Commission**, 1952.

### 1952-5

**Geneva conference**, 1955, divided Vietnam into North and South after a Communist victory at **Dien Bien Phu** had forced the French forces to withdraw.
**Opposition to British and French imperialism** brought terrorist campaigns in Algeria, Kenya, Cyprus and Malaya.
**The USSR** opposed the reunification of Germany, 1954, and the **Warsaw Pact** united the Soviet satellites in reaction to West Germany's incorporation in NATO, 1955.

### 1955-8

**The Soviet leader, Nikita Khrushchev**, 1894-1971, denounced Stalinist principles, 1956; a Sino-Soviet split resulted. Soviet troops invaded **Hungary**, to crush a nationalist rising, 1956.
**President Nasser**, 1918-70, of Egypt nationalized the Suez Canal Company, 1956, provoking Britain, France and Israel to military intervention.
**The Treaty of Rome**, 1957, established the **Common Market** in western Europe.

### 1958-60

**Discontent in France** over the Algerian war brought **Charles de Gaulle**, 1890-1970, to power in 1958.
**China's Great Leap Forward**, an economic push in agriculture and industry, 1958, ended in economic chaos, after the withdrawal of Soviet aid, 1960.
**World opinion** was aroused by the Sharpeville massacre, 1960.
**Fidel Castro**, 1927- , a Marxist, controlled **Cuba**, 1959.
**The Belgian Congo's** independence, 1960, led to anarchy.

## National events

**Britain granted independence to most of her empire and aligned herself with the US and Europe, but after the prosperity of the 1950s and 1960s governments have faced increasing violence in Northern Ireland while mounting inflation and worsening industrial relations prompted a questioning of the Welfare State.**

### 1950-2

**Hugh Gaitskell**, 1906-63, imposed health service charges in 1951 to meet defence costs.
**Labour** lost the October election.

### 1952-5

**Britain** exploded her first atomic bomb, 1952. **Churchill's ministry**, 1951-5, de-nationalized road transport and steel.
**Food rationing** ended, 1954.

### 1955-8

**Britain lost prestige** in the Suez crisis, 1956, but exploded hydrogen bombs, 1957.
**The Campaign for Nuclear Disarmament** began, 1958.

### 1958-60

**Cyprus** was given her independence, 1960.
**Britain** agreed to join the European Free Trade Association, 1960.

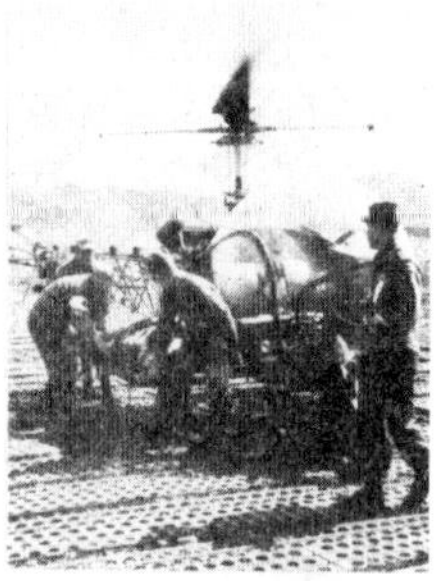

Medivac in the Korean War

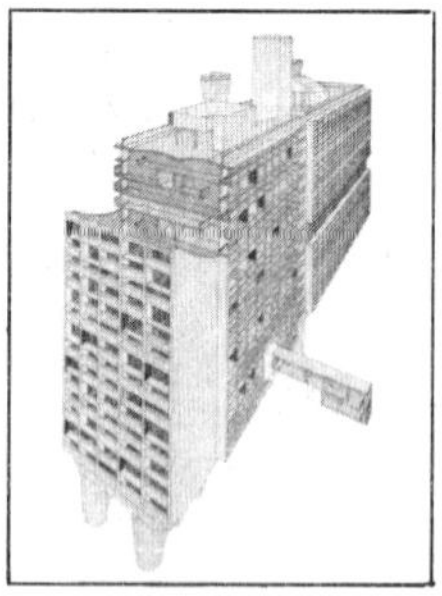

Le Corbusier: design

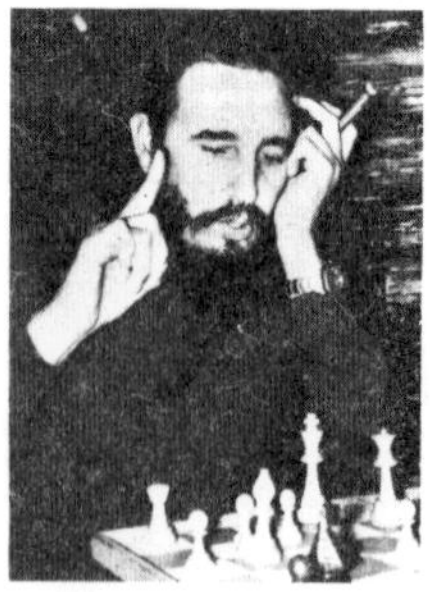

Fidel Castro

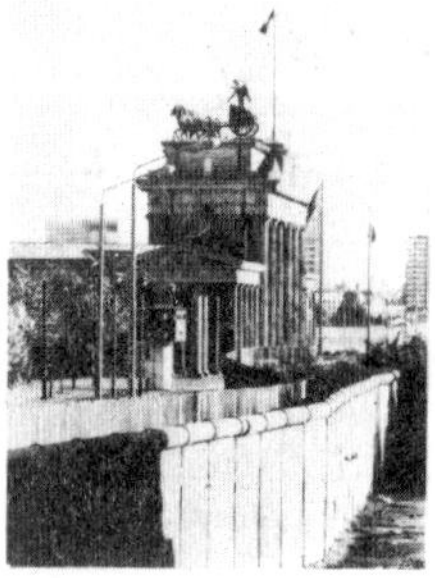

The Berlin Wall

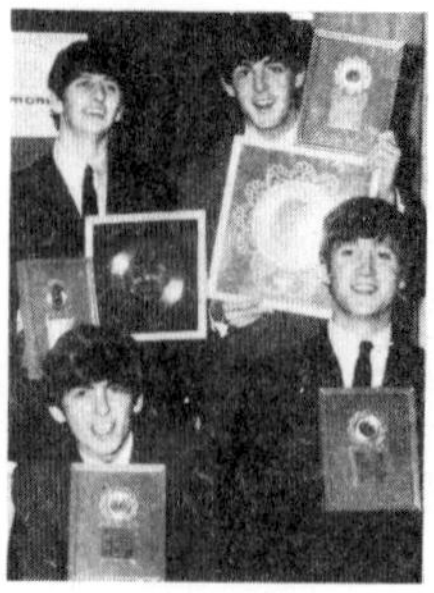

The Beatles, 1963

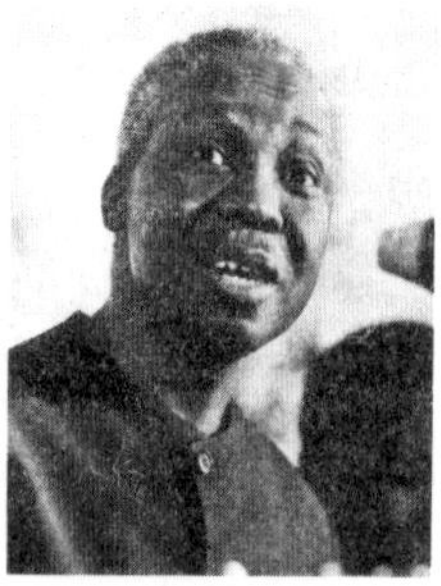

Nyerere of Tanzania

## Religion and philosophy

**American sociology has been dominant in the West since World War II, expanding the use of surveys and other observational techniques into a major tool of government policy and developing in the work of Talcott Parsons a complex schema for the understanding of whole societies. Many of the general trends of thought seen in the industrialized countries also originated in the United States, whether in the work of theorists such as Marcuse, in the radical opposition to the Vietnam War or in the hippy movement, with its rejection of political activism and search for increased personal awareness and communal living.**

**In the same period Third World theorists have produced an analysis of the processes and effects of colonialism and the means of eradicating it.**

**The Christian churches have tried to overcome some of their differences, and in the Third World become linked with progressive social policies.**

### 1950-2

**Frantz Fanon**, 1925-61, a West Indian, analysed the psychological and social repression of the black man in *Black Skin, White Masks*, 1952. He advocated an independent and socialist Third World.
**Talcott Parsons**, 1902- , an American, developed structural functional sociology in *The Social System*, setting out to construct a general model for societies, showing the interdependence of their institutions and emphasizing shared values.

### 1952-5

**Joseph McCarthy**, 1908-57, led an American witch-hunt against liberals and Marxists as a result of Cold War tension.
**The Oxford School of Ordinary Language Philosophy**, including **Gilbert Ryle**, 1900- , and **J. L. Austin**, 1911-60, followed Wittgenstein's later ideas.
In *Dilemmas*, 1954, Ryle tried to show that problems in philosophy derive from conceptual confusion and would be dissolved if we kept to the normal meaning of words.

### 1955-8

**Noam Chomsky**, 1928- , an American, revolutionized linguistics by analysing the structure of language. He showed in *Syntactic Structures*, 1957, that grammatical speech depends upon a system of rules too complex to be learned by example.
**Paul Tillich**, 1886-1965, a Protestant, sought to fuse traditional religious values with a modern emphasis on individual responsibility in the *Dynamics of Faith*, 1957.

### 1958-60

**Structuralism**, the attempt to find basic patterns or "structures" for a scientific study of man, was developed by the Frenchman **Claude Levi-Strauss**, 1908- in his *Structural Anthropology*, 1958. **Michel Foucault**, 1926- has applied this method to the history of ideas.
**Jean-Paul Sartre**, 1905- , tried to link **Existentialism** and **Marxism** in the *Critique of Dialectical Reason*, 1960.

## Literature

**The rise of a worldwide reading public and of cheap and widely distributed books has allowed the writer greater freedom of experimentation. Increasingly confessional novels reflecting a sense of the isolation of the individual, and the use of a journalistic approach to deal with contemporary events have challenged the very concept of fiction, which has traditionally required a distance between the author and his subject. At the same time the beat writers, in seeking to celebrate the spontaneous, have questioned artistic form.**

**However, traditional literary forms remain the main vehicle for Third World writers, who have set out to portray the conflicts aroused in the individual by the colonization.**

### 1950-2

**The Theatre of the Absurd**, which saw man as a helpless creature in a meaningless universe, was explored by **Samuel Beckett**, 1906- , **Eugene Ionesco**, 1912- , and **Jean Genet**, 1910-
The "new novel", without form or plot, was developed in the work of **Alain Robbe-Grillet**, 1922- and **Nathalie Sarraute**, 1900-

### 1952-5

**Black American writers** gained status with *The Invisible Man*, by **Ralph Ellison**, 1914- , and the writings of **James Baldwin**, 1924- . The Swiss dramatists **Max Frisch**, 1911- , and **Friedrich Dürrenmatt**, 1921- , and the Frenchman **Jean Anouilh**, 1910- , share a preoccupation with the tragi-comic and grotesque aspects of life.

### 1955-8

**English drama** was active in the 1950s. Disillusionment with contemporary Britain was vented by **John Osborne**, 1929- in his play *Look Back in Anger*, 1956. **Harold Pinter**, 1930- wrote *The Birthday Party*, 1958, which he followed with more "comedies of menace"
**Arnold Wesker**, 1932- , wrote socialist plays including *Roots*, 1958.

### 1958-60

The work of **Jack Kerouac**, 1922-69, epitomizes the outlook of the American beat generation. Its writers include **William Burroughs**, 1914- , and **Henry Miller**, 1891- , and the poets **Allen Ginsberg**, 1926- , and **Lawrence Ferlinghetti**, 1919- , all of whom sought "spontaneous living" and the means to express it.

## Art and architecture

**Although America still dominates the visual arts, the increasingly international nature of the market has brought a new uniformity of style most clearly seen in architecture, where monumental concrete styles are found throughout the world.**

**In painting, attempts to explore the fundamentals of visual language have produced an ever-simplified abstract style and the breakdown of traditional distinctions between the disciplines and even between art and life; while Pop-art has incorporated into art the mass-produced images of consumer society.**

**The emergence in many parts of the world, including South America, India and eastern Europe, of the art film, aiming more at expression than at profit, has challenged the domination of Hollywood and forced the adoption of new formal styles and greater individual freedom in American commercial cinema, as well as a more critical view of modern society.**

### 1950-2

**Skyscraper building** in the US revived after World War I, with a new reliance on glass and steel, seen in Lever House, New York, 1952.
**Le Corbusier** designed **Chandigarh**, the new capital of the Punjab, 1950, in rough cast concrete.
**The growth of film festivals** after 1945 led to a less commercial cinema, and brought the work of the Japanese **Kurosawa**, 1910- , and the Indian **Satyajit Ray**, 1921- , to the West.

### 1952-5

**Pier Luigi Nervi**, 1891- , regarded as the most brilliant concrete designer of his age, helped design the UNESCO building in Paris, 1954-8.
**The International Style** in architecture can be seen, postwar, at its most elegant in the Rødovre Town Hall, Copenhagen, begun in 1955 by **Arne Jacobsen**, 1902-71.
**"Brutalism"** in architecture was a term coined, 1953, for a functional style which, for example, let electric ducts be clearly seen.

### 1955-8

**Pop-art** emerged in London in 1956 in the works of **Richard Hamilton**, 1922- , **Peter Blake**, 1932- , and **Eduardo Paolozzi**, 1924- , using motifs from commercial art.
**Hard-edge painting** with large, clearly defined areas of bright colour, was conceived in New York, 1958, and explored by **Ellsworth Kelly**, 1923-
**Kinetic art** made use of light and movement for its effects as in *Mobile*, 1958, by **Alexander Calder**, 1898-1976

### 1958-60

**Brazilian architecture** centred on the building of a new capital, **Brasilia**. Its cathedral, 1959, by **Oscar Niemeyer**, 1907- , uses graceful curved concrete structures.
**The New Wave of French cinema** emerged in 1959 in reaction to the clichés of Hollywood. *400 Blows*, 1959 by **François Truffaut**, 1932- and *Breathless*, by **Jean-Luc Godard**, 1930- , introduced stylistic innovations on a low budget.

## Music

**New elements have appeared in Western music, stemming from new ways of producing sound and of organizing the music. The open texture of Eastern music began to make its mark in the West as Western music, in turn, reached the East. Rock music began simply in the 1950s and soon became highly creative.**

### 1950-2

**Traditional methods** lived on in the operas of **Benjamin Britten**, 1913-76, and the symphonies of **Dimitri Shostakovitch**, 1906-75, who created personal styles of music by conventional means.

### 1952-5

**John Cage**, 1912- , pioneered a music in which the score is a set of directions delineating a musical process, giving much freedom to performers. His notorious *4' 33"*, 1954, is all silence.

### 1955-8

**Musique concrète** widened musical horizons after World War II in France, involving a collage of sounds, both musical and natural, processed into a recording.

### 1958-60

**Rock music** promoted a strong eight-note beat over a static harmony in popular music. At first played on guitars by groups with a lead singer, it later became far more complex.

## Science and technology

**Scientific institutions set up by governments or industries have taken over from the individual experimenter, as the scale on which scientific research is conducted has mushroomed. The growth in prosperity in industrialized countries since 1945 has been accompanied by a boom in technologically sophisticated goods available to the general public; in particular, electronic equipment has been improved by miniaturization.**

**Much scientific research has been related to the rival arms and space programmes of the USSR and the US. But since the completion of the American Apollo Moon programme, the emphasis in the US has shifted to the ecological problems which man must solve if he is to have a future on Earth. The hunt for new energy resources has been stimulated by a rise in oil prices, and new foods have been developed to help cope with expanding population. Small-scale, technological innovations have benefited Third World economies.**

### 1950-2

**Magnetic recording** developed during the 1950s. Modern sound and video recording as well as computer operations depend on storing electrical signals in the form of magnetic patterns according to principles discovered by the Danish inventor **Valdemar Poulsen**, 1869-1942, in 1898.
**Soya-bean farming** increased, *c.* 1950, following a growing demand for vegetable oil during World War II.
**The first hydrogen bomb** was tested by the United States in 1952.

### 1952-5

**The structure of DNA** was found in 1953, leading to closer understanding of protein synthesis in the body and the inheritance of characteristics by the next generation.
**Polio vaccine** was developed, 1953-5.
**Oral contraception** followed from the investigations in the 1950s into the role that sex hormones play in reproduction.
**The link between smoking and lung cancer** was first proposed in 1952.

### 1955-8

**The neutrino**, a fundamental particle predicted in 1931, was detected in 1956.
**Nuclear power** was first generated on a viable industrial scale in Britain from 1956.
**Britain** introduced a **Clean Air Act**, 1956, after 4,000 died in a London smog, 1952.
**International Geophysical Year**, an international venture to investigate the Earth, took place, 1957-8.
**The first artificial satellite**, Sputnik 1, was launched by the USSR in 1957.

### 1958-60

**Explorer 1**, the first American satellite, was launched, 1958, and detected radiation belts above the Earth.
**Stereophonic records** first became available in 1958.
**The hovercraft** was demonstrated in 1959.
**Computers** entered into commercial use, 1955, and were common by 1960.
**The kidney machine** was developed in the US *c.* 1960.

## 1960-3

**South Africa** left the British Commonwealth, 1961, after Britain accepted the trend of decolonization in Africa, 1960. **The Russians** built the Berlin Wall, 1961. After **Joyhn F. Kennedy**, 1917–63, the US president, intervened in the Cuban civil war, 1961. Soviet missile supplies to Cuba provoked a world crisis, 1962. Kennedy supported the **Civil Rights Movement**, encouraging the march on Washington, 1963. **Algeria** won her independence.

**Harold Macmillan**, 1894- accepted decolonization and racial equality within the expanded Commonwealth. **Labour** debated nationalization.

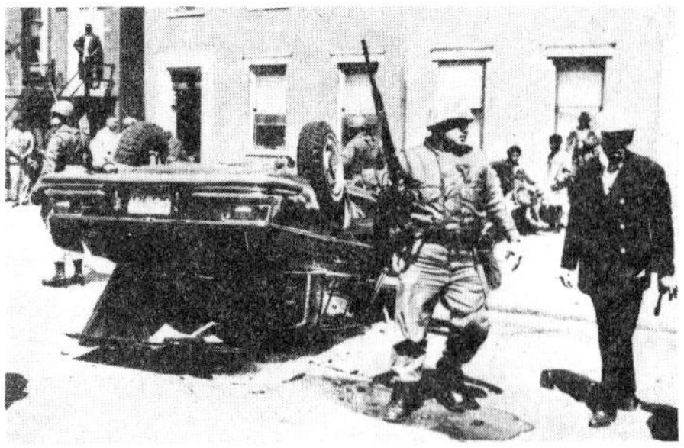

Riots in Washington at the death of Martin Luther King

**R. D. Laing**, 1927- , studied schizophrenia in a personal rather than clinical way in *The Divided Self*, 1960, and developed a humanistic school of anti-psychology. **The Ecumenical Movement** for Christian unity began in 1961-2 when the Eastern Orthodox and Catholic churches met with Protestants at the World Council of Churches, while the Vatican Council, 1962, tried to reconcile differences within Catholicism.

The damaging effects of Western civilization in African culture are examined in the novels of **Chinua Achebe**, 1930- , and the plays of **Wole Soyinka**, 1934- , both Nigerians. The West Indian novelist **V. S. Naipaul**, 1932- , wrote of poverty in Trinidad with delicate irony in *A House for Mr Biswas*, 1961.

**Distorted human forms** confined within a claustrophobic space characterize the work of the Briton **Francis Bacon**, 1910- seen in his "Red Figure", 1962. **A move towards formalism** is seen in the dramatic use of curved concrete at the TWA buildings, Kennedy Airport, 1961, by **Eero Saarinen**, 1910-61. **Japanese architecture** united traditional forms with the new materials of steel and concrete in the work of **Tange**, 1913-

**Graphic notation** of symbols to portray sound became widespread in the 1960s as composers sought new sounds and effects from electronic and conventional instruments.

**The bathyscape *Trieste*** descended 11km (7miles) to the deepest part of the ocean, 1960. **The laser** was invented in 1960, and used for precision cutting and optical surgery. **Tiros I**, the first weather satellite, was placed in orbit by the United States in 1960. **Manned space flight** began in 1961 with a one-orbit mission by the Russian cosmonaut **Yuri Gagarin** 1934-68. **Telstar** the first communications satellite, was launched by the US in 1962.

## 1963-5

**The Nuclear Test Ban Treaty** was signed by the US, USSR and Britain, 1963, but China exploded her first bomb in 1964. **After Kennedy's assassination**, **Lyndon B. Johnson**, 1908-73, passed civil rights bills and built up US forces in Vietnam to oppose the Communist rebels. **Britain** granted independence to **Kenya**, 1963, and **Malawi**, 1964. But Rhodesia declared her own independence under white rule.

**Following Tory leadership disputes** and a Labour victory in the election of 1964, the steel industry was nationalized, 1965.

**Herbert Marcuse**, 1898- , associated with the "Frankfurt" School of Sociology, argued in *One Dimensional Man*, 1964, that in modern industrial society there is a process of "repressive tolerance" which diverts the creative impulses in man by satisfying his material needs. **Julius Nyerere**, president of Tanzania since 1964, set out to weaken Western influence by political non-alignment, to develop a village-based socialism, and to foster African nationalism.

**Postwar German society** was explored in the writings of **Günter Grass**, 1927- and **Heinrich Böll**, 1917-. **The American novel** flourished with many Jewish writers becoming prominent, among them **Saul Bellow**, 1915- , **Philip Roth**, 1933- and **Norman Mailer**, 1923- who also satirized politics in a journalistic style.

Two exponents of **Op-art**, who studied the effect of optical illusions juxtaposing colours and forms, were the Hungarian **Victor Vasarely**, 1908- , and the Briton **Bridget Riley**, 1931-. **Pop-art in America** in the 1960s took images from cartoon comics as in *Whaam*, 1963, by **Roy Lichtenstein**, 1923- , and from commercial advertising in the work of **Andy Warhol**, 1930-. **The Chinese sculpture** "Rent Collection Yard", 1965, depicted the miseries of the empire.

**Simplicity and space** marked the experimental music of the 1960s. Composers like **Terry Riley**, 1935- use simple repeated phrases that overlap in ever-changing patterns, as in his *In C*, 1964.

**Syncom**, the first communications satellite which is constantly available for use, was put into orbit by the US in 1964. **Radiation** at a wavelength of 7 centimetres was first detected from space in 1965, providing support for the big bang theory. **The development of integrated circuits** in the 1960s brought new possibilities of miniaturization, stimulating the rise of the electronics industry in the US and making electronic equipment common in the West.

## 1965-8

**The Chinese Cultural Revolution** aimed to weaken the bureaucracy and stimulate more public participation, 1966-8. **Growing American military activity** in Vietnam failed to bring victory. **Biafran** secessionist claims led to civil war in Nigeria. **Israel** defeated the Arab states in the 1967 **Six Days War** and extended her frontiers. **France** withdrew from military commitments to NATO in 1966.

**Under Harold Wilson**, 1916- , British policies on racial equality were rejected by the white minority of Southern Rhodesia, which claimed independence, 1965.

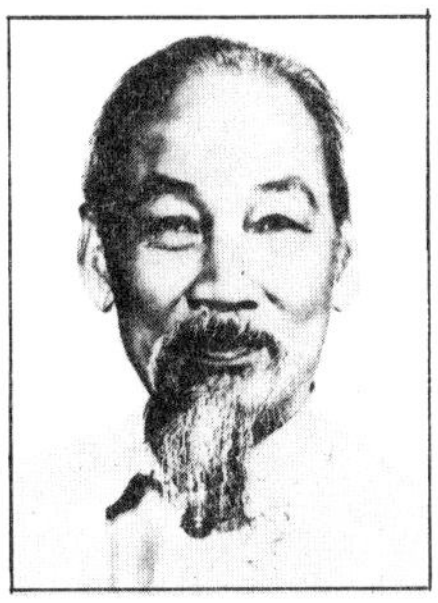

Ho Chi Minh

**The American Civil Rights Movement** against racial intolerance of Negroes was led by **Martin Luther King**, 1929-68, who believed in the use of moral forces. In the mid-60s, however, black leaders such as **Eldridge Cleaver**, turned to violence. **The "flower-power" movement**, originating with American students in 1967, seeking awareness with the aid of mind-expanding drugs. A US counter-culture grew up, based on communes and anarchism.

**South American literature** reached the West with translations of established writers. The Columbian **Gabriel García Marquéz**, 1928- , described the history of a family in a tropical town in *One Hundred Years of Solitude*, 1967. **Mexico's dual heritage** of savagery and civilization is the theme of the surrealistic poetry of **Octavio Paz**, 1914-

**The "Happening"**, the creation of an environment simulating the effects of hallucinatory drugs, often with rock music and shifting patterns of colour, was pioneered in the US, *c.* 1965. **Realism** in British painting was exemplified in the works of **Lucian Freud** 1922- , whose portraits and townscapes show detailed draughtsmanship, and in the figure paintings of **David Hockney**, 1937- , like "Peter getting out of Nick's pool", 1966.

**The tape recorder**, invented in 1942, made all kinds of artificial sound reproduction possible. It was used creatively in popular music, as in the song "Sergeant Pepper", 1967, by the **Beatles**.

**Plate tectonics** developed as a theory to explain continental drift from 1965. **Mariner 4**, an American space probe, flew past Mars in 1965 and sent back the first pictures of another planet. **The first heart transplant** was performed in 1966. **Research into plant genetics** and soil fertility led to the **Green Revolution** in many Third World countries, 1966-70. **The Rance estuary power station** in France, harnessing tidal energy, was set up 1967.

## 1968-70

**Student revolt** in France, 1968, was reflected throughout Europe. After referendum defeat, 1969, de Gaulle resigned. **Soviet troops** invaded Czechoslovakia to end liberal reforms. **Richard Nixon**, 1913- , resumed bombing North Vietnam, after peace talks and troop withdrawals, 1970. **Tanzania and Zambia** secured Chinese support for a railway linking the copperbelt to the sea.

**The Labour government** faced continued economic problems in spite of devaluation, 1967. **Immigration** restrictions were introduced, 1968.

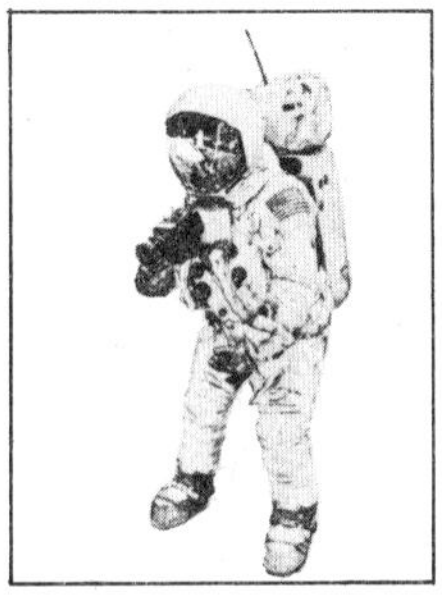

Apollo astronaut

**The radical student movement** of 1968, originating in America and Europe in opposition to the Vietnam War, stressed individual liberation from the constraints of capitalism, influenced by Third World revolutionaries such as **Che Guevara**, 1928-67, and the writings of **Marcuse**. **Pope Paul VI**, *r.* 1963-1978 condemned the use of artificial methods of birth control, 1968, arousing widespread criticism.

*Change of Skin* by the Mexican **Carlos Fuentes**, 1928- , is an "open novel" describing the fluctuations of experience. **Criticism of the Soviet regime** in the *Gulag Archipelago*, led to the exile of **Alexander Solzhenitsyn**, 1918-. **The Japanese postwar generation** is described in the novels of **Yukio Mishima**, 1925-70.

**Land Art** and **"Arte Povera"**, emerged in 1969 as an avant-garde movement which was concerned with art as assemblages of simple elements such as earth and rocks. **A politically committed documentary style** of film-making arose in Britain, seen in *Kes*, 1969, by the directors **Tony Garnett**, 1936- , and **Kenneth Loach**, 1936-

**Poet-musicians** became popular in the late 1960s, singing their own often highly individual compositions. Most influential was **Bob Dylan**, 1941-

**DDT** was banned in the US, 1969, following concern about its harmful side-effects. **The first Moon landing** was made in 1969 by members of the US Apollo 11 space mission. Space research has facilitated **invisible light astronomy**, and assisted **meteorology**. Spin-offs with industrial or domestic use include aluminium foil, and teflon, convenient for cooking utensils.

## 1970–4

**US invaded Cambodia**, 1970. **Biafra surrendered** in the Nigerian civil war. **China joined the UN**, 1971. **Bangladesh** was set up. **US President Nixon** visited China, fostering detente, 1972. **Palestinian guerrillas** killed 11 Israeli athletes at the 1972 Olympic Games. **Chile's President Allende** was killed in a rightwing coup, 1973. **US troops** left Vietnam, 1973. **The Nixon administration** fell as a result of the Watergate scandal.

**Britain** entered the EEC. Heath imposed a three-day week in response to the miners' strike, and faced growing violence in **Northern Ireland.**

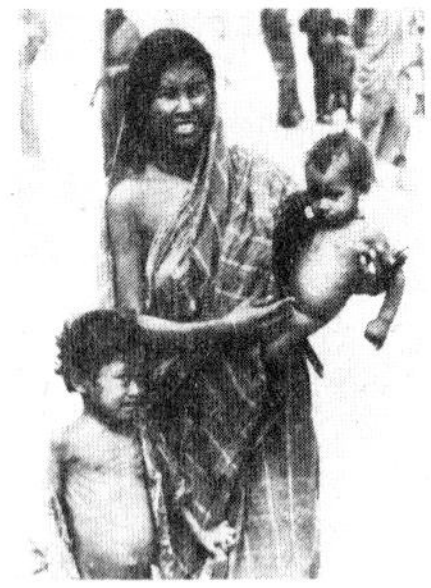

Bangladesh famine victims

**Western religious groups** stressing personal awareness included the "Jesus Freaks" and the Divine Light Mission, which has Hindu elements. **The Conservation Movement's** *The Limits to Growth*, 1973, predicted the imminent disappearance of natural resources. **The Vatican** reaffirmed its anti-divorce stance, 1974. **Dr Donald Cogan** succeeded Dr Ramsay as Archbishop of Canterbury.

**Science fiction** was popular; notably the works of Kurt Vonnegut Jr. 1922–, and Isaac Asimov 1920–. **Carlos Castaneda** published his *Journey to Ixtlan*, the last of a series of accounts of his meetings with a Mexican shaman. **Joseph Heller,** author of *Catch–22*, produced *Something Happened*, 1974.

**An exhibition** in London and Paris, 1973, of Chinese art treasures, including archaeological discoveries made during the Cultural Revolution, restored cultural contacts between China and the West. **The Hong Kong film industry**, specializing in kung-fu and karate films, won immense popularity in the West after 1973 with films such as *Fist of Fury*, 1973, starring Bruce Lee, 1940–73.

**Jamaican music,** reggae, gained popularity in the 1970s in Britain, and became a vehicle for Rastifarian expression with its excursions into 'dub'.

**Earth resources satellites** were first launched by the US in 1971 to detect and map the world's resources. **Germ warfare** was banned by international convention, 1972. **Fear over limited fuel supplies,** and their cost led to the investigation of alternatives such as tidal, solar and geophysical energy. **Micro-computers** were developed in the US.

## 1974–9

**World energy crisis** grew more acute as OPEC increased prices. **Portuguese colonies** broke up as a result of a coup, 1974. **Turkey** invaded Cyprus, 1974. **Chinese leader** Mao Tse-tung died, 1976. **Ethiopia** repulsed a Somali invasion, 1977. **Egypt and Israel** initiated Middle East peace talks, 1978. **Iran's religious leader** the Ayatollah Khomeini returned from exile after the Shah left the country, 1979.

**Britain's first referendum,** under a Labour Government (1974), approved entry into the EEC, 1975. Ulster terrorism extended to London.

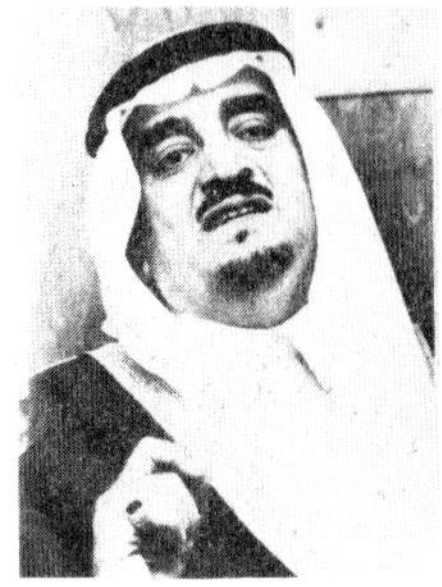

Prince Fahd of Saudi Arabia

**Developing countries' populations** were the subject of a campaign to introduce birth control to the Third World, 1974. **International Women's Year** was called by the UN, 1975. **The Vatican** suspended Mgr Lefebvre for championing the Tridentine Mass, 1976. **Ugandan Anglican Archbishop** was reportedly killed in a car crash; Amin later banned 27 religious organizations, 1977. **John Paul II** was the first non-Italian Pope since 1522, 1978.

**English drama** was represented by Tom Stoppard 1937– and David Storey 1933–. **Anthony Powell's** Proustian novel-sequence *A Dance to the Music of Time* concluded with the publication of *Hearing Secret Harmonies*, 1975. **American novelists** produced grim, closely-written works like Patricia Highsmith's *Edith's Diary* and Hubert Selby's *The Demon*, 1977.

**Conceptual art** rejected conventional art in favour of experiences and ideas related to ideals. These were communicated by combinations of words, three-dimensional objects and audience participation. **Francis Bacon's** *Reclining Man with Sculpture* fetched £89,000, breaking the record for a painting by a living artist. **An art sale** at Mentmore Towers, England, realized £6.4 million, 1977.

**Rock music** became bland, easy-listening, gaining a world audience and becoming a multi-million dollar industry. **Disco** was the trend of 1978.

**The US Moon Programme** ended, 1974, releasing scientific resources for environmental research. Space probes transmitted pictures from Mars. **Russian and US spacecraft** linked in space, 1975. **British scientists** discovered the complete genetic structure of a virus, 1977. **The world's first test-tube baby** was born in Britain, 1978.

# INDEX

# Bibliography

**General**  
Bonhoeffer, D.; *Christology*; Fontana, 1971  
*Cambridge History of the British Empire*; Cambridge U.P., 1940–59 (3 vols)  
Grubel, H. G.; *International Monetary System*; Penguin, 1969  
Gutteridge, J.; *United Nations in a Changing World*; Manchester U.P., 1970  
Jansen, G. H.; *Afro-Asia and Non-Alignment*; Faber, 1966  
Kinch, F. W. (Ed.); *Sociology in the World Today*; Addison, 1971  
Lijphart, A.; *Trauma of Decolonization*; Yale U.P., 1966  
Mar, A. D.; *History of Monetary Systems*; Kelley, 1969  
Myrdal, K. G.; *Economic Theory and Underdeveloped Regions*; Duckworth, 1957  
Patton, J.; *How the Depression Hit the West*; McClelland, 1974  
Pelikan, I (Ed ); *20th Century Theology in the Making*; Fontana, 1970 (3 vols)  
Tetlow, E.; *United Nations: First 25 Years*; P. Owen, 1970  
Worsley, P.; *Third World*; Weidenfeld & Nicolson, 1967  
**Africa**  
Hallett, R.; *Africa to 1875: A Modern History*; Univ. of Michigan Press, 1970  
Hallett, R.; *Africa since 1875: A Modern History*; Univ. of Michigan Press, 1970  
Martin, P. M.; *External Trade of the Loango Coast 1576–1870*; Oxford U.P., 1972  
Sagay, J. O.; *Africa: A Modern History*; Evans Bros., 1978  
Wilson, M. & L. M. Thompson; *Oxford History of S. Africa*; Oxford U.P., 1969–71 (2 vols)  
**North America**  
Billington, R. A. & H. E. Huntingdom; *Westward Expansion*; Collier-Macmillan, 1974  
Creighton, D. G.; *Story of Canada*; Faber, 1971  
Galbraith, K.; *Affluent Society*; Penguin, 1970  
McNaught, K.; *Pelican History of Canada*; Penguin, 1970  
Randall, J. G. & D. Donald; *Civil War and Reconstruction*; Heath, 1968  
Smith, H. N.; *Virgin Land: American West*; Harvard U.P., 1972  
Thistlethwaite, F.; *Great Experiment*; Cambridge U.P., 1955  
Wright, E.; *American Revolution*; Leicester U.P., 1967  
**Central America**  
Parry, J. H. & P. M. Sherlock; *Short History of the West Indies*; Macmillan, 1968  
Prescott, W. H.; *History of the Conquest of Mexico*; Dent, 1970 (2 vols)  
**South America**  
Diaz, B.; *Conquest of New Spain*; Penguin, 1969  
Furtado, C.; *Economic Development of Latin America*; Cambridge U.P., 1970  
Glade, W. P., *Latin American Economies*; Van Nost. Reinhold, 1969  
Hemming, J.; *Conquest of the Incas*; Sphere, 1972  
Lambert, J.; *Latin America: Social Structure and Political Institutions*; Univ. of California Press, 1969  
Prescott, W. H.; *History of the Conquest of Peru*; Modern Library, 1973  
**Asia**  
  *General*  
Crowley, J. B. (Ed.); *Modern E. Asia*; Harcourt Brace, 1970  
Fitzgerald, C. P.; *Concise History of E. Asia*; Penguin, 1974  
Miller, D. B. (Ed.); *Peasants and Politics: Grass Roots Reaction to Change in Asia*; E. Arnold, 1979  
  *China*  
Gittings, J.; *Chinese View of China*; BBC, 1973  
Han Suyin; *Morning Deluge: Mao and the Chinese Revolution*; Panther, 1976 (2 vols)  
McAleavy, H.; *Modern History of China*; Weidenfeld & Nicolson, 1968  
Myrdal, J.; *Report from a Chinese Village*; Pan, 1975  
Schram, S.; *Mao Tse-Tung*; Penguin, 1970  
Schram, S.; *Mao Tse-Tung Unrehearsed*; Penguin, 1974  
Schurmann, F. & O. Schell; *Imperial China*; Penguin, 1967  
Snow, E.; *China's Long Revolution*; Penguin, 1975  
Snow, E.; *Red China Today*; Penguin, 1970  
Snow, E.; *Red Star over China*; Penguin, 1972  
  *India*  
Brown, J. M.; *Gandhi's Rise to Power*; Cambridge U.P., 1974  
Gopal, S.; *British Policy in India 1858–1905*; Cambridge U.P., 1965  
Spear, P.; *History of India II*; Penguin, 1970  
Woodruff, P.; *Men who Ruled India: The Founders*; Cape, 1963  
Woodruff, P.; *Men who Ruled India: The Guardians*; Cape, 1963  
  *Japan*  
Beasley, W. G.; *Modern History of Japan*; Weidenfeld & Nicolson, 1973  
Sansom, Sir G.; *Western World and Japan*; Barrie & Jenkins, 1966  
Storry, R.; *History of Modern Japan*; Penguin, 1969  
  *Vietnam*  
Duncanson, D. J.; *Government and Revolution in Vietnam*; Oxford U.P., 1968  
Porter, G.; *Peace Denied: US, Vietnam and the Paris Agreement*; Indiana U.P., 1976  
**Australasia**  
Marais, J. S.; *Colonization of New Zealand*; Dawsons, 1968  
Mills, R. C.; *Colonization of Australia 1829–42*; Dawsons, 1968  
Shaw, A. G. L.; *Story of Australia*; Faber, 1973  
Sinclair, K.; *History of New Zealand*; Penguin, 1970  
**Middle East**  
al-Otaiba, M. S.; *OPEC and the Petroleum Industry*; Croom Helm, 1975  
Robinson, M.; *Israel and the Arabs*; Penguin, 1973  
**Europe**  
  *General*  
Addison, P.; *Road to 1945*; Cape, 1975  
Anderson, M. S.; *Eastern Question 1774–1923*; Macmillan, 1966  
Andrews, S.; *18th Century Europe*; Longman, 1965  
Aster, S.; *Making of the Second World War*; Deutsch, 1974  
Bainton, R. H.; *Age of Reformation*; Van Nost. Reinhold, 1956  
Bainton, R. H.; *Erasmus of Christendom*; Collins, 1970

Bainton, R. H.; *Here I Stand: Life of Martin Luther*; New American Library, 1950  
Barnes, H. E. (Ed.); *Introduction to the History of Sociology*; Univ. Chicago Press, 1966  
Becker, C. L.; *Heavenly City of the 18th Century Philosophers*; Yale U.P., 1932  
Birnie, A.; *Economic History of Europe 1760–1939*; Methuen, 1967  
Calvocoressi, P. & G. Wint; *Total War*; Penguin, 1974  
Cameron, R.; *Europe since 1945*; Arnold, 1976  
Carsten, F.; *Rise of Fascism*; Methuen, 1970  
Clark, Sir G.; *17th Century*; Oxford U.P., 1960  
Cole, G. D. H.; *History of Socialist Thought*; Macmillan 1953–60 (5 vols)  
Dickens, A. G.; *Counter-Reformation*; Thames & Hudson, 1968  
Dickens, A. G.; *Reformation and Society in 16th Century Europe*; Thames & Hudson, 1966  
Elton, G. R.; *Reformation Europe 1517–99*; Fontana, 1969  
Fejto, F.; *History of the People's Democracies: E. Europe since Stalin*; Penguin, 1974  
Fieldhouse, D. K.; *Economics and Empire*; Weidenfeld & Nicolson, 1976  
Gollwitzer, H.; *Europe in the Age of Imperialism*; Thames & Hudson, 1969  
Green, V. H. H.; *Renaissance and Reformation*; E. Arnold, 1964  
Grenville, J. A. S.; *Europe Re-shaped 1848–78*; Fontana, 1976  
Hampson, N.; *Enlightenment*; Penguin, 1968  
Hartung, F.; *Enlightened Despotism*; Historical Association, 1964  
Hayek, F. A. (Ed.); *Capitalism and the Historians*; Univ. Chicago Press, 1954  
Hazard, P.; *European Mind 1680–1715*; Penguin, 1973  
Keynes, J. M.; *Economic Consequences of the Peace*; Macmillan, 1971  
Knapp, W.; *Unity and Nationalism in Europe since 1945*; Pergamon, 1969  
Knight, F.; *Exploration*; Benn, 1973  
Koebner, R.; *Empire*; Cambridge U.P., 1961  
Koenigsberger, N. G. & G. D. Mosse; *Europe in the 16th Century*; Longman, 1971  
Laqueur, W. (Ed.); *Fascism: A Reader's Guide*; Wildwood House, 1977  
Lichteim, G.; *Short History of Socialism*; Fontana, 1975  
Liddell-Hart, B. H.; *History of the First World War*; Pan, 1972  
Namier, Sir L.; *1848 – Revolution of the Intellectuals*; Oxford U.P., 1971  
Nicolson, H.; *Congress of Vienna*; Methuen, 1946  
Reid, A.; *Concise Encyclopaedia of the Second World War*; Osprey, 1974  
Robertson, E. M. (Ed.); *Origins of the Second World War*; Macmillan, 1971  
Sherover, C. M.; *Development of the Democratic Idea*; Mentor, 1974  
Smith, D. & D. Newton; *Exploration*; Schofield, 1971  
Smith, W. H. C.; *20th Century Europe*; Longman, 1970  
Stoye, J.; *Europe Unfolding 1648–88*; Fontana, 1969  
Sumner, W. G.; *History of Banking in all the Leading Nations*; Kelley, 1970  
Tawney, R. H.; *Religion and the Rise of Capitalism*; Penguin, 1969  
Taylor, A. J. P.; *Origins of the Second World War*; Penguin, 1961  
Taylor, A. J. P.; *Struggle for Mastery in Europe 1848–1914*; Oxford U.P., 1971  
Watkins, F. M.; *Age of Ideology: 1790–Present*; Prentice-Hall, 1964  
Wendel, F.; *Calvin*; Fontana, 1965  
  *Britain (c. 1500–c. 1600)*  
Dickens, A. G.; *English Reformation*; Fontana, 1967  
Donaldson, G.; *James V – James VII*; Oliver & Boyd, 1965  
Edwards, D.; *Ireland in the Age of the Tudors*; Crown Helm, 1977  
Elton, G. R.; *England Under the Tudors*; Methuen, 1974  
Elton, G. R.; *Tudor Revolution in Government*; Cambridge U.P., 1953  
Hakluyt, R.; *Voyages and Documents*; Oxford U.P., 1958  
Lydan, J. F.; *Ireland in the Later Middle Ages*; Gill, 1973  
Mattingly, G.; *Defeat of the Spanish Armada*; Cape, 1970  
Neale, J. E.; *Elizabeth I and Her Parliaments*; Cape, 1953  
Neale, J. E.; *Queen Elizabeth I*; Cape, 1967  
Nicholson, R.; *Scotland: The Later Middle Ages*; Oliver & Boyd, 1973  
Rowse, A. L.; *England of Elizabeth*; Macmillan, 1950  
Scarisbrick, J. J.; *Henry VIII*; Eyre Methuen, 1976  
Wernham, R. B.; *Before the Armada*; Cape, 1966  
Williamson, J. A.; *Age of Drake*; Black, 1965  
  *Britain (c. 1600 – c. 1700)*  
Bryant, Sir A.; *Samuel Pepys*; Collins, 1967 (3 vols)  
Cipolla, C. M.; *Before the Industrial Revolution*; Methuen, 1976  
Clark, Sir G.; *Later Stuarts 1660–1714*; Oxford U.P., 1956  
Fraser, A.; *Cromwell, Our Chief of Men*; Panther, 1975  
Hill, C.; *Century of Revolution 1603–1714*; Cardinal, 1974  
Hill, C.; *God's Englishman: Oliver Cromwell and the English Revolution*; Penguin, 1972  
Lamont, W. M.; *Godly Rule*; Macmillan, 1969  
Mitchison, R.; *History of Scotland*; Methuen, 1970  
Ogg, D.; *England in the Reign of Charles II*; Oxford U.P., 1967  
Stone, L.; *Crisis of the Aristocracy 1558–1641*; Oxford U.P., 1965  
Wedgwood, C. V.; *King's Peace 1637–41*; Collins, 1955  
Wedgwood, C. V.; *King's War 1641–47*; Collins, 1958  
  *Britain (c. 1700–c. 1800)*  
Ashton, T. S.; *Industrial Revolution*; Oxford U.P., 1969  
Barnes, D. G.; *George III and William Pitt*; Cass, 1967  
Cannon, J.; *Parliamentary Reform 1640–1832*; Cambridge U.P., 1973  
Chambers, J. D. & G. E. Mingay; *Agricultural Revolution*; Batsford, 1969  
Chandler, D.; *Art of Warfare in the Age of Marlborough*; Batsford, 1976  
Churchill, W.; *Marlborough*; Harrap, 1970  
Ferguson, W.; *Scotland 1689 to the Present*; Oliver & Boyd, 1968  
Hamilton, H.; *Economic History of Scotland in the 18th Century*; Oxford U.P., 1963  
James, F. G.; *Ireland in the Empire 1688–1770*; Harvard U.P., 1973  
Mathias, P.; *First Industrial Nation*; Methuen, 1969  
Pares, R.; *King George III and the Politicians*; Oxford U.P., 1968  
Plumb, J. H.; *Sir Robert Walpole*; Allan Lane, 1972 (2 vols)  
Seeley, Sir J. R.; *Expansion of England*; Univ. Chicago Press, 1973

Smout, T. C.; *History of the Scottish People 1560–1830*; Fontana, 1972
Williams, E. E.; *Capitalism and Slavery*; Deutsch, 1964
*Britain (c. 1800 – c. 1900)*
Blake, R.; *Disraeli*; Methuen, 1969
Briggs, A.; *Victorian Cities*; Penguin, 1968
Dyos, H. J. & M. Wolff (Eds.); *Victorian City: Images and Realities*; Routledge, 1973
Hayes, P.; *19th Century*; Black, 1975
Hobsbawm, E. J.; *Industry and Empire*; Weidenfeld & Nicolson, 1968
Hunter, J.; *Making of the Crofting Community*; Donald, 1976
Longford, E.; *Victoria RI*; Pan, 1966
Longford, E.; *Wellington*; ; Panther, 1971 & 1975 (2 vols)
Magnus, Sir P.; *Gladstone*; J. Murray, 1954
Midwinter, E. C.; *Victorian Social Reform*; Longman, 1968
Morton, A. L. & G. Tate; *British Labour Movement 1770–1920*; Lawrence, 1956
Robinson, R. & J. Gallagher; *Africa and the Victorians*; Macmillan, 1966
Roderick, A. J.; *Wales through the Ages Vol II, 1845–1900*; C. Davies, 1971
Samuel, R. (Ed.); *Village Life and Labour*; Routledge, 1975
Seton-Watson, R.; *Britain in Europe 1789–1914*; Cambridge U.P., 1937
Shepherd, T. H. & J. Elmes; *Metropolitan Improvements, or London in the 19th Century*; Arno, 1976
Slaven, A.; *Development of the West of Scotland*; Routledge, 1975
Southey, R.; *Life of Nelson*; Dent
Stewart, R.; *Foundation of the Conservative Party*; Longman, 1978
*Britain (c. 1900–present)*
Branson, N. & M. Heinemann; *Britain in the 1930s*; Weidenfeld & Nicolson, 1975
Frankel, J.; *British Foreign Policy 1945–73*; Oxford U.P., 1975
Freeman-Grenville, G. S.; *Chronology of World History*; R. Collings, 1975
Freeman-Grenville, G. S.; *Queen's Lineage*; R. Collings, 1977
Harvie, C.; *Scotland and Nationalism*; Allen & Unwin, 1977
Mansergh, N.; *Commonwealth Experience*; Weidenfeld & Nicolson, 1969
Marwick, A.; *Home Front: British and the Second World War*; Thames & Hudson
Medlicott, W. M.; *Contemporary England 1914–64*; Longman, 1976
Morgan, D.; *Suffragists and Liberals*; Blackwell, 1975
Mowat, C. L.; *Britain between the Wars 1918–40*; Methuen, 1968
Murphy, J. A.; *Ireland in the 20th Century*; Gill, 1975
Orwell, G.; *Road to Wigan Pier*; Penguin, 1970
Richards, D. & A. Quick; *20th Century Britain*; Longman, 1968
Rothstein, A.; *British Foreign Policy and its Critics*; Lawrence, 1969
Rumpf, E. & A. Hepburn; *Nationalism and Socialism in 20th Century Ireland*; Liverpool U.P., 1977
Taylor, A. J. P.; *English History 1914–45*; Penguin, 1970
Williams, D.; *History of Modern Wales*; J. Murray, 1977
*France*
Behrens, C. B. A.; *Ancien Regime*; Thames & Hudson, 1967
Goodwin, A.; *French Revolution*; Hutchinson, 1966
Goodwin, A. (Ed.); *American and French Revolutions 1763–93*; Cambridge U.P., 1976
Goubert, P.; *Ancien Regime: French Society 1600–1750*; Weidenfeld & Nicolson, 1973
Hampson, N.; *First European Revolution 1776–1815*; Thames & Hudson, 1969
Hatton, R. M.; *Europe in the Age of Louis XIV*; Thames & Hudson, 1969
Lefebvre, G.; *Napoleon*; Routledge, 1969 (2 vols)
Lefebvre, G.; *French Revolution*; Routledge, 1964 (2 vols)
Ogg, D.; *Louis XIV*; Oxford U.P., 1967
*Germany*
Fischer, F.; *Germany's Aims in the First World War*; Chatto, 1967
Taylor, A. J. P.; *Bismarck*; New English Library, 1974
*Italy*
Smith, D. M.; *Garibaldi*; Prentice-Hall, 1969
*Spain*
Elliot, J. H.; *Imperial Spain 1469–1716*; E. Arnold, 1963
Parry, J. H.; *Spanish Seaborne Empire*; Hutchinson, 1966
*USSR*
Auty, R. & D. Obolensky (Eds.); *Introduction to Russian History*; Cambridge U.P., 1976
Carr, E. H.; *Russian Revolution*; Macmillan, 1950–53 (3 vols)
Deutscher, I.; *Stalin: A Political Biography*; Oxford U.P., 1972
Florinsky, M. T.; *Russia: History and Interpretation*; Collier-Macmillan, 1953 (2 vols)
Raeff, M.; *Catherine the Great*; Macmillan, 1972
Riasanovsky, N. V.; *History of Russia*; Oxford U.P., 1969
Schapiro, L. B.; *Communist Party of the Soviet Union*; Methuen, 1970
Seton-Watson, H.; *Russian Empire*; Oxford U.P., 1967
Tatu, M.; *Power in the Kremlin*; Collins, 1968
Trotsky, L.; *Stalin School of Falsification*; New Park, 1974
Ulam, A. B.; *Lenin and the Bolsheviks*; Secker & Warburg, 1966
Vernadsky, G.; *Kievan Russia*; Yale U.P., 1973
Vernadsky, G.; *Mongols and Russia*; Yale U.P., 1953
Vernadsky, G.; *Russia at the Dawn of the Modern Age*; Yale U.P., 1959
Wolfe, B. D.; *Three who made a Revolution*; Penguin, 1966

## Major contributors and advisers to The Joy of Knowledge

Fabian Acker CEng, MIEE, MIMarE; Professor Leslie Alcock; Professor H. C. Allen MC; Leonard Amey OBE; Neil Ardley BSc; Professor H. R. V. Arnstein DSc, PhD, FIBiol; Russell Ash BA (Dunelm), FRAI; Norman Ashford PhD, CEng, MICE, MASCE, MCIT; Professor Robert Ashton; B. W. Atkinson BSc, PhD; Anthony Atmore BA; Professor Philip S. Bagwell BSc(Econ), PhD; Peter Ball MA; Edwin Banks MIOP; Professor Michael Banton; Dulan Barber; Harry Barrett; Professor J. P. Barron MA, DPhil, FSA; Professor W. G. Beasley FBA; Alan Bender PhD, MSc, DIC, ARCS; Lionel Bender BSc; Israel Berkovitch PhD, FRIC, MIChemE; David Berry MA; M. L. Bierbrier PhD; A. T. E. Binsted FBBI (Dipl); David Black; Maurice E. F. Block BA, PhD(Cantab); Richard H. Bomback BSc (London), FRPS; Basil Booth BSc (Hons), PhD, FGS, FRGS; J. Harry Bowen MA(Cantab), PhD(London); Mary Briggs MPS, FLS; John Brodrick BSc(Econ); J. M. Bruce ISO, MA, FRHistS, MRAeS; Professer D. A. Bullough MA, FSA, FRHistS; Tony Buzan BA(Hons) UBC; Dr Alan R. Cane; Dr J. G. de Casparis; Dr Jeremy Catto MA; Denis Chamberlain; E. W. Chanter MA; Professor Colin Cherry DSc(Eng), MIEE; A. H. Christie MA, FRAI, FRAS; Dr Anthony W. Clare MPhil(London), MB, BCh, MRCPI, MRCPsych; Professor Aidan Clarke MA, PhD, FTCD; Sonia Cole; John R. Collis MA, PhD; Professor Gordon Connell-Smith BA, PhD, FRHistS; Dr A. H. Cook FRS; Professor A. H. Cook FRS; J. A. L. Cooke MA, DPhil; R. W. Cooke BSc, CEng, MICE; B. K. Cooper; Penelope J. Corfield MA; Robin Cormack MA, PhD, FSA; Nona Coxhead; Patricia Crone BA, PhD; Geoffrey P. Crow BSc(Eng), MICE, MIMunE, MInstHE, DIPTE; J. G. Crowther; Professor R. B. Cundall FRIC; Noel Currer-Briggs MA, FSG; Christopher Cviic BA(Zagreb), BSc(Econ, London); Gordon Daniels BSc(Econ, London), DPhil(Oxon); George Darby BA; G. J. Darwin; Dr David Delvin; Robin Denselow BA; Professor Bernard L. Diamond; John Dickson; Paul Dinnage MA; M. L. Dockrill BSc(Econ), MA, PhD; Patricia Dodd BA; James Dowdall; Anne Dowson MA(Cantab); Peter M. Driver BSc, PhD, MIBiol; Rev Professor C. W. Dugmore DD; Herbert L. Edlin BSc, Dip in Forestry; Pamela Egan MA(Oxon); Major S. R. Elliot CD, BComm; Professor H. J. Eysenck PhD, DSc; Dr Peter Fenwick BA, MB, BChir, DPM, MRCPsych; Jim Flegg BSc, PhD, ARCS, MBOU; Andrew M. Fleming MA; Professor Antony Flew MA(Oxon), DLitt (Keele); Wyn K. Ford FRHistS; Paul Freeman DSc(London); G. S. P. Freeman-Grenville DPhil, FSA, FRAS, G. E. Fussell DLitt, FRHistS; Kenneth W. Gatland FRAS, FBIS; Norman Gelb BA; John Gilbert BA(Hons, London); Professor A. C. Gimson; John Glaves-Smith BA; David Glen; Professor S. J. Goldsack BSc, PhD, FInstP, FBCS; Richard Gombrich MA, DPhil; A. F. Gomm; Professor A. Goodwin MA; William Gould BA(Wales); Professor J. R. Gray; Christopher Green PhD; Bill Gunston; Professor A. Rupert Hall DLitt; Richard Halsey BA(Hons, UEA); Lynette K. Hamblin BSc; Norman Hammond; Peter Harbison MA, DPhil; Professor Thomas G. Harding PhD; Professor D. W. Harkness; Richard Harris; Dr Randall P. Harrison; Cyril Hart MA, PhD, FRICS, FIFor; Anthony P. Harvey; Nigel Hawkes BA(Oxon); F. P. Heath; Peter Hebblethwaite MA (Oxon), LicTheol; Frances Mary Heidensohn BA; Dr Alan Hill MC, FRCP; Robert Hillenbrand MA, DPhil; Catherine Hills PhD; Professor F. H. Hinsley; Dr Richard Hitchcock; Dorothy Hollingsworth OBE, BSc, FRIC, FIBiol, FIFST, SRD; H. P. Hope BSc(Hons, Agric); Antony Hopkins CBE, FRCM, LRAM, FRSA; Brian Hook; Peter Howell BPhil, MA(Oxon); Brigadier K. Hunt; Peter Hurst BDS, FDS, LDS, RSCEd, MSc(London); Anthony Hyman MA, PhD; Professor R. S. Illingworth MD, FRCP, DPH, DCH; Oliver Impey MA, DPhil; D. E. G. Irvine PhD; L. M. Irvine BSc; E. W. Ives BA, PhD; Anne Jamieson cand mag(Copenhagen), MSc (London); Michael A. Janson BSc; G. H. Jenkins PhD; Professor P. A. Jewell BSc (Agric), MA, PhD, FIBiol; Hugh Johnson; Commander I. E. Johnston RN; I. P. Jolliffe BSc, MSc, PhD, ComplCE, FGS; Dr D. E. H. Jones ARCS, FCS; R. H. Jones PhD, BSc, CEng, MICE, FGS, MASCE, Hugh Kay; Dr Janet Kear; Sam Keen; D. R. C. Kempe BSc, DPhil, FGS; Alan Kendall MA(Cantab); Michael Kenward; John R. King BSc(Eng), DIC, CEng, MIProdE; D. G. King-Hele FRS; Professor J. F. Kirkaldy DSc; Malcolm Kitch; Michael Kitson MA; B. C. Lamb BSc, PhD; Nick Landon; Major J. C. Larminie QDG, Retd; Diana Leat BSc(Econ), PhD; Roger Lewin BSc, PhD; Harold K. Lipset; Norman Longmate MA(Oxon); John Lowry; Kenneth E. Lowther MA; Diana Lucas BA(Hons); Keith Lye BA, FRGS; Dr Peter Lyon; Dr Martin McCauley; Sean McConville BSc; D. F. M. McGregor BSc, PhD(Edin); Jean Macqueen PhD; William Baird MacQuitty MA(Hons), FRGS, FRPS; Professor Rev F. X. Martin OSA; Jonathan Martin MA; Rev Cannon E. L. Mascall DD; Christopher Maynard MSc, DTh; Professor A. J. Meadows; Dr T. B. Millar; John Miller MA, PhD; J. S. G. Miller MA, DPhil, BM, BCh; Alaric Millington BSc, DipEd, FIMA; Rosalind Mitchison MA, FRHistS; Peter L. Moldon; Patrick Moore OBE; Robin Mowat MA, DPhil; J. Michael Mullin BSc; Alistair Munroe BSc, ARCS; Professor Jacob Needleman, John Newman MA, FSA; Professor Donald M. Nicol MA PhD; Gerald Norris; Professor F. S. Northedge PhD; Caroline E. Oakman BA(Hons, Chinese); S. O'Connell MA(Cantab), MInstP; Dr Robert Orr; Michael Overman; Di Owen BSc; A. R. D. Pagden MA, FRHistS; Professor E. J. Pagel PhD; Liam de Paor MA; Carol Parker BA(Econ), MA (Internat. Aff.); Derek Parker; Julia Parker DFAstrolS; Dr Stanley Parker; Dr Colin Murray Parkes MD, FRC(Psych), DPM; Professor Geoffrey Parrinder MA, PhD, DD(London), DLitt(Lancaster); Moira Paterson; Walter C. Patterson MSc; Sir John H. Peel KCVO, MA, DM, FRCP, FRCS, FRCOG; D. J. Penn; Basil Peters MA, MInstP, FBIS; D. L. Phillips FRCR, MRCOG; B. T. Pickering PhD, DSc; John Picton; Susan Pinkus; Dr C. S. Pitcher MA, DM, FRCPath; Alfred Plaut FRCPsych; A. S. Playfair MRCS, LRCP, DObst, RCOG; Dr Antony Polonsky; Joyce Pope BA; B. L. Potter NDA, MRAC, CertEd; Paulette Pratt; Antony Preston; Frank J. Pycroft; Margaret Quass; Dr John Reckless; Trevor Reese BA, PhD, FRHistS; M. M. Reese MA (Oxon); Derek A. Reid BSc, PhD; Clyde Reynolds BSc; John Rivers; Peter Roberts; Colin A. Ronan MSc, FRAS; Professor Richard Rose BA(Johns Hopkins), DPhil (Oxon); Harold Rosenthal; T. G. Rosenthal MA(Cantab); Anne Ross MA, MA(Hons, Celtic Studies), PhD, (Archaeol and Celtic Studies, Edin); Georgina Russell MA; Dr Charles Rycroft BA (Cantab), MB(London), FRCPsych; Susan Saunders MSc(Econ); Robert Schell PhD; Anil Seal MA, PhD(Cantab); Michael Sedgwick MA(Oxon); Martin Seymour-Smith BA(Oxon), MA(Oxon); Professor John Shearman; Dr Martin Sherwood; A. C. Simpson BSc; Nigel Sitwell; Dr Alan Sked; Julie and Kenneth Slavin FRGS, FRAI; Professor T. C. Smout; Alec Xavier Snobel BSc(Econ); Terry Snow BA, ATCL; Rodney Steel; Charles S. Steinger MA, PhD; Geoffrey Stern BSc(Econ); Maryanne Stevens BA(Cantab), MA(London); John Stevenson DPhil, MA; J. Sidworthy MA; D. Michael Stoddart BSc, PhD; Bernard Stonehouse DPhil, MA, BSc, MInst Biol; Anthony Storr FRCP, FRCPsych; Richard Storry; Charles Stuart-Jervis; Professor John Taylor; John W. R. Taylor FRHistS, MRAeS, FSLAET; R. B. Taylor BSc(Hons, Microbiol); J. David Thomas MA, PhD; D. Thompson BSc(Econ); Harvey Tilker PhD; Don Tills PhD, MPhil, MIBiol, FIMLS; Jon Tinker; M. Tregear MA; R. W. Trender; David Trump MA, PhD, FSA; M. F. Tuke PhD; Christopher Tunney MA; Laurence Urdang Associates (authentication and fact check); Sally Walters BSc; Christopher Wardle; Dr D. Washbrook; David Watkins; George Watkins MSc; J. W. N. Watkins; Anthony J. Watts; Dr Geoff Watts; Melvyn Westlake; Anthony White MA(Oxon), MAPhil(Columbia); Dr Ruth D. Whitehouse; P. J. S. Whitmore MBE, PhD; Professor G. R. Wilkinson; Rev H. A. Williams CR; Christopher Wilson BA; Professor David M. Wilson; John B. Wilson BSc, PhD, FGS, FLS; Philip Windsor BA, DPhil(Oxon), Roy Wolfe BSc(Econ), MSc; Donald Wood MA PhD; Dr David Woodings MA, MRCP, MRCPath; Bernard Yallop PhD, BSc, ARCS, FRAS Professor John Yudkin MA, MD, PhD(Cantab), FRIC, FIBiol, FRCP.

(*continuation of picture credits*)

Mansell Collection; [7] Radio Times Hulton Picture Library; [8] Mansell Collection; [9] Radio Times Hulton Picture Library. **54–5** [Key] Radio Times Hulton Picture Library; [2] Mary Evans Picture Library; [4] Woodmansterne; [5] Popperfoto; [7] National Portrait Gallery; [8] Radio Times Hulton Picture Library; [9] Weidenfeld & Nicolson Archives/Labour Party Photo Library. **56–7** [1] Eileen Tweedy/National Library of Wales; [2] Welsh Folk Museum/National Museum of Wales; [3] Eileen Tweedy/National Library of Wales; [4] National Museum of Wales; [5] Radio Times Hulton Picture Library; [6] Eileen Tweedy/ National Library of Wales; [7] Eileen Tweedy/National Library of Wales; [8] National Portrait Gallery. **58–9** [Key] Novosti Press Agency; [1] Radio Times Hulton Picture Library; [2] Radio Times Hulton Picture Library; [3] John R. Freeman; [4] Novosti Press Agency; [5] Courtesy of Cultural Relations with the USSR; [6] Novosti Press Agency; [8] Radio Times Hulton Picture Library; [9] Novosti Press Agency; [10] Novosti Press Agency. **60–1** [Key] Mansell Collection; [1] Punch Publications Ltd; [3] From the John Gorman Collection; [4] Radio Times Hulton Picture Library; [5] Giraudon; [6] British Red Cross Society; [7] Radio Times Hulton Picture Library. **62–3** [Key] Mansell Collection; [2] Manchester Public Libraries; [3A] Radio Times Hulton Picture Library; [3B] Radio Times Hulton Picture Library; [3C] Mansell Collection; [5A] Giraudon; [5B] Angelo Hornak/V & A. **64–5** [Key] Ronan Picture Library; [1] Mary Evans Picture Library; [3] Ullstein Bilderdienst; [5] Österreichische Nationalbibliothek; [6] Source unknown; [7] Snark International; [8] Radio Times Hulton Picture Library. **66–7** [Key] National Portrait Gallery; [1] Photographie Giraudon; [2] Mary Evans Picture Library; [3] Radio Times Hulton Picture Library; [4] Mansell Collection; [6] Mansell Collection; [7] Punch Publications Ltd; [8] Popperfoto; [9] London School of Economics. **68–9** [Key] Source unknown; [1] Mansell Collection; [2] Cyril & Methodius National Library, Sofia, Bulgaria; [3] Mansell Collection; [4] Archiv für Kunst & Geschichte; [6] IBA, Zurich; [8] Radio Times Hulton Picture Library. **70–1** [Key] Roger Viollet; [1] Radio Times Hulton Picture Library; [2] Ullstein Bilderdienst; [7] Source unknown; [8] Ullstein Bilderdienst. **72–3** [Key] Imperial War Museum; [7] Robert Hunt Library; [10] Image Press. **74–5** [1] Imperial War Museum; [3] Heeresgeschichtliches Museum, Vienna; [5] Image Press; [6] Chaz Bowyer; [7] Ullstein Bilderdienst; [9] Image Press. **76–7** [Key] Roger Viollet; [4] Roger Viollet; [5] Radio Times Hulton Picture Library; [8] Mansell Collection; [9] Ullstein Bilderdienst. **78–9** [Key] Mansell Collection; [1] Radio Times Hulton Picture Library; [2] Radio Times Hulton Picture Library; [3] Eileen Tweedy/IWM; [4] Camera Press; [5] Wilfred Owen Estate; [8] Mansell Collection; [9] Radio Times Hulton Picture Library; [10] Radio Times Hulton Picture Library. **80–1** [Key] Novosti Press Agency; [1] Novosti Press Agency; [2] Mansell Collection; [3] Bettmann Archive; [4] Novosti Press Agency; [5] Novosti Press Agency; [6] Radio Times Hulton

Picture Library; [7] Novosti Press Agency; [8] Snark International; [9] Geoff Goode/Courtesy The School of Slavonic Studies; [11] Radio Times Hulton Picture Library. **82–3** [Key] Camera Press; [1] Radio Times Hulton Picture Library; [2] Radio Times Hulton Picture Library; [4] Radio Times Hulton Picture Library; [5] Popperfoto; [8] Radio Times Hulton Picture Library; [9] Life © Time Inc. 1976/Colorific; [10] Radio Times Hulton Picture Library; [11] Robert Hunt Library. **84–5** [Key] Bettmann Archive; [4] Woolf, Laing, Christie & Partners; [5] Bettmann Archive; [6] Radio Times Hulton Picture Library; [7] Picturepoint; [9] Bettmann Archive. **86–7** [Key] London School of Economics; [1] Radio Times Hulton Picture Library; [2] Radio Times Hulton Picture Library; [3] Radio Times Hulton Picture Library; [5] Radio Times Hulton Picture Library; [6] Radio Times Hulton Picture Library; [7] Syndication International; [8] Radio Times Hulton Picture Library. **88–9** [Key] TUC Archive; [1] Mansell Collection; [2] Radio Times Hulton Picture Library; [3] Radio Times Hulton Picture Library; [4] Roger Viollet; [5] Roger Viollet; [7] Bettmann Archive; [8] Radio Times Hulton Picture Library; [9] Maurice Rickards. **90–1** [Key] Camera Press; [1] Source unknown; [3] Radio Times Hulton Picture Library; [4] Keystone Press; [5] Camera Press; [7] Keystone Press; [9] Robert Hunt Library. **92–3** [Key] Radio Times Hulton Picture Library; [1] Radio Times Hulton Picture Library; [2] National Army Museum; [3] Popperfoto; [4] Camera Press; [5] Mansell Collection; [6] Geoslides; [7] National Army Museum; [8] Robert Hunt Library; [10] Keystone Press. **94–5** [Key] Popperfoto; [1] Popperfoto; [2] ZEFA; [3] National Portrait Gallery; [4] Popperfoto; [7] Black Star Publishing Ltd; [8] Keystone Press Agency Ltd; [9] Popperfoto; [10] Camera Press. **96–7** [Key] Daily Mirror; [2] Trustees of the National Portrait Gallery; [3] Radio Times Hulton Picture Library; [5] Keystone Press; [6] Camera Press; [7] Royal Commonwealth Institute; [8] Associated Press. **98–9** [Key] Internationale Bildagentur; [2] Ullstein Bilderdienst; [3] Ullstein Bilderdienst; [5] Ullstein Bilderdienst; [6] International Bilderagentur; [8] Snark International. **100–1** [Key] Popperfoto; [1] Radio Times Hulton Picture Library; [2] Radio Times Hulton Picture Library; [3] Radio Times Hulton Picture Library; [4] British Airways; [5] Radio Times Hulton Picture Library; [6] Graham Newell; [7] Butlins; [8] Radio Times Hulton Picture Library; [9] Radio Times Hulton Picture Library; [10] Radio Times Hulton Picture Library. **102–3** [Key] Keystone Press; [1] Keystone Press; [2] Robert Hunt Library/Associated Press; [4] Archiv für Kunst und Geschichte; [7] Robert Hunt Library; [8] Cartoon by David Low by arrangement with the Trustees of the London *Evening Standard;* [9] Robert Hunt Library. **104–5** [2A] Robert Hunt Library; [2B] Robert Hunt Library; [2C] Imperial War Museum; [4] Robert Hunt Library; [6] Robert Hunt Library; [8] Robert Hunt Library/Imperial War Museum. **106–7** [1] Documentation Française; [2] Image Press; [3] Image Press; [4]

Novosti Press Agency; [5] Popperfoto; [6] Imperial War Museum; [7] Official USAF Photo; [8] Imperial War Museum; [9] Popperfoto; [10] Australian War Memorial. **108–9** [Key] Radio Times Hulton Picture Library; [1] Radio Times Hulton Picture Library; [2] Radio Times Hulton Picture Library; [3] Imperial War Museum; [4] Fox Photos; [5] Roger Viollet; [6] Roger Viollet; [7] Angelo Hornak/Imperial War Museum; [8] Novosti Press Agency; [9] Orion Press/Camera Press; [10] Snark International; [11] IBA, Zurich; [12] Snark International. **110–11** [Key] Novosti Press Agency; [1] Robert Hunt Library; [2] Radio Times Hulton Picture Library; [3] IBA, Zurich; [4] Associated Press; [6] Keystone Press Agency; [7] IBA, Zurich; [8] Popperfoto; [9] Popperfoto. **112–13** [Key] Popperfoto; [1] Popperfoto; [2] Punch Publications Ltd; [3] Radio Times Hulton Picture Library; [5] Graham Nash/Conservative Party Archives; [6] Fox Photos; [7] Radio Times Hulton Picture Library; [8] Popperfoto; [9] Popperfoto. **114–15** [Key] Picturepoint; [1] Popperfoto; [2] David Strickland; [3] Popperfoto; [5] Camera Press; [6] Camera Press; [7] Rolls-Royce Motors Ltd; [8] Camera Press; [9] Picturepoint. **116–17** [Key] Novosti Press Agency; [1] Popperfoto; [2] Popperfoto; [3] John F. Freeman; [5] Popperfoto; [8] Colorsport. **118–19** [Key] Camera Press; [2] Popperfoto; [3] Camera Press; [4] Associated Press; [5] Popperfoto; [6] Ginette Laborde, Paris; [7] Picturepoint. **120–1** [Key] Eastfoto; [1] Henri Cartier Bresson/John Hillelson Agency; [2] Eastfoto; [4] Camera Press; [6A] Sally and Richard Greenhill; [6B] Camera Press; [7] Camera Press; [9] Magnum Distribution. **122–3** [Key] Popperfoto; [2] Camera Press; [4] Popperfoto; [5] Camera Press; [6] Camera Press; [7] Australian News & Information Bureau. **124–5** [Key] Picturepoint; [1] Australian News & Information Bureau; [2] Anne-Marie Ehrlich; [5] Australian News & Information Bureau; [6] Popperfoto; [7] Popperfoto; [8] Camera Press; [9] Australian News & Information Bureau; [10] Australian News & Information Bureau. **126–7** [1] Weekly News; [2] New Zealand Herald; [3] Housing Corporation of New Zealand/Alexander Turnbull Library; [4] New Zealand Herald; [5] Weekly News; [6] New Zealand Forest Products Ltd, Auckland; [7] New Zealand Dairy Board; [8] Air New Zealand; [9] Frank Wallis. **128–9** [Key] Popperfoto; [1] Popperfoto; [2] De Beers Consolidated Mines Ltd; [3] National Portrait Gallery; [4] South Africa House; [5] Camera Press; [6] Camera Press; [7] Popperfoto; [8] Popperfoto; [9] Popperfoto. **130–1** [Key] Source unknown; [2] Camera Press; [3] Camera Press; [4] Associated Press; [5] Popperfoto; [7] Camera Press; [8] Keystone Press; [9] United Nations; [10] Agency for Public Information/Errol Harvey. **132–3** [Key] General Secretariat, Organization of American States; [1] National Palace of Mexico; [2] Radio Times Hulton Picture Library; [3] Camera Press; [4] Robert Cundy/Robert Harding Associates; [5] Associated Press; [7] G. A. Mather/Robert Harding Associates; [8] Romano Cagnoni; [9] Douglas Botting; [10] Associated Press. **134–5** [Key] Associated Press; [1] Roger

Viollet; [2] Popperfoto; [4A] Roger Viollet; [4B] Roger Viollet; [6] Associated Press; [7] Associated Press; [9] Camera Press; [10] Associated Press. **136–7** [Key] Popperfoto; [1] The Archives, Glasgow University; [2] Radio Times Hulton Picture Library; [3] Popperfoto; [5] Camera Press; [6] Picturepoint; [7] Picturepoint; [8] Picturepoint; [9] Camera Press; [10] Picturepoint. **138–9** [Key] Picturepoint; [1] Mansell Collection; [3] Radio Times Hulton Picture Library; [4] MB photograph; [5] Camera Press; [6] Welsh Arts Council; [7] Camera Press. **140–1** [Key] Shostal; [2A] Camera Press; [2B] Camera Press; [2C] Camera Press; [2D] Camera Press; [2E] Camera Press; [2F] Camera Press; [2G] Camera Press; [4] Associated Press. **142–3** [Key] Margaret Murray; [2] Geoff Goode; [3] Kibbutz Representatives; [4] Scottish New Towns Development Board; [6] Keystone Press; [7] Ted Lau, Fortune © Time Inc 1976/Colorific; [9] Camera Press; [10] Camera Press. **144–5** [Key] Romano Cagnoni; [2] Popperfoto; [3] Camera Press; [4] Camera Press; [5] Camera Press; [9] Camera Press; [10] Popperfoto. **146–7** [1] Mansell Collection; [2] Tony O'Malley Pictures Ltd; [3] Green Studio, Dublin; [4] Harland & Wolff Ltd; [5] Camera Press; [6] Camera Press; [7] Camera Press; [8] Arthur Guinness Son & Co (Dublin) Ltd; [9] Camera Press; [10] Popperfoto. **148–9** [Key] Institute of Contemporary History/Weiner Library/Geoff Goode; [3] Central Zionist Archives; [4] Central Press; [5] Camera Press. **150–1** [Key] United Nations; [1] Associated Press; [2] Associated Press; [4A] United Nations; [4B] United Nations; [4C] United Nations; [4D] United Nations; [6] Camera Press; [7] Keystone Press; [8] Camera Press. **152–3** [Key] Terry Kirk/Financial Times; [3] Régis Bossu/Copyright SYGMA/Magnum. **154–5** [Key] Camera Press; [4] Paolo Koch; [5] C. Gascoigne/Robert Harding Associates; [6] Picturepoint; [7] Margaret Murray/Ikon Productions; [8] Peter Fraenkel. **156–7** [Key] Popperfoto; [1] World Council of Churches; [2] Camera Press; [4] Camera Press; [5] Associated Press; [6] Shostal; [7] Camera Press; [8] Associated Press; [9] Chris Steele Perkins. **158–9** [Key] Associated Press; [2] Associated Press; [3] Elliot Erwitt/Magnum; [4] Associated Press; [5] Associated Press; [6] Associated Press; [7] Neal Boenzi/The New York Times/John Hillelson Agency; [9] Camera Press; [10] Popperfoto.

The map on p.57 is based on information in *An Historical Atlas of Wales* by William Rees, published by Faber and Faber. The map on p.18 is based on information in *South African Atlas,* by G. S. P. Freeman-Grenville, published by Rex Collings.

182